Family in Transition

Family in Transition

SEVENTEENTH EDITION

Arlene S. Skolnick

New York University

Jerome H. Skolnick

New York University

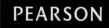

Boston   Columbus   Indianapolis   New York   San Francisco   Upper Saddle River
Amsterdam   Cape Town   Dubai   London   Madrid   Milan   Munich   Paris   Montréal   Toronto
Delhi   Mexico City   São Paulo   Sydney   Hong Kong   Seoul   Singapore   Taipei   Tokyo

Editor in Chief: Ashley Dodge
Publisher: Nancy Roberts
Editorial Assistant: Molly White
Director of Marketing: Brandy Dawson
Executive Marketing Manager: Kelly May
Marketing Coordinator: Courtney Stewart
Managing Editor: Denise Forlow
Program Manager: Mayda Bosco
Senior Operations Supervisor: Mary Fischer
Operations Specialist: Diane Peirano
Art Director: Jayne Conte

Cover photo: Diana Ong/Getty Images
Cover design: Bruce Kenselaar
Director of Digital Media: Brian Hyland
Digital Media Project Manager:
 Tina Gagliostro
**Full-Service Project Management and
 Composition:** PreMediaGlobal/Anju Joshi
Printer/Binder: RR Donnelley
Cover Printer: RR Donnelley
Text Font: JansonTextLTStd 10/12

Credits and acknowledgments borrowed from other sources and reproduced, with permission, in this textbook appear on page 487.

Library of Congress Cataloging-in-Publication Data

Family in transition / [edited by] Arlene S. Skolnick, New York University, Jerome H. Skolnick, New York University. — Seventeeth edition.
  pages cm
  ISBN-13: 978-0-205-21597-3
  ISBN-10: 0-205-21597-1
1. Families.   I. Skolnick, Arlene S., 1933-   II. Skolnick, Jerome H.
  HQ518.F336 2014
  306.85—dc23

                                              2013009352

10 9 8 7 6 5 4 3

ISBN 10: 0-205-21597-1
ISBN 13: 978-0-205-21597-3

Contents

v

8 Growing Up 249

PART IV • Families in Society 303

9 Work and Family Life 309

Preface

This edition of *Family in Transition* is once again aimed at helping students make sense of current trends in family life. It presents recent important research findings in articles that are scholarly and yet readable for an audience of undergraduates.

Among the new readings are the following:

NEW TO THIS EDITION

- **Richard A. Settersten, Jr.** and **Barbara Ray** explore a fundamental shift in family life: Today's parents play much larger roles in the lives of their young adult children than in the past. Without supportive parents, young people are less likely to succeed in a highly risky and competitive world.
- **Arlene Skolnick** examines the precarious economic lives of middle-class families in today's "high risk, high stress," winner-take-all economy. The costs of middle-class living standards have risen faster than middle-class incomes, while the security of jobs and benefits has declined.
- **Kathryn Edin**, **Timothy Nelson**, and **Joanna Miranda Reed** report that low-income urban fathers no longer fit the "package deal" model of fatherhood in which a man's bond to his child depends on his relationship with the mother. Today, these men seek to be involved in their children's lives even if they are not connected to the mothers romantically.
- **Joan C. Williams** explains that while the media focuses on professional women "opting out" from high-pressure careers, low income employees are typically only "one sick child away from being fired."
- **Judith Stacey** shows how widespread gay fatherhood is overturning traditional concepts of parenthood.
- **Demie Kurz** examines the debate over domestic violence: Should it be seen as a family issue or a problem of violence against women?

STUDENT AND TEACHER RESOURCES

This text is available in a variety of formats—digital and print. To learn more about our programs, pricing options, and customization, visit www.pearsonhighered.com.

MySearchLab with eText

A passcode-protected website that provides engaging experiences that personalize learning, MySearchLab contains an eText that is just like the printed text. Students can highlight and add notes to the eText online or download it to an iPad. MySearchLab also provides a wide range of writing, grammar, and research tools plus access to a variety of academic journals, census data, Associated Press news feeds, and discipline-specific readings to help hone writing and research skills.

Test Bank (0-205-21598-X)

For each reading in the text, this valuable resource provides test questions in multiple choice, true/false, and essay formats; the answers are page-referenced to the text.

MyTest (0-205-90642-7)

This computerized software allows instructors to create their own personalized exams, to edit any or all of the existing test questions, and to add new questions. Other special features of this program include the random generation of test questions, the creation of alternative versions of the same test, scrambling question sequences, and test previews before printing.

ACKNOWLEDGMENTS

We would like to thank all those who have helped us with suggestions in this edition, as well as the previous ones. Special thanks to Rifat Salem, assistant professor of sociology at the BMCC campus of the City University of New York, for her suggestions on revising the previous edition. Also, many thanks to the reviewers: Erica Hunter, University at Albany; Antoinette Livingston, West Virginia University; Teresa Mayors, Northeastern University; Amanda Moske, University of North Texas; Dennis McGrath, Community College of Philadelphia; and Rosalind Fisher, University of West Florida.

Arlene S. Skolnick
Jerome H. Skolnick

Introduction

The aim of this book is to help the reader make sense of American family life in the early twenty-first century. Most important, it aims to make clear the complicated links between families and the larger society. Contrary to most students' expectations, "the family" is not an easy topic to study. One reason is that we know too much about it, because virtually everyone has grown up in a family. As a result there is a great temptation to generalize from our own experiences.

Another difficulty is that the family is a subject that arouses intense emotions. Not only are family relationships themselves deeply emotional, but family issues are also entwined with strong moral and religious beliefs. In the past several decades, "family values" have become a central battleground in American politics. Abortion, sex education, single parenthood, and gay rights are some of the issues that have been debated since the 1980s.

Still another problem is that the current state of the family is always being portrayed as "in decline" compared with the way families used to be. The trouble is, most people tend to have an idealized image of families in "the good old days." No era ever looked like a golden age of family life to people actually living through it. That includes the 1950s, which many Americans now revere as the high point of American family life.

Finally, it is difficult to make sense of the state of the family from the statistics presented in the media. For example, the Pew Research Center reported that in 2010, married couples made up only 51 percent of American households. Only 9 percent of 18 to 24 year olds were married, compared to almost 50 percent in 1960. The headlines seemed to suggest that marriage is becoming obsolete. But in fact, 90 percent of Americans are expected to marry eventually, according to the Census Bureau. Another example: before Father's Day in 2003, the Census Bureau issued a press release headlined "Two Married Parents the Norm." It went on to state that, according to the Bureau's most recent survey, about 70 percent of children live with their two parents. Two months earlier, however, a report by a respected social science research organization contained the following

1

headlines: "Americans Increasingly Opting Out of Marriage" and "Traditional Families Account for Only 7 Percent of U.S. Households."

These are just a few examples of the confusing array of headlines and statistics about the family that the media are constantly serving up. Most often, the news tells of yet another fact or shocking incident that shows the alarming decline of the family. But every once in a while, the news is that the traditional family is making a comeback. No wonder one writer compared the family to a "great intellectual Rorschach blot" (Featherstone, 1979).

Everyone agrees that families have changed dramatically over the past several decades, but there is no consensus on what the changes mean. The majority of women, including mothers of young children, are now working outside the home. Divorce rates have risen sharply (although they have leveled off since 1979). Twenty-eight percent of children are living in single-parent families. Cohabitation—once called "shacking up" or "living in sin"—is a widespread practice. The sexual double standard—the norm that demanded virginity for the bride, but not the groom—has largely disappeared from mainstream American culture. There are mother-only families, father-only families, grandparents raising grandchildren, and gay and lesbian families.

Indeed, the growing public acceptance of homosexuals is one of the most striking trends of recent time. Local governments and leading corporations have granted gays increasing recognition as domestic partners entitled to spousal benefits. In June 2003, the Supreme Court struck down the last state laws that made gay sex a crime. The following November 18, the Massachusetts Supreme Judicial Court ruled that gays have the right to marry. As of early 2013 nine states allow same-sex couples to marry, and more are likely to follow. In 2011, the military dropped its "don't ask, don't tell" policy, allowing gays and lesbians to serve openly.

All these shifts in family life are part of an ongoing global revolution. All industrialized nations, and many of the emerging ones, have experienced similar changes. In no other Western country, however, has family change been as traumatic and divisive as in the United States. For example, the two-earner family is the most common family pattern in the United States; 75 percent of mothers of children under age 18 and more than 60 percent of those with young children work outside the home. Yet the question of whether mothers *should* work is still a fiercely debated issue.

Family issues have been at the center of our electoral politics. Thus, the typical pattern for public discussion of family issues is a polarized, either–or debate. Is single motherhood the main cause of our social problems, such as poverty crime, drug use, school failure? Is divorce so damaging to children and their futures that the government should make it harder to get? This kind of argument makes it difficult to discuss the issues and problems facing the family in a realistic way. It doesn't describe the range of views among family scholars, and it doesn't fit the research evidence. For example, the right question to ask about divorce is "Under what circumstances is divorce harmful or beneficial to children?" How can parents make divorce less harmful for their children? (Amato, 1994). In most public debates about divorce, however, that question is never asked, and the public never hears the useful information they should.

Still another problem with popular discourse about the family is that it exaggerates the amount of change that has actually occurred. For example, consider the previous statement that only 7 percent of American households fit the model of the traditional family. This number, or something like it, is often cited by conservatives as proof that the institution is in danger of disappearing unless the government steps in to restore marriage and the two-parent family. At the opposite end of the political spectrum are those who celebrate the alleged decline of the traditional family and welcome the new family forms that have supposedly replaced it.

But is it true that only 7 percent of American households are traditional families? It all depends, as the saying goes, on how you define *traditional*. The statement is true if you count only families with children under age 18 in which only the husband works outside the home. But if the wife works too, as most married women now do, the family doesn't count as "traditional" by that definition. Neither does the recently married couple who do not have children yet. The couple whose youngest child turns 18 is no longer counted as a "traditional" family either.

Despite the current high divorce rates (actually down from 1979), Americans have not abandoned the institution of marriage. The United States has the highest marriage rate in the industrial world. About 90 percent of Americans marry at some point in their lives, and virtually all who do either have, or want children. Further, surveys repeatedly show that family is central to the lives of most Americans. Family ties are their deepest source of satisfaction and meaning, as well as the source of their greatest worries (Mellman, Lazarus, and Rivlin, 1990). In sum, family life in the United States is a complex mixture of continuity and change, satisfaction and trouble.

While the transformations of the past three decades do not mean the end of family life, they have brought a number of new difficulties. For example, although most families now depend on the earnings of wives and mothers, the rest of our institutions have not caught up to the new realities. For example, most schools are out of step with parents' working hours—they let out at 3:00 p.m., and still maintain the long summer vacations that once allowed children to work on the family farm. Most jobs, especially well-paying ones, are based on the male model—that is, a worker who can work full time or longer without interruptions. Workers can be fired if they take time off to attend to a sick child.

An earnings gap persists between men and women in both blue-collar and white-collar jobs. Employed wives and mothers still bear most of the workload at home. And since the financial meltdown of 2008 and the start of the Great Recession, millions of families continue to face joblessness, pay cuts, losses of funds saved for children's education or their own retirement.

UNDERSTANDING THE CHANGING FAMILY

During the same years in which the family was becoming the object of public anxiety and political debate, a torrent of new research on the family was pouring forth. The study of the family had come to excite the interest of scholars in a range of disciplines—history, demography, economics, law, and psychology. We now have much more information available about families of the past, as well as current families, than we have ever had before.

The main outcome of this research has been to debunk myths about family life, both past and present. Nevertheless, the myths persist and help to fuel the cultural wars over family change.

The Myth of Universality

In some ways, families are the same everywhere. Yet families also vary in many ways—in who is included as a family member, emotional environments, living arrangements, ideologies, social and kinship networks, and economic and other functions. Although anthropologists have tried to come up with a single definition of family that would hold across time and place, they generally have concluded that doing so is not useful (Geertz, 1965; Stephens, 1963).

For example, although marriage is virtually universal across cultures, the definition of marriage is not the same, and living arrangements vary. Although many cultures have weddings and notions of monogamy and permanence, some lack one or more of these attributes. In some cultures, the majority of people mate and have children without legal marriage and often without living together. In other societies, husbands, wives, and children do not live together under the same roof.

In U.S. society, the assumption of universality has usually defined what is normal and natural both for research and therapy and has subtly influenced our thinking to regard deviations from the nuclear family as sick, perverse, or immoral. As Suzanne Keller (1971) once observed, "The fallacy of universality has done students of behavior a great disservice by leading us to seek and hence to find a single pattern that has blinded us to historical precedents for multiple legitimate family arrangements."

The Myth of Family Harmony

"Happy families are all alike; each unhappy family is unhappy in its own way." This well-known quotation from Leo Tolstoy is a good example of the widespread tendency to divide families into two opposite types—happy or unhappy, good or bad, normal or abnormal. The sitcom families of the 1950s—*Ozzie and Harriet*, *Leave It to Beaver*, and the rest—still serve as "ideal" models for how families should be.

But few families, then or now, fit neatly into either category. Even the most loving relationships inevitably involve negative feelings as well as positive ones. It is this ambivalence that sets close relationships apart from less intimate ones. Indeed, from what we have learned about the Nelson family over the years, the real Ozzie and Harriet did not have an Ozzie and Harriet family.

Only in fairly recent times has the darker side of family life come to public attention. For example, child abuse was only "discovered" as a social problem in the 1960s. In recent years, family scholars have been studying family violence such as child or spousal abuse to better understand the normal strains of family life. More police officers are killed and injured dealing with family fights than in dealing with any other kind of situation. In addition, of all the relationships between murderers and their victims, the family relationship is most common. Studies of family violence reveal that it is much more widespread than had been assumed, cannot easily be attributed to mental illness, and is not confined to the lower classes. Family violence seems to be a product of psychological tensions and external stresses that can affect all families at all social levels.

The study of family interaction has also undermined the traditional image of the happy, harmonious family. About three decades ago, researchers and therapists began to bring schizophrenic patients and their families together to watch how they behaved with one another. Oddly, researchers had not studied whole family groups before. At first, the family interactions were interpreted as pathogenic: a parent expressing affection in words but showing nonverbal hostility; alliances being made between different family members; families having secrets; or one family member being singled out as a scapegoat to be blamed for the family's troubles. As more and more families were studied, however, such patterns were found in many families, not just in those families with a schizophrenic child. Although this line of research did not uncover the cause of schizophrenia, it revealed that normal, ordinary families can often seem dysfunctional, or, in the words of one study, they may be "difficult environments for interaction."

The Myth of Parental Determinism

The kind of family a child grows up in leaves a profound, lifelong impact. But a growing body of studies shows that early family experience is not the all-powerful, irreversible influence it has sometimes been thought to be. An unfortunate childhood does not doom a person to an unhappy adulthood. Nor does a happy childhood guarantee a similarly blessed future (Emde and Harmon, 1984; Macfarlane, 1964; Rubin, 1996).

Any parent knows that child rearing is not like molding clay or writing on a blank slate. Rather, it's a two-way process in which both parent and child influence each other. Children come into this world with their own temperaments and other characteristics. Moreover, from a very early age, children are active perceivers and thinkers. Finally, parents and children do not live in a social vacuum; children are also influenced by the world around them and the people in it—relatives, family friends, their neighborhoods, other children, their schools, as well as the media.

The traditional view of parental determinism has been challenged by the extreme opposite view. Psychologist Judith Rich Harris asserts that parents have very little impact on their children's development. In her book, *The Nurture Assumption: Why Children Turn Out the Way They Do* (1998), Harris argues that genetics and peer groups, not parents, determine how a child will develop. As in so many debates about the family, both extremes oversimplify complex realities.

The Myth of a Stable Past

As we have seen, laments about the current state of decay of the family imply some earlier era when the family was more stable and harmonious. Historians have not, in fact, located a golden age of the family. Nor have they found any time or place when families did not vary in many ways from whatever the standard model was. Indeed, they have found that premarital sexuality, illegitimacy, and generational conflict can best be studied as a part of family life itself rather than as separate categories of deviation.

The most shocking finding of recent years is the prevalence of child abandonment and infanticide throughout European history. It now appears that infanticide provided a major means of population control in all societies lacking reliable contraception, Europe included, and that it was practiced by families on legitimate children (Hrdy, 1999).

Rather than being a simple instinctive trait, having profound love for a newborn child seems to require two things: the infant must have a decent chance of surviving, and the parents must feel that the infant is not competing with them and their older children in a struggle for survival. Throughout many centuries of European history, both of these conditions were lacking.

Another myth about the family is that it has been a static, unchanging form until recently, when it began to come apart. In reality, families have always been in flux; when the world around them changes, families have to change in response. At periods when a whole society undergoes some major transformation, family change may be especially rapid and dislocating.

In many ways, the era we are living through now resembles two earlier periods of family crisis and transformation in U.S. history (see Skolnick, 1991). The first occurred in the early nineteenth century, when the industrial era moved work out of the home (Ryan, 1981). In the older pattern, most people lived on farms. A father was not only the head of the household, but also boss of the family enterprise. The mother, children, and hired hands worked under his supervision.

When work moved out, however, so did the father and the older sons and daughters, leaving behind the mother and the younger children. These dislocations unleashed an era of personal stress and cultural confusion. Eventually, a new model of family emerged that not only reflected the new separation of work and family, but also glorified it.

The household now became idealized as "home sweet home," an emotional and spiritual shelter from the heartless world outside. Many of our culture's most basic ideas about the family and gender were formed at this time. The mother-at-home, father-out-at-work model that most people think of as "traditional" was in fact the first version of the modern family.

Historians label this nineteenth century model of the family "Victorian" because it became influential in England and Western Europe, as well as in the United States, during the reign of Queen Victoria. It reflected, in idealized form, the nineteenth-century middle-class family. The Victorian model became the prevailing cultural definition of family, but few families could live up to the ideal in all its particulars. Working-class, black, and ethnic families, for example, could not get by without the economic contributions of wives, mothers, and daughters. Even for middle-class families, the Victorian ideal prescribed a standard of perfection that was virtually impossible to fulfill (Demos, 1986).

Eventually, social change overtook the Victorian model. Beginning around the 1880s, another period of rapid economic, social, and cultural change unsettled Victorian family patterns, especially their gender arrangements. Several generations of "new women" challenged Victorian notions of femininity. They became educated, pursued careers, became involved in political causes—including their own—and created the first wave of feminism. This ferment culminated in the victory of the women's suffrage movement—the movement was followed by the 1920s jazz-age era of flappers and flaming youth—the first, and probably the major, sexual revolution of the twentieth century.

Another cultural crisis ensued, until a new cultural blueprint emerged—the companionate model of marriage and the family. The new model was a modern, more relaxed version of the Victorian family; companionship and sexual intimacy were now defined as central to marriage.

This highly abbreviated history of family and cultural change forms the necessary backdrop for understanding the family upheavals of the late twentieth and early twenty-first centuries. As in earlier times, major changes in the economy and society have destabilized an existing model of family life and the everyday patterns and practices that have sustained it.

In the last half of the twentieth century, we experienced a triple revolution: first, the move toward a postindustrial service and information economy; second, a life course revolution brought about by reductions in mortality and fertility; and third, a psychological transformation rooted mainly in rising educational levels. Although these shifts have profound implications for everyone, women have been the pacesetters of change. Most women's lives and expectations over the past three decades, inside and outside the family, have departed drastically from those of their own mothers. Men's lives today are also different from their fathers' generation, but to a much lesser extent.

THE TRIPLE REVOLUTION

The Postindustrial Family

A service and information economy produces large numbers of jobs that, unlike factory work, seem suitable for women. Yet as Jessie Bernard (1982) once observed, the transformation of a housewife into a paid worker outside the home sends tremors through every family relationship. It blurs the sharp contrast between men's and women's roles that mark the breadwinner–homemaker pattern. It also reduces women's economic dependence on men, thereby making it easier for women to leave unhappy marriages.

Beyond drawing women out of the home, shifts in the nature of work and a rapidly changing globalized economy have unsettled the lives of individuals and families at all class levels. The well-paying industrial jobs that once enabled a blue-collar worker to own a home and support a family have disappeared. The once steady secure jobs that sustained the "organization men" and their families in the 1950s and 1960s have been made shaky by downsizing, outsourcing, an unstable economy, corporate takeovers, and a rapid pace of technological change.

The new economic uncertainty has also made the transition to adulthood increasingly problematic. In the postwar years, particularly in the United States, young people entered adulthood in one giant step. They found jobs, often out of high school, married young, left home, and had children quickly. Today, few young adults can afford to marry and have children in their late teens or early twenties. In an economy where a college degree is necessary to earn a living wage, early marriage impedes education for both men and women.

Those who do not go on to college have little access to jobs that can sustain a family. Particularly in the inner cities of the United States, growing numbers of young people have come to see no future for themselves in the ordinary world of work. In middle-class families, a narrowing opportunity structure has increased anxieties about downward mobility for offspring and parents as well. Because of the new economic and social realities, a new stage of life has opened up between adolescence and adulthood. It is simply impossible for most young people in today's postindustrial societies to become financially and emotionally independent at the same ages as earlier generations did.

This new stage of life is so new it doesn't have an agreed-on name. It has been called "arrested development," "adultolescence," or "emerging adulthood." And many people assume that today's younger generations are simply slackers—unwilling to grow up, get jobs, and start their own families. But the fact is that today's economy demands more schooling than ever before, and jobs that can sustain a family are fewer and less permanent than ever before. These difficulties did not begin with the Great Recession, but the economic outlook for young adults has grown worse since the financial meltdown of 2008.

The Life Course Revolution

It's not just the rise of a new economy that has reshaped the stages of life. The basic facts of life and death changed drastically in the twentieth century. In 1900, average life expectancy was 47 years. Infants had the highest mortality rates, but young and middle-aged adults were often struck down by infectious diseases. Before the turn of the twentieth century, only 40 percent of women lived through all the stages of a normal life course: growing up, marrying, having children, and surviving with a spouse to the age of 50 (Uhlenberg, 1980).

Declining mortality rates have had a profound effect on women's lives. Women today are living longer and having fewer children. When infant and child mortality rates fall, women no longer have five, seven, or nine children to ensure that two or three will survive to adulthood. After rearing children, the average woman can look forward to three or four decades without maternal responsibilities.

One of the most important changes in contemporary marriage is the potential length of marriage and the number of years spent without children in the home. Our current high divorce rates may be a by-product of this shift. By the 1970s, the statistically average couple spent only 18 percent of their married lives raising young children, compared with 54 percent a century ago (Bane, 1976). As a result, marriage is becoming defined less as a union between parents raising a brood of children and more as a personal relationship between two individuals.

A Psychological Revolution

The third major transformation is a set of psychocultural changes that might be described as *psychological gentrification* (Skolnick, 1991). That is, cultural advantages once enjoyed by only the upper classes—in particular, education—have been extended to those lower down on the socioeconomic scale. Psychological gentrification also involves greater leisure time, travel, and exposure to information, as well as a general rise in the standard of living. Despite the persistence of poverty, unemployment, and economic insecurity in the industrialized world, far less of the population than in the historical past is living at the level of sheer subsistence.

Throughout Western society, rising levels of education and related changes have been linked to a complex set of shifts in personal and political attitudes. One of these is a more psychological approach to life—greater introspectiveness and a yearning for warmth and intimacy in family and other relationships (Veroff, Douvan, and Kulka, 1981). There is also evidence of an increasing preference on the part of both men and women for a more companionate ideal of marriage and a more democratic family. More broadly, these changes in attitude have been described as a shift to "postmaterialist values," emphasizing self-expression, tolerance, equality, and a concern for the quality of life (Inglehart, 1990).

The multiple social transformations of our era have brought both costs and benefits: Family relations have become both more fragile and more emotionally rich; longevity has brought us a host of problems as well as the gift of extended life. Although change has brought greater opportunities for women, persisting gender inequality means women have borne a large share of the costs of these gains. We cannot turn the clock back to the family models of the past.

Despite the upheavals of recent decades, the emotional and cultural significance of the family persists. Family remains the center of most people's lives and, as numerous surveys show, is a cherished value. Although marriage has become more fragile, the parent–child relationship—especially the mother–child relationship—remains a core attachment across the life course (Rossi and Rossi, 1990). The family, however, can be both "here to stay" and beset with difficulties.

Most European countries have recognized for some time that governments must play a role in supplying an array of supports to families, such as health care, children's allowances, and housing subsidies. Working parents are offered child care, parental leave, and shorter workdays. Services are provided for the elderly.

Each country's response to these changes, as we noted earlier, has been shaped by its own political and cultural traditions. The United States remains embroiled in a cultural war over the family; many social commentators and political leaders have promised to reverse the recent trends and restore the "traditional" family. In contrast, other Western nations, including Canada and other English-speaking countries, have responded to family change by trying to remedy the problems brought about by economic and social transformations. These countries have been spared much of the poverty and other social ills that have plagued the United States in recent decades.

Looking Ahead

The world in the early twenty-first century is vastly different from what it was at the beginning, or even the middle, of the last century. Our public and private policies have not kept up with the new realities of family life. Ironically, despite all the changes, despite all the talk about the "decline of the family" family ties are more important than ever.

Far from having "lost its functions," as some social theorists used to put it, the family plays a critical role in the health and well-being of its members, the education and life chances of its children. But families are not the freestanding, self-sufficient foundation stones of society our political rhetoric assumes them to be. They live in an entire socio-economic and cultural landscape from the Internet to fast food to a fast-changing global economy in which few jobs are steady, most do not support middle-class living standards, and the great majority of mothers have to work outside the home.

Still, there is no reason to be nostalgic for some earlier golden age. Our current troubles inside and outside the family are genuine, but we should never forget that many of the most vexing issues confronting us derive from benefits of modernization few of us would be willing to give up—for example, longer, healthier lives, and the ability to choose how many children to have and when to have them.

When most people died before they reached age 50, there was no problem of a large elderly population to care for. Nor was adolescence a difficult stage of life when children worked education was a privilege of the rich, and a person's place in society was determined by heredity rather than choice.

In short, family life is bound up with the social, economic, and cultural circumstances of particular times and places. We are no longer peasants, Puritans, or even suburbanites in the 1950s. We are all pioneers, facing a world earlier generations could hardly imagine, and we must struggle to find new ways to cope with it.

A NOTE ON *THE FAMILY*

Some family scholars have suggested that we drop the term *the family* and replace it with *families* or *family life*. They argue that the problem with *the family* is that it calls to mind the stereotyped image of the Ozzie and Harriet kind of family—two parents and their two or three minor children. But those other terms don't always work. In our own writing we use the term *the family* in much the same way we use *the economy*—a set of institutional arrangements through which particular tasks are carried out in a society. The economy deals with the production, distribution, and consumption of goods and services. The family deals with reproduction and care and support for children and adults.

References

Amato, P. R. 1994. Life span adjustment of children to their parents' divorce. *The Future of Children* 4, no. 1 (Spring).

Bane, M. J. 1976. *Here to Stay*. New York: Basic Books.

Bernard, J. 1982. *The Future of Marriage*. New York: Bantam.

Demos, J. 1986. *Past, Present, and Personal*. New York: Oxford University Press.

Emde, R. N., and R. J. Harmon, eds. 1984. *Continuities and Discontinuities in Development*. New York: Plenum Press.

Featherstone, J. 1979. Family matters. *Harvard Educational Review* 49, no. 1: 20–52.

Geertz, G. 1965. The impact of the concept of culture on the concept of man. In *New Views of the Nature of Man*, edited by J. R. Platt. Chicago: University of Chicago Press.

Harris, J. R. 1998. *The Nurture Assumption: Why Children Turn Out the Way They Do*. New York: Free Press.

Hrdy, S. B. 1999. *Mother Nature*. New York: Pantheon Books.

Inglehart, R. 1990. *Culture Shift*. Princeton, NJ: Princeton University Press.

Keller, S. 1971. Does the family have a future? *Journal of Comparative Studies*, Spring.

Macfarlane, J. W. 1964. Perspectives on personality consistency and change from the guidance study. *Vita Humana* 7: 115–126.

Mellman, A., E. Lazarus, and A. Rivlin. 1990. Family time, family values. In *Rebuilding the Nest*, edited by D. Blankenhorn, S. Bayme, and J. Elshtain. Milwaukee, WI: Family Service America.

Rossi, A. S., and P. H. Rossi. 1990. *Of Human Bonding: Parent–Child Relations across the Life Course*. Hawthorne, NY: Aldine de Gruyter.

Rubin, L. 1996. *The Transcendent Child*. New York: Basic Books.

Ryan, M. 1981. *The Cradle of the Middle Class*. New York: Cambridge University Press.

Skolnick, A. 1991. *Embattled Paradise: The American Family in an Age of Uncertainty*. New York: Basic Books.

Stephens, W. N. 1963. *The Family in Cross-Cultural Perspective*. New York: World.

Uhlenberg, P. 1980. Death and the family. *Journal of Family History* 5, no. 3: 313–320.

Veroff, J., E. Douvan, and R. A. Kulka. 1981. *The Inner American: A Self-Portrait from 1957 to 1976*. New York: Basic Books.

The Changing Family

Over the past four decades, family matters have been much in the news. For much of the time, the media have supplied an endless stream of stories and statistics that seem to document the decline and fall of marriage and the family as we knew them in the past. Conservatives denounce family change, blaming it on a loss of "values." They warn that recent changes in marriage and family patters threaten the survival of American society.

Social scientists have been arguing for many years about how to define the family, even before the dramatic changes of the past four decades. Now the question of how to define the family has become a hot political issue. Are a mother and her child a family? A cohabiting couple? A cohabiting couple with children? A married couple without children? A grandmother who is raising her grandchildren? A gay couple? A gay couple with children?

In fact, despite all the changes and diversity, most Americans still marry and have children at some point in their lives. However, as William J. Good argues in his classic article, "The Theoretical Importance of the Family," we should not think of "family" as particular kind of group living together under one roof. Rather, he defines family as a special *kind* of relationship between people. He argues that in all known societies, and under many social conditions, people develop family-like social patterns—a "familistic package."

What is in this "familistic package"? One essential element is continuity—the expectation that the relationship will last through time. This makes it possible to share money and goods and offer help to the other person, knowing that in the future that person will reciprocate. In addition, familiarity is another benefit; family members know one another and their likes and dislikes, such as how each person likes their coffee or tea. One of the most important elements in the package is that the family is something like a mutual aid society. It helps individuals meet their multiple needs, and also serves as an insurance policy in times of sickness or other troubles. Finally, family members develop emotion bonds with one another, stronger and yet more ambivalent than with people outside the group.

But family relationships do not take place in a social vacuum. They are profoundly affected by the world outside the home—from the immediate neighborhood, to government policies, to events such as wars, disasters and depressions, or other aspects of the historical times they are living in.

Several of the selections hear explain these links. For example, Anthony Giddens argues we are living through a major historical transition, a wave of technological and economic modernization that is having a profound impact on personal life. Giddens labels this wave of large scale change "globalization"; others call it the shift from industrial to postindustrial society. As a result, he argues, there is "global revolution" going on in sexuality, in marriage and the family, and in how people think of themselves and their relationships.

Further, Giddens sees a strong parallel between the ideals of a democratic society and the emerging new ideals of family relationships. For example, a good marriage is coming to be seen as a relationship between equals. Giddens recognizes that many of the changes in family life are worrisome, but we can't go back to the family patterns of an earlier time.

Nor would most of us really want to step into a time machine. Nostalgic images of the family in earlier times typically omit the high mortality rates that prevailed before the twentieth century. Death could strike at any age, and was a constant threat to family stability. No historian has located a past golden age of family happiness that we have sadly lost.

Nevertheless, people continue to worry about the state of the family in the Unites States. Often this worry has little to do with the realities of family life, or the serious problems that plague too many families, such as economic hardship or the lack of health care. Indeed, economists and others have been warning about growing income inequality for the past three decades. Yet the problem has only recently been noticed by the media and politicians, mostly because of the noisy demonstrations of the Occupy Movement and their slogan targeting the "1" versus the "99."

One persistent worry in the United States is that the "social fabric" is shredding, and individuals are becoming more and more isolated from friends and family. Every so often the media trumpet a bit of research that seems to prove the decline in social ties. Claude Fischer has examined a large body of survey data from 1970 to the 2000s to see how valid these worries are. It seems that once again the media have been too eager to announce dramatic trends. Fischer finds very few noteworthy trends. Despite all the changes in demography, technology, and society, relationships with family and friends continue to offer both emotional and material support.

Another worry is the unsettled place of women in postindustrial society. As women increasingly participate in the paid workforce, argues Sharon Hays, they find themselves caught up in a web of cultural contradictions that remain unresolved and indeed have deepened over the years. There is no way, she says, for contemporary women to get it "just right." Both stay-at-home and working mothers maintain an intensive commitment to motherhood. Women who stay at home no longer feel comfortable and fulfilled being defined by themselves and others as "mere housewives." And, working women are typically anxious about the time away from children and the complexities of balancing parental duties with the demands of the job.

The cultural contradictions that trouble motherhood can be seen as a part of the larger "cultural war" over the family. But there are more than two sides in the family wars. Janet Z. Giele carefully draws three positions on the family: the conservative, the liberal, and the feminist. The latter, for Giele, is the most promising for developing public policies that would combine conservative and liberal perspectives. The feminist vision, she argues, appreciates both the "premodern nature of the family" with the inevitable interdependence of family and a modern, fast-changing economy.

1

Families Past and Present

The Theoretical Importance of the Family

William J. Goode

Through the centuries, thoughtful people have observed that the family was disintegrating. In the past several decades, this idea has become more and more common. Many analysts have reported that the family no longer performs tasks once entrusted to it—production, education, protection, for example. From these and other data we might conclude that the family is on its way out.

But almost everyone who lives out an average life span enters the married state. Most eventually have children, who will later do the same. Of the increasing number who divorce, many will hopefully or skeptically marry again. In the Western nations, a higher percentage of people marry than a century ago. Indeed, the total number of years spent within marriage by the average person is higher now than at any previous time in the history of the world. In all known societies, almost everyone lives enmeshed in a network of family rights and obligations. People are taught to accept these rules through a long period of childhood socialization. That is, people come to feel that these family patterns are both right and desirable.

At the present time, human beings appear to get as much joy and sorrow from the family as they always have, and seem as bent as ever on taking part in family life. In most of the world, the traditional family may be shaken, but the institution will probably enjoy a longer life than any nation now in existence. The family does not seem to be a powerful institution, like the military, the church, or the state, but it seems to be the most resistant to conquest, or to the efforts people make to reshape it. Any specific family may appear to be fragile or unstable, but the family system as a whole is tough and resilient.

THE FAMILY: VARIOUS VIEWS

The intense emotional meaning of family relations for almost everyone has been observed throughout history. Philosophers and social analysts have noted that any society is a structure made up of families linked together. Both travelers and anthropologists often describe the peculiarities of a given society by outlining its family relations.

.The earliest moral and ethical writings of many cultures assert the significance of the family.Within those commentaries, the view is often expressed that a society loses its strength if people do not fulfill family obligations. Confucius thought that happiness and prosperity would prevail if everyone would behave "correctly" as a family member. This meant primarily that no one should fail in his filial obligations. That is, the proper relationship between ruler and subjects was like that between a father and his children. The cultural importance of the family is also emphasized in the Old Testament. The books of Exodus, Deuteronomy, Ecclesiastes, Psalms, and Proverbs, for example, proclaim the importance of obeying family rules. The earliest codified literature in India, the Rig-Veda, which dates from about the last half of the second millennium B.C., and the Law of Manu, which dates from about the beginning of the Christian era, devote much attention to the family. Poetry, plays, novels, and short stories typically seize upon family relationships as the primary focus of human passion, and their ideas and themes often grow from family conflict. Even the great epic poems of war have subthemes focusing on problems in family relations.[1]

From time to time, social analysts and philosophers have presented plans for societies that *might* be created (these are called utopias) in which new family roles (rights and obligations of individual members) are offered as solutions to traditional social problems. Plato's *Republic* is one such attempt. Plato was probably the first to urge the creation of a society in which all members, men and women alike, would have an equal opportunity to develop their talents to the utmost, and to achieve a position in society solely through merit. Since family patterns in all societies prevent selection based entirely on individual worth, to Plato's utopia the tie between parents and children would play no part, because knowledge of that link would be erased. Approved conception would take place at the same time each year at certain hymeneal festivals; children born out of season would be eliminated (along with those born defective). All children would be taken from their parents at birth and reared by specially designated people.

Experimental or utopian communities like Oneida, the Shakers, the Mormons, and modern communes have typically insisted that changes in family relations were necessary to achieve their goals. Every fundamental political upheaval since the French Revolution of 1789 has offered a program that included profound changes in family relations. Since World War II, most countries of the world have written new constitutions. In perhaps all of them, but especially in all the less developed nations, these new laws have been far more advanced than public opinion in those countries. They have aimed at creating new family patterns more in conformity with the leaders' views of equality and justice, and often antagonistic to traditional family systems. This wide range of commentary, analysis, and political action, over a period of twenty-five hundred years, suggests that throughout history we have been at least implicitly aware of the importance of family patterns as a central element in human societies.

THE CENTRAL POSITION OF THE FAMILY IN SOCIETY

In most tribal societies, kinship patterns form the major part of the whole social structure. By contrast, the family is only a small part of the social structure of modern industrial societies. It is nevertheless a key element in them, specifically linking individuals with other social institutions, such as the church, the state, or the economy. Indeed modern society, with its complex advanced technology and its highly trained bureaucracy, would collapse without the contributions of this seemingly primitive social agency. The class system, too, including its restrictions on education and opportunity, its high or low social mobility rates, and its initial social placement by birth, is founded on the family.

Most important, it is within the family that the child is first socialized to serve the needs of the society, and not only its own needs. A society will not survive unless its needs are met, such as the production and distribution of commodities, protection of the young and old or the sick and the pregnant, conformity to the law, and so on. Only if individuals are motivated to serve these needs will the society continue to operate, and the foundation for that motivation is laid by the family. Family members also participate in informal social control processes. Socialization at early ages makes most of us wish to conform, but throughout each day, both as children and as adults, we are often tempted to deviate. The formal agencies of social control (such as the police) are not enough to do more than force the extreme deviant to conform. What is needed is a set of social pressures that provide feedback to the individual whenever he or she does well or poorly and thus support internal controls as well as the controls of the formal agencies. Effectively or not, the family usually takes on this task.

The family, then, is made up of individuals, but it is also a social unit, and part of a larger social network. Families are not isolated, self-enclosed social systems; and the other institutions of society, such as the military, the church, or the school system, continually rediscover that they are not dealing with individuals, but with members of families. Even in the most industrialized and urban of societies, where it is sometimes supposed that people lead rootless and anonymous lives, most people are in continual interaction with other family members. Men and women who achieve high social position usually find that even as adults they still respond to their parents' criticisms, are still angered or hurt by a sibling's scorn. Corporations that offer substantial opportunities to rising executives often find that their proposals are turned down because of objections from family members.

So it is through the family that the society is able to elicit from the individual his or her contributions. The family, in turn, can continue to exist only if it is supported by the larger society. If these two, the smaller and the larger social system, furnish each other the conditions necessary for their survival, they must be interrelated in many important ways. Thus, the two main themes in this [reading] will be the relations among family members, and the relations between the family and the society.

PRECONCEPTIONS ABOUT THE FAMILY

The task of understanding the family presents many difficulties, and one of the greatest barriers is found in ourselves. We are likely to have strong emotions about the family. Because of our own deep involvement in family relationships, objective analysis is not easy. When we read about other types of family behavior, in other classes or societies, we are likely to feel that they are odd or improper. We are tempted to argue that this or that type of family behavior is wrong or right, rather than to analyze it. Second, although we have observed many people in some of their family behavior, usually we have had very limited experience with what goes on behind the walls of other homes. This means that our sample of observations is very narrow. It also means that for almost any generalization we create or read about, we can often find some specific experience that refutes it, or fits it. Since we feel we "already know," we may not feel motivated to look for further data against which to test generalizations.

However, many supposedly well-known beliefs about the family are not well grounded in fact. Others are only partly true and must be studied more precisely if they are to be understood. One such belief is that "children hold the family together." Despite repeated attempts to affirm it, this generalization does not seem to be very strong. A more correct view seems to be that there is a modest association between divorce and not having children, but it is mostly caused by the fact that people who do not become well adjusted, and who may for some reasons be prone to divorce, are also less likely to have children.

Another way of checking whether the findings of family sociology are obvious is to present some research findings, and ask whether it was worth the bother of discovering them since "everybody knew them all along." Consider the following set of facts. Suppose a researcher had demonstrated those facts. Was it worthwhile to carry out the study, or were the facts already known?

1. Because modern industrial society breaks down traditional family systems, one result is that the age of marriage in Western nations (which was low among farmers) has risen greatly over many generations.
2. Because of the importance of the extended family in China and India, the average size of the household has always been large, with many generations living under one roof.
3. In polygynous societies, most men have several wives, and the fertility rate is higher than in monogamous societies.

Although these statements sound plausible to many people, and impressive arguments have been presented to support them, in fact they are all false. For hundreds of years, the age at marriage among farmers in Western nations has been relatively high (25–27 years), and though it rises and falls somewhat over time, there seems to be no important trend in any particular direction. With reference to multifamily households, every survey of Chinese and Indian households has shown that even generations ago they were relatively modest in size (from four to six persons, varying by region and time period). Only under special historical circumstances will large, extended households be common. As to polygyny, the fact is that except under special circumstances, almost all men in all societies must be content with only one wife, and the fertility rate of polygynous marriages (one man married to several wives) is lower than that for monogamous marriages. Thus we see that with reference to the incorrect findings just cited, common beliefs did require testing, and they were wrong.

On the other hand, of course, many popular beliefs about how families work *are* correct. We cannot assume their correctness, however. Instead, we have to examine our observations, and make studies on our own to see how well these data fit in order to improve our understanding of the dynamics of family processes in our own or in other societies. If we emphasize the problems of obtaining facts, we should not lose sight of the central truth of any science: vast quantities of figures may be entirely meaningless, unless the search is guided by fruitful hypotheses or broad conceptions of social behavior. What we seek is organized facts, a structure of propositions, in which theory and fact illuminate one another. If we do not seek actual observation, we are engaged in blind speculation. If we seek facts without theoretical guidance, our search is random and often yields findings that have no bearing on anything. Understanding the family, then, requires the same sort of careful investigation as any other scientific endeavor.

WHY THE FAMILY IS THEORETICALLY SIGNIFICANT

Because the family is so much taken for granted, we do not often stop to consider the many traits that make it theoretically interesting. A brief consideration of certain peculiarities of the family will suggest why it is worthwhile exploring this social unit.

The family is the only social institution other than religion that is formally developed in all societies: a specific social agency is in charge of a great variety of social behaviors and activities. Some have argued that legal systems did not exist in preliterate or technologically less developed tribes or societies because there was no formally organized legislative body or judiciary. Of course, it is possible to abstract from concrete behavior the legal *aspects* of action, or the economic aspects, or the political dynamics, even when there are no explicitly labeled agencies formally in control of these areas in the society. However, kinship statuses and their responsibilities are the object of both formal and informal attention in societies at a high or a low technological level.

Family duties are the direct role responsibility of everyone in the society, with rare exceptions. Almost everyone is both born into a family and founds one of his or her own. Each individual is kin to many others. Many people, by contrast, may escape the religious duties others take for granted, or military or political burdens. Moreover, many family role responsibilities cannot usually be delegated to others, while in a work situation specialized obligations can be delegated.

Taking part in family activities has the further interesting quality that though it is not backed by the formal punishments supporting many other obligations, almost everyone takes part nonetheless. We must, for example, engage in economic or productive acts, or face starvation. We must enter the army, pay taxes, and appear before courts, or face money penalties and force. Such punishments do not usually confront the individual who does not wish to marry, or refuses to talk with his father or brother. Nevertheless, so pervasive are the social pressures, and so intertwined with indirect or direct rewards and punishments, that almost everyone conforms, or claims to conform, to family demands.

Although the family is usually thought of as an *expressive* or emotional social unit, it serves as an *instrumental* agency for the larger social structures, and all other institutions and agencies depend upon its contributions. For example, the role behavior learned within the family becomes the model or prototype for behavior required in other segments of the society. Inside the family, the content of the *socialization* process is the cultural tradition of the larger society. Families are also themselves *economic* units with respect to production and allocation. With reference to *social control*, each person's total range of behavior, and how his or her time and energies are budgeted, is more easily visible to family members than to outsiders. They can evaluate how the individual is allocating his or her time and money, and how well he or she is carrying out various duties. Consequently, the family acts as a source of pressure on the individual to adjust—to work harder and play less, or go to church less and study more. In all these ways, the family is partly an instrument or agent of the larger society. If it fails to perform adequately, the goals of the larger society may not be effectively achieved.

Perhaps more interesting theoretically is the fact that the various *tasks of the family are all separable* from one another, but in fact are not separated in almost all known family systems. Here are some of the contributions of the family to the larger society: reproduction of young, physical maintenance of family members, social placement of the child, socialization, and social control.

Let us consider how these activities could be separated. For example, the mother could send her child to be fed in a neighborhood mess hall, and of course some harassed mothers do send their children to buy lunch in a local snack bar. Those who give birth to a child need not socialize the child. They might send the child to specialists, and indeed specialists do take more responsibility for this task as the child grows older. Parents might, as some eugenicists have suggested, be selected for their breeding qualities, but these might not include any great talent for training the young. Status placement might be accomplished by random drawing of lots, by IQ tests or periodic examinations in physical and intellectual skills, or by popularity polls. This assignment of children to various social positions could be done without regard to an individual's parents, those who socialized or fed the child, or others who might supervise the child's daily behavior.

Separations of this kind have been suggested from time to time, and a few hesitant attempts have been made here and there in the world to put them into operation. However, three conclusions relevant to this kind of division can be drawn: (1) In all known societies, the *ideal* (with certain qualifications to be noted) is that the family be entrusted with all these functions. (2) When one or more family tasks are entrusted to another agency by a revolutionary or utopian society, the change can be made only with the support of much ideological fervor, and usually political pressure as well. (3) These experiments are also characterized by a gradual return to the more traditional type of family. In both the Israeli *kibbutzim* and the Russian experiments in relieving parents of child care, the ideal of completely communal living was once urged. Husband and wife were to have only a personal and emotional tie with one another: divorce would be easy. The children were to see their parents at regular intervals but look to their nursery attendants and mother surrogates for affection and direction during work hours. Each individual was to contribute his or her best skills to the cooperative unit without regard to family ties or sex status (there would be few or no "female" or "male" tasks). That ideal was attempted in a modest way, but behavior gradually dropped away from the ideal. The only other country in which the pattern has been attempted on a large scale is China. Already Chinese communes have retreated from their high ambitions, following the path of the *kibbutz* and the Russian *kolkhoz*.

Various factors contribute to these deviations from attempts to create a new type of family, and the two most important sets of pressures cannot easily be separated from each other. First is the problem, also noted by Plato, that individuals who develop their own attitudes and behaviors in the usual Western (European and European-based) family system do not easily adjust to the communal "family" even when they believe it is the right way. The second is the likelihood that when the family is radically changed, the various relations between it and the larger society are changed. New strains are created, demanding new kinds of adjustments on the part of the individuals in the society. Perhaps the planners must develop somewhat different agencies, or a different blueprint, to transform the family.

These comments have nothing to do with "capitalism" in its current political and economic argument with "communism." They merely describe the historical fact that though various experiments in separating the major functions of the family from one another have been conducted, none of these evolved from a previously existing family system. In addition, the several modern important attempts at such a separation, including the smaller communes that were created in the United States during the 1960s and 1970s, mostly exhibit a common pattern, a movement *away* from the utopian blueprint of separating the various family activities and giving each of them to a different social unit.

It is possible that some of these activities (meals) can be more easily separated than others; or that some family systems (for example, matrilineal systems) might lend themselves to such a separation more easily than others. On the other hand, we have to begin with the data that are now available. Even cautiously interpreted, they suggest that the family is a rather stable institution. On the other hand, we have not yet analyzed what this particular institution is. In the next section we discuss this question.

DEFINING THE FAMILY: A MATTER OF MORE OR LESS

Since thousands of publications have presented research findings on the family, one might suppose that there must be agreement on what this social unit is. In fact, sociologists and anthropologists have argued for decades about how to define it. Indeed, creating a clear, formal definition of any object of study is sometimes more difficult than making a study of that object. If we use a *concrete* definition, and assert that "a family is a social unit made up of father, mother, and children," then only about 35 percent of all U.S. households can be classed as a family. Much of the research on the family would have to exclude a majority of residential units. In addition, in some societies, one wife may be married to several husbands, or one husband to several wives. The definition would exclude such units. In a few societies there have been "families" in which the "husband" was a woman; and in some, certain "husbands" were not expected to live with their "wives." In the United States, millions of households contain at least one child, but only one parent. In a few communes, every adult male is married to all other adult females. That is, there are many kinds of social units that seem to be like a family, but do not fit almost any concrete definition that we might formulate.

We can escape such criticisms in part by claiming that most adults eventually go through such a *phase* of family life; that is, almost all men and women in the

United States marry at some time during their lives, and most of them eventually have children. Nevertheless, analysis of the family would be much thinner if we focused only on that one kind of household. In ordinary language usage, people are most likely to agree that a social unit made up of father, mother, and child or children is a genuine family. They will begin to disagree more and more, as one or more of those persons or social roles is missing. Few people would agree that, at the other extremes, a household with only a single person in it is a family. Far more would think of a household as a family if it comprised a widow and her several children. Most people would agree that a husband-wife household is a family if they have children, even if their children are now living somewhere else. However, many would not be willing to class a childless couple as a family, especially if that couple planned never to have children. Very few people would be willing to accept a homosexual couple as a family.

What can we learn from such ordinary language usage? First, that *family* is not a single thing, to be captured by a neat verbal formula. Second, many social units can be thought of as "more or less" families, as they are more or less similar to the traditional type of family. Third, much of this graded similarity can be traced to the different kinds of role relations to be found in that traditional unit. Doubtless the following list is not comprehensive, but it includes most of those relationships: (1) At least two adult persons of opposite sex reside together. [In the United States and some European countries, same sex marriage has been advancing in both public opinion and the law.] (2) They engage in some kind of division of labor; that is, they do not both perform exactly the same tasks. (3) They engage in many types of economic and social exchanges; that is, they do things for one another. (4) They share many things in common, such as food, sex, residence, and both goods and social activities. (5) The adults have parental relations with their children, as their children have filial relations with them; the parents have some authority over their children, and both share with one another, while also assuming some obligation for protection, cooperation, and nurturance. (6) There are sibling relations among the children themselves, with, once more, a range of obligations to share, protect, and help one another. When all these conditions exist, few people would deny that the unit is a family. As we consider households in which more are missing, a larger number of people would express some doubt as to whether it really is a family. Thus, if two adults live together, but do nothing for each other, few people would agree that it is a family. If they do not even live together, fewer still would call the couple a family.

Individuals create all sorts of relations with each other, but others are more or less likely to view them as a family to the extent that their continuing social relations exhibit some or all of the role patterns noted above. Most important for our understanding of the family is that in all known societies, and under a wide range of social conditions, some kinds of familistic living arrangements seem to emerge, with some or all of these traits. These arrangements can emerge in prisons (with homosexual couples as units), under the disorganized conditions of revolution, conquest, or epidemic; or even when political attempts are made to reduce the importance of the family, and instead to press people to live in a more communal fashion. That is, people create and re-create some forms of familistic social patterns even when some of those traditional elements are missing.

This raises the inevitable question: Why does this happen? Why do people continue to form familistic relations, even when they are not convinced that it is the ideal social arrangement? Why is *this* and not some *other* social pattern so widespread? Of course, this is not an argument for the *universality* of the conjugal family. Many other kinds of relations between individuals are created. Nevertheless, some approximation of these familistic relationships do continue to occur in the face of many alternative temptations and opportunities as well as counterpressures. Unless we are willing to assert that people are irrational, we must conclude that these relationships must offer some *advantages*. What are they?

ADVANTAGES OF THE "FAMILISTIC PACKAGE"

We suppose that the most fundamental set of advantages is found in the division of labor and the resulting possibility of social exchanges between husband and wife (or members of a homosexual couple), as well as between children and parents. This includes not only economic goods, but help, nurturance, protection, and affection. It is often forgotten that the modern domestic household is very much an *economic* unit even if it is no longer a farming unit. People are actually producing goods and services for one another. They are buying objects in one place, and transporting them to the household. They are transforming food into meals. They are engaged in cleaning, mowing lawns, repairing, transporting, counseling—a wide array of services that would have to be paid for in money if some member of the family did not do them.

Families of all types also enjoy some small economies of scale. When there are two or more members of the household, various kinds of activities can be done almost as easily for everyone as for a single person; it is almost as easy to prepare one meal for three or four people as it is to prepare a similar meal for one person. Thus, the cost of a meal is less per person within a family. Families can cooperate to achieve what an individual cannot, from building a mountain cabin to creating a certain style of life. Help from all members will make it much easier to achieve that goal than it would be for one person.

All the historic forms of the family that we know, including communal group marriages, are also attractive because they offer *continuity*. Thus, whatever the members produce together, they expect to be able to enjoy together later. Continuity has several implications. One is that members do not have to bear the costs of continually searching for new partners, or for new members who might be "better" at various family tasks. In addition, husband and wife, as well as children, enjoy a much longer line of social credit than they would have if they were making exchanges with people outside the family. This means that an individual can give more at one time to someone in the family, knowing that in the longer run this will not be a loss: the other person will remain long enough to reciprocate at some point, or perhaps still another member will offer help at a later time.

Next, the familistic mode of living offers several of the advantages of any informal group.[2] It exhibits, for example, a very short line of communication; everyone is close by, and members need not communicate through intermediaries. Thus they can respond quickly in case of need. A short line of communication makes cooperation much easier. Second, everyone has many idiosyncratic needs and wishes. In day to day interaction with outsiders, we need not adjust to these very much, and they may be a nuisance;

others, in turn, are likely not to adjust to our own idiosyncracies. However, within the familistic mode of social interaction, people learn what each other's idiosyncratic needs are. Learning such needs can and does make life together somewhat more attractive because adjusting to them may not be a great burden, but does give pleasure to the other. These include such trivia as how strong the tea or coffee should be, how much talk there will be at meals, sleep and work schedules, levels of noise, and so on. Of course with that knowledge we can more easily make others miserable, too, if we wish to do so.

Domestic tasks typically do not require high expertise, and as a consequence most members of the family can learn to do them eventually. Because they do learn, members derive many benefits from one another, without having to go outside the family unit. Again, this makes a familistic mode of living more attractive than it would be otherwise. In addition, with reference to many such tasks, there are no outside experts anyway (throughout most of world history, there have been no experts in childrearing, taking care of small cuts or bruises, murmuring consoling words in response to some distress, and so on). That is, the tasks within a family setting are likely to be tasks at which insiders are at least as good as outsiders, and typically better.

No other social institutions offer this range of complementarities, sharing, and closely linked, interwoven advantages. The closest possible exception might be some ascribed, ritual friendships in a few societies, but even these do not offer the range of exchanges that are to be found in the familistic processes.

We have focused on advantages that the *members* of families obtain from living under this type of arrangement. However, when we survey the wide range of family patterns in hundreds of societies, we are struck by the fact that this social unit is strongly supported by *outsiders*—that is, members of the larger society.

It is supported by a structure of norms, values, laws, and a wide range of social pressures. More concretely, other members of the society believe such units are necessary, and they are concerned about how people discharge their obligations within the family. They punish members of the family who do not conform to ideal behavior, and praise those who do conform. These intrusions are not simply whimsical, or a matter of oppression. Other members of the society do in fact have a stake in how families discharge their various tasks. More broadly, it is widely believed that the collective needs of the whole society are served by some of the activities individual families carry out. In short, it is characteristic of the varieties of the family that participants on an average enjoy more, and gain more comfort, pleasure, or advantage from being in a familistic arrangement than from living alone; and *other* members of the society view that arrangement as contributing in some measure to the survival of the society itself. Members of societies have usually supposed it important for most *other* individuals to form families, to rear children, to create the next generation, to support and help each other—whether or not individual members of specific families do in fact feel they gain real advantages from living in a familistic arrangement. For example, over many centuries, people opposed legal divorces, whether or not they themselves were happily married, and with little regard for the marital happiness of others.

This view of what makes up the "familistic social package" explains several kinds of widely observable social behavior. One is that people experiment with different kinds of arrangements, often guided by a new philosophy of how people ought to live. They do so because their own needs have not been adequately fulfilled in the traditional modes of family arrangements available to them in their own society. Since other people have a stake in the kinds of familistic arrangements people make, we can also expect that when some individuals or groups attempt to change or experiment with the established system, various members of the society will object, and may even persecute them for it. We can also see why it is that even in a high-divorce society such as our own, where millions of people have been dissatisfied or hurt by their marriages and their divorces, they nevertheless move back into a marital arrangement. That is, after examining various alternatives, the familistic social package still seems to offer a broader set of personal advantages, and the outside society supports that move. And, as noted earlier, even when there are strong political pressures to create new social units that give far less support for the individual family, as in China, Russia, and the Israeli *kibbutzim*, we can expect that people will continue to drift back toward some kind of familistic arrangement.

A SOCIOLOGICAL APPROACH TO FAMILY RESEARCH

The unusual traits the family exhibits as a type of social subsystem require that some attention be paid to the analytic approach to be used in studying it. First, neither ideal nor reality can be excluded from our attention. It would, for example, be naïve to suppose that because some 40 percent of all U.S. couples now marrying will eventually divorce, they do not cherish the ideal of remaining married to one person. Contemporary estimates suggest that about half of all married men engage in extramarital intercourse at some time, but public opinion surveys report that a large majority of both men and women in the United States, even in these permissive times, approve of the ideal of faithfulness. On a more personal level, every reader of these lines has lied at some time, but nevertheless most believe in the ideal of telling the truth.

A sociologist ascertains the ideals of family systems partly because they are a rough guide to behavior. Knowing that people prefer to have their sons and daughters marry at least at the same class level, we can expect them to try to control their children's mate choices if they can do so. We can also specify some of the conditions under which they will have a greater or lesser success in reaching that goal. We also know that when a person violates the ideal, he or she is likely to conceal the violation if possible. If that is not possible, people will try to find some excuse for the violation, and are likely to be embarrassed if others find out about it.

The sociology of the family cannot confine itself only to contemporary urban (or suburban) American life. Conclusions of any substantial validity or scope must include data from other societies, whether these are past or present, industrial or nonindustrial, Asian or European. Data from the historical past, such as Periclean Athens or imperial Rome, are not often used because no sociologically adequate account of their family systems has as yet been written.[3] On the other hand, the last two decades have seen the appearance of many studies about family systems in various European cities of the last five centuries.

The study of customs and beliefs from the past yields a better understanding of the possible range of social behavior. Thereby, we are led to deny or at least to qualify a finding that might be correct if limited only to modern American life (such as the rise in divorce rates over several decades). The use of data from tribal societies of the past or present helps us in testing conclusions about family systems that are not found at all in Western society, such as matrilineal systems or polygyny. Or, an apparently simple relationship may take a different form in other societies. For example, in the United States most first marriages are based on a love relationship (whatever else they may be based on), and people are reluctant to admit that they have married someone with whom they were not in love. By contrast, though people fall in love in other societies, love may play a small or a large part in the marriage system. . . .

It is possible to study almost any phenomenon from a wide range of viewpoints. We may study the economic aspects of family behavior, or we may confine ourselves to the biological factors in family patterns. A full analysis of any concrete object is impossible. Everything can be analyzed from many vantage points, each of them yielding a somewhat different but still limited picture. Everything is infinitely complex. Each science limits its perspective to the range of processes that it considers important. Each such approach has its own justification. Here we examine the family mainly from a sociological perspective.

The sociological approach focuses on the family as a social institution, the peculiar and unique quality of family interaction as *social*. For example, family systems exhibit the characteristics of legitimacy and authority, which are not biological categories at all. The values and the prescribed behavior to be found in a family, or the rights and duties of family statuses such as father or daughter, are not psychological categories. They are peculiar to the theoretical approach of sociology. Personality theory is not very useful in explaining the particular position of the family in Chinese and Japanese social structures, although it may help us understand how individuals respond emotionally to those rights and obligations. If we use a consistently sociological approach, we will miss some important information about concrete family interaction. The possible gain when we stay on one theoretical level may be the achievement of some increased systematization, and some greater rigor.

At a minimum, however, when an analyst moves from the sociological to the psychological level of theory, he or she ought at least to be conscious of it. If the investigation turns to the impact of biological or psychological factors on the family, they should be examined with reference to their *social* meaning. For example, interracial marriage appears to be of little biological significance, but it has much social impact on those who take part in such a marriage. A sociologist who studies the family is not likely to be an expert in the *psychodynamics* of mental disease, but is interested in the effect of mental disease on the social relations in a particular family or type of family, or in the adjustment different family types make to it.

Notes _____

1. See in this connection Nicholas Tavuchis and William J. Goode (eds.), *The Family through Literature* (Oxford University Press, 1973).
2. For further comparisons of bureaucracy and informal groups, see Eugene Litwak, "Technical Innovation and Theoretical Functions of Primary Groups and Bureaucratic Structures," *American Journal of Sociology*, 73 (1968), 468–481.
3. However, Keith Hopkins has published several specialized studies on various aspects of Roman families. See his *Conquerors and Slaves* (Cambridge University Press, 1978).

■ READING 2

The Global Revolution in Family and Personal Life

Anthony Giddens

Among all the changes going on today, none are more important than those happening in our personal lives—in sexuality, emotional life, marriage and the family. There is a global revolution going on in how we think of ourselves and how we form ties and connections with others. It is a revolution advancing unevenly in different regions and cultures, with many resistances.

As with other aspects of the runaway world, we don't know what the ratio of advantages and anxieties will turn out to be. In some ways, these are the most difficult and disturbing transformations of all. Most of us can tune out from larger problems for much of the time. We can't opt out, however, from the swirl of change reaching right into the heart of our emotional lives.

There are few countries in the world where there isn't intense discussion about sexual equality, the regulation of sexuality and the future of the family. And where there isn't open debate, this is mostly because it is actively repressed by authoritarian governments or fundamentalist groups. In many cases, these controversies are national or local—as are the social and political reactions to them. Politicians and pressure groups will suggest that if only family policy were modified, if only divorce were made harder or easier to get in their particular country, solutions to our problems could readily be found.

But the changes affecting the personal and emotional spheres go far beyond the borders of any particular country, even one as large as the United States. We find the same issues almost everywhere, differing only in degree and according to the cultural context in which they take place.

In China, for example, the state is considering making divorce more difficult. In the aftermath of the Cultural Revolution, very liberal marriage laws were passed. Marriage is a working contract, that can be dissolved, I quote: "when husband and wife both desire it."

Even if one partner objects, divorce can be granted when "mutual affection" has gone from the marriage. Only a two week wait is required, after which the two pay $4 and are henceforth independent. The Chinese divorce rate is still low as compared with Western countries, but it is rising rapidly—as is true in the other developing Asian societies. In Chinese cities, not only divorce, but cohabitation is becoming more frequent.

In the vast Chinese countryside, by contrast, everything is different. Marriage and the family are much more traditional—in spite of the official policy of limiting childbirth through a mixture of incentives and punishment. Marriage is an arrangement between two families, fixed by the parents rather than the individuals concerned.

A recent study in the province of Gansu, which has only a low level of economic development, found that 60% of marriages are still arranged by parents. As a Chinese saying has it: "meet once, nod your head and marry." There is a twist in the tail in modernising China. Many of those currently divorcing in the urban centres were married in the traditional manner in the country.

In China there is much talk of protecting the family. In many Western countries the debate is even more shrill. The family is a site for the struggles between tradition and modernity, but also a metaphor for them. There is perhaps more nostalgia surrounding the lost haven of the family than for any other institution with its roots in the past. Politicians and activists routinely diagnose the breakdown of family life and call for a return to the traditional family.

Now the "traditional family" is very much a catch-all category. There have been many different types of family and kinship systems in different societies and cultures. The Chinese family, for instance, was always distinct from family forms in the West. Arranged marriage was never as common in most European countries, as in China, or India. Yet the family in non-modern cultures did, and does, have some features found more or less everywhere.

The traditional family was above all an economic unit. Agricultural production normally involved the whole family group, while among the gentry and aristocracy, transmission of property was the main basis of marriage. In mediaeval Europe, marriage was not contracted on the basis of sexual love, nor was it regarded as a place where such love should flourish. As the French historian, Georges Duby, puts it, marriage in the Middle Ages was not to involve "frivolity, passion, or fantasy."

The inequality of men and women was intrinsic to the traditional family. I don't think one could overstate the importance of this. In Europe, women were the property of their husbands or fathers—chattels as defined in law.

In the traditional family, it wasn't only women who lacked rights—children did too. The idea of enshrining children's rights in law is in historical terms relatively recent. In premodern periods, as in traditional cultures today, children weren't reared for their own sake, or for the satisfaction of the parents. One could almost say that children weren't recognised as individuals.

It wasn't that parents didn't love their children, but they cared about them more for the contribution they made to the common economic task than for themselves. Moreover, the death rate of children was frightening. In Colonial America nearly one in four infants died in their first year. Almost 50% didn't live to age 10.

Except for certain courtly or elite groups, in the traditional family sexuality was always dominated by reproduction. This was a matter of tradition and nature combined. The absence of effective contraception meant that for most women sexuality was inevitably closely connected with childbirth. In many traditional cultures, including in Western Europe up to the threshold of the 20th Century, a woman might have 10 or more pregnancies during the course of her life.

Sexuality was regulated by the idea of female virtue. The sexual double standard is often thought of as a creation of the Victorian period. In fact, in one version or another it was central to almost all non-modern societies. It involved a dualistic view of female sexuality—a clear cut division between the virtuous woman on the one hand and the libertine on the other.

Sexual promiscuity in many cultures has been taken as a positive defining feature of masculinity. James Bond is, or was, admired for his sexual as well as his physical heroism. Sexually adventurous women, by contrast, have nearly always been beyond the pale, no matter how much influence the mistresses of some prominent figures might have achieved.

Attitudes towards homosexuality were also governed by a mix of tradition and nature. Anthropological surveys show that homosexuality—or male homosexuality at any rate—has been tolerated, or openly approved of, in more cultures than it has been outlawed.

Those societies that have been hostile to homosexuality have usually condemned it as specifically unnatural. Western attitudes have been more extreme than most; less than half a century ago homosexuality was still widely regarded as a perversion and written up as such in manuals of psychiatry.

Antagonism towards homosexuality is still widespread and the dualistic view of women continues to be held by many—of both sexes. But over the past few decades the main elements of people's sexual lives in the West have changed in an absolutely basic way. The separation of sexuality from reproduction is in principle complete. Sexuality is for the first time something to be discovered, moulded, altered. Sexuality, which used to be defined so strictly in relation to marriage and legitimacy, now has little connection to them at all. We should see the increasing acceptance of homosexuality not just as a tribute to liberal tolerance. It is a logical outcome of the severance of sexuality from reproduction. Sexuality which has no content is by definition no longer dominated by heterosexuality.

What most of its defenders in Western countries call the traditional family was in fact a late, transitional phase in family development in the 1950's. This was a time at which the proportion of women out at work was still relatively low and when it was still difficult, especially for women, to obtain divorce without stigma. On the other hand, men and women by this time were more equal than they had been previously, both in fact and in law. The family had ceased to be an economic entity and the idea of romantic love as basis for marriage had replaced marriage as an economic contract.

Since then, the family has changed much further. The details vary from society to society, but the same trends are visible almost everywhere in the industrialised world. Only a minority of people now live in what might be called the standard 1950's family—both parents living together with their children of the marriage, where the mother is a full time housewife, and the father the breadwinner. In some countries, more than a third of all births happen outside wedlock, while the proportion of people living alone has gone up steeply and looks likely to rise even more.

In most societies, like the U.S., marriage remains popular—the U.S. has aptly been called a high divorce, high marriage society. In Scandinavia, on the other hand, a large proportion of people living together, including where children are involved, remain unmarried. Moreover, up to a quarter of women aged between 18 and 35 in the U.S. and Europe say they do not intend to have children—and they appear to mean it.

Of course in all countries older family forms continue to exist. In the U.S., many people, recent immigrants particularly, still live according to traditional values. Most family life, however, has been transformed by the rise of the couple and coupledom.

Marriage and the family have become what I termed in an earlier lecture "shell institutions." They are still called the same, but inside their basic character has changed.

In the traditional family, the married couple was only one part, and often not the main part, of the family system. Ties with children and other relatives tended to be equally or even more important in the day to day conduct of social life. Today the couple, married or unmarried, is at the core of what the family is. The couple came to be at the centre of family life as the economic role of the family dwindled and love, or love plus sexual attraction, became the basis of forming marriage ties.

A couple once constituted has its own exclusive history, its own biography. It is a unit based upon emotional communication or intimacy. The idea of intimacy . . . sounds old but in fact is very new. Marriage was never in the past based upon intimacy—emotional communication. No doubt this was important to a good marriage but it was not the foundation of it. For the couple, it is. Communication is the means of establishing the tie in the first place and it is the chief rationale for its continuation.

We should recognise what a major transition this is. "Coupling" and "uncoupling" provide a more accurate description of the arena of personal life now than do "marriage and the family." A more important question for us than "are you married?" is "how good is your relationship?"

The idea of a relationship is also surprisingly recent. Only 30 or so years ago, no one spoke of "relationships." They didn't need to, nor did they need to speak in terms of intimacy and commitment. Marriage at that time was the commitment, as the existence of shotgun marriages bore witness. While statistically marriage is still the normal condition, for most people its meaning has more or less completely changed. Marriage signifies that a couple is in a stable relationship, and may indeed promote that stability, since it makes a public declaration of commitment. However, marriage is no longer the chief defining basis of coupledom.

The position of children in all this is interesting and somewhat paradoxical. Our attitudes towards children and their protection have altered radically over the past several generations. We prize children so much partly because they have become so much rarer, and partly because the decision to have a child is very different from what it was for previous generations. In the traditional family, children were an economic benefit. Today in Western countries a child, on the contrary, puts a large financial burden on the parents. Having a child is more of a distinct and specific decision than it used to be, and it is a decision guided by psychological and emotional needs. The worries we have about the effects of divorce upon children, and the existence of many fatherless families, have to be understood against the background of our much higher expectations about how children should be cared for and protected.

There are three areas in which emotional communication, and therefore intimacy, are replacing the old ties that used to bind together people's personal lives—in sexual and love relations, parent-child relations and in friendship.

To analyse these, I want to use the idea of what I call the "pure relationship." I mean by this a relationship based upon emotional communication, where the rewards derived from such communication are the main basis for the relationship to continue.

I don't mean a sexually pure relationship. Also I don't mean anything that exists in reality. I'm talking of an abstract idea that helps us understand changes going on in the world. Each of the three areas just mentioned—sexual relationships, parent-child relations and friendship—is tending to approximate to this model. Emotional communication or intimacy, in other words, are becoming the key to what they are all about.

The pure relationship has quite different dynamics from more traditional social ties. It depends upon processes of active trust—opening oneself up to the other. Self-disclosure is the basic condition of intimacy.

The pure relationship is also implicitly democratic. When I was originally working on the study of intimate relationships, I read a great deal of therapeutic and self-help literature on the subject. I was struck by something I don't believe has been widely noticed or remarked upon. If one looks at how a therapist sees a good relationship—in any of the three spheres just mentioned—it is striking how direct a parallel there is with public democracy.

A good relationship, of course, is an ideal—most ordinary relationships don't come even close. I'm not suggesting that our relations with spouses, lovers, children or friends aren't often messy, conflictful and unsatisfying. But the principles of public democracy are ideals too, that also often stand at some large distance from reality.

A good relationship is a relationship of equals, where each party has equal rights and obligations. In such a relationship, each person has respect, and wants the best, for the other. The pure relationship is based upon communication, so that understanding the other person's point of view is essential.

Talk, or dialogue, are the basis of making the relationship work. Relationships function best if people don't hide too much from each other—there has to be mutual trust. And trust has to be worked at, it can't just be taken for granted.

Finally, a good relationship is one free from arbitrary power, coercion or violence.

Every one of these qualities conforms to the values of democratic politics. In a democracy, all are in principle equal, and with equality of rights and responsibilities comes mutual respect. Open dialogue is a core property of democracy. Democratic systems substitute open discussion of issues—a public space of dialogue—for authoritarian power, or for the sedimented power of tradition. No democracy can work without trust. And democracy is undermined if it gives way to authoritarianism or violence.

When we apply these principles—as ideals, I would stress again—to relationships, we are talking of something very important—the possible emergence of what I shall call, a democracy of the emotions in everyday life. A democracy of the emotions, it seems to me, is as important as public democracy in improving the quality of our lives.

This holds as much in parent-child relations as in other areas. These can't, and shouldn't, be materially equal. Parents must have authority over children, in everyone's interests. Yet they should presume an in-principle equality. In a democratic family, the authority of parents should be based upon an implicit contract. The parent in effect says to the child: "If you were an adult, and knew what I know, you would agree that what I ask you to do is legitimate."

Children in traditional families were—and are—supposed to be seen and not heard. Many parents, perhaps despairing of their children's rebelliousness, would dearly like to resurrect that rule. But there isn't any going back to it, nor should there be. In a democracy of the emotions, children can and should be able to answer back.

An emotional democracy doesn't imply lack of discipline, or absence of authority. It simply seeks to put them on a different footing.

Something very similar happened in the public sphere, when democracy began to replace arbitrary government and the rule of force. And like public democracy the democratic family must be anchored in a stable, yet open, civil society. If I may coin a phrase—"It takes a village."

A democracy of the emotions would draw no distinctions of principle between heterosexual and same-sex relationships. Gays, rather than heterosexuals, have actually been pioneers in discovering the new world of relationships and exploring its possibilities. They have had to be, because when homosexuality came out of the closet, gays weren't able to depend upon the normal supports of traditional marriage. They have had to be innovators, often in a hostile environment.

To speak of fostering an emotional democracy doesn't mean being weak about family duties, or about public policy towards the family. Democracy, after all, means the acceptance of obligations, as well as rights sanctioned in law. The protection of children has to be the primary feature of legislation and public policy. Parents should be legally obliged to provide for their children until adulthood, no matter what living arrangements they enter into. Marriage is no longer an economic institution, yet as a ritual commitment it can help stabilise otherwise fragile relationships. If this applies to heterosexual relationships, I don't see why it shouldn't apply to homosexual ones too.

There are many questions to be asked of all this—too many to answer in a short lecture. I have concentrated mainly upon trends affecting the family in Western countries. What about areas where the traditional family remains largely intact, as in the example of China with which I began? Will the changes observed in the West become more and more global?

I think they will—indeed that they are. It isn't a question of whether existing forms of the traditional family will become modified, but when and how. I would venture even further. What I have described as an emerging democracy of the emotions is on the front line in the struggle between cosmopolitanism and fundamentalism that I described in the last lecture. Equality of the sexes, and the sexual freedom of women, which are incompatible with the traditional family, are anathema to fundamentalist groups. Opposition to them, indeed, is one of the defining features of religious fundamentalism across the world.

There is plenty to be worried about in the state of the family, in Western countries and elsewhere. It is just as mistaken to say that every family form is as good as any other, as to argue that the decline of the traditional family is a disaster.

I would turn the argument of the political and fundamentalist right on its head. The persistence of the traditional family—or aspects of it—in many parts of the world is more worrisome than its decline. For what are the most important forces promoting democracy and economic development in poorer countries? Well, they are the equality and education of women. And what must be changed to make these possible? Most importantly, what must be changed is the traditional family.

In conclusion, I should emphasise that sexual equality is not just a core principle of democracy. It is also relevant to happiness and fulfilment.

Many of the changes happening to the family are problematic and difficult. But surveys in the U.S. and Europe show that few want to go back to traditional male and female roles, much less to legally defined inequality.

If ever I were tempted to think that the traditional family might be best after all, I remember what my great aunt said. She must have had one of the longest marriages of anyone. She married young, and was with her husband for over 60 years. She once confided to me that she had been deeply unhappy with him the whole of that time. In her day there was no escape.

2

Public Debates and Private Lives

■READING 3

The Mommy Wars: Ambivalence, Ideological Work, and the Cultural Contradictions of Motherhood

Sharon Hays

I have argued that all mothers ultimately share a recognition of the ideology of intensive mothering. At the same time, all mothers live in a society where child rearing is generally devalued and the primary emphasis is placed on profit, efficiency, and "getting ahead." If you are a mother, both logics operate in your daily life.

But the story is even more complicated. Over half of American mothers participate directly in the labor market on a regular basis; the rest remain at least somewhat distant from that world as they spend most of their days in the home. One might therefore expect paid working mothers to be more committed to the ideology of competitively maximizing personal profit and stay-at-home mothers to be more committed to the ideology of intensive mothering. As it turns out, however, this is not precisely the way it works.

Modern-day mothers are facing two socially constructed cultural images of what a good mother looks like. Neither, however, includes the vision of a cold, calculating businesswoman—that title is reserved for childless career women. If you are a good mother, you *must* be an intensive one. The only "choice" involved is whether you *add* the role of paid working woman. The options, then, are as follows. On the one side there is the portrait of the "traditional mother" who stays at home with the kids and dedicates her energy to the happiness of her family. This mother cheerfully studies the latest issue of *Family Circle*, places flowers in every room, and has dinner waiting when her husband comes home. This mother, when she's not cleaning, cooking, sewing, shopping, doing the laundry, or comforting her mate, is focused on attending to the children and ensuring their proper development. On the other side is the image of the successful "supermom." Effortlessly juggling home and work, this mother can push a stroller with one hand and carry a briefcase in the other. She is always properly coiffed, her nylons have no runs, her suits are freshly pressed, and her home has seen the white tornado. Her children are immaculate and well mannered but not passive, with a strong spirit and high self-esteem.[1]

Although both the traditional mom and the supermom are generally considered socially acceptable, their coexistence represents a serious cultural ambivalence about how mothers should behave. This ambivalence comes out in the widely available indictments of the failings of both groups of women. Note, for instance, the way Mecca, a welfare mother, describes these two choices and their culturally provided critiques:

> The way my family was brought up was, like, you marry a man, he's the head of the house, he's the provider, and you're the wife, you're the provider in the house. Now these days it's not that way. Now the people that stay home are classified, quote, "lazy people," we don't "like" to work.
>
> I've seen a lot of things on TV about working mothers and nonworking mothers. People who stay home attack the other mothers 'cause they're, like, bad mothers because they left the kids behind and go to work. And, the other ones aren't working because we're lazy. But it's not lazy. It's the lifestyle in the 1990s it's, like, too much. It's a demanding world for mothers with kids.

The picture Mecca has seen on television, a picture of these two images attacking each other with ideological swords, is not an uncommon one.

It is this cultural ambivalence and the so-called choice between these paths that is the basis for what Darnton (1990) has dubbed the "mommy wars."[2] Both stay-at-home and paid working mothers, it is argued, are angry and defensive; neither group respects the other. Both make use of available cultural indictments to condemn the opposing group. Supermoms, according to this portrait, regularly describe stay-at-home mothers as lazy and boring, while traditional moms regularly accuse employed mothers of selfishly neglecting their children.

My interviews suggest, however, that this portrait of the mommy wars is both exaggerated and superficial. In fact, the majority of mothers I spoke with expressed respect for one another's need or right to choose whether to go out to work or stay at home with the kids. And, as I have argued, they also share a whole set of similar concerns regarding appropriate child rearing. These mothers have not formally enlisted in this war. Yet the rhetoric of the mommy wars draws them in as it persists in mainstream American culture, a culture that is unwilling, for various significant reasons, to unequivocally embrace either vision of motherhood, just as it remains unwilling to embrace wholeheartedly the childless career woman.[3] Thus, the charges of being lazy and bored, on the one hand, or selfish and money-grubbing, on the other, are made available for use by individual mothers and others should the need arise.

What this creates is a no-win situation for women of child-bearing years. If a woman voluntarily remains childless, some will say that she is cold, heartless, and unfulfilled as a woman. If she is a mother who works too hard at her job or career, some will accuse her of neglecting the kids. If she does not work hard enough, some will surely place her on the "mommy track" and her career advancement will be permanently slowed by the claim that her commitment to her children interferes with her workplace efficiency (Schwartz 1989). And if she stays at home with her children, some will call her unproductive and useless. A woman, in other words, can never fully do it right.

At the same time that these cultural images portray all women as somehow less than adequate, they also lead many mothers to feel somehow less than adequate in their daily lives. The stay-at-home mother is supposed to be happy and fulfilled, but how can she be when she hears so often that she is mindless and bored? The supermom is supposed to be able to juggle her two roles without missing a beat, but how can she do either job as well as she is expected if she is told she must dedicate her all in both directions? In these circumstances, it is not surprising that many supermoms feel guilty about their inability to carry out both roles to their fullest, while many traditional moms feel isolated and invisible to the larger world.

Given this scenario, both stay-at-home and employed mothers end up spending a good deal of time attempting to make sense of their current positions. Paid working mothers, for instance, are likely to argue that there are lots of good reasons for mothers to work in the paid labor force; stay-at-home mothers are likely to argue that there are lots of good reasons for mothers to stay at home with their children. These arguments are best understood not as (mere) rationalizations or (absolute) truths but rather as socially necessary "ideological work." Berger (1981) uses this notion to describe the way that all people make use of available ideologies in their "attempt to cope with the relationship between the ideas they bring to a social context and the practical pressures of day-to-day living in it" (15). People, in other words, select among the cultural logics at their disposal in order to develop some correspondence between what they believe and what they actually do.[4] For mothers, just like others, ideological work is simply a means of maintaining their sanity.

The ideological work of mothers, as I will show, follows neither a simple nor a straightforward course. First, as I have pointed out, both groups face two contradictory cultural images of appropriate mothering. Their ideological work, then, includes a recognition and response to both portraits. This duality is evident in the fact that the logic the traditional mother uses to affirm her position matches the logic that the supermom uses to express ambivalence about her situation, and the logic that the employed mother uses to affirm her position is the same logic that the stay-at-home mother uses to express ambivalence about hers. Their strategies, in other words, are mirror images, but they are also incomplete—both groups are left with some ambivalence. Thus, although the two culturally provided images of mothering help mothers to make sense of their own positions, they simultaneously sap the strength of mothers by making them feel inadequate in one way or the other. It is in coping with these feelings of inadequacy that their respective ideological strategies take an interesting turn. Rather than taking divergent paths, as one might expect, both groups attempt to resolve their feelings of inadequacy by returning to the logic of the ideology of intensive mothering.

THE FRUMPY HOUSEWIFE AND THE PUSH
TOWARD THE OUTSIDE WORLD

Some employed mothers say that they go out to work for pay because they need the income.[5] But the overwhelming majority also say that they *want* to work outside the home. First, there's the problem of staying inside all day: "I decided once I started working that I need that. I need to work. Because I'll become like this big huge hermit frumpy person if I stay home." Turning into a "big huge hermit frumpy person" is connected to the feeling of being confined to the home. Many women have had that experience at one time or another and do not want to repeat it:

> When I did stay home with him, up until the time when he was ten months old, I wouldn't go out of the house for three days at a time. Ya know, I get to where I don't want to get dressed, I don't care if I take a shower. It's like, what for? I'm not going anywhere.

Not getting dressed and not going anywhere are also tied to the problem of not having a chance to interact with other adults:

> I remember thinking, "I don't even get out of my robe. And I've gotta stay home and breast-feed and the only adult I hear is on *Good Morning America*—and he's not even live!" And that was just for a couple of months. I don't even know what it would be like for a couple of years. I think it would be really difficult.

Interacting with adults, for many paid working mothers, means getting a break from the world of children and having an opportunity to use their minds:

> When I first started looking for a job, I thought we needed a second income. But then when I started working it was like, this is great! I do have a mind that's not *Sesame Street!* And I just love talking with people. It's just fun, and it's a break. It's tough, but I enjoyed it; it was a break from being with the kids.

If you don't get a break from the kids, if you don't get out of the house, if you don't interact with adults, and if you don't have a chance to use your mind beyond the *Sesame Street* level, you might end up lacking the motivation to do much at all. This argument is implied by many mothers:

> If I was stuck at home all day, and I did do that 'cause I was waiting for day care, I stayed home for four months, and I went crazy, I couldn't stand it. I mean not because I didn't want to spend any time with her, but because we'd just sit here and she'd just cry all day and I couldn't get anything done. I was at the end of the day exhausted, and feeling like shit.

Of course, it is exhausting to spend the day meeting the demands of children. But there's also a not too deeply buried sense in all these arguments that getting outside the home and using one's mind fulfill a longing to be part of the larger world and to be recognized by it. One mother made this point explicitly:

[When you're working outside the home] you're doing something. You're using your mind a little bit differently than just trying to figure out how to make your day work with your kid. It's just challenging in a different way. So there's part of me that wants to be, like, *recognized*. I think maybe that's what work does, it gives you a little bit of a sense of recognition, that you don't feel like you get [when you stay home].

Most employed mothers, then, say that if they stay at home they'll go stir-crazy, they'll get bored, the demands of the kids will drive them nuts, they won't have an opportunity to use their brains or interact with other adults, they'll feel like they're going nowhere, and they'll lose their sense of identity in the larger world. And, for many of these mothers, all these points are connected:

> Well, I think [working outside is] positive, because I feel good about being able to do the things that I went to school for, and keep up with that, and use my brain. As they grow older, [the children are] going to get into things that they want to get into, they're going to be out with their friends and stuff, and I don't want to be in a situation where my whole life has been wrapped around the kids. That's it. Just some outside interests so that I'm not so wrapped up in how shiny my floor is. [She laughs.] Just to kind of be out and be stimulated. Gosh, I don't want this to get taken wrong, but I think I'd be a little bit bored. And the other thing I think of is, I kind of need a break, and when you're staying at home it's constant. It's a lot harder when you don't have family close by, [because] you don't get a break.

In short, paid working mothers feel a strong pull toward the outside world. They hear the world accusing stay-at-home moms of being mindless and unproductive and of lacking an identity apart from their kids, and they experience this as at least partially true. Stay-at-home mothers also worry that the world will perceive them as lazy and bored and watching television all day as children scream in their ears and tug at their sleeves. And sometimes this is the way they feel about themselves. In other words, the same image that provides working mothers with the reasons they should go out to work accounts for the ambivalence that stay-at-home mothers feel about staying at home.

A few stay-at-home mothers seem to feel absolutely secure in their position, but most do not.[6] Many believe that they will seek paid work at some point, and almost all are made uncomfortable by the sense that the outside world does not value what they do. In all cases, their expressions of ambivalence about staying at home mimic the concerns of employed mothers. For instance, some women who stay at home also worry about becoming frumpy: "I'm not this heavy. I'm, like, twenty-seven pounds overweight. It sounds very vain of me, in my situation. It's like, I'm not used to being home all the time, I'm home twenty-four hours. I don't have that balance in my life anymore." And some stay-at-home mothers feel as if they are physically confined inside the home. This mother, for example, seems tired of meeting the children's demands and feels that she is losing her sense of self:

> There's a hard thing of being at home all the time. You have a lot of stress, because you're constantly in the house. I think having a job can relieve some of that stress and to make it a lot more enjoyable, to want to come home all the time. . . . My outings are [limited]. I'm excited when I have to go grocery shopping. Everything I pick is what they eat,

everything they like, or what they should eat. Me, I'm just *there*. I'm there for them. I feel that I'm here for them.

Both of these stay-at-home mothers, like over one-third of the stay-at-home mothers in my sample, plan to go out to work as soon as they can find paid employment that offers sufficient rewards to compensate (both financially and ideologically) for sending the kids to day care. Most of the remaining mothers are committed to staying at home with the children through what they understand as formative years. The following mother shares that commitment, while also echoing many paid working mothers in her hopes that one day she will have a chance to be around adults and further her own growth:

> Well, we could do more, we'd have more money, but that's really not the biggest reason I'd go back to work. I want to do things for myself, too. I want to go back and get my master's [degree] or something. I need to grow, and be around adults, too. I don't know when, but I think in the next two years I'll go back to work. The formative years—their personality is going to develop until they're about five. It's pretty much set by then. So I think it's pretty critical that you're around them during those times.

One mother stated explicitly that she can hardly wait until the kids are through their formative years:

> At least talking to grown-ups is a little more fulfilling than ordering the kids around all day. My life right now is just all theirs. Sometimes it's a depressing thought because I think, "Where am I? I want my life back." . . . I mean, they are totally selfish. It's like an ice cream. They just gobble that down and say, "Let me have the cinnamon roll now."
>   . . . [But] I had them, and I want them to be good people. So I've dedicated myself to them right now. Later on I get my life back. They won't always be these little sponges. I don't want any deficiency—well, nobody can cover all the loopholes—but I want to be comfortable in myself to know that I did everything that I could. It's the least I can do to do the best I can by them.

Mothers, she seems to be saying, are like confections that the kids just gobble down—and then they ask for more.

Thus, many stay-at-home moms experience the exhaustion of meeting the demands of children all day long, just as employed mothers fear they might. And many stay-at-home mothers also experience a loss of self. Part of the reason they feel like they are losing their identity is that they know the outside world does not recognize a mother's work as valuable. This woman, committed to staying at home until her youngest is at least three years old, explains:

> You go through a period where you feel like you've lost all your marbles. Boy, you're not as smart as you used to be, and as sharp as you used to be, and not as respected as you used to be. And those things are really hard to swallow. But that's something I've discussed with other mothers who are willing to stay home with their kids, and we've formed a support group where we've said, "Boy, those people just don't know what they're talking about." We're like a support group for each other, which you have to have if you've decided to

stay at home, because you have so many people almost pushing you to work, or asking "Why don't you work?" You're not somehow as good as anybody else 'cause you're staying at home; what you're doing isn't important. We have a lot of that in this society.

Another mother, this one determined to stay at home with her kids over the long haul, provides a concrete example of the subtle and not-so-subtle ways in which society pushes mothers to participate in the paid labor force, and of the discomfort such mothers experience as a result:

> As a matter of fact, somebody said to me (I guess it was a principal from one of the schools.) . . . "Well, what do you *do?* Do you have a *job?*" And it was just very funny to me that he was so uncomfortable trying to ask me what it was in our society that I did. I guess that they just assume that if you're a mom at home that it means nothing. I don't know, I just don't consider it that way. But it's kind of funny, worrying about what you're gonna say at a dinner party about what you do.

And it's not just that these mothers worry about being able to impress school principals and people at cocktail parties, of course. The following mother worries about being "interesting" to other women who do not have children:

> I find myself, now that I'm not working, not to have as much in common [with other women who don't have children]. We don't talk that much because I don't have that much to talk about. Like I feel I'm not an interesting person anymore.

In short, the world presents, and mothers experience, the image of the lazy, mindless, dull housewife—and no mother wants to be included in that image.

THE TIME-CRUNCHED CAREER WOMAN AND THE PULL TOWARD HOME

Stay-at-home mothers use a number of strategies to support their position and combat the image of the frumpy housewife. Many moms who are committed to staying at home with their kids often become part of formal or informal support groups, providing them an opportunity to interact with other mothers who have made the same commitment. Others, if they can afford the cost of transportation and child care, engage in a variety of outside activities—as volunteers for churches, temples, and community groups, for instance, or in regular leisure activities and exercise programs. They then have a chance to communicate with other adults and to experience themselves as part of a larger social world (though one in which children generally occupy a central role).

But the primary way that stay-at-home mothers cope with their ambivalence is through ideological work. Like paid working mothers, they make a list of all the good reasons they do what they do. In this case, that list includes confirming their commitment to good mothering, emphasizing the importance of putting their children's needs ahead of their own, and telling stories about the problems that families, and especially children, experience when mothers go out to work for pay.

Many stay-at-home mothers argue that kids require guidance and should have those cookies cooling on the kitchen counter when they come home from school:

> The kids are the ones that suffer. The kids need guidance and stuff. And with two parents working, sometimes there isn't even a parent home when they come home from school. And that's one thing that got me too. I want to be home and I want to have cookies on the stove when they come home from school. Now we eat meals together all the time. It's more of a homey atmosphere. It's more of a *home* atmosphere.

Providing this homey atmosphere is difficult to do if one works elsewhere all day. And providing some period of so-called quality time in the evening, these mothers tell me, is not an adequate substitute. One mother elaborates on this point in response to a question about how she would feel if she was working outside the home:

> Oh, guilty as anything. I know what I'm like after dinner, and I'm not at my best. And neither are my kids. And if that's all the time I had with them, it wouldn't be, quote, "quality time." I think it's a bunch of b.s. about quality time.

And quality time, even if it *is* of high quality, cannot make up for children's lack of a quantity of time with their mothers. This argument is often voiced in connection with the problem of paid caregiver arrangements. Most mothers, whether they work for pay or not, are concerned about the quality of day care, but stay-at-home mothers often use this concern to explain their commitment to staying at home. This mother, for example, argues that children who are shuffled off to a series of day-care providers simply will not get the love they need:

> I mean, if I'm going to have children I want to *raise* them. I feel really strongly about that. Really strongly. I wish more people did that. Myself, I think it's very underestimated the role the mother plays with the child. I really do. From zero to three [years], it's like their whole self-image. [Yet, working mothers will say,] "Well, okay, I've got a caretaker now," "Well, that nanny didn't work out." So by the time the children are three years old they've had four or five people who have supposedly said "I'll love you forever," and they're gone. I think that's really tough on the kids.[7]

Since paid caregivers lack that deep and long-lasting love, I'm told, they won't ever be as committed to ministering to the child's needs as a mom will:

> I don't think anybody can give to children what a mother can give to her own children. I think there's a level of willingness to put up with hard days, crying days, cranky days, whining days, that most mothers are going to be able to tolerate just a little bit more than a caretaker would. I think there's more of a commitment of what a mother wants to give her children in terms of love, support, values, etcetera. A caretaker isn't going to feel quite the same way.

Stay-at-home mothers imply that all these problems of kids who lack guidance, love, and support are connected to the problem of mothers who put their own interests ahead of the interests of their children. A few stay-at-home mothers will explicitly argue, as this one does, that employed mothers are allowing material and power interests to take priority over the well-being of their kids:

> People are too interested in power, they just aren't interested in what happens to their kids. You know, "Fine, put them in day care." And I just feel sad. If you're so interested in money or a career or whatever, then why have kids? Why bring them into it?

Putting such interests ahead of one's children is not only somehow immoral; it also produces children with real problems. The following mother, echoing many stories about "bad mothers" that we have heard before, had this to say about her sister:

> My sister works full-time—she's a lawyer. And her kids are the most obnoxious, whiny kids. I can't stand it. They just hang on her. She thinks she's doing okay by them because they're in an expensive private school and they have expensive music lessons and they have expensive clothes and expensive toys and expensive cars and an expensive house. I don't know. Time will tell, I guess. But I can't believe they're not going to have some insecurities. The thing that gets me is, they don't need it. I mean, he's a lawyer too. Basically, it's like, "Well, I like you guys, but I don't really want to be there all day with you, and I don't want to have to do the dirty work."

These are serious indictments indeed.

It is just these sorts of concerns that leave paid working mothers feeling inadequate and ambivalent about *their* position. Many of them wonder at times if their lives or the lives of their children might actually be better if they stayed at home with the kids. Above all, many of them feel guilty and wonder, "Am I doing it right?" or "Have I done all I can do?" These are the mothers who, we're told, have it all. It is impossible to have it all, however, when "all" includes two contradictory sets of requirements. To begin to get a deeper sense of how these supermoms do not always feel so super, two examples might be helpful.

Angela is a working-class mother who had expected to stay home with her son through his formative years. But after nine months she found herself bored, lonely, and eager to interact with other adults. She therefore went out and got a full-time job as a cashier. She begins by expressing her concern that she is not living up to the home-making suggestions she reads in *Parenting* magazine, worrying that she may not be doing it right:

> I get *Parenting* magazine and I read it. I do what is comfortable for me and what I can do. I'm not very creative. Where they have all these cooking ideas, and who has time to do that, except for a mother who stays home all day? Most of this is for a mother who has five, six hours to spend with her child doing this kind of thing. I don't have time for that.
>
> So then that's when I go back to day care. And I know that she's doing this kind of stuff with him, teaching him things. You know, a lot of the stuff that they have is on schooling kinds of things, flash cards, that kind of thing. Just things that I don't do. That makes me feel bad. Then I think, "I should be doing this" and "Am I doing the right thing?" I know I have a lot of love for him.

Although she loves her son and believes that this is probably "the most important thing," she also feels guilty that she may not be spending a sufficient amount of time with him, simply because she gets so tired:

> I think sometimes that I feel like I don't spend enough time with him and that's my biggest [concern]. And when I am with him, sometimes I'm not really up to being with him. Even though I am with him, sometimes I want him to go away because I've been working all day and I'm exhausted. And I feel sometimes I'll stick him in bed early because I just don't want to deal with him that day. And I feel really guilty because I don't spend enough time with him as it is. When I do have the chance to spend time with him, I don't want to spend time with him, because I'm so tired and I just want to be with myself and by myself.

Even though Angela likes her paid work and does not want to give it up, the problems of providing both a quantity of time and the idealized image of quality time with her child, just like the challenge of applying the creative cooking and child-rearing ideas she finds in *Parenting* magazine, haunt her and leave her feeling both inadequate and guilty.

Linda is a professional-class mother with a well-paying and challenging job that gives her a lot of satisfaction. She spent months searching for the right preschool for her son and is relieved that he is now in a place where the caregivers share her values. Still, she worries and wonders if life might be better if she had made different choices:

> I have a friend. She's a very good mom. She seems very patient, and I never heard her raise her voice. And she's also not working. She gets to stay home with her children, which is another thing I admire. I guess I sort of envy that too. There never seems to be a time where we can just spend, like, playing a lot. I think that's what really bothers me, that I don't feel like I have the time to just sit down and, in a relaxing way, play with him. I can do it, but then I'm thinking "Okay, well I can do this for five minutes." So that's always in the back of my mind. Time, time, time. So I guess that's the biggest thing.
>
> And just like your question, "How many hours a day is he at preschool and how many hours do you spend per day as the primary caregiver?" just made me think, "Oh my gosh!" I mean they're watching him grow up more than I am. They're with him more than I am. And that makes me feel guilty in a way, and it makes me feel sad in a way. I mean I can just see him, slipping, just growing up before me. Maybe it's that quality-time stuff. I don't spend a lot of time, and I don't know if the time I do spend with him is quality.
>
> [But] if I just stay at home, I'll kind of lose, I don't know if I want to say my sense of identity, but I guess I'll lose my career identity. I'm afraid of that I guess. . . . My friend who stays at home, she had a career before she had her children, but I forget what it was. So that whole part of her, I can't even identify it now.

On the one hand, Linda envies and admires stay-at-home moms and worries about not spending enough quality time with her son, or enough play time. She is also upset that her day-care provider spends more hours with her son each day than she can. On the other hand, Linda worries that if she did stay at home she'd lose her identity as a professional and a member of the larger society. "Time, time, time," she says, there's never enough time to do it all—or at least to do it all "right."

The issue of time is a primary source of paid working mothers' ambivalence about their double shift. Attempting to juggle two commitments at once is, of course, very difficult and stressful. This mother's sense of how time pressures make her feel that she is always moving too fast would be recognizable to the majority of paid working mothers:

> I can see when I get together with my sister [who doesn't have a paid job] . . . that she's so easygoing with the kids, and she takes her time, and when I'm with her, I realize how stressed out I am sometimes trying to get things done.
>   And I notice how much faster I move when I shop. . . . She's so relaxed, and I think I kind of envy that.

The problem of moving too fast when shopping is connected to the problem of moving too fast when raising children. Many paid working mothers envy those who can do such things at a more relaxed pace.

For a few employed mothers (two out of twenty in my sample) the problems of quality and quantity time outweigh the rewards of paid work, and they intend to leave their jobs as soon as they can afford to do so. This woman is one example:

> I believe there's a more cohesive family unit with maybe the mother staying at home. Because a woman tends to be a buffer, mediator, you name it. She pulls the family together. But if she's working outside the home, sometimes there's not that opportunity anymore for her to pull everyone together. She's just as tired as the husband would be and, I don't know, maybe the children are feeling like they've been not necessarily abandoned but, well, I'm sure they accept it, especially if that's the only life they've seen. But my daughter has seen a change, even when I was only on maternity leave. I've seen a change in her and she seemed to just enjoy it and appreciate us as a family more than when I was working. So now she keeps telling me, "Mom, I miss you."

When this mother hears her daughter say "I miss you," she feels a tremendous pull toward staying at home. And when she talks about the way a family needs a mother to bring its members together, she is pointing to an idealized image of the family that, like quality and quantity time, weighs heavily in the minds of many mothers.

The following paid working mother also wishes she could stay at home with the kids and wishes she could be just like the television mom of the 1950s who bakes cookies every afternoon. But she knows she has to continue working for financial reasons:

> Yes. I want to be Donna Reed, definitely. Or maybe Beaver Cleaver's mother, Jane Wyatt. Anybody in an apron and a pretty hairdo and a beautiful house. Yes. Getting out of the television set and making the most of reality is really what I have to do. Because I'll always have to work.

But the majority of paid working mothers, as I have stated, not only feel they need to work for financial reasons but also *want* to work, as Angela and Linda do. Nonetheless, their concerns about the effects of the double shift on their children match the concerns of those employed moms who wish they could stay at home as well as mimicking those of mothers who actually do stay at home. This mother, for instance, loves her paid work and does not want to give it up, but she does feel guilty, wondering if she's depriving her kids of the love and stimulation they need, particularly since she does not earn enough to justify the time she spends away:

> Honestly, I don't make that much money. So that in itself brings a little bit of guilt, 'cause I know I work even though we don't have to. So there's some guilt associated. If kids are coming home to an empty house every day, they're not getting the intellectual stimulation [and] they're not getting the love and nurturing that other mothers are able to give their kids. So I think in the long run they're missing out on a lot of the love and the nurturing and the caring.

And this mother does not want it to seem that she is putting her child second, but she feels pressure to live up to the image of a supermom:

> I felt really torn between what I wanted to do. Like a gut-wrenching decision. Like, what's more important? Of course your kids are important, but you know, there's so many outside pressures for women to work. Every ad you see in magazines or on television shows this working woman who's coming home with a briefcase and the kids are all dressed and clean. It's such a lie. I don't know of anybody who lives like that.
>
> There's just a lot of pressure that you're not a fulfilled woman if you're not working outside of the home. But yet, it's just a real hard choice.

This feeling of being torn by a gut-wrenching decision comes up frequently:

> I'm constantly torn between what I feel I should be doing in my work and spending more time with them. . . . I think I would spend more time with them if I could. Sometimes I think it would be great not to work and be a mom and do that, and then I think, "well?"
>
> I think it's hard. Because I think you do need to have contact with your kid. You can't just see him in the morning and put him to bed at night because you work all day long. I think that's a real problem. You need to give your child guidance. You can't leave it to the schools. You can't leave it to churches. You need to be there. So, in some ways I'm really torn.

The overriding issue for this mother is guidance; seeing the children in the morning and putting them to bed at night is just not enough.

This problem, of course, is related to the problem of leaving kids with a paid caregiver all day. Paid working mothers do not like the idea of hearing their children cry when they leave them at day care any more than any other mother does. They are, as we have seen, just as concerned that their children will not get enough love, enough nurturing, enough of the right values, enough of the proper education, and enough of the right kind of discipline if they spend most of their time with a paid caregiver. To this list of concerns, paid working mothers add their feeling that when the kids are with a paid caregiver all day, it feels as if someone else is being the mother. One woman (who stayed at home until her son was two years old) elaborates:

> Well, I think it's really sad that kids have to be at day care forty hours a week. Because basically the person who's taking care of them is your day-care person. They're pretty much

being the mother. It's really sad that this other person is raising your child, and it's basically like having this other person *adopting* your child. It's *awful* that we have to do that. I just think it's a crime basically. I wish we didn't have to do it. I wish everybody could stay home with their kids and have some kind of outlet. . . .

And I think having a career is really important, but I think when it comes time to have children, you can take that time off and spend it with your kid. Because you can't go backwards, and time does fly with them. It's so sad . . . I hear people say, "Oh, my day-care lady said that so-and-so walked today or used a spoon or something." I mean it's just so devastating to hear that you didn't get to see that.

Leaving one's child with a paid caregiver for hours on end is therefore a potential problem not only because that "other mother" may not be a good mother but also because the real mother misses out on the joys that come from just being with the child and having a chance to watch him or her grow. This is a heart rending issue for many mothers who work outside the home.

Once again, the arguments used by stay-at-home mothers to affirm their commitment to staying home are mimicked by the arguments paid working mothers use to express their ambivalence about the time they spend away from their children. And again, though the reasoning of these women is grounded in their experiences, it is also drawn from a widely available cultural rhetoric regarding the proper behavior of mothers.

THE CURIOUS COINCIDENCE OF PAID WORK AND THE IDEOLOGY OF INTENSIVE MOTHERING

Both paid working moms and stay-at-home moms, then, do the ideological work of making their respective lists of the reasons they should work for pay and the reasons they should stay at home. Yet both groups also continue to experience and express some ambivalence about their current positions, feeling pushed and pulled in two directions. One would assume that they would cope with their ambivalence by simply returning to their list of good reasons for doing what they do. And stay-at-home mothers do just that: they respond to the push toward work in the paid labor force by arguing that their kids need them to be at home. But, as I will demonstrate, working mothers do not use the mirror strategy. The vast majority of these women do not respond to the pull toward staying at home by arguing that kids are a pain in the neck and that paid work is more enjoyable. Instead, they respond by creating a new list of all the reasons that they are good mothers even though they work outside the home. In other words, the ideological work meant to resolve mothers' ambivalence generally points in the direction of intensive mothering.

Most paid working mothers cope with the ambivalence by arguing that their participation in the labor force is ultimately good for their kids. They make this point in a number of ways. For instance, one mother thinks that the example she provides may help to teach her kids the work ethic. Another says that with the "outside constraints" imposed by her work schedule, she's "more organized and effective" as a mom.[8] Yet another mother suggests that her second child takes just as much time and energy away from her first child as her career does:

> I think the only negative effect [of my employment] is just [that] generally when I'm over-stressed I don't do as well as a mother. But work is only one of the things that gets me over-stressed. In fact it probably stresses me less than some other things. I think I do feel guilty about working 'cause it takes time away from [my oldest daughter]. But it struck me that it's acceptable to have a second child that takes just as much time away from the other child. *That* I'm not supposed to feel guilty about. But in some ways this [pointing to the infant she is holding] takes my time away from her more than my work does. Because this is constant.

More often, however, paid working mothers share a set of more standard explanations for why their labor-force participation is actually what's best for their kids. First, just as Rachel feels that her income provides for her daughter's toys, clothing, outings, and education, and just as Jacqueline argues, "I have weeks when I don't spend enough time with them and they suffer, but those are also the weeks I bring home the biggest paychecks," many mothers point out that their paid work provides the financial resources necessary for the well-being of their children:

> How am I supposed to send her to college without saving up? And also the money that I make from working helps pay for her toys, things that she needs, clothes. I never have to say, "Oh, I'm on a budget, I can't go buy this pair of shoes." I want the best for her.

Some mothers express a related concern—namely, what would happen to the family if they did not have paying jobs and their husbands should die or divorce them? One woman expressed it this way:

> Well, my dad was a fireman, so I guess there was a little bit of fear, well, if anything happened to him, how are we gonna go on? And I always kind of wished that [my mother] had something to fall back on. I think that has a lot to do with why I continue to work after the kids. I've always just felt the need to have something to hold on to.

The second standard argument given by employed mothers is that paid caregiver arrangements can help to further children's development. With respect to other people's kids, I'm told, these arrangements can keep them from being smothered by their mothers or can temporarily remove them from bad family situations. With reference to their own children, mothers emphasize that good day care provides kids with the opportunity to interact with adults, gives them access to "new experiences" and "different activities," "encourages their independence," and allows them to play with other kids—which is very important, especially now that neighborhoods no longer provide the sort of community life they once did:

> They do say that kids in preschool these days are growing up a little more neurotic, but I don't think that my daughter would have had a better life. In fact I think her life would have been a thousand times worse if I was a low-income mother who stayed home and she only got to play with the kids at the park. Because I think that preschool is really good for them. Maybe not a holding tank, but a nice preschool where they play nice games with them and they have the opportunity to play with the same kids over and over again.

I think that's really good for them. Back in the 1950s, everybody stayed home and there were kids all over the block to play with. It's not that way now. The neighborhoods are deserted during the week.

Third, several mothers tell me that the quality of the time they spend with their kids actually seems to increase when they have a chance to be away from them for a part of the day. Listen to these mothers:

> When I'm with them too long I tend to lose my patience and start yelling at them. This way we both get out. And we're glad to see each other when we come home.
>
> If women were only allowed to work maybe ten to fifteen hours a week, they would appreciate their kids more and they'd have more quality time with them, rather than having to always just scold them.
>
> I think I have even less patience [when I stay home with the children], because it's like, "Oh, is this all there is?" . . . Whereas when I go to work and come home, I'm glad to see him. You know, you hear people say that they're better parents when they work because they spend more quality time, all those clichés, or whatever. For me that happens to be true.
>
> And now when I come home from work (although I wish I could get off earlier from work), I think I'm a better mom. There you go! Because when I come home from work, I don't have *all* day, just being with the kids. It's just that when I'm working I feel like I'm competent, I'm a person!

Getting this break from the kids, a break that reinforces your feeling of competence and therefore results in more rewarding time with your children is closely connected to the final way paid working mothers commonly attempt to resolve their ambivalence. Their children's happiness, they explain, is dependent upon their *own* happiness as mothers. One hears this again and again: "Happy moms make happy children"; "If I'm happy in my work then I think I can be a better mom"; and "I have to be happy with myself in order to make the children happy." One mother explains it this way:

> In some ways working is good. It's definitely got its positive side, because I get a break. I mean, now what I'm doing [working part-time] is perfect. I go to work. I have time to myself. I get to go to the bathroom when I need to go to the bathroom. I come home and I'm very happy to see my kids again. What's good for the mother and makes the mother happy is definitely good for the kids.

In all these explanations for why their participation in the paid labor force is actually good for their kids, these mothers want to make it clear that they still consider children their primary interest. They are definitely not placing a higher value on material success or power, they say. Nor are they putting their own interests above the interests of their children. They want the children to get all they need. But part of what children need, they argue, is financial security, the material goods required for proper development, some time away from their mothers, more quality time when they are with their mothers, and mothers who are happy in what they do. In all of these statements, paid working mothers clearly recognize the ideology of intensive mothering and testify that they are committed to fulfilling its requirements.

To underline the significance of this point, let me remind the reader that these paid working mothers use methods of child rearing that are just as child-centered, expert-guided, emotionally absorbing, labor-intensive, and financially expensive as their stay-at-home counterparts; they hold the child just as sacred, and they are just as likely to consider themselves as primarily responsible for the present and future well-being of their children. These are also the very same mothers who put a tremendous amount of time and energy into finding appropriate paid caregiver arrangements. Yet for all that they do to meet the needs of their children, they still express some ambivalence about working outside the home. And they still resolve this ambivalence by returning to the logic of intensive mothering and reminding the observer that ultimately they are most interested in what is best for their kids. This is striking.

CONTINUING CONTRADICTIONS

All this ideological work is a measure of the power of the pushes and pulls experienced by American mothers today. A woman can be a stay-at-home mother and claim to follow tradition, but not without paying the price of being treated as an outsider in the larger public world of the market. Or a woman can be a paid worker who participates in that larger world, but she must then pay the price of an impossible double shift. In both cases, women are enjoined to maintain the logic of intensive mothering. These contradictory pressures mimic the contradictory logics operating in this society, and almost all mothers experience them. The complex strategies mothers use to cope with these contradictory logics highlight the emotional, cognitive, and physical toll they take on contemporary mothers.

As I have argued, these strategies also highlight something more. The ways mothers explain their decisions to stay at home or work in the paid labor force, like the pushes and pulls they feel, run in opposite directions. Yet the ways they attempt to resolve the ambivalence they experience as a result of those decisions run in the *same* direction. Stay-at-home mothers, as I have shown, reaffirm their commitment to good mothering, and employed mothers maintain that they are good mothers even though they work. Paid working mothers do not, for instance, claim that child rearing is a relatively meaningless task, that personal profit is their primary goal, and that children are more efficiently raised in child-care centers. If you are a mother, in other words, although both the logic of the workplace and the logic of mothering operate in your life, the logic of intensive mothering has a *stronger* claim.

This phenomenon is particularly curious. The fact that there is no way for either type of mother to get it right would seem all the more reason to give up the logic of intensive mothering, especially since both groups of mothers recognize that paid employment confers more status than motherhood in the larger world. Yet images of freshly baked cookies and *Leave It to Beaver* seem to haunt mothers more often than the housewives' "problem that has no name" (Friedan 1963), and far more often than the image of a corporate manager with a big office, a large staff, and lots of perks. Although these mothers do not want to be defined as "mere" housewives and do want to achieve recognition in the outside world, most would also like to be there when the kids come home from school. Mothers surely try to balance their own desires against the requirements of appropriate child rearing, but in the world of mothering, it is socially unacceptable for them (in word if not in deed) to place their own needs above the needs of their children. A good mother certainly would never simply put her child aside for her own convenience. And placing material wealth or power on a higher plane than the well-being of children is strictly forbidden. It is clear that the two groups come together in holding these values as primary, despite the social devaluation of mothering and despite the glorification of wealth and power.

The portrait of the mommy wars, then, is overdrawn. Although the ideological strategies these groups use to explain their choice of home or paid work include an implicit critique of those "on the other side," this is almost always qualified, and both groups, at least at times, discuss their envy or admiration for the others. More important, as should now be abundantly clear, both groups ultimately share the same set of beliefs and the same set of concerns. Over half the women in my sample explicitly state that the choice between home and paid work depends on the individual woman, her interests, desires, and circumstances. Nearly all the rest argue that home is more important than paid work because children are simply more important than careers or the pursuit of financial gain. The paid working women in my sample were actually twice as likely as their stay-at-home counterparts to respond that home and children are more important and rewarding than paid work.[9] Ideologically speaking, at least, home and children actually seem to become more important to a mother the more time she spends away from them.

There *are* significant differences among mothers—ranging from individual differences to more systematic differences of class, race, and employment. But in the present context, what is most significant is the commitment to the ideology of intensive mothering that women share in spite of their differences. In this, the cultural contradictions of motherhood persist.

The case of paid working mothers is particularly important in this regard, since these are the very mothers who, arguably, have the most to gain from redefining motherhood in such a way as to lighten their load on the second shift. As we have seen, however, this is not exactly what they do. It is true, as Gerson (1985) argues, that there are ways in which paid working mothers do redefine motherhood and lighten their load—for instance, by sending their kids to day care, spending less time with them than their stay-at-home counterparts, legitimating their paid labor-force participation, and engaging in any number of practical strategies to make child-rearing tasks less energy- and time-consuming.[10] But, as I have argued, this does not mean that these mothers have given up the ideology of intensive mothering. Rather, it means that, whether or not they actually do, they feel they should spend a good deal of time looking for appropriate paid caregivers, trying to make up for the lack of quantity time by focusing their energy on providing quality time, and remaining attentive to the central tenets of the ideology of intensive child rearing. It also means that many are left feeling pressed for time, a little guilty, a bit inadequate, and somewhat ambivalent about their position. These stresses and the strain toward compensatory strategies should actually be taken as a measure of the persistent strength of the ideology of intensive mothering.

To deepen the sense of paradox further, one final point should be repeated. There are reasons to expect middle-class mothers to be in the vanguard of transforming ideas about child rearing away from an intensive model. First, middle-class women were historically in the vanguard of transforming child-rearing ideologies. Second, while many poor and working-class women have had to carry a double shift of wage labor and domestic chores for generations, middle-class mothers have had little practice, historically speaking, in juggling paid work and home and therefore might be eager to avoid it. Finally, one could argue that employed mothers in the middle class have more to gain from reconstructing ideas about appropriate child rearing than any other group—not only because their higher salaries mean that more money is at stake, but also because intensive mothering potentially interferes with their career trajectories in a more damaging way than is true of less high-status occupations. But, as I have suggested, middle-class women are, in some respects, those who go about the task of child rearing with the greatest intensity.

When women's increasing participation in the labor force, the cultural ambivalence regarding paid working and stay-at-home mothers, the particular intensity of middle-class mothering, and the demanding character of the cultural model of appropriate child rearing are taken together, it becomes clear that the cultural contradictions of motherhood have been deepened rather than resolved. The history of child-rearing ideas demonstrates that the more powerful the logic of the rationalized market became, so too did its ideological opposition in the logic of intensive mothering. The words of contemporary mothers demonstrate that this trend persists in the day-to-day lives of women.

Notes

1. It seems to me that the popular-culture images of both the traditional mother and the supermom tend to be portraits of professional-class women; the life-styles of working-class and poor women are virtually ignored. Hochschild (1989) does a particularly nice job of describing the image of a professional-class supermom, an image that our society pastes on billboards and covers in full-page ads in popular magazines: "She has that working-mother look as she strides forward, briefcase in one hand, smiling child in the other. Literally and figuratively, she is moving ahead. Her hair, if long, tosses behind her; if it is short, it sweeps back at the sides, suggesting mobility and progress. There is nothing shy or passive about her. She is confident, active, 'liberated.' She wears a dark tailored suit, but with a silk bow or colorful frill that says, 'I'm really feminine underneath.' She has made it in a man's world without sacrificing her femininity. And she has done this on her own. By some personal miracle, this image suggests, she has managed to combine what 150 years of industrialization have split wide apart—child and job, frill and suit, female culture and male" 1).

2. Women's decisions to remain childless or to become stay-at-home mothers or paid working mothers are based in social-structural circumstances. Kathleen Gerson's *Hard Choices: How Women Decide about Work, Career, and Motherhood* (1985) focuses precisely on this issue.

3. For discussions of this war in its various forms, see, for instance, Berger and Berger (1983); Gerson (1985); Ginsburg (1989); Hunter (1991, 1994); Klatch (1987); and Luker (1984).

4. The fact that people use ideological work to come to terms with their social circumstances does not mean that people's ideas are purely the result of their social position. An individual's ideas may well be the reason he or she came to that position in the first place. There is, as Berger points out, a dialectical relationship between ideas and circumstances. And neither one's ideas nor one's position is a matter of completely "free" or individual choice. Both are socially shaped.

5. A full half of the paid working women in my sample were employed only part-time. Nationally, approximately 33 percent of the married mothers employed in 1992 worked part-time; the remaining 67 percent worked full-time, that is, 35 hours or more per week (Hayghe and Bianche 1994). When one adds to this reality the facts that a number of stay-at-home mothers engage in forms of temporary or hidden paid work (such as child care for others) and that all mothers tend to move in and out of the labor force over time, it becomes clear that there is actually a *continuum* rather than a sharp divide between the statuses of paid working mothers and stay-at-home

mothers. Nonetheless, the mothers in my sample systematically defined themselves as either paid working mothers or stay-at-home mothers and focused on the divide rather than on the continuum, as their arguments in this chapter make clear.

6. Over one-third of the stay-at-home mothers I talked to planned to enter the paid labor force within the next five years, one-third were not sure if they would or not, and just under one-third felt sure that they would stay at home for at least another five years. These figures compare with the eighteen of twenty paid working mothers who planned to continue working outside the home; only two hoped they would at some point be able to stay at home with the kids.

    Two of the eighteen stay-at-home mothers in my sample wanted to stay home *indefinitely*. Here's how one of them explained her position: "I don't want to go to work. I enjoy being [at home]. I enjoy it. I don't mind if somebody would call me a housewife or a homemaker. It doesn't bother me. I'm not a feminist. There's no need for me to be out there. For the amount of money I made, it's not worth it." Her concluding remark is, of course, telling. But poorly paid jobs are not the only reason that mothers want to stay home. . . . It should also be recognized that many women want to work outside the home even if their jobs pay poorly.

7. This can be hard on a mother too. For instance: "[My friend] was working full-time, and she came to the baby-sitter's, and her daughter was just kind of clinging to the baby-sitter and wouldn't come to her. And that was it for her. She quit her job."

8. This same argument is also found in popular-press pieces such as "The Managerial Mother" (Schneider 1987). Since the time of these interviews a number of the middle-class employed mothers I know (nearly all of whom are academics) have made this same argument: that they are more "organized, efficient, and effective" as moms because their paid work trains them to develop those skills, just as their double shift forces them to be organized, efficient, and effective *all* the time. In fact, many of these mothers argue that the professionalism they learn as working women explains their intensive mothering. The problem with this explanation is that the ideology of intensive motherhood, as I have shown, is not confined to middle-class, paid-working mothers. Many other women argue that it is mothering itself that teaches them to be more organized, efficient, and effective as mothers and as workers.

    But there is some truth in what my paid professional women friends say. Although intensive mothering has a much broader social basis, there are reasons why middle-class mothers on the one side, and paid working women on the other, are, in some respects, more intensive in their mothering. It makes sense that women who are both middle-class and paid professionals add to this an overlay of training in organization and focused commitment to their assigned tasks. But this only explains differences in degree; it does not explain the larger social grounding for the ideology of intensive mothering.

9. My sample is too small to make any definitive comment on this, but the numbers are as follows: half of the paid working mothers in my study say that children and home are more important for a woman than work, whereas only one-quarter of the stay-at-home mothers respond in this way (with the remainder providing the "it depends" response). And, it is interesting to note, professional-class and affluent paid-working mothers are the group most likely to say that home and children are more important and rewarding than careers; nearly three-quarters of them respond this way.

10. While the historical increase in the use of day-care facilities and alternative caregivers might be seen as an attempt to lessen the cultural contradictions of motherhood, it should be recognized that, historically speaking, mothers rarely did the job of raising children alone: rural families often had live-in help and relied on older siblings to take care of the younger ones; working-class women in urban areas also relied on older children as well as on friends and neighbors; and many upper-class women depended upon servants, nannies, and nursemaids. Although there does seem to have been a period during the 1950s and 1960s when families were less able to obtain and less likely to use help in raising children, today's alternatives to exclusively maternal care are probably in large measure a simple *substitute* for the help that was previously available. Furthermore, it is important to note that the expectations for the task are much higher today than they once were, that mothers must therefore expend much time and energy seeking out and assuring the maintenance of the proper day-care situation, and that the use of day care coexists with increased expectations for mothers to make up for the hours their children spend under the care of others.

References_____

Berger, Bennett. 1981. *Survival of a Counterculture*. Berkeley: University of California Press.
Berger, Brigitte, and Peter Berger. 1983. *The War over the Family: Capturing the Middle Ground*. Garden City, NY: Anchor.
Darnton, Nina. 1990. "Mommy vs. Mommy." *Newsweek*, June 4.
Friedan, Betty. 1963. *The Feminine Mystique*. New York: Dell.
Gerson, Kathleen. 1985. *Hard Choices: How Women Decide about Work, Career, and Motherhood*. Berkeley: University of California Press.
Schwartz, Felice. 1989. "Management Women and the New Facts of Life." *Harvard Business Review* 67 (1): 65–77.

■ **READING 4**

Decline of the Family: Conservative, Liberal, and Feminist Views

Janet Z. Giele

In the 1990s the state of American families and children became a new and urgent topic. Everyone recognized that families had changed. Divorce rates had risen dramatically. More women were in the labor force. Evidence on rising teenage suicides, high rates of teen births, and disturbing levels of addiction and violence had put children at risk.

Conservatives have held that these problems can be traced to a culture of toleration and an expanding welfare state that undercut self-reliance and community standards. They focus on the family as a caregiving institution and try to restore its strengths by changing the culture of marriage and parenthood. Liberals center on the disappearance of manual jobs that throws less educated men out of work and undercuts their status in the family as well as rising hours of work among the middle class that makes stable two-parent families more difficult to maintain. Liberals argue that structural changes are needed outside the family in the public world of employment and schools.

The feminist vision combines both the reality of human interdependence in the family and individualism of the workplace. Feminists want to protect diverse family forms that allow realization of freedom and equality while at the same time nurturing the children of the next generation.

THE CONSERVATIVE EXPLANATION: SELFISHNESS AND MORAL DECLINE

The new family advocates turn their spotlight on the breakdown in the two-parent family, saying that rising divorce, illegitimacy, and father absence have put children at greater risk of school failure, unemployment, and antisocial behavior. The remedy is to restore religious faith and family commitment as well as to cut welfare payments to unwed mothers and mother-headed families.

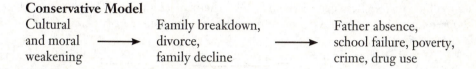

Conservative Model

Cultural and moral weakening $\longrightarrow$ Family breakdown, divorce, family decline $\longrightarrow$ Father absence, school failure, poverty, crime, drug use

Cultural and Moral Weakening

To many conservatives, the modern secularization of religious practice and the decline of religious affiliation have undermined the norms of sexual abstinence before marriage and the prohibitions of adultery or divorce thereafter. Sanctions against illegitimacy or divorce have been made to seem narrow-minded and prejudiced. In addition, daytime television and the infamous example of Murphy Brown, a single mother having a child out of wedlock, helped to obscure simple notions of right and wrong. Barbara Dafoe Whitehead's controversial article in the *Atlantic* entitled "Dan Quayle Was Right" is an example of this argument.[1]

Gradual changes in marriage law have also diminished the hold of tradition. Restrictions against waiting periods, race dissimilarity, and varying degrees of consanguinity were gradually disappearing all over the United States and Europe.[2] While Mary Ann Glendon viewed the change cautiously but relativistically—as a process that waxed and waned across the centuries—others have interpreted these changes as a movement from status to contract (i.e., from attention to the particular individual's characteristics to reliance on the impersonal considerations of the market place).[3] The resulting transformation lessened the family's distinctive capacity to serve as a bastion of private freedom against the leveling effect and impersonality of public bureaucracy.

Erosion of the Two-Parent Family

To conservatives, one of the most visible causes of family erosion was government welfare payments, which made fatherless families a viable option. In *Losing Ground*, Charles Murray used the rise in teenage illegitimate births as proof that government-sponsored welfare programs had actually contributed to the breakdown of marriage.[4] Statistics on rising divorce and mother-headed families appeared to provide ample proof that the two-parent family was under siege. The proportion of all households headed by married couples fell from 77 percent in 1950 to 61 percent in 1980 and 55 percent in 1993.[5] Rising cohabitation, divorce rates, and births out of wedlock all contributed to the trend. The rise in single-person households was also significant, from only 12 percent of all households in 1950 to 27 percent in 1980, a trend fed by rising affluence and the undoubling of living arrangements that occurred with the expansion of the housing supply after World War II.[6]

The growth of single-parent households, however, was the most worrisome to policymakers because of their strong links to child poverty. In 1988, 50 percent of all children were found in mother-only families compared with 20 percent in 1950. The parental situation of children in poverty changed accordingly. Of all poor children in 1959, 73 percent had two parents present and 20 percent had a mother only. By 1988, only 35 percent of children in poverty lived with two parents and 57 percent lived with a mother only. These developments were fed by rising rates of divorce and out-of-wedlock births. Between 1940 and 1990, the divorce rate rose from 8.8 to 21 per thousand married women. Out-of-wedlock births exploded from 5 percent in 1960 to 26 percent in 1990.[7]

To explain these changes, conservatives emphasize the breakdown of individual and cultural commitment to marriage and the loss of stigma for divorce and illegitimacy. They understand both trends to be the result of greater emphasis on short-term gratification and on adults' personal desires rather than on what is good for children. A young woman brings a child into the world without thinking about who will support it. A husband divorces his wife and forms another household, possibly with other children, and leaves children of the earlier family behind without necessarily feeling obliged to be present in their upbringing or to provide them with financial support.

Negative Consequences for Children

To cultural conservatives there appears to be a strong connection between erosion of the two-parent family and the rise of health and social problems in children. Parental investment in children has declined—especially in the time available for supervision and companionship. Parents had roughly 10 fewer hours per week for their children in 1986 than in 1960, largely because more married women were employed (up from 24 percent in 1940 to 52 percent in 1983) and more mothers of young children (under age six) were working (up from 12 percent in 1940 to 50 percent in 1983). By the late 1980s just over half of mothers of children under a year old were in the labor force for at least part of the year.[8] At the same time fathers were increasingly absent from the family because of desertion, divorce, or failure to marry. In 1980, 15 percent of white children, 50 percent of black children, and 27 percent of children of Hispanic origin had no father present. Today 36 percent of children are living apart from their biological fathers compared with only 17 percent in 1960.[9]

Without a parent to supervise children after school, keep them from watching television all day, or prevent them from playing in dangerous neighborhoods, many more children appear to be falling by the wayside, victims of drugs, obesity, violence, suicide, or failure in school. During the 1960s and 1970s the suicide rate for persons aged fifteen to nineteen more than doubled. The proportion of obese children between the ages of six and eleven rose from 18 to 27 percent. Average SAT scores fell, and 25 percent of all high school students failed to graduate.[10] In 1995 the Council on Families in America reported, "Recent surveys have found that children from broken homes, when they become teenagers, have 2 to 3 times more behavioral and psychological problems than do children from intact homes."[11] Father absence is blamed by the fatherhood movement for the rise in violence among young males. David Blankenhorn and others reason that the lack of a positive and productive male role model has contributed to an uncertain masculine identity which then uses violence and aggression to prove itself. Every child deserves a father and "in a good society, men prove their masculinity not by killing other people, impregnating lots of women, or amassing large fortunes, but rather by being committed fathers and loving husbands."[12]

Psychologist David Elkind, in *The Hurried Child*, suggests that parents' work and time constraints have pushed down the developmental timetable to younger ages so that small children are being expected to take care of themselves and perform at levels which are robbing them of their childhood. The consequences are depression, discouragement, and a loss of joy at learning and growing into maturity.[13]

Reinvention of Marriage

According to the conservative analysis, the solution to a breakdown in family values is to revitalize and reinstitutionalize marriage. The culture should change to give higher priority to marriage and parenting. The legal code should favor marriage and encourage parental responsibility on the part of fathers as well as mothers. Government should cut back welfare programs which have supported alternate family forms.

The cultural approach to revitalizing marriage is to raise the overall priority given to family activities relative to work, material consumption, or leisure. Marriage is seen as the basic building block of civil society, which helps to hold together the fabric of volunteer activity and mutual support that underpins any democratic society.[14] Some advocates are unapologetically judgmental toward families who fall outside the two-parent mold. According to a 1995 *Newsweek* article on "The Return of Shame," David Blankenhorn believes "a stronger sense of shame about illegitimacy and divorce would do more than any tax cut or any new governmental program to maximize the life circumstances of children." But he also adds that the ultimate goal is "to move beyond stigmatizing only teenage mothers toward an understanding of the terrible message sent by all of us when we minimize the importance of fathers or contribute to the breakup of families."[15]

Another means to marriage and family revitalization is some form of taking a "pledge." Prevention programs for teenage pregnancy affirm the ideal of chastity before marriage. Athletes for Abstinence, an organization founded by a professional basketball player, preaches that young people should "save sex for marriage." A Baptist-led national program called True Love Waits has gathered an abstinence pledge from hundreds of thousands of teenagers since it was begun in the spring of 1993. More than 2,000 school districts now offer an abstinence-based sex education curriculum entitled "Sex Respect." Parents who are desperate about their children's sexual behavior are at last seeing ways that society can resist the continued sexualization of childhood.[16]

The new fatherhood movement encourages fathers to promise that they will spend more time with their children. The National Fatherhood Initiative argues that men's roles as fathers should not simply duplicate women's roles as mothers but should teach those essential qualities which are perhaps uniquely conveyed by fathers—the ability to take risks, contain emotions, and be decisive. In addition, fathers fulfill a time-honored role of providing for children as well as teaching them.[17]

Full-time mothers have likewise formed support groups to reassure themselves that not having a job and being at home full-time for their children is an honorable choice, although it is typically undervalued and perhaps even scorned by dual-earner couples and women with careers. A 1994 *Barron's* article claimed that young people in their twenties ("generation X") were turning away from the two-paycheck family and scaling down their consumption so that young mothers could stay at home. Although Labor Department statistics show no such trend but only a flattening of the upward rise of women's employment, a variety of poll data does suggest that Americans would rather spend less time at work and more time with their families.[18] Such groups as Mothers at Home (with 15,000 members) and Mothers' Home Business Network (with 6,000 members) are trying to create a sea change that reverses the priority given to paid work outside the home relative to unpaid caregiving work inside the family.[19]

Conservatives see government cutbacks as one of the major strategies for strengthening marriage and restoring family values. In the words of Lawrence Mead, we have "taxed Peter to pay Paula."[20] According to a *Wall Street Journal* editorial, the "relinquishment of personal responsibility" among people who bring children into the world without any visible means of support is at the root of educational, health, and emotional problems of children from one-parent families, their higher accident and mortality rates, and rising crime.[21]

The new congressional solution is to cut back on the benefits to young men and women who "violate social convention by having children they cannot support."[22] Sociologist Brigitte Berger notes that the increase in children and women on welfare coincided with the explosion of federal child welfare programs—family planning, prenatal and postnatal care, child nutrition, child abuse prevention and treatment, child health and guidance, day care, Head Start, and Aid to Families with Dependent Children (AFDC), Medicaid, and Food Stamps. The solution is to turn back the debilitating culture of welfare dependency by decentralizing the power of the federal government and restoring the role of intermediary community institutions such as the neighborhood and the church. The mechanism for change would be block grants to the states which would change the welfare culture from the ground up.[23] Robert Rector of the American Heritage Foundation explains that the states would use these funds for a wide variety of alternative programs to discourage illegitimate births and to care for children born out of wedlock, such as promoting adoption, closely supervised group homes for unmarried mothers and their children, and pregnancy prevention programs (except abortion).[24]

Government programs, however, are only one way to bring about cultural change. The Council on Families in America puts its hope in grassroots social movements to change the hearts and minds of religious and civil leaders, employers, human service professionals, courts, and the media and entertainment industry. The Council enunciates four ideals: marital permanence, childbearing confined to marriage, every child's right to have a father, and limitation of parents' total work time (60 hours per week) to permit adequate time with their families.[25] To restore the cultural ideal of the two-parent family, they would make all other types of family life less attractive and more difficult.

ECONOMIC RESTRUCTURING: LIBERAL ANALYSIS OF FAMILY CHANGE

Liberals agree that there are serious problems in America's social health and the condition of its children. But they pinpoint economic and structural changes that have placed new demands on the family without providing countervailing social supports.

The economy has become ever more specialized with rapid technological change undercutting established occupations. More women have entered the labor force as their child-free years have increased due to a shorter childbearing period and longer lifespan. The family has lost economic functions to the urban workplace and socialization functions to the school. What is left is the intimate relationship between the marital couple, which, unbuffered by the traditional economic division of labor between men and women, is subject to even higher demands for emotional fulfillment and is thus more vulnerable to breakdown when it falls short of those demands.

Liberal Model

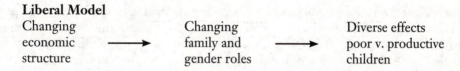

| Changing economic structure | → | Changing family and gender roles | → | Diverse effects poor v. productive children |

The current family crisis thus stems from structural more than cultural change—changes in the economy, a pared-down nuclear family, and less parental time at home. Market forces have led to a new ethic of individual flexibility and autonomy. More dual-earner couples and single-parent families have broadened the variety of family forms. More single-parent families and more working mothers have decreased the time available for parenting. Loss of the father's income through separation and divorce has forced many women and children into poverty with inadequate health care, poor education, and inability to save for future economic needs. The solution that most liberals espouse is a government-sponsored safety net which will facilitate women's employment, mute the effects of poverty, and help women and children to become economically secure.

Recent Changes in the Labor Market

Liberals attribute the dramatic changes in the family to the intrusion of the money economy rather than cultural and moral decline. In a capitalist society individual behavior follows the market. Adam Smith's "invisible hand" brings together buyers and sellers who maximize their satisfaction through an exchange of resources in the marketplace. Jobs are now with an employer, not with the family business or family farm as in preindustrial times. The cash economy has, in the words of Robert Bellah, "invaded" the diffuse personal relationships of trust between family and community members and transformed them into specific impersonal transactions. In an agricultural economy husbands and wives and parents and children were bound together in relationships of exchange that served each others' mutual interests. But modern society erodes this social capital of organization, trust among individuals, and mutual obligation that enhances both productivity and parenting.[26]

The market has also eroded community by encouraging maximum mobility of goods and services. Cheaper labor in the South, lower fuel prices, and deeper tax breaks attracted first textile factories, then the shoe industry, and later automobile assembly plants which had begun in the North. Eventually, many of these jobs left the country. Loss of manufacturing jobs has had dramatic consequences for employment of young men without a college education and their capacity to support a family. In the 1970s,

68 percent of male high school graduates had a full-time, year-round job compared with only 51 percent in the 1980s. Many new jobs are located in clerical work, sales, or other service occupations traditionally associated with women. The upshot is a deteriorating employment picture for less well educated male workers at the same time that there are rising opportunities for women. Not surprisingly, even more middle income men and women combine forces to construct a two-paycheck family wage.[27]

Changing Family Forms

Whereas the farm economy dictated a two-parent family and several children as the most efficient work group, the market economy gives rise to a much wider variety of family forms. A woman on the frontier in the 1800s had few other options even if she were married to a drunken, violent, or improvident husband. In today's economy this woman may have enough education to get a clerical job that will support her and her children in a small apartment where the family will be able to use public schools and other public amenities.[28]

Despite its corrosive effect on family relations, the modern economy has also been a liberating force. Women could escape patriarchal domination; the young could seek their fortune without waiting for an inheritance from their elders—all a process that a century ago was aligned with a cultural shift that Fred Weinstein and Gerald Platt termed "the wish to be free."[29] Dramatic improvements took place in the status of women as they gained the right to higher education, entry into the professions, and the elective franchise.[30] Similarly, children were released from sometimes cruel and exploitive labor and became the object of deliberate parental investment and consumption.[31] Elders gained pensions for maintenance and care that made them economically independent of their adult children. All these developments could be understood as part of what William J. Goode has referred to as the "world revolution in family patterns" which resulted in liberation and equality of formerly oppressed groups.[32]

The current assessment of change in family forms is, however, mostly negative because of the consequences for children. More parental investment in work outside the family has meant less time for children. According to liberals, parents separate or divorce or have children outside of marriage because of the economic structure, not because they have become less moral or more selfish. Young women have children out of wedlock when the young men whom they might marry have few economic prospects and when the women themselves have little hope for their own education or employment.[33] Change in the family thus begins with jobs. Advocates of current government programs therefore challenge the conservatives' assertion that welfare caused the breakup of two-parent families by supporting mothers with dependent children. According to William Julius Wilson, it is partly the lack of manual labor jobs for the would-be male breadwinner in inner-city Chicago—the scarcity of "marriageable males"—which drives up the illegitimacy rate.[34]

Among educated women, it is well known that the opportunity costs of foregone income from staying home became so high during the 1950s and 1960s that ever increasing numbers of women deserted full-time homemaking to take paid employment.[35] In the 1990s several social scientists have further noted that Richard Easterlin's prediction that women will return to the home during the 1980s never happened. Instead, women continued in the labor force because of irreversible normative changes surrounding women's equality and the need for women's income to finance children's expensive college education.[36] Moreover, in light of globalization of the economy and increasing job insecurity in the face of corporate downsizing, economists and sociologists are questioning Gary Becker's thesis that the lower waged worker in a household (typically the woman) will tend to become a full-time homemaker while the higher waged partner becomes the primary breadwinner. Data from Germany and the United States on the trend toward women's multiple roles suggests that uncertainty about the future has made women invest more strongly than ever in their own careers. They know that if they drop out for very long they will have difficulty reentering if they have to tide over the family when the main breadwinner loses his job.[37]

Consequences for Children

The ideal family in the liberal economic model, according to political philosopher Iris Young, is one which has sufficient income to support the parents and the children and "to foster in those children the emotional and intellectual capacities to acquire such well-paid, secure jobs themselves, and also sufficient to finance a retirement."[38] Dependent families do not have self-sufficient income but must rely on friends, relatives, charity, or the state to carry out their contribution to bringing up children and being good citizens.

Among liberals there is an emerging consensus that the current economic structure leads to two kinds of underinvestment in children that are implicated in their later dependency—material poverty, characteristic of the poor, and "time" poverty, characteristic of the middle class.

Thirty years ago Daniel Patrick Moynihan perceived that material poverty and job loss for a man put strain on the marriage, sometimes to the point that he would leave. His children also did less well in school.[39] Rand Conger, in his studies of Iowa families who lost their farms during the 1980s, found that economic hardship not only puts strain on the marriage but leads to harsh parenting practices and poorer outcomes for children.[40] Thus it appears possible that poverty may not just be the result of family separation, divorce, and ineffective childrearing practices; it may also be the *cause* of the irritability, quarrels, and violence which lead to marital breakdown. Material underinvestment in children is visible not just with the poor but in the changing ratio of per capita income of children and adults in U.S. society as a whole. As the proportion of households without children has doubled over the last century (from 30 to 65 percent), per capita income of children has fallen from 71 percent of adult income in 1870 to 63 percent in 1930 and 51 percent in 1983.[41]

The problem of "time" poverty used to be almost exclusively associated with mothers' employment. Numerous studies explored whether younger children did better if their mother was a full-time homemaker rather than employed outside the home but found no clear results.[42] Lately the lack of parental time for children has become much more acute because parents are working a total of twenty-one hours more per week than in 1970 and because there are more single-parent families. In 1965 the average child spent about thirty hours a week interacting with a parent, compared with seventeen hours in the 1980s.[43] Moreover, parents are less dependent on their children to provide support for them during old age, and children feel less obligated to do so. As skilled craftsmanship, the trades, and the family farms have disappeared, children's upbringing can no longer be easily or cheaply combined with what parents are already doing. So adults are no longer so invested in children's futures. The result is that where the social capital of group affiliations and mutual obligations is the lowest (in the form of continuity of neighborhoods, a two-parent family, or a parent's interest in higher education for her children), children are 20 percent more likely to drop out of high school.[44]

It is not that parents prefer their current feelings of being rushed, working too many hours, and having too little time with their families. Economist Juliet Schor reports that at least two-thirds of persons she surveyed about their desires for more family time versus more salary would take a cut in salary if it could mean more time with their families. Since this option is not realistically open to many, what parents appear to do is spend more money on their children as a substitute for spending more time with them.[45]

Fixing the Safety Net

Since liberals believe in a market economy with sufficient government regulation to assure justice and equality of opportunity, they support those measures which will eradicate the worst poverty and assure the healthy reproduction of the next generation.[46] What particularly worries them, however, is Charles Murray's observation that since 1970 the growth of government welfare programs has been associated with a *rise* in poverty among children. Payments to poor families with children, while not generous, have nevertheless enabled adults to be supported by attachment to their children.[47] Society is faced with a dilemma between addressing material poverty through further government subsidy and time poverty through policies on parental leave and working hours. It turns out that the United States is trying to do both.

Measures for addressing material poverty would stimulate various kinds of training and job opportunities. The Family Support Act of 1988 would move AFDC mothers off the welfare rolls by giving them job training and requiring them to join the labor force. Such action would bring their economic responsibility for supporting their children into line with their parental authority. A whole program of integrated supports for health insurance, job training, earned income tax credits for the working poor, child support by the noncustodial parent, and supported work is put forward by economist David Ellwood in *Poor Support*.[48] An opposite strategy is to consolidate authority over children with the state's economic responsibility for their care by encouraging group homes and adoption for children whose parents cannot support them economically.[49]

Means for addressing time poverty are evident in such legislative initiatives as the Family and Medical Leave Act of 1993. By encouraging employers to grant parental leave or other forms of flexible work time, government policy is recognizing the value of parents having more time with their children, but the beneficiaries of such change are largely middle-class families who can afford an unpaid parental leave.[50] Another tactic is to reform the tax law to discourage marital splitting. In a couple with two children in which the father earns $16,000 annually and the mother $9,000, joint tax filing gives them no special consideration. But if they file separately, each taking one child as a dependent, the woman will receive about $5,000 in Earned Income Tax Credit and an extra $2,000 in food stamps.[51] Changing the tax law to remove the incentives for splitting, establishing paternity of children born out of wedlock, and intensifying child support enforcement to recover economic support from fathers are all examples of state efforts to strengthen the kinship unit.

INTERDEPENDENCE: THE FEMINIST VISION OF WORK AND CAREGIVING

A feminist perspective has elements in common with both conservatives and liberals: a respect for the family as an institution (shared with the conservatives) and an appreciation of modernity (valued by the liberals). In addition, a feminist perspective grapples with the problem of women's traditionally subordinate status and how to improve it through both a "relational" and an "individualist" strategy while also sustaining family life and the healthy rearing of children.[52] At the same time feminists are skeptical of both conservative and liberal solutions. Traditionalists have so often relied on women as the exploited and underpaid caregivers in the family to enable men's activities in the public realm. Liberals are sometimes guilty of a "male" bias in focusing on the independent individual actor in the marketplace who does not realize that his so-called "independence," is possible only because he is actually *dependent* on all kinds of relationships that made possible his education and life in a stable social order.[53]

By articulating the value of caregiving along with the ideal of women's autonomy, feminists are in a position to examine modern capitalism critically for its effects on families and to offer alternative policies that place greater value on the quality of life and human relationships. They judge family strength not by their *form* (whether they have two-parents) but by their functioning (whether they promote human satisfaction and development) and whether both women and men are able to be family caregivers as well as productive workers. They attribute difficulties of children less to the absence of the two-parent family than to low-wage work of single mothers, inadequate child care, and inhospitable housing and neighborhoods.

Feminist Model

| Lack of cooperation among community, family, and work | → | Families where adults are stressed and overburdened | → | Children lack sufficient care and attention from parents |

Accordingly, feminists would work for reforms that build and maintain the social capital of volunteer groups, neighborhoods, and communities because a healthy civil society promotes the well-being of families and individuals as well as economic prosperity and a democratic state. They would also recognize greater role flexibility across the life cycle so that both men and women could engage in caregiving, and they would encourage education and employment among women as well as among men.

Disappearance of Community

From a feminist perspective, family values have become an issue because individualism has driven out the sense of collective responsibility in our national culture. American institutions and social policies have not properly implemented a concern for all citizens. Comparative research on family structure, teenage pregnancy, poverty, and child outcomes in other countries demonstrates that where support is generous to help *all* families and children, there are higher levels of health and general education and lower levels of violence and child deviance than in the United States.[54]

Liberal thinking and the focus on the free market have made it seem that citizens make their greatest contribution when they are self-sufficient, thereby keeping themselves off the public dole. But feminist theorist Iris Young argues that many of the activities that are basic to a healthy democratic society (such as cultural production, caretaking, political organizing, and charitable activities) will never be profitable in a private market. Yet many of the recipients of welfare and Social Security such as homemakers, single mothers, and retirees are doing important volunteer work caring for children and helping others in their communities. Thus the social worth of a person's contribution is not just in earning a paycheck that allows economic independence but also in making a social contribution. Such caretaking of other dependent citizens and of the body politic should be regarded as honorable, not inferior, and worthy of society's support and subsidy.[55]

In fact it appears that married women's rising labor force participation from 41 percent in 1970 to 58 percent in 1990 may have been associated with their withdrawal from unpaid work in the home and community.[56] Volunteer membership in everything from the PTA to bowling leagues declined by over 25 percent between 1969 and 1993. There is now considerable concern that the very basis that Alexis de Tocqueville thought necessary to democracy is under siege.[57] To reverse this trend, social observers suggest that it will be necessary to guard time for families and leisure that is currently being sucked into the maw of paid employment. What is needed is a reorientation of priorities to give greater value to unpaid family and community work by both men and women.

National policies should also be reoriented to give universal support to children at every economic level of society, but especially to poor children. In a comparison of countries in the Organization for Economic Cooperation and Development, the United States ranks at the top in average male wages but near the bottom in its provision for disposable income for children. In comparison with the $700 per month available to children in Norway, France, or the Netherlands in 1992, U.S. children of a single nonemployed mother received only slightly under $200.[58] The discrepancy is explained by very unequal distribution of U.S. income, with the top quintile, the "fortunate fifth," gaining 47 percent of the national income while the bottom fifth receives only 3.6 percent.[59] This sharp inequality is, in turn, explained by an ideology of individualism that justifies the disproportionate gains of the few for their innovation and productivity and the meager income of the poor for their low initiative or competence. Lack of access to jobs and the low pay accruing to many contingent service occupations simply worsen the picture.

Feminists are skeptical of explanations that ascribe higher productivity to the higher paid and more successful leading actors while ignoring the efforts and contribution of the supporting cast. They know that being an invisible helper is the situation of many women. This insight is congruent with new ideas about the importance "social capital" to the health of a society that have been put forward recently by a number of social scientists.[60] Corporations cannot be solely responsible for maintaining the web of community, although they are already being asked to serve as extended family, neighborhood support group, and national health service.

Diversity of Family Forms

Those who are concerned for strengthening the civil society immediately turn to the changing nature of the family as being a key building block. Feminists worry that seemingly sensible efforts to reverse the trend of rising divorce and single parenthood will privilege the two-parent family to the detriment of women; they propose instead that family values be understood in a broader sense as valuing the family's unique capacity for giving emotional and material support rather than implying simply a two-parent form.

The debate between conservatives, liberals, and feminists on the issue of the two-parent family has been most starkly stated by sociologist Judith Stacey and political philosopher Iris Young.[61] They regard the requirement that all women stay in a marriage as an invitation to coercion and subordination and an assault on the principles of freedom and self-determination that are at the foundation of democracy. Moreover, as Christopher Jencks and Kathryn Edin conclude from their study of several hundred welfare families, the current welfare reform rhetoric that no couple should have a child unless they can support it, does not take into account the uncertainty of life in which people who start out married or with adequate income [do] not always remain so. In the face of the worldwide dethronement of the two-parent family (approximately one-quarter to one-third of all families around the globe are headed by women), marriage should not be seen as the cure for child poverty. Mothers should not be seen as less than full citizens if they are not married or not employed (in 1989 there were only 16 million males between the ages of 25 and 34 who made over $12,000 compared with 20 million females of the same age who either had a child or wanted one).[62] National family policy should instead begin with a value on women's autonomy and self-determination that includes the right to bear children. Mother-citizens are helping to reproduce the next generation for the whole society, and in that responsibility they deserve at least partial support.

From a feminist perspective the goal of the family is not only to bring up a healthy and productive new generation; families also provide the intimate and supportive group of kin or fictive kin that foster the health and well-being of every person—young or old, male or female, heterosexual, homosexual, or celibate. Recognition as "family" should therefore not be confined to the traditional two-parent unit connected by blood, marriage, or adoption, but should be extended to include kin of a divorced spouse (as Stacey documented in her study of Silicon Valley families), same-sex partnerships, congregate households of retired persons, group living arrangements, and so on.[63] Twenty years ago economist Nancy Barrett noted that such diversity in family and household form was already present. Among all U.S. households in 1976, no one of the six major types constituted more than 15–20 percent: couples with and without children under eighteen with the wife in the labor force (15.4 and 13.3 percent respectively); couples with or without children under 18 with the wife not in the labor force (19.1 and 17.1 percent); female- or male-headed households (14.4 percent); and single persons living alone (20.6 percent).[64]

Such diversity both describes and informs contemporary "family values" in the United States. Each family type is numerous enough to have a legitimacy of its own, yet no single form is the dominant one. As a result the larger value system has evolved to encompass beliefs and rules that legitimate each type on the spectrum. The regressive alternative is "fundamentalism" that treats the two-parent family with children as the only legitimate form, single-parent families as unworthy of support, and the nontraditional forms as illegitimate. In 1995 the general population appears to have accepted diversity of family forms as normal. A Harris poll of 1,502 women and 460 men found that only 2 percent of women and 1 percent of men defined family as "being about the traditional nuclear family." One out of ten women defined family values as loving, taking care of, and supporting each other, knowing right from wrong or having good values, and nine out of ten said society should value all types of families.[65] It appears most Americans believe that an Aunt Polly single-parent type of family for a Huck Finn that provides economic support, shelter, meals, a place to sleep and to withdraw, is better than no family at all.

Amidst gradual acceptance of greater diversity in family form, the gender-role revolution is also loosening the sex-role expectations traditionally associated with bread-winning and homemaking. Feminists believe that men and women can each do both.[66] In addition, women in advanced industrial nations have by and large converged upon a new life pattern of multiple roles by which they combine work and family life. The negative outcome is an almost universal "double burden" for working women in which they spend eighty-four hours per week on paid and family work, married men spend seventy-two hours, and single persons without children spend fifty hours.[67] The positive consequence, however, appears to be improved physical and mental health for those women who, though stressed, combine work and family roles.[68] In addition, where a woman's husband helps her more with the housework, she is less likely to think of getting a divorce.[69]

The Precarious Situation of Children

The principal remedy that conservatives and liberals would apply to the problems of children is to restore the two-parent family by reducing out-of-wedlock births, increasing the presence of fathers, and encouraging couples who are having marital difficulties to avoid divorce for the sake of their children. Feminists, on the other hand, are skeptical that illegitimacy, father absence, or divorce are the principal culprits they are made out to be. Leon Eisenberg reports that over half of all births in Sweden and one-quarter of births in France are to unmarried women, but without the disastrous correlated effects observed in the United States. Arlene Skolnick and Stacey Rosencrantz cite longitudinal studies showing that most children recover from the immediate negative effects of divorce.[70]

How then, while supporting the principle that some fraction of women should be able to head families as single parents, do feminists analyze the problem of ill health, antisocial behavior, and poverty among children? Their answer focuses on the *lack of institutional supports* for the new type of dual-earner and single-parent families that are more prevalent today. Rather than attempt to force families back into the traditional mold, feminists note that divorce, lone-mother families, and women's employment are on the rise in every industrialized nation. But other countries have not seen the same devastating decline in child well-being, teen pregnancy, suicides and violent death, school failure, and a rising population of children in poverty. These other countries have four key elements of social and family policy which protect all children and their mothers: (1) work guarantees and other economic supports; (2) child care; (3) health care; and (4) housing subsidies. In the United States these benefits are scattered and uneven; those who can pay their way do so; only those who are poor or disabled receive AFDC for economic support, some help with child care, Medicaid for health care, and government-subsidized housing.

A first line of defense is to raise women's wages through raising the minimum wage, then provide them greater access to male-dominated occupations with higher wages. One-half of working women do not earn a wage adequate to support a family of four above the poverty line. Moreover, women in low-wage occupations are subject to frequent lay-offs and lack of benefits. Training to improve their human capital, provision of child care, and broadening of benefits would help raise women's capacity to support a family. Eisenberg reports that the Human Development Index of the United Nations (HDI), which ranks countries by such indicators as life expectancy, educational levels, and per capita income, places the United States fifth and Sweden sixth in the world. But when the HDI is recalculated to take into account equity of treatment of women, Sweden rises to first place and the United States falls to ninth. Therefore, one of the obvious places to begin raising children's status is to "raise the economic status and earning power of their mothers."[71]

A second major benefit which is not assured to working mothers is child care. Among school-age children up to thirteen years of age, one-eighth lack any kind of after-school child care. Children come to the factories where their mothers work and wait on the lawn or in the lobby until their mothers are finished working. If a child is sick, some mothers risk losing a job if they stay home. Others are latchkey kids or in unknown circumstances such as sleeping in their parents' cars or loitering on the streets. Although 60 percent of mothers of the 22 million preschool children are working, there are only 10 million child care places available, a shortfall of one to three million slots.[72] Lack of good quality care for her children not only distracts a mother, adds to her absences from work, and makes her less productive, it also exposes the child to a lack of attention and care that leads to violent and antisocial behavior and poor performance in school.

Lack of medical benefits is a third gaping hole for poor children and lone-parent families. Jencks and Edin analyze what happens to a Chicago-area working woman's income if she goes off welfare. Her total income, in 1993, dollars on AFDC (with food stamps, unreported earnings, help from family and friends) adds up to $12,355, in addition to which she receives Medicaid and child care. At a $6 per hour full-time job, however, without AFDC, with less than half as much from food stamps, with an Earned Income Tax Credit, and help from relatives, her total income would add to $20,853. But she would have to pay for her own medical care, bringing her effective income down to $14,745 if she found free child care, and $9,801 if she had to pay for child care herself.[73]

Some housing subsidies or low-income housing are available to low-income families. But the neighborhoods and schools are frequently of poor quality and plagued by violence. To bring up children in a setting where they cannot safely play with others introduces important risk factors that cannot simply be attributed to divorce and single parenthood. Rather than being protected and being allowed to be innocent, children must learn to be competent at a very early age. The family, rather than being child-centered, must be adult-centered, not because parents are selfish or self-centered but because the institutions of the society have changed the context of family life.[74] These demands may be too much for children, and depression, violence, teen suicide, teen pregnancy, and school failure may result. But it would be myopic to think that simply restoring the two-parent family would be enough to solve all these problems.

Constructing Institutions for the Good Society

What is to be done? Rather than try to restore the two-parent family as the conservatives suggest or change the economy to provide more jobs as recommended by the liberals, the feminists focus on the need to revise and construct institutions to accommodate the new realities of work and family life. Such an undertaking requires, however, a broader interpretation of family values, a recognition that families benefit not only their members but the public interest, and fresh thinking about how to schedule work and family demands of everyday life as well as the entire life cycle of men and women.

The understanding of family values has to be extended in two ways. First, American values should be stretched to embrace all citizens, their children and families, whether they are poor, white, or people of color, or living in a one-parent family. In 1977, Kenneth Keniston titled the report of the Carnegie Commission on Children *All Our Children*. Today many Americans still speak and act politically in ways suggesting that they *disown* other people's children as the next generation who will inherit the land and support the economy. Yet in the view of most feminists and other progressive reformers, all these children should be embraced for the long-term good of the nation.[75] By a commitment to "family values" feminists secondly intend to valorize the family as a distinctive intimate group of many forms that is needed by persons of all ages but especially children. To serve the needs of children and other dependent persons, the family must be given support and encouragement by the state to carry out its unique functions. Iris Young contends that marriage should not be used to reduce the ultimate need for the state to serve as a means to distribute needed supports to the families of those less fortunate.[76] Compare the example of the GI Bill of Rights after World War II, which provided educational benefits to those who had served their country in the military. Why should there not be a similar approach to the contribution that a parent makes in raising a healthy and productive youngster?[77]

At the community level families should be embraced by all the institutions of the civil society—schools, hospitals, churches, and employers—as the hidden but necessary complement to the bureaucratic and impersonal workings of these formal organizations. Schools rely on parents for the child's "school readiness." Hospitals send home patients who need considerable home care before becoming completely well. The work of the church is carried out and reinforced in the family; and when families fail, it is the unconditional love and intimacy of family that the church tries to replicate. Employers depend on families to give the rest, shelter, emotional support, and other maintenance of human capital that will motivate workers and make them productive. Increasingly, the professionals and managers in these formal organizations are realizing that they need to work more closely with parents and family members if they are to succeed.

Feminists would especially like to see the reintegration of work and family life that was torn apart at the time of the industrial revolution when productive work moved out of the home and into the factory. Several proposals appear repeatedly: parental leave (which now is possible through the Family and Medical Leave Act of 1993); flexible hours and part-time work shared by working parents but without loss of benefits and promotion opportunities; home-based work; child care for sick children and after-school supervision. Although some progress has been made, acceptance of these reforms has been very slow. Parental leave is still *unpaid*. The culture of the workplace discourages many persons from taking advantage of the more flexible options which do exist because they fear they will be seen as less serious and dedicated workers. In addition, most programs are aimed at mothers and at managers, although there is growing feeling that fathers and hourly workers should be included as well.[78]

Ultimately these trends may alter the shape of women's and men's life cycles. Increasingly, a new ideal for the life course is being held up as the model that society should work toward. Lotte Bailyn proposes reorganization of careers in which young couples trade off periods of intense work commitment with each other while they establish their families so that either or both can spend more time at home.[79] Right now both women and men feel they must work so intensely to establish their careers that they have too little time for their children.[80] For the poor and untrained, the problem is the opposite: childbearing and childrearing are far more satisfying and validating than a low-paying, dead-end job. The question is how to reorient educators or employers to factor in time with family as an important obligation to society (much as one would factor in military service, for example). Such institutional reorganization is necessary to give families and childrearing their proper place in the modern postindustrial society.

CONCLUSION

A review of the conservative, liberal, and feminist perspectives on the changing nature of the American family suggests that future policy should combine the distinctive contributions of all three. From the conservatives comes a critique of modernity that recognizes the important role of the family in maintaining child health and preventing child failure. Although their understanding of "family values" is too narrow, they deserve credit for raising the issue of family function and form to public debate. Liberals see clearly the overwhelming power of the economy to deny employment, make demands on parents as workers, and drive a wedge between employers' needs for competitiveness and families' needs for connection and community.

Surprising although it may seem, since feminists are often imagined to be "way out," the most comprehensive plan for restoring family to its rightful place is put forward by the feminists who appreciate both the inherently premodern nature of the family and at the same time its inevitable interdependence with a fast-changing world economy. Feminists will not turn back to the past because they know that the traditional family was often a straightjacket for women. But they also know that family cannot be turned into a formal organization or have its functions performed by government or other public institutions that are incapable of giving needed succor to children, adults, and old people which only the family can give.

The feminist synthesis accepts both the inherent particularism and emotional nature of the family and the inevitable specialization and impersonality of the modern economy. Feminists are different from conservatives in accepting diversity of the family to respond to the needs of the modern economy. They are different from the liberals in recognizing that intimate nurturing relationships such as parenting cannot all be turned into a safety net of formal care. The most promising social policies for families and children take their direction from inclusive values that confirm the good life and the well-being of every individual as the ultimate goal of the nation. The policy challenge is to adjust the partnership between the family and its surrounding institutions so that together they combine the best of private initiative with public concern.

Notes

1. Barbara Dafoe Whitehead, "Dan Quayle Was Right," *Atlantic Monthly* (April 1993): 47. Her chapter in [*Promises to Keep: Decline and Renewal of Marriage in America*, edited by D. Popenoe, J. B. Elshtain, and D. Blankenhorn] on the "Story of Marriage" continues the theme of an erosion of values for cultural diversity.
2. Mary Ann Glendon, "Marriage and the State: The Withering Away of Marriage," *Virginia Law Review* 62 (May 1976): 663–729.
3. See chapters by Milton Regan and Carl Schneider in [*Promises to Keep: Decline and Renewal of Marriage in America*, edited by D. Popenoe, J. B. Elshtain, and D. Blankenhorn].
4. Charles A. Murray, *Losing Ground: American Social Policy: 1950–1980* (New York: Basic Books, 1984). Critics point out that the rise in out-of-wedlock births continues, even though welfare payments have declined in size over the last several decades, thereby casting doubt on the perverse incentive theory of rising illegitimacy.
5. U.S. Bureau of the Census. *Statistical Abstract of the United States: 1994*, 114th ed. (Washington, DC: 1994), 59.
6. Suzanne M. Bianchi and Daphne Spain, *American Women in Transition* (New York: Russell Sage Foundation, 1986), 88.
7. Donald J. Hernandez, *America's Children: Resources from Family, Government, and the Economy* (New York: Russell Sage Foundation, 1993), 284, 70. Janet Zollinger Giele, "Woman's Role Change and Adaptation: 1920–1990," in *Women's Lives through Time: Educated American Women of the Twentieth Century*, ed. K. Hulbert and D. Schuster (San Francisco: Jossey-Bass. 1993), 40.
8. Victor Fuchs, "Are Americans Underinvesting in Children?" in *Rebuilding the Nest*, ed. David Blankenhorn, Stephen Bayme, and Jean Bethke Elshtain (Milwaukee: Family Service America, 1990), 66. Bianchi and Spain, *American Women in Transition*, 141, 201, 226. Janet Zollinger Giele, "Gender and Sex Roles," in *Handbook of Sociology*, ed. N. J. Smelser (Beverly Hills, CA: Sage Publications, 1988), 300.
9. Hernandez, *America's Children*, 130. Council on Families in America, *Marriage in America* (New York: Institute for American Values. 1995), 7.
10. Fuchs, "Are Americans Underinvesting in Children?" 61. Some would say, however, that the decline was due in part to a larger and more heterogeneous group taking the tests.

11. Council on Families in America, *Marriage in America*, 6. The report cites research by Nicholas Zill and Charlotte A. Schoenborn, "Developmental, Learning and Emotional Problems: Health of Our Nation's Children, United States, 1988." *Advance Data*, National Center for Health Statistics, Publication #120, November 1990. See also, Sara McLanahan and Gary Sandefur, *Growing Up with a Single Parent* (Cambridge, MA: Harvard University Press, 1994).
12. Edward Gilbreath, "Manhood's Great Awakening," *Christianity Today* (February 6, 1995): 27.
13. David Elkind, *The Hurried Child: Growing Up Too Fast Too Soon* (Reading, MA: Addison-Wesley, 1981).
14. Jean Bethke Elshtain, *Democracy on Trial* (New York: Basic Books, 1995).
15. Jonathan Alter and Pat Wingert, "The Return of Shame," *Newsweek* (February 6, 1995): 25.
16. Tom McNichol, "The New Sex Vow: 'I won't' until 'I do'," *USA Weekend*, March 25–27, 1994, 4 ff. Lee Smith. "The New Wave of Illegitimacy," *Fortune* (April 18, 1994): 81 ff.
17. Susan Chira, "War over Role of American Fathers," *New York Times* (June 19, 1994): 22.
18. Juliet Schor, "Consumerism and the Decline of Family and Community: Preliminary Statistics from a Survey on Time, Money, and Values." Harvard Divinity School, Seminar on Families and Family Policy, April 4, 1995.
19. Karen S. Peterson, "In Balancing Act, Scale Tips toward Family," *USA Today*, (January 25, 1995).
20. Lawrence Mead, "Taxing Peter to Pay Paula," *Wall Street Journal*, (November 2, 1994).
21. Tom G. Palmer, "English Lessons: Britain Rethinks the Welfare State," *Wall Street Journal*, (November 2, 1994).
22. Robert Pear, "G.O.P. Affirms Plan to Stop Money for Unwed Mothers," *New York Times*, (January 21, 1995), 9.
23. Brigitte Berger. "Block Grants: Changing the Welfare Culture from the Ground Up," *Dialogue* (Boston: Pioneer Institute for Public Policy Research), no. 3, March, 1995.
24. Robert Rector, "Welfare," *Issues '94: The Candidate's Briefing Book* (Washington, DC: American Heritage Foundation, 1994), chap. 13.
25. Council on Families in America, *Marriage in America*, 13–16.
26. Robert Bellah, "Invasion of the Money World," in *Rebuilding the Nest*, ed. David Blankenhorn, Steven Bayme, and Jean Bethke Elshtain (Milwaukee: Family Service America, 1990), 227–36. James Coleman, *Foundations of Social Theory* (Cambridge, MA: Harvard University Press, 1990).
27. Sylvia Nasar, "More Men in Prime of Life Spend Less Time Working," *New York Times*, (December 1, 1994), Al.
28. John Scanzoni, *Power Politics in the American Marriage* (Englewood Cliffs, NJ: Prentice-Hall, 1972). Ruth A. Wallace and Alison Wolf, *Contemporary Sociological Theory* (Englewood Cliffs, NJ: Prentice-Hall, 1991), 176.
29. Fred Weinstein and Gerald M. Platt, *The Wish to Be Free: Society, Psyche, and Value Change* (Berkeley, CA: University of California Press, 1969).
30. Kingsley Davis, "Wives and Work: A Theory of the Sex-Role Revolution and Its Consequences," in *Feminism, Children, and the New Families*, ed. S. M. Dornbusch and M. H. Strober (New York: Guilford Press. 1988), 67–86. Janet Zollinger Giele, *Two Paths to Women's Equality: Temperance, Suffrage, and the Origins of American Feminism* (New York: Twayne Publishers, Macmillan, 1995).
31. Vivianna A. Zelizer, *Pricing the Priceless Child: The Changing Social Value of Children* (New York: Basic Books, 1985).
32. William J. Goode, *World Revolution in Family Patterns* (New York: The Free Press, 1963).
33. Constance Willard Williams, *Black Teenage Mothers: Pregnancy and Child Rearing from Their Perspective* (Lexington, MA: Lexington Books, 1990).
34. William Julius Wilson, *The Truly Disadvantaged: The Inner City, the Underclass, and Public Policy* (Chicago: University of Chicago Press, 1987).
35. Jacob Mincer, "Labor-Force Participation of Married Women: A Study of Labor Supply," in *Aspects of Labor Economics*, Report of the National Bureau of Economic Research (Princeton, NJ: Universities-National Bureau Committee of Economic Research, 1962). Glen G. Cain, *Married Women in the Labor Force: An Economic Analysis* (Chicago: University of Chicago Press, 1966).
36. Richard A. Easterlin, *Birth and Fortune: The Impact of Numbers on Personal Welfare* (New York: Basic Books, 1980). Valerie K. Oppenheimer, "Structural Sources of Economic Pressure for

Wives to Work—Analytic Framework," *Journal of Family History* 4, no. 2 (1979): 177–99. Valerie K. Oppenheimer, *Work and the Family: A Study in Social Demography* (New York: Academic Press, 1982).

37. Janet Z. Giele and Rainer Pischner, "The Emergence of Multiple Role Patterns Among Women: A Comparison of Germany and the United States," *Vierteljahrshefte zur Wirtschaftsforschung* (Applied Economics Quarterly) (Heft 1–2, 1994). Alice S. Rossi, "The Future in the Making," *American Journal of Orthopsychiatry* 63, no. 2 (1993): 166–76. Notburga Ott, *Intrafamily Bargaining and Household Decisions* (Berlin: Springer-Verlag, 1992).

38. Iris Young, "Mothers, Citizenship and Independence: A Critique of Pure Family Values," *Ethics* 105, no. 3 (1995): 535–56. Young critiques the liberal stance of William Galston, *Liberal Purposes* (New York: Cambridge University Press, 1991).

39. Lee Rainwater and William L. Yancey, *The Moynihan Report and the Politics of Controversy* (Cambridge, MA: MIT Press, 1967).

40. Glen H. Elder, Jr., *Children of the Great Depression* (Chicago: University of Chicago Press, 1974). Rand D. Conger, Xiao-Jia Ge, and Frederick O. Lorenz, "Economic Stress and Marital Relations," in *Families in Troubled Times: Adapting to Change in Rural America*, ed. R. D. Conger and G. H. Elder, Jr. (New York: Aldine de Gruyter, 1994), 187–203.

41. Coleman, *Foundations of Social Theory*, 590.

42. Elizabeth G. Menaghan and Toby L. Parcel, "Employed Mothers and Children's Home Environments," *Journal of Marriage and the Family* 53, no. 2 (1991): 417–31. Lois Hoffman, "The Effects on Children of Maternal and Paternal Employment," in *Families and Work*, ed. Naomi Gerstel and Harriet Engel Gross (Philadelphia: Temple University Press, 1987), 362–95.

43. Juliet Schor, *The Overworked American: The Unexpected Decline of Leisure* (New York: Basic Books, 1991). Robert Haveman and Barbara Wolfe, *Succeeding Generations: On the Effects of Investments in Children* (New York: Russell Sage Foundation, 1994), 239.

44. Coleman, *Foundations of Social Theory*, 596–97.

45. Schor, "Consumerism and Decline of Family."

46. Iris Young, "Mothers, Citizenship and Independence," puts Elshtain, Etzioni, Galston, and Whitehead in this category.

47. Coleman, *Foundations of Social Theory*, 597–609.

48. Sherry Wexler, "To Work and To Mother: A Comparison of the Family Support Act and the Family and Medical Leave Act" (Ph.D. dissertation draft, Brandeis University, 1995). David T. Ellwood, *Poor Support: Poverty in the American Family* (New York: Basic Books, 1988).

49. Coleman, *Foundations of Social Theory*, 300–21. Coleman, known for rational choice theory in sociology, put forward these theoretical possibilities in 1990, fully four years ahead of what in 1994 was voiced in the Republican Contract with America.

50. Wexler, "To Work and To Mother."

51. Robert Lerman, "Marketplace," National Public Radio, April 18, 1995.

52. Karen Offen, "Defining Feminism: A Comparative Historical Approach," *Signs* 14, no. 1 (1988): 119–51.

53. Young, "Mothers, Citizenship and Independence."

54. Robert N. Bellah et al., *Habits of the Heart* (Berkeley, CA: University of California Press, 1985), 250–71. Gosta Esping-Andersen, *The Three Worlds of Welfare Capitalism* (Princeton, NJ: Princeton University Press, 1990). Susan Pedersen, *Family, Dependence, and the Origins of the Welfare State: Britain and France, 1914–1945* (New York: Cambridge University Press, 1993).

55. Young, "Mothers, Citizenship and Independence."

56. Giele, "Woman's Role Change and Adaptation" presents these historical statistics.

57. Elshtain, *Democracy on Trial*. Robert N. Bellah et al., *The Good Society* (New York: Knopf, 1991), 210. Robert D. Putnam, "Bowling Alone: America's Declining Social Capital," *Journal of Democracy* 4, no. 1 (1995): 65–78.

58. Heather McCallum, "Mind the Gap" (paper presented to the Family and Children's Policy Center colloquium, Waltham, MA, Brandeis University, March 23, 1995). The sum was markedly better for children of employed single mothers, around $700 per mother in the United States. But this figure corresponded with over $1,000 in eleven other countries, with only Greece and

Portugal lower than the U.S. Concerning the high U.S. rates of teen pregnancy, see Planned Parenthood advertisement, "Let's Get Serious About Ending Teen Childbearing," *New York Times*, April 4, 1995, A25.

59. Ruth Walker, "Secretary Reich and the Disintegrating Middle Class," *Christian Science Monitor*, (November 2, 1994): 19.

60. For reference to "social capital," see Coleman, *Foundations of Social Theory*; Elshtain, *Democracy on Trial*; and Putnam, "Bowling Alone." For "emotional capital," see Arlie Russell Hochschild, *The Managed Heart: The Commercialization of Human Feeling* (Berkeley, CA: University of California Press, 1983). For "cultural capital," see work by Pierre Bourdieu and Jurgen Habermas.

61. Judith Stacey, "Dan Quayle's Revenge: The New Family Values Crusaders," *The Nation*, (July 25/August 1, 1994): 119–22. Iris Marion Young, "Making Single Motherhood Normal," *Dissent* (Winter 1994): 88–93.

62. Christopher Jencks and Kathryn Edin, "Do Poor Women Have a Right to Bear Children," *The American Prospect* (Winter 1995): 43–52.

63. Stacey, "Dan Quayle's Revenge." Arlene Skolnick and Stacey Rosencrantz, "The New Crusade for the Old Family," *The American Prospect* (Summer 1994): 59–65.

64. Nancy Smith Barrett, "Data Needs for Evaluating the Labor Market Status of Women," in *Census Bureau Conference on Federal Statistical Needs Relating to Women*, ed. Barbara B. Reagan (U.S. Bureau of the Census, 1979), Current Population Reports, Special Studies, Series P-23, no. 83, pp. 10–19. These figures belie the familiar but misleading statement that "only 7 percent" of all American families are of the traditional nuclear type because "traditional" is defined so narrowly—as husband and wife with two children under 18 where the wife is not employed outside the home. For more recent figures and a similar argument for more universal family ethic, see Christine Winquist Nord and Nicholas Zill, "American Households in Demographic Perspective," working paper no. 5, Institute for American Values, New York, 1991.

65. Tamar Levin, "Women Are Becoming Equal Providers," *New York Times*, (May 11, 1995), A27.

66. Marianne A. Ferber and Julie A. Nelson, *Beyond Economic Man: Feminist Theory and Economics* (Chicago: University of Chicago Press, 1993).

67. Fran Sussner Rodgers and Charles Rodgers, "Business and the Facts of Family Life," *Harvard Business Review*, no. 6 (1989): 199–213, especially 206.

68. Ravenna Helson and S. Picano, "Is the Traditional Role Bad for Women?" *Journal of Personality and Social Psychology* 59 (1990): 311–20. Rosalind C. Barnett, "Home-to-Work Spillover Revisited: A Study of Full-Time Employed Women in Dual-Earner Couples," *Journal of Marriage and the Family* 56 (August 1994): 647–56.

69. Arlie Hochschild, "The Fractured Family," *The American Prospect* (Summer 1991): 106–15.

70. Leon Eisenberg, "Is the Family Obsolete?" *The Key Reporter* 60, no. 3 (1995): 1–5. Arlene Skolnick and Stacey Rosencrantz, "The New Crusade for the Old Family," *The American Prospect* (Summer 1994): 59–65.

71. Roberta M. Spalter-Roth, Heidi I. Hartmann, and Linda M. Andrews, "Mothers, Children, and Low-Wage Work: The Ability to Earn a Family Wage," in *Sociology and the Public Agenda*, ed. W. J. Wilson (Newbury Park, CA: Sage Publications, 1993), 316–38.

72. Louis Uchitelle, "Lacking Child Care, Parents Take Their Children to Work," *New York Times*, (December 23, 1994), 1.

73. Jencks and Edin, "Do Poor Women Have a Right," 50.

74. David Elkind, *Ties That Stress: The New Family in Balance* (Boston: Harvard University Press, 1994).

75. It is frequently noted that the U.S. is a much more racially diverse nation than, say, Sweden, which has a concerted family and children's policy. Symptomatic of the potential for race and class division that impedes recognition of all children as the nation's children is the book by Richard J. Herrnstein and Charles A. Murray, *The Bell Curve: Intelligence and Class Structure in American Life* (New York: The Free Press, 1994).

76. Young, "Making Single Motherhood Normal," 93.

77. If the objection is that the wrong people will have children, as Herrnstein and Murray suggest in *The Bell Curve*, then the challenge is to find ways for poor women to make money or have some

other more exciting career that will offset the rewards of having children, "such as becoming the bride of Christ or the head of a Fortune 500 corporation," to quote Jencks and Edin, "Do Poor Women Have a Right," 48.

78. Beth M. Miller, "Private Welfare: The Distributive Equity of Family Benefits in America" (Ph.D. thesis, Brandeis University, 1992). Sue Shellenbarger, "Family-Friendly Firms Often Leave Fathers Out of the Picture," *Wall Street Journal*, (November 2, 1994). Richard T. Gill and T. Grandon Gill, *Of Families, Children, and a Parental Bill of Rights* (New York: Institute for American Values, 1993). For gathering information on these new work-family policies, I wish to acknowledge help of students in my 1994–95 Family Policy Seminar at Brandeis University, particularly Cathleen O'Brien, Deborah Gurewich, Alissa Starr, and Pamela Swain, as well as the insights of two Ph.D. students, Mindy Fried and Sherry Wexler.

79. Lotte Bailyn, *Breaking the Mold: Women, Men and Time in the New Corporate World* (New York: The Free Press, 1994).

80. Penelope Leach, *Children First: What Our Society Must Do and Is Doing* (New York: Random House, 1994).

II

Sex and Gender

The United States, along with other advanced countries, has experienced both a sexual revolution and a gender revolution. The first has liberalized attitudes toward erotic behavior and expression; the second has changed the roles and status of women and men in the direction of greater equality. Both revolutions have been brought about by the rapid social changes in recent years, and both revolutions have challenged traditional conceptions of marriage.

A persistent debate about both gender and sexuality concerns the relative importance of biological versus psychological and social factors. This nature-nurture debate has been dominated by an argument between two extreme views. On the one extreme, there are the strict biological determinists who declare that anatomy is destiny. In other words, they argue "men are from Mars and women from Venus," or that there is a male brain and female brain. On the other extreme, there are those who argue that all aspects of gender differences are learned.

There are two essential points to be made about the nature versus nurture argument. First, modern genetic theory views biology and environment as interacting, not opposing, forces. Second, both biological determinists and their opponents assume that if a biological force exists, it must be overwhelmingly strong. But the most sophisticated evidence concerning both gender development and erotic arousal suggests that physiological forces are less than powerful. Despite all the media stories about a "gay gene" or "a gene for lung cancer," the scientific reality is more complicated. As one researcher puts it, "The scientists have identified a number of genes that may, under certain circumstances, make an individual more or less susceptible to the action of a variety of environmental agents" (as cited in Berwick, 1998, p. 4).

Many sociologists and psychologists used to take it for granted that women's roles and functions in society reflect universal physiological and temperamental traits. Since in practically every society men have been considered superior to women, inequality was interpreted as an inescapable necessity of organized social life. Such analysis suffered from the same flaw as the idea that discrimination against nonwhites implies their innate inferiority. All such explanations failed to look at the social institutions and forces producing and supporting the observed differences.

As Robert M. Jackson points out, over the past 150 years modern economic and political institutions have been moving gradually toward gender equality, whether or not the men who have traditionally run these institutions wanted that outcome or not. The driving force behind this transformation has been the shift of work away from the household, and the reorganization of economics and politics away from family and gender. Jackson divides the decline of gender inequality in American society into three periods. First, is the era of Separate Spheres, from around 1840–1890, with men defined as family breadwinners, forced to make their way in the harsh world outside the home; women were defined as homemakers and nurturers. Sexuality was repressive. The second era from 1890–1940 was what Jackson calls the Era of Egalitarian Illusions; women won the right to vote, were increasingly able to go to college, and were beginning to enter the workplace, but were limited in many ways. From 1940–1990 was the Era of Assimilation; sex discrimination in the workplace, education, and other institutions became illegal, professional careers opened to women, and marital equality became a cultural idea. From 1990 on, we have been living through the era of "Residual inequities"; there seems to be a "glass ceiling" and relatively few women are in high political offices, or top executive positions. Women have not yet attained full equality, but in Jackson's view, the trend in that direction is irreversible.

People born since the 1970s have grown up in a more equal society than their parents' generation. Kathleen Gerson reports on a number of findings from her interviews with 18- to 30-year-old "children of the gender revolution." She finds that young men and women share similar hopes; both would like to be able to combine work and family life in an egalitarian way. But they also recognize that in today's world, such aspirations will be hard to fulfill. Jobs require long hours, and good child-care options are scarce and expensive.

In the face of such obstacles, young women and men pursue different second choices or "fall-back strategies." Men are willing to fall back on a more "traditional" arrangement where he is the main breadwinner in the family, and his partner is the main caregiver. Young women, however, find this situation much less attractive; they are wary of giving up their ability to support themselves and their children, should the need arise. Gerson concludes that the lack of institutional supports for today's young families creates tensions between the partners that may undermine marriage itself.

In their article here, Elizabeth Armstrong, Laura Hamilton, and Paula England investigate the realities of the "hooking-up" scene on college campuses. In recent years, the media have become obsessed with the casual sex practices of young adults. They portray hooking up as a wild sexual free-for-all, a sudden and shocking change in young people's sexual behavior, and especially dangerous to the emotional health of young women. Some journalists warn that hookups have replaced relationship.

Armstrong et al, citing their own and other researchers' findings, challenge these claims. Hooking up isn't radically new, doesn't happen that often, the sex tends to be "light," and it hasn't replaced long-term relationships. In fact, they find that being in a relationship while in college brings its own problems. A good relationship takes time and energy away from academic work. Further, a bad relationship can be more emotionally "costly" painful than a bad hookup.

These authors do find some support for the notion that hooking up can be worse for women than for men. A major reason is persisting the sexual double standard: a man can have sex with as many women as he wants, with no harm to his reputation, but a woman is in danger of being labeled a "slut" no matter what she does.

The idea that marriage is dead, dying, or in steep decline, is a persistent theme in the media. Statistics on premarital sex, cohabitation, single mothers, divorce, the growing numbers of people living alone—all seem clear evidence for the collapse of the institution. End of story. But as Mark Regnerus and Jeremy Uecker show, the real story is far more complicated. Using both survey data and in-depth interviews of young adults from age 18 to 23, they find no evidence that today's young people have abandoned the idea of marriage.

Times and cultural norms have clearly changed, and sex before marriage is "no big deal." But practically all the young men and women in the study—93 to 96 percent—want to marry someday. They are not, however, in a rush to do so, although more women are eager to marry than men. Most young adults have a much clearer idea of their educational and career plans than their plans for marriage. However, a minority of young adults do marry early. The major factors in early marriage are religion and having parents with lower socioeconomic status.

Looking at American marriage more broadly, Andrew J. Cherlin describes the forces, both economic and cultural, that have transformed family life in recent decades. The shift toward a postindustrial economy has had a profound impact on family life. Economic change has made women less dependent on men; it has drawn women into the workplace and deprived less-educated men of the blue-collar jobs that once enabled them to support their families. Getting married and staying married have become increasingly optional. Despite all the changes, however, Americans value marriage more than people in other developed countries, and the two-parent family remains the most common living arrangement for raising children.

So marriage remains a cherished U.S. institution. The Census Bureau estimates that 90 percent of Americans will marry at some point in their lives. Hardly anyone goes to the altar expecting that the marriage will end in divorce. So what makes a marriage break down? In her article here, Arlene Skolnick shows that in recent years researchers have found out a great deal about couple relationships, and some of the findings are contrary to widespread beliefs. For example, happy families are not all alike. And every marriage contains within it two marriages—a happy one and an unhappy one. The key to a successful marriage is the balance between the two. The good marriage must outweigh the bad one.

Did no-fault divorce laws lead to skyrocketing divorce rates of the 1970s? Laurence M. Friedman shows that the "divorce revolution" of the 1970s—when many states passed no-fault divorce laws—did not spring up suddenly out of nowhere. Nor was it the result of feminism or any other public protest movement. Divorce reform has a long history. In the first half of the twentieth century, a dual system of divorce prevailed; the official law allowed divorce only on the basis of "fault"—one partner had to be proven guilty of adultery or cruelty or some other offense. But most divorces were actually "collusive"—the result of a deal between husbands and wives, who would concoct a story, to permit a divorce to be granted. Legal reformers proposed no-fault divorce to remedy what they saw as a mockery of the law.

As divorce has become a common experience for Americans, there has been a backlash against divorce, especially for couples with children. The media have featured dramatic stories about the devastating, life-long scars that parental divorce supposedly inflicts on children. Legislators in some states have been considering making divorce more difficult. Given the bad press divorce gets these days, Virginia Rutter asks, "Is there a case for divorce?" Are there some situations where divorce leads to better outcomes than if the couple stayed together?

Rutter observes there is often a large gap between stories about divorce that appear in the media, and what the research actually shows. She points to a number of questions anyone should ask about reports of alarming findings on divorce. For example, readers should ask, who are the children of divorce being compared to? Sometimes, there are no comparison groups. Sometimes, the comparison is with presumably happy marriages. But those are not the families that get divorced in the first place. In addition, readers should beware of what researchers call "selection effects": People who get divorced may not be a random sample of the married population; they may have preexisting problems that lead to marital problems, and also to negative outcomes after divorce.

Because most divorced people remarry, more children will live with stepparents than in the recent past. As Mary Ann Mason points out in her article, stepfamilies are a large and growing part of American family life, but their roles in the family are not clearly defined. Moreover, stepfamilies are largely ignored by public policymakers, and they exist in a legal limbo. She suggests a number of ways to remedy the situation.

Despite all its difficulties, marriage is not likely to go out of style in the near future. Ultimately we agree with Jessie Bernard (1982), who, after a devastating critique of traditional marriage from the point of view of a sociologist, who is also a feminist, said: "The future of marriage is as assured as any social form can be. . . . For men and women will continue to want intimacy, they will continue to want to celebrate their mutuality, to experience the mystic unity which once led the church to consider marriage a sacrament. . . . There is hardly any probability such commitments will disappear or that all relationships between them will become merely casual or transient" (p. 301).

References

Bernard, Jessie. 1982. *The Future of Marriage*. New York: World Publishing.
Berwick, Robert C. 1998. "The Doors of Perception." *The Los Angeles Times Book Review*, March 15.
Gagnon, J. R., and W. Simon. 1970. *The Sexual Scene*. Chicago: Aldine Transaction.

3

Changing Gender Roles

■ READING 5

Destined for Equality

Robert M. Jackson

Over the past two centuries, women's long, conspicuous struggle for better treatment has masked a surprising condition. Men's social dominance was doomed from the beginning. Gender inequality could not adapt successfully to modern economic and political institutions. No one planned this. Indeed, for a long time, the impending extinction of gender inequality was hidden from all.

In the middle of the nineteenth century, few said that equality between women and men was possible or desirable. The new forms of business, government, schools, and the family seemed to fit nicely with the existing division between women's roles and men's roles. Men controlled them all, and they showed no signs of losing belief in their natural superiority. If anything, women's subordination seemed likely to grow worse as they remained attached to the household while business and politics became a separate, distinctively masculine, realm.

Nonetheless, 150 years later, seemingly against all odds, women are well on the way to becoming men's equals. Now, few say that gender equality is impossible or undesirable. Somehow our expectations have been turned upside down.

Women's rising status is an enigmatic paradox. For millennia women were subordinate to men under the most diverse economic, political, and cultural conditions. Although the specific content of gender-based roles and the degree of inequality between the sexes varied considerably across time and place, men everywhere held power and status over women. Moreover, people believed that men's dominance was a natural and unchangeable part of life. Yet over the past two centuries, gender inequality has declined across the world.

The driving force behind this transformation has been the migration of economic and political power outside households and its reorganization around business and political interests detached from gender. Women (and their male supporters) have fought against prejudice and discrimination throughout American history, but social conditions governed the intensity and effectiveness of their efforts. Behind the very visible conflicts between women and male-dominated institutions, fundamental processes concerning economic and political organization have been paving the way for women's success. Throughout these years, while many women struggled to improve their status and many men resisted those efforts, institutional changes haltingly, often imperceptibly, but persistently undermined gender inequality. Responding to the emergent imperatives of large-scale, bureaucratic organizations, men with economic or political power intermittently adopted policies that favored greater equality, often without anticipating the implications of their actions. Gradually responding to the changing demands and possibilities of households without economic activity, men acting as individuals reduced their resistance to wives and daughters extending their roles, although men rarely recognized they were doing something different from their fathers' generation.

Social theorists have long taught us that institutions have unanticipated consequences, particularly when the combined effect of many people's actions diverges from their individual aims. Adam Smith, the renowned theorist of early capitalism, proposed that capitalist markets shared a remarkable characteristic. Many people pursuing only selfish, private interests could further the good of all. Subsequently, Karl Marx, considering the capitalist economy, proposed an equally remarkable but contradictory assessment. Systems of inequality fueled by rational self-interest, he argued, inevitably produce irrational crises that threaten to destroy the social order. Both ideas have suffered many critical blows, but they still capture our imaginations by their extraordinary insight. They teach us how unanticipated effects often ensue when disparate people and organizations each follow their own short-sighted interests.

Through a similar unanticipated and uncontrolled process, the changing actions of men, women, and powerful institutions have gradually but irresistibly reduced gender inequality. Women had always resisted their constraints and inferior status. Over the past 150 years, however, their individual strivings and organized resistance became increasingly effective. Men long continued to oppose the loss of their privileged status. Nonetheless, although men and male-controlled institutions did not adopt egalitarian values, their actions changed because their interests changed. Men's resistance to women's aspirations diminished, and they found new advantages in strategies that also benefited women.

Modern economic and political organization propelled this transformation by slowly dissociating social power from its allegiance to gender inequality. The power over economic resources, legal rights, the allocation of positions, legitimating values, and setting priorities once present in families shifted into businesses and government organizations. In these organizations, profit, efficiency, political legitimacy, organizational stability, competitiveness, and similar considerations mattered more than male privileges vis-à-vis females. Men who had power because of their positions in these organizations gradually adopted policies ruled more by institutional interests than by personal prejudices. Over the long run, institutional needs and opportunities produced policies that worked against gender inequality. Simultaneously, ordinary men (those without economic or political power) resisted women's advancements less. They had fewer resources to use against the women in their lives, and less to gain from keeping women subordinate. Male politicians seeking more power, businessmen pursuing wealth and success, and ordinary men pursuing their self-interest all contributed to the gradual decline of gender inequality.

Structural developments produced ever more inconsistencies with the requirements for continued gender inequality. Both the economy and the state increasingly treated people as potential workers or voters without reference to their family status. To the disinterested, and often rationalized, authority within these institutions, sex inequality was just one more consideration with calculating strategies for profit and political advantage. For these institutions, men and women embodied similar problems of control, exploitation, and legitimation.

Seeking to further their own interests, powerful men launched institutional changes that eventually reduced the discrimination against women. Politicians passed laws giving married women property rights. Employers hired women in ever-increasing numbers. Educators opened their doors to women. These examples and many others show powerful men pursuing their interests in preserving and expanding their economic and political power, yet also improving women's social standing.

The economy and state did not systematically oppose inequality. On the contrary, each institution needed and aggressively supported some forms of inequality, such as income differentials and the legal authority of state officials, that gave them strength. Other forms of inequality received neither automatic support nor automatic opposition. Over time, the responses to other kinds of inequality depended on how well they met institutional interests and how contested they became.

When men adopted organizational policies that eventually improved women's status, they consciously sought to increase profits, end labor shortages, get more votes, and increase social order. They imposed concrete solutions to short-term economic and political problems and to conflicts associated with them. These men usually did not envision, and probably did not care, that the cumulative effect of these policies would be to curtail male dominance.

Only when they were responding to explicitly egalitarian demands from women such as suffrage did men with power consistently examine the implications of their actions for gender inequality. Even then, as when responding to women's explicit demands for legal changes, most legislators were concerned more about their political interests than the fate of gender inequality. When legislatures did pass laws responding to public pressure about women's rights, few male legislators expected the laws could dramatically alter gender inequality.

Powerful men adopted various policies that ultimately would undermine gender inequality because such policies seemed to further their private interests and to address inescapable economic, political, and organizational problems. The structure and integral logic of development within modern political and economic institutions shaped the problems, interests, and apparent solutions. Without regard to what either women or men wanted, industrial capitalism and rational legal government eroded gender inequality.

MAPPING GENDER INEQUALITY'S DECLINE

When a band of men committed to revolutionary change self-consciously designed the American institutional framework, they did not imagine or desire that it would lead toward gender equality. In 1776 a small group of men claimed equality for themselves and similar men by signing the Declaration of Independence. In throwing off British sovereignty, they inaugurated the American ideal of equality. Yet after the success of their revolution, its leaders and like-minded property-owning white men created a nation that subjugated women, enslaved blacks, and withheld suffrage from men without property.

These men understood the egalitarian ideals they espoused through the culture and experiences dictated by their own historical circumstances. Everyone then accepted that women and men were absolutely and inalterably different. Although Abigail Adams admonished her husband that they should "remember the ladies," when these "fathers" of the American nation established its most basic rights and laws, the prospect of fuller citizenship for women was not even credible enough to warrant the effort of rejection. These nation builders could not foresee that their political and economic institutions would eventually erode some forms of inequality much more emphatically than had their revolutionary vision. They could not know that the social structure would eventually extend egalitarian social relations much further than they might ever have thought desirable or possible.

By the 1830s, a half-century after the American Revolution, little had changed. In the era of Jacksonian democracy, women still could not vote or hold political office. They had to cede legal control of their inherited property and their income to their husbands. With few exceptions, they could not make legal contracts or escape a marriage through divorce. They could not enter college. Dependence on men was perpetual and inescapable. Household toil and family welfare monopolized women's time and energies. Civil society recognized women not as individuals but as adjuncts to men. Like the democracy of ancient Athens, the American democracy limited political equality to men.

Today women enjoy independent citizenship; they have the same liberty as men to control their person and property. If they choose or need to do so, women can live without a husband. They can discard an unwanted husband to seek a better alternative. Women vote and occupy political offices. They hold jobs almost as often as men do. Ever more women have managerial and professional positions. Our culture has adopted more affirmative images for women, particularly as models of such values as independence, public advocacy, economic success, and thoughtfulness. Although these changes have not removed all inequities, women now have greater resources, more choices in life, and a higher social status than in the past.

In terms of the varied events and processes that have so dramatically changed women's place in society, the past 150 years of American history can be divided into three half-century periods. The *era of separate spheres* covers roughly 1840–1890, from the era of Jacksonian democracy to the Gilded Age. The *era of egalitarian illusions*, roughly 1890–1940, extends from the Progressive Era to the beginning of World War II. The third period, the *era of assimilation*, covers the time from World War II to the present (see Table 5.1).

TABLE 5.1   *The Decline of Gender Inequality in American Society*

	1840–1890 *The Era of Separate Spheres*	1890–1940 *The Era of Egalitarian Illusions*	1940–1990 *The Era of Assimilation*	1990–? *Residual Inequities*
Legal and political status	Formal legal equality instituted	Formal political equality instituted	Formal economic equality instituted	Women rare in high political offices
Economic opportunity	Working-class jobs for single women only	Some jobs for married women and educated women	All kinds of jobs available to all kinds of women	"Glass ceiling" and domestic duties hold women back
Higher education	A few women admitted to public universities and new women's colleges	Increasing college; little graduate or professional education	Full access at all levels	Some prestigious fields remain largely male domains
Divorce	Almost none, but available for dire circumstances	Increasingly available, but difficult	Freely available and accepted	Women typically suffer greater costs
Sexuality and reproductive control	Repressive sexuality; little reproductive control	Positive sexuality but double standard; increasing reproductive control	High sexual freedom; full reproductive control	Sexual harassment and fear of rape still widespread
Cultural image	Virtuous domesticity and subordination	Educated motherhood, capable for employment & public service	Careers, marital equality	Sexes still perceived as inherently different

Over the three periods, notable changes altered women's legal, political, and economic status, women's access to higher education and to divorce, women's sexuality, and the cultural images of women and men. Most analysts agree that people's legal, political, and economic status largely define their social status, and we will focus on the changes in these. Of course, like gender, other personal characteristics such as race and age also define an individual's status, because they similarly influence legal, political, and economic rights and resources. Under most circumstances, however, women and men are not systematically differentiated by other kinds of inequality based on personal characteristics, because these other differences, such as race and age, cut across gender lines. Educational institutions have played an ever-larger role in regulating people's access to opportunities over the last century. Changes in access to divorce, women's sexuality, and cultural images of gender will not play a central role in this study. They are important indicators of women's status, but they are derivative rather than formative. They reveal inequality's burden.

The creation of separate spheres for women and men dominated the history of gender inequality during the first period, 1840–1890. The cultural doctrine of separate spheres emerged in the mid-nineteenth century. It declared emphatically that women and men belonged to different worlds. Women were identified with the household and maintenance of family life. Men were associated with income-generating employment and public life. Popular ideas attributed greater religious virtue to women but greater civic virtue to men. Women were hailed as guardians of private morality while men were regarded as the protectors of the public good. These cultural and ideological inventions were responses to a fundamental institutional transition, the movement of economic activity out of households into independent enterprises. The concept of separate spheres legitimated women's exclusion from the public realm, although it gave them some autonomy and authority within their homes.

Women's status was not stagnant in this period. The cultural wedge driven between women's and men's worlds obscured diverse and significant changes that did erode inequality. The state gave married women the right to control their property and income. Jobs became available for some, mainly single, women, giving them some economic independence and an identity apart from the household. Secondary education similar to that offered to men became available to women, and colleges began to admit some women for higher learning. Divorce became a possible, though still difficult, strategy for the first time and led social commentators to bemoan the increasing rate of marital dissolution. In short, women's opportunities moved slowly forward in diverse ways.

From 1890 to 1940 women's opportunities continued to improve, and many claimed that women had won equality. Still, the opportunities were never enough to enable women to transcend their subordinate position. The passage of the Woman Suffrage Amendment stands out as the high point of changes during this period, yet women could make little headway in government while husbands and male politicians belittled and rejected their political aspirations. Women entered the labor market in ever-increasing numbers, educated women could get white-collar positions for the first time, and employers extended hiring to married women. Still, employers rarely considered women for high-status jobs, and explicit discrimination was an accepted practice. Although women's college opportunities became more like men's, professional and advanced degree programs still excluded women. Married women gained widespread access to effective contraception. Although popular opinion expected women to pursue and enjoy sex within marriage, social mores still denied them sex outside it. While divorce became more socially acceptable and practically available, laws still restricted divorce by demanding that one spouse prove that the other was morally repugnant. Movies portrayed glamorous women as smart, sexually provocative, professionally talented, and ambitious, but even they, if they were good women, were driven by an overwhelming desire to marry, bear children, and dedicate themselves to their homes.

Writing at the end of this period, the sociologist Mirra Komarovsky captured its implications splendidly. After studying affluent college students during World War II, Komarovsky concluded that young women were beset by "serious contradictions between two roles." The first was the feminine role, with its expectations of deference to men and a future focused on familial activities. The second was the "modern" role that "partly obliterates the differentiation in sex," presumably because the emphasis on education made the universal qualities of ability and accomplishment seem the only reasonable limitations on future activities. Women who absorbed the egalitarian implications of modern education felt confused, burdened, and irritated by the contrary expectations that they display a subordinate femininity. The intrinsic contradictions between these two role expectations could only end, Komarovsky declared, when women's real adult role was redefined to make it "consistent with the socioeconomic and ideological modern society."[1]

Since 1940, many of these contradictions have been resolved. At an accelerating pace, women have continually gained greater access to the activities, positions, and statuses formerly reserved to men.

Despite the tremendous gains women have experienced, they have not achieved complete equality, nor is it imminent. The improvement of women's status has been uneven, seesawing between setbacks and advances. Women still bear the major responsibility for raising children. They suffer from lingering harassment, intimidation, and disguised discrimination. Women in the United States still get poorer jobs and lower income. They have less access to economic or political power. The higher echelons of previously male social hierarchies have assimilated women slowest and least completely. For example, in blue-collar hierarchies they find it hard to get skilled jobs or join craft unions; in white-collar hierarchies they rarely reach top management; and in politics the barriers to women's entry seem to rise with the power of the office they seek. Yet when we compare the status of American women today with their status in the past, the movement toward greater equality is striking.

While women have not gained full equality, the formal structural barriers holding them back have largely collapsed and those left are crumbling. New government policies have discouraged sex discrimination by most organizations and in most areas of life outside the family. The political and economic systems have accepted ever more women and have promoted them to positions with more influence and higher status. Education at all levels has become equally available to women. Women have gained great control over their reproductive processes, and their sexual freedom has come to resemble that of men. It has become easy and socially acceptable to end unsatisfactory marriages with divorce. Popular culture has come close to portraying women as men's legitimate equal. Television, our most dynamic communication media, regularly portrays discrimination as wrong and male abuse or male dominance as nasty. The prevailing theme of this recent period has been women's assimilation into all the activities and positions once denied them.

This book [this reading was taken from] focuses on the dominant patterns and the groups that had the most decisive and most public roles in the processes that changed women's status: middle-class whites and, secondarily, the white working class. The histories of gender inequality among racial and ethnic minorities are too diverse to address adequately here.[2] Similarly, this analysis neglects other distinctive groups, especially lesbians and heterosexual women who avoided marriage, whose changing circumstances also deserve extended study.

While these minorities all have distinctive histories, the major trends considered here have influenced all groups. Every group had to respond to the same changing political and economic structures that defined the opportunities and constraints for all people in the society. Also, whatever their particular history, the members of each group understood their gender relations against the backdrop of the white, middle-class family's cultural preeminence. Even when people in higher or lower-class positions or people in ethnic communities expressed contempt for these values, they were familiar with the middle-class ideals and thought of them as leading ideas in the society. The focus on the white middle classes is simply an analytical and practical strategy. The history of dominant groups has no greater inherent or moral worth. Still, except in cases of open, successful rebellion, the ideas and actions of dominant groups usually affect history much more than the ideas and actions of subordinate groups. This fact is an inevitable effect of inequality.

THE MEANING OF INEQUALITY AND ITS DECLINE

We will think differently about women's status under two theoretical agendas. Either we can try to evaluate how short from equality women now fall, or we can try to understand how far they have come from past deprivations.

Looking at women's place in society today from these two vantage points yields remarkably different perspectives. They accentuate different aspects of women's status by altering the background against which we compare it. Temporal and analytical differences separate these two vantage points, not distinctive moral positions, although people sometimes confuse these differences with competing moral positions.

If we want to assess and criticize women's disadvantages today, we usually compare their existing status with an imagined future when complete equality reigns. Using this ideal standard of complete equality, we would find varied shortcomings in women's status today. These shortcomings include women's absence from positions of political or economic power, men's preponderance in the better-paid and higher-status occupations, women's lower average income, women's greater family responsibilities, the higher status commonly attached to male activities, and the dearth of institutions or policies supporting dual-earner couples.

Alternatively, if we want to evaluate how women's social status has improved, we must turn in the other direction and face the past. We look back to a time when women were legal and political outcasts, working only in a few low-status jobs, and always deferring to male authority. From this perspective, women's status today seems much brighter. Compared with the nineteenth century, women now have a nearly equal legal and political status, far more women hold jobs, women can succeed at almost any occupation, women usually get paid as much as men in the same position (in the same firm), women have as much educational opportunity as men, and both sexes normally expect women to pursue jobs and careers.

As we seek to understand the decline of gender inequality, we will necessarily stress the improvements in women's status. We will always want to remember, however, that gender inequality today stands somewhere between extreme inequality and complete equality. To analyze the modern history of gender inequality fully, we must be able to look at this middle ground from both sides. It is seriously deficient when measured against full equality. It is a remarkable improvement when measured against past inequality.

Notes

1. Mirra Komarovsky, "Cultural Contradictions and Sex Roles," pp. 184, 189. Cf. Helen Hacker, "Women as a Minority Group."
2. For studies of these various groups see, e.g., Paula Giddings, *When and Where I Enter*; Alfredo Mirande and Evangelina Enriquez, *La Chicana*; Evelyn Nakana Glen, *Issei, Nisei, War Bride*; Jacqueline Jones, *Labor of Love, Labor of Sorrow*.

References

Komarovsky, Mirra. "Cultural Contradictions and Sex Roles." *American Journal of Sociology* 52 (1946): 184–189.

■ **READING 6**

Falling Back on Plan B: The Children of the Gender Revolution Face Uncharted Territory

Kathleen Gerson

Young adults today grew up with mothers who marched into the workplace and parents who forged innovative alternatives to traditional marriage. These "children of the gender revolution" now face a world that is far different than that of their parents or grandparents. While massive changes in work and family arrangements have expanded their options, these changes also pose new challenges to crafting a marriage, rearing children, and building a career. Members of this new generation walk a fine line between their desire to achieve egalitarian, sharing relationships that can meld with satisfying work and succumbing to the realities of gender conflict, fragile relationships, and uncertain job prospects. The choices they are able to make will shape work and family life for decades to come.

Social forecasters have reached starkly different conclusions about what these choices will be. Some proclaim that the recent upturn in "opt out" mothers foreshadows a wider return to tradition among younger women.[1] Others believe the rising number of single adults foretells a deepening "decline of commitment" that is threatening family life and the social fabric.[2] While there is little doubt that tumultuous changes have shaped the lives of a new generation, there is great disagreement about how. Does the diversification of families into two-earner, single-parent, and cohabiting forms represent a waning of family life or the growth of more flexible relationships? Will this new generation integrate family and work in new ways, or will older patterns inexorably pull them back?

To find out how members of the first generation to grow up in diversifying families look back on their childhoods and forward to their own futures, I conducted in-depth, life history interviews with a carefully selected group of young people between 18 and 32. These young women and men experienced the full range of changes that have taken place in family life, and most lived in some form of "nontraditional" arrangement at some point in their childhood.[3] My interviews reveal a generation that does not conform to prevailing media stereotypes, whether they depict declining families or a return to strict gender divisions in caretaking and breadwinning.

In contrast to popular images of twenty- and thirty-somethings who wish to return to tradition or reject family life altogether, the young women and men I interviewed are more focused on *how well* their parents met the challenges of providing economic and emotional support than on *what form* their families took. Now facing their own choices, women and men share a set of lofty aspirations. Despite their varied family experiences, most hope to blend the traditional value of lifelong commitment with the modern value of flexible sharing. In the best of all possible worlds, the majority would like to create a lasting marriage (or a "marriage like" relationship) that allows them to blend home and work in a flexible, egalitarian way.

Yet young people are also developing strategies to prepare for "second best" options in a world where time-demanding workplaces, a lack of child care, and fragile relationships may place their ideals out of reach. Concerned about the difficulty of finding a reliable and egalitarian partner to help them integrate work with family caretaking, most women see work as essential to their own and their children's survival, whether or not they marry. Worried about time-greedy workplaces, most men feel they must place work first and will need to count on a partner at home. As they prepare for second best options, the differing fallback positions of "self-reliant" women and "neo-traditional" men may point to a new gender divide. But this divide does not reflect a new generation's highest aspirations.

GROWING UP IN CHANGING FAMILIES

Even though theorists and social commentators continue to debate the merits of various family forms, my informants did not focus on their family's "structure."[4] Instead, I found large variation among children who grew up in apparently similar family types. Those who grew up in families with a homemaking mother and breadwinning father hold divided assessments. While a little more than half thought this was the best arrangement, close to a half reached a different conclusion. When domesticity appeared to undermine a mother's satisfaction, disturb the household's harmony, or threaten its economic security, the children concluded that it would have been better if their mothers had pursued a sustained commitment to work.

Many of those who grew up in a single-parent home also expressed ambivalence about their parents' breakups. Slightly more than half wished their parents had stayed together, but close to half believed that a breakup, while not ideal, was better than continuing to live in a conflict-ridden or silently unhappy home. The longer-term consequences of a breakup shaped the lessons children drew.[5] If their parents got back on their feet and created better lives, children developed surprisingly positive outlooks on the decision to separate.

Those who grew up in a dual-earner home were the least ambivalent about their parents' arrangements. More than three-fourths believed that having two work-committed parents provided increased economic resources and also promoted marriages that seemed more egalitarian and satisfying.[6] If, however, the pressures of working long hours or coping with blocked opportunities and family-unfriendly workplaces took their toll, some children concluded that having overburdened, time-stressed caretakers offset these advantages.

In short, growing up in this era of diverse families led children to focus more on how well—or poorly—parents (and other caretakers) were able to meet the twin challenges of providing economic and emotional support than on its form. Even more important, children experienced family life as a dynamic process that changed over time. Since family life is a film, not a snapshot, the key to understanding young people's views lies in charting the diverse paths their families took.

FAMILY PATHS AND GENDER FLEXIBILITY

Families can take different paths from seemingly common starting points, and similar types of families can have travel toward different destinations. When young adults reflect on their families, they focus on how their homes either came to provide stability and support or failed to do so. About a third reported growing up in a stable home, while a quarter concluded that their families grew more supportive as time passed. In contrast, just under one in ten reported living in a chronically insecure home, while a bit more than a third felt that family support eroded as they grew up. Why, then, do some children look back on families that became supportive and secure, while others experienced a decline in their family's fortunes?

Parents' strategies for organizing breadwinning and caretaking hold the key to understanding a family's pathway.[7] Flexible strategies, which allowed mothers, fathers, and other caretakers to transcend rigid gender boundaries, helped families prevail in the face of unexpected economic and interpersonal crises. Inflexible responses, in contrast, left families ill-equipped to cope with eroding supports for a strict division in mothers' and fathers' responsibilities.

RISING FAMILY FORTUNES

The sources of expanding support differed by family situation, but all reflect a flexible response to unexpected difficulties. Sometimes marriages became more equal as demoralized mothers went to work and pushed for change or helped overburdened fathers. Josh, for example, reported that his mother's decision to go to work gave her the courage to insist that his father tackle his drug addiction:[8]

> My parents fought almost constantly. Then my mom got a job. They separated about five, six, seven months. Even though I was upset, I thought it was for the best. That's when (my dad) got into some kind of program and my mom took him back. That changed

the whole family dynamic. We got extremely close. A whole new relationship developed with my father.

Chris recalled how his mother's job allowed his father to quit a dead-end job and train for a more satisfying career:

> Between 7th and 8th grade, my dad had a business which didn't work. It was a dead-end thing, and he came home frustrated, so my mom got him to go to school. It was hard financially, but it was good because he was actually enjoying what he was doing. He really flourished. A lot of people say, "Wow, your mom is the breadwinner, and that's strange." It's not. It is a very joint thing.

Parental breakups that relieved domestic conflict or led to the departure of an unstable parent also helped caretaking parents get back on their feet. Connie recounted how her mother was able to create a more secure home after separating from an alcoholic husbands and finding a job that offered a steady income and a source of personal esteem:

> My father just sat in the corner and once in a while got angry at us, but (my mom)—I don't know if it was him or the money, but she didn't stand up for herself as much as I think she should. The tension with my dad never eased, and my mom had gotten sick with multiple bleeding ulcers. That was her real turning point. It was building inside of her to leave, 'cause she'd got a job and started to realize she had her own money . . . (She) became a much happier person. And because she was better, I was better. I had a weight taken off of me.

More stable and egalitarian remarriages could also give children the economic and emotional support they had not previously received. Having never known her biological father, Shauna recalled about how her stepfather became a devoted caretaker and the "real" father she always wanted:

> At first, I was feeling it was a bad change because I wanted my mom to myself. Then my mom said, "Why don't you call him daddy?" The next thing I was saying "Daddy!" I remember the look on his face and his saying "She called me daddy!" I was so happy. After that, he's always been my dad, and there's never been any question about it. . . . (He) would get home before my mom, so he would cook the dinner and clean. My dad spoiled me for any other man, because this is the model I had.
>
> When Isabella's parents divorced, her grandfather became a treasured caretaker: It's not like I didn't have a father, because my grandfather was always there. He was there to take me to after-school clubs and pick me up. I was sheltered—he had to take me to the library, wait till I finished all my work, take me home. I call him dad. Nobody could do better.

And when Antonio's single mother lost her job, his grandparents provided essential income that kept the family afloat:

> My mom and grandparents were the type of people that even if we didn't have (money), we was gonna get it. Their ideal is, "I want to give you all the things I couldn't have when

I was young." My grandparents and my mother thought like that, so no matter how much in poverty we were living, I was getting everything I wanted.

Despite their obvious differences, the common ingredient in these narratives is the ability of parents and other caretakers to reorganize child rearing and breadwinning in a more flexible, less gender-divided way. Mothers going to work, fathers becoming more involved in child rearing, and others joining in the work of family life—all of these strategies helped families overcome unexpected difficulties and create more economically secure, emotionally stable homes. Growing flexibility in how parents met the challenges of a earning needed income and caring for children nourished parental morale, increased a home's financial security, and provided inspiring models of adult resilience. While children acknowledged the costs, they valued these second chances and gleaned lessons from watching parents find ways to create a better life. Looking back, they could conclude that "all's well that end's well."

DECLINING FAMILY FORTUNES

For some children, however, home life followed a downward slope. Here, too, the key to their experiences lies in the work and caretaking strategies of those entrusted with their care; but in this case, gender inflexibility in the face of domestic difficulties left children with less support than they had once taken for granted. Faced with a father's abandonment or a stay-at-home mother's growing frustration, children described how their parents' resistance to more flexible strategies for apportioning paid and domestic work left them struggling to meet children's economic and emotional needs. Over time, deteriorating marriages, declining parental morale, and financial insecurity shattered a once rosy picture of family stability and contentment.

When parents became stuck in a rigid division of labor, with unhappy mothers and fathers ill-equipped to support the household, traditional marriages could deteriorate. Sarah explains how her mother became increasingly depressed and "over-involved" after relinquishing a promising career to devote all of her time to child rearing:

> When my sister was born, (my mom's) job had started up, career-wise, so she wasn't happy (but) she felt she had to be home. She had a lot of conflicts about work and home and opted to be really committed to family, but also resented it. . . . She was the super-mom, but just seemed really depressed a lot of time . . . (It came) with an edge to it—"in return, I want you to be devoted to me." If we did something separate from her, that was a major problem. So I was making distance because I felt I had to protect myself from this invasion. . . . She thought she was doing something good to sacrifice for us. . . . but it would have been better if my mother was happier working.

Megan recalls her father's mounting frustration as his income stagnated and he endured the complaints of a wife who expected to him to provide a "better lifestyle":

> My mother was always dissatisfied. She wanted my father to be more ambitious, and he wasn't an ambitious man. As long as he was supporting the family, it didn't matter if it was

a bigger house or a bigger car. Forty years of being married to a woman saying, "Why don't we have more money?"—I think that does something to your self-esteem.

Unresolved power struggles in dual-earner marriages could also cause problems, as wives felt the weight of "doing it all" and fathers resisted egalitarian sharing. For Justin, juggling paid and domestic work left his mother exhausted, while a high-pressured job running a restaurant left his father with no time to attend nightly dinners or even Little League games:

> I was slightly disappointed that I could not see my father more—because I understood but also because it depends on the mood he's in. And it got worse as work (went) downhill . . . (So) I can't model my relationship on my parents. My mother wasn't very happy. There was a lot of strain on her.

Harmful breakups, where fathers abandoned their children and mothers could not find new ways to support the family or create an identity beyond wife and mother, also eroded family support. Nina remembers how her father's disappearance, combined with her mother's reluctance to seek a job and create a more independent life, triggered descent from a comfortable middle-class existence to one of abiding poverty:

> My mother ended up going on welfare. We went from a nice place to living in a really cruddy building. And she's still in the same apartment. To this day, my sister will not speak to my father because of what he's done to us.

Children (and their parents) sometimes lost the support of other caretakers. Shortly after Jasmine's father left to live with another woman and her mother fell into a deep depression, she suffered the loss of a "third parent" when her beloved grandmother died:

> It seemed like I had everything I wanted. My mom worked at a good paying job and was doing great. My dad worked at night, so he was around when I'd get home from school. I just thought of it as the way it was supposed to be. I was used to him being there, cooking dinner for us. So after he moved in with another woman and her children, it made me feel worse 'cause I felt that he was leaving me to be with other kids. I miss him, and I know he misses me.

The events that propelled families on a downward track—including rising financial instability, declining parental involvement and morale, and a dearth of other supportive caretakers—share a common element. Whether parents faced marital impasses or difficult breakups, resistance to more flexible gender arrangements left them unable to sustain an emotionally or economically secure home. Their children concluded that all did *not* end well.

In sum, sustained parental support and economic security were more important to my informants than the form their families took. Since any family type holds potential pitfalls if parents do not or cannot prevail over the difficulties that arise, conventional categories that see families as static "forms" cannot account for the ways that families change as children grow to adulthood. Instead, young women and men from diverse family backgrounds recounted how parents and other family members who transcended gender boundaries and developed flexible strategies for breadwinning and caretaking were better able to cope with marital crises, economic insecurities, and other unanticipated challenges.

A range of social trends—including the erosion of single-earner paychecks, the fragility of modern marriages, and the expanding options and pressures for women to work—require varied and versatile ways of earning and caring. These institutional shifts make gender flexibility increasingly desirable and even essential. Flexible approaches to work and parenting help families adapt, while inflexible ones leave them ill-prepared to cope with new economic and social realities.

CONVERGING IDEALS, DIVERGING FALLBACKS

How are young adults using the lessons of growing up in changing families to formulate their own plans for the future? Women and men from diverse family backgrounds share a set of lofty aspirations. Whether or not their parents stayed together, more than nine out of ten hope to rear children in the context of a satisfying lifelong bond. Far from rejecting the value of commitment, almost everyone wants to create a lasting marriage or "marriage-like" partnership. This does not, however, reflect a desire for a traditional relationship. Most also aspire to build a committed bond where both paid work and family caretaking are shared. Three-fourths of those who grew up in dual-earner homes want their spouses to share breadwinning and caretaking; but so do more that two-thirds of those from traditional homes, and close to nine-tenths of those with single parents. While four-fifths of women want an egalitarian relationship, but so do two-thirds of men. In short, most share an ideal that stresses the value of a lasting, flexible, and egalitarian partnership with considerable room for personal autonomy. Amy, an Asian American with two working parents, thus explains that:

> I want a fifty-fifty relationship, where we both have the potential of doing everything—both of us working and dealing with kids. With regard to career, if neither has flexibility, then one of us will have to sacrifice for one period, and the other for another.

And Wayne, an African American raised by a single mother, expresses the essentially same hopes when he says that:

> I don't want the '50s type of marriage, where I come home and she's cooking. I want her to have a career of her own. I want to be able to set my goals, and she can do what she wants, too.

While most of my interviewees hope to strike a flexible breadwinning and caretaking balance with an egalitarian partner, they are also skeptical about their chances of achieving this ideal. Women and men both worry that work demands, a lack of child rearing supports, and the fragility of modern relationships will undermine their desire to forge an enduring, egalitarian partnership. In the face of barriers to equality, most have concluded that they have little choice but to prepare for options that may fall substantially short of their ideals. Despite their shared aspirations, however, men and women are facing different institutional obstacles and cultural pressures, which are prompting divergent fallback strategies. If they cannot find a supportive partner, most women prefer self-reliance over economic dependence within a traditional marriage. Most men, if they cannot strike an equal balance between work and parenting, prefer a neo-traditional arrangement that allows them to put work first and rely on a partner for the lion's share of caregiving. In the event that Plan A proves unreachable, women and men are thus pursuing a different Plan B as insurance against their "worst case" fears. These divergent fallback strategies point toward the emergence of a new gender divide between young women, most of whom who see a need for self-reliance, and young men, who are more inclined to retain a modified version of traditional expectations.

WOMEN'S PLAN B

Torn between high hopes for combining work and family and worries about sustaining a lasting and satisfying partnership, young women are navigating uncertain waters. While some are falling back on domesticity, most prefer to find a more independent base than traditional marriage provides. In contrast to the media-driven message that young women are turning away from work and career in favor of domestic pursuits, the majority of my interviewees are determined to seek financial and emotional self-reliance, whether or not they also forge a committed relationship. Regardless of class, race, or ethnicity, most are reluctant to surrender their autonomy in a traditional marriage. When the bonds of marriage are so fragile, relying on a husband for economic security seems foolhardy. And if a relationship deteriorates, economic dependence on a man leaves few means of escape. Danisha, an African American who grew up in an inner-city, working-class neighborhood, and Jennifer, who was raised in a middle-class, predominantly white suburb, agree. Danisha proclaims that:

> Let's say that my marriage doesn't work. Just in case, I want to establish myself, because I don't ever want to end up, like, "What am I going to do?" I want to be able to do what I have to do and still be okay.

Jennifer agrees:

> I will have to have a job and some kind of stability before considering marriage. Too many of my mother's friends went for that—"Let him provide everything"—and they're stuck in a very unhappy relationship, but can't leave because they can't provide for themselves or the children they now have. So it's either welfare or putting up with somebody else's c–p.

Hoping to avoid being trapped in an unhappy marriage or left by an unreliable partner without a way to survive, almost three-fourths of women plan to build a non-negotiable base of self-reliance and an independent identity in the world of paid work. But they do not view this strategy as incompatible with the search for a life partner. Instead, it reflects their determination to set a high standard for a worthy relationship. Economic self-reliance and personal independence make it possible to resist "settling" for anything less than a satisfying, mutually supportive bond.

Women from all backgrounds have concluded that work provides indispensable economic, social, and emotional resources. They have drawn lessons about the rewards of self-reliance and the perils of domesticity from their mothers, other women, and their own experiences growing up. When the bonds of marriage are fragile, relying on a husband for economic security seems foolhardy. They are thus seeking alternatives to traditional marriage by establishing a firm tie to paid work, by redesigning motherhood to better fit their work aspirations, and by looking to kin and friends as a support network to enlarge and, if needed, substitute, for an intimate relationship. These strategies do not preclude finding a life partner, but they reflect a determination to set a high standard for choosing one. Maria, who grew up in a two-parent home in a predominantly white, working-class suburb, declares:

> I want to have this person to share [my] life with—(someone) that you're there for as much as they're there for you. But I can't settle.

And Rachel, whose Latino parents separated when she was young, shares this view:

> I'm not afraid of being alone, but I am afraid of being with somebody's who's a jerk. I want to get married and have children, but it has to be under the right circumstances, with the right person.

Maria and Rachel also agree that if a worthy relationship ultimately proves out of reach, then remaining single need not mean social disconnection. Kin and friends provide a support network that enlarges and, if needed, even substitutes for an intimate relationship. Maria explains:

> If I don't find (a relationship), then I cannot live in sorrow. It's not the only thing that's ultimately important. If I didn't have my family, if I didn't have a career, if I didn't have friends, I would be equally unhappy. (A relationship) is just one slice of the pie.

And Rachel concurs:

> I can spend the rest of my life on my own, and as long as I have my sisters and my friends, I'm okay.

By blending support from friends and kin with financial self-sufficiency, these young women are pursuing a strategy of autonomy rather than placing their own fate or their children's in the hands of a traditional relationship.[9] Whether or not this strategy ultimately leads to marriage, it appears to offer the safest and most responsible way to prepare for the uncertainties of relationships and the barriers to men's equal sharing.

MEN'S PLAN B

Young men, in contrast, face a different dilemma: Torn between women's pressures for an egalitarian partnership and their own desire to succeed—or at least survive—in time-demanding workplaces, they are more inclined to fall back on a modified traditionalism that contrasts vividly with women's search for self-reliance. While they do not want or expect to return to a 1950s model of fathers as the only breadwinner, most men prefer a modified traditionalism that recognizes a mother's right (and need) to work, but puts his own career first. Although Andrew grew up in a consistently two-income home, he distinguished between a woman's "choice" to work and a man's "responsibility" to support his family:

> I would like to have it be equal—just from what I was exposed to and what attracts me—but I don't have a set definition for what that would be like. I would be fine if both of us were working, but if she thought, "At this point in my life, I don't want to work," then it would be fine.

Because equality may prove to be too costly to their careers, seven out of ten men are pursuing a strategy that positions them as the main breadwinner, even if it allows for two working spouses. When push comes to shove, and the demands of work collide with the needs of children, this approach allows men to resist equal caretaking, even in a two-earner context. Like women, men from a range of family, class, and ethnic backgrounds fall back on neo-traditionalism. They favor retaining a clear boundary between a breadwinning father and a caretaking mother, even when she holds a paid job. This neo-traditional strategy stresses women's primary status as mothers and defines equality as a woman's "choice" to add work onto mothering.

By making room for two earners, these strategies offer the financial cushion of a second income, acknowledge women's desire for a life beyond the home, and allow for more involved fatherhood. But this vision, which still claims separate spheres of responsibility for women and men, does not challenge a man's position as the primary earner or undermine the claim that his work prospects should come first. Although James's mother became too mentally ill to care for her children or herself, Josh plans to leave the lion's share of caretaking to his wife:

> All things being equal, it (caretaking) should be shared. It may sound sexist, but if somebody's going to be the breadwinner, it's going to be me. First of all, I make a better salary, and I feel the need to work, and I just think the child really needs the mother more than the father at a young age.

Men are thus more likely to favor a fallback arrangement that retains the gender boundary between breadwinning and caretaking, even when mothers hold paid jobs. From young men's perspective, this modified but still gendered household offers women the chance to earn income and establish an identity at the workplace without imposing the costs of equal parenting on men. Granting a mother's "right" to work supports women's claims for independence, but does not undermine men's claim that their work prospects should come first. Acknowledging men's responsibilities at home provides for more involved fatherhood, but does not envision domestic equality. And making room for two earners provides a buffer against the difficulties of living on one income, but does not challenge men's position as the primary earner. Modified traditionalism thus appears to be a good compromise when the career costs of equality remain so high.[10] New economic insecurities, coupled with women's growing desire for equality, are creating dilemmas for men, even if they take a different form than the ones confronting women. Ultimately, however, men's desire to protect work prerogatives collides with women's growing desire for equality and need for independence.

ACROSS THE GENDER DIVIDE

In contrast to the popular images of a generation who feels neglected by working mothers, unsettled by parental breakups, and wary of equality, these life stories show strong support for working mothers, a greater concern with the quality of a relationship, and a shared desire to create lasting, flexible, and egalitarian partnerships. The good news is that most young women and men had largely positive experiences with mothers who worked and parents who strove for flexibility and equality. Those who grew up with a caring support network and sufficient economic security, whether in a single or a two-parent household, did well. Young women and men both recounted how gender flexibility in breadwinning and caretaking helped their parents (and other caretakers) overcome such increasingly prevalent family crises as the loss of a father's income or the decline of a mother's morale. By letting go of rigid patterns that once narrowly defined women's and men's "proper" places in the family and the wider world, all kinds of families were able to overcome unexpected challenges and create more financially stable and emotionally supportive homes. And most, even among those who lived in less flexible families, hope to build on the gains of their parents' generation by seeking equality and flexibility in their own lives.

The bad news, however, is that most young adults remain skeptical about their chances of achieving their ideals. Amid their shared desire to transcend gender boundaries and achieve flexibility in their own lives, however, young women and men harbor strong concerns that their aspirations will prove impossible to reach. Faced with the many barriers to egalitarian relationships and fearful that they will not find the right partner to help them integrate work with family caretaking, they are also preparing for options that may fall substantially short of their ideals. Reversing the argument that women are returning to tradition, however, these divergent fallback strategies suggest that a new divide is emerging between "self-reliant" women, who see work, an independent income, and emotional autonomy as essential to their survival, and "neo-traditional" men, who grant women's "choice" to work but also feel the need and pressure to be a primary breadwinner.

While women are developing more innovative strategies than are men, the underlying story is one of a resilient, but realistic generation that has changed far more than the institutions it has inherited. Whether they grew up in a flexible home or one with more rigid definitions of women's and men's proper places, their hard won lessons about the need for new, more egalitarian options for building relationships and caring for children are outpacing their ability to implement these aspirations.

Yet young men and women still hope to reach across the divide that separates them. Aware that traditional job ladders and traditional marriages are both waning, they are seeking more flexible ways to build careers, care for families, and integrate the two.[11] Convinced that the "organized career" is a relic of the past, most hope to craft a "personal career" that is not bound by a single employer or work organization. Most men as well as women are trying to redefine the "ideal worker" to accommodate the ebb and flow of family life, even if that means sacrificing some income for a more balanced life.[12] They hope to create a shared "work-family" career that interweaves breadwinning and caretaking.

Growing up in changing families and facing uncertainty in their own lives has left this generation weary of rigid, narrowly framed "family values" that moralize about their personal choices or those of others. They are searching for a morality without moralism that balances an ethic of tolerance and inclusiveness with the core values of behaving responsibly and caring for others. The clash between self-reliant women and neo-traditional men may signal a new divide, but it stems from intensifying work-family dilemmas, not from a decline of laudable values.

Since new social realties are forcing young adults to seek new ways to combine love and work, the best hope for bridging new gender divides lies in creating social policies that will allow 21st century Americans to pursue the flexible, egalitarian gender strategies they want rather than forcing them to fall back on less desirable—and ultimately less workable—options. Whether the goal is equal opportunity or a healthy family landscape, the best family values can only be achieved by creating the social supports for gender flexibility in our communities, homes, and workplaces.

Notes

1. Anecdotal, but high profile stories have touted an "opt out revolution," to use Lisa Belkin's term (2003), although a number of analysts have shown that "revolution" is a highly misleading and exaggerated term to describe the recent slight downturn in young mothers' labor force participation (Boushey, 2008; Williams, 2007). Most well-educated women are not leaving the workforce, and even though mothers with infants have shown a small downturn from their 1995 peak, mothers with children over the age of one are still just as likely as other women to hold a paid job. Even mothers with children under one show levels of employment that are much higher than the 1960's levels, which averaged 30 percent. Moreover, Williams (2007), Stone (2007), Bennetts (2007), and Hirshman (2006) also point out that the metaphor of "opting out" obscures the powerful ways that mothers are, in Williams words, "pushed out."
2. Recent overviews of the rise of single adults can be found in Pew Research Center (2007a and 2007b) and Roberts (2007). Prominent proponents of the "family decline" perspective include Blankenhorn (1995), Popenoe (1988, 1996), Poponoe et al. (1996), and Whitehead (1997). Waite and Gallagher (2000) focus on the personal and social advantages of marriage. For rebuttals to the "family decline" perspective, see Bengtson et al. (2002), Coontz (2005), Moore et al. (2002), Skolnick and Rosencrantz (1994), and Stacey (1996).
3. Randomly chosen from a broad range of city and suburban neighborhoods dispersed throughout the New York metropolitan region, the group includes 120 respondents from diverse race and class backgrounds and all parts of the country. In all, 54 percent identified as non-Hispanic white, 21 percent as African American, 18 percent as Latino, and 7 percent as Asian. About 43 percent grew up in middle and upper-middle class homes, while 43 percent lived in homes that were solidly working class, and another 15 percent lived in or on the edge of poverty. With an average age of 24, they are evenly divided between women and men, and about 5 percent identified as either lesbian or gay. As a group, they reflect the demographic contours of young adults throughout metropolitan America. See Gerson (2006 and forthcoming) for a full description of my sample and methods.

4. Most research shows that diversity *within* family types, however defined, is as large as the differences *between* them. Acock and Demo (1994) argue that family type does not predict children's well-being. Parcel and Menaghan (1994) make the same case for different forms of parental employment.

5. In the case of one vs. two-parent homes, children living with both biological parents do appear on average to fare better, but most of the difference disappears after taking account of the family's financial resources and the degree of parental conflict prior to a break-up (Amato and Booth, 1997; Amato and Hohmann-Marriott, 2007; Booth and Amato, 2001; Furstenberg and Cherlin, 1991; Hetherington, 1999; McLanahan and Sandefur, 1994). In a recent study of the effects of divorce on children's behavior, Li (2007) shows that "while certain divorces harm children, others benefit them."

6. Decades of research have shown that children do not suffer when their mothers work outside the home. A mother's satisfaction with her situation, the quality of care a child receives, and the involvement of fathers and other caretakers are far more important factors (Galinsky, 1999; Harvey, 1999; Hoffman, 1987; Hoffman et al., 1999). Bianchi, Robinson, and Milkie (2006) report that parents are actually spending more time with their children. Recent research on the effects of daycare have found only small, temporary differences. Barnett and Rivers (1996) demonstrate a range of advantages for two-income couples, and Springer (2007) reports significant health benefits for men whose wives work.

7. Hochschild (1989) refers to dual earner couples' "gender strategies," although she focuses more on how these strategies reproduce gender divisions than on when, how, and why they might undermine gender distinctions. See Lorber (1994), Risman (1998), and West and Zimmerman (1987) for discussions of the social construction of gender. Zerubavel (1991) analyzes the social roots of mental flexibility.

8. All of the names have been changed to protect confidentiality, and some quotes have been shortened or lightly edited to remove extraneous phrases.

9. About a quarter of women concluded that if work and family collide, they would rather make a more traditional compromise. These women worried about inflexible workplaces and the difficulty finding an equal partner. Yet they still hoped to fit work into their lives. This outlook, too, reflects the dilemmas facing young women who lack the supports to share work and caretaking equally. (See Gerson, forthcoming, for a full analysis of the variation in women's fallback strategies.)

10. About three in ten men stress independence over traditional marriage, but autonomy has a different meaning for them than it does for women. Poor work prospects left them determined to remain single unless they find a partner who does not expect financial support. Unlike self-reliant women, who hoped to support themselves and their children, autonomous men worried about their ability to earn enough to support a family. (See Gerson, forthcoming, for a full analysis of men's varied strategies.)

11. See Moen and Roehling (2005).

12. See Williams (2000).

References

Acock, Alan C. and David H. Demo. 1994. *Family Diversity and Well-being*. Thousand Oaks, CA: Sage.

Amato, Paul R. and Alan Booth. 1997. *A Generation at Risk: Growing Up in an Era of Family Upheaval*. Cambridge, MA: Harvard University Press. (Cited twice)

Amato, Paul R. and Bryndl Hohmann-Marriott. 2007. "A Comparison of High- and Low-Distress Marriages That End in Divorce." *Journal of Marriage and Family* 69(3): 621–638.

Barnett, Rosalind C. and Caryl Rivers. 1996. *She works/He works: How Two-income Families Are Happier, Healthier, and Better-off*. San Francisco, CA: Harper.

Belkin, Lisa. 2003. "The Opt Out Revolution." *The New York Times Magazine*.

Bengtson, Vern L., Timothy J. Biblarz and Robert E. L. Roberts. 2002. *How Families Still Matter: A Longitudinal Study of Youth in Two Generations*. New York: Cambridge University Press.

Bennetts, Leslie. 2007. *The Feminine Mistake: Are We Giving Up Too Much?* New York: Voice/Hyperion.

Bianchi, Suzanne M., John P. Robinson and Melissa A. Milkie. 2006. *Changing Rhythms of American Family Life*. New York: Russell Sage Foundation.

Blankenhorn, David. 1995. *Fatherless America: Confronting Our Most Urgent Social Problem*. New York: BasicBooks.

Booth, Alan and Paul R. Amato. 2001. "Parental Predivorce Relations and Offspring Postdivorce Well-Being." *Journal of Marriage and the Family* 63(1): 197–212.

Boushey, Heather. 2008. ""Opting out"? The Effect of Children on Women's Employment in the United States." *Feminist Economics* 14(1): 1–36.

Coontz, Stephanie. 2005. *Marriage, a History: From Obedience to Intimacy, or How Love Conquered Marriage*. New York: Viking.

Furstenberg, Frank F. and Andrew J. Cherlin. 1991. *Divided Families: What Happens to Children When Parents Part*. Cambridge, MA: Harvard University Press.

Galinsky, Ellen. 1999. *Ask the Children: What America's Children Really Think about Working Parents*. New York: William Morrow.

Gerson, Kathleen. Forthcoming. *Blurring Boundaries: How the Children of the Gender Revolution are Remaking Family and Work*. New York: Oxford University Press.

———. 2006. "Families as Trajectories: Children's Views of Family Life in Contemporary America." In *Families Between Flexibility and Dependability: Perspectives for a Life Cycle Family Policy*, edited by Hans Bertram et al. Farmington Hills, MI: Verlag Barbara Budrich.

Harvey, Lisa. 1999. "Short-Term and Long-Term Effects of Early Parental Employment on Children of the National Longitudinal Study of Youth." *Developmental Psychology* 35(2): 445–459.

Hetherington, E. M. 1999. *Coping with Divorce, Single Parenting, and Remarriage: A Risk and Resiliency Perspective*. Mahwah, NJ: Lawrence Erlbaum Associates.

Hirshman, Linda. 2006. *Get to Work*. New York: Viking.

Hochschild, Arlie R. 1989. *The Second Shift: Working Parents and the Revolution at Home*. New York: Viking.

Hoffman, Lois. 1987. "The Effects on Children of Maternal and Paternal Employment." pp. 362–395 in *Families and Work*, edited by N. Gerstel and H. E. Gross. Philadelphia: Temple University Press.

Hoffman, Lois, Norma Wladis and Lise M. Youngblade. 1999. *Mothers at Work: Effects on Children's Well-being*. New York: Cambridge University Press.

Li, Allen J. 2007. "The Kids are OK: Divorce and Children's Behavior Problems." Santa Monica, CA: Rand Working Paper WR 489.

Lorber, Judith. 1994. *Paradoxes of Gender*. New Haven: Yale University Press.

McLanahan, Sara and Gary D. Sandefur. 1994. *Growing Up with a Single Parent: What Hurts, What Helps*. Cambridge, MA: Harvard University Press.

Moen, Phyllis and Patricia Roehling. 2005. *The Career Mystique: Cracks in the American Dream*. Lanham, MD: Rowman & Littlefield Publishers.

Moore, Kristin A., Rosemary Chalk, Juliet Scarpa and Sharon Vandiverre. 2002. *Family Strengths: Often Overlooked, But Real*. Washington, DC: Annie E. Casey Foundation.

Parcel, Toby L. and Elizabeth G. Menaghan. 1994. *Parents' Jobs and Children's Lives*. New York: A. de Gruyter.

Pew Research Center. 2007a. "As Marriage and Parenthood Drift Apart, Public Is Concerned about Social Impact." Retrieved June 19, 2008 (http://pewresearch.org/pubs/526/marriage-parenthood).

———. 2007b. "How Young People View Their Lives, Futures and Politics: A Portrait of the "Generation Next"" Retrieved June 19, 2008 (http://people-press.org/reports/pdf/300.pdf).

Popenoe, David. 1996. *Life without Father: Compelling New Evidence that Fatherhood and Marriage Are Indispensable for the Good of Children and Society*. New York: Martin Kessler Books.

———. 1988. *Disturbing the Nest: Family Change and Decline in Modern Societies*. New York: A. de Gruyter.

Popenoe, David, Jean B. Elshtain and David Blankenhorn. 1996. *Promises to Keep: Decline and Renewal of Marriage in America*. Lanham, MD: Rowman & Littlefield Publishers.

Risman, Barbara J. 1998. *Gender Vertigo: American Families in Transition*. New Haven, CT: Yale University Press.

Roberts, Sam. 2007. "Fifty-one percent of Women are Now Living without Spouse." *The New York Times*, January 16.

Skolnick, Arlene and Stacy Rosencrantz. 1994. "The New Crusade for the Old Family." *The American Prospect*, p. 59.

Springer, Kristen W. 2007. "Research or Rhetoric? A Response to Wilcox and Nock." *Sociological Forum* 22(1): 111–116.

Stacey, Judith. 1996. *In the Name of the Family: Rethinking Family Values in the Postmodern Age*. Boston: Beacon Press.

Stone, Pamela. 2007. *Opting Out? Why Women Really Quit Careers and Head Home*. Berkeley: University of California Press.

Waite, Linda J. and Maggie Gallagher. 2000. *The Case for Marriage: Why Married People Are Happier, Healthier, and Better off Financially*. New York: Doubleday.

Whitehead, Barbara D. 1997. *The Divorce Culture*. New York: Alfred A. Knopf: Distributed by Random House.

West, Candace and Don H. Zimmerman. 1987. "Doing Gender." *Gender & Society* 1(2): 125–151.

Williams, Joan. 2007. "The Opt-Out Revolution Revisited." *The American Prospect* (March): A12–A15.

———. 2000. *Unbending Gender: Why Family and Work Conflict and What to Do About It*. New York: Oxford University Press.

Zerubavel, Eviatar. 1991. *The Fine Line: Making Distinctions in Everyday Life*. Chicago: University of Chicago Press.

Sexuality and Society

■ READING 7

Is Hooking Up Bad for Women?

Elizabeth A. Armstrong, Laura Hamilton,
and Paula England

"Girls can't be guys in matters of the heart, even though they think they can," says Laura Sessions Stepp, author of *Unhooked: How Young Women Pursue Sex, Delay Love, and Lose at Both*, published in 2007. In her view, "hooking up"—casual sexual activity ranging from kissing to intercourse—places women at risk of "low self-esteem, depression, alcoholism, and eating disorders." Stepp is only one of half a dozen journalists currently engaged in the business of detailing the dangers of casual sex.

On the other side, pop culture feminists such as Jessica Valenti, author of *The Purity Myth: How America's Obsession with Virginity is Hurting Young Women* (2010), argue that the problem isn't casual sex, but a "moral panic" over casual sex. And still a third set of writers like Ariel Levy, author of *Female Chauvinist Pigs: Women and the Rise of Raunch Culture* (2005), questions whether it's empowering for young women to show up at parties dressed to imitate porn stars or to strip in "Girls Gone Wild" fashion. Levy's concern isn't necessarily moral, but rather that these young women seem less focused on their own sexual pleasure and more worried about being seen as "hot" by men.

Following on the heels of the mass media obsession, sociologists and psychologists have begun to investigate adolescent and young adult hookups more systematically. In this essay, we draw on systematic data and studies of youth sexual practices over time to counter claims that hooking up represents a sudden and alarming change in youth sexual culture.

The research shows that there is some truth to popular claims that hookups are bad for women. However, it also demonstrates that women's hookup experiences are quite varied and far from uniformly negative and that monogamous, long-term relationships are not an ideal alternative. Scholarship suggests that pop culture feminists have correctly zeroed in on sexual double standards as a key source of gender inequality in sexuality.

THE RISE OF LIMITED LIABILITY HEDONISM

Before examining the consequences of hooking up for girls and young women, we need to look more carefully at the facts. *Unhooked* author Stepp describes girls "stripping in the student center in front of dozens of boys they didn't know." She asserts that "young people have virtually abandoned dating" and that "relationships have been replaced by the casual sexual encounters known as hookups." Her sensationalist tone suggests that young people are having more sex at earlier ages in more casual contexts than their Baby Boomer parents.

This characterization is simply not true. Young people today are not having more sex at younger ages than their parents. The sexual practices of American youth changed in the 20th century, but the big change came with the Baby Boom cohort who came of age more than 40 years ago. The National Health and Social Life Survey—the gold standard of American sexual practice surveys—found that those born after 1942 were more sexually active at younger ages than those born from 1933–42. However, the trend toward greater sexual activity among young people appears to halt or reverse among the youngest cohort in the NHSLS, those born from 1963–72. Examining the National Survey of Family Growth, Lawrence B. Finer, Director of Domestic Research for the Guttmacher Institute, found that the percent of women who have had premarital sex by age 20 (65–76 percent) is roughly the same for all cohorts born after 1948. He also found that the women in the youngest cohort in this survey—those born from 1979–1984—were less likely to have premarital sex by age 20 than those born before them. The Centers for Disease Control, reporting on the results of the National Youth Risk Behavior Survey, report that rates of sexual intercourse among 9th–12th graders decreased from 1991–2007, as did numbers of partners. Reports of condom use increased. So what are young people doing to cause such angst among Boomers?

The pervasiveness of *casual* sexual activity among today's youth may be at the heart of Boomers' concerns. England surveyed more than 14,000 students from 19 universities and colleges about their hookup, dating, and relationship experiences. Seventy-two percent of both men and women participating in the survey reported at least one hookup by their senior year in college. What the Boomer panic may gloss over, however, is the fact that college students don't, on average, hook up that much. By senior year, roughly 40 percent of those who ever hooked up had engaged in three or fewer hookups, 40 percent between four and nine hookups, and only 20 percent in ten or more hookups. About 80 percent of students hook up, on average, less than once per semester over the course of college.

In addition, the sexual activity in hookups is often relatively light. Only about one third engaged in intercourse in their most recent hookup. Another third had engaged in oral sex or manual stimulation of the genitals. The other third of hookups only involved kissing and non-genital touching. A full 20 percent of survey respondents in their fourth year of college had never had vaginal intercourse. In addition, hookups between total strangers are relatively uncommon, while hooking up with the same person multiple times is common. Ongoing sexual relationships without commitment are labeled as "repeat," "regular," or "continuing" hookups, and sometimes as "friends with benefits." Often there is friendship or socializing both before and after the hookup.

Hooking up hasn't replaced committed relationships. Students often participate in both at different times during college. By their senior year, 69 percent of heterosexual students had been in a college relationship of at least six months. Hookups sometimes became committed relationships and vice versa; generally the distinction revolved around the agreed upon level of exclusivity and the willingness to refer to each other as "girlfriend/boyfriend."

And, finally, hooking up isn't radically new. As suggested above, the big change in adolescent and young adult sexual behavior occurred with the Baby Boomers. This makes sense, as the forces giving rise to casual sexual activity among the young—the availability of birth control pill, the women's and sexual liberation movements, and the decline of *in loco parentis* on college campuses—took hold in the 1960s. But changes in youth sexual culture did not stop with the major behavioral changes wrought by the Sexual Revolution.

Contemporary hookup culture among adolescents and young adults may rework aspects of the Sexual Revolution to get some of its pleasures while reducing its physical and emotional risks. Young people today—particularly young whites from affluent families—are expected to delay the commitments of adulthood while they invest in careers. They get the message that sex is okay, as long as it doesn't jeopardize their futures; STDs and early pregnancies are to be avoided. This generates a sort of limited liability hedonism. For instance, friendship is prioritized a bit more than romance, and oral sex appeals because of its relative safety. Hookups may be the most explicit example of a calculating approach to sexual exploration. They make it possible to be sexually active while avoiding behaviors with the highest physical and emotional risks (e.g., intercourse, intense relationships). Media panic over hooking up may be at least in part a result of adult confusion about youth sexual culture—that is, not understanding that oral sex and sexual experimentation with friends are actually some young people's ways of balancing fun and risk.

Even though hooking up in college isn't the rampant hedonistic free-for-all portrayed by the media, it does involve the movement of sexual activity outside of relationships. When *Contexts* addressed youth sex in 2002, Barbara Risman and Pepper Schwartz speculated that the slowdown in youth sexual activity in the 1990s might be a result of "girls' increasing control over the conditions of sexual intercourse," marked by the restriction of sex to relationships. They expressed optimism about gender equality in sexuality on the grounds that girls are more empowered in relationship sex than casual sex. It appears now that these scholars were overly optimistic about the progress of the gender revolution in sex. Not only is casual sex common, it seems that romantic relationships themselves are riddled with gender inequality.

HOOKUP PROBLEMS, RELATIONSHIP PLEASURES

Hookups are problematic for girls and young women for several related reasons. As many observers of American youth sexual culture have found, a sexual double standard continues to be pervasive. As one woman Hamilton interviewed explained, "Guys can have sex with all the girls and it makes them more of a man, but if a girl does then all of a sudden she's a 'ho' and she's not as quality of a person." Sexual labeling among adolescents and young adults may only loosely relate to actual sexual behavior; for example, one woman complained in her interview that she was a virgin the first time she was called a "slut." The lack of clear rules about what is "slutty" and what is not contribute to women's fears of stigma.

On college campuses, this sexual double standard often finds its most vociferous expression in the Greek scene. Fraternities are often the only venues where large groups of underage students can readily access alcohol. Consequently, one of the easiest places to find hookup partners is in a male-dominated party context. As a variety of scholars have observed, fraternity men often use their control of the situation to undermine women's ability to freely consent to sex (e.g., by pushing women to drink too heavily, barring their exit from private rooms, or refusing them rides home). Women report varying degrees of sexual disrespect in the fraternity culture, and the dynamics of this scene predictably produce some amount of sexual assault.

The most commonly encountered disadvantage of hookups, though, is that sex in relationships is far better for women. England's survey revealed that women orgasm more often and report higher levels of sexual satisfaction in relationship sex than in hookup sex. This is in part because sex in relationships is more likely to include sexual activities conducive to women's orgasm. In hookups, men are much more likely to receive fellatio than women are to receive cunnilingus. In relationships, oral sex is more likely to be reciprocal. In interviews conducted by England's research team, men report more concern with the sexual pleasure of girlfriends than hookup partners, while women seem equally invested in pleasing hookup partners and boyfriends.

The continuing salience of the sexual double standard mars women's hookup experiences. In contrast, relationships provide a context in which sex is viewed as acceptable for women, protecting them from stigma and establishing sexual reciprocity as a basic expectation. In addition, relationships offer love and companionship.

RELATIONSHIP PROBLEMS, HOOKUP PLEASURES

Relationships are good for sex but, unfortunately, they have a dark side as well. Relationships are "greedy," getting in the way of other things that young women want to be doing as adolescents and young adults, and they are often characterized by gender inequality—sometimes even violence.

Talking to young people, two of us (Hamilton and Armstrong) found that committed relationships detracted from what women saw as main tasks of college. The women we interviewed complained, for example, that relationships made it difficult to meet people. As a woman who had just ended a relationship explained:

> I'm happy that I'm able to go out and meet new people . . . I feel like I'm doing what a college student should be doing. I don't need to be tied down to my high school boyfriend for two years when this is the time to be meeting people.

Women also complained that committed relationships competed with schoolwork. One woman remarked, "[My boyfriend) doesn't understand why I can't pick up and go see him all the time. But I have school . . . I just want to be a college kid." Another told one of us (Hamilton) that her major was not compatible with the demands of a boyfriend. She said, "I wouldn't mind having a boyfriend again, but it's a lot of work. Right now with [my major] and everything . . . I wouldn't have time even to see him." Women feared that they would be devoured by relationships and sometimes struggled to keep their self-development projects going when they did get involved.

Subjects told us that relationships were not only time-consuming, but also marked by power inequalities and abuse. Women reported that boyfriends tried to control their social lives, the time they spent with friends, and even what they wore. One woman described her boyfriend, saying, "He is a very controlling person . . . He's like, 'What are you wearing tonight?' . . . It's like a joke but serious at the same time." Women also became jealous. Coping with jealousy was painful and emotionally absorbing. One woman noted that she would "do anything to make this relationship work." She elaborated, "I was so nervous being with Dan because I knew he had cheated on his [prior] girlfriend . . . [but] I'm getting over it. When I go [to visit him] now . . . I let him go to the bar, whatever. I stayed in his apartment because there was nothing else to do." Other women changed the way they dressed, their friends, and where they went in the hope of keeping boyfriends.

When women attempted to end relationships, they often reported that men's efforts to control them escalated. In the course of interviewing 46 respondents, two of us (Hamilton and Armstrong) heard ten accounts of men using abuse to keep women in relationships. One woman spent months dealing with a boyfriend who accused her of cheating on him. When she tried to break up, he cut his wrist in her apartment. Another woman tried to end a relationship, but was forced to flee the state when her car windows were broken and her safety was threatened. And a third woman reported that her ex-boyfriend stalked her for months—even showing up at her workplace, showering her with flowers and gifts, and blocking her entry into her workplace until the police arrived. For most women, the costs of bad hookups tended to be less than costs of bad relationships. Bad hookups were isolated events, while bad relationships wreaked havoc with whole lives. Abusive relationships led to lost semesters, wrecked friendships, damaged property, aborted pregnancies, depression, and time-consuming involvement with police and courts.

The abuse that women reported to us is not unusual. Intimate partner violence among adolescents and young adults is common. In a survey of 15,000 adolescents conducted in 2007, the Centers for Disease Control found that 10 percent of students had been "hit, slapped, or physically hurt on purpose by their boyfriend or girlfriend" in the last 12 months.

If relationships threaten academic achievement, get in the way of friendship, and can involve jealousy, manipulation, stalking, and abuse, it is no wonder that young women sometimes opt for casual sex. Being open to hooking up means being able to go out and fit into the social scene, get attention from young men, and learn about sexuality. Women we interviewed gushed about parties they attended and attention they received from boys. As one noted, "Everyone was so excited. It was a big fun party." They reported turning on their "make out radar," explaining that "it's fun to know that a guy's attracted to you and is willing to kiss you." Women reported enjoying hookups, and few reported regretting their last hookup. Over half the time women participating in England's survey reported no relational interest before or after their hookup, although more women than men showed interest in a relationship both before and after hookups. The gender gap in relationship interest is slightly larger after the hookup, with 48 percent of women and 36 percent of men reporting interest in a relationship.

TOWARD GENDER EQUALITY IN SEX

Like others, Stepp, the author of *Unhooked*, suggests that restricting sex to relationships is the way to challenge gender inequality in youth sex. Certainly, sex in relationships is better for women than hookup sex. However, research suggests two reasons why Stepp's strategy won't work: first, relationships are also plagued by inequality. Second, valorizing relationships as the ideal context for women's sexual activity reinforces the notion that women shouldn't want sex outside of relationships and stigmatizes women who do. A better approach would challenge gender inequality in both relationships and hookups. It is critical to attack the tenacious sexual double standard that leads men to disrespect their hookup partners. Ironically, this could improve relationships because women would be less likely to tolerate "greedy" or abusive relationships if they were treated better in hookups. Fostering relationships among young adults should go hand-in-hand with efforts to decrease intimate partner violence and to build egalitarian relationships that allow more space for other aspects of life—such as school, work, and friendship.

*Recommended Resources*_____

Paula England, Emily Fitzgibbons Shafer, and Alison C. K. Fogarty. "Hooking Up and Forming Romantic Relationships on Today's College Campuses." In M. Kimmel and A. Aronson (eds.). *The Gendered Society Reader*, 3rd edition (Oxford University Press, 2008). Overview of the role of gender in the college hookup scene.

Laura Hamilton and Elizabeth A. Armstrong. "Double Binds and Flawed Options: Gendered Sexuality in Early Adulthood," *Gender & Sexuality* (2009), 23: 589-616. Provides methodological details of Hamilton and Armstrong's interview study and elaborates on costs and benefits of hookups and relationships for young women.

■ READING 8

Sex and Marriage in the Minds of Emerging Adults

Mark Regnerus and Jeremy Uecker

> It isn't tying himself to one woman that a man dreads when he thinks of marrying; it's separating himself from all the others.
>
> —*Helen Rowland*

SOME OUTSIDE OBSERVERS look at the relationship scene among young adults, consider it entirely about short-term hookups, and presume that the majority of emerging adults are avoiding lasting and meaningful intimate relationships in favor of random sex. While certainly the times have changed and so have our sexual norms, there's no evidence to suggest that emerging adults are disinterested in relationships that last, including marriage. In fact, they want to marry. In our interview study, in the online CSLS, and in lots of other studies, nearly all young women and men tell us they would like to get married someday. We're not talking half or even 80 percent, but more like 93–96 percent. Most just don't want to marry *now* or any time soon. They feel no rush. The slow-but-steady increase in average age at first marriage—to its present-day 26 for women and 28 for men—suggests that the *purpose* of dating or cross-sex romantic relationships is changing or has changed. Most sexual relationships among emerging adults neither begin with marital intentions nor end in marriage or even cohabitation. They just begin and end.

Reasons for their termination are numerous, of course, but one overlooked possibility is that many of them don't know how to get or stay married to the kind of person they'd like to find. For not a few, their parents provided them with a glimpse into married life, and what they saw at the dinner table—if they dined with their parents much at all—didn't look very inviting. They hold the institution of marriage in high regard, and they put considerable pressure—probably too much—on what their own eventual marriage ought to look like. And yet it seems that there is little effort from any institutional source aimed at helping emerging adults consider how their present social, romantic, and sexual experiences shape or war against their vision of marriage—or even how marriage might fit in with their other life goals. In fact, talk of career goals seems increasingly divorced from the relational context in which many emerging adults may eventually find themselves. They speak of the MDs, JDs, and PhDs they intend to acquire with far more confidence than they speak of committed relationships or marriage. The former seem attainable, the latter unclear or unreliable. To complicate matters, many educated emerging adults are skeptical of possible relational constraints on their career goals.

We should admit here that we think the institution of marriage remains a foundational good for individuals and communities, even if all of us have plenty of anecdotal examples of poor and failed marriages. Even the best marriages endure regular challenges. Yet many Americans—and westerners in general—underestimate the *collective benefits* of marriage at their peril. Most would still agree that it's the optimal setting for child-rearing. Married people also tend to accumulate more wealth than people who are single or cohabiting. Marriage consolidates expenses—like food, child care, electricity, and gas—and over the life course drastically reduces the odds of becoming indigent or dependent on the state. And since the vast majority of single emerging adults still hope to marry someday, how they think about marriage in their future seems like a topic worth exploring here.

Since emerging adults esteem the idea of marriage and yet set it apart as inappropriate for their age, waiting until marriage for a fulfilling sex life is considered not just quaint and outdated but quite possibly foolish. It's certainly not a big deal anymore. Sex *outside relationships* might still be disparaged by many, but not sex *before marriage*. And yet creating successful sexual relationships—ones that last a very long time or even into marriage—seems only a modest priority among many in this demographic group. Jeffrey Arnett, the developmental psychologist of emerging adulthood, notes the absence of relationship permanence as a *value* in the minds of emerging adults:

> Finding a love partner in your teens and continuing in a relationship with that person through your early twenties, culminating in marriage, is now viewed as unhealthy, a mistake, a path likely to lead to disaster. Those who do not experiment with different partners are warned that they will eventually wonder what they are missing, to the detriment of their marriage.

Arnett's right. The majority of young adults in America not only think they should explore different relationships, they believe it may be foolish and wrong not to.

Instead, there is value placed upon *flexibility*, *autonomy*, *change*, and the potential for *upgrading*. Allison, an 18-year-old from Illinois, characterizes this value when she describes switching from an older, long-term boyfriend (and sexual partner) to a younger one: "I really liked having a steady boyfriend for a long time, but then it just got to the point when it was like, 'Okay, I need something different.' It wasn't that I liked him any less or loved or cared about him any less, I just needed a change." Many emerging adults—especially men—conduct their relationship with a nagging sense that there may still be someone better out there.

SETTLING DOWN: IS MARRIAGE THE DEATH OR THE BEGINNING OF REAL LIFE?

Despite the emphasis on flexibility and freedom, most emerging adults wish to fall in love, commit, and marry someday. And some already have. (More about them shortly.) The vast majority of those that haven't married believe themselves to be too young to "settle down" yet. They are definitely *not* in a hurry. In a recent nationwide survey of young men, 62 percent of unmarried 25- to 29-year-olds (and 51 percent of 30- to 34-year-olds) said they were "not interested in getting married any time soon." While their reticence could be for good reasons, their widespread use of this phrase is an interesting one, suggesting a tacitly antagonistic perspective about marriage. "Settling down" is something people do when it's time to stop having fun and get serious—when it's time to get married and have children, two ideas that co-occur in the emerging-adult mind. In the same national survey of men we just noted, 81 percent of unmarried men aged 25–29 agreed that "at this stage in your life, you want to have fun and freedom." (Even 74 percent of single 30- to 34-year-olds still agreed.) That figure would have been even higher had they interviewed men in their early 20s.

Trevor, a 19-year-old virgin from North Carolina, agrees wholeheartedly with this sentiment. He would like to marry someday. When asked if there were certain things people should accomplish before they're ready to marry, he lists the standard economic criteria. But he also conveys a clear understanding that his best days would be behind him: "I'd say before you're married, make sure you have a place to live. Don't have a child before marriage. . . . Have a decent paying job, because, I mean, it's only going to get worse."

Sex Is for Singles

A distinctive fissure exists in the minds of young Americans between the carefree single life and the married life of economic pressures and family responsibilities. The one is sexy, the other is sexless. In the minds of many, sex is for the young and single, while marriage is for the old. Marriage is quaint, adorable.

A key developmental task, then, for Juan, a 19-year-old from southern California, is to consume his fill of sex before being content with a fixed diet. His advice would be to "get a lot of stuff out of your system, like messing around with girls and stuff, or partying. . . . Once you get married, you won't be able to do all that stuff." When and whether the task of "getting it out of your system" can be successfully accomplished is anyone's guess. (A look at the continuing sexual dalliances of politicians suggests it may not be so easy.)

Likewise, Megan (22, from Texas) doesn't conceive of parenthood as a sexual life stage, the irony of it aside. She captures what very many young men and women believe to be a liability of marriage: the end of good sex. The last omnibus sex study of Americans—issued in 1994—disputes Megan's conclusion, as do our interviews with married emerging adults. But the power of surveys and statistics are nothing compared to the strength of a compelling story in the minds of so many people. We asked Megan whether married life would be less sexual than her single life:

> Probably. [*Because?*] Just, as you age, your sex drive goes down. [*Okay.*] I mean not because you want to be less sexual, that could be the case, but I won't know till I'm older. [*Um, so some people say when you get married, you settle down, like it's literally a settling down. Do you look at marriage and married sex as being like, "That's off in the future; it might be a disappointment. Now I'm having a better time"?*] Yeah. [*Do you?*] Yes. [*Why?*] Why do I think it might be a disappointment? [*Sure.*] Um, just because of the horror stories of getting married. Nobody wants to have sex anymore. [*Where do you hear these stories?*] Movies, other people. . . . [*Like what? Can you think of one?*] Um, there's plenty. Like the movie that just came out—*License to Wed*—there's this one scene where the guy is sitting on top of a roof with his best friend talking about how his wife doesn't want to have sex anymore.

Although Megan enjoys sex for its own sake and predicts a declining sex life in her future marriage, it's not the death of sex that frightens her about marriage: "It's living with a guy that freaks me out." Author Laura Sessions Stepp claims that today's young adults are so self-centered that they don't have time for "we," only for "me." They begrudge the energy that real relationships require. If that's true—and we suspect that's a journalistic overgeneralization—Megan should get together with Patrick. While he's so far slept with six women, Patrick informed us that he cannot imagine being married, and yet he too plans to do exactly that someday:

> Well, I don't want to get married now. I guess, like, I do want to find a girl but I just can't see myself being married. . . . [*And you can't see yourself getting married or being married because?*] Um, I guess I just don't like the idea of being real tied down.

His current girlfriend is someone to hang out with, have sex with, and generally enjoy her company. Imagining more than that frightens him: "You sacrifice like so much stuff to be in a relationship that, um, that I guess I'm just not ready to make that huge sacrifice yet." Nor is Gabriela (23, Texas):

> Once you get married, your responsibilities change. It's no longer, "Oh, I want to go to China next year. I have to save up money." No. Now you have to pay for the house. . . . or you have a job and you have, you can't just leave, because your husband can't get that day off. And things like that. It doesn't just become you, it becomes you and another person." [*So what do you think of that?*] I think that it's fine when I'm older. [*Which will be when?*] At least 30.

For many emerging adults, the idea of marriage is a sexual letdown—something to do only after they've sampled the cornucopia of flesh that's out there. After that, sexual vitality and freedom must be traded for the different pleasures and pressures of family life. It'll be worth it, they believe. Eventually. Amber, a 22-year-old from Arkansas, notes that someday, along with a marriage, she would like to have children, because they're "what makes your life like, full, after like, you are done with your life, I guess." Marriage and children would then become her life.

Devon, a 19-year-old from Washington, does most of his peers one better. Getting married—which he too eventually plans to do—is not just about "settling down" from the vibrant sex life of his late teen years. It signifies a death, albeit a scripted and necessary one. When asked what he wanted out of marriage, he said, "Just to have a good ending to my life, basically." Chen, a 20-year-old from Illinois, agrees: "I don't really plan on getting married for a while, or settling down for a while. I'd like to do all my living when I'm young. Like, save all the rest of life—falling in love, and having a family—for later." He does wish to marry, though, because he doesn't expect his current self-focused life to satisfy him forever:

> I don't want to die alone. That's the number one thing. It's like, especially after I'm done living my life, that would be like the worst thing for me. I'd like to have a kid eventually, but there's always time for that later on. I'll settle with a kid when I'm 40, 45. . . . The time to live a selfish life is while you're young, and the time to live a giving life is when you're older, when you have kids. I'd rather live for myself while I have the time to.

Such perspectives fly in the face of lots of empirical evidence about the satisfactions of marriage. That is, marriage tends to be good for emotional intimacy as well as sexual intimacy. Married people have access to more regular, long-term sex than do serially monogamous single adults. But that doesn't *feel* true to many emerging adults. Many perceive their parents as having modest or poor sex lives, and movie sex largely features singles. Indeed, relational instability and immaturity are perceived by some as *sexual values*. That is, sex is thought to be better when a relationship is new or tenuous, when it might not exist in the future. It's an erotic thought to some, including Tara (20, Louisiana), whose relationship with David was currently on the rocks. When asked if they were still sleeping together, even as she made plans to move out of the apartment they shared, she not only replied affirmatively but also noted a heightened quality to their sex: "It's actually been better, too. [*Why?*] I don't know. Just more like, passionate, I guess you could say. [*Why?*] I feel like it's mainly because of me . . . I am more into it than I was."

Not every emerging adult pictures marriage as a necessary but noble death, of course. Elizabeth (20, New York) likewise saw her 20s as about having fun. But her 30s (and marriage) would not be simply about settling down; they would be the time "when your life is really gonna kick into gear." We suspect that contemporary male and female perspectives on marriage, sexuality, and fertility are indeed different, on average—that many men anticipate the institution as necessary and good for them, but with less enthusiasm for it than women express. For emerging-adult men, the single life is great, and married life could be good. For women, the single life is good but married life is potentially better. Ironically, after years of marriage, men tend to express slightly higher marital satisfaction (on average) than women. Moreover, marriage seems to be particularly important in civilizing men, turning their attention away from dangerous, antisocial, or self-centered activities and toward the needs of a family. Married men drink less, fight less, and are less likely to engage in criminal activity than are their single peers. Married husbands and fathers are significantly more involved and affectionate with their wives and children than are men in cohabiting relationships (with and without children). The norms, status rewards, and social support offered to men by marriage all combine to help men walk down the path of adult responsibility.

No wonder the idea of marriage can feel like a death to them. It is—the demise of unchecked self-centeredness and risk-taking. Plenty elect to delay it as long as seems feasible to them, marrying on average around age 28. That's hardly an old age, of course, but remember that age 28 is their median (or statistical middle) age at first marriage, meaning that half of all men marry then or later. Their decision to delay makes sense from a sexual economics perspective: they can access sex relatively easily outside of marriage, they can obtain many of the perceived benefits of marriage by cohabiting rather than marrying, they encounter few social pressures from peers to marry, they don't wish to marry someone who already has a child, and they want to experience the joys and freedoms of singleness as long as they can.

WHO MARRIES EARLY AND WHY

A good deal more is known about why people are *not* marrying in early adulthood than why some still do. And yet a minority marry young—and even more wish they were married—despite the fact that cohabitation and premarital sex are increasingly normative and socially acceptable. While the majority of emerging adults have no wish to be married at present, more than we expected actually harbor this desire. Just under 20 percent of unmarried young men and just under 30 percent of such women said they would like to be married at present. Understandably, religious emerging adults are more apt to want to be married. And those emerging adults who are in a romantic or sexual relationship are nearly twice as likely to want to be married right now than those who aren't in a relationship. Cohabiters are more than *four times as likely* as those who are single to want to be married. In fact, just under half of cohabiting young women and 40 percent of cohabiting young men said they'd like to be married right now.

Those who marry younger face a variety of hurdles, no doubt, including potential impediments to their educational attainment, a more economically modest beginning, and possibly becoming parents ahead of their peers. Among all the 18- to 23-year-olds in the Add Health study's third wave—the group about whom we've been talking in this book—19 percent of women and 11 percent of men report having ever been married. This is a snapshot of emerging adulthood taken at one point in time. However, since plenty of 18- to 19-year-olds will get married before the end of their 23rd year, we have to reach beyond this age group to get a better, retrospective portrait of just how many emerging adults actually marry before they turn 24, and what they're like. According to Table 8.1, 31 percent of women and 23 percent of men reported being married before they turned 24. We'll call this marrying "early," since the median age for men and women is 28 and 26, respectively.

Marriage in early adulthood is clearly patterned by race: only 15 percent of African American women marry before age 24. White and Hispanic women have the highest rates of early marriage at 36 and 30 percent, respectively (although Hispanic women are not significantly more likely to marry by this point than are Asian women). Among men, African Americans are likewise the least likely to marry young, at 15 percent, compared with 22 percent of Asian men and 24 percent of white men. Hispanic men are the most likely to marry early; nearly three in ten of them are married before the end of their 23rd year.

Given the historical proximity of the institutions of religion and family, it's no surprise that religion continues to distinguish earlier marriages from later ones. In the Add Health as well as other studies, the results are similar: on the later end of the age spectrum are Catholics, Jews, and the religiously unaffiliated. Mainline Protestants appear in the middle, and evangelical Protestants and Mormons are the most likely to marry young.

Parental socioeconomic status (SES) is a major factor in younger marriages. Only about 13 percent of young women with two college-educated parents, and just about 11 percent of such young men, marry before turning 24, compared with 36 percent and 26 percent of young women and men (respectively) with no college-educated parent at all. Indeed, educated parents may be quicker to socialize their daughters to wait for marriage than they are their sons. Young women who come from a household where neither parent earned a college degree are 167 percent more likely to marry early than are women from households where at least one parent has a college degree. Among men, the difference is 131 percent, suggesting that, whether intentional or not, parents' class-based wait-to-marry messages may resonate more with women than men.

Emerging adults whose families seem best poised to financially assist them are the very ones most disinterested in marrying relatively young. In one sense, it's ironic: those

TABLE 8.1 *Percent of Young Adults Married before Age 24, Split by Gender, 24- to 28-Year-Olds*

	Women	Men
Overall	30.8	23.1
Race/Ethnicity		
White	35.7	24.4
Black	14.8	15.1
Hispanic	30.3	29.9
Asian	29.4	21.7
Region		
Lives in the South	38.4	29.7
Lives outside the South	26.2	18.5
Urbanicity		
Lives in urban area	28.6	21.9
Lives in suburban area	27.9	21.2
Lives in rural area	45.1	31.3
Parents' Educational Attainment		
Resident parent(s) have college degree	13.4	11.3
One parent has college degree	23.1	16.6
No parent has college degree	35.8	26.1
Structure of Family of Origin		
Biological parents married	29.9	25.3
Single-parent family	28.4	16.4
Stepfamily	32.8	26.4
Other family structure	36.0	22.1
Religious Affiliation		
Conservative Protestant	48.8	36.2
Black Protestant	16.2	14.3
Mainline Protestant	38.5	22.6
Catholic	20.5	19.4
Mormon	53.7	30.7
Other religion	40.9	31.9
No religion	27.8	18.5
Educational Attainment		
Earned high-school diploma	31.5	23.9
Did not earn high-school diploma	26.9	19.2
Family Income (from family of origin)		
Family income below $30,000	33.4	24.1
Family income $30,000 or higher	29.9	22.8

(continued)

TABLE 8.1 *Continued*

	Women	Men
Parent's Age at Marriage		
Parent married at age 18 or younger	42.7	31.5
Parent married at age 19 or 20	34.0	25.7
Parent married at age 21 or 22	27.6	15.4
Parent married at age 23 or older, or never married	19.2	15.3

Source: Add Health

Note: There were too few Jewish young adults to establish a stable estimate.

who could, don't. (It's an extension of the demographic-economic paradox we noted in Chapter 2.) On the other hand, their choices make perfect sense and bear witness to the power of social learning or mimicking: because one's parents have succeeded economically, they're more apt to nudge their children toward the best possible routes for their own economic success. And marrying in the early 20s is seldom part of that formula. Maximizing education and focusing on individual skill-building, however, is.

Another example of mimicking is the connection between parents who married young and children who do the same. Given the increasing age at first marriage, this connection is becoming more tenuous over time. Most emerging adults getting married today are doing so later than their parents did. Indeed, about two out of three Add Health respondents who married before age 24 still married later than their parents did. But a strong link remains, and it's nearly linear in effect: the younger a respondent's parents were when *they* married, the more likely the respondent was to be married themselves.

Other predictable characteristics of marrying young also emerge. More than 38 percent of all women who live in the South marry before turning 24, as do about 45 percent of those from rural areas. Considerably fewer rural men marry by then—31 percent—but still far more than their urban or suburban counterparts. Sonja, a 23-year-old from Missouri, married when she was 19. Why so young?

> It was one of those things where we would [either] get married or live together without being married, and neither wanted to do that. Out of high school, I went to college for a year, and he went off to basic training. And he was coming here, so we just got married.

Since Sonja's answer isn't very illuminating, we let the variables do the talking. She fit a variety of types that marry when younger: she's Hispanic, from a military family, and lives in a small town. Her parents were supportive, not oppositional. Sonja does, however, fracture at least one stereotype about early marriage—that it's poisonous to higher education. She completed her bachelor's degree in nursing both after marrying and in a timely manner.

None of this is terribly surprising. For all the rebelling that emerging adults think they're doing against their parents, parents are having the last laugh. They appear to be very successful at transmitting their ideas about marriage and appropriate marital timing—whatever those ideas are—to their children.

EARLY MARRIAGE: GUARANTEED DIVORCE?

As obvious as it might sound, getting married introduces the risk of getting divorced. And that very specter remains a key mental barrier to relationship commitment among emerging adults. Six in ten unmarried men in their late 20s—who are already beginning to lag behind the median age at marriage—report that one of their biggest concerns about marriage is that it will end in divorce. Thus getting married young is increasingly frowned upon not just as unwise but as a *moral mistake* in which the odds of failure are perceived as too high to justify the risk. This conventional wisdom is at work in journalist Paula Kamen's interview with a 24-year-old woman who claims she knows her boyfriend far better than her parents knew each other when they married. But would she marry him? No: "Like, are you stupid? Have you read the statistics lately?"

Emerging adults claim to be very stats-savvy about marriage. They are convinced that half of all marriages end in divorce, suggesting that the odds of anyone staying married amounts to a random flip of a coin. In reality, of course, divorce is hardly a random event. Some couples are more likely to divorce than others: people who didn't finish high school, people with little wealth or income, those who aren't religious, African Americans, couples who had children before they married, those who live in the South, those who cohabited before marrying, and those who live in neighborhoods that exhibit elevated crime and poverty rates. Lots of emerging adults have a few of these risk factors for divorce, but most don't exhibit numerous factors. And yet the compelling idea in the minds of many is that any given marriage's chance of success—however defined—is only 50/50, and worse if you marry early. In fact, most Americans who cite the statistics argument against considering marriage in early adulthood tend to misunderstand what exactly "early marriage" is. Most sociological evaluations of early marriage note that the link between age-at-marriage and divorce is strongest among those who marry *as teenagers* (in other words, before age 20). Marriages that begin at age 20, 21, or 22 are not nearly so likely to end in divorce as most Americans presume. Data from the 2002 National Study of Family Growth suggest that the probability of a marriage lasting at least 10 years—hardly a long-term success, we realize, but a good benchmark of endurance—hinges not only on age-at-marriage but also gender.

- Men and women who marry at or before age 20 are by far the worst bets for long-term success.
- The likelihood of a marriage (either a man's or a woman's) lasting 10 years stably exceeds 60 percent beginning at age 21.
- Starting around age 23 (until at least 29), the likelihood of a woman's marriage lasting 10 years improves by about three percent with each added year of waiting.
- However, no such linear "improvement" pattern appears among men.

To reiterate, then, the most *significant* leap in avoiding divorce occurs by simply waiting to marry until you're 21. The difference in success between, say, marrying at 23 and marrying at 28 are just not as substantial as many emerging adults believe them to be. And among men, there are really no notable differences to speak of. While sociologist Tim Heaton finds that teenage marriage—and perhaps marriage among 20- and

21-year-olds—carries a higher risk of marital disruption, he too notes that "increasing the age at marriage from 22 to 30 would not have much effect on marital stability."

Still, to most of us, marital success is more than just managing to avoid a divorce. It's about having a *good* marriage. Sociologist Norval Glenn's study of marital success, where "failure" is defined as either divorce or being in an unhappy marriage, reveals a curvilinear relationship between age at marriage and marital success. Women who marry before 20 or after 27 report lower marital success, while those marrying at ages 20–27 report higher levels of marital success. The pattern is a bit different for men. Men who marry before age 20 appear to have only a small chance at a successful marriage, while those who marry between ages 20 and 22 or after age 27 face less daunting—but still acute—challenges for a successful marriage. The best odds for men are in the middle, at ages 23–27. In a meta-analysis of *five different surveys* that explored marriage outcomes, researchers note that respondents who marry between ages 22 and 25 express greater marital satisfaction than do those who marry later than that. In other words, the conventional wisdom about the obvious benefits (to marital happiness) of delayed marriage overreaches. Why it is that people who wait into their late 20s and 30s may experience *less* marital success rather than more is not entirely clear—and the finding itself is subject to debate. But it may be a byproduct of their greater rates of cohabitation. While relationship quality typically declines a bit over the course of marriage, the same process is believed to occur during cohabitation. If so, for many couples who marry at older ages, the "honeymoon" period of their relationship may have ended *before* they married, not after.*

All these findings, however, are largely lost on emerging adults because of the compelling power of the popular notion in America that marriages carry a 50 percent risk of divorce. End of story. Indeed, what matters most is what people *think* reality is like, not how reality really is. Human beings think and act based on what they *believe* to be true, often with little regard to alternative possibilities that may stick closer to empirical accuracies. They have faith in the conventional wisdom about marriage—and especially about early marriage. Consequently, marriage is considered off-limits to many emerging adults, especially those in the middle of college or building a career. Thus while research suggests that adults who are married and in monogamous relationships report more global happiness, more physical satisfaction with sex, and more emotional satisfaction with sex, emerging adults don't believe it. Such claims just don't *feel* true. And why should they? When's the last time you watched a romantic film about a happily married 40-year-old couple?

---

*Later research suggests that marrying after age 27 does not necessarily lead to a drop in satisfaction. (Eds.)

Courtship and Marriage

■ READING 9

American Marriage in the Early Twenty-First Century

Andrew J. Cherlin

The decline of American marriage has been a favorite theme of social commentators, politicians, and academics over the past few decades. Clearly the nation has seen vast changes in its family system—in marriage and divorce rates, cohabitation, childbearing, sexual behavior, and women's work outside the home. Marriage is less dominant as a social institution in the United States than at any time in history. Alternative pathways through adulthood—childbearing outside of marriage, living with a partner without ever marrying, living apart but having intimate relationships—are more acceptable and feasible than ever before. But as the new century begins, it is also clear that despite the jeremiads, marriage has not faded away. In fact, given the many alternatives to marriage now available, what may be more remarkable is not the decline in marriage but its persistence. What is surprising is not that fewer people marry, but rather that so *many* still marry and that the desire to marry remains widespread. Although marriage has been transformed, it is still meaningful. In this [reading] I review the changes in American marriage, discuss their causes, compare marriage in the United States with marriage in the rest of the developed world, and comment on how the transformation of marriage is likely to affect American children in the early twenty-first century.

CHANGES IN THE LIFE COURSE

To illuminate what has happened to American marriage, I begin by reviewing the great demographic changes of the past century, including changes in age at marriage, the share of Americans ever marrying, cohabitation, non-marital births, and divorce.

Recent Trends

Figure 9.1 shows the median age at marriage—the age by which half of all marriages occur—for men and women from 1890 to 2002. In 1890 the median age was relatively high, about twenty-six for men and twenty-two for women. During the first half of the twentieth century the typical age at marriage dropped—gradually at first, and then precipitously after World War II. By the 1950s it had reached historic lows: roughly twenty-three for men and twenty for women. Many people still think of the 1950s as the standard by which to compare today's families, but as Figure 9.1 shows, the 1950s were the anomaly: during that decade young adults married earlier than ever before or since. Moreover, nearly all young adults—about 95 percent of whites and 88 percent of African Americans—eventually married.[1] During the 1960s, however, the median age at marriage began to climb, returning to and then exceeding that prevalent at the start of the twentieth century. Women, in particular, are marrying substantially later today than they have at any time for which data are available.

What is more, unmarried young adults are leading very different lives today than their earlier counterparts once did. The late-marrying young women and men of the early 1900s typically lived at home before marriage or paid for room and board in someone else's home. Even when they were courting, they lived apart from their romantic interests and, at least among women, the majority abstained from sexual intercourse until they were engaged or married. They were usually employed, and they often turned over much of their paycheck to their parents to help rear younger siblings. Few went to college; most had not even graduated from high school. As recently as 1940, only about one-third of adults in their late twenties had graduated from high school and just one in sixteen had graduated from college.[2]

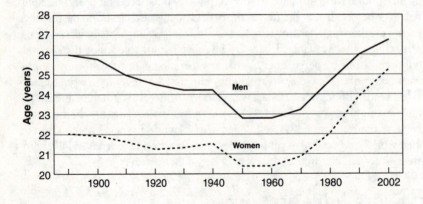

FIGURE 9.1 *Median Age at Marriage, 1890–2002*

Source: U.S. Bureau of the Census, "Estimated Median Age at First Marriage, by Sex: 1890 to Present," 2003, www.census.gov/population/socdemo/hh-fam/tabMS-2.pdf (accessed July 23, 2004).

Today's unmarried young adults are much more likely to be living independently, in their own apartments. Five out of six young adults graduate from high school, and about one-third complete college.[3] They are more likely than their predecessors to spend their wages on themselves. Their sexual and intimate lives are also very different from those of earlier generations. The vast majority of unmarried young adults have had sexual intercourse. In fact, most women who married during the 1990s first had intercourse five years or more before marrying.[4]

About half of young adults live with a partner before marrying. Cohabitation is far more common today than it was at any time in the early- or mid-twentieth century (although it was not unknown among the poor and has been a part of the European family system in past centuries). Cohabitation today is a diverse, evolving phenomenon. For some people, it is a prelude to marriage or a trial marriage. For others, a series of cohabiting relationships may be a long-term substitute for marriage. (Thirty-nine percent of cohabiters in 1995 lived with children of one of the partners.) It is still rare in the United States for cohabiting relationships to last long—about half end, through marriage or a breakup, within a year.[5]

Despite the drop in marriage and the rise in cohabitation, there has been no explosion of nonmarital births in the United States. Birth rates have fallen for unmarried women of all reproductive ages and types of marital status, including adolescents. But because birth rates have fallen faster for married women than for unmarried women, a larger share of women who give birth are unmarried. In 1950, only 4 percent of all births took place outside of marriage. By 1970, the figure was 11 percent; by 1990, 28 percent; and by 2003, 35 percent. In recent years, then, about one-third of all births have been to unmarried women—and that is the statistic that has generated the most debate.[6] Of further concern to many observers is that about half of all unmarried first-time mothers are adolescents. Academics, policymakers, and private citizens alike express unease about the negative consequences of adolescent childbearing, both for the parents and for the children, although whether those consequences are due more to poverty or to teen childbearing per se remains controversial.

When people think of nonmarital or "out-of-wedlock" childbearing, they picture a single parent. Increasingly, however, nonmarital births are occurring to cohabiting couples—about 40 percent according to the latest estimate.[7] One study of unmarried women giving birth in urban hospitals found that about half were living with the fathers of their children. Couples in these "fragile families," however, rarely marry. One year after the birth of the child, only 15 percent had married, while 26 percent had broken up.[8]

Marriage was not an option for lesbians and gay men in any U.S. jurisdiction until Massachusetts legalized same-sex marriage in 2004. Cohabitation, however, is common in this group. In a 1992 national survey of sexual behavior, 44 percent of women and 28 percent of men who said they had engaged in homosexual sex in the previous year reported that they were cohabiting.[9] The Census Bureau, which began collecting statistics on same-sex partnerships in 1990, does not directly ask whether a person is in a romantic same-sex relationship; rather, it gives people the option of saying that a housemate is an "unmarried partner" without specifying the nature of the partnership. Because some people may not wish to openly report a same-sex relationship to the Census Bureau, it is hard to determine how reliable these figures are. The bureau reports, however, that in 2000, 600,000 households were maintained by same-sex partners. A substantial share—33 percent of female partnerships and 22 percent of male partnerships—reported the presence of children of one or both of the partners.[10]

As rates of entry into marriage were declining in the last half of the twentieth century, rates of exit via divorce were increasing—as they have been at least since the Civil War era. At the beginning of the twentieth century, about 10 percent of all marriages ended in divorce, and the figure rose to about one-third for marriages begun in 1950.[11] But the rise was particularly sharp during the 1960s and 1970s, when the likelihood that a married couple would divorce increased substantially. Since the 1980s the divorce rate has remained the same or declined slightly. According to the best estimate, 48 percent of American marriages, at current rates, would be expected to end in divorce within twenty years.[12] A few percent more would undoubtedly end in divorce after that. So it is accurate to say that unless divorce risks change, about half of all marriages today would end in divorce. (There are important class and racial-ethnic differences, which I will discuss below.)

The combination of more divorce and a greater share of births to unmarried women has increased the proportion of children who are not living with two parents. Figure 9.2 tracks the share of children living, respectively, with two parents, with one parent, and with neither parent between 1968 and 2002. It shows a steady decline in the two-parent share and a corresponding increase in the one-parent share. In 2002, 69 percent of children were living with two parents, including families where one biological (or adoptive) parent had remarried. Not counting step- or adoptive families, 62 percent, according to the most recent estimate in 1996, were living with two biological parents.[13] Twenty-seven percent of American children were living with one parent; another 4 percent, with neither parent.[14] Most in the latter group were living with relatives, such as grandparents.

Where do all these changes leave U.S. marriage patterns and children's living arrangements in the early twenty-first century? As demographers have noted, many of the above trends have slowed over the past decade, suggesting a "quieting" of family

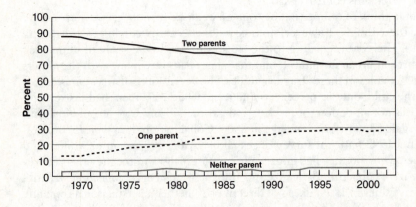

FIGURE 9.2   *Living Arrangements of U.S. Children, 1968–2002*

Source: U.S. Bureau of the Census, "Living Arrangements of U.S. Children under 18 Years Old: 1960 to Present," 2003, www.census.gov/population/socdemo/hh-fam/tabCH-1.pdf (accessed July 23, 2004).

change.[15] Marriage remains the most common living arrangement for raising children. At any one time, most American children are being raised by two parents. Marriage, however, is less dominant in parents' and children's lives than it once was. Children are more likely to experience life in a single-parent family, either because they are born to unmarried mothers or because their parents divorce. And children are more likely to experience instability in their living arrangements as parents form and dissolve marriages and partnerships. Although children are less likely to lose a parent through death today than they once were, the rise in nonmarital births and in divorce has more than compensated for the decline in parental death.[16] From the adult perspective, the overall drop in birth rates and the increases in nonmarital childbearing and divorce mean that, at any one time, fewer adults are raising children than in the past.

Class and Racial-Ethnic Divergence

To complete this portrait of American marriage one must take note of class and racial-ethnic variations, for the overall statistics mask contrasting trends in the lives of children from different racial-ethnic groups and different social classes. In fact, over the past few decades, the family lives of children have been diverging across class and racial-ethnic lines.[17] A half-century ago, the family structures of poor and non-poor children were similar: most children lived in two-parent families. In the intervening years, the increase in single-parent families has been greater among the poor and near-poor.[18] Women at all levels of education have been postponing marriage, but less-educated women have postponed childbearing less than better-educated women have. The divorce rate in recent decades appears to have held steady or risen for women without a college education but fallen for college-educated women.[19] As a result, differences in family structure according to social class are much more pronounced than they were fifty years ago.

Consider the share of mothers who are unmarried. Throughout the past half-century, single motherhood has been more common among women with less education than among well-educated women. But the gap has grown over time. In 1960, 14 percent of mothers in the bottom quarter of the educational distribution were unmarried, as against 4.5 percent of mothers in the top quarter—a difference of 9.5 percentage points. By 2000, the corresponding figures were 43 percent for the less-educated mothers and 7 percent for the more educated—a gap of 36 percentage points.[20] Sara McLanahan argues that societal changes such as greater opportunities for women in the labor market, a resurgence of feminist ideology, and the advent of effective birth control have encouraged women to invest in education and careers. Those who make these investments tend to delay childbearing and marriage, and they are more attractive in the marriage market.[21] Put another way, women at the top and bottom of the educational distribution may be evolving different reproductive strategies. Among the less educated, early childbearing outside of marriage has become more common, as the ideal of finding a stable marriage and then having children has weakened, whereas among the better educated, the strategy is to delay childbearing and marriage until after investing in schooling and careers.

One result of these developments has been growth in better-educated, dual-earner married-couple families. Since the 1970s these families have enjoyed much greater income growth than have breadwinner-homemaker families or single-parent families.

What we see today, then, is a growing group of more fortunate children who tend to live with two parents whose incomes are adequate or ample and a growing group of less fortunate children who live with financially pressed single parents. Indeed, both groups at the extremes—the most and the least fortunate children—have been expanding over the past few decades, while the group of children in the middle has been shrinking.[22]

The family lives of African American children have also been diverging from those of white non-Hispanic children and, to a lesser extent, Hispanic children. African American family patterns were influenced by the institution of slavery, in which marriage was not legal, and perhaps by African cultural traditions, in which extended families had more influence and power compared with married couples. As a result, the proportion of African American children living with single parents has been greater than that of white children for a century or more.[23] Nevertheless, African American women married at an earlier age than did white women through the first half of the twentieth century.[24]

But since the 1960s, the decline of marriage as a social institution has been more pronounced among African Americans than among whites. The best recent estimates suggest that at current rates only about two-thirds of African American women would be expected ever to marry.[25] Correspondingly, the share of African American children born outside of marriage has risen to 69 percent.[26] In fact, about three-fifths of African American children may never live in a married-couple family while growing up, as against one-fifth of white children.[27] The greater role of extended kin in African American families may compensate for some of this difference, but the figures do suggest a strikingly reduced role of marriage among African Americans.

The family patterns of the Hispanic population are quite diverse. Mexican Americans have higher birth rates than all other major ethnic groups, and a greater share of Mexican American births than of African American births is to married women.[28] Moreover, Mexican American families are more likely to include extended kin.[29] Consequently, Mexican Americans have more marriage-based, multigenerational households than do African Americans. Puerto Ricans, the second largest Hispanic ethnic group and the most economically disadvantaged, have rates of nonmarital childbearing second only to African Americans.[30] But Puerto Ricans, like many Latin Americans, have a tradition of consensual unions, in which a man and woman live together as married but without approval of the church or a license from the state. So it is likely that more Puerto Rican "single" mothers than African American single mothers are living with partners.

EXPLAINING THE TRENDS

Most analysts would agree that both economic and cultural forces have been driving the changes in American family life over the past half-century. Analysts disagree about the relative weight of the two, but I will assume that both have been important.

Economic Influences

Two changes in the U.S. labor market have had major implications for families.[31] First, demand for workers increased in the service sector, where women had gained a foothold earlier in the century while they were shut out of manufacturing jobs. The rising demand encouraged women to get more education and drew married women into the workforce—initially, those whose children were school-aged, and later, those with younger children. Single mothers had long worked, but in 1996 major welfare reform legislation further encouraged work by setting limits on how long a parent could receive public assistance. The increase in women's paid work, in turn, increased demand for child care services and greatly increased the number of children cared for outside their homes.

The second work-related development was the decline, starting in the 1970s, in job opportunities for men without a college education. The flip side of the growth of the service sector was the decline in manufacturing. As factory jobs moved overseas and industrial productivity increased through automated equipment and computer-based controls, demand fell for blue-collar jobs that high school–educated men once took in hopes of supporting their families. As a result, average wages in these jobs fell. Even during the prosperous 1990s, the wages of men without a college degree hardly rose.[32] The decline in job opportunities had two effects. It decreased the attractiveness of non-college-educated men on the marriage market—made them less "marriageable" in William Julius Wilson's terms—and thus helped drive marriage rates down among the less well educated.[33] It also undermined the single-earner "family wage system" that had been the ideal in the first half of the twentieth century and increased the incentive for wives to take paying jobs.

Cultural Developments

But economic forces, important as they were, could not have caused all the changes in family life noted above. Declines in the availability of marriageable men, for example, were not large enough to account, alone, for falling marriage rates among African Americans.[34] Accompanying the economic changes was a broad cultural shift among Americans that eroded the norms both of marriage before childbearing and of stable, lifelong bonds after marriage.

Culturally, American marriage went through two broad transitions during the twentieth century. The first was described famously by sociologist Ernest Burgess as a change "from institution to companionship."[35] In institutional marriage, the family was held together by the forces of law, tradition, and religious belief. The husband was the unquestioned head of the household. Until the late nineteenth century, husband and wife became one legal person when they married—and that person was the husband. A wife could not sue in her own name, and her husband could dispose of her property as he wished. Until 1920 women could not vote; rather, it was assumed that almost all women would marry and that their husbands' votes would represent their views. But as the forces of law and tradition weakened in the early decades of the twentieth century, the newer, companionate marriage arose. It was founded on the importance of the emotional ties between wife and husband—their companionship, friendship, and romantic love. Spouses drew satisfaction from performing the social roles of breadwinner, homemaker, and parent. After World War II, the spouses in companionate marriages, much to everyone's surprise, produced the baby boom: they had more children per family than any other generation in the twentieth century. The typical age at marriage fell to its lowest point since at least the late nineteenth century, and the share of all people who ever married rose. The decade of the 1950s was the high point of the breadwinner-homemaker, two-, three-, or even four-child family.

Starting around 1960, marriage went through a second transition. The typical age at marriage returned to, and then exceeded, the high levels of the early 1900s. Many young adults stayed single into their mid- to late twenties or even their thirties, some completing college educations and starting careers. Most women continued working for pay after they married. Cohabitation outside marriage became much more acceptable. Childbearing outside marriage became less stigmatized. The birth rate resumed its long decline and sank to an all-time low. Divorce rates rose to unprecedented levels. Same-sex partnerships found greater acceptance as well.

During this transition, companionate marriage waned as a cultural ideal. On the rise were forms of family life that Burgess had not foreseen, particularly marriages in which both husband and wife worked outside the home and single-parent families that came into being through divorce or through childbearing outside marriage. The roles of wives and husbands became more flexible and open to negotiation. And a more individu-alistic perspective on the rewards of marriage took root. When people evaluated how satisfied they were with their marriages, they began to think more in terms of developing their own sense of self and less in terms of gaining satisfaction through building a family and playing the roles of spouse and parent. The result was a transition from the compan-ionate marriage to what we might call the individualized marriage.[36]

THE CURRENT CONTEXT OF MARRIAGE

To be sure, the "companionate marriage" and the "individualized marriage" are what sociologists refer to as ideal types. In reality, the distinctions between the two are less sharp than I have drawn them. Many marriages, for example, still follow the compan-ionate ideal. Nevertheless, as a result of the economic and cultural trends noted above, marriage now exists in a very different context than it did in the past. Today it is but one among many options available to adults choosing how to shape their personal lives. More forms of marriage and more alternatives to it are socially acceptable. One may fit marriage into life in many ways: by first living with a partner, or sequentially with several partners, without explicitly considering whether to marry; by having children with one's eventual spouse or with someone else before marrying; by (in some jurisdictions) marry-ing someone of the same gender and building a shared marital world with few guidelines to rely on. Within marriage, roles are more flexible and negotiable, although women still do more of the household work and childrearing.

The rewards that people seek through marriage and other close relationships have also shifted. Individuals aim for personal growth and deeper intimacy through more open communication and mutually shared disclosures about feelings with their partners. They may insist on changes in a relationship that no longer provides them with individ-ualized rewards. They are less likely than in the past to focus on the rewards gained by fulfilling socially valued roles such as the good parent or the loyal and supportive spouse. As a result of this changing context, social norms about family and personal life count for less than they did during the heyday of companionate marriage and far less than during the era of institutional marriage. Instead, personal choice and self-development loom large in people's construction of their marital careers.

But if marriage is now optional, it remains highly valued. As the practical importance of marriage has declined, its symbolic importance has remained high and may even have increased.[37] At its height as an institution in the mid-twentieth century, marriage was almost required of anyone wishing to be considered a respectable adult. Having children outside marriage was stigmatized, and a person who remained single through adulthood was suspect. But as other lifestyle options became more feasible and acceptable, the need to be married diminished. Nevertheless, marriage remains the preferred option for most people. Now, however, it is not a step taken lightly or early in young adulthood. Being "ready" to marry may mean that a couple has lived together to test their compatibility, saved for a down payment on a house, or possibly had children to judge how well they parent together. Once the foundation of adult family life, marriage is now often the capstone.

Although some observers believe that a "culture of poverty" has diminished the value of marriage among poor Americans, research suggests that the poor, the near-poor, and the middle class conceive of marriage in similar terms. Although marriage rates are lower among the poor than among the middle class, marriage as an ideal remains strong for both groups. Ethnographic studies show that many low-income individuals subscribe to the capstone view of marriage. In a study of low-income families that I carried out with several collaborators, a twenty-seven-year-old mother told an ethnographer:[38]

> I was poor all my life and so was Reginald. When I got pregnant, we agreed we would marry some day in the future because we loved each other and wanted to raise our child together. But we would not get married until we could afford to get a house and pay all the utility bills on time. I have this thing about utility bills. Our gas and electric got turned off all the time when we were growing up and we wanted to make sure that would not happen when we got married. That was our biggest worry. . . . We worked together and built up savings and then we got married. It's forever for us.

The poor, the near-poor, and the middle class also seem to view the emotional rewards of marriage in similar terms. Women of all classes value companionship in marriage: shared lives, joint childrearing, friendship, romantic love, respect, and fair treatment. For example, in a survey conducted in twenty-one cities, African Americans were as likely as non-Hispanic whites to rate highly the emotional benefits of marriage, such as friendship, sex life, leisure time, and a sense of security; and Hispanics rated these benefits somewhat higher than either group.[39] Moreover, in the "fragile families" study of unmarried low- and moderate-income couples who had just had a child together, Marcia Carlson, Sara McLanahan, and Paula England found that mothers and fathers who scored higher on a scale of relationship supportiveness were substantially more likely to be married one year later.[40] Among the items in the scale were whether the partner "is fair and willing to compromise" during a disagreement, "expresses affection or love," "encourages or helps," and does not insult or criticize. In a 2001 national survey of young adults aged twenty to twenty-nine conducted by the Gallup

Organization for the National Marriage Project, 94 percent of never-married respondents agreed that "when you marry, you want your spouse to be your soul mate, first and foremost." Only 16 percent agreed that "the main purpose of marriage these days is to have children."[41]

As debates over same-sex marriage illustrate, marriage is also highly valued by lesbians and gay men. In 2003 the Massachusetts Supreme Court struck down a state law limiting marriage to opposite-sex couples, and same-sex marriage became legal in May 2004 (although opponents may eventually succeed in prohibiting it through a state constitutional amendment). Advocates for same-sex marriage argued that gay and lesbian couples should be entitled to marry so that they can benefit from the legal rights and protections that marriage brings. But the Massachusetts debate also showed the symbolic value of marriage. In response to the court's decision, the state legislature crafted a plan to enact civil unions for same-sex couples. These legally recognized unions would have given same-sex couples most of the legal benefits of marriage but would have withheld the status of being married. The court rejected this remedy, arguing that allowing civil unions but not marriage would create a "stigma of exclusion," because it would deny to same-sex couples "a status that is specially recognized in society and has significant social and other advantages." That the legislature was willing to provide legal benefits was not sufficient for the judges, nor for gay and lesbian activists, who rejected civil unions as second-class citizenship. Nor would it be enough for mainstream Americans, most of whom are still attached to marriage as a specially recognized status.

PUTTING U.S. MARRIAGE IN INTERNATIONAL PERSPECTIVE

How does the place of marriage in the family system in the United States compare with its place in the family systems of other developed nations? It turns out that marriage in the United States is quite distinctive.

A Greater Attachment to Marriage

Marriage is more prevalent in the United States than in nearly all other developed Western nations. Figure 9.3 shows the total first marriage rate for women in the United States and in six other developed nations in 1990. (Shortly after 1990, the U.S. government stopped collecting all the information necessary to calculate this rate.) The total first marriage rate provides an estimate of the proportion of women who will ever marry.[42] It must be interpreted carefully because it yields estimates that are too low if calculated at a time when women are postponing marriage until older ages, as they were in 1990 in most countries. Thus, all the estimates in Figure 9.3 are probably too low. Nevertheless, the total first marriage rate is useful in comparing countries at a given time point, and I have selected the nations in Figure 9.3 to illustrate the variation in this rate in the developed world. The value of 715 for the United States—the highest of any country—implies that 715 out of 1,000 women were expected to marry. Italy had a relatively high

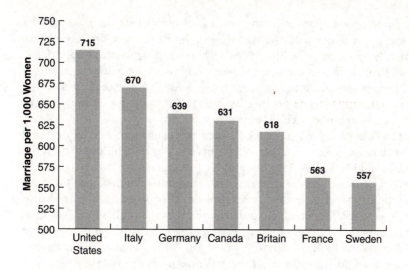

FIGURE 9.3 *Total First Marriage Rates of Women, Selected European and English-Speaking Countries, 1990*

Sources: Alain Monnier and Catherine de Guibert-Lantoine, "The Demographic Situation of Europe and Developed Countries Overseas: An Annual Report," *Population: An English Selection* 8 (1996): 235–50; U.S. National Center for Health Statistics, "Advance Report of Final Marriage Statistics, 1989 and 1990," *Monthly Vital Statistics Report* 43, no. 12, supp. (Government Printing Office, 1995).

value, while France and Sweden had the lowest. In between were Britain, Canada, and Germany.

Not only is marriage stronger demographically in the United States than in other developed countries, it also seems stronger as an ideal. In the World Values Surveys conducted between 1999 and 2001, one question asked of adults was whether they agreed with the statement, "Marriage is an outdated institution." Only 10 percent of Americans agreed—a lower share than in any developed nation except Iceland. Twenty-two percent of Canadians agreed, as did 26 percent of the British, and 36 percent of the French.[43] Americans seem more attached to marriage as a norm than do citizens in other developed countries.

This greater attachment to marriage has a long history. As Alexis de Tocqueville wrote in the 1830s, "There is certainly no country in the world where the tie of marriage is more respected than in America or where conjugal happiness is more highly or worthily appreciated."[44] Historian Nancy Cott has argued that the nation's founders viewed Christian marriage as one of the building blocks of American democracy. The marriage-based family was seen as a mini-republic in which the husband governed with the consent of the wife.[45] The U.S. government has long justified laws and policies that support marriage. In 1888, Supreme Court justice Stephen Field wrote, "marriage, as creating the most important relation in life, as having more to do with the morals and civilization of a people than any other institution, has always been subject to the control of the legislature."[46]

The conspicuous historical exception to government support for marriage was the institution of slavery, under which legal marriage was prohibited. Many slaves nevertheless married informally, often using public rituals such as jumping over a broomstick.[47] Some scholars also think that slaves may have retained the kinship patterns of West Africa, where marriage was more a process that unfolded over time in front of the community than a single event.[48] The prospective husband's family, for example, might wait until the prospective wife bore a child to finalize the marriage.

The distinctiveness of marriage in the United States is also probably related to greater religious participation. Tocqueville observed, "there is no country in the world where the Christian religion retains a greater influence over the souls of men than in America."[49] That statement is still true with respect to the developed nations today: religious vitality is greatest in the United States.[50] For instance, in the World Values Surveys, 60 percent of Americans reported attending religious services at least monthly, as against 36 percent of Canadians, 19 percent of the British, and 12 percent of the French.[51] Americans look to religious institutions for guidance on marriage and family life more than do the citizens of most Western countries. Sixty-one percent of Americans agreed with the statement, "Generally speaking, do you think that the churches in your country are giving adequate answers to the problems of family life?" Only 48 percent of Canadians, 30 percent of the British, and 28 percent of the French agreed.[52]

Moreover, family policies in many European nations have long promoted births, whereas American policies generally have not. This emphasis on pronatalism has been especially prominent in France, where the birth rate began to decline in the 1830s, decades before it did in most other European nations.[53] Since then, the French government has been concerned about losing ground in population size to potential adversaries such as Germany.[54] (The Germans felt a similar concern, which peaked in the Nazis' pronatalist policies of the 1930s and early 1940s.)[55] As a result, argues one historian, French family policy has followed a "parental logic" that places a high priority on supporting parents with young children—even working wives and single parents.[56] These policies have included family allowances prorated by the number of children, maternity insurance, and maternity leave with partial wage replacement. In contrast, policies in Britain and the United States followed a "male breadwinner logic" of supporting married couples in which the husband worked outside the home and the wife did not.[57] Pronatalist pressure has never been strong in the United States, even though the decline in the U.S. birth rate started in the early 1800s, because of the nation's openness to increasing its population through immigration.

More Transitions Into and Out of Marriage

In addition to its high rate of marriage, the United States has one of the highest rates of divorce of any developed nation. Figure 9.4 displays the total divorce rate in 1990 for the countries shown in Figure 9.3. The total divorce rate, which provides an estimate of the number of marriages that would end in divorce, has limits similar to those of the total marriage rate but is likewise useful in international comparisons.[58] Figure 9.4 shows that the United States had a total divorce rate of 517 divorces per 1,000 marriages, with just

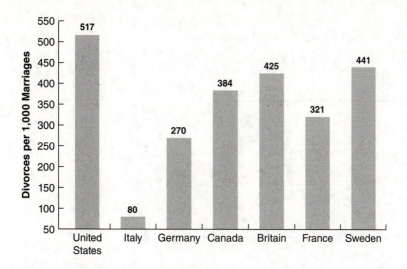

FIGURE 9.4   *Total Divorce Rates, Selected European and English-Speaking Countries, 1990*

Sources: Monnier and de Guibert-Lantoine, "The Demographic Situation of Europe and the Developed Countries Overseas" (see Figure 9.3); U.S. National Center for Health Statistics, "Advance Report of Final Divorce Statistics, 1989 and 1990," *Monthly Vital Statistics Report* 43, no. 9, supp. (Government Printing Office, 1995).

over half of all marriages ending in divorce. Sweden had the second highest total divorce rate, and other Scandinavian countries had similar levels. The English-speaking countries of Britain and Canada were next, followed by France and Germany. Italy had a very low level of predicted divorce.

Both entry into and exit from marriage are indicators of what Robert Schoen has called a country's "marriage metabolism": the number of marriage- and divorce-related transitions that adults and their children undergo.[59] Figure 9.5, which presents the sum of the total first marriage rate and the total divorce rate, shows that the United States has by far the highest marriage metabolism of any of the developed countries in question.[60] Italy, despite its high marriage rate, has the lowest metabolism because of its very low divorce rate. Sweden, despite its high divorce rate, has a lower metabolism than the United States because of its lower marriage rate. In other words, what makes the United States most distinctive is the combination of high marriage and high divorce rates—which implies that Americans typically experience more transitions into and out of marriages than do people in other countries.

A similar trend is evident in movement into and out of cohabiting unions. Whether in marriage or cohabitation, Americans appear to have far more transitions in their live-in relationships. According to surveys from the mid-1990s, 5 percent of women in Sweden had experienced three or more unions (marriages or cohabiting relationships) by age thirty-five. In the rest of Europe, the comparable figure was 1 to 3 percent.[61] But in the United States, according to a 1995 survey, 9 percent of women

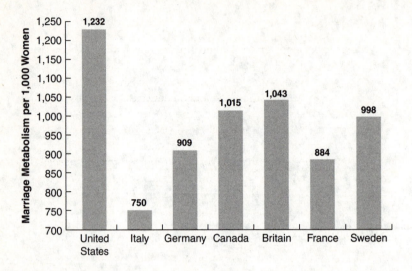

FIGURE 9.5   *Marriage Metabolism, Selected European and English-Speaking Countries, 1990*

Sources: See Figures 9.3 and 9.4.

aged thirty-five had experienced three or more unions, nearly double the Swedish figure and far higher than that of other European nations.[62] By 2002, the U.S. figure had climbed to 12 percent.[63] No other comparable nation has such a high level of multiple marital and cohabiting unions.

American children are thus more likely to experience multiple transitions in living arrangements than are children in Europe. Another study using the same comparative data from the mid-1990s reported that 12 percent of American children had lived in three or more parental partnerships by age fifteen, as against 3 percent of children in Sweden, which has the next highest figure.[64] As transitions out of partnerships occur, children experience a period of living in a single-parent family. And although American children, in general, are more likely to live in a single-parent family while growing up than are children elsewhere, the trend differs by social class. As Sara McLanahan shows in a comparison of children whose mothers have low or moderate levels of education, American children are much more likely than those in several European nations to have lived with a single mother by age fifteen. The cross-national difference is less pronounced among children whose mothers are highly educated.[65]

Also contributing to the prevalence of single-parent families in the United States is the relatively large share of births to unmarried, noncohabiting women—about one in five.[66] In most other developed nations with numerous nonmarital births, a greater share of unmarried mothers lives with the fathers of their children. In fact, the increases in nonmarital births in Europe in recent decades largely reflect births to cohabiting couples rather than births to single parents.[67] As noted, the United States is seeing a similar trend toward births to cohabiting couples, but the practice is still less prevalent in the United States than in many European nations.

Greater Economic Inequality

Children in the United States experience greater inequality of economic well-being than children in most other developed nations. One recent study reported that the gap between the cash incomes of children's families in the lowest and highest 10 percent was larger in the United States than in twelve other developed countries.[68] The low ranking of the United States is attributable both to the higher share of births to single parents and to the higher share of divorce. But even when the comparison is restricted to children living in single-parent families, children in the United States have the lowest relative standard of living. For example, one comparative study reported that 60 percent of single-mother households in the United States were poor, as against 45 percent in Canada, 40 percent in the United Kingdom, 25 percent in France, 20 percent in Italy, and 5 percent in Sweden.[69] The differences are caused by variations both in the income earned by single parents and in the generosity of government cash transfers. In other words, having a high share of single-parent families predisposes the United States to have a higher poverty rate, but other countries compensate better for single parenthood through a combination of social welfare spending and supports for employed parents, such as child care.

More Controversy over Gay and Lesbian Partnerships

Other developed countries tend to be more open to gay and lesbian partnerships than is the United States. Two European nations, Belgium and the Netherlands, have legalized same-sex marriage. By 2005, courts in seven Canadian provinces had ruled that laws restricting marriage to opposite-sex couples were discriminatory, and the Canadian federal government had introduced a bill to legalize gay marriage nationwide. Many other developed nations, including all the Scandinavian countries and Germany, have amended their family laws to include legal recognition of same-sex partnerships.[70]

France enacted its somewhat different form of domestic partnership, the *pacte civil de solidarité* (PACS), in 1999. Originally conceived in response to the burden placed on gay couples by the AIDS epidemic, the 1999 legislation was not restricted to same-sex partnerships.[71] In fact, it is likely that more opposite-sex partners than same-sex partners have chosen this option.[72] The PACS does not provide all the legal benefits of marriage. It is a privately negotiated contract between two persons who are treated legally as individuals unless they have children. Even when they have children, the contract does not require one partner to support the other after a dissolution, and judges are reluctant to award joint custody. Moreover, individuals in a same-sex PACS do not have the right to adopt children or to use reproductive technology such as in vitro fertilization.

For the most part, the issue of marriage has been less prominent in European than in North American debates about same-sex partnerships. To this point, no serious movement for same-sex marriage has appeared in Britain.[73] The French debate, consistent with the nation's child-oriented social policies, has focused more on the kinship rights and relationships of the children of the partners than on whether the legal form of partnership should include marriage.[74] In 2004, the mayor of Bogles, France, created a furor—similar to that seen in the United States following the granting of marriage licenses in San Francisco—by marrying a gay couple. But marriage remains less central to the politics of same-sex partnerships in France and elsewhere in Europe than it is in North America.

MARRIAGE TRANSFORMED

Marriage remains an important part of the American family system, even if its dominance has diminished. Sentiment in favor of marriage appears to be stronger in the United States than elsewhere in the developed world, and the share of adults who are likely to marry is higher—as is, however, their propensity to get divorced. Increasingly, gay and lesbian activists are arguing, with some success, that they, too, should be allowed to marry. Even poor and near-poor Americans, who are statistically less likely to marry, hold to marriage as an ideal. But the contemporary ideal differs from that of the past in two important ways.

The Contemporary Ideal

First, marriage is now more optional in the United States than it has ever been. Until recently, family formation rarely occurred outside of marriage. Now, to a greater extent than ever before, one can choose whether to have children on one's own, in a cohabiting relationship, or in a marriage. Poor and working-class Americans have radically separated the timing of childbearing and marriage, with many young adults having children many years before marrying. At current rates, perhaps one-third of African Americans will never marry. To be sure, some of the increase in seemingly single-parent families reflects a rise in the number of cohabiting couples who are having children, but these cohabiting relationships often prove unstable. How frequently the option of marriage becomes a reality depends heavily on one's race, ethnicity, or social class. African Americans and less well-educated Americans, for example, still value marriage highly but attain it less frequently than whites and better-educated Americans.

Second, the rewards of marriage today are more individualized. Being married is less a required adult role and more an individual achievement—a symbol of successful self-development. And couples are more prone to dissolve a marriage if their individualized rewards seem inadequate. Conversely, marriage is less centered on children. Today, married couples in the United States are having fewer children than couples have had at any time in the nation's history except during the Great Depression.

The changes in marriage, however, have not been solely cultural in origin. It is still the norm that a man must be able to provide a steady income to be seen as a good prospect for marriage. He no longer need earn all the family's income, but he must make a substantial, stable contribution. As the labor market position of young men without a college education has eroded, their attractiveness in the marriage market has declined. Many of their potential partners have chosen to have children outside marriage early in adulthood rather than to wait for the elusive promise of finding a spouse. Moreover, the introduction of the birth control pill and the legalization of abortion have allowed young women and men to become sexually active long before they think about marriage.

When the American family system is viewed in international perspective, it is most distinctive for the many transitions into and out of marital and cohabiting unions. Americans are more likely to experience multiple unions over the course of their lives than are Europeans. Moreover, cohabiting relationships in the United States still tend to be rather short, with a median duration (until either marriage or dissolution) of about one year. The median duration of cohabiting unions is about four years in Sweden and France and two or more years in most other European nations.[75] All this means that American children probably face greater instability in their living arrangements than children anywhere else in the developed world. Recent research has suggested that changes in family structure, regardless of the beginning and ending configurations, may cause problems for children.[76] Some of these apparent problems may reflect preexisting family difficulties, but some cause-and-effect association between instability and children's difficulties probably exists. If so, the increase in instability over the past decades is a worrisome trend that may not be receiving the attention it deserves.

Positive Developments

This is not to suggest that all the trends in marriage in America have been harmful to children. Those who live with two parents or with one well-educated parent may be doing better than comparable children a few decades ago. As noted, income growth has been greater in dual-career families, and divorce rates may have fallen among the college educated. In addition, the time spent with their parents by children in two-parent families has gone up, not down, and the comparable time spent by children with single parents has not changed, even though mothers' work outside the home has increased.[77] Working mothers appear to compensate for time spent outside the home by cutting back on housework and leisure—and, for those who are married, relying on modest but noticeable increases in husbands' housework—to preserve time with children.[78]

Meanwhile, the decline in fertility means that there are fewer children in the home to compete for their parents' attention. Middle-class parents engage in an intensive childrearing style that sociologist Annette Lareau calls "concerted cultivation": days filled with organized activities and parent-child discussions designed to enhance their children's talents, opinions, and skills.[79] While some social critics decry this parenting style, middle-class children gain skills that will be valuable to them in higher education and in the labor market. They learn how to communicate with professionals and other adults in positions of authority. They develop a confident style of interaction that Lareau calls "an emerging sense of entitlement," compared with "an emerging sense of constraint" among working-class and lower-class youth.

MARRIAGE AND PUBLIC POLICY

Because marriage has been, and continues to be, stronger in the United States than in much of Europe, American social welfare policies have focused more on marriage than have those of many European countries. That emphasis continues. George W. Bush's administration advocates marriage-promotion programs as the most promising way to assist families. No European country has pursued a comparable policy initiative. Moreover, the issue of gay marriage has received more attention in the United States than in most of Europe. This greater emphasis on marriage in public policy reflects the history and culture of the United States. Policies that build on and support marriage are likely to be popular with American voters because they resonate with American values. Europe's more generous public spending on children, regardless of their parents' marital status, is rooted in concerns about low population growth that have never been strong in the United States. Such public spending on single-parent families also reflects the lesser influence of religion in Europe. So it is understandable that American policymakers wishing to generate support for new family policy initiatives might turn to marriage-based programs.

Yet the relatively high value placed on marriage in the United States coexists with an unmatched level of family instability and large numbers of single-parent families. This, too, is part of the American cultural heritage. The divorce rate appears to have been higher in the United States than in most of Europe since the mid-nineteenth century.[80]

This emblematic American pattern of high marriage and divorce rates, cohabiting unions of short duration, and childbearing among unpartnered women and men makes it unrealistic to think that policymakers will be able to reduce rates of multiple unions and of single parenthood in the United States to typical European levels. Consequently, a family policy that relies too heavily on marriage will not help the many children destined to live in single-parent and cohabiting-parent families—many of them economically disadvantaged—for some or all of their formative years. Only assistance directed to needy families, regardless of their household structure, will reach them. Such policies are less popular in the United States, as the widespread disdain for cash welfare and the popularity of the 1996 welfare reform legislation demonstrate. Moreover, some American policymakers worry that programs that support all parents without regard to partnership status may decrease people's incentive to marry.[81] The dilemma for policymakers is how to make the trade-off between marriage-based and marriage-neutral programs. A careful balance of both is needed to provide adequate support to American children.

Notes

1. W. C. Rodgers and A. Thornton, "Changing Patterns of First Marriage in the United States," *Demography* 22 (1985): 265–79; Joshua R. Goldstein and Catherine T. Kenney, "Marriage Delayed or Marriage Forgone? New Cohort Forecasts of First Marriage for U.S. Women," *American-Sociological Review* 66 (2001): 506–19.
2. U.S. Bureau of the Census, "Percent of People 25 Years Old and Over Who Have Completed High School or College, by Race, Hispanic Origin and Sex: Selected Years 1940 to 2002," 2003, table A-2, www.census.gov/population/socdemo/education/tabA-2.pdf (accessed June 24, 2004).
3. Ibid.
4. U.S. National Center for Health Statistics, "Fertility, Family Planning, and Women's Health: New Data from the 1995 National Survey of Family Growth," *Vital and Health Statistics* 23, no. 19 (1997), available at www.cdc.gov/nchs/data/series/sr_23/sr23_019.pdf (accessed July 13, 2004).
5. Larry L. Bumpass and Hsien-Hen Lu, "Trends in Cohabitation and Implications for Children's Family Contexts in the United States," *Population Studies* 54 (2000): 29–41. They note that 49 percent of women aged thirty to thirty-four years old in the 1995 National Survey of Family Growth reported ever cohabiting.
6. U.S. National Center for Health Statistics, "Number and Percent of Births to Unmarried Women, by Race and Hispanic Origin: United States, 1940–99," *Vital Statistics of the United States, 1999*, vol. 1, *Natality*, table 1-17 (available at www.cdc.gov/nehs/data/statab/t99lxl7.pdf [accessed January 12, 2005]); and U.S. National Center for Health Statistics, "Births: Preliminary Data for 2002," *National Vital Statistics Report* 53, no. 9, www.cdc.gov/nchs/data/nvsr/nvsr53/nvsr53_09.pdf

(accessed January 12, 2005). For 2003, the figures were 34.6 percent overall, 23.5 percent for non-Hispanic whites, 68.5 percent for non-Hispanic blacks, and 45 percent for Hispanics.

7. Ibid.

8. Marcia Carlson, Sara McLanahan, and Paula England, "Union Formation in Fragile Families," *Demography* 41 (2004): 237–61.

9. Dan Black and others, "Demographics of the Gay and Lesbian Population in the United States: Evidence from Available Systematic Data," *Demography* 37 (2000): 139–54.

10. U.S. Bureau of the Census, "Married-Couple and Unmarried-Partner Households: 2000" (Government Printing Office, 2003).

11. Andrew Cherlin, *Marriage, Divorce, Remarriage* (Harvard University Press, 1992).

12. Matthew Bramlett and William D. Mosher, *Cohabitation, Marriage, Divorce and Remarriage in the United States*, series 22, no. 2 (U.S. National Center for Health Statistics, Vital and Health Statistics, 2002), available at www.cdc.gov/nchs/data/series/sr_23/sr23_022.pdf (accessed June 2003).

13. U.S. Bureau of the Census. "Detailed Living Arrangements of Children by Race and Hispanic Origin, 1996," 2001, www.census.gov/population/socdemo/child/p70-74/tab01.pdf (accessed June 28, 2004). The data are from the 1996 Survey of Income and Program Participation, wave 2.

14. Some of the one-parent families contain an unmarried cohabiting partner, whom the Census Bureau normally does not count as a "parent." According to the 1996 estimates cited in the previous note, about 2.5 percent of children live with a biological or adoptive parent who is cohabiting.

15. Lynne Casper and Suzanne M. Bianchi, *Continuity and Change in the American Family* (Thousand Oaks, CA: Sage, 2002).

16. David Ellwood and Christopher Jencks, "The Uneven Spread of Single-Parent Families: What Do We Know? Where Do We Look for Answers?" in *Social Inequality*, edited by Kathryn M. Neckerman (New York: Russell Sage Foundation, 2004), pp. 3–118.

17. Sara McLanahan, "Diverging Destinies: How Children Are Faring under the Second Demographic Transition," *Demography* 41 (2004): 607–27.

18. Ellwood and Jencks, "The Uneven Spread of Single-Parent Families" (see note 16).

19. Steven P. Martin, "Growing Evidence for a 'Divorce Divide'? Education and Marital Dissolution Rates in the U.S. since the 1970s," Working Paper on Social Dimensions of Inequality (New York: Russell Sage Foundation, 2004).

20. McLanahan, "Diverging Destinies" (see note 17).

21. Ibid.

22. Isabel Sawhill and Laura Chadwick, *Children in Cities: Uncertain Futures* (Brookings, 1999); and Donald J. Hernandez, *America's Children: Resources from Family, Government, and Economy* (New York: Russell Sage Foundation, 1993).

23. S. Philip Morgan and others, "Racial Differences in Household and Family Structure at the Turn of the Century," *American Journal of Sociology* 98 (1993): 798–828.

24. Cherlin, *Marriage, Divorce, Remarriage* (see note 11).

25. Goldstein and Kenney, "Marriage Delayed or Marriage Forgone?" (see note 1).

26. U.S. National Center for Health Statistics, "Births: Preliminary Data" (see note 6).

27. Bumpass and Lu, "Trends in Cohabitation" (see note 5).

28. U.S. National Center for Health Statistics, "Revised Birth and Fertility Rates for the 1990s and New Rates for the Hispanic Populations, 2000 and 2001: United States," *National Vital Statistics Reports* 51, no. 12 (Government Printing Office, 2003); and U.S. National Center for Health Statistics, "Births: Final Data for 2000," *National Vital Statistics Report* 50, no. 5 (Government Printing Office, 2002).

29. Frank D. Bean and Marta Tienda, *The Hispanic Population of the United States* (New York: Russell Sage Foundation, 1987).

30. U.S. National Center for Health Statistics, "Births: Final Data for 2000" (see note 28).

31. McLanahan, "Diverging Destinies" (see note 17).

32. Elise Richer and others, *Boom Times a Bust: Declining Employment among Less-Educated Young Men* (Washington: Center for Law and Social Policy, 2003); available at www.clasp.org/DMS/Documents/1058362464.08/Boom_Times.pdf (accessed July 13, 2004).

33. William J. Wilson, The Truly Disadvantaged: The Inner City, the Underclass, and Public Policy (University of Chicago Press, 1987).

34. Robert D. Mare and Christopher Winship, "Socioeconomic Change and the Decline in Marriage for Blacks and Whites," in *The Urban Underclass*, edited by Christopher Jencks and Paul Peterson (Brookings, 1991), pp. 175–202; and Daniel T. Lichter, Diane K. McLaughlin, and David C. Ribar, "Economic Restructuring and the Retreat from Marriage," *Social Science Research* 31 (2002): 230–56.

35. Ernest W. Burgess and Harvey J. Locke, *The Family: From Institution to Companionship* (New York: American Book Company, 1945).

36. Andrew J. Cherlin, "The Deinstitutionalization of American Marriage," *Journal of Marriage and the Family* 66 (2004): 848–61.

37. Ibid.

38. Linda Burton of Pennsylvania State University directed the ethnographic component of the study. For a general description, see Pamela Winston and others, "Welfare, Children, and Families: A Three-City Study Overview and Design," 1999, www.jhu.edu\~welfare\overviewanddesign.pdf (accessed July 10, 2004).

39. M. Belinda Tucker, "Marital Values and Expectations in Context: Results from a 21-City Survey," in *The Ties That Bind: Perspectives on Marriage and Cohabitation*, edited by Linda J. Waite (New York: Aldine de Gruyter, 2000), pp. 166–87.

40. Carlson, McLanahan, and England, "Union Formation" (see note 8).

41. Barbara Dafoe Whitehead and David Popenoe, "Who Wants to Marry a Soul Mate?" in *The State of Our Unions, 2001*, The National Marriage Project, Rutgers University, pp. 6–16, 2001, available at marriage.rutgers.edu/Publications/SOOU/NMPAR200l.pdf (accessed February 12, 2004).

42. The estimate assumes that the age-specific marriage rates in the year of calculation (in this case, 1990) will remain unchanged in future years. Since this assumption is unrealistic, the total marriage rate is unlikely to predict the future accurately. But it does demonstrate the rate of marriage implied by current trends.

43. Ronald Inglehart and others, Human Beliefs and Values: A Cross-Cultural Soureebook Based on the 1999–2002 Values Surveys (Mexico City: Siglo Veintiuno Editores, 2004).

44. Alexis de Tocqueville, *Democracy in America*, vol. 1 (New York: Knopf, Everyman's Library, 1994), p. 304.

45. Nancy Cott, *Public Vows: A History of Marriage and the Nation* (Harvard University Press, 2000).

46. Quoted in ibid., pp. 102–03.

47. Herbert G. Gutman, *The Black Family in Slavery and Freedom, 1750–1925* (New York: Pantheon, 1976).

48. Jacqueline Jones, Labor of Love, Labor of Sorrow: Black Women and the Family from Slavery to the Present (New York: Basic Books, 1985).

49. Tocqueville, *Democracy in America* (see note 44), p. 303.

50. Grace Davie, "Patterns of Religion in Western Europe: An Exceptional Case," in *The Blackwell Companion to the Sociology of Religion*, edited by Richard K. Fenn (Oxford: Blackwell, 2001), pp. 264–78; and Seymour Martin Lipset, "American Exceptionalism Reaffirmed," *Tocqueville Review* 10 (1990): 3–35.

51. Inglehart and others, *Human Beliefs and Values* (see note 43).

52. Ibid.

53. See the discussion in Ron J. Lesthaeghe, *The Decline of Belgian Fertility, 1800–1970* (Princeton University Press, 1977), p. 304.

54. Alisa Klaus, "Depopulation and Race Suicide: Maternalism and Pronatalist Ideologies in France and the United States," in *Mothers of a New World: Maternalist Politics and the Origins of the Welfare State*, edited by Seth Koven and Sonya Michel (New York: Routledge, 1993), pp. 188–212.

55. Paul Ginsborg, "The Family Politics of the Great Dictators," in *Family Life in the Twentieth Century*, edited by David I. Kertzer and Marzio Barbagli (Yale University Press, 2003), pp. 188–97.

56. Susan Pedersen, Family, Dependence, and the Origins of the Welfare State: Britain and France, 1914–1945 (Cambridge University Press, 1993).

57. Ibid.

58. The total divorce rate is formed by summing duration-specific divorce rates prevalent in the year of observation—in this case, 1990. It therefore assumes that the duration-specific rates of 1990 will remain the same in future years. It shares the limits of the total marriage rate (see note 42).

59. Robert Schoen and Robin M. Weinick, "The Slowing Metabolism of Marriage: Figures from 1988 U.S. Marital Status Life Tables," *Demography* 39 (1993): 737–46. Schoen and Weinick used life table calculations to establish the marriage and divorce probabilities for American men and women. Unfortunately, only total marriage rates and total divorce rates are available for other countries. Consequently, I calculated a total divorce rate for the United States from published duration-specific divorce rates for 1990. I then summed the total first marriage rate and total divorce rate for the United States and the other countries displayed in Figure 9.4. Although this procedure is not as accurate as using rates generated by life tables, the difference is unlikely to alter the relative positions of the countries in the figure.

60. Strictly speaking, I should use the total divorce rate for people in first marriages (as opposed to including people in remarriages), but the available data do not allow for that level of precision.

61. Alexia Fürnkranz-Prskawetz and others, "Pathways to Stepfamily Formation in Europe: Results from the FFS," *Demographic Research* 8 (2003): 107–49.

62. Author's calculation from the 1995 National Survey of Family Growth microdata file.

63. Author's calculation from the 2002 National Survey of Family Growth microdata file.

64. Patrick Heuveline, Jeffrey M. Timberlake, and Frank F. Furstenberg Jr., "Shifting Childrearing to Single Mothers: Results from 17 Western Countries," *Population and Development Review* 29 (2003): 47–71. The figures quoted appear in note 6.

65. McLanahan, "Diverging Destinies" (see note 17).

66. About one-third of all births are to unmarried mothers, and Bumpass and Lu report that about 60 percent of unmarried mothers in 1995 were not cohabiting ($0.33 \times 0.60 = 0.198$). Bumpass and Lu, "Trends in Cohabitation" (see note 5).

67. Kathleen Kiernan, "European Perspectives on Nonmarital Childbearing," in *Out of Wedlock: Causes and Consequences of Nonmarital Fertility*, edited by Lawrence L. Wu and Barbara Wolfe (New York: Russell Sage Foundation, 2001), pp. 77–108.

68. Lars Osberg, Timothy M. Smeeding, and Jonathan Schwabish, "Income Distribution and Public Social Expenditure: Theories, Effects, and Evidence," in *Social Inequality*, edited by Kathryn M. Neckerman (New York: Russell Sage Foundation, 2004), pp. 821–59.

69. Poverty was defined as having a family income of less than half of the median income for all families. Bruce Bradbury and Markus Jäntti, "Child-Poverty across the Industrialized World: Evidence from the Luxembourg Income Study," in *Child Well-Being, Child Poverty and Child Policy in Modern Nations: What Do We Know?* edited by Koen Vleminckx and Timothy M. Smeeding (Bristol, England: Policy Press, 2000), pp. 11–32.

70. Marzio Barbagli and David I. Kertzer, "Introduction," and Paulo Ronfani, "Family Law in Europe," in *Family Life in the Twentieth Century*, edited by David I. Kertzer and Marzio Barbagli (Yale University Press, 2003), respectively, pp. xi–xliv and 114–51.

71. Claude Martin and Irène Théry, "The Pacs and Marriage and Cohabitation in France," *International Journal of Law, Policy and the Family* 15 (2001): 135–58.

72. Patrick Festy, "The 'Civil Solidarity Pact' (PACS) in France: An Impossible Evaluation," *Population et Sociétés*, no. 369 (2001): 1–4.

73. John Eekelaar, "The End of an Era?" *Journal of Family History* 28 (2003): 108–22.

74. Eric Fassin, "Same Sex, Different Politics: 'Gay Marriage' Debates in France and the United States," *Popular Culture* 13 (2001): 215–32.

75. Kathleen Kiernan, "Cohabitation in Western Europe," *Population Trends* 96 (Summer 1999): 25–32.

76. See, for example, Lawrence L. Wu and Brian C. Martinson, "Family Structure and the Risk of Premarital Birth," *American Sociological Review* 59 (1993): 210–32; Jake M. Najman and others, "Impact of Family Type and Family Quality on Child Behavior Problems: A Longitudinal Study," *Journal of the American Academy of Child and Adolescent Psychiatry* 36 (1997): 1357–65.

77. John F. Sandberg and Sandra D. Hofferth, "Changes in Children's Time with Parents, U.S. 1981–1997," *Demography* 38 (2001): 423–36.

78. Suzanne M. Bianchi, "Maternal Employment and Time with Children: Dramatic Change or Surprising Continuity?" *Demography* 37 (2000): 401–14.
79. Annette Lareau, *Unequal Childhoods: Class, Race, and Family Life* (University of California Press, 2003).
80. Gören Therborn, Between Sex and Power: Family in the World, 1900–2000 (London: Routledge, 2004).
81. This proposition is similar to what David Ellwood has called the "assistance-family structure conundrum." David T. Ellwood, *Poor Support: Poverty and the American Family* (New York: Basic Books, 1988).

■ **READING 10**

Grounds for Marriage: How Relationships Succeed or Fail

Arlene Skolnick

> The home made by one man and one woman bound together "until death do ye part" has in large measure given way to trial marriage.
>
> —*Chauncey J. Hawkins (1907)*

> Marriage has universally fallen into awful disrepute.
>
> —*Martin Luther (1522)*

On June 2, 1986, *Newsweek* magazine featured a cover story that proclaimed that a woman over 40 had a greater chance of being "killed by a terrorist" than of getting married. The story, based on one study, set off a media blitz, along with a wave of alarm and anxiety among single women. Eventually, however, after the furor died down, other researchers pointed to serious flaws in the study *Newsweek* had relied on for the story. The study had relied on trends in earlier generations of women to make predictions about the future of unmarried women today.

In the summer of 1999, another report about the alarming state of marriage was released (National Marriage Project, 1999). Exhibit A was a finding that, between 1960 and 1990, the marriage rate among young adults had gone down 23 percent. Again a widely publicized "finding" had to be corrected. The problem this time was including teenagers as young as 15 as "young adults" in 1960 and 1996. Teenagers were far more likely to get married in the 1950s than the 1990s or at any previous time in American history.

The death of marriage has been proclaimed many times in American history, but in the first years of the twenty-first century, the institution is still alive. Despite today's high divorce rates, the rise in one-parent families, and other trends, the United

States today has the highest marriage rate among the advanced industrial countries. The Census Bureau estimates that about 90 percent of Americans will eventually marry.

The combination of both high marriage and high divorce rates seems paradoxical, but actually represents two sides of the same coin: the importance of the emotional relationship between the partners. Marriage for love was not unknown in earlier eras, but other, more practical considerations usually came first—economic security, status, and the interests of parents and kin.

Even in the 1950s, the heyday of the marital "togetherness" ideal, researchers found that so-called "empty shell" or "disengaged" marriages were widespread. Such couples lived under one roof, but seemed to have little or no emotional connection to one another. Some of these spouses considered themselves happily married, but others, particularly women, lived in quiet desperation.

Couples today have much higher expectations. Between the 1950s and the 1970s, American attitudes toward marriage changed dramatically as part of what has been called a "psychological revolution"—a transformation in the way people look at marriage, parenthood, and their lives in general (Veroff, Donvan, and Kulka, 1981). In 1957, people judged themselves and their partners in terms of how well the partners fulfilled their social roles in marriage. Is he a good provider? Is she a good homemaker?

By the 1970s, people had become more psychologically oriented, seeking emotional warmth and intimacy in marriage. Why the change? The shift is linked to higher educational levels. In the 1950s, the psychological approach to relationships was found among the relatively few Americans who had been to college. By the 1970s the psychological approach to marriage and family life had become, as the authors put it, "common coin."

In an era when divorce has lost its stigma and remaining married has become as much a choice as getting married in first place, it's not surprising that a loving and rewarding relationship has become the gold standard for marital success. Although they know the statistics, few if any couples go to the altar expecting that their own relationship will break down. How do relationships become unhappy? What is the process that transforms happy newlyweds into emotional strangers? In the rest of this paper, I discuss my own research on marriage in the context of what others have been learning in answer to these questions.

THE STUDY OF MARRIAGE PAST AND PRESENT

In recent years, there have been great advances in the study of couple relationships. Until the 1970s there were many studies of what was called marital "adjustment," "happiness," "success," or "satisfaction." This research was usually based on large surveys in which people's ratings of their own marital happiness were correlated with other characteristics. The best-established correlates were demographic factors, such as occupation, education, income, age at marriage, religious participation, and the like. There was little theorizing about why these links might exist.

The use of self-reported ratings to study marriage came under a lot of criticism. Some researchers argued that the concept of marital happiness was hopelessly vague; others questioned the validity of simply asking people to rate their own marriages.

But there were deeper problems with these earlier studies. Even the best self-report measure can hardly capture what goes on in the private psychosocial theater of married life.

In the 1970s, a new wave of marital research began to breach the wall of marital privacy. Psychologists, clinicians, and social scientists began to observe families interacting with one another in laboratories and clinics, usually through one-way mirrors. The new technology of videotaping made it possible to preserve these interactions for later analysis. Behavioral therapists and researchers began to produce a literature describing the behavior of happy and unhappy couples. At the same time, social psychologists began to study close relationships of various kinds.

During this period I began my own research into marriage, using couples who had taken part in the longitudinal studies carried out at the Institute of Human Development (IHD) at the University of California at Berkeley. One member of the couple had been part of the study since childhood, and had been born either in 1921 or 1928. Each spouse had been interviewed in depth in 1958, when the study members were 30 or 37 years old. They were interviewed again in 1970 and 1982.

Despite the richness of the longitudinal data, it did not include observations of the spouses interacting with one another, a method of research that did not come on the scene until the study was decades old. On the other hand, few of the new observational studies of marriage have included the kind of in-depth material on the couples' lives as did the longitudinal study. It seemed to me that the ideal study of marriage, assuming cost was not an issue, would include both observational and interview data as well as a sort of ethnography of the couples' lives at home. A few years ago, I was offered the opportunity to be involved in a small version of such a project in a study of the marriages of police officers. I will discuss this study later on.

The new wave of research has revealed a great deal about the complex emotional dynamics of marriage, and perhaps most usefully, revealed that some widespread beliefs about couple relations are incorrect. But there is still a great deal more to learn. There is as yet no grand theory of marriage, no one royal road to understanding marriage, no one size fits all prescriptions for marital success. But we have gained some important insights to marital (and marriage-like) relationships. And there seems to be a striking convergence of findings emerging from different approaches to studying couples. Here are some of these insights.

For Better and For Worse

The sociologist Jesse Bernard argued that every marriage contains two marriages, the husband's and the wife's (1972), and that his is better than hers. Bernard's claims have been controversial, but in general, her idea that husbands and wives have different perspectives on their marriage has held up over time.

But apart from gender differences, marital relationships also seem to divide in two another way: every marriage contains within it both a good marriage and bad marriage. Early studies of marital quality assumed that all marriages could be lined up along a single dimension of satisfaction, adjustment or happiness—happy couples would be at one end of the scale, unhappy ones at the other, and most couples would fall somewhere in between.

More recently, marriage researchers have found that that you need two separate dimensions to capture the quality of a relationship, a positive dimension and a negative one. The key to marital happiness is the balance between the good marriage and the bad one. The finding emerges in different ways in studies using different methods.

In my own research, I came across this same "good marriage-bad marriage" phenomenon among the Berkeley longitudinal couples (Skolnick, 1981). First, we identified couples ranging from high and low in marital satisfaction based on ratings of the marriage each spouse had made, combined with ratings made by clinical interviewers who had seen each separately. Later we examined transcripts of the clinical interviews to see how people who had scored high or low on measures of marital quality described their marriages. In the course of the interview, each person was asked about his or her satisfactions and dissatisfactions in the relationship.

Surprisingly, looking only at statements about dissatisfaction, it was hard to tell the happily married from their unhappy counterparts. None of the happy spouses were without some complaints or irritations. One husband went on at length at what a terrible homemaker his wife was. The wife in one of the most highly rated marriages reported having "silent arguments"—periods of not speaking to one another—which lasted about a week. "People always say you should talk over your differences," the wife said, "but it doesn't work in our family."

Only in descriptions of the satisfactions of the marriage did the contrast emerge. The happy couples described close, affectionate, and often romantic relationships. One man remarked after almost 30 years of marriage, "I still have stars in my eyes." A woman said, "I just can't wait for him to get home every night; just having him around is terrific."

The most systematic evidence for this good marriage/bad marriage model emerges from the extensive program of studies of marital interaction carried out by Gottman, Levenson, and associates (1992, 1998). Their research is based on videotaped observations of couple discussions in a laboratory setting. These intensive studies not only record facial expressions, gestures, and tone of voice, but also monitor heart rates and other physiological indicators of stress.

Surprisingly, these studies do not confirm the widespread notion that anger is the great destroyer of marital relationships. Among the indicators that do predict marital distress and eventual divorce are high levels of physiological arousal, that is stress, as couples interact with one another, a tendency for quarrels to escalate in intensity, and a tendency to keep the argument going even after the other person has tried to "make up" and end it.

As noted earlier, the key factor in the success of a marriage is not the amount of anger or other negative emotion in the relationship—no marriage always runs smoothly and cheerfully—but the balance between positive and negative feelings and actions. Indeed, Gottman gives a precise estimate of this ratio in successful marriages—five to one. In other words, the "good" marriage has to be five times better than the "bad" marriage is bad.

It seems as if the "good" marriage acts like a reservoir of positive feelings that can keep arguments from escalating out of control. In virtually every marriage and family, "emotional brushfires" are constantly breaking out. Whether these flare-ups develop into major bonfires depends on the balance between the good marriage and the bad one.

Gottman identifies a set of four behavioral patterns, that he calls "the four horsemen of the apocalypse"; they constitute a series of escalating signs of marital breakdown.

These include: criticism (not just complaining about a specific act, but denouncing the spouse's whole character); contempt (insults, name calling, mockery); then defensiveness (each spouse feeling hurt, mistreated and misunderstood by the other); and finally, stonewalling (one or both partners withdraws into silence and avoidance).

Tolstoy Was Wrong: Happy Marriages Are Not All Alike

The most common approach to understanding marriage, as we have seen, is to correlate ratings of marital happiness with other variables. But focusing on *variables* masks an enormous amount of *individual* variation. Some studies over the years, however, have looked at differences among marriages at a given level of satisfaction. Among the first was a widely cited study published in 1965. John Cuber and Peggy Harroff interviewed 437 successful upper-middle-class men and women about their lives and marriages. These people had been married for at least 15 years to their original spouses, and reported themselves as being satisfied with their marriages. Yet the authors found enormous variation in marital style among these stable, contented upscale couples.

Only one out of six marriages in the sample conformed to the image of what marriage is supposed to be—that is, a relationship based on strong emotional bonds of love and friendship. The majority of others, however, did not fit the ideal model. Some couples were "conflict habituated," the bickering, battling spouses often portrayed in plays, movies, and television. Yet they were content with their marriages and did not define their fighting as a problem.

A second group of couples were in "devitalized" marriages; starting out in close, loving relationships, they had drifted apart over the years. In the third "passive congenial" type of relationship, the partners were never in love or emotionally close in the first place. Marriage for these couples was a comfortable and convenient lifestyle, leaving them free to devote their energy to their careers or other interests.

The most recent studies of marital types come from the research of John Gottman and his colleagues, described earlier. Along with identifying early warning signs of later marital trouble and divorce, Gottman also observed that happy, successful marriages were not all alike. Moreover, he also found that much of the conventional wisdom about marriage is misguided.

For example, marital counselors and popular writings on marriage often advocate what Gottman calls a "validation" or "active-listening" model. They recommend that when couples have a disagreement, they should speak to one another as a therapist speaks to a client. For example, a wife is supposed to state her complaints directly to the husband, in the form of "I" statements: "I feel you're not doing your share of the housework." Then he is supposed to calmly respond by paraphrasing what she has said, and empathize with her feelings, "Sounds like you're upset about this."

To their surprise, Gottman and his colleagues found that very few couples actually fit this therapeutically approved, "validating" model of marriage. Like Cuber and Harroff, they found that people can be happily married even if they fight a lot; Gottman calls these "volatile" marriages. At the opposite extreme, were "avoidant" couples, who did not argue or even talk about their conflicts. These happily married couples also defied conventional wisdom about the importance of "communication" in marriage.

In my own study, I too found a great deal of variation among the longitudinal couples. Apart from the deep friendship that typified all the happy couples they differed in many other ways. Some spent virtually 24 hours a day together, others went their own ways, going off to parties or weekends alone. Some were very traditional in their gender patterns, others egalitarian. Some were emotionally close to their relatives, some were distant. Some had a wide circle of friends, some were virtual hermits.

They could come from happy or unhappy families. The wife in one of the happiest marriages had a very difficult relationship with her father; she grew up "hating men" and planned never to marry. Her husband also grew up in an unhappy home where the parents eventually divorced. In short, if the emotional core of marriage is good, it seems to matter very little what kind of lifestyle the couple chooses to follow.

Marriage Is a Movie, Not a Snapshot

The ancient Greek philosopher Heroclitis once said that you can never step into the same river twice, because it is always moving. The same is true of marriage. A variety of studies show that over a relatively short period of time, marriages and families can change in the ways they interact and in their emotional atmosphere. In studies of police officer couples, to be described in more detail later, the same marriage could look very different from one laboratory session to the next, depending on how much stress the officer had experienced on each day.

The IHD longitudinal studies made it possible to follow the same couples over several decades. Consider the following examples, based on the first two adult follow-ups around 1960 and the early 1970s (Skolnick, 1981).

Seen in 1960, when they were in their early 30s, the marriage of Jack and Ellen did not look promising. Jack was an aloof husband and uninvolved father. Ellen was overwhelmed by caring for three small children. She had a variety of physical ailments, and needed a steady dose of tranquilizers to calm her anxieties. Ten years later, however, she was in good health and enjoying life. She and Jack had become a warm, loving couple.

Martin and Julia were a happily married couple in 1960. They had two children they adored, an active social life, and were fixing up a new home they had bought. Martin was looking forward to a new business venture. A decade later, Martin had developed a severe drinking problem that had disrupted every aspect of their relationship. Thinking seriously about divorce, Julia said it all had started when the business had started to fail and ultimately went bankrupt.

Perhaps the most striking impression from following these marriages through long periods of time is the great potential for change in intimate relationships. Those early interviews suggest that many couples had what would today be called "dysfunctional" marriages. At the time, it seemed to the spouses, as well as to the interviewers, that the source of the trouble was psychological problems in the husband or wife or both, or else that they were incompatible.

For some couples, such explanations were valid: at later interviews the same emotional or personality difficulties were clear. Some people, however, had divorced and married again to people with whom they were a better fit. One man who had seemed emotionally immature all his life finally found happiness in his third marriage.

He married a younger woman who was both nurturing to him and yet a "psychological age mate," as he put it.

Although close to a third of the IHD marriages eventually did end in divorce, all the IHD couples were married years before the divorce revolution of the 1970s made divorce legally easier to obtain, as well as more common and socially acceptable. Many unhappy couples remained married long enough to outgrow their earlier difficulties, or advance past the circumstances that were causing the difficulties in the first place. Viewed from a later time, marital distress at one period or stage in life seemed to be rooted in situational factors: problems at work, trouble with in-laws or money, bad housing, or too many babies too close together. In the midst of these strains, however, it was easy to blame problems on a husband's or a wife's basic character. Only later, when the situation had changed, did it seem that there was nothing inherently wrong with the couple's relationship.

The Critical Events of a Marriage May Not Be inside the Marriage

The longitudinal data, as noted earlier, revealed a striking amount of change for better or worse depending on a large variety of life circumstances. While the impact of such external factors remains a relatively understudied source of marital distress, there has been growing interest in the impact of work and working conditions—especially job stress—on family life. One of the most stressful occupations, police work, also suffers from very high rates of divorce, domestic violence, and alcoholism. In 1997, Robert Levenson and I took part in collaboration between the University of California and a West Coast urban police department (Levenson, Roberts, and Bellows, 1998; Skolnick, 1998). We focused on job stress and marriage. This was a small, exploratory study, using too few couples—eleven—for statistical analysis, but it yielded some striking preliminary findings.

Briefly, Levenson's part of the study looked at the impact of stress on couple interaction in the laboratory. His procedures called for each spouse to keep a stress diary every day for 30 days. Once a week for four weeks, the couples came to the laboratory at the end of the work day, after eight hours of being apart. Their interaction was videotaped, and physiological responses of each spouse were monitored continuously.

In my part of the project, we used an adaptation of the IHD clinical interview with officers and their wives in their homes. (The sample did not include female officers or police couples.) The aim was to examine their perceptions of police work and its impact on their marriages, their general life circumstances, and the sources of stress and support in their lives. I discovered that these officers and their wives were making heroic efforts to do well in their work and family lives against enormous odds. The obvious dangers and disasters police must deal with are only part of the story; sleep deprivation, frustration with the department bureaucracy, and inadequate equipment were some of the other factors adding up to an enormous stress.

In spite of their difficult lives, these couples seemed to have good, well-functioning marriages, at home and in the laboratory, except on high stress days. Levenson's study was able to examine the direct effects of different levels of stress on the face-to-face interaction of these couples—something that had not been done before. The findings were striking. Variations in the husband's work stress had a marked impact on both couple interaction and the physiological indicators of emotional arousal.

More surprising, it was not just the police officer who showed evidence of stress, but the partner as well. Even before either partner had said a word, while they were just sitting quietly, both the officer and the spouse showed signs of physiological arousal. In particular, there was a kind of "paralysis of the positive emotion system" in both partners (Levenson, Roberts, and Bellows, 1998). Looking at the videotapes, you didn't need the physiological measures to see what was going on. The husband's restless agitation was clear, as was the wife's tense and wary response to it. The wives seemed frozen in their seats, barely able to move. In fact, just watching the couples on videotape is enough to make a viewer also feel tense and uneasy.

Recall that these couples did not look or act this way on the days they were not under high job stress. However, on high stress days, the couples were showing the same warning signs that Gottman and Levenson had found in their earlier studies to be predictors of divorce. The "paralysis of the positive emotion system" means that the "good" aspects of the marriage were unavailable just when they were most needed. Repeated often enough, such moments can strain even a good marriage; they create an emotional climate where tempers can easily flare, hurtful things may be said, and problems go unsolved. Police work may be an extreme example of a high-pressure occupation, but it is far from the only one. "What's the difference between a stressed-out business executive and a stressed-out police officer?" asked a New York columnist not long ago, after a terrible case of domestic violence in a police family. "The officer," he went on, "brings home a loaded gun."

CAN MARRIAGE BE SAVED?

The notion that marriage is a dying institution is remarkably persistent among the American public. Politicians and social critics, particularly conservative ones, insist that divorce, cohabitation, single parenthood, and other recent trends signal moral decline and the unraveling of the social fabric. Some family scholars agree with these pessimistic conclusions. Others argue that marriage and the family are not collapsing but simply becoming more diverse.

A third possibility is that American families are passing through a cultural lag, a difficult in-between period, as they adapt to new social and economic conditions. While a rapidly changing world outside the home has moved towards greater gender equality, the roles of men and women inside the home have changed relatively little. Across the twentieth century, schools, businesses, the professions, and other institutions have become increasingly neutral about gender. Moreover, legal and political trends in modern democracies have undermined the legitimacy of gender and other forms of caste-like inequality, at least in principle.

To be sure, we have not yet achieved full equality. But we have become used to seeing women in the workplace, even in such formerly all-male institutions as the police, the military, the Congress, and the Supreme Court. The family remains the one institution still based on separate and distinct roles for men and women. Despite the vast social and economic changes that have transformed our daily lives, the old gender roles remain deeply rooted in our cultural assumptions and definitions of masculinity and femininity. At the same time, a more equal or "symmetrical" model of marriage is struggling to be born. Surveys show that most Americans, especially young people, favor equal rather than traditional marriage.

But the transition to such a model has been difficult, even for those committed to the idea of equal partnerships. The difficulties of raising children, and men's continuing advantages in the workplace, make it hard for all but the most dedicated couples to live up to their own ideals.

Adding to the difficulties are the economic shifts of recent years—growing economic inequality, the demise of the well-paying blue-collar job, and the end of the stable career of the 1950s "organization man." The long hours and working weeks that have replaced the nine-to-five corporate workplace take their toll on relationships.

Traditionally, marriage has always been linked to economic opportunity—a young man had to be able to support a wife to be considered eligible to marry. The high rates of marriage in the 1950s were sustained in part by rising wages and a relatively low cost of living; the average 30-year-old man could afford to buy an average-priced house for less than 20 percent of his salary. Today, marriage is becoming something of a "luxury item," a form of "having" available mainly to those already enjoying economic advantages (Furstenberg, 1996). The vast majority of low income men and women would like the "luxury" model, but feel they can't afford it.

Inside marriage, conflicts stemming from gender issues have become the leading cause of divorce (Nock, 1999). Studies of couples married since the 1970s reveal the dynamics of these conflicts. Arlie Hochchild, for example, has found that the happiest marriages are those where the husband does his share of the "second shift," the care of home and children. Another recent study shows that today's women also expect their husbands to do their share of the emotional work of marriage—monitoring and talking about the relationship itself; this "marital work ethic" has emerged in middle class couples married since the 1970s, in response to easy and widespread divorce (Hackstaff, 2000).

Dominance is another sore point in many of today's marriages. Gottman and his colleagues (1998) have found that a key factor in predicting marital happiness and divorce is a husband's willingness to accept influence from his wife; but to many men, the loss of dominance in marriage doesn't feel like equality, it feels more like a shift in power that leaves their wives dominant over them. Studies of battered women show that domestic violence may be the extreme form of this common problem—the man's attempt to assert what he sees as his prerogative to dominate and control his partner.

Still, change is happening, even while men lag behind in the gender revolution. Today's men no longer expect to be waited on in the home the way their grandfathers were by their grandmothers. Middle class norms demand a more involved kind of father than those of a generation ago. The sight of a man with a baby in his arms or on his back is no longer unusual.

In sum, marriage today is passing through a difficult transition to a new economy and a new ordering of gender relations. Those who sermonize about "family values" need to recall that the family is also about "bread and butter" issues and back up their words with resources. And while some people believe that equality and stable marriage are incompatible, the evidence seems so far to show the opposite. As one therapist and writer puts it:

> The feminist revolution of this century has provided the most powerful challenge to traditional patterns of marriage. Yet paradoxically, it may have strengthened the institution by giving greater freedom to both partners, and by allowing men to accept some of traditionally female values. (Rubinstein, 1990)

References

Bernard, J. 1972. *The Future of Marriage*. New York: Bantam Books.

Furstenberg, F. 1996. The future of marriage. *American Demographics* (June): 34–40.

Gottman, J. M. and R. W. Levenson. 1992. Marital processes predictive of later dissolution: Behavior, physiology and health. *Journal of Personality and Social Psychology* 63: 221–33.

Gottman, J. M., J. Coan, S. Carrere, and C. Swanson. 1998. Predicting marital happiness and stability from newlywed interactions. *Journal of Marriage and the Family* 60: 5–22.

Hackstaff, K. 2000. *Marriage in a Culture of Divorce*. Boston: Beacon Press.

Levenson, R. W., N. Roberts, and S. Bellows. 1998. Report on police marriage and work stress study. Unpublished paper, University of California, Berkeley.

National Marriage Project. 1999. *Report on Marriage*. Rutgers University.

Nock, S. L. 1999. The problem with marriage. *Society* 36, No. 5 (July/August).

Rubinstein, H. 1990. *The Oxford Book of Marriage*. New York: Oxford University Press.

Skolnick, A. 1981. Married lives: longitudinal perspectives on marriage. In *Present and Past in Middle Life*, edited by D. H. Eichorn, J. A. Clausen, N. Haan, M. P. Honzik, and P. H. Mussen, 269–298. New York: Academic Press.

———. 1993. His and her marriage in longitudinal perspective. In *Feminine/Masculine: Gender and Social Change*. Compendium of Research Summaries. New York: The Rockefeller Foundation.

———. 1998. Sources and processes of police marital stress. Paper presented at National Conference on Community Policing. November. Arlington, VA.

Veroff, J. G., E. Douvan, and R. A. Kulka. 1981. *The Inner American: A Self-Portrait from 1957–1976*. New York: Basic Books.

6

Divorce and Remarriage

Divorce: The "Silent Revolution"

Lawrence M. Friedman

In the first half of the twentieth century . . . [t]he vast majority of divorces were in fact collusive; they resulted from a deal between husband and wife. (Whether the deal was really "consensual"—that is, a bargain between equals, between two people who both wanted a divorce—is . . . another question.) Collusive divorces were, strictly speaking, illegal. . . . But the official law was a living lie. In Illinois, for example, if the court found that the parties colluded, "no divorce shall be decreed," according to the statute. This was . . . standard doctrine. But according to a study published in the 1950s, almost all divorce cases in Illinois were actually collusive—they came about as a result of "agreement by the parties to the divorce as such." The "testimony" in these cases was usually cut and dried. The typical plaintiff complained of cruelty: her husband beat her, slapped her, abused her. As the author of the study remarked sarcastically, the "number of cruel spouses in Chicago . . . who strike their marriage partners in the face exactly twice . . . is remarkable." To back up her story, the plaintiff almost always brought along her mother or a sister or brother.[1]

Deep into the twentieth century, the formal law, stubbornly insisted that an agreement "between husband and wife that suit shall be brought and no defense entered" was unacceptable; and such a case had to be dismissed. The "policy of our law favors marriage, and disfavors divorce," as a New Jersey judge put it in 1910.[2] In Indiana as late as the 1950s, according to the law, if the defendant failed to make an appearance, the judge was supposed to notify the prosecutor, and the duty of the prosecutor was to enter and defend the case; this was also to happen if the judge suspected any sort of collusion. But these were empty strictures. In practice, almost all cases in Indiana were still uncontested, no defense was made by anybody, the prosecutor never intervened, and plaintiffs could have their divorce virtually "for the asking."[3] In New York, where adultery was the only practical grounds for divorce, a bizarre form of collusion was commonplace. The husband would check into a hotel. A woman hired to play his lover would join him in the room. Both of them would take off some or all of their clothes. A study of 500 divorce cases conducted in the 1930s actually counted how often the man was nude (23), in a nightgown (8), in "B.V.D. or underwear (119)" or in pajamas (227). The woman was nude more often (55 times); in a nightgown 126 times; in a "kimono" 68 times. At this point of undress, a maid would arrive with towels, or a bellboy with a telegram. Suddenly, a photographer would burst into the room and take pictures. Then the man would pay the woman; she then thanked him and left. The photographs would be shown in court as "evidence" of adultery.[4] In England, too, adultery was the only grounds for divorce before 1938; and, as in New York, hotel evidence of this phony type was used in many cases.[5] There were occasional scandals and crackdowns, but the system always went back to normal, after some decent interval.

In the nineteenth century, the British government had been less complacent about collusion than the states. Divorce was socially unacceptable, especially for the lower orders. In 1860, only three years after the divorce law was passed, a new statute created the office of the Queen's Proctor. This officer had the duty of sniffing out collusion and protecting the interests of society in divorce cases. The point was to prevent consensual divorce. On the whole, the experiment did not succeed.[6] The rigid class system of the British did provide some support for a tough regime of divorce; but slowly, the same forces that overwhelmed American divorce overwhelmed the British system as well.

What seems clear is that everywhere in the developed world there was a tremendous, pent-up demand for divorce—a powerful force that simply had to find an outlet. Change or reform remained difficult, if not impossible; respectable society (and legislatures frightened of some of their voters) simply did not permit "easy" divorce. The result was the dual system—collusion and migratory divorce. Another outlet for the divorce demand, at least in New York state, was annulment. In New York, the law, as we have seen, was unusually severe, allowing divorce only for adultery. As a result, New York became the annulment capital of the United States. An annulled marriage, legally speaking, never existed. It was dead from the start because of some grave impediment or fraud. In most states, annulments were much less common than divorces. They were used mostly by Roman Catholics, whose church did not recognize divorce. In San Mateo County, California, in the 1950s, 12 percent of the petitions to end a marriage were petitions for annulment; in the period 1890–1910, only 1 or 2 percent of such petitions in Alameda County, California, were petitions for annulment.[7]

But in New York the situation was entirely different. Annulments were exceedingly common. The New York statute allowed annulment of a marriage if the "consent" of one party was "obtained by force, duress, or fraud" or if "one of the parties was physically incapable of entering into the marriage state" or was a "lunatic."[8] There was nothing unusual about this statute. But in most states, the courts interpreted annulment laws rather strictly. Fraud was not easy to prove. Joel Bishop, writing in the late nineteenth century, found annulment cases "inherently" embarrassing (and "not numerous").[9] It is one thing to want to get rid of a spouse, quite another to accuse that spouse of fraud (or even worse, of total impotence or frigidity). In New York, however, the courts stretched the concept of "fraud" almost beyond recognition, and in general they opened up the legal grounds of annulment to an astonishing degree. By 1950, in ten counties in New York, there were more annulments than divorces; for the state as a whole, there were two-thirds as many annulments as decrees of divorce.[10] To be sure, the appellate courts were not always willing to grant annulments in dubious cases. The case law was quite involute and complex.[11] Loretta Coiley Pawloski failed to get an annulment for fraud against her husband, Alex John; she claimed he lied about his name and told her he was "German" when in fact he was Polish. Loretta "did not care much for Polish people." They had been married over twenty years. This "fraud," even if proven, did not "go to the essence" of the marriage contract, said the court.[12]

Still, it says something that Loretta even *thought* she had a chance at annulment. In most states, her claim would have gotten exactly nowhere. And in many other cases, the New York appellate courts were more willing to discover "fraud" and other impediments. In a 1923 case, James Truiano told Florence Booth, a schoolteacher, that he was a U.S. citizen; in fact he was not. The court granted an annulment.[13] And a young man was able to get an annulment in 1935, when he claimed that his (foreign) wife married him only to get his money, as part of a "scheme" of European "nobility" to "inveigle" wealthy Americans into marriage. The man, said the court, was "unaccustomed to dealing with the workings of a shrewd and cunning European mind"; he had been "deceived and defrauded." The marriage was duly wiped off the books.[14] Most annulment cases, one must remember, were never appealed. They began and ended in the trial courts. They were just as consensual as the thousands of divorces in other states. The New York annulment statistics speak for themselves on this point.

Contemporary Chile is another jurisdiction where annulments have been terrifically and abnormally common. Chile, until 2004, was the only major Western country that still did not recognize absolute divorce. (In that year, the legislature finally enacted such a law.)[15] Annulment was an obvious escape hatch. People used all sorts of tricks and stratagems . . . in their quest for an annulment. In both Chile and New York state, the official law said one thing, and the ordinary lower-level courts did something quite different. Both jurisdictions were trapped in a situation of historic stalemate.

The stalemate, however, came to an end in New York, and in the United States in general, in the second half of the twentieth century. Up to that point, official reform was slow and difficult. But underneath, the dual system was simply rotting away. Divorce became more and more common. Its stigma slowly evaporated. As a judge in Chicago put it around 1950, most people thought divorce was nobody's business, except that of the man and woman in question. Getting a divorce was, or should be, like getting a marriage license: a couple was "entitled to a marriage license for a certain fee" and a blood test, and nothing else. Why not make getting a divorce equally easy? This judge thought "Hollywood" was to blame for the change in attitudes, for the loss of "scandal and shame."[16] This was surely giving Hollywood too much credit (or blame). Movie stars got divorces, of course, but the movies themselves were quite skittish on the subject; indeed, for a while in the 1930s and 1940s they almost never dealt with divorce at all.[17] The judge might even have been somewhat off base in his reading of general public opinion. But there is no doubt that the winds were shifting; even the official law began to evolve, though in a rather gingerly way. New Mexico was bolder than most states: from

1933 on, its divorce statute specifically listed "incompatibility" as grounds for divorce.[18] "Incompatibility" means basically that two people do not and cannot get along. As far as traditional divorce law was concerned, this was rank heresy.

New Mexico was unusual. But in a fair number of states, the law began to ease the path to divorce in a different way. Divorce became available, even without "grounds," if the couple had been separated for a specific number of years—from two to ten, depending on the state. By 1950, about twenty states had a provision of this sort. In Arizona, Idaho, Kentucky, and Wisconsin, the period was five years; in Rhode Island, it was ten; in Arkansas and Nevada, it was three years; in Louisiana and North Carolina, two years.[19] These statutes, too, were heretical. They plainly recognized that some marriages were dead and gone. It was only decent to give them a proper burial and let people get on with their lives. In fact, in many of these states few couples took advantage of this device. Why wait two, five or ten years when a few harmless lies could bring about a divorce right away?[20]

In many states, a spouse was entitled to a divorce if the other spouse had become "incurably insane" or the like. Sometimes the statute required actual confinement in an insane asylum—for five years in Vermont and Kansas.[21] A spouse also commonly had the right to a divorce if the other spouse was in prison on a felony charge. These seem fairly obvious grounds; but in fact they contradicted the theory of traditional marriage—the promise to cleave together in sickness and in health; in good times and in bad. Cancer or heart disease were never grounds for divorce. Why then insanity? or imprisonment, for a crime not committed against the spouse? Neither of these was technically desertion. But from the standpoint of the sane spouse, or the spouse not in prison, the marriage was a hollow shell and a daily frustration.

There were a few cracks in the armor at the level of appellate courts. In California, a 1952 case, *De Burgh v. De Burgh*,[22] was an important sign of oncoming change. Daisy and Albert De Burgh were suffering through what was obviously a rotten marriage. Albert beat her, bragged about his other women, was often drunk, was lavish with waiters but stingy with Daisy. This was her story. His story was different. He claimed she was spreading lies about him; she was trying to ruin him in business and wreck his reputation, sending letters to partners and associates, accusing him of "dishonesty and homosexuality." Under standard legal doctrine, if both parties were cruel or otherwise at fault, there could be no divorce. The Superior Court, accordingly, denied the divorce and dismissed the case. The California Supreme Court reversed. The family, wrote Justice Roger Traynor, "is the core of our society," and the state should "foster and preserve marriage." But when a marriage "has failed, and the family has ceased to be a unit," the couple should be able to end it through divorce. The evidence in the case showed a "total and irremedial breakdown of the marriage." Traynor sent the case back to trial; the trial judge was instructed to "determine whether the legitimate objects of matrimony have been destroyed" and whether the marriage could be "saved." Theoretically, the judge had the power to deny the divorce; but Traynor's words made that very unlikely.

In the last third of the twentieth century, what Herbert Jacob has called a "silent revolution" finally destroyed the dual system.[23] The "silent revolution" refers to the passage of no-fault divorce laws. Jacob called this revolution a "silent" one because, though it seemed like a radical change, it was accomplished with little discussion and even less controversy. It was as if no-fault crept into the law like a thief in the night. Technocrats drafted the laws, and they were adopted almost without serious debate. A system that had lasted a century vanished in the twinkling of an eye.

Socially, if not legally, the old system had simply rotted away. In the age of individualism and the sexual revolution, in the age of the enthronement of choice, people felt there was no point saving marriages that no longer satisfied either husband or wife or both. They had a right to a divorce whenever the marriage "just didn't work out." Demand for recognition of this social fact finally overwhelmed the forces that held traditional views. And, of course, nobody ever really liked the collusive system. It was corrupt, dirty, and expensive. It demeaned everybody involved in the process—lawyers, judges, and the parties to the divorce themselves.

What came out of California was the so-called no-fault divorce. No-fault divorce is not consensual divorce; it goes far beyond that. It is really unilateral divorce, divorce at will, divorce when either partner, husband or wife, wants a divorce and asks for it. Under a no-fault system, there are absolutely no defenses to an action for divorce. There are no longer any "grounds" for divorce. No-fault reconstructs divorce in the image of marriage; marriage and divorce become parallel, legally speaking. For a marriage to take place, two people have to agree to get married. Breach of promise has been abolished. Both the man and the woman have a veto, then; each one has a right to back out of marriage, up to the very moment when someone pronounces them man and wife. In movie after movie—*The Graduate* is one of the best known—somebody in fact does pull out in the very shadow of the altar. Under no-fault, this veto power continues after marriage. Either partner can decide if the marriage goes on or comes to an end. Either one can break the marriage off, at any time, for any reason—or for no reason at all. This is the practical meaning of a no-fault system—the way it actually operates.

The first no-fault divorce law took effect in California in 1970. The old "grounds" for divorce were eliminated, except for two: total insanity, and "irreconcilable differences, which have caused the irremediable breakdown of the marriage."[24] Interestingly, the experts and jurists who wrote the reports and drafted the law never intended a no-fault system. They wanted to get rid of the old dual system; they wanted to clean house, eliminate hypocrisy and fraud, end the dirty business of collusion, and allow consensual divorce— divorce by mutual agreement. This was already the living law, and they wanted to make it official. They never intended to make divorce easy or automatic, and certainly not unilateral. Marriages were a good thing, they felt; and if at all possible, marriages should be saved. They wanted, for example, a system of marriage counseling. They wanted the courts to mend sick marriages and, if possible, cure them. Their notion was to give more power and resources to family courts; couples in trouble could find help, advice, and perhaps a certain amount of therapy.[25] Herma Hill Kay, a scholar and expert in family law active in the reform movement, suggested remodeling family court in the image of juvenile court. Husband and wife would meet with a counselor; they would explore together whether the marriage could be saved. An important role would be played by "professional caseworkers," psychiatrists, and "experienced supervisors." There would be no "coercion." Ultimately, the court would decide whether "the legitimate objects of matrimony have been destroyed."[26] None of Kay's proposals, as it turned out, would actually stir into life.

Still, the original California law, taken literally, contemplated something other than what actually happened. The law asked a question of fact: are there "irreconcilable differences," and has the marriage completely broken down? Presumably, it would be up to a judge to decide this factual question. But almost immediately the law came to mean something radically different. It took on a life of its own. Divorce became simply automatic. Judges never inquired into reasons; they never actually asked whether a marriage had "irretrievably broken down," or broken down at all. They merely signed the papers. What is more, the no-fault "revolution" swept the country. State after state adopted a no-fault statute—or, more accurately, a statute that turned out to mean no-fault. The details varied from state to state, but almost everywhere no-fault made its mark on the statute book. Some states, like California, were "pure" no-fault states—in Rhode Island, for example, divorce was to be "decreed, irrespective of the fault of either party, on the ground of irreconcilable differences which have caused the irremediable breakdown of the marriage."[27] In some states, the legislature simply added no-fault to the list of "grounds," even though this was in a way illogical, since no-fault meant that the grounds were no longer important.[28] Utah and Tennessee, for example, added "irreconcilable differences" to their list. In Ohio, what was added was "incompatibility, unless denied by either party."[29] But in most states, divorce became automatic, just as in California. Either party could end the marriage. Judges never did any looking, questioning, or counseling. They became a rubber stamp, nothing more.

To be sure, tough issues of property rights and custody of children remained to plague family law. Many hotly contested cases turned on these issues. They provide plenty of business for divorce lawyers. But the divorce itself was no longer something to fight and contest. No-fault is the epitome of what used to be called "easy" divorce. In fact, divorce is almost never easy, psychologically speaking. But no-fault made the legal part of it much less painful—and cheaper, too. This is especially true if the duration of the marriage was short, no children were born, and there either was no money to divide or no argument about how to divide it. Divorce can even be, for some people, a do-it-yourself project. Nowadays one can buy books that tell readers how to get rid of a spouse in ten easy lessons, without paying for the time and services of a lawyer.

Changes in sexual mores, in the social meaning of marriage and divorce, and in the relationship of men and women underlay the no-fault movement. These factors were more or less common to all developed countries. All of them have moved in the same direction. Some countries in Europe and Latin America—those that are strongly Catholic by tradition—resisted divorce altogether. Italy, Spain, and Ireland for a long time had no laws allowing absolute divorce at all (they did recognize legal separation, however). Gordon Ireland and Jesus de Galindez surveyed divorce laws in the countries of the Western hemisphere just after the end of the Second World War.[30] At that time, there was still no such thing as absolute divorce in Argentina, Brazil, Chile, Colombia, and Paraguay. Divorce had had a long history in some of the republics of Latin America; in others it had come only later—in Uruguay, for example, in 1907, and in Bolivia only in 1932. With the exception of Chile (where absolute divorce, as we saw, was not legally available until 2004), every Latin American country by 2000 had provisions for breaking the bonds of matrimony. Brazil adopted a divorce law in 1977. Strongly Catholic countries in Europe, too, eventually came to adopt divorce laws, though often in the teeth of furious opposition. Italy began to allow divorce in 1970; Spain did so in 1981, after the end of the Franco regime. Divorce is now available in Ireland as well.

Moreover, many countries have modified their laws along paths roughly similar to that of the United States. Brazil, as mentioned, had no divorce at all until 1977; and its first divorce law was quite restrictive (for example, no one was allowed to get divorced twice). In 1992, however, a more modern, consensual divorce law was enacted.[31] In some countries—France, for example—divorce by mutual consent has become available, along with a no-fault system (if the couple had a long-time separation). Germany in the late 1970s adopted a no-fault system; divorce is available whenever the marriage has simply broken down. Sweden, too, has a no-fault system.[32] Most countries have not gone to the same extreme as the United States. But even so conservative a state as Switzerland has liberalized its divorce laws. A new law, in force as of 2000, allowed for divorce by mutual agreement of the parties; and either party can ask for divorce after four years of separation. The law in Austria is quite similar: a couple can get a divorce after six months of separation, if both declare that their marriage has broken down.[33] In England, despite waves of reform, it is still the law as of 2003 that a divorce is allowed only if a marriage has "irretrievably" broken down. In practice, however, as Stephen Cretney has put it, "divorce is readily and quickly available if both parties agree"; and even if one does not, the marriage is basically over. After all, there is no point "denying that the marriage has broken down if one party firmly asserts that it has."[34] Divorce rates have also risen in almost all Western countries. The ropes that bind married people together have gotten weaker; for millions, they are altogether gone.

Notes

1. Maxine B. Virtue, *Family Cases in Court* (1956), pp. 90–91.
2. The case is *Sheehan v. Sheehen*, 77, N. J. Eq. 411, 77 A. 1063 (Ct. of Chancery of N. J., 1910).
3. Virtue, *Family Cases*, pp. 118, 140.
4. The study is reported in a note, "Collusive and Consensual Divorce and the New York Anomaly," *Col. L. Rev.* 36:1121, 1131 (1936); see Lawrence M. Friedman, "A Dead Language: Divorce Law and Practice before No-Fault," *Va. L. Rev.* 86:1497, 1512–1513 (2000).
5. Colin S. Gibson, *Dissolving Wedlock* (1994), pp. 96–97.
6. On the Queen's Proctor, see Wendie Ellen Schneider, "Secrets and Lies: The Queen's Proctor and Judicial Investigation of Party-Controlled Narratives," *Law and Social Inquiry* 27:449 (2002). The situation in Canada in the first part of the twentieth century was also complex. There was probably plenty of collusion, but the courts were less willing to close their eyes to it. As in England, the "king's proctor" was an official who acted on behalf of the state in divorce cases, snooping about to see if there was conniving or colluding. In Nova Scotia, this official was called a "watching counsel." These busybodies appear to have been at least somewhat effective. See James G. Snell, *In the Shadow of the Law: Divorce in Canada, 1900–1939* (1991), pp. 104–106.
7. I am indebted to Albert Lopez for the figures on San Mateo County. For Alameda County, see Joanna Grossman and Chris Guthrie, "The Road Less Taken: Annulment at the Turn of the Century," *Am. J. of Legal History* 40:307 (1996).
8. *Thompson's Laws of New York* (1939), Part 2, N.Y. Civil Practice Act, sec. 1137, 1139, 1141.
9. Bishop, *New Commentaries*, vol. 1, p. 193.
10. Paul H. Jacobson, *American Marriage and Divorce* (1959), p. 113.
11. See William E. Nelson, *The Legalist Reformation: Law, Politics, and Ideology in New York, 1920–1980* (2001), pp. 51–54, 231–236.
12. *Pawloski v. Pawloski*, 65 N.Y.S. 2d 413 (Sup. Ct., Cayuga County, 1946).
13. *Truiano v. Truiano*, 121 Misc. Rep. 635, 201 N.Y.S. 573 (Sup. Ct., Special Term, Warren County, 1923). In fairness to Florence, it has to be said that under a federal statute at the time of the marriage, she would have lost her citizenship (and taken on her husband's citizenship). This would have cost her job. After the couple separated, the law was changed, in 1922, under the

Married Women's Citizenship Act, 42 Stat. 1021 (act of Sept. 12, 1922). This was in effect at the time of the Truiano annulment case; but this fact, said the court, "cannot relieve defendant of the fraud, or cause denial to the plaintiff of the relief which she asks," since she would not have married James had she known of his blemish.

14. *Ryan v. Ryan*, 156 Misc. 251, 281 N.Y.S. 709 (Sup. Ct., Spec. Term, N.Y. County, 1935).
15. Jen Ross, "Separate Ways: Divorce to Become Legal," *Washington Post*, Mar. 30, 2004, p. C1. Malta apparently still does not allow absolute divorce.
16. Cited in Virtue, *Family Cases*, pp. 145–146.
17. Michael Asimow, "Divorce in the Movies: From the Hays Code to *Kramer vs. Kramer*," *Legal Studies Forum* 24: 221 (2000).
18. Act of March 3, 1933, ch. 62, sec. 1.
19. J. Herbie DiFonzo, *Beneath the Fault Line: The Popular and Legal Culture of Divorce in Twentieth-Century America* (1997), pp. 78–79.
20. Friedman, "A Dead Language," p. 1497.
21. Vt. Laws 1933, ch. 140, sec. 3117; Gen'l Stats. Kansas 1935, sec. 60–1501 (11).
22. 39 Cal. 2d 858, 250 P 2d 598 (1952).
23. Herbert Jacob, *Silent Revolution: The Transformation of Divorce Law in the United States* (1988).
24. Cal. Civ. Code, sec. 4506.
25. See DiFonzo, *Beneath the Fault Line*, pp. 112–137.
26. Herma Hill Kay, "A Family Court: The California Proposal," *Cal. L. Rev.* 56:1205, 1230 (1968).
27. Rhode Island Rev. Stats., sec. 15-5-3.1.
28. Jacob, *Silent Revolution*, p. 102.
29. Utah Code Ann. (1998), sec. 30-3-1; Tenn. Code sec. 36-4-101. Ohio Rev. Code (2000), sec. 3105.01.
30. Gordon Ireland and Jesus de Galindez, *Divorce in the Americas* (1947).
31. I am indebted to Eliane B. Junqueiro for this information about Brazil. See also Eliane B. Junqueiro, "Brazil: The Road of Conflict Bound for Total Justice," in Lawrence M. Friedman and Rogelio Perez-Perdomo, eds., *Legal Culture in the Age of Globalization: Latin America and Latin Europe* (2003), pp. 64, 74–75.
32. Mary Ann Glendon, *Abortion and Divorce in Western Law. American Failures, European Challenges* (1987), pp. 71–76.
33. For Switzerland, see Andrea Büchler, "Family Law in Switzerland: Recent Reforms and Future Issues—an Overview," *European J. of Law Reform* 3: 275, 279 (2001); for Austria, see Monika Hinteregger, "The Austrian Matrimonial Law—a Patchwork Pattern of History," *European J. of Law Reform* 3:199, 212 (2001).
34. Stephen Cretney, *Family Law in the Twentieth Century: A History* (2003), p. 391.

■ READING 12

Divorce in Research vs. Divorce in Media

Virginia E. Rutter

The U.S. divorce rate did not start increasing in the 1960s. Our divorce statistics began to be recorded in 1880, and starting then, our rate of divorce increased steadily for the next 80 years (Ruggles 1997). It then doubled between 1960 and 1980. By the end of that period, about half of marriages ended in divorce. Since 1980, our 50 percent divorce rate has leveled off, and we haven't seen much change (Goldstein 1999).

Divorce, then, is a fixture in family life—and a 'problem' to be understood, interpreted, analyzed, and fixed (Coltrane & Adams 2003). But what exactly is the problem? A better understanding of divorce—and divorce research—clarifies the reasoning behind making a 'case for divorce'. By extension, this understanding informs us about the realities faced by contemporary families. Some perceptions of divorce as a problem emerge because research fails to ask a simple question: Divorce is a problem, but compared to what?

Put another way, the case for divorce asks: Are there some cases where divorce is a *better* outcome than remaining married? Using research developments from three distinct time periods, this paper demonstrates that research on the impact on adults and children points to yes. These three episodes also provide an opportunity to understand *why* 'a case for divorce' is being made. Each of these three episodes involves paired research results. Studies that include a comparison group (that analytically represents that divorce is a choice made most often in already bad circumstances) are paired in each of three cases with studies that do not provide a comparison. The discussion of the three episodes includes description of media coverage of the work.

A second, related question is: Do we have reasons why we value divorce, as part of our liberal democracy? The history of divorce goes hand in hand with our history of individual rights that have improved the status of women, minorities, workers, and people without property throughout our history. Since the shift in divorce laws in the 1960s and 1970s to allow unilateral divorce ('no-fault divorce') in the United States, the rate of suicide among wives, domestic violence, and spousal homicide have declined (Stevenson & Wolfers 2006). Meanwhile, part and parcel with declining fertility rates in the United States, the number of children involved in any given divorce has gone from 1.34 children to less than 1 child per divorce (Cowen 2007). Hence, there is a decline in the impact of any given divorce on children. These data do suggest that divorce is associated with outcomes that we value in a liberal democracy.

DIVORCE RESEARCH: TWO THEMES

In research and public conversations, researchers and journalists have earnestly parsed the causes and consequences of divorce in light of the hastened growth of divorce between 1960 and 1980. Researchers find that divorce's impact depends on what the comparison is: compared to a happy marriage, divorce is associated with many disadvantages for the divorced couple and their children; compared to a harsh marriage, however, the research generally shows that divorce has benefits. Meanwhile, policy makers and general audiences alike get their information about divorce research via the news media, where the negative consequences of divorce tend to be exaggerated, especially when comparisons are neglected. At least some of the time, this neglect is advanced by special interest groups seeking to promote a conservative family agenda. Over the past 20 years, U.S. news coverage of divorce illustrates two key intertwined topics: moral entrepreneurship using divorce as an issue and divorce research using (or not) careful methods of comparison. Three cases discussed below (in 1988–1989, 2002–2004, and 2008) make the case.

Moral Entrepreneurs

What information about divorce enters into popular awareness? Over the years, when research results produce apparently conflicting results, the more alarming (and simpler) results consistently get more ink. In the context of divorce research, sociologists Scott Coltrane and Michele Adams (2003) have argued that *moral entrepreneurs* act to heighten collective anxiety in order to promote 'family values' and their more traditional gender norms.

Moral entrepreneurs (Becker 1973) seek to adopt or maintain a norm or tradition. Enterprising opinion leaders seek to shape public awareness about the 'case against divorce' by making *knowledge claims* grounded in a version of social science that, especially in the most conservative cases, reinforces traditional, two-parent, in-tact, biologically related families. A knowledge claim is a statement that we know something is a *fact*. Where research shows that divorce harms children or women or the economy, the case *seems* to be clear. In the cases presented here, the claims against divorce are made based on research that fails to make reasonable comparisons or to provide representative samples.

Organizations–ranging from the more moderate Institute for American Values to the more conservative Heritage Foundation—have skillfully spread the word about research—the kind that supports their concerns about the way they believe that divorce has contributed to the decay of American family life. From the perspective of moral entrepreneurship, worry is good for business—and consistent with a moral agenda that questions changes in family organization. Family historian Steven Mintz (2004) describes case after case of Americans' fondness for the story of decay, and the penchant for worry about divorce is like hand wringing about teen sexuality, delinquency, the corrupting force of television, the problem of working mothers, the problem of mothers not working, etc. Indeed, worry about divorce is not new. As Mintz describes, moral entrepreneurs raved about the scourge of divorce, for example, from 1890 to 1920.

Research Methods: Look for Comparison Groups

Scientists reviewing research will always ask whether or not it makes a logical and reasonable comparison. When researchers examine, 'divorce compared to what?' they are searching for *selection bias* or preceding factors that may explain a given set of results. People who end up divorcing may be different from people who remain married and it may be these pre-marriage differences between the two groups—and not divorce itself—that explain differences in health and mental health outcomes after divorce. This type of selection bias may influence results and the interpretation of results. In diverse studies, several factors suggest that the divorced group is, indeed, already different from the stably married group. For example, divorced couples are younger in age at first marriage, more likely to be living in poverty, and less likely to have a college degree. Researchers must also answer the question about how whether and, if so, how, divorce *causes* problems for adults or their children?

1988–2008: DUELING DIVORCE COVERAGE

Three episodes of divorce research in the news—in 1988–1989, 2002–2004, and 2008—exemplify themes of *moral entrepreneurship* and *research issues with* they were civil. Hetherington was able to analyze the well-being of children in extremely distressed married families versus children of divorce and children in harmonious, married families. By adding comparisons about the level of distress in all the families, she observed that children in harmonious, married families fared better than children in divorced families, *and* in distressed married families. By making comparisons based on the quality of the intact marriages in her study, she was able to make an important distinction: The worst kind of family for a child to be raised in, in terms of mental health and behavior, was a *distressed, married* family (Hetherington 1999).

Several key pieces of research extended Hetherington's results by using comparison groups and a prospective design. In 1991, demographer Andrew Cherlin and colleagues wrote about longitudinal studies in Great Britain and the United States in the journal *Science*. The studies included data from parents, children, and teachers over time. At the first time point, age 7, all the children's parents were married. Over the study period, some went on to divorce, and some did not. Cherlin confirmed Hetherington's findings: while about 10 percent of children overall were at risk for adjustment and mental health problems, children of divorce were at 20–25 percent at risk for problems.

Cherlin also found that the difference between the children of divorce versus stable marriages existed *prior* to the divorce. These were *predisruption effects*, a term that highlights that parents who end up divorcing (but are not yet divorced) are different from parents who don't end up divorcing. They relate to each other differently, they relate to their children differently, and their children relate to them differently. Cherlin had identified selection bias, or a case of selection into divorce:

In 1998, Cherlin and colleagues offered an update on their continuing research, which modified his conclusions. Respondents analyzed in the 1991 study had gotten older, so he had more information. While the 1991 paper highlighted predisruption effects, this one reported that in addition, there were *postdisruption* effects (negative effects after the divorce) that accumulated and made life more difficult for children of divorce. Financial hardship and the loss of paternal involvement were key culprits. He called this phenomenon the 'cascade of negative life events', and emphasized, as he had back in 1991, the importance of social and institutional supports for children in disrupted and remarried families.

Starting with Hetherington in the 1980s, and following through Cherlin's parallel work in the 1990s, research designs that included comparison groups helped bring to light three points: first, using a population-based rather than a clinical sample provided a rate of distress among children of divorce that exemplified their *resilience:* approximately 80 percent were doing well, versus 90 percent of children in the general population. Second, difficulties—*pre-disruption effects*—found in longitudinal, prospective studies, meant that children in families where their parents were headed for divorce were having troubles prior to the break-up. *Postdisruption effects*—and the cascade of negative life events—also played a role and suggested that institutions and communities can do more to support these families. Third, severely distressed marriages were more damaging to children than divorces. This last point foreshadowed the results in the studies of adults that I describe in the next section.

At the same time, the 'adult child of divorce' research remained popular in mainstream reporting. This trope showed the robustness of uncertainty about the impact of divorce and the extensiveness of anxiety about changes to family life, of which divorce was a part. (It also helped to create it.) Above all, such discourse represented a missed opportunity for people to know in greater detail where the hazards of divorce actually lie.

DOES DIVORCE MAKE YOU HAPPY?

The question of well-being among adults who divorce provides additional evidence for the case for divorce—and the case for research methods.

In 2002, the Institute for American Values released a paper by Linda Waite, a demographer at the University of Chicago, and several of her colleagues. The paper was titled, 'Does Divorce Make You Happy?' Around that time, other, similar research, 'The Case for Divorce: Under What Conditions Is Divorce Beneficial and for Whom?' (Rutter 2004), also sought to examine emotional consequences of divorcing versus staying married.

Both researchers asked: how does people's level of well-being change when they divorce (versus when they stay married)? Both projects relied on the same data set; they both used a longitudinal design where all subjects were married at the first time point, and some of them went on to divorce by the second time point. The results, however, were divergent. According to Rutter, adults who exited unhappy marriages were less depressed than those who stayed. According to Waite, there were no differences in happiness between those who stayed married and those who divorced.

In order to understand the divergence of these results, we can examine the research methods. The overarching research question is: 'divorce, compared to what?' (Or: is there a *selection bias?*) Were divorced individuals compared to people staying in a happy marriage? Were the divorced compared to those staying in a stressed-out marriage? One difference between Rutter's and Waite's studies was that Rutter used a more stringent measure of marital distress that was more likely to identify which couples were more likely candidates for divorce. Rutter also took severe domestic violence into account and measured depression rather than 'happiness'.

These distinctions—whether the marriage is in serious distress, whether respondents have debilitating emotional problems—made a difference.[1] When comparing how people in a truly distressed marriage fare compared to divorced people, the divorced were better off (less depressed). Rutter's additional statistical tests (which accounted for 'fixed effects', discussed below) confirmed that marital distress, not other factors, accounted for the differences in depression between the married and divorced groups.

More recent research has examined how the accumulation of marital transitions—a divorce, a cohabitation, a break up, perhaps a remarriage—may be an additional important way to examine the impact of divorce on adults. The approach is to examine 'relationship trajectories'. Meadows and colleagues (2008) examined the consequence of such transitions for women who started as single mothers, and found that women who face continuous instability—rather than a single transition—have worse health. Such research allows for even more complexity, and requires that we compare higher levels of disruption with lower levels of disruption, including divorce, in parents' and children's life stories.

Why Marital Quality Matters

Why does marital quality make a difference? The benefits of marriage accrue only to people in happy and well-functioning marriages. For example, studies on the 'psychophysiology of marriage' show that when men and women are in distressed marriages—with, for example, contempt, criticism, defensiveness, stonewalling—their immune systems decline over time (Gottman 1994; Kiekolt-Glaser et al. 1988; Robles & Kiekolt-Glaser 2003). These people are less healthy and less happy. Troubled marriages have immediate costs; they also have downstream health costs.

When researchers measure marital distress in terms of level of conflict, or they use multiple measures of distress, they find that divorce is a relief to those couples. This parallels what Hetherington found for children: that divorce is better than living in a high-conflict family. It is easy enough to ask, 'how was marital distress measured?' in order to learn whether a measure of general sentiment that captures more transient feelings of satisfaction was used, or whether a measure of serious distress or conflict, which tends to tell us which couples would be 'candidates' for divorce if they considered divorce an option, was used.

On Happiness

The Waite and Rutter studies had in common looking at the personal costs of divorcing. While Waite measured 'happiness', Rutter's outcome measure was 'depression'. Does it matter how we specify 'personal well-being'? In brief, the answer is yes. While happiness and depression are correlated (van Hemert et al. 2002), there is a difference. Out of hundreds of correlational studies catalogued in the World Database of Happiness (Veenhoven 2004), there are scarcely any gender differences in happiness. Nor does happiness have the major correlates to race or poverty that have been well established for depression.

All these differences suggest that 'happiness' is measuring something psychologically different from 'distress' or 'depression'. The societal implications are quite different between these two measures: unhappy people are not usually functionally impaired; depression, however, involves costs in terms of lost wages, productivity, and negative impact on children (Greenberg et al. 1993a, b).

For media, Waite's study had sufficient scientific authority. Reporters, such as those at *USA Today* and the Today Show, covered the results. The news coverage 'punchline': divorce isn't going to make you any happier, so stay married! But other studies showed that the case for divorce is more complex. Such coverage helps sustain public 'uncertainty' related to any case for divorce.

WHERE'S THE COMPARISON GROUP? REDUX

In April 2008, the questions about the impact of divorce and its costs continued to be alive and well: Two studies were released the very same week on the topic. What, these studies asked, is the impact of divorce? A research brief from the researchers' think-tank Council on Contemporary Families (2008)[2] was based on demographer Allen Li's Rand Corporation working paper (Li 2007). The other paper by economist Ben Scafidi was released by the Institute for American Values (Scafidi 2008). Li's paper pertained to the emotional impact of divorce on children, while Scafidi's paper addressed the economic impact of divorce across America. Comparing these papers, we can examine the sponsors, the media coverage, and the research content of the work.

The results were completely divergent. Li asked, what is the impact of divorce on children? He found that divorce itself does not explain the difference we see between children with divorced versus married parents. Yes, he found differences between the two groups (on average)—just as researchers had been finding since the 1980s. With increasingly refined research techniques, however, Li was able to show that *selection bias* accounts for the difference.

The technique included testing for 'fixed effects'. 'Fixed effects' refers to time-invariant characteristics of individuals that may be correlated with both the outcomes of interest (psychological-well-being, for example) and explanatory variables in the statistical model (divorce, for example) producing biased results. Longitudinal data—multiple observations on the same individual over time—can allow researchers to control for these effects. Fixed-effects models test whether there are aspects of the individuals that are not measured explicitly but that can account for results. This method helped to reveal that the children in Li's study whose parents ended up divorcing were getting a different kind of parenting all along the way than the children whose parents stayed married.

Meanwhile, Scafidi asked, what does divorce cost the general public? By his calculations, divorce—plus single parenthood—cost taxpayers 112 billion dollars. To calculate this, he assumed that divorce and single parenthood *cause* poverty. In other words, he neglected the notion that selection bias could play a role in who ends up as a single parent or divorced. But, in a 2002 report, economist Nancy Folbre and historian Stephanie Coontz were among many who examined the problems with making this assumption (Folbre and Coontz 2002). While there is a correlation between single parenthood and poverty, they explained, the correlation does not imply that single parenthood *causes* poverty. *Causation* is complex and challenging to establish, but the evidence for causality going in the other direction—that poverty *causes* or precedes single parenthood is to many minds a lot stronger. As Stevenson and Wolfers (in Li 2008) point out, Scafidi neglected comparisons in another way as well: while some women end up losing financially following divorce, others actually *gain*. According to Ananat and Michael 2008 (cited by Stevenson & Wolfers), the gains actually *exceed* the losses. Scafidi did not include these economic gains in his calculations.

Li's and Scafidi's results were divergent because of their fundamental differences in thinking about 'what causes what?' While Li's article asks, divorce, *compared to what?*, Scafidi did not assess the costs of divorce relative to, for example, remaining in a distressed, tumultuous, or violent family situation. Scafidi didn't test the assumption that divorce (and single parenthood) cause economic problems. He assumed that.

Li's results were not isolated. Like Li, other researchers continue to find selection bias accounts for some if not all of the differences between children whose parents divorce and those who don't. For example, Fomby and Cherlin (2007) found that selection effects—the characteristics of the mother that precede the divorce—helped explain the reduced cognitive outcomes for children of divorce. They also found that the divorce itself, rather than just selection bias or pre-disruption effects, was associated with behavioral problems sometimes seen in children of divorce. Just as research on relationship trajectories may help us understand in finer detail how and when divorce is difficult on adults, this same promising line of research can further examine the postdisruption effects of divorce on children: children exposed to multiple transitions—a divorce, then a cohabitation and break up, then perhaps another marriage—may be at elevated risk relative to children exposed only to one transition. In a study that focuses on single parents, Osborne and McLanahan (2007) found that the accumulation of mother's relationship transitions adds to children's troubles.[3]

How were the Li and Scafidi articles covered? Both studies were reported in *USA Today*. While Scafidi received more coverage (such as the *Associated Press*, *Newsweek*, the *Washington Times*, the *Wall Street Journal*) than Li did, still a review of the coverage shows us that news coverage may be turning a bit.

Another change over the past 20 years of discussing results of divorce research also looks promising: when searching the blogosphere on the most recent divorce research, many researchers, scientists, and citizens commented on the problematic research methods of Scafidi and the case of 'advocacy science' (or 'moral entrepreneurship'). Granted, the blogosphere also included many discussions applauding Scafidi, and others castigating Li. Thus, the Internet offers much opportunity for people to speak out and have a dialogue about moral entrepreneurship and science on the one hand, and research methods on the other. While popular dialogue on the Internet is promising for telling a more complicated story of the case for divorce, now more than ever we need citizens who can ask whether they are reading a case of moral entrepreneurship and who have a good understanding of the basics of research design—including selection bias.

LESSONS LEARNED

Students of sociology have learned that knowledge is socially constructed—social forces such as our modern interest in individual psychology (Illouz 2008), technological breakthroughs in data collection that ease longitudinal and prospective studies, and policy interest in family structure that has followed the increases in divorces between 1960 and 1980, all play a role in what we learn about families.

Sociologists, like good contextualists (Pepper 1942), recognize that just because knowledge is socially constructed, this does not pre-empt our capacity to judge science on its merits. We can still evaluate research in terms of best practices. What the story of divorce research shows is that the tools of science can help us to read the research and assess where we *really* stand on the impact of divorce.

IN SUM: WHAT IS A CASE FOR DIVORCE, AND WHY MAKE IT?

What is the impact of divorce on children? There is no arguing that the lives of children of divorce are different from the lives of children whose parents remain married. But in order to understand what happens to children (and adults), one must consider their situation relative to the alternatives available to them. This article details the process of discovery by social scientists over time—through the application of new research methods—that has given us an increasingly fine-grained understanding of divorce. The plot culminates in current research that examines how parents' relationship careers may help us understand the details of when, where, and under what conditions divorce is stressful to children.

This case for divorce involves a review of research over time and a recognition of its complexity. While researchers who use comparisons, and control for selection bias, who measure marital adjustment carefully, and who take domestic violence into account, will disagree about exactly how children of divorce differ from children of married parents (are 20 percent affected? are 25 percent affected?), there is agreement about the resilience of children of divorce. Researchers may disagree about whether the impact of divorce is neutral, as Allen Li contends, or whether some of the impact of divorce is due to pre-existing factors, but that some of the impact of divorce can still be attributed to post-disruption factors, as Andrew Cherlin argues; or that relationship trajectory research will yield more finely grained knowledge. Still, scientists agree that comparing married families to divorced families without taking selection bias into account is a case of comparing apples to oranges, and will get us nowhere in terms of helping families. As Rutter, Hawkins and Booth, and Hetherington show, failing to take the quality of the marriages seriously limits our capacity to understand the linkages between the experience of marriage and the experience of divorce. The distressed marriage is where most people considering divorce start.

Finally, *why* a 'case' for divorce? The phrase itself refers back to Waite and Gallagher's *The Case for Marriage* (2000); this in turn is reminiscent of William Eskridge's *The Case for Same-Sex Marriage* (1996). In one sense, only *The Case for Same-Sex Marriage* had a 'case' to make, given the status of same-sex marriage in the United States at the time of its publication. Yet, as these three examples from 1988 to 2008 highlight, popular understanding of divorce's impact remains contested and uncertain. In another sense, both *The Case for Marriage* and 'The Case for Divorce' draw upon this trope to conduct a literature review for the purposes of focusing attention on social institutions that are currently in flux both demographically and symbolically.

The Case for Marriage was not written because the legal rights of heterosexual people to access marriage or the fondness of Americans for marriage was under threat (though it had been declining). The book was an effort to re-organize common understanding of marriage as beneficial for men, women, children, and communities by drawing our attention to the wealth of social scientific research on the health and economic benefits associated with marriage. In a time of perceived uncertainty, *The Case for Marriage* was associated with drawing policy makers' attention to their opportunity to use the authors' data-based understanding of marriage in order to create policies shaped by the compassionate insight that marriage is associated with a good life for many. *The Case for Marriage* was also associated with a related *cultural* mission of compassion, to help refocus attention on the benefits of marriage that can make lives better. Similarly 'The Case for Divorce' seeks to re-focus common understanding of divorce by reporting on and drawing parallels across diverse times and types of divorce research, and to guide readers through the uncertainty that persists simultaneously in the understanding of the data and in the culture. This too is a mission of compassion.

Notes

1. Other longitudinal studies, including Hawkins and Booth (2005), found similar results: the more carefully marital distress is measured, the more pronounced are the psychological advantages of leaving over staying.
2. The Council on Contemporary Families is a non-partisan, non-profit organization of family scholars and clinicians whose mission is to disseminate the latest research and best-practice findings on the changing experiences and needs of today's diverse families. Authors of briefing reports receive no funding, in-kind support, or reimbursement for contributions.
3. A July 2008 briefing report (D'Onofrio 2008) at the website for the Institute for American Values offers a discussion of research on the impact of divorce on children.

References

Ananat, E. and G. Michaels 2008. 'The Effect of Marital Breakup on the Income Distribution of Women and Children.' *Journal of Human Resources*. Forthcoming, url: http://eprints.lse.ac.uk/4643/ Retrieved online June 24, 2008.

Becker, Howard S. 1973. *Outsiders: Studies in the Sociology of Deviance*. New York, NY: The Free Press, pp. 147–153.

Cherlin, A. J., Furstenberg, F. F., Chase-Lansdale, P. L. et al. 1991. 'Longitudinal Studies of Effects of Divorce on Children in Great Britain and the U.S.' *Science* **252**: 1386–89.

Cherlin, A. J., Chase-Lansdale, P. Lindsay and Christine McRae 1998. 'Effects of Parental Divorce on Mental Health through the Life Course,' *American Sociological Review* **63**: 239–249.

Coltrane, Scott and Michele Adams 2003. 'The Social Construction of the Divorce "Problem": Morality, Child Victims, and the Politics of Gender.' *Family Relations* **52**: 363–372.

Cowen, Tyler 2007. 'Matrimony Has Its Benefits, and Divorce Has a Lot to do With That.' *The New York Times* April 19. url: http://www.nytimes.com/2007/04/19/business/19scene.html?emc=eta1 Retrieved online on June 20, 2008.

D'Onofrio, Brian 2008. 'Divorce, Dads, and the Well-Being of Children: Answers to Common Research Questions.' Research Brief #12, July. Washington, D.C.: Institute for American Values, url: http://center.americanvalues.org/?p=76 Retrieved online December 22, 2008.

Eskridge, William 1996. *The Case for Same-Sex Marriage: From Sexual Liberty to Civilized Commitment*. New York, NY: Free Press.

Folbre, N. and S. Coontz 2002. 'Marriage, Poverty, and Public Policy.' A briefing paper from the Council on Contemporary Families, url: http://www.contemporaryfamilies.org/public/briefing.html (April). Retrieved online on June 24, 2008.

Fomby, Paula and Andrew Cherlin 2007. 'Family Instability and Child Well-Being.' *American Sociological Review* **72**: 181–204.

Goldstein, J. R. 1999. The Leveling of Divorce in the United States,' *Demography*, **36**: 409–414.

Gottman, J. M. 1994. *What Predicts Divorce?* New Jersey: Erlbaum.

Greenberg, P. E., Stiglin, L. E., Finkelstein, S. N. and E. R. Berndt 1993a. 'Depression: A Neglected Major Illness.' *Journal of Clinical Psychiatry* **54**: 419–424.

Greenberg, P. E., Stiglin, L. E., Finkelstein, S. N. and E. R. Berndt 1993b. 'The Economic Burden of Depression in 1990.' *Journal of Clinical Psychiatry* **54**: 405–418.

Hawkins, Daniel N. and Alan Booth 2005. 'Unhappily Ever After: Effects of Long-Term, Low-Quality Marriages on Well-Being.' *Social Forces* **84**: 451–471.

Hetherington, E. Mavis 1988. 'The Impact of Divorce.' *Keynote Address at the Annual Conference of American Association for Marriage and Family Therapy*. New Orleans, LA: October.

Hetherington, E. M. and John Kelly 2002. *For Better or For Worse: Divorce Reconsidered*. New York, NY: W.W. Norton.

Hetherington, E. M. 1999. 'Should We Stay Together for the Sake of the Children?' pp. 93–116 in *Coping with Divorce, Single Parenting, and Remarriage: A Risk and Resiliency Perspective*, edited by E. Mavis Hetherington. Mahwah, NJ: Lawrence Erlbaum Associates.

Hetherington, E. M. and P. Stanley-Hagan 1997. 'Divorce and the Adjustment of Children: A risk and resiliency perspective.' *Journal of Child Psychology & Psychiatry* **40**: 129–140.

Illouz, E. 2008. *Saving the modern Soul: Therapy, Emotions, and the Culture of Self-Help*. Berkeley, CA: University of California Press.

Kiekolt-Glaser, J. K., Kennedy, S., Malkoff, S., Fisher, L., Speicher, C. E. and R. Glaser 1988. 'Marital Discord and Immunity in Males.' *Psychosomatic Medicine* **50**: 213–299.

Li, Jui-Chung Allen 2007. 'The Kids Are OK: Divorce and Children's Behavior Problems.' RAND Labor and Population Working Paper No. WR-489. RAND, Santa Monica, CA.

Li, Jui-Chung Allen 2008. 'New findings on an old question: Does divorce cause children's behavior problems?' *A Briefing Paper from the Council on Contemporary Families*, url: http://www.contemporaryfamilies.org/public/briefing.html (April 24). Retrieved online June 24, 2008.

Meadows, S. O., McLanahan, S. and J. Brooks-Gunn 2008. 'Stability and Change in Family Structure and Maternal Health Trajectories.' *American Sociological Review* **73**: 314–334.

Mintz, Steven 2004. *Huck's Raft: A History of American Childhood*. Cambridge, MA: Harvard University Press.

Osborne, C. and S. McLanahan 2007. 'Partnership Instability and Child Well-Being.' *Journal of Marriage and Family* **69**: 1065–1083.

Pepper, Stephen C. 1942. *World Hypotheses: A Study in Evidence*. Berkeley, CA: University of California Press.

Robles, T. F. and J. K. Kiekolt-Glaser 2003. 'The Physiology of Marriage: Pathways to Health.' *Physiology and Behavior* **79**: 409–16.

Ruggles, Steven 1997. 'The Rise of Divorce and Separation in the United States 1880–1990.' *Demography* **34**(4): 455–466.

Rutter, Virginia E. 2004. *The Case for Divorce: Under What Conditions Is Divorce Beneficial and for Whom?* PhD thesis, University of Washington.

Scafidi, B. 2008. *The Taxpayer Costs of Divorce: First-Ever Estimates for the Nation and All Fifty States*. New York, NY: Institute for American Values.

Stevenson, B. and J. Wolfers 2006. 'Bargaining in the Shadow of Divorce Laws and Family Distress.' *Quarterly Journal of Economics* **121**: 267–288.

van Hemert, Dianne A., Vijver, F. J. R. vande and Ype H. Poortinga 2002. 'The Beck Depression Inventory as a Measure of Subjective Well-Being: A Cross-National Study.' *Journal of Happiness Studies* **3**(3): 257–286.

Veenhoven, Ruut 2004. *World Database of Happiness: Continuous Register of Scientific Research on Subjective Appreciation of Life*. Rotterdam, The Netherlands: Erasmus University, url: http://www2.eur.nl/fsw/research/happiness/.

Waite, Linda J. and Maggie Gallagher 2000. *The Case for Marriage: Why Married People Are Happier, Healthier and Better Off Financially*. New York, NY: Doubleday.

Waite, Linda J., Browning, Don, Doherty, William J., Gallagher, Maggie, Luo, Ye and Scott M. Stanley 2002. *Does Divorce Make People Happy? Findings From a Study of Unhappy Marriages*. New York, NY: Institute for American Values.

Wallerstein, J. 1989. 'Children after Divorce.' *The New York Times* January 22. url: http://query. nytimes.com/gst/fullpage.html?res=950DE2DF123BF931A15752C0A96F948260&sec=&spon=. Retrieved online June 20, 2008.

Wallerstein, J. and Sandra Blakeslee 1988. *Second Chances: Men, Women, and Children a Decade after Divorce: Who Wins, Who Loses, and Why.* New York, NY: Ticknor & Fields.

*Correspondence address: Department of Sociology, Framingham State College, 100 State Street, Framingham, MA 01701, USA. Email: vrutter@framingham.edu.

■READING 13

The Modern American Stepfamily: Problems and Possibilities

Mary Ann Mason

Cinderella had one, so did Snow White and Hansel and Gretel. Our traditional cultural myths are filled with the presence of evil stepmothers. We learn from the stories read to us as children that stepparents, particularly stepmothers, are not to be trusted. They may pretend to love us in front of our biological parent, but the moment our real parent is out of sight they will treat us cruelly and shower their own children with kindnesses. Few modern children's tales paint stepparents so harshly, still the negative image of stepparents lingers in public policy. While the rights and obligations of biological parents, wed or unwed, have been greatly strengthened in recent times, stepparents have been virtually ignored. At best it is fair to say that as a society we have a poorly formed concept of the role of stepparents and a reluctance to clarify that role.

Indeed, the contrast between the legal status of stepparents and the presumptive rights and obligations of natural parents is remarkable. Child support obligations, custody rights, and inheritance rights exist between children and their natural parents by virtue of a biological tie alone, regardless of the quality of social or emotional bonds between parent and child, and regardless of whether the parents are married. In recent years policy changes have extended the rights and obligations of natural parents, particularly in regard to unwed and divorced parents, but have not advanced with regard to stepparents. Stepparents in most states have no obligation during the marriage to support their step-children, nor do they enjoy any right of custody or control. Consistent with this pattern, if the marriage terminates through divorce or death, they usually have no rights to custody or even visitation, however longstanding their relationship with their stepchildren. Conversely, stepparents have no obligation to pay child support following divorce, even if their stepchildren have depended on their income for many years. In turn, stepchildren have no right of inheritance in the event of the stepparent's death (they are, however, eligible for Social Security benefits in most cases).[1]

Policymakers who spend a great deal of time worrying about the economic and psychological effects of divorce on children rarely consider the fact that about 70 percent of mothers are remarried within six years. More over, about 28 percent of children are born to unwed mothers, many of whom eventually marry someone who is not the father of their child. In a study including all children, not just children of divorce, it was estimated that one-fourth of the children born in the United States in the early 1980s will live with a stepparent before they reach adulthood.[2] These numbers are likely to increase in the future, at least as long as the number of single-parent families continues to grow. In light of these demographic trends, federal and state policies affecting families and children, as well as policies governing private-sector employee benefits, insurance, and other critical areas of everyday life, may need to be adapted to address the concerns of modern stepfamilies.

In recent years stepfamilies have received fresh attention from the psychological and social sciences but little from legal and policy scholars. We now know a good deal about who modern stepfamilies are and how they function, but there have been few attempts to apply this knowledge to policy. This [reading] first of all reviews the recent findings on the everyday social and economic functioning of today's stepfamilies, and then examines current state and federal policies, or lack of them in this arena. Finally, the sparse set of current policy recommendations, including my own, are presented. These proposals range from active discouragement of stepfamilies[3] to a consideration of stepparents as de facto parents, with all the rights and responsibilities of biological parents during marriage, and a limited extension of these rights and responsibilities following the breakup of marriage or the death of the stepparent.[4]

THE MODERN STEPFAMILY

The modern stepfamily is different and more complex than Cinderella's or Snow White's in several important ways. First, the stepparent who lives with the children is far more likely to be a stepfather than a stepmother, and in most cases the children's biological father is still alive and a presence, in varying degrees, in their lives. Today it is divorce, rather than death, which usually serves as the background event for the formation of the stepfamily, and it is the custodial mother who remarries (86 percent of stepchildren live primarily with a custodial mother and stepfather),[5] initiating a new legal arrangement with a stepfather.[6]

Let us take the case of the Jones-Hutchins family. Sara was eight and Josh five when their mother and father, Martha and Ray Jones divorced. Three years later Martha married Sam Hutchins, who had no children. They bought a house together and the children received health and other benefits from Sam's job, since Martha was working part time at a job with no benefits.

Theoretically, this new parental arrangement was a triangle, since Ray was still on the scene and initially saw the children every other weekend. In most stepfamilies the noncustodial parent, usually the father, is still alive (only in 25 percent of cases is the noncustodial parent dead, or his whereabouts unknown). This creates the phenomenon of more than two parents, a situation that conventional policymakers are not well equipped to address. However, according to the National Survey of Families and Households (NSFH), a nationally representative sample of families, contact between stepchildren and their absent natural fathers is not that frequent. Contact falls into four broad patterns: roughly one-quarter of all stepchildren have no association at all with their fathers and receive no child support; one-quarter see their fathers only once a year or less often and receive no child support; one-quarter have intermittent contact or receive some child support; and one-quarter may or may not receive child support but have fairly regular contact, seeing their fathers once a month or more. Using these data as guides to the quality and intensity of the father-child relationship, it appears that relatively few stepchildren are close to their natural fathers or have enough contact with them to permit the fathers to play a prominent role in the children's upbringing. Still, at least half of natural fathers do figure in their children's lives to some degree.[7] The presence of the noncustodial parent usually precludes the option of stepparent adoption, a solution that would solve the legal ambiguities, at least, of the stepparent's role.

In size, according to the National Survey of Families and Households, modern residential stepfamilies resemble modern nondivorced families and single-parent families, with an average of two children per family. Only families with two stepparents (the rarest type of stepfamily, in which both parents had children from previous relationships, and both are the custodial parents) are larger, with an average of 3.4 children per household. In part because divorce and remarriage take time, children are older. In the NSFH households, the youngest stepchildren in families are, on average, aged eleven, while the youngest children in nondivorced families are six and a half.[8]

There are also, of course, nonresidential stepparents (the spouses of noncustodial parents), usually stepmothers. In our case, Ray married again, the year after Martha married Sam. Ray's new wife, Leslie, was the custodial parent of Audrey, age twelve. This marriage complicated the weekend visits. The Jones children were resentful of their new stepmother, Leslie, and her daughter, Audrey. Ray found it easier to see them alone, and his visits became less frequent.

Some children may spend a good deal of time with nonresidential stepparents, and they may become significant figures in the children's lives, unlike Leslie in our example. But for our purpose of reassessing the parental rights and obligations of stepparents, we will focus only on residential stepparents, since they are more likely to be involved in the everyday support and care of their stepchildren. Moreover, the wide variety of benefits available to dependent children, like Social Security and health insurance, are usually attached only to a residential stepparent.

The modern stepfamily, like those of Cinderella and Snow White, also has stresses and strains. This was certainly true for the Jones-Hutchins family. Sara was eleven and Josh seven when their mother married Sam. At first Sara refused to talk to Sam and turned her face away when he addressed her. Josh was easier. He did not say much, but was willing to play catch or go an on errand with Sam if encouraged by Sam to do so. Sara grew only slightly more polite as she developed into adolescence. She spoke to Sam only if she needed something. But, as her mother pointed out to Sam, she hardly spoke to her either. Josh continued to be pleasant, if a little distant, as he grew older. He clearly preferred his mother's attention.

The classic longitudinal studies by Heatherington and colleagues,[9] spanning the past two decades, provide a rich source of information on how stepfamilies function. Heatherington emphasizes that stepchildren are children who have experienced several marital transitions. They have usually already experienced the divorce of their parents (although the number whose mothers have never before wed is increasing) and a period of life in a single-parent family before the formation of the stepfamily. In the early stages of all marital transitions, including divorce and remarriage, child-parent relations are often disrupted and parenting is less authoritative than in nondivorced families. These early periods, however, usually give way to a parenting situation more similar to nuclear families.[10]

The Heatherington studies found that stepfathers vary in how enthusiastically and effectively they parent their stepchildren, and stepchildren also vary in how willingly they permit a parental relationship to develop. Indeed, many stepfather-stepchild relationships are not emotionally close. Overall, stepfathers in these studies are most often disengaged and less authoritative as compared with nondivorced fathers. The small class of residential stepmothers exhibits a similar style.[11] Conversely, adolescent children tend to perceive their stepfathers negatively in the early stages of remarriage, but over time, they too become disengaged. In an interesting twist on fairy tale lore, adolescent children in stepfamilies experience less conflict with their residential stepmothers than do children in nondivorced families with their own mothers.[12]

The age and gender of the child at the time of stepfamily formation are critical in his or her adjustment. Early adolescence is a difficult time in which to have remarriage occur, with more sustained difficulties in stepfather-stepchild relations than in remarriages where the children are younger. Young (preadolescent) stepsons, but not necessarily stepdaughters, develop a closer relationship to their stepfathers after a period of time; this is not as likely with older children.[13]

Other researchers have found that in their lives outside the family, stepchildren do not perform as well as children from nondivorced families, and look more like the children from single-parent families. It seems that divorce and remarriage (or some factors associated with divorce and remarriage) increase the risk of poor academic, behavioral, and psychological outcomes.[14]

The difficulties of the stepfamily relationship are evident in the high divorce rate of such families. About one-quarter of all remarrying women separate from their new spouses within five years of the second marriage, and the figure is higher for women with children from prior relationships. A conservative estimate is that between 20 percent and 30 percent of stepchildren will, before they turn eighteen, see their custodial parent and stepparent divorce.[15] This is yet another disruptive marital transition for children, most of whom have already undergone at least one divorce.

Other researchers look at the stepfamily more positively. Amato and Keith analyzed data comparing intact, two-parent families with stepfamilies and found that while children from two-parent families performed significantly better on a multifactored measure of well-being and development, there was a significant overlap. A substantial number of children in stepfamilies actually perform as well or better than children in intact two-parent families. As Amato comments, "Some children grow up in well-functioning intact families in which they encounter abuse, neglect, poverty, parental mental illness, and parental substance abuse. Other children grow up in well-functioning stepfamilies and have caring stepparents who provide affection, effective control and economic support."[16] Still other researchers suggest that it may be the painful transitions of divorce and economically deprived single-parenthood which usually precede the formation of the stepfamily that explain the poor performance of stepchildren.[17]

Perhaps a fairer comparison of stepchildren's well-being is against single-parent families. Indeed, if there were no remarriage (or first marriage, in the case of unmarried birth mothers), these children would remain a part of a single-parent household. On most psychological measures of behavior and achievement, stepchildren look more like children from single-parent families than children from never-divorced families, but on economic measures it is a different story. The National Survey of Families and Households (NSFH) data show that stepparents have slightly lower incomes and slightly less education than parents in nuclear families, but that incomes of all types of married families with children are three to four times greater than the incomes of single mothers. Custodial mothers in stepfamilies have similar incomes to single mothers (about $12,000 in 1987). If, as seems plausible, their personal incomes are about the same before they married as after, then marriage has increased their household incomes more than threefold. Stepfathers' incomes are, on average, more than twice as great as their wives', and account for nearly three-fourths of the family's income.[18]

In contrast to residential stepparents, absent biological parents only rarely provide much financial or other help to their children. Some do not because they are dead or cannot be found; about 26 percent of custodial, remarried mothers and 28 percent of single mothers report that their child's father is deceased or of unknown whereabouts. Yet even in the three-quarters of families where the noncustodial parent's whereabouts are known, only about one-third of all custodial mothers (single and remarried) receive child support or alimony from former spouses, and the amounts involved are small compared to the cost of raising children. According to NSFH data, remarried women with awards receive on average $1780 per year, while single mothers receive $1383. Clearly, former spouses cannot be relied on to lift custodial mothers and their children out of poverty.[19]

The picture is still more complex, as is true with all issues relating to stepfamilies. Some noncustodial fathers, like Ray Jones in our scenario, have remarried and have stepchildren themselves. These relationships, too, are evident in the NSFH data. Nearly one-quarter (23 percent) of residential stepfathers have minor children from former relationships living elsewhere. Two-thirds of those report paying child support for their children.[20] In our case, Ray Jones did continue his child support payments, but he felt squeezed by the economic obligation of contributing to two households. This is a growing class of fathers who frequently feel resentful about the heavy burden of supporting two households, particularly when their first wife has remarried.

In sum, although we have no data that precisely examine the distribution of resources within a stepfamily, it is fair to assume that stepfathers' substantial contributions to family income improve their stepchildren's material well-being by helping to cover basic living costs. For many formerly single-parent families, stepfathers' incomes provided by remarriage are essential in preventing or ending poverty among custodial mothers and their children. (The data are less clear for the much smaller class of residential stepmothers.)

While legal dependency usually ends at eighteen, the economic resources available to a stepchild through remarriage could continue to be an important factor past childhood. College education and young adulthood are especially demanding economic events. The life-course studies undertaken by some researchers substantiate the interpersonal trends seen in stepfamilies before the stepchildren leave home. White reports that viewed from either the parent's or the child's perspective, relationships over the life-course between stepchildren and stepparents are substantially weaker than those between biological parents and children. These relationships are not monolithic, however; the best occur when the stepparent is a male, there are no stepsiblings, the stepparent has no children of his own, and the marriage between the biological parent and the stepparent is intact.[21] On the other end, support relationships are nearly always cut off if the stepparent relationship is terminated because of divorce or the death of the natural parent.

The Jones children were fortunate. Martha and Sam enjoyed a good marriage, in spite of the stress of stepparenting, and Sam was glad to help them with college expenses. Their biological father, Ray, felt he had his own family to support; his stepdaughter, Audrey, also needed money for college. As Sara grew older she grew more accepting of Sam. And after her first child was born, she seemed happy to accept Sam as a grandfather for her child. Josh continued on good terms with Sam.

Again, one might ask to compare these findings to single-parent households where there are no stepparents to provide additional support. The data here are less available. While we do know that stepchildren leave home earlier and are less likely to attend college than children from intact families, the comparison with single-parent families is not clear.[22] One study of perceived normative obligation to stepparents and stepchildren suggests that people in stepfamilies have weaker, but still important, family ties than do biological kin.[23] In terms of economic and other forms of adult support, even weak ties cannot be discounted. They might, instead, become the focus of public policy initiatives.

STEPFAMILIES IN LAW AND PUBLIC POLICY

Both state and federal law set policies that affect stepfamilies. Overall, these policies do not reflect a coherent policy toward stepparents and stepchildren. Two competing models are roughly evident. One, a "stranger" model, followed by most states, treats the residential stepparent as if he or she were a legal stranger to the children, with no rights and no responsibilities. The other, a "dependency" model, most often followed by federal policymakers, assumes the residential stepfather is, in fact, supporting the stepchildren and provides benefits accordingly. But there is inconsistency in both state and federal policy. Some states lean at times toward a dependency model and require support in some instances, and the federal government sometimes treats the stepparent as if he or she were a stranger to the stepchildren, and ignores them in calculating benefits.

State law governs the traditional family matters of marriage, divorce, adoption, and inheritance, while federal law covers a wide range of programs and policies that touch on the lives of most Americans, including stepfamilies. As the provider of benefits through such programs as Temporary Aid for Needy Families (TANF) and Social Security, the federal government sets eligibility standards that affect the economic well-being of many stepfamilies. In addition, as the employer of the armed forces and civil servants, the federal government establishes employee benefits guidelines for vast numbers of American families. And in its regulatory role, the federal government defines the status of stepfamilies for many purposes ranging from immigration eligibility to tax liability.

Not covered in this [reading] or, to my knowledge, yet systematically investigated are the wide range of private employee benefit programs, from medical and life insurance through educational benefits. These programs mostly take their lead from state or federal law. Therefore, it is fair to guess that they suffer from similar inconsistencies.

State Policies

State laws generally give little recognition to the dependency needs of children who reside with their stepparent; they are most likely to treat the stepparent as a stranger to the children, with no rights or obligations. In contrast to the numerous state laws obligating parents to support natural children born out of wedlock or within a previous marriage, only a few states have enacted statutes which specifically impose an affirmative duty on stepparents. The Utah stepparent support statute, for example, provides simply that, "A stepparent shall support a stepchild to the same extent that a natural or adoptive parent is required to support a child."[24] This duty of support ends upon the termination of the marriage. Most states are silent on the obligation to support stepchildren.[25]

A few states rely on common law, the legal tradition stemming from our English roots. The common law tradition leans more toward a dependency model. It dictates that a stepparent can acquire the rights and duties of a parent if he or she acts *in loco parentis* (in the place of a parent). Acquisition of this status is not automatic; it is determined by the stepparent's intent. A stepparent need not explicitly state the intention to act as a parent; he or she can "manifest the requisite intent to assume responsibility by actually providing financial support or by taking over the custodial duties."[26] Courts, however, have been reluctant to grant *in loco* parental rights or to attach obligations to unwilling stepparents. In the words of one Wisconsin court, "A good Samaritan should not be saddled with the legal obligations of another and we think the law should not with alacrity conclude that a stepparent assumes parental relationships to a child."[27]

At the extreme, once the status of *in loco parentis* is achieved, the stepparent "stands in the place of the natural parent, and the reciprocal rights, duties, and obligations of parent and child subsist." These rights, duties, and obligations include the duty to provide financial support, the right to custody and control of the child, immunity from suit by the stepchild, and, in some cases, visitation rights after the dissolution of the marriage by death or divorce.

Yet stepparents who qualify as *in loco parentis* are not always required to provide support in all circumstances. A subset of states imposes obligation only if the stepchild is in danger of becoming dependent on public assistance. For example, Hawaii provides that:

> A stepparent who acts in loco parentis is bound to provide, maintain, and support the stepparent's stepchild during the residence of the child with the stepparent if the legal parents desert the child or are unable to support the child, thereby reducing the child to destitute and necessitous circumstances.[28]

Just as states do not regularly require stepparents to support their stepchildren, they do not offer stepparents the parental authority of custody and control within the marriage. A residential stepparent generally has fewer rights than a legal guardian or a foster parent. According to one commentator, a stepparent "has no authority to make decisions about the child—no authority to approve emergency medical treatment or even to sign a permission slip for a field trip to the fire station."[29]

Both common law and state statutes almost uniformly terminate the stepparent relationship upon divorce or the death of the custodial parent. This means that the support obligations, if there were any, cease, and that the stepparent has no rights to visitation or custody. State courts have sometimes found individual exceptions to this role, but they have not created any clear precedents. Currently only a few states authorize stepparents to seek visitation rights, and custody is almost always granted to a biological parent upon divorce. In the event of the death of the stepparent's spouse, the noncustodial, biological parent is usually granted custody even when the stepparent has, in fact, raised the child. In one such recent Michigan case, *Henrickson v. Gable*,[30] the children, aged nine and ten when their mother died, had lived with their stepfather since infancy and had rarely seen their biological father. In the ensuing custody dispute, the trial court left the children with their stepfather, but an appellate court, relying upon a state law that created a strong preference for biological parents, reversed this decision and turned the children over to their biological father.

Following the stranger model, state inheritance laws, with a few complex exceptions, do not recognize the existence of stepchildren. Under existing state laws, even a dependent stepchild whose stepparent has supported and raised the child for many years is not eligible to inherit from the stepparent if there is no will. California provides the most liberal rule for stepchild recovery when there is no will, but only if the stepchild meets relatively onerous qualifications. Stepchildren may inherit as the children of a deceased stepparent only if "it is established by clear and convincing evidence that the stepparent would have adopted the person but for a legal barrier."[31] Very few stepchildren have been able to pass this test. Similarly a stepchild cannot bring a negligence suit for the accidental death of a stepparent. In most instances, then, only a biological child will inherit or receive legal compensation when a stepparent dies.

Federal Policies

The federal policies that concern us here are of two types: federal benefit programs given to families in need, including TANF and Supplemental Security Income (SSI), and general programs not based on need, including Social Security as well as civil service and military personnel employee benefits. Most of these programs follow the dependency model. They go further than do most states in recognizing or promoting the actual family relationship of residential stepfamilies. Many of them (although not all) assume that residential stepparents support their stepchildren and accordingly make these children eligible for benefits equivalent to those afforded to other children of the family.

Despite the fact that federal law generally recognizes the dependency of residential stepchildren, it remains wanting in many respects. There is a great deal of inconsistency in how the numerous federal programs and policies treat the stepparent-stepchild relationship, and the very definitions of what constitutes a stepchild are often quite different across programs. Most of the programs strive for a dependency-based definition, such as living with or receiving 50 percent of support from a stepparent. However, some invoke the vague definition, "actual family relationship," and some do not attempt any definition at all, thus potentially including nonresidential stepchildren among the beneficiaries. In some programs the category of stepchild is entirely absent or specifically excluded from the list of beneficiaries for some programs.

Even where program rules permit benefits for dependent stepchildren as for natural children, the benefits to stepchildren are typically severed by death or divorce.[32] While Social Security does cover dependent stepchildren in the event of death, several programs specifically exclude stepchildren from eligibility for certain death benefits. Under the Federal Employees' Retirement System, stepchildren are explicitly excluded from the definition of children in determining the default beneficiary, without concern for the stepchild's possible dependency. All stepchildren are similarly excluded from eligibility for lump-sum payments under the Foreign Service Retirement and Disability System and the CIA Retirement and Disability program.[33]

Stepchildren are even more vulnerable in the event of divorce. Here the stranger model is turned to. As with state law, any legally recognized relationship is immediately severed upon divorce in nearly all federal programs. The children and their stepparents become as strangers. Social Security does not provide any cushion for stepchildren if the deceased stepparent is divorced from the custodial parent. Under Social Security law, the stepparent-stepchild relationship is terminated immediately upon divorce and the stepchild is no longer eligible for benefits even if the child has in fact been dependent on the insured stepparent for the duration of a very long marriage.[34] If the divorce were finalized the day before the stepparent's death the child would receive no benefits.

In sum, current federal policy goes part way toward defining the role of the stepparent by assuming a dependency model in most programs, even when state law does not, and providing benefits to stepchildren based on this assumption of stepparent support. However, as described, existing federal stepparent policy falls short in several critical areas. And state laws and policies fall far short of federal policies in their consideration of stepfamilies, for the most part treating stepparents as strangers with regard to their stepchildren.

NEW POLICY PROPOSALS

Proposals for policy reform regarding stepfamilies are scant in number and, so far, largely unheard by policymakers. Most of the proposals come from legal scholars, a few from social scientists. Stepparents have not been organized to demand reform, nor have child advocates. All the reforms have some disagreements with the existing stranger and dependency models, but few offer a completely new model.

All of the proposals I review base their arguments to a greater or lesser degree on social science data, although not always the same data. The proposers may roughly be divided into three camps. The first, and perhaps smallest camp, I call *negativists*. These are scholars who view stepfamilies from a sociobiological perspective, and find them a troublesome aberration to be actively discouraged. The second, and by far largest group of scholars, I term *voluntarists*. This group acknowledges both the complexity and the often distant nature of stepparent relationships, and largely believes that law and policy should leave stepfamilies alone, as it does now. If stepparents wish to take a greater role in their stepchildren's lives, they should be encouraged to do so, by adoption or some other means. The third camp recognizes the growing presence of stepfamilies as an alternate family form and believes they should be recognized and strengthened in some important ways. This group, I call them *reformists*, believes the law should take the lead in providing more rights or obligations to stepparents. The few policy initiatives from this group range from small specific reforms regarding such issues as inheritance and visitation to my own proposal for a full-scale redefinition of stepparents' rights and obligations.

The negativist viewpoint on stepparenting, most prominently represented by sociologist David Popenoe, relies on a sociobiological theory of reproduction. According to this theory, human beings will give unstintingly to their own biological children, in order to promote their own genes, but will be far less generous to others. The recent rise in divorce and out-of-wedlock births, according to Popenoe, has created a pattern of essentially fatherless households that cannot compete with the two-biological-parent families.

Popenoe believes the pattern of stepparent disengagement revealed by many researchers is largely based on this biological stinginess.

> If the argument . . . is correct, and the family is fundamentally rooted in biology and at least partly activated by the "genetically selfish" activities of human beings, childbearing by non relatives is inherently problematic. It is not that unrelated individuals are unable to do the job of parenting, it is just that they are not as likely to do the job well. Stepfamily problems, in short, may be so intractable that the best strategy for dealing with them is to do everything possible to minimize their occurrence.

Moreover, Popenoe cites researchers on the greatly increased incidence of child abuse by stepfathers over natural fathers, who suggest that "stepchildren are not merely 'disadvantaged' but imperiled."[35] This argument is not so farfetched, he claims, in fact it is the stuff of our folk wisdom. Snow White and Hansel and Gretel had it right; stepparents are not merely uncaring, they may be dangerous.

Popenoe goes beyond the stranger model, which is neutral as to state activity, and suggests an active discouragement of stepparent families. He believes the best way to obstruct stepfamilies is to encourage married biological two-parent families. Premarital and marital counseling, a longer waiting period for divorce, and a redesign of the current welfare system so that marriage and family are empowered rather than denigrated are among his policy recommendations.] He is heartened by what he calls the "new familism," a growing recognition of the need for strong social bonds, which he believes can best be found in the biological two-parent family.[36]

The second group of scholars, whom I call voluntarists, generally believe that the stepparent relationship is essentially voluntary and private and the stranger model most clearly reflects this. The legal bond formed by remarriage is between man and wife—stepchildren are incidental; they are legal strangers. Stepparents may choose, or not choose, to become more involved with everyday economic and emotional support of their stepchildren; but the law should not mandate this relationship, it should simply reflect it. These scholars recognize the growth of stepfamilies as a factor of modern life and neither condone nor condemn this configuration. Family law scholar David Chambers probably speaks for most scholars in this large camp when he says,

> In most regards, this state of the law nicely complements the state of stepparent relationships in the United States. Recall the inescapable diversity of such relationships—residential and non-residential, beginning when the children are infants and when they are teenagers, leading to comfortable relationships in some cases and awkward relationships in others, lasting a few years and lasting many. In this context it seems sensible to permit those relationships to rest largely on the voluntary arrangements among stepparents and biologic parents. The current state of the law also amply recognizes our nation's continuing absorption with the biologic relationship, especially as it informs our sensibilities about enduring financial obligations.[37]

Chambers is not enthusiastic about imposing support obligations on stepparents, either during or following the termination of a marriage, but is interested in promoting voluntary adoption. He would, however, approve some middle ground where biological parents are not completely cut off in the adoption process.

Other voluntarists are attracted by the new English model of parenting, as enacted in the Children Act of 1989. Of great attraction to American voluntarists is the fact that under this model a stepparent who has been married at least two years to the biological parent may voluntarily petition for a residence order for his or her spouse's child. With a residence order the stepparent has parental responsibility toward the child until the age of sixteen. But this order does not extinguish the parental responsibility of the noncustodial parent.[38] In accordance with the Children Act of 1989, parents, biological or otherwise, no longer have parental rights, they have only parental responsibilities, and these cannot be extinguished upon the divorce of the biological parents. In England, therefore, it is possible for three adults to claim parental responsibility. Unlike biological parental responsibility, however, stepparent responsibility does not usually extend following divorce. The stepparent is not normally financially responsible following divorce, but he or she may apply for a visitation order.

The third group, whom I call reformists, believe that voluntary acts on the part of stepparents are not always adequate, and that it is necessary to reform the law in some way to more clearly define the rights and responsibilities of stepparents. The American Bar Association Family Law Section has been working for some years on a proposed Model Act to suggest legislative reforms regarding stepparents' obligations to provide child support and rights to discipline, visitation, and custody. A Model Act is not binding anywhere; it is simply a model for all states to consider. Traditionally, however, Model Acts have been very influential in guiding state legislative reform. In its current form, the ABA Model Act would require stepparents to assume a duty of support during the duration of the remarriage only if the child is not adequately supported by the custodial and noncustodial parent. The issue is ultimately left to the discretion of the family court, but the Model Act does not require that the stepparent would need to have a close relationship with a stepchild before a support duty is imposed. The Model Act, however, does not describe what the rule should be if the stepparent and the custodial parent divorce.

The proposed statute is rather more complete in its discussion of stepparent visitation or custody rights following divorce. It takes a two-tiered approach, first asking if the stepparent has standing (a legal basis) to seek visitation and then asking if the visitation would be in the best interests of the child. The standing question is to be resolved with reference to five factors, which essentially examine the role of the stepparent in the child's life (almost an *in loco parentis* question), the financial support offered by the stepparent, and the detriment to the child from denying visitation. The court, if it finds standing, then completes the analysis with the best interests standard of the jurisdiction. The Model Act's section on physical custody also requires a two-tiered test, requiring standing and increasing the burden on the stepparent to present clear and convincing proof that he or she is the better custodial parent.

The ABA Model Act is a worthwhile start, in my opinion, but it is little more than that. At most it moves away from a stranger model and provides a limited concept of mandatory stepparent support during a marriage, acknowledging that stepchildren are at least sometimes dependent. It also gives a stepparent a fighting chance for visitation or custody following a divorce. It fails to clarify stepparents' rights during the marriage, however, and does not deal with the issue of economic support at the period of maximum vulnerability, the termination of the marriage through death and divorce. Moreover, the Model Act, and, indeed, all the existing reform proposals, deal only with traditional legal concepts of parenthood defined by each state and do not consider the vast range of federal programs, or other public and private programs, that define the stepparent-stepchild relationship for purposes of benefits, insurance, or other purposes.

I propose, instead, a new conceptualization of stepparent rights and responsibilities, a de facto parent model, that will cover all aspects of the stepparent-stepchild relationship and will extend to federal and private policy as well. My first concern in proposing a new framework is the welfare of the stepchildren, which is not adequately dealt with in either the stranger or the dependency model. The failure of state and, to a lesser extent, federal policy to address coherently the financial interdependencies of step relationships, described earlier in this [reading], means that children dependent upon a residential stepparent may not receive adequate support or benefits from that parent during the marriage, and they may not be protected economically in the event of divorce or parental death.

The longitudinal studies of families described earlier in this [reading] suggest that the most difficult periods for children are those of marital transition, for example, divorce and remarriage. Families with a residential stepfather have a much higher family income than mother-headed single families; indeed, their household incomes look much like nuclear families.[39] However, research demonstrates that stepfamilies are fragile and are more likely to terminate in divorce than biological families. The event of divorce can quite suddenly pull the resources available for the children back to the single-parent level. Currently children are at least financially cushioned by child support following the divorce of their biological parents, but have no protective support following the breakup of their stepfamily. Nor are they protected in the event of the death of the stepparent, which is certainly another period of vulnerability (as discussed earlier, only a small minority continue to receive support from noncustodial parents).

A second reason for proposing a new framework is to strengthen the relationship of the stepparent and stepchildren. While research generally finds that stepparents are less engaged in parenting than natural parents, research studies do not explain the causes; others must do so. In addition to the sociobiologists' claim for stingy, genetically driven behavior, sociologists have posited the explanation of "incomplete institutionalization."[40] This theory is based on the belief that, by and large, people act as they are expected to act by society. In the case of stepfamilies, there are unclear or absent societal norms and standards for how to define the remarried family, especially the role of the stepparent in relation to the stepchild.

Briefly, my new model requires, first of all, dividing stepparents into two subclasses: those who are de facto parents and those who are not. De facto parents would be defined as "those stepparents legally married to a natural parent who primarily reside with their stepchildren, or who provide at least 50 percent of the stepchild's financial support." Stepparents who do not meet the de facto parent requirements would, in all important respects, disappear from policy.

For the purposes of federal and state policy, under this scheme, a de facto parent would be treated virtually the same as a natural parent during the marriage. The same rights, obligations, and presumptions would attach vis-à-vis their stepchildren, including the obligation of support. These rights and duties would continue in some form, based on the length of the marriage, following the custodial parent's death or divorce from the stepparent, or the death of the stepparent. In the event of divorce the stepparent would have standing to seek custody or visitation but the stepparent could also be obligated for child support of a limited duration. Upon the death of a stepparent, a minor stepchild would be treated for purposes of inheritance and benefits as would a natural child.

So far this proposal resembles the common law doctrine of *in loco parentis*, described earlier, where the stepparent is treated for most purposes (except inheritance) as a parent on the condition that he or she voluntarily agrees to support the child. In the de facto model, however, support is mandatory, not voluntary, on the grounds both that it is not fair to stepchildren to be treated by the law in an unequal or arbitrary manner, and that child welfare considerations are best met by uniform support of stepchildren. Furthermore, in the traditional common law *in loco parentis* scenario, the noncustodial parent had died, and was not a factor to be reckoned with. Under this scheme, creating a de facto parent category for stepparents would not invalidate the existing rights and obligations of a noncustodial biological parent. Rather, this proposal would empower a stepparent as an additional parent.

Multiple parenting and the rights and obligations of the stepparent and children following divorce or death are controversial and difficult policy matters that require more detailed attention than the brief exposition that can be offered here. Multiple parenting is the barrier upon which many family law reform schemes, especially in custody and adoption, have foundered. It is also one of the reasons that there has been no consistent effort to reformulate the role of stepparents. Working out the details is critical. For instance, mandating stepparent support raises a central issue of fairness. If the stepparent is indeed required to support the child, there is a question about the support obligations of the noncustodial parent. Traditionally, most states have not recognized the stepparent contribution as an offset to child support.[41] While this policy promotes administrative efficiency, and may benefit some children, it may not be fair to the noncustodial parent. An important advance in recognizing the existence of multiple parents in the nonlinear family is to recognize multiple support obligations. The few states that require stepparent obligation have given limited attention to apportionment of child support obligations, offering no clear guidelines. I propose that state statutory requirements for stepparent obligation as de facto parents also include clear guidelines for apportionment of child support between the noncustodial natural parent and the stepparent.

Critics of this proposal may say that if the custodial parent's support is reduced, the child will have fewer resources. For some children, this may be true, but as discussed earlier in this [reading], only about 25 percent of all stepchildren receive child support and the average amount is less than $2000 per year.[42] Therefore, a reduction of this small amount of support to a minority of stepchildren would not have a large overall effect compared with the increased resources of living with a stepparent that most stepchildren enjoy. And, certainly, the additional safety net of protection in the event of the death of the stepparent or divorce from the custodial parent would benefit all stepchildren. In addition, under the de facto scheme, the reduction of the support payment for the noncustodial parent may help to sweeten the multiple parenting relationship.

Let us apply this model to the Jones-Hutchins family introduced earlier. If Ray Jones, the noncustodial parent, were paying $6000 a year support for his two children (on the high end for noncustodial parents according to the National Survey for Children and Families), his payments could be reduced by as much as half, since Sam Hutchins's income is $50,000 per year and he has no other dependents. It should be emphasized, however, that in most stepfamilies there would be no reduction in support, because the noncustodial parent is paying no support. In the Jones-Hutchins family the $3000 relief would certainly be welcome to Ray, who is also now living with and helping to support his new wife's child. The relief would likely make him somewhat friendlier toward Sam, or at least more accepting of his role in his children's lives. It also might make him more likely to continue support past eighteen, since he would not feel as financially pinched over the years. More important, while the children would lose some support, they would have the security that if Sam died they would be legal heirs and default beneficiaries to his life insurance. They could also ask for damages if his death were caused by negligence or work-related events. And if he and their mother divorced, they could continue for a time to be considered dependents on his health and other benefits and to receive support from him.

Another facet of multiple parenting is legal authority. If stepparents are required to accept parental support obligations, equal protection and fairness concerns dictate that they must also be given parental rights. Currently, state laws, as noted earlier, recognize only natural or adoptive parents; a stepparent currently has no legal authority over a stepchild, even to authorize a field trip. If stepparents had full parental rights, in some cases, as when the parents have shared legal custody, the law would be recognizing the parental rights of three parents, rather than two. While this sounds unusual, it is an accurate reflection of how many families now raise their children. Most often, however, it would be only the custodial parent and his or her spouse, the de facto parent, who would have authority to make decisions for the children in their home.

In the Jones-Hutchins family this policy would give Sam more recognition as a parent. Schools, camps, hospitals, and other institutions that require parental consent or involvement would now automatically include him in their consideration of the children's interests. Since Sam is the more day-to-day parent, their biological father, Ray, may not mind at all. If he did mind, the three of them would have to work it out (or in an extreme event, take it to mediation or family court). In fact, since only a minority of noncustodial dads see their children on a regular basis, three-parent decision making would be unusual.

Critics of this scheme may argue that adoption, not the creation of the legal status of de facto parent, is the appropriate vehicle for granting a stepparent full parental rights and responsibilities.[43] If, as discussed earlier, nearly three-quarters of stepchildren are not being supported by their noncustodial parents, policy initiatives could be directed to terminating the nonpaying parents' rights and promoting stepparent adoption. Adoption is not possible, however, unless the parental rights of the absent natural parent have been terminated—a difficult procedure against a reluctant parent. Normally, the rights of a parent who maintains contact with his or her child cannot be terminated even if that parent is not contributing child support. And when parental rights are terminated, visitation rights are terminated as well in most states. It is by no means clear that it is in the best interests of children to terminate contact with a natural parent, even if the parent is not meeting his or her obligation to support.[44] As discussed earlier, a large percentage (another 25 percent or so), of noncustodial parents continue some contact with their children, even when not paying support.[45] And while stepparent adoption should be strongly encouraged when it is possible, this solution will not resolve the problem of defining the role of stepparents who have not adopted.

Extending, in some form, the rights and obligations following the termination of the marriage by divorce or death is equally problematical. Currently, only a few courts have ruled in favor of support payments following divorce, and these have been decided on an individual basis. Only one state, Missouri, statutorily continues stepparent support obligations following divorce.[46] It would clearly be in the best interests of the child to experience continued support, since a significant number of children may sink below the poverty line upon the dissolution of their stepfamily.[47]

Since the de facto model is based on dependency, not blood, a fair basis for support following divorce or the death of the custodial parent might be to require that a stepparent who qualified as a de facto parent for at least one year must contribute child support for half the number of years of dependency until the child reached majority. If a child resided with the stepparent for four years, the stepparent would be liable for support for two years. If the biological noncustodial parent were still paying support payments, the amount could be apportioned. While it may be said that this policy would discourage people from becoming stepparents by marrying, it could also be said to discourage divorce once one has become a stepparent. Stepparents might consider working harder at maintaining a marriage if divorce had some real costs.

Conversely, stepparents should have rights as well as responsibilities following divorce or the death of the custodial parent. Divorced or widowed stepparents should be able to pursue visitation or custody if they have lived with and supported the child for at least one year. Once again, multiple parent claims might sometimes be an issue, but these could be resolved, as they are now, under a primary caretaker, or a best interest standard.

The death of a stepparent is a particular period of vulnerability for stepchildren for which they are unprotected by inheritance law. While Social Security and other federal survivor benefits are based on the premise that a stepchild relies on the support of the residential stepparent and will suffer the same hardship as natural children if the stepparent dies, state inheritance laws, notoriously archaic, decree that only biology, not dependency, counts. State laws should assume that a de facto parent would wish to have all his dependents receive a share of his estate if he died without a will. If the step-children are no longer dependent, that assumption would not necessarily prevail. The same assumption should prevail for insurance policies and compensation claims following an accidental death. A dependent stepchild, just as a natural child, should have the right to sue for loss of support.

On the federal front, a clear definition of stepparents as de facto parents would eliminate the inconsistencies regarding stepparents which plague current federal policies and would clarify the role of the residential stepparent. For the duration of the marriage, a stepchild would be treated as a natural child for purposes of support and the receipt of federal benefits. This treatment would persist in the event of the death of the stepparent. The stepchild would receive all the survivor and death benefits that would accrue to a natural child.[48]

In the case of divorce, the issue of federal benefits is more complicated. Stepchildren and natural children should not have identical coverage for federal benefits following divorce, again, but neither is it good policy to summarily cut off children who have been dependent, sometimes for many years, on the de facto parent. A better policy is to extend federal benefits for a period following divorce, based on a formula that matches half the number of years of dependency, as earlier suggested for child support. For instance, if the stepparent resided with the stepchild for four years, the child would be covered by Social Security survivor benefits and other federal benefits, including federal employee benefits, for a period of two years following the divorce. This solution would serve children by at least providing a transitional cushion. It would also be relatively easy to administer. In the case of the death of the biological custodial parent, benefits could be similarly extended, or continued indefinitely if the child remains in the custody of the stepparent.

All other private benefits programs would similarly gain from the application of a clear definition of the rights and obligations of residential stepparents. While these nongovernmental programs, ranging from eligibility for private health and life insurance and annuities to access to employee child care, are not reviewed in this [reading], they almost surely reflect the same inconsistencies or silences evident in federal and state policies.

Ultimately, state law defines most of these stepfamily relationships, and it is difficult, if not impossible to achieve uniform reform on a state-by-state basis. In England it is possible to pass a single piece of national legislation, such as the Children Act of 1989, which completely redefines parental roles. In America, the process of reform is slower and less sure. Probably the first step in promoting a new policy would be for the federal government to insist all states pass stepparent general support obligation laws requiring stepparents acting as de facto parents (by my definition) to support their stepchildren as they do their natural children. This goal could be accomplished by making stepparent general support obligation laws a prerequisite for receiving federal welfare grants. Federal policy already assumes this support in figuring eligibility in many programs, but it has not insisted that states change their laws. Precedent for this strategy has been set by the Family Support Acts of 1988 in which the federal government mandated that states set up strict child support enforcement laws for divorced parents and unwed fathers at TANF levels in order to secure AFDC funding.[49] The second, larger step would be to require limited stepparent support following divorce, as described previously. Once the basic obligations were asserted, an articulation of basic rights would presumably follow.

CONCLUSION

Stepfamilies compose a large and growing sector of American families that is largely ignored by public policy. Social scientists tell us that these families have problems. Stepparent-stepchildren relationships, poorly defined by law and social norms, are not as strong or nurturing as those in nondivorced families, and stepchildren do not do as well in school and in other outside settings. Still, stepfamily relationships are important in lifting single-parent families out of poverty. When single or divorced mothers marry, the household income increases by more than threefold, rising to roughly the same level as nuclear families. A substantial portion of these families experiences divorce, however, placing the stepchildren at risk of falling back into poverty. It makes good public policy sense then, both to strengthen these stepfamily relationships and to cushion the transition for stepchildren should the relationship end.

Notes

1. Mary Ann Mason and David Simon, "The Ambiguous Stepparent: Federal Legislation in Search of a Model," *Family Law Quarterly* 29: 446–448, 1995.
2. E. Mavis Heatherington and Kathleen M. Jodl, "Stepfamilies as Settings for Child Development," in Alan Booth and Judy Dunn (eds.), *Stepfamilies: Who Benefits? Who Does Not?* (Hillsdale, N.J.: L. Erlbaum 1994), 55; E. Mavis Heatherington, "An Overview of the Virginia Longitudinal Study of Divorce and Remarriage: A Focus on Early Adolescence," *Journal of Family Psychology* 7: 39–56, 1993.
3. David Popenoe, "Evolution of Marriage and Stepfamily Problems," in Booth and Dunn (eds.), *Stepfamilies*, 3–28.
4. Mason and Simon, "The Ambiguous Stepparent," 467–482; Mary Ann Mason and Jane Mauldon, "The New Stepfamily Needs a New Public Policy," *Journal of Social Issues* 52(3), Fall 1996.
5. U.S. Bureau of Census, 1989.

6. Divorce is not always the background event. An increasing, but still relatively small number of custodial mothers have not previously wed.

7. Mason and Mauldon, "The New Stepfamily," 5.

8. Ibid., 6.

9. Heatherington and Jodl, "Stepfamilies," 55–81.

10. Ibid., 76.

11. E. Mavis Heatherington and William Clingempeel, "Coping with Marital Transitions: A Family Systems Perspective," *Monographs of the Society for Research in Child Development* 57: 2–3, Serial No. 227, New York: 1992; E. Thomson, Sara McLanahan, and R. B. Curtin, "Family Structure, Gender, and Parental Socialization," *Journal of Marriage and the Family* 54: 368–378, 1992.

12. Heatherington and Jodl, "Stepfamilies," 69.

13. Ibid., 64–65.

14. Thomson, McLanahan, and Curtin, "Family Structure," 368–378.

15. L. Bumpass and J. Sweet, *American Families and Households* (New York: Russell Sage Foundation, 1987), 23.

16. Paul Amato, "The Implications of Research Findings on Children in Stepfamilies," in Booth and Dunn (eds.), *Stepfamilies*, 84.

17. Nicholas Zill, "Understanding Why Children in Stepfamilies Have More Learning and Behavior Problems Than Children in Nuclear Families," in Booth and Dunn (eds.), *Stepfamilies*, 89–97.

18. Mason and Mauldon, "The New Stepfamily Needs a New Public Policy," 7.

19. Ibid., 8.

20. Ibid.

21. Lynn White, "Stepfamilies over the Lifecourse: Social Support," in Booth and Dunn (eds.), *Stepfamilies*, 109–139.

22. Ibid., 130.

23. A. S. Rossi and P. H. Rossi, *Of Human Bonding: Parent-Child Relations Across the Life Course* (New York: A. de Gruyter, 1990).

24. Utah Code Ann. 78-45-4.1.

25. Margaret Mahoney, *Stepfamilies and the Law* (Ann Arbor: University of Michigan Press, 1994), 13–47.

26. Miller v. United States, 123 F.2d 715, 717 (8th Cir, 1941).

27. Niesen v. Niesen, 157 N. W.2d 660 664 (Wis. 1968).

28. Hawaii Revised Stat. Ann., Title 31, Sec. 577–4.

29. David Chambers, "Stepparents, Biologic Parents, and the Law's Perceptions of 'Family' after Divorce," in S. Sugarman and H. H. Kay (eds.), *Divorce Reform at the Crossroads* (New Haven: Yale University Press, 1990), 102–129.

30. Henrickson v. Gable.

31. Cal. Prob. Code, Sec. 6408.

32. Mason and Simon, "The Ambiguous Stepparent: Federal Legislation in Search of a Model," 449.

33. Ibid., p. 460–466.

34. 42. U.S.C. sec. 416(e), 1994.

35. M. Daly and M. Wilson, *Homicide* (New York: Aldine de Gruyter, 1988), 230.

36. Barbara Whitehead, "A New Familism?" *Family Affairs*, Summer, 1992.

37. Chambers, "Stepparents, Biologic Parents, and the Law's Perceptions of 'Family' after Divorce," 26.

38. Mark A. Fine, "Social Policy Pertaining to Stepfamilies: Should Stepparents and Stepchildren Have the Option of Establishing a Legal Relationship?" in Booth and Dunn (eds.), *Stepfamilies*, 199.

39. Mason and Mauldon, "The New Stepfamily," 5.

40. Andrew Cherlin, "Remarriage as an Incomplete Institution," *American Journal of Sociology* 84: 634–649, 1978.

41. S. Ramsey and J. Masson, "Stepparent Support of Stepchildren: A Comparative Analysis of Policies and Problems in the American and British Experience," *Syracuse Law Review* 36: 649–666, 1985.

42. Mason and Mauldon, "The New Stepfamily," 7.

43. Joan Hollinger (ed.) et al., *Adoption Law and Practice* (New York: Matthew Bender, 1988).
44. Katherine Bartlett, "Re-thinking Parenthood as an Exclusive Status: The Need for Alternatives When the Premise of the Nuclear Family Has Failed," *Virginia Law Review* 70: 879–903, 1984.
45. Mason and Mauldon, "The New Stepfamily," 5.
46. Vernon's Ann. Missouri Stats. 453.400, 1994.
47. Mason and Mauldon, "The New Stepfamily," 5.
48. Mason and Simon, "The Ambiguous Stepparent," 471.
49. 100 P.L. 485; 102 Stat. 2343 (1988).

III

Parents and Children

No aspect of family life seems more natural, universal, and changeless than the relationship between parents and children. Yet we know from history and from cross-cultural evidence that major changes have taken place in terms of how people think and feel about children and childhood. And the nature of relationships between children and parents has also changed. For example, the shift from an agrarian to an industrial and then a postindustrial society over the past 200 years has revolutionized parent-child relations and the conditions of child development.

Among the changes associated with this transformation of childhood are: the decline of farming as a way of life, the elimination of child labor, the fall in infant death rates, the spread of literacy and mass schooling, and a focus on childhood as a distinct and valuable stage of life. As a result of these changes, modern parents bear fewer children, make greater emotional and economic investments in them and expect little. Farm families were bound together by economic necessity: children were an essential source of labor in the family economy and a source of support in old age. Today, almost all children are economic liabilities when they are young, and they need financial help well into young adulthood. But children now have deep emotional significance for parents. Thus, although today's children have become economically "useless," they have become emotionally "priceless" (Zelizer, 1985).

No matter how eagerly an emotionally priceless child is awaited, becoming a parent is usually experienced as one of life's major "normal" crises. In a classic article, Alice Rossi (1968) was one of the first to point out that the transition to parenthood is often one of life's difficult passages. Since Rossi's article first appeared more than four decades ago, a large body of research literature has developed, most of which supports her view that the early years of parenting can be a period of stress and change as well as joy.

As Philip and Carolyn Cowan observe in their article here that becoming a parent may be more difficult now than it used to be, even for two parent, middle-class families. The Cowans studied couples before and after the births of their first children. They conclude that because of the rapid and dramatic social changes of the past decades, young parents today are like pioneers in a new, uncharted territory. For example, the vast majority of today's couples come to parenthood with both husband and wife in the workforce, and most have expectations of a more egalitarian relationship than their own parents had. But the balance in their work lives and their own relationship has to shift dramatically after the baby is born.

Most couples can't afford the "traditional" pattern of the wife staying home full time, even if they would prefer that arrangement. But this traditional pattern has its own cost: the Cowans found that mothers who stay home full time are more likely to become depressed than those who go back to work. Young families thus face more burdens than in the past, yet they lack the supportive services for new parents, such as visiting nurses, paid parental leave, quality child care, and other family policies widely available in other countries. The Cowans suggest that workplace flexibility, combined with these policies would go a long way to easing the strains in new families.

The focus of public concern about the family mostly pertains to those in high-risk situations like those studied by Kathryn Edin, Timothy Nelson, and Joanna M. Reed. These researchers report on an in-depth study of unmarried, low-income fathers and their relationships with their children. Most of these men, it turned out, have radically different ideas about family life than men who came of age in previous decades. Earlier researchers found that fatherhood tended to be a "package deal": the father's relationship with the child depended on his relationship with the mother. If the man was not involved with the mother, he would not be involved with the child or try to meet his or her obligations.

But Armstrong and her coresearchers found a very marked change from this "package deal" model of fatherhood. For the men they studied, the father-child bond is central; it holds men in couple relationships they might not otherwise have even formed. And even men who are not involved with the mothers may still carry on a relationship with their child. "Daddy Baby: Momma, Maybe" according to Edin, et al. is a good statement about the worldviews of many of the fathers they studied.

Diversity in American family life is not new, but openly gay and lesbian families are a new addition to the mix. Of all the new- and not-so-new family arrangements in today's America, no one expected that gay fathers would become part of social landscape. But they have. The acceptance of gay people and gay marriage has been remarkably swift; by 2012, a majority of Americans told pollsters they were in favor of gay marriage. Once there was a strong backlash against homosexual rights; now there is a backlash against the backlash.

In her article here, Judith Stacey examines the gay fatherhood community in Los Angeles. Unless they have children of their own from former marriages, gay men who live together and want to be parents have to navigate a variety of expensive choices and hurdles. Gay male parents are typically white, middle class, and affluent but the children who are available for adoption are disproportionately poorer, darker, and born to alcohol and drug addicted women. Nevertheless, those gay would-be fathers who succeed in adopting are usually happy and devoted parents.

Much of the worry about family life today is about children, and it is deeply nostalgic. Usually we compare troubling images of children now with rosy images of children growing up in past times. But as historian Steven Mintz explains, public thinking about the history of American childhood is clouded by a series of myths. One is the myth of a carefree childhood. We cling to a fantasy that once upon a time childhood and youth were years of carefree adventure; however, for most children in the past, growing up was anything but easy. Disease, family disruption, and having to go to work at a very young age were typical aspects of family life.

The notion of a long, secure childhood, devoted to education and free from adult-like responsibilities, is a very recent invention—one that only became a reality for a majority of children during the period of relative prosperity that followed World War II. During the last quarter of the twentieth century, however, poverty and inequality grew. In addition, social mobility—the ability of a poor child to rise into the middle class—declined.

In his article here, Frank F. Furstenberg, looks in more detail at how social class differences shape a child's development in the course of growing up. By early adulthood, he finds there are huge gaps between children growing up in advantaged and disadvantaged families. These realities go against the "rags to riches" idea that anyone can rise from the bottom to the top of the social ladder. Furstenberg argues that while the nation has never fully lived up to its billing as the land of opportunity, Americans have tended to ignore class differences. Even social scientists now emphasize gender race and ethnicity, rather than socioeconomic differences.

Furstenberg shows how social class begins to influence development even before a child is born; for example, it affects the diet and medical care of the mother-to-be, and the health care the new baby receives. The emotional and financial resources of the parents affect the skills the child learns at preschool, as well as his or her readiness to succeed in school. These differences matter now more than ever because young people need more education than the previous generations, and they need help from their parents for a longer time.

Indeed, in today's postindustrial society a whole new stage of life has emerged between adolescence and adulthood. Indeed it is no longer clear what turns a twenty- or thirty something into an adult. The standard markers of adulthood are finishing school, leaving home, finding work, getting married, having children. In the 1950s and 60s, most young people passed all these milestones in their early twenties.

In recent decades, this pattern has changed dramatically. Instead of settling down into jobs, marriage, and parenthood in a relatively short period after leaving adolescence, young adults now move into a lengthened period of transition that may last through the twenties and thirties and even beyond. Living at home with parents, or moving back and forth from home, is a common pattern. Many social critics see this shift simply as a refusal to grow up, as "arrested development" or "adultolescence" on a mass scale.

But this new and meandering road to adulthood doesn't reflect any major change in the psychology of today's young adults. Rather, it is a by-product of globalization and the information age. In different countries around the world, these large scale shifts have reduced job opportunities for young adults, increased the need and demand for education, and driven up the costs of housing.

The generations that came of age in the mass prosperity of 1950s and 60s could find steady, family-supporting work with just a high school diploma, or even less. Those born since the 1970s face new and difficult realities: you need a college degree or even more to get a decent job, but most average middle-class jobs don't pay very well. The affluent blue-collar workers of the postwar years have disappeared, along with the factories. Few jobs, even those that pay well, guarantee steady work. Settersten and Ray in their article argue that these new realities put strains on young people as well as their families and other institutions.

7

Parenthood

■ **READING 14**

New Families: Modern Couples as New Pioneers

Philip Cowan and Carolyn Pape Cowan

Mark and Abby met when they went to work for a young, ambitious candidate who was campaigning in a presidential primary. Over the course of an exhilarating summer, they debated endlessly about values and tactics. At summer's end they parted, returned to college, and proceeded to forge their individual academic and work careers. When they met again several years later at a political function, Mark was employed in the public relations department of a large company and Abby was about to graduate from law school. Their argumentative, passionate discussions about the need for political and social change gradually expanded to the more personal, intimate discussions that lovers have.

They began to plan a future together. Mark moved into Abby's apartment. Abby secured a job in a small law firm. Excited about their jobs and their flourishing relationship, they talked about making a long-term commitment and soon decided to marry. After the wedding, although their future plans were based on a strong desire to have children, they were uncertain about when to start a family. Mark raised the issue tentatively, but felt he did not have enough job security to take the big step. Abby was fearful of not being taken seriously if she became a mother too soon after joining her law firm.

Several years passed. Mark was now eager to have children. Abby, struggling with competing desires to have a baby *and* to move ahead in her professional life, was still hesitant. Their conversations about having a baby seemed to go nowhere but were dramatically interrupted when they suddenly discovered that their birth control method had failed: Abby was unmistakably pregnant. Somewhat surprised by their own reactions, Mark and Abby found that they were relieved to have the timing decision taken out of their hands. Feeling readier than they anticipated, they became increasingly excited as they shared the news with their parents, friends, and coworkers.

Most chapters [in the book from which this reading is taken] focus on high-risk families, a category in which some observers include all families that deviate from the traditional two-parent, nonteenage, father-at-work-mother-at-home "norm." The increasing prevalence of these families has been cited by David Popenoe, David Blankenhorn, and others[1] as strong evidence that American families are currently in a state of decline. In the debate over the state of contemporary family life, the family decline theorists imply that traditional families are faring well. This view ignores clear evidence of the pervasive stresses and vulnerabilities that are affecting most families these days—even those with two mature, relatively advantaged parents.

In the absence of this evidence, it appears as if children and parents in traditional two-parent families do not face the kinds of problems that require the attention of family policymakers. We will show that Abby and Mark's life, along with those of many modern couples forming new families, is less ideal and more subject to distress than family observers and policymakers realize. Using data from our own and others' studies of partners becoming parents, we will illustrate how the normal process of becoming a family *in this culture, at this time* sets in motion a chain of potential stressors that function as risks that stimulate moderate to severe distress for a substantial number of parents. Results of a number of recent longitudinal studies make clear that if the parents' distress is not addressed, the quality of their marriages and their relationships with their children are more likely to be compromised. In turn, conflictful or disengaged family relationships during the family's formative years foreshadow later problems for the children when they reach the preschool and elementary school years. This means that substantial numbers of new two-parent families in the United States do not fit the picture of the ideal family portrayed in the family decline debate.

In what follows we: (1) summarize the changing historical context that makes life for many modern parents more difficult than it used to be; (2) explore the premises underlying the current debate about family decline; (3) describe how conditions associated with the transition to parenthood create risks that increase the probability of individual, marital, and family distress; and (4) discuss the implications of this family strain for American family policy. We argue that systematic information about the early years of family life is critical to social policy debates in two ways: first, to show how existing laws and regulations can be harmful to young families, and second, to provide information about promising interventions with the potential to strengthen family relationships during the early childrearing years.

HISTORICAL CONTEXT: CHANGING FAMILIES IN A CHANGING WORLD

From the historical perspective of the past two centuries, couples like Mark and Abby are unprecedented. They are a modern, middle-class couple attempting to create a different kind of family than those of their parents and grandparents. Strained economic conditions and the shifting ideology about appropriate roles for mothers and fathers pose new challenges for these new pioneers whose journey will lead them through unfamiliar terrain. With no maps to pinpoint the risks and hardships, contemporary men and women must forge new trails on their own.

Based on our work with couples starting families over the past twenty years, we believe that the process of becoming a family is more difficult now than it used to be. Because of the dearth of systematic study of these issues, it is impossible to locate hard evidence that modern parents face more challenges than parents of the past. Nonetheless, a brief survey of the changing context of family life in North America suggests that the transition to parenthood presents different and more confusing challenges for modern couples creating families than it did for parents in earlier times.

Less Support = More Isolation

While 75 percent of American families lived in rural settings in 1850, 80 percent were living in urban or suburban environments in the year 2000. Increasingly, new families are created far from grandparents, kin, and friends with babies the same age, leaving parents without the support of those who could share their experiences of the ups and downs of parenthood. Most modern parents bring babies home to isolated dwellings where their neighbors are strangers. Many women who stay home to care for their babies find themselves virtually alone in the neighborhood during this major transition, a time when we know that inadequate social support poses a risk to their own and their babies' well-being.[2]

More Choice = More Ambiguity

Compared with the experiences of their parents and grandparents, couples today have more choice about whether and when to bring children into their lives. In addition to the fact that about 4.5 percent of women now voluntarily remain forever childless (up from 2.2 percent in 1980), partners who do become parents are older and have smaller families—only one or two children, compared to the average of three, forty years ago. The reduction in family size tends to make each child seem especially precious, and the decision about whether and when to become parents even more momentous. Modern birth control methods give couples more control over the timing of a pregnancy, in spite of the fact that many methods fail with some regularity, as they did for Mark and Abby. Although the legal and moral issues surrounding abortion are hotly debated, modern couples have a choice about whether to become parents, even after conception begins.

Once the baby is born, there are more choices for modern couples. Will the mother return to work or school, which most were involved in before giving birth, and if so, how soon and for how many hours? Whereas only 18 percent of women with a child under six were employed outside the home in 1960, according to the 2000 census, approximately 55 percent of women with a child *under one* now work at least part time. Will the father take an active role in daily child care, and if so, how much? Although having these new choices is regarded by many as a benefit of modern life, choosing from among alternatives with such far-reaching consequences creates confusion and uncertainty for both men and women—which itself can lead to tension within the couple.

New Expectations for Marriage = New Emotional Burdens

Mark and Abby, like many other modern couples, have different expectations for marriage than their forebears. In earlier decades, couples expected marriage to be a working partnership in which men and women played unequal but clearly defined roles in terms of family and work, especially once they had children. Many modern couples are trying to create more egalitarian relationships in which men and women have more similar and often interchangeable family and work roles.

The dramatic increase of women in the labor force has challenged old definitions of what men and women are expected to do inside and outside the family. As women have taken on a major role of contributing to family income, there has been a shift in *ideology* about fathers' greater participation in housework and child care, although the *realities* of men's and women's division of family labor have lagged behind. Despite the fact that modern fathers are a little more involved in daily family activities than their fathers were, studies in every industrialized country reveal that women continue to carry the major share of the burden of family work and care of the children, even when both partners are employed full time.[3] In a detailed qualitative study, Arlie Hochschild notes that working mothers come home to a "second shift." She describes vividly couples' struggle with contradictions between the values of egalitarianism and traditionalism, and between egalitarian ideology and the constraints of modern family life.

As husbands and wives struggle with these issues, they often become adversaries. At the same time, they expect their partners to be their major suppliers of emotional warmth and support.[4] These demanding expectations for marriage as a haven from the stresses of the larger world come naturally to modern partners, but this comfort zone is difficult to create, given current economic and psychological realities and the absence of helpful models from the past. The difficulty of the task is further compounded by the fact that when contemporary couples feel stressed by trying to work and nurture their children, they feel torn by what they hear from advocates of a "simpler," more traditional version of family life. In sum, we see Abby and Mark as new pioneers because they are creating a new version of family life in an era of greater challenges and fewer supports, increased and confusing choices about work and family arrangements, ambiguities about men's and women's proper roles, and demanding expectations of themselves to be both knowledgeable and nurturing partners and parents.

POLITICAL CONTEXT: DOES FAMILY CHANGE MEAN FAMILY DECLINE?

A number of writers have concluded that the historical family changes we described have weakened the institution of the family. One of the main spokespersons for this point of view, David Popenoe,[5] interprets the trends as documenting a "retreat from the traditional nuclear family in terms of a lifelong, sexually exclusive unit, with a separate-sphere division of labor between husbands and wives." He asserts, "Nuclear units are losing ground to single-parent families, serial and stepfamilies, and unmarried and homosexual couples."[6] The main problem in contemporary family life, he argues, is a shift in which familism as a cultural value has lost ground to other values such as individualism, self-focus, and egalitarianism.[7]

Family decline theorists are especially critical of single-parent families whether created by divorce or out-of-wedlock childbirth.[8] They assume that two-parent families of the past functioned with a central concern for children that led to putting children's needs first. They characterize parents who have children under other arrangements as putting themselves first, and they claim that children are suffering as a result.

The primary index for evaluating the family decline is the well-being of children. Family decline theorists repeatedly cite statistics suggesting that fewer children are being born, and that a higher proportion of them are living with permissive, disengaged, self-focused parents who ignore their physical and emotional needs. Increasing numbers of children show signs of mental illness, behavior problems, and social deviance. The remedy suggested? A social movement and social policies to promote "family values" that emphasize nuclear families with two married, monogamous parents who want to have children and are willing to devote themselves to caring for them. These are the families we have been studying.

Based on the work of following couples starting families over the past twenty years, we suggest that there is a serious problem with the suggested remedy, which ignores the extent of distress and dysfunction in this idealized family form. We will show that in a surprisingly high proportion of couples, the arrival of the first child is accompanied by increased levels of tension, conflict, distress, and divorce, not because the parents are self-centered but because it is inherently difficult in today's world to juggle the economic and emotional needs of all family members, even for couples in relatively "low-risk" circumstances. The need to pay more attention to the underside of the traditional family myth is heightened by the fact that we can now (1) identify in advance those couples most likely to have problems as they make the transition to parenthood, and (2) intervene to reduce the prevalence and intensity of these problems. Our concern with the state of contemporary families leads us to suggest remedies that would involve active support to enable parents to provide nurturance and stability for their children, rather than exhortations that they change their values about family life.

REAL LIFE CONTEXT: NORMAL RISKS ASSOCIATED WITH BECOMING A FAMILY

To illustrate the short-term impact of becoming parents, let us take a brief look at Mark and Abby four days after they bring their daughter, Lizzie, home from the hospital.

It is 3 A.M. Lizzie is crying lustily. Mark had promised that he would get up and bring the baby to Abby when she woke, but he hasn't stirred. After nudging him several times, Abby gives up and pads across the room to Lizzie's cradle. She carries her daughter to a rocking chair and starts to feed her. Abby's nipples are sore and she hasn't yet been able to relax while nursing. Lizzie soon stops sucking and falls asleep. Abby broods silently, the quiet broken only by the rhythmic squeak of the rocker. She is angry at Mark for objecting to her suggestion that her parents come to help. She fumes, thinking about his romantic image of the three of them as a cozy family. "Well, Lizzie and I are cozy all right, but where is Mr. Romantic now?" Abby is also preoccupied with worry. She is intrigued and drawn to Lizzie but because she hasn't experienced the "powerful surge of love" that she thinks "all mothers" feel, she worries that something is wrong with her. She is also anxious because she told her boss that she'd be back to work shortly, but she simply doesn't know how she will manage. She considers talking to her best friend, Adrienne, but Adrienne probably wouldn't understand because she doesn't have a child.

Hearing what he interprets as Abby's angry rocking, Mark groggily prepares his defense about why he failed to wake up when the baby did. Rather than engaging in conversation, recalling that Abby "barked" at him when he hadn't remembered to stop at the market and pharmacy on the way home from work, he pretends to be asleep. He becomes preoccupied with thoughts about the pile of work he will face at the office in the morning.

We can see how two well-meaning, thoughtful people have been caught up in changes and reactions that neither has anticipated or feels able to control. Based on our experience with many new parent couples, we imagine that, if asked, Abby and Mark would say that these issues arousing their resentment are minor; in fact, they feel foolish about being so upset about them. Yet studies of new parents suggest that the stage is set for a snowball effect in which these minor discontents can grow into more troubling distress in the next year or two. What are the consequences of this early disenchantment? Will Mark and Abby be able to prevent it from triggering more serious negative outcomes for them or for the baby?

To answer these questions about the millions of couples who become first-time parents each year, we draw on the results of our own longitudinal study of the transition to parenthood and those of several other investigators who also followed men and women from late pregnancy into the early years of life with a first child.[9] The samples in these studies were remarkably similar: the average age of first-time expectant fathers was about thirty years, of expectant mothers approximately one year younger. Most investigators studied urban couples, but a few included rural families. Although the participants' economic level varied from study to study, most fell on the continuum from working class, through lower-middle, to upper-middle class. In 1995 we reviewed more than twenty longitudinal studies of this period of family life; we included two in Germany by Engfer and Schneewind[10] and one in England by Clulow,[11] and found that results in all but two reveal an elevated risk for the marriages of couples becoming parents.[12] A more recent study and review comes to the same conclusion.[13]

We talk about this major normative transition in the life of a couple in terms of risk, conflict, and distress for the relationship because we find that the effects of the transition to parenthood create disequilibrium in each of five major domains of family life: (1) the parents' sense of self; (2) parent-grandparent relationships; (3) the parent-child relationships; (4) relationships with friends and work; and (5) the state of the marriage. We find that "fault lines" in any of these domains before the baby arrives amplify marital tensions during the transition to parenthood. Although it is difficult to determine precisely when the transition to parenthood begins and ends, our findings suggest that it encompasses a period of more than three years, from before conception until at least two years after the first child is born. Since different couples experience the transition in different ways, we rely here not only on Mark and Abby but also on a number of other couples in our study to illustrate what happens in each domain when partners become parents.

Parents' Sense of Self

Henry, aged 32, was doing well in his job at a large computer store. Along with Mei-Lin, his wife of four years, he was looking forward to the birth of his first child. Indeed, the first week or two found Henry lost in a euphoric haze. But as he came out of the clouds and went back to work, Henry began to be distracted by new worries. As his coworkers kept reminding him, he's a father now. He certainly feels like a different person, though he's not quite sure what a new father is supposed to be doing. Rather hesitantly, he confessed his sense of confusion to Mei-Lin, who appeared visibly relieved. "I've been feeling so fragmented," she told him. "It's been difficult to hold on to my sense of *me*. I'm a wife, a daughter, a friend, and a teacher, but the Mother part seems to have taken over my whole being."

Having a child forces a redistribution of the energy directed to various aspects of parents' identity. We asked expectant parents to describe themselves by making a list of the main aspects of themselves, such as son, daughter, friend, worker, and to divide a circle we called *The Pie* into pieces representing how large each aspect of self feels. Men and women filled out *The Pie* again six and eighteen months after their babies were born. As partners became parents, the size of the slice labeled *parent* increased markedly until it occupied almost one-third of the identity of mothers of eighteen-month-olds. Although men's *parent* slice also expanded, their sense of self as father occupied only one-third the "space" of their wives'. For both women and men, the *partner* or *lover* part of their identities got "squeezed" as the *parent* aspect of self expanded.

It is curious that in the early writing about the transition to parenthood, which E. E. LeMasters claimed constituted a crisis for a couple,[14] none of the investigators gathered or cited data on postpartum depression—diagnosed when disabling symptoms of depression occur within the first few months after giving birth. Accurate epidemiological estimates of risk for postpartum depression are difficult to come by. Claims about the incidence in women range from .01 percent for serious postpartum psychosis to 50 percent for the "baby blues." Results of a study by Campbell and her colleagues suggest that approximately 10 percent of new mothers develop serious clinical depressions that interfere with their daily functioning in the postpartum period.[15] There are no epidemiological estimates of the incidence of postpartum depression in new fathers. In our study of 100 couples, one new mother and one new father required medical treatment for disabling postpartum depression. What we know, then, is that many new parents like Henry and Mei-Lin experience a profound change in their view of themselves after they have a baby, and some feel so inadequate and critical of themselves that their predominant mood can be described as depressed.

Relationships with Parents and In-Laws

Sandra, one of the younger mothers in our study, talked with us about her fear of repeating the pattern from her mother's life. Her mother gave birth at sixteen, and told her children repeatedly that she was too young to raise a family. "Here I am with a beautiful little girl, and I'm worrying about whether I'm really grown up enough to raise her." At the same time, Sandra's husband, Daryl, who was beaten by his stepfather, is having flashbacks about how helpless he felt at those times: "I'm trying to maintain the confidence I felt when Sandra and I decided to start our family, but sometimes I get scared that I'm not going to be able to avoid being the kind of father I grew up with."

Psychoanalytically oriented writers[16] focusing on the transition to parenthood emphasize the potential disequilibration that is stimulated by a reawakening of intrapsychic conflicts from new parents' earlier relationships. There is considerable evidence that having a baby stimulates men's and women's feelings of vulnerability and loss associated with their own childhoods, and that these issues play a role in their emerging sense of self as parents. There is also evidence that negative relationship patterns tend to be repeated across the generations, despite parents' efforts to avoid them;[17] so Sandra and Daryl have good reason to be concerned. However, studies showing that a strong, positive couple relationship can provide a buffer against negative parent-child interactions suggest that the repetition of negative cycles is not inevitable.[18]

We found that the birth of a first child increases the likelihood of contact between the generations, often with unanticipated consequences. Occasionally, renewed contact allows the expectant parents to put years of estrangement behind them if their parents are receptive to renewed contact. More often, increased contact between the generations stimulates old and new conflicts—within each partner, between the partners, and between the generations. To take one example: Abby wants her mother to come once the baby is born but Mark has a picture of beginning family life on their own. Tensions between them around this issue can escalate regardless of which decision they make. If Abby's parents do visit, Mark may have difficulty establishing his place with the baby. Even if Abby's parents come to help, she and Mark may find that the grandparents need looking after too. It may be weeks before Mark and Abby have a private conversation. If the grandparents do not respond or are not invited, painful feelings between the generations are likely to ensue.

The Parent-Child Relationship

Few parents have had adequate experience in looking after children to feel confident immediately about coping with the needs of a first baby.

Tyson and Martha have been arguing, it seems, for days. Eddie, their six-month-old, has long crying spells every day and into the night. As soon as she hears him, Martha moves to pick him up. When he is home, Tyson objects, reasoning that this just spoils Eddie and doesn't let him learn how to soothe himself. Martha responds that Eddie wouldn't be crying if something weren't wrong, but she worries that Tyson may be right; after all, she's never looked after a six-month-old for more than an evening of baby-sitting. Although

Tyson continues to voice his objections, he worries that if Martha is right, *his* plan may not be the best for his son either.

To make matters more complicated, just as couples develop strategies that seem effective, their baby enters a new developmental phase that calls for new reactions and routines. What makes these new challenges difficult to resolve is that each parent has a set of ideas and expectations about how parents should respond to a child, most based on experience in their families of origin. Meshing both parents' views of how to resolve basic questions about child rearing proves to be a more complex and emotionally draining task than most couples had anticipated.

Work and Friends

Dilemmas about partners' work outside the home are particularly salient during a couple's transition to parenthood.

> Both Hector and Isabel have decided that Isabel should stay home for at least the first year after having the baby. One morning, as Isabel is washing out José's diapers and hoping the phone will ring, she breaks into tears. Life is not as she imagined it. She misses her friends at work. She misses Hector, who is working harder now to provide for his family than he was before José was born. She misses her parents and sisters who live far away in Mexico. She feels strongly that she wants to be with her child full time, and that she should be grateful that Hector's income makes this possible, but she feels so unhappy right now. This feeling adds to her realization that she has always contributed half of their family income, but now she has to ask Hector for household money, which leaves her feeling vulnerable and dependent.
>
> Maria is highly invested in her budding career as an investment counselor, making more money than her husband, Emilio. One morning, as she faces the mountain of unread files on her desk and thinks of Lara at the child care center almost ready to take her first steps, Maria bursts into tears. She feels confident that she and Emilio have found excellent child care for Lara, and reminds herself that research has suggested that when mothers work outside the home, their daughters develop more competence than daughters of mothers who stay home. Nevertheless, she feels bereft, missing milestones that happen only once in a child's life.

We have focused on the women in both families because, given current societal arrangements, the initial impact of the struggle to balance work and family falls more heavily on mothers. If the couple decides that one parent will stay home to be the primary caretaker of the child, it is almost always the mother who does so. As we have noted, in contemporary America, about 50 percent of mothers of very young children remain at home after having a baby and more than half return to work within the first year. Both alternatives have some costs and some benefits. If mothers like Isabel want to be home with their young children, and the family can afford this arrangement, they have the opportunity to participate fully in the early day-to-day life of their children. This usually has benefits for parents and children. Nevertheless, most mothers who stay home face limited opportunities to accomplish work that leads them to feel competent, and staying home deprives them of emotional support that coworkers and friends can provide, the kinds of support that play a significant role in how parents fare in the early postpartum years. This leaves women like Isabel at risk for feeling lonely and isolated from friends and family.[19] By contrast, women like Maria who return to work are able to maintain a network of adults to work with and talk with. They may feel better about themselves and "on track" as far as their work is concerned, but many become preoccupied with worry about their children's well-being, particularly in this age of costly but less than ideal child care. Furthermore, once they get home, they enter a "second shift" in which they do the bulk of the housework and child care.[20]

We do not mean to imply that all the work-family conflicts surrounding the transition to parenthood are experienced by women. Many modern fathers feel torn about how to juggle work and family life, move ahead on the job, and be more involved with their children than their fathers were with them. Rather than receive a reduction in workload, men tend to work longer hours once they become fathers, mainly because they take their role as provider even more seriously now that they have a child.[21] In talking to more than 100 fathers in our ongoing studies, we have become convinced that the common picture of men as resisting the responsibilities and workload involved in family life is seriously in error. We have become painfully aware of the formidable obstacles that bar men from assuming more active roles as fathers and husbands.

First, parents, bosses, and friends often discourage men's active involvement in the care of their children ("How come you're home in the middle of the day?" "Are you really serious about your work here?" "She's got you baby-sitting again, huh?"). Second, the economic realities in which men's pay exceeds women's, make it less viable for men to take family time off. Third, by virtue of the way males and females are socialized, men rarely get practice in looking after children and are given very little support for learning by trial and error with their new babies.

> In the groups that we conducted for expectant and new parents, to which parents brought their babies after they were born, we saw and heard many versions of the following: we are discussing wives' tendency to reach for the baby, on the assumption that their husbands will not respond. Cindi describes an incident last week when little Samantha began to cry. Cindi waited. Her husband, Martin, picked up Samantha gingerly, groped for a bottle, and awkwardly started to feed her. Then, according to Martin, within about sixty seconds, Cindi suggested that Martin give Samantha's head more support and prop the bottle in a different way so that the milk would flow without creating air bubbles. Martin quickly decided to hand the baby back to "the expert" and slipped into the next room "to get some work done."

The challenge to juggle the demands of work, family, and friendship presents different kinds of stressors for men and women, which propels the spouses even farther into separate worlds. When wives stay at home, they wait eagerly for their husbands to return, hoping the men will go "on duty" with the child, especially on difficult days. This leaves tired husbands who need to unwind facing tired wives who long to talk to an adult who will respond intelligibly to them. When both parents work outside the family, they must coordinate schedules, arrange child care, and decide how to manage when their child is ill. Parents' stress from these dilemmas about child care and lack of rest often spill over into the workday—and their work stress, in turn, gets carried back into the family atmosphere.[22]

The Marriage

It should be clearer now why we say that the normal changes associated with becoming a family increase the risk that husbands and wives will experience increased marital dissatisfaction and strain after they become parents. Mark and Abby, and the other couples we have described briefly, have been through changes in their sense of themselves and in their relationships with their parents. They have struggled with uncertainties and disagreements about how to provide the best care for their child. Regardless of whether one parent stays home full or part time or both work full days outside the home, they have limited time and energy to meet conflicting demands from their parents, bosses, friends, child, and each other, and little support from outside the family to guide them on this complex journey into uncharted territory. In almost every published study of the transition conducted over the last four decades, men's and women's marital satisfaction declined. Belsky and Rovine found that from 30 percent to 59 percent of the participants in their Pennsylvania study showed a decline between pregnancy and nine months postpartum, depending on which measure of the marriage they examined.[23] In our study of California parents, 45 percent of the men and 58 percent of the women showed declining satisfaction with marriage between pregnancy and eighteen months postpartum. The scores of approximately 15 percent of the new parents moved from below to above the clinical cutoff that indicates serious marital problems, whereas only 4 percent moved from above to below the cutoff.

Why should this optimistic time of life pose so many challenges for couples? One key issue for couples becoming parents has been treated as a surefire formula for humor in situation comedies—husband-wife battles over the "who does what?" of housework, child care, and decision making. Our own study shows clearly that, regardless of how equally family work is divided before having a baby, or of how equally husbands and wives *expect* to divide the care of the baby, the roles men and women assume tend to be gender-linked, with wives doing more family work than they had done before becoming a parent and substantially more housework and baby care than their husbands do. Furthermore, the greater the discrepancy between women's predicted and actual division of family tasks with their spouses, the more symptoms of depression they report. The more traditional the arrangements—that is, the less husbands are responsible for family work—the greater fathers' *and* mothers' postpartum dissatisfaction with their overall marriage.

Although theories of life stress generally assume that *any* change is stressful, we found no correlation between sheer *amount* of change in the five aspects of family life and parents' difficulties adapting to parenthood. In general, parenthood was followed by increasing discrepancies between husbands' and wives' perceptions of family life and their descriptions of their actual family and work roles. Couples in which the partners showed the greatest increase in those discrepancies—more often those with increasingly traditional role arrangements—described increasing conflict as a couple and greater declines in marital satisfaction.

These findings suggest that whereas family decline theorists are looking at statistics about contemporary families through 1950 lenses, actual families are responding to the realities of life in the twenty-first century. Given historical shifts in men's and women's ideas about family roles and present economic realities, it is not realistic to expect them to simply reverse trends by adopting more traditional values and practices. Contemporary families in which the parents' arrangements are at the more traditional end of the spectrum are *less* satisfied with themselves, with their relationships as couples, and with their role as parents, than those at the more egalitarian end.

DO WE KNOW WHICH FAMILIES WILL BE AT RISK?

The message for policymakers from research on the transition to parenthood is not only that it is a time of stress and change. We and others have found that there is predictability to couples' patterns of change: this means that it is possible to know whether a couple is at risk for more serious problems before they have a baby and whether their child will be at risk for compromised development. This information is also essential for purposes of designing *preventive* intervention. Couples most at risk for difficulties and troubling outcomes in the early postpartum years are those who were in the greatest individual and marital distress before they became parents. Children most at risk are those whose parents are having the most difficulty maintaining a positive, rewarding relationship as a couple.

The "Baby-Maybe" Decision

Interviews with expectant parents about their process of making the decision to have a baby provide one source of information about continuity of adaptation in the family-making period. By analyzing partners' responses to the question, "How did the two of you come to be having a baby at this time?" we found four fairly distinct types of decision making in our sample of lower-middle- to upper-middle-class couples, none of whom had identified themselves as having serious relationship difficulties during pregnancy: (1) The *Planners*—50 percent of the couples—agreed about whether and when to have a baby. The other 50 percent were roughly evenly divided into three patterns: (2) The *Acceptance of fate couples*—15 percent—had unplanned conceptions but were pleased to learn that they were about to become parents; (3) The *Ambivalent couples*—another 15 percent—continually went back and forth about their readiness to have a baby, even late in pregnancy; and (4) The *Yes-No couples*—the remaining 15 percent—claimed not to be having relationship difficulties but nonetheless had strong disagreements about whether to complete their unplanned pregnancy.

Alice, thirty-four, became pregnant when she and Andy, twenty-seven, had been living together only four months. She was determined to have a child, regardless of whether Andy stayed in the picture. He did not feel ready to become a father, and though he dearly loved Alice, he was struggling to come to terms with the pregnancy. "It was the hardest thing I ever had to deal with," he said. "I had this idea that I wasn't even going to have to think about being a father until I was over thirty, but here it was, and I had to decide now. I was concerned about my soul. I didn't want, under any circumstances, to compromise myself, but I knew it would be very hard on Alice if I took action that would result in her being a single parent. It would've meant that I'm the kind of person who turns his back on someone I care about, and that would destroy me as well as her." And so he stayed.[24]

The *Planners* and *Acceptance of fate couples* experienced minimal decline in marital satisfaction, whereas the *Ambivalent couples* tended to have lower satisfaction to begin with and to decline even further between pregnancy and two years later. The greatest risk was for couples who had serious disagreement—more than ambivalence—about having a first baby. In these cases, one partner gave in to the other's wishes in order to remain in the relationship. The startling outcome provides a strong statement about the wisdom of this strategy: all of the *Yes-No couples* like Alice and Andy were divorced by the time their first child entered kindergarten, and the two *Yes-No couples* in which the wife was the reluctant partner reported severe marital distress at every postpartum assessment. This finding suggests that partners' unresolved conflict in making the decision to have a child is mirrored by their inability to cope with conflict to both partners' satisfaction once they become parents. Couples' styles of making this far-reaching decision seem to be a telling indicator of whether their overall relationship is at risk for instability, a finding that contradicts the folk wisdom that having a baby will mend serious marital rifts.

Additional Risk Factors for Couples

Not surprisingly, when couples reported high levels of outside-the-family life stress during pregnancy, they are more likely to be unhappy in their marriages and stressed in their parenting roles during the early years of parenthood. When there are serious problems in the relationships between new parents and their own parents the couples are more likely to experience more postpartum distress.[25] Belsky and colleagues showed that new parents who recalled strained relationships with their own parents were more likely to experience more marital distress in the first year of parenthood.[26] In our study, parents who reported early childhoods clouded by their parents' problem drinking had a more stressful time on every indicator of adjustment in the first two years of parenthood—more conflict, less effective problem solving, less effective parenting styles, and greater parenting stress.[27] Although the transmission of maladaptive patterns across generations is not inevitable, these data suggest that without intervention, troubled relationships in the family of origin constitute a risk factor for relationships in the next generation.

Although it is never possible to make perfect predictions for purposes of creating family policies to help reduce the risks associated with family formation, we have been able to identify expectant parents at risk for later individual, marital, and parenting difficulties based on information they provided during pregnancy. Recall that the participants in the studies we are describing are the two-parent intact families portrayed as ideal in the family decline debate. The problems they face have little to do with their family values. The difficulties appear to stem from the fact that the visible fault lines in couple relationships leave their marriages more vulnerable to the shake-up of the transition-to-parenthood process.

Risks for Children

We are concerned about the impact of the transition to parenthood not only because it increases the risk of distress in marriage but also because the parents' early distress can have far-reaching consequences for their children. Longitudinal studies make it clear that parents' early difficulties affect their children's later intellectual and social adjustment. For example, parents' well-being or distress as individuals and as couples during pregnancy predicts the quality of their relationships with their children in the preschool period.[28] In turn, the quality of both parent-child relationships in the preschool years is related to the child's academic and social competence during the early elementary school years.[29] Preschoolers whose mothers and fathers had more responsive, effective parenting styles had higher scores on academic achievement and fewer acting out, aggressive, or withdrawn behavior problems with peers in kindergarten and Grade 1.[30] When we receive teachers' reports, we see that overall, five-year-olds whose parents reported making the most positive adaptations to parenthood were the ones with the most successful adjustments to elementary school.

Alexander and Entwisle[31] suggested that in kindergarten and first grade, children are "launched into achievement trajectories that they follow the rest of their school years." Longitudinal studies of children's academic and social competence[32] support this hypothesis about the importance of students' early adaptation to school: children who are socially rejected by peers in the early elementary grades are more likely to have academic problems or drop out of school, to develop antisocial and delinquent behaviors, and to have difficulty in intimate relationships with partners in late adolescence and early adulthood. Without support or intervention early in a family's development, the children with early academic, emotional, and social problems are at greater risk for later, even more serious problems.

POLICY IMPLICATIONS

What social scientists have learned about families during the transition to parenthood is relevant to policy discussions about how families with young children can be strengthened.

We return briefly to the family values debate to examine the policy implications of promoting traditional family arrangements, of altering workplace policies, and of providing preventive interventions to strengthen families during the early childrearing years.

The Potential Consequences of Promoting Traditional Family Arrangements

What are the implications of the argument that families and children would benefit by a return to traditional family arrangements? We are aware that existing data are not adequate to provide a full test of the family values argument, but we believe that some systematic information on this point is better than none. At first glance, it may seem as if studies support the arguments of those proposing that "the family" is in decline. We have documented the fact that a substantial number of new two-parent families are experiencing problems of adjustment—parents' depression, troubled marriages, inter-generational strain, and stress in juggling the demands of work and family. Nevertheless, there is little in the transition to parenthood research to support the idea that parents' distress is attributable to a decline in their family-oriented *values*. First, the populations studied here are two-parent, married, nonteenage, lower-middle- to upper-middle-class families, who do not represent the "variants" in family form that most writers associate with declining quality of family life.

Second, threaded throughout the writings on family decline is the erroneous assumption that because these changes in the family have been occurring at the same time as increases in negative outcomes for children, the changes are the *cause* of the problems. These claims are not buttressed by systematic data establishing the direction of causal influence. For example, it is well accepted (but still debated) that children's adaptation is poorer in the period after their parents' divorce.[33] Nevertheless, some studies suggest that it is the unresolved conflict between parents prior to and after the divorce, rather than the divorce itself, that accounts for most of the debilitating effects on the children.[34]

Third, we find the attack on family egalitarianism puzzling when the fact is that, despite the increase in egalitarian ideology, modern couples move toward more traditional family role arrangements as they become parents—despite their intention to do otherwise. Our key point here is that traditional family and work roles in families of the last three decades tend to be associated with *more* individual and marital distress for parents. Furthermore, we find that when fathers have little involvement in household and child care tasks, both parents are less responsive and less able to provide the structure necessary for their children to accomplish new and challenging tasks in our project playroom. Finally, when we ask teachers how all of the children in their classrooms are faring at school, it is the children of these parents who are less academically competent and more socially isolated. There is, then, a body of evidence suggesting that a return to strictly traditional family arrangements may not have the positive consequences that the proponents of "family values" claim they will.

Family and Workplace Policy

Current discussions about policies for reducing the tensions experienced by parents of young children tend to be polarized around two alternatives: (1) Encourage more mothers to stay home and thereby reduce their stress in juggling family and work; (2) Make the workplace more flexible and "family friendly" for both parents through parental leave policies, flextime, and child care provided or subsidized by the workplace. There is no body of systematic empirical research that supports the conclusion that when mothers work outside the home, their children or husbands suffer negative consequences.[35] In fact, our own data and others' suggest that (1) children, especially girls, benefit from the model their working mothers provide as productive workers, and (2) mothers of young children who return to work are less depressed than mothers who stay home full time.

Thus it is not at all clear that a policy designed to persuade contemporary mothers of young children to stay at home would have the desired effects, particularly given the potential for depression and the loss of one parent's wages in single paycheck families. Unless governments are prepared, as they are in Sweden and Germany, for example, to hold parents' jobs and provide *paid* leave to replace lost wages, a stay-at-home *policy* seems too costly for the family on both economic and psychological grounds.

We believe that the issue should not be framed in terms of policies to support single-worker *or* dual-worker families, but rather in terms of support for the well-being of all family members. This goal could entail financial support for families with very young children so that parents could choose to do full-time or substantial part-time child care themselves *or* to have support to return to work.

What about the alternative of increasing workplace flexibility? Studies of families making the transition to parenthood suggest that this alternative may be especially attractive and helpful when children are young, if it is accompanied by substantial increases in the availability of high-quality child care to reduce the stress of locating adequate care or making do with less than ideal caretakers. Adults and children tend to adapt well when both parents work *if both parents support that alternative*. Therefore, policies that support paid family leave along with flexible work arrangements could enable families to choose arrangements that make most sense for their particular situation.

Preventive Services to Address Family Risk Points

According to our analysis of the risks associated with the formation of new families, many two-parent families are having difficulty coping on their own with the normal challenges of becoming a family. If a priority in our society is to strengthen new families, it seems reasonable to consider offering preventive programs to reduce risks and distress and enhance the potential for healthy and satisfying family relationships, which we know lead to more optimal levels of adjustment in children. What we are advocating is analogous to the concept of Lamaze and other forms of childbirth preparation, which are now commonly sought by many expectant parents. A logical context for these programs would be existing public and private health and mental health delivery systems in which services could be provided for families who wish assistance or are already in difficulty. We recognize that there is skepticism in a substantial segment of the population about psychological services in general, and about services provided for families by government in particular. Nonetheless, the fact is that many modern families are finding parenthood unexpectedly stressful and they typically have no access to assistance. Evidence from intervention trials suggests that when preventive programs help parents move their family relationships in more positive directions, their children have fewer academic, behavioral, and emotional problems in their first years of schooling.[36]

Parent-Focused Interventions. Elsewhere, we reviewed the literature on interventions designed to improve parenting skills and parent-child relationship quality in families at different points on the spectrum from low-risk to high-distress.[37] For parents of children already identified as having serious problems, home visiting programs and preschool and early school interventions, some of which include a broader family focus, have demonstrated positive effects on parents' behavior and self-esteem and on children's academic and social competence, particularly when the intervention staff are health or mental health professionals. However, with the exception of occasional classes, books, or tapes for parents, there are few resources for parents who need to learn more about how to manage small problems before they spiral out of their control.

Couple-Focused Interventions. Our conceptual model of family transitions and results of studies of partners who become parents suggest that family-based interventions might go beyond enhancing parent-child relationships to strengthen the relationship *between* the parents. We have seen that the couple relationship is vulnerable in its own right around the decision to have a baby and increasingly after the birth of a child. We know of only one pilot program that provided couples an opportunity to explore mixed feelings about the "Baby-Maybe" decision.[38] Surely, services designed to help couples resolve their conflict about whether and when to become a family—especially "Yes-No" couples—might reduce the risks of later marital and family distress, just as genetic counseling helps couples make decisions when they are facing the risk of serious genetic problems.

In our own work, we have been systematically evaluating two preventive interventions for couples who have not been identified as being in a high-risk category. Both projects involved work with small groups of couples who met weekly over many months, in one case expectant couples, in the other, couples whose first child is about to make the transition to elementary school.[39] In both studies, staff couples who are mental health professionals worked with *both parents* in small groups of four or five couples. Ongoing discussion over the months of regular meetings addressed participants' individual, marital, parenting, and three-generational dilemmas and problems. In both cases we found promising results when we compared adjustment in families with and without the intervention.

By two years after the Becoming a Family project intervention, new parents had avoided the typical declines in role satisfaction and the increases in marital disenchantment reported in almost every longitudinal study of new parents. There were no separations or divorces in couples who participated in the intervention for the first three years of parenthood, whereas 15 percent of comparable couples with no intervention had already divorced. The positive impact of this intervention was still apparent five years after it had ended.

In the Schoolchildren and Their Families project intervention, professional staff engaged couples in group discussions of marital, parenting, and three-generational problems and dilemmas during their first child's transition to school. Two years after the intervention ended, fathers and mothers showed fewer symptoms of depression and less conflict in front of their child, and fathers were more effective in helping their children with difficult tasks than comparable parents with no intervention. These positive effects on the parents' lives and relationships had benefits for the children as well: children of parents who worked with the professionals in an ongoing couples group showed greater academic improvement and fewer emotional and behavior problems in the first five years of elementary school than children whose parents had no group intervention.[40]

These results suggest that preventive interventions in which clinically trained staff work with "low-risk" couples have the potential to buffer some of the parents' strain, slow down or stop the spillover of negative and unrewarding patterns from one relationship to another, enhance fathers' responsiveness to their children, and foster the children's ability both to concentrate on their school work and to develop more rewarding relationships with their peers. The findings suggest that *without intervention*, there is increased risk of spillover from parents' distress to the quality of the parent-child relationships. This means that preventive services to help parents cope more effectively with their problems have the potential to enhance their responsiveness to their children *and* to their partners, which, in turn, optimizes their children's chances of making more successful adjustments to school. Such programs have the potential to reduce the long-term negative consequences of children's early school difficulties by setting them on more positive developmental trajectories as they face the challenges of middle childhood.

CONCLUSION

The transition to parenthood has been made by men and women for centuries. In the past three decades, the notion that this transition poses risks for the well-being of adults and, thus, potentially for their children's development, has been greeted by some with surprise, disbelief, or skepticism. Our goal has been to bring recent social science findings about the processes involved in becoming a family to the attention of social scientists, family policymakers, and parents themselves. We have shown that this often-joyous time is normally accompanied by changes and stressors that increase risks of relationship difficulty and compromise the ability of men and women to create the kinds of families they dream of when they set out on their journey to parenthood. We conclude that there is cause for concern about the health of "the family"—even those considered advantaged by virtue of their material and psychological resources.

Most chapters in this book focus on policies for families in more high-risk situations. We have argued that contemporary couples and their children in two-parent lower- to upper-middle-class families deserve the attention of policymakers as well. We view these couples as new pioneers, because, despite the fact that partners have been having babies for millennia, contemporary parents are journeying into uncharted terrain, which appears to hold unexpected risks to their own and their children's development.

Like writers describing "family decline," we are concerned about the strength and hardiness of two-parent families. Unlike those who advocate that parents adopt more traditional family values, we recommend that policies to address family health and well-being allow for the creation of programs and services for families in diverse family arrangements, with the goal of enhancing the development and well-being of all children. We recognize that with economic resources already stretched very thin, this is not an auspicious time to recommend additional collective funding of family services. Yet research suggests that without intervention, there is a risk that the vulnerabilities and problems of the parents will spill over into the lives of their children, thus increasing the probability of the transmission of the kinds of intergenerational problems that erode the quality of family life and compromise children's chances of optimal development. This will be very costly in the long run.

We left Mark and Abby, and a number of other couples, in a state of animated suspension. Many of them were feeling somewhat irritable and disappointed, though not ready to give up on their dreams of creating nurturing families. These couples provide a challenge—that the information they have offered through their participation in scores of systematic family studies in many locales will be taken seriously, and that their voices will play a role in helping our society decide how to allocate limited economic and social resources for the families that need them.

Notes

1. D. Blankenhorn, S. Bayme, and J. B. Elshtain (eds.), *Rebuilding the Nest: A New Commitment to the American Family* (Milwaukee, WI: Family Service America, 1990), 3–26; D. Popenoe, "American Family Decline, 1960–1990," *Journal of Marriage and the Family* 55: 527–541, 1993.
2. S. B. Crockenberg, "Infant Irritability, Mother Responsiveness, and Social Support Influences on Security of Infant-Mother Attachment," *Child Development* 52: 857–865, 1981; C. Cutrona, "Non-psychotic Postpartum Depression: A Review of Recent Research," *Clinical Psychology Review* 2: 487–503, 1982.
3. A. Hochschild, *The Second Shift: Working Parents and the Revolution at Home* (New York: Viking Penguin, 1989); J. H. Pleck, "Fathers and Infant Care Leave," in E. F. Zigler and M. Frank (eds.), *The Parental Leave Crisis: Toward a National Policy* (New Haven, CT: Yale University Press, 1988).
4. A. Skolnick, *Embattled Paradise: The American Family in an Age of Uncertainty* (New York: Basic Books, 1991).
5. D. Popenoe, *Disturbing the Nest: Family Change and Decline in Modern Societies* (New York: Aldine de Gruyter, 1988); Popenoe, "American Family Decline."
6. Popenoe, "American Family Decline." 41–42. Smaller two-parent families and larger one-parent families are both attributed to the same mechanism: parental self-focus and selfishness.
7. D. Blankenhorn, "American Family Dilemmas," in D. Blankenhorn, S. Bayme, and J. B. Elshtain (eds.), *Rebuilding the Nest. A New Commitment to the American Family* (Milwaukee, WI: Family Service America, 1990), 3–26.
8. Although the proportion of single-parent families is increasing, the concern about departure from the two-parent form may be overstated. Approximately 70 percent of American babies born in the 1990s come home to two parents who are married. If we include couples with long-term commitments who are not legally married, the proportion of modern families that *begins* with two parents is even higher. The prevalence of two-parent families has declined since 1956, when 94 percent of newborns had married parents, but, by far, the predominant family form in the nonteenage population continues to be two parents and a baby.
9. J. Belsky, M. Lang, and M. Rovine, "Stability and Change across the Transition to Parenthood: A Second Study," *Journal of Personality and Social Psychology* 50: 517–522, 1985; C. P. Cowan, P. A. Cowan, G. Heming, E. Garrett, W. S. Coysh, H. Curtis-Boles, and A. J. Boles, "Transitions to Parenthood: His, Hers, and Theirs," *Journal of Family Issues* 6: 451–481, 1985; M. J. Cox, M. T. Owen, J. M. Lewis, and V. K. Henderson, "Marriage, Adult Adjustment, and Early Parenting," *Child Development* 60: 1015–1024, 1989; F. Grossman, L. Eiehler, and S. Winickoff, *Pregnancy, Birth, and Parenthood* (San Francisco: Jossey-Bass, 1980); C. M. Heinicke, S. D. Diskin, D. M. Ramsay-Klee, and D. S. Oates, "Pre- and Postbirth Antecedents of 2-year-old Attention, Capacity for Relationships and Verbal Expressiveness," *Developmental Psychology* 22: 777–787, 1986; R. Levy-Shiff, "Individual and Contextual Correlates of Marital Change Across the Transition to Parenthood," *Developmental Psychology* 30: 591–601, 1994.

10. A. Engfer, "The Interrelatedness of Marriage and the Mother-Child Relationship," in R. A. Hinde and J. Stevenson-Hinde (eds.), *Relationships within Families: Mutual Influences* (Cambridge, UK: Cambridge University Press, 1988), 104–118; K. A. Schneewind, "Konsequenzen der Erstelternschaft" [Consequences of the Transition to Parenthood: An Overview], *Psychologie in Erziehung and Unterricht* 30: 161–172, 1983.

11. C. F. Clulow, *To Have and to Hold: Marriage, the First Baby and Preparing Couples for Parenthood* (Aberdeen, Scotland: Aberdeen University Press, 1982).

12. C. P. Cowan and P. A. Cowan, "Interventions to Ease the Transition to Parenthood: Why They Are Needed and What They Can Do," *Family Relations* 44: 412–423, 1995.

13. A. F. Shapiro, J. M. Gottman, and S. Carrere, "The Baby and the Marriage. Identifying Factors that Buffer against Decline in Marital Satisfaction after the First Baby Arrives. *Journal of Family Psychology*, 14: 59–70, 2000.

14. E. E. LeMasters, "Parenthood as Crisis," *Marriage and Family Living* 19: 352–365, 1957.

15. S. B. Campbell, J. F. Cohn, C. Flanagan, S. Popper, and T. Myers, "Course and Correlates of Postpartum Depression during the Transition to Parenthood," *Development and Psychopathology* 4: 29–48, 1992.

16. T. Benedek, "Parenthood during the Life Cycle," in E. J. Anthony and T. Benedek (eds.), *Parenthood: Its Psychology and Psychopathology* (Boston: Little, Brown, 1970); J. D. Osofsky and H. J. Osofsky, "Psychological and Developmental Perspectives on Expectant and New Parenthood," in R. D. Parke (ed.), *Review of Child Development Research 7: The Family* (Chicago: University of Chicago Press, 1984), 372–397.

17. A. Caspi and G. H. Elder, Jr. "Emergent Family Patterns: The Intergenerational Construction of Problem Behavior and Relationships," in R. A. Hinde and J. Stevenson-Hinde (eds.), *Relationships Within Families: Mutual Influences* (Oxford: Clarendon Press, 1988), 218–241; M. H. van Ijzendoorn, F. Juffer, M. G. Duyvesteyn, "Breaking the Intergenerational Cycle of Insecure Attachment: A Review of the Effects of Attachment-based Interventions on Maternal Sensitivity and Infant Security," *Journal of Child Psychology & Psychiatry & Allied Disciplines* 36: 225–248, 1995.

18. D. A. Cohn, P. A. Cowan, C. P. Cowan, and J. Pearson, "Mothers' and Fathers' Working Models of Childhood Attachment Relationships, Parenting Styles, and Child Behavior," *Development and Psychopathology* 4: 417–431, 1992.

19. Crockenberg, "Infant Irritability."

20. Hochschild, *The Second Shift.*

21. C. P. Cowan and P. A. Cowan, *When Partners Become Parents: The Big Life Change for Couples* (Mahwah, NJ: Lawrence Erlbaum, 2000).

22. M. S. Schulz, "Coping with Negative Emotional Arousal: The Daily Spillover of Work Stress into Marital Interactions," Unpublished doctoral dissertation. University of California, Berkeley, 1994; R. Repetti and J. Wood, "Effects of Daily Stress at Work on Mothers' Interactions with Preschoolers," *Journal of Family Psychology*, 11: 90–108, 1997.

23. J. Belsky and M. Rovine, "Patterns of Marital Change across the Transition to Parenthood," *Journal of Marriage and the Family* 52: 109–123, 1990.

24. We interviewed the couples in the mid-to-late stages of pregnancy. We were not, therefore, privy to the early phases of decision making of these couples, whether wives became pregnant on purpose, or whether husbands were coercive about the baby decision. What we saw in the Yes-No couples, in contrast with the Ambivalent couples, was that the decision to go ahead with the pregnancy, an accomplished fact, was still an unresolved emotional struggle.

25. M. Kline, P. A. Cowan, and C. P. Cowan, "The Origins of Parenting Stress during the Transition to Parenthood: A New Family Model," *Early Education and Development* 2: 287–305, 1991.

26. J. Belsky and R. A. Isabella, "Marital and Parent-Child Relationships in Family of Origin and Marital Change Following the Birth of a Baby: A Retrospective Analysis," *Child Development* 56: 342–349, 1985; C. P. Cowan, P. A. Cowan, and G. Heming, "Adult Children of Alcoholics:

Adaptation during the Transition to Parenthood." Paper presented to the National Council on Family Relations, 1988.

27. Cowan, Cowan, and Heming; "Adult Children of Alcoholics."

28. Belsky, Lang, and Rovine, "Stability and Change across the Transition to Parenthood"; Cowan and Cowan, *When Partners Become Parents*; Cox, Owen, Lewis, and Henderson, "Marriage, Adult Adjustment, and Early Parenting"; Heinicke, Diskin, Ramsay-Klee, and Oates, "Pre- and Postbirth Antecedents of 2-Year-Old Attention, Capacity for Relationships and Verbal Expressiveness."

29. D. Baumrind, "The Development of Instrumental Competence through Socialization," in A. D. Pick (ed.), *Minnesota Symposia on Child Psychology*, vol. 7 (Minneapolis: University of Minnesota Press, 1979); J. H. Block and J. Block, "The Role of Ego-Control and Ego-Resiliency in the Organization of Behavior," in W. A. Collins (ed.), *Minnesota Symposia on Child Psychology*, vol. 13 (Hillsdale, NJ: Erlbaum, 1980).

30. P. A. Cowan, C. P. Cowan, M. Schulz, and G. Heming, "Prebirth to Preschool Family Factors Predicting Children's Adaptation to Kindergarten," in R. Parke and S. Kellam (eds.), *Exploring Family Relationships with Other Social Contexts: Advances in Family Research*, vol. 4 (Hillsdale, NJ: Erlbaum, 1994), 75–114.

31. K. L. Alexander and D. Entwisle, "Achievement in the First 2 Years of School: Patterns and Processes," *Monographs of the Society for Research in Child Development* 53: 2, Serial No. 218, 1988.

32. S. Asher and J. D. Coie (eds.), *Peer Rejection in Childhood* (Cambridge: Cambridge University Press, 1990); S. G. Kellam, M. B. Simon, and M. E. Ensminger, "Antecedents in First Grade of Teenage Drug Use and Psychological Well-Being: A Ten-Year Community-wide Prospective Study," in D. Ricks and B. Dohrenwend (eds.), *Origins of Psychopathology: Research and Public Policy* (New York: Cambridge, 1982); N. Lambert, "Adolescent Outcomes for Hyperactive Children: Perspectives on General and Specific Patterns of Childhood Risk for Adolescent Educational, Social, and Mental Health Problems," *American Psychologist* 43: 786–799, 1988; E. A. Carlson, L. A. Sroufe et al. "Early Environment Support and Elementary School Adjustment as Predictors of School Adjustment in Middle Adolescence," *Journal of Adolescent Research* 14: 72–94, 1999.

33. E. M. Hetherington and J. Kelly, *For Better or for Worse: Divorce Reconsidered* (New York: W. W. Norton, 2002); J. Wallerstein and J. Kelly, *Surviving the Breakup* (New York: Basic Books, 1980).

34. E. M. Cummings and P. T. Davies, *Children and Marital Conflict: The Impact of Family Dispute and Resolution* (New York: Guilford Press, 1994).

35. M. Moorehouse, "Work and Family Dynamics," in P. A. Cowan, D. Field, D. A. Hansen, A. Skolnick, and G. E. Swanson (eds.), *Family, Self, and Society: Toward a New Agenda for Family Research* (Hillsdale, NJ: Erlbaum, 1993).

36. P. A. Cowan and C. P. Cowan, "What an Intervention Design Reveals about How Parents Affect Their Children's Academic Achievement and Behavior Problems," in J. G. Borkowski, S. Ramey, and M. Bristol-Power (eds.), *Parenting and the Child's World: Influences on Intellectual, Academic, and Social-Emotional Development* (Mahwah, NJ: Lawrence Erlbaum, 2002).

37. P. A. Cowan, D. Powell, and C. P. Cowan, "Parenting Interventions: A Family Systems View of Enhancing Children's Development," in I. E. Sigel and K. A. Renninger (eds.), *Handbook of Child Psychology*, 5th ed. vol. 4: *Child Psychology in Practice* (New York: Wiley, 1997).

38. L. Potts, "Considering Parenthood: Group Support for a Critical Life Decision," *American Journal of Orthopsychiatry* 50: 629–638, 1980.

39. P. A. Cowan, C. P. Cowan, and T. Heming. "Two Variations of a Preventive Intervention for Couples: Effects on Parents and Children during the Transition to Elementary School," in P. A. Cowan, C. P. Cowan, J. Ablow, V. K. Johnson, and J. Measelle (eds.), *The Family Context of Parenting in Children's Adaptation to Elementary School* (Mahwah, NJ: Lawrence Erlbaum Associates, in press).

40. Ibid.

Daddy, Baby; Momma, Maybe: Low-Income Urban Fathers and the "Package Deal" of Family Life

Kathryn Edin, Timothy Nelson, and Joanna Miranda Reed

Economically disadvantaged fathers are far less likely to marry before having children than middle-class fathers are, and they have them far earlier (Nock 2007). When they do marry, they are more likely to divorce (Martin 2004). In the absence of a marital tie, the government assigns them financial obligations, which most do not satisfy fully (Grail 2007). Thus, such men's fathering behavior attracts a good deal of attention from both scholars and policymakers.

Little attention is paid, however, to these men's roles as romantic partners. Qualitative studies have been an exception to this trend, both the classic community studies (i.e., Drake and Cayton 1945; Liebow 1967; Hannerz 1969; Hollingshead 1949; Moreland 1958; Powdermaker 1939; Rainwater 1970; 1960) and more recent qualitative work (Nelson, Clampet-Lundquist, and Edin 2002; Furstenberg 2001; Hill 2007; Reed 2007; Roy et al. 2008; Waller 2008; 2002; Wilson 1996). As these studies have repeatedly shown, economically disadvantaged men do engage in romantic relationships; this is the context into which most of their children are born (though some children are the product of nonrelationships, i.e., one-night stands) (Augustine, Nelson, and Edin 2009). New survey research reveals that fully eight in ten nonmarital children now enter the world with a mother and father who describe themselves as "romantically involved"; up to half of those parents live together, and at least 70 percent of both mothers and fathers say there is at least a 50-50 chance they'll marry each other. Yet it is also true that fewer than a third of such couples are still together by the time the child turns 5 (Center for Research on Child Wellbeing 2007). Low-income couples who marry before having children are fragile as well—much more so than middle-class married couples are—but they still function as partners for a considerable period of time (Martin 2004; McLanahan 2004).

We offer the reader two portraits of the romantic partnerships of such men. The first is of a relatively large group of very economically disadvantaged white and black men (with earnings below the poverty line for a family of four in the formal economy over the prior year) who live in poor and struggling working-class neighborhoods throughout the Philadelphia metropolitan area and have biological children, most of them outside of marriage. All were fathers of at least one minor child outside of a marital tie when we interviewed them. The second comes from a longitudinal, qualitative study of forty-eight unmarried couples who were first interviewed just after the birth of a nonmarital child and followed through the child's fourth birthday. These couples are not sampled according to their economic status or neighborhood characteristics, though most (like the population they represent) are nonetheless quite disadvantaged.

By exploring in depth the texture of their romantic lives and worldviews, we show that the function of the romantic tie for the father role departs radically from the traditional 1950s "package deal" conception of family life. Furstenberg and Cherlin (1991), and more recently Nicholas Townsend (2002), point to the family behaviors of men who came of age in an earlier generation, arguing that for these men fatherhood flowed through, and was contingent upon, men's relationship with the children's mother (see also Liebow 1967). Furstenberg and Cherlin coined the term "package deal" to explain the very low rates of father involvement among the divorced fathers they observed. In this view, the tie between the mother and father is central and serves to bind men to their obligations to their children—obligations they would otherwise ignore (e.g., in the case of divorce).[1]

Two of us (Edin and Nelson) and a multiracial team of graduate students spent seven years observing and interviewing low-income fathers residing in high-poverty neighborhoods in Philadelphia and its poorest inner suburb, Camden, New Jersey. All three of us, along with a large research team, participated in a four-year qualitative study of forty-eight unmarried couples, a subsample of respondents to a large representative survey of nonmarital births in three cities, Chicago, Milwaukee, and New York. We began interviewing these couples in the hospital right after the mother had given birth to a nonmarital child. The fathers in both studies were not only quite economically disadvantaged and fathering outside of a marital tie; they also came of age several decades later than the divorced men Furstenberg and Cherlin (1991) observed, or the 1972 high school graduates Townsend (2002) was writing about. Our average respondent reached adulthood (21) in the mid- to late 1990s.

For the men we have studied, notions of family life are radically different than the portrait that Furstenberg, Cherlin, and Townsend provide. In our story, the *father-child* relationship is typically what is viewed as central, and is what binds men to couple relationships—relationships that might not have otherwise formed or been maintained (see also Edin et al. 2007; Reed 2007; Roy et al. 2008). This is not to say that such men are child-centric to the degree that mothers are (Edin and Kefalas 2005), only that in the realm of family relations, "Daddy, baby; momma maybe" is a fair representation of the worldview of many of the fathers we studied.

METHOD

The Philadelphia/Camden Fathers Study (PCFS)

We began the Philadelphia/Camden Father's Study with two and a half years of participant observation in one of the eight low-income communities (census tract clusters where at least 20 percent of the population lived in poverty in 1990) selected for the study. Based on this fieldwork, which began in 1995, we constructed an interview guide that we administered in systematic, repeated, in-depth interviews with 110 white and African American men between 1997 and 2002. We sampled equal numbers of blacks and non-Hispanic whites. To offer more of a life-course view, roughly half of our fathers were under 30 and the rest were older. During the prior year, the earnings of all of them were below the poverty line for a family of four in the formal economy. In the course of our conversations with these men, we collected detailed life histories. Our data come from these life histories (e.g., "Tell me how it was for you coming up," "Tell me the whole story of that relationship from the time you first met until now"), and from their answers to questions formulated to capture their worldview (e.g., "What should fathers do for their children?" "In your view, what makes for a good father?").

The Time, Love, and Cash among Couples with Children Study (TLC3)

As part of the Fragile Families and Child Wellbeing Survey, a birth cohort study of mostly nonmarital children that is representative of births to women living in large cities, we conducted repeated, in-depth interviews with a stratified random subsample of couples in three cities. We targeted even numbers of blacks, Hispanics, and non-Hispanic whites. We excluded parents who were not romantically involved at the time of the child's birth and whose household income was more than $60,000 per year (30 percent of the survey sample). After conducting the survey in the hospital, couples who agreed to also participate in TLC3 were interviewed in their homes around the time when their child reached the following benchmarks: two to three months of age, and the first, second, and fourth birthdays. In each wave, the couple was interviewed together and each parent was also interviewed separately. Response rates were high, both in the initial wave and over time. Eighty-three percent of those asked agreed to participate; 100 percent of these completed couple interviews and 91 percent completed individual interviews at the time their babies were born (baseline). Round two response rates were 75 percent for couples and 81 percent for individuals from the original sample. Rates for round three were 69 percent for couples and 85 percent for individuals, and for round four 61 percent and 81 percent of the original sample, respectively. Couple response rates were lower, in part because about a third of the couples broke up during the course of the study. In our conversations with these parents, we collected detailed relationship histories and asked nearly identical questions about parents' worldviews as we had asked of the PCFS fathers. For added richness, we draw from both the individual and couple narratives here.

In the pages that follow, we begin with an analysis of the PCFS data, followed by a parallel analysis of the TLC3 couple-level data. The PCFS findings capture the worldview of a very disadvantaged group of fathers (by virtue of their income and neighborhood context) living in a single metropolitan area (Philadelphia/Camden). The TLC sample, drawn from three cities (Chicago, Milwaukee, and New York), imposed only modest income—and no neighborhood—criteria restrictions. The sample also captured an unusually large proportion of cohabiters. Thus the TLC3 sample is considerably more advantaged, both economically and in terms of their relationship characteristics, than the fathers in PCFS. A limitation of the samples is that they are both from large urban areas.

FINDINGS

The Philadelphial/Camden Father's Study

In PCFS, we asked each father to tell us "the whole story" of how he got together with the mothers of each of his children, and how these relationships developed over time. Typically, the pre-pregnancy narrative was noticeably succinct: the couple met, began to "affiliate," and then "came up pregnant." Men seldom even mentioned, much less discussed, any special qualities of their partners or any common tastes or values that drew the two together. Usually, the woman lived on his block, hung out on his corner, worked at the same job, was a friend of his sister, or the girlfriend of a friend, and she was simply willing to "affiliate" with him. Hanging out on the stoop, an occasional outing to a bar or a club, a window-shopping trip to a hot venue such as the downtown Gallery or the popular South Street strip, and fantasizing about shared children is what constituted romance (see also Townsend 2002: 42).

In the case of couples with a first birth together, the length of the courtship before conception was usually exceedingly brief—typically well under a year. As Furstenberg points out in Chapter 8 of this volume, exceedingly brief courtships were also a feature of the 1950s postwar marriage boom, often because a baby was on the way. Not surprisingly then, a common feature of men's narratives about the period before pregnancy is the ambiguous nature of the relational tie (see also Augustine, Nelson, and Edin 2009; Edin et al. 2007; Reed 2007; Roy et al. 2008). Only rarely did such couples "fall in love," get engaged, or get married before conceiving a child together, though some did so later. Instead, they meet, they "associate," "affiliate," "communicate" begin to "kick it," "talk to each other," "get with each other," or "end up together." Then, "one thing leads to another." Consistent with England, McClintock, and Shafer's account in Chapter 1 of this volume, planned pregnancies were rare, yet the contraceptive practices that couples usually engaged in initially seldom continued for long (see also Edin and Kefalas 2005; Edin et al. 2008; Augustine, Nelson, and Edin 2009). Then the inevitable occurred: the woman "comes up pregnant" (see also Davis, Gardner, and Gardner 1941: 127).

John, a 24-year-old white father of one, described the sequencing of his relationship with his child's mother in this way: "Actually she was dating a friend of mine and somehow . . . she wanted me. . . . Eventually, I just got stuck with her for a little while." John didn't feel that he had found the ideal match—he "got stuck" with his baby's mother "for a little while." No language of love or even attraction (except her attraction to him) entered into this narrative, although there may well have been attraction involved. Nor does the phrase "a little while" indicate much commitment.

Thirty-nine-year-old Amin, a black father of two, described the development of his relationship with his youngest son's mother, a coworker in the dietary department of a local hospital, in this way: "She was attractive to me when I first saw her and I made my approach and we begin to socialize and communicate and then from there we began to affiliate at some point and time we became intimate and my son was born." As Amin told it, attraction, affiliation, and intimacy quite naturally—and inevitably—led to a son being born.

Despite the vague and bureaucratic language often used to describe these relationships (e.g., "affiliation"), almost no father had much trouble pinpointing when his relationship with his baby's mother began; they knew the point at which they got "to-gether" with their baby's mother (though a small number of pregnancies do occur outside of relationships). Being together generally means that the couple is spending regular time together and defines the relationship as something more than a casual encounter or a one-night stand. Unlike a mere "hook-up," which has no distinct beginning or end, the termination of these relationships generally involve a "breakup." Furthermore, those who maintained outside liaisons usually viewed their own behavior as "cheating," though this did not mean that such relationships did not occur.

The verbs "affiliate," "associate," and "get with" suggest a bond that is more than a casual liaison, but not exactly a boyfriend/girlfriend relationship. Few of these men were consciously "courting" or searching for a life partner. Indeed, there is little evidence that they were even attempting to discriminate much based on who would be a suitable mother for their child. Many recalled that they did very much want children and fairly soon, even if not right then. Yet, as was the case with Furstenberg's 1950s couples (Chapter 8, this volume), who were propelled by an impending pregnancy into so-called lifelong marital commitments with partners they barely knew, the partnering process was far more haphazard than discriminating.

Bruce was a white father of 2-year-old twins. At 42, Bruce met a "new girl," Debbie. He didn't use protection because "Every time I had any kind of relationship there is no babies born so I didn't believe in safe sex. Next thing I knew, this girl Debbie, she was pregnant." Debbie made the announcement that she was seven weeks pregnant after the two had been together for only four months. Bruce told her, "'I am shooting blanks, you cant be pregnant . . . !' Then we went for a DNA test and that was when she found out that I was the father and she was the mother." Here a "family" was formed through a pregnancy brought to term in a relationship that was neither casual nor serious. Yet for Bruce, and most other men in our study, this was not viewed as a problem.

Tim, a white 23-year-old father of two, got a woman pregnant after only two months of being "together." "She used to go out with my friend. My friend was trying to get back with her, and I ended up getting with her. . . . We were only together for about two months, and she was getting pregnant. I didn't mind at all." Tim didn't choose his baby's mother; he "ended up" with her. Yet he "didn't mind" when he learned she was pregnant.

Children, while usually desired, were only rarely explicitly planned, according to the narratives of men in PCFS (see Augustine, Nelson, and Edin, 2009). Yet contraception and other attempts to avoid pregnancy faded quickly as the couple began "affiliating." According to England and her coauthors, these fertility patterns are typical of less-educated men (Chapter 1, this volume). Once she became pregnant and decided to take the pregnancy to term (this decision is generally ceded to the woman), the bond between the two typically coalesced into more of a "relationship," though often in dramatic fits and starts (see also Edin and Kefalas 2005).

David, a black 30-year-old, was the father of five children by three women. In the months just before conceiving his fifth child, he was both "with" Deborah and "seeing" Kathy on the side. He went to Kathy whenever he and Deborah argued (though Deborah didn't know about Kathy). Which woman he should choose became a dilemma. However, when Deborah ended up pregnant, he decided to "do what was right" and chose her.

[When I was first with Deborah] I had a girlfriend on the side too. Kathy. She's some-body that I met at a NA meeting. We got close and we were helping each other [with our addictions]. One thing led to another, and we got intimate. . . . Me and Deborah would get into an argument, she'd tell me to leave, I'd go stay with Kathy. (So how did you end it with Kathy?) Deborah got pregnant, and I had to do what was right, stand by Deborah.

Monte, a white 21-year-old, had three children by the same woman.

I had just come out of a juvenile institution. I think I just turned 17 . . . and I started going with her friend. And then one day she came around and we started talking, then I went with her and left her friend, and me and her got together and started having kids together and then we got closer and closer. Then we started living together.

Monte's story illustrates well a typical sequence of events among men in our study: attraction and a moderate level of couple cohesion produced a pregnancy that was taken to term. It was at this point that the real relationship commenced; it was an outgrowth of the pregnancy, not the impetus. "Getting closer and closer" and then "living together" were things these couples generally accomplished *after* they conceived children, not before.

For Jack, a 33-year-old white father of two, his babies' mother was just one of several "girls" he met on a weekend home from college. She was already married to someone else, but left her husband for Jack that very day. Three months later she was pregnant, yet Jack saw nothing remarkable about the process by which he first became a father.

[After high school] I went to college. . . . My grades weren't great but I was getting through. I was going back home every other weekend. . . . Met some girls. In turn, met my [baby's mother]. Shortly afterwards, she became pregnant, so I quit school, got a job.

Kahlid, a 28-year-old black father of one, said that it was just a few months into the relationship with his child's mother that the pair conceived. Despite the fact that the outside observer might read his narrative as a classic example of putting the cart before the horse, Kahlid, like Jack, viewed the sequence of events leading up to the pregnancy as unexceptional.

(How long were you and your girlfriend together before she got pregnant?) Six, seven months. (What went through your mind?) I was happy! I came [over after] work and she said that she was getting symptoms and I was like, "What you talking about?" Morning sickness, throwing up, like this. So she went to the hospital. She took the test and she says she was pregnant . . . and I was excited. It was my first child. And she was going to keep the baby, and I was happy. I knew I had to keep a job and take care of my responsibilities.

Evidence from the Fragile Families survey—the longitudinal birth cohort survey that is representative of nonmarital births to couples living in large cities we mentioned earlier—offers additional support for the idea that the couple relationship is often gal-vanized by pregnancy (Rainwater 1970: 210–11). First, recall the high rate of couple cohesion at the time of a typical nonmarital birth (80 percent). Second, roughly six in ten couples giving birth outside of marriage cohabit between the time of conception and the child's first birthday (Center for Research on Child Wellbeing 2007).

The glories of the delivery room are the high point of many fathers' life histories in PCFS. But the arrival of a child introduces a sharp contradiction. On the one hand, fathers' narratives offer evidence that they are making some effort to sustain a relationship with their babies' mothers—often motivated by the desire to live with or be intensely involved with the children. But they also recognize, at least in part, that they are trying to live out the dream of being part of a real "family unit" against almost impossible odds. Thus, while working to solidify these relationships, they are also often deeply fatalistic about their chances of staying together over the long term. This fatalism, which, as we will show, is fueled by men's fears about their ongoing ability to provide and their utter conviction that their babies' mothers will leave them if they fail, often rendered men's relational efforts half-hearted.

With only a few exceptions, fathers emphatically said that their relationship with their children ought not be contingent on their relationship with their child's mother—and outright rejected the package deal. Yet they nonetheless realized that due to normative and legal practices governing the custody of nonmarital children, as well as their own limited economic prospects, their relationship to the mother was their conduit to the child.

Lavelle was the 34-year-old black father of a 4-year-old girl he called Little Toya. Little Toya's mother, also named Toya, didn't inform him that he'd become a father until his child was nearly 2. Lavelle, who had no other children, fell head over heels in love—with Little Toya. Nonetheless, once "Big Toya" made it clear she was going to restrict access to his daughter—to "try and play if off as a package deal," in Lavelle's words—he made considerable efforts to invest in a romantic relationship he had had little interest in previously.

Over the two year period that we observed Lavelle "dealing" with Toya, we watched as he first tried to get visitation (she told him she would not allow her daughter to visit or go on outings with him unless she could come too), then proposed marriage (she turned him down, saying she didn't want to lose her freedom, her welfare benefits, or her Section 8 certificate), and then finally convinced her to let him call her his fiancée. What did he get out of the deal? She was willing to spend weekends with him in Camden (she lived about thirty minutes away), with Little Toya in tow. Lavelle confided that he would never have chosen Toya if she hadn't given birth to his child.

> I would have had to get visitation to see her [which is why] I'm still with the mother. 'Cause she wants to play it off like a package deal: "You can't go here without me." "You can't take her here without me." "You can't take her there without me." [First,] I said, "Okay, then I'm going to get visitation so I can take her when I want to take her. . . ." It is [difficult negotiating with Toya about little Toya]. She [feels] she gave birth to her so it's her way or the highway.

Self, a South Jersey black youth who was 21, knew he was to become a father as soon as his girlfriend learned of the pregnancy, but had such a fractious relationship with his baby's mother during the pregnancy that he didn't even visit the child until almost a year after she was born. The emotional connection he built with his daughter on the week-long visit was so compelling that he abandoned plans to attend college in Florida and decided instead to move in with the mother of his child.

> Almost a year after the child was born, finally I went to go visit her. . . . I was going to go away and whatnot. But [after that week], we decided that we would stay together. . . . I decided not to go to school, I decided to stay. We made the decision that I would search for proper employment and stay in the city and we would work together.

Across the income distribution, most couples now stay together, at least in part, because they share common interests and values. Owing to the lightning speed of the courtship period, disadvantaged couples who bear children together often find they have little in common, as we show below. But childbirth offers a vital new shared interest—a child—and this often brings some measure of emotional closeness. Consider the story of 38-year-old Tony, father of one.

> (How do you think the birth of Alyssa affected your relationship?) Um, I think in the beginning it brought us a lot closer together. (Why would it bring you closer together?) It just—being with this little baby that's just a part of both of us—it was amazing.

Bucket, a black father of two children by the same woman, described how the birth of his first child made things even a "little better."

> (How'd you all get along during the rest of the pregnancy?) We had a good time man. While she was pregnant, I couldn't go *nowhere*. Shoot! She wanted me to do this, wanted me to do that, I was like a puppy anyway, I waited on her. I did certain things that she wanted me to do. I was *glad* man. (How did the birth of your child affect your relationship with her?) It didn't affect it at all. See like, when the baby was born and we had a *baby*, it seemed like things got a little better and stuff.

Yet men like Bucket have powerful reasons *not* to invest in the relationship as well. The ethnographic literature typically focuses on how much women mistrust men. What is less well known is how little men trust women (for exceptions, see Waller 2008; Hannertz 1969: 100–102; Liebow 1967: 137–60; Rainwater 1970: 209). The chief source of power (outside of physical violence) in these relationships is control over the child. In the context of a nonmarital birth, women have much greater power in this regard. Because men view children as their most precious resource (Nelson and Edin, forthcoming), they are, on the one hand, eager to hang on, and expect to be actively involved in parenting the child. Furstenberg, in Chapter 8 of this volume, shows that this desire for paternal engagement is consonant with their partner's expectations. Yet they are often very apprehensive about their ability to satisfy the economic demands they also know their children's mothers will place on them over time, and most are convinced that a woman's love for a man will come to an abrupt halt the minute he fails to provide (see also Drake and Cayton 1945: 564–99; Rainwater 1970: 216).

Men on the economic edge, even those in multi-year partnerships with several children, often obsessed about the younger guy with the nicer car who had a better job and might turn their partner's head. Most were convinced that, for women, "there is no source of commitment in a relationship." Donald was certain that a woman would dump any man if he failed to provide. This black 37-year-old found himself always "feuding and fightin'"—with his child's mother during their eight-year on-again-off-again relationship, which he blamed on the fact that she was too controlling, plus the fact that "I was not committed to really being with her" (see also Roy 2008; Waller 2008). Reading between the lines of his narrative, we can assume that spotty employment and drug use were probably also a cause. After their breakup, Donald's ex-partner went on to have two additional children by two other men and had just married a third man, who was trying to play the role of father to his 14-year-old daughter while her mother was trying to push Donald out of their lives. Listen to the deep cynicism in Donald's view of women:

> Yeah, their whole thing is, "What can you give me?" and "What can I get from you and how fast can I get it?" More of less money-wise. There is no commitment to a real relationship. Particularly in black women, their whole goal is let me see how much I can get for it and how good I can look and you know . . . To be honest, yeah, I do [have a theory]. A lot of them are caught up in, "I want to look good." "I want to be independent." "I don't want to be dependent upon you." "I want to be able to be with you, but not like that." There is no source of commitment in a relationship. [It is not] just men [that aren't committed], but anybody [nowadays]. In a relationship it is about, "We are in it 50-50 commitment," and so forth. They are not here. Their thing is, "When things go bad, I am out of here." To me, that was my experience and I am not taking it [anymore].

Amin (introduced earlier), was similarly convinced that money was necessary to sustain a relationship and that "situations"—such as unemployment—would almost certainly bring a relationship to an end. Because he lacked confidence that he could remain stably employed, Amin felt that he couldn't even contemplate marriage, and worried he might not even be able to sustain a long-term relationship.

> So you just have to explain to individuals that this is your situation for the present time and I would appreciate it if you would bear with me and understand that you know that when I was able to provide, this is what I did. And there are periods where things are going to be rough and the things are going to be not as plentiful. So I am hoping that you would bear with me and understand. . . . My confidence level was a good advantage and my relationship with my former girlfriend was at an advantage [when I was working full-time] because when you have money and you are helping to support a family, women feel a lot better about a man when he is doing that. . . . When a woman is a woman and she accepts a man for who he is and not necessarily what he does and doesn't have, then she will stand by a man regardless. But when a woman starts to allow the fact that he is not bringing as much money into the home affect her relationship and her attitude towards him then that is a problem. . . . And that is another reason why I have not considered marriage because . . . there is not too many women out there that is really ready themselves to honestly fulfill the covenant of the words that you recite when you are at the podium.

Jeff, a black 47-year-old father of two, also believed a woman's love was contingent on money. He also saw this mercenary strain in his daughter.

[My daughter's mother taught me that] love is like running water. It turns off and on. I really believe that behind the fact that they can love you when you're doing, but when you don't do, they don't love. . . . My daughter had told me on numerous occasions that this [or that] individual does more for her than I do and I felt hurt. Regardless if this person is doing something for you or not, he can't fill my shoes. I'm still your father regardless. If I give you a million dollars or I give you a penny, I'm still your father.

Bill, a white 31-year-old father of six, similarly emphasized the nearly ubiquitous belief that love and engagement are not enough; relationships take money. Bill was deeply in love with his girlfriend of a decade and the mother of all of his children, but he had just lost his job tending bar and she had kicked him out. While working to get back into her good graces, Bill feared that in the meantime she would be wooed by a "younger guy."

I hear a lot of people say that love is good but I am telling you, money will rule over a relationship real quick. [If that is gone, the love is gone] and a lot of women will do that to you, they do, and I don't know what it is. Don't get me wrong, there might be maybe two relationships out of a hundred that will survive without money. . . . It is all about that fashion statement too. . . . Women don't want to be sitting around thinking, even if a man works part-time and he is doing what he has to do, he could be the greatest man in the world and a woman will overlook that for somebody driving in a new car, a young guy. He might have a little bit of money now, but sooner or later down the line he could wind up like I am at anytime, no guarantees at all. Yo, that concerns me a lot. I love my girl-friend a lot. I call her my wife because we have been together for ten years off and on and we have six kids and I still say she is my wife basically, even though we are not married.

Tom, a white father of three, believed that when a man is "down and out" a woman could easily be attracted away by a guy who was doing better or "has a nicer car." In his case, a slowdown at work while the mother of his younger two children was pregnant the second time led to unbearable conflict.

I was working every day and I was paying the bills. I did everything that I possibly could. I came home, I took care of the kids, I would put the kids to bed, just so we would have some [alone] time. . . . Her father had got me a job doing the roofing. . . . We saved money and we moved into the house and things were good and we were splitting the rent. Then I lost the job and I couldn't afford them payments anymore. . . . Yeah, it got real slow and the winter time came and there was just no work, so I didn't know what to do. I couldn't collect unemployment because I wasn't on the books. . . . She was already pregnant with the second baby and that is when I couldn't deal with her anymore and we couldn't get along.

We asked Tom, "Only money? No other problems?"

Exactly. Only money. [It was] only a money issue. That is what I don't understand, why don't they understand, why don't they understand . . . ? They might see other people doing better or a guy that has a nicer car and I am sure that plays on their conscience, "I can have that. That could be me. Why am I [with this guy]?" And it is all about money in my eyes, I can see it.

Monte, the white father we introduced earlier, doesn't cite specific fears that are behind his mistrust of women he just doesn't trust them period. Girls that appear "honest and nice" might start "act[ing] like a fool" without warning. As soon as a couple begins living together, a woman's "real self starts to come out," Monte says. That's why he isn't taking a chance on love.

I'm just afraid [to trust women], you know. You can't judge a book by its cover, you know. I've known these girls who are so honest and nice, but I've also learned that when you meet a girl and she's real nice and honest and everything like that, when, [after] talking and getting to know each other and you're there every day and all night with each other, things start to change. Her real self starts to come out. So I'm not taking that chance. It just ain't worth it.

The Time, Love, and Cash among Couples with Children Study

George and Tamika met through a chance encounter at a downtown department store. They started talking at the jewelry counter, a conversation that lasted for hours. Tamika, a black 29-year-old, wasn't so sure about George, who was also black and 30. After he began deluging her with phone calls, flowers, and presents, the two did begin seeing each other now and then. Meanwhile, George was seeing other women as well, but he knew he wanted to "settle down" with Tamika. It had been two months since they had last seen each other when Tamika called George and told him she was pregnant. She too was shocked by the pregnancy—she had thought she was infertile so they had never used contraception. George said they went through "that scary stage" of considering abortion before deciding to have the baby. They broke up once during the pregnancy, according to George, because of Tamika's "hormones." When they reconciled, they decided to "step up" their relationship and try to stay together for the sake of the child. Tamika moved into George's apartment just before Kaylee, Tamika's first child and George's second, was born.

"I had doubts, first of all [about] living with somebody . . . because that was something I said I would never do," reported Tamika a few months into cohabitation with George. Ideally, she said, parents should marry before they have a baby. She and George had their ups and downs in the four months they lived together after Kaylee's birth. George said that they moved in together because "we just wanted to put the baby in the best situation. And that was over here as opposed to her mom's house because there wasn't much space."

When we spoke with Tamika a few months later, she and Kaylee had moved back to her mother's house because "we wasn't really getting along," but she and George were still together and continued to see a lot of each other. George talked about getting married, but Tamika held back—"there's a lot of personal things with him that he needs to work on. And money-wise also, I think he's bad with his money. . . . He has a lot that he needs to clean up. I don't know what it would take [for us to get married]."

They were still living apart when we spoke with them the following, year. Tamika said she was considering giving him another chance, because he was "trying really hard," and by the time we spoke with him they were living together again. They had recently been robbed at gunpoint while out one evening with their daughter, and the trauma of this experience in large part motivated them to try and make things work. George still talked about wanting to marry Tamika, but she was far from sure that he was the one, She said, "I just know that if [Kaylee] wasn't around, I wouldn't have been with him. But you know, because she was there, I wanted to stay together."

Around Kaylee's third birthday, things had reached the nadir with Tamika and George. Their renewed attempt at cohabitation had not gone well. Tamika was planning to move back to her mother's house, and George planned to move to another city, where his mother lived, and visit Kaylee on weekends. Tamika was relieved, she said, to finally realize that "it is OK, that I am not a bad person that this is not going to work out." She felt that they were incompatible from the start, and alleged he had a bad temper that erupted during arguments and that she was now afraid of him. She also said George was resigned to the relationship ending, although he still would like to get married. He told us that she "closes [me] out," and felt he had tried very hard to please her, but "nothing is enough."

The last time we spoke with them, George lived in another city and had visited Kaylee once or twice during the past year. He said that he felt bad about the breakup with Tamika but had started to date other women. Tamika was dating an ex-boyfriend. She said this relationship ended the first time because he had got someone else pregnant, but now he really wanted to marry her. She said they would have to "work out some personality conflicts" before she considered marriage.

From the above narrative it is clear that George and Tamika's relationship had a very rocky start. Although he pursued her, he was still seeing other women. She had reservations about the relationship almost from the very beginning. This is a couple who might never have gotten together except for the fact that Tamika got pregnant with Kaylee. The couple's subsequent decision to move in together and to "step up" the relationship was undertaken purely as an experiment, for the sake of the baby. It became clear very quickly, particularly to Tamika, that this impetus was not going to be enough to sustain the relationship, especially given her dissatisfaction with George's behavior. This story of a relationship in its infancy put to the test by a quick and unexpected pregnancy followed by a longer period of relational problems is echoed in the next example, though with even more volatility and a less conclusive ending.

Jazz, a black 21-year-old, and Keisha, who was 19, joked that their relationship "was supposed to be a one-night stand." Just after that first meeting with Jazz, Keisha became pregnant with another man's child but quickly miscarried. Meanwhile, she and Jazz had already gotten "together." When Jazz was put on house arrest, he moved in with Keisha and her mother to serve his sentence. Soon after that, Keisha learned she was pregnant by Jazz.

Jazz's legal troubles, financial problems, and weak willpower when it came to other women made her leery about taking their pregnancy to term, but in the end she decided to have the baby. Keisha said it was hard for her to stay with Jazz, but she did because "I guess this baby, I wanted him to have a father." Jazz offered to pay for an abortion, and was not involved with Keisha during the pregnancy, but had a dramatic change of heart right after his son, Jalani, was born.

> I didn't never want any kids because I didn't want to put those kids in a world and take them through the things my mama and them took me through. But now that I got them it's a blessing. . . . He makes me feel proud to be a father . . . and he'll show his love for me and that makes me really happy.

After Jalani's birth, Jazz and Keisha moved into his uncle's house. Here they could have their own room—more space than the two had had at Keisha's mother's house during Jazz's house arrest. Keisha was glad they were living together and said when a couple has children together, "I would say moving in together would be a good idea. 'Cause all the bills would either be put together and you would get help with them." She still had a general mistrust of men, though, and of Jazz in particular, and said men couldn't be counted on for long.

Keisha preferred to stay together with Jazz, but wasn't sure what would happen. Jazz said that his and Keisha's relationship "is cool but . . . she isn't the type I'd marry. . . . Just ain't what I'm looking for right now." Keisha thought she might marry him, but only "on the terms that he is a good man to me." Financially things were tough: Keisha was on welfare, and Jazz was working only sporadically. He found that there wasn't much money left over after buying the things the baby needed, yet he remained optimistic. "We can go without for a long time," he asserted.

The couple had ongoing problems with mistrust, and Jazz admitted he had cheated from the beginning of the relationship. "I ain't going to lie. I have cheated. I don't think she will cheat. . . . [Our] last argument was about . . . jealousy, that's all. I was jealous, and she was jealous. I made her even more jealous than she made me." The following year they were still a couple and living together, moving between different relatives. But Jazz suspected Keisha of cheating on him because a man called and she wouldn't tell Jazz who it was. In response, Jazz got so angry he pulled the phone out of the wall.

Keisha suspected that Jazz was cheating again when she realized she was pregnant with their second child. Neither she nor Jazz had wanted to have another child, but decided to bring the pregnancy to term. Despite their problems, Keisha said she thought they might marry in the future, if Jazz could spend more time with the family and work on improving communication with her. Jazz said he was not interested in marriage, but wanted to stay together with Keisha. Although their relationship began casually, Jazz told us he fell in love with Keisha after their first child was born. "This was the first woman that I had loved or had feelings for. Because [before] I was more like a bachelor. I be your friend . . . we can be sex partners. That will basically be it."

By the third year of the study, Jazz and Keisha had a new baby boy, Dajon, and Keisha was pregnant with their third child. Seeking a better life outside of Chicago, Keisha and Jazz moved to Iowa, along with Jazz's sister, and the two were able to afford their own place for the first time. Nine months later, Jazz was arrested for selling drugs and no family member was able to make bail. Stunned by this course of events, Keisha had "no idea" whether she and Jazz were still together or not. She was willing to give him another chance once he was released, but said "he's gonna need to grow up and get a [real] job . . . [start] being a man and paying the bills."

When we caught up with Jazz, he was living in a halfway house while serving the rest of his sentence. Explaining his descent into crime, he said, "times got rough" and "I tried to make some fast money." He felt that "a lot of time has been lost" and wanted to turn his life around. He had just gotten a job at a nearby meat processing plant where he made $11 an hour and was very optimistic about a future with Keisha, who had visited him regularly while he was incarcerated. He claimed he wanted to get married now, mostly as a tribute to Keisha's loyalty. "She's been there for me through thick and thin and not only that. I know how she feel about me. We got kids together. We a family . . . and we love each other the way we do. Every woman got their dream. They want to get married. . . . I feel I owe that to her."

We spoke to Jazz one last time a few months later. He had been released from the halfway house and the family was living together again. Keisha and Jazz were now both working at the local meat processing plant. They liked Iowa and saw "lots of opportunities here," but for Jazz it was "maybe too quiet." He claimed things between the two were going well, but also that old problems related to past infidelities and the resulting mistrust had resurfaced. "Like we might call each other a couple of names . . . , I might get jealous because I feel she's around a certain male." In a recent trip to Chicago, Jazz confided, he had had an affair with an old school friend, the same woman he had been with during Keisha's pregnancy with Jalani.

Jazz and Keisha's story exemplifies the mistrust that often pervades relations between men and women in poor neighborhoods (and also show that there is some basis for this). This mistrust makes maintaining a relationship initiated in the face of an unexpected pregnancy a nearly impossible strain, especially when motivated primarily by the desire for the baby to "have a father," in Keisha's words. But even when not plagued by such serious problems as infidelity and mistrust, couples whose relationships are forged "for the sake of the baby" often have difficulty maintaining their relationships, much less moving forward to marriage, as the story of Suzanne and Myron shows.

Suzanne and Myron met through mutual friends right after high school graduation. Suzanne, a white 22-year-old, and Myron, who was 23, had been together off and on for about four years and had just gotten back together when Suzanne learned she was pregnant. She was "shocked" about the pregnancy, and Myron was "in denial phase" until she started showing. They brought their son, Joey, home from the hospital to Suzanne's mother's foreclosed house, where they planned to live rent-free until the bank evicted them. When we met them the first time, both Suzanne and Myron said they wanted to get married but that it was not the right time and were wary of taking such a big step before they felt ready.

Before she got pregnant, Suzanne lived with her mom and stepfather, and Myron stayed there sporadically. Suzanne said that, ideally, she would have wanted to get married and then have a baby, "but I didn't have those thoughts when I was 18 . . . I just think we got too serious too fast." Myron thought couples should move in together only once they got engaged, but that a baby can change things. "If [our son] was born of course I'd move in, even if we weren't engaged." Although Myron thought there was a 90–95 percent chance he and Suzanne would marry, having a child together is not a good reason to do so, in his view. "I want to keep Joey completely out of that, we should get married because mommy and daddy love each other not because we have [him]."

Suzanne agreed, saying, "living together, well it was kind of just something that happened . . . because of Joey. I mean we want to be together. And if there weren't some financial issues and stuff and just the circumstances, we'd probably already be married." (What circumstances?) "I'm not ready to commit to him until his past, until he's done working on it. . . . I think he has to mature in some different ways." Myron said that he loved Suzanne, but disliked that she was jealous and needy; as evidence, he described how she found the phone number of a female work colleague in his bureau drawer and "started going nuts." It was completely innocent, she learned, and they eventually resolved it, "but it kind of scared me for a little bit because every time I imagine us breaking up I imagine me not being around my son all the time, this and that. It kind of scares me."

When we visited them again, Myron said that Suzanne really wanted to get married and was "looking at rings." Rings were expensive, he countered, and he told Suzanne that they should save the money and try to buy a house and get a ring later. He also wanted her to work with a counselor about her "need" problem before they married. For his part, he was working on keeping to a monthly budget and said he was getting better with finances. He believed he would be happier if they married because then they would be "doing things right, the way things are supposed to be done." Suzanne also wanted to marry, but still had mixed feelings about Myron. "Myron and I are very committed to each other," but he was still "living too much of the single life" and had serious credit problems due to overspending in the past.

By the third year of our study, Myron and Suzanne had just had their second child, a daughter. They had also joined a church and were actively discussing what their wedding would be like. When they were married, Myron said, "she won't constantly ask me when are we getting married," and "[we will be] more respected in society." He admitted they hadn't made marriage a priority before, but now wanted to do it "the right way," with a reception, rings, and all the trimmings. Suzanne said she felt like they were married already; "we just haven't gone through the whole ceremony and everything." She predicted that nothing would change in terms of their daily lives, but "I probably would be a little bit happier if we were married."

The final time we spoke with this couple, Suzanne had enrolled in community college and Myron was working for the local cable company. They had recently moved to a brand new duplex where they "just got by" on his income of around $2,800 a month. Suzanne claimed she lived alone, and was thus able to claim food stamps for her and the children, but Myron had to comply with the child-support system. Suzanne was thinking of going back to work, and they were considering moving to Texas to be closer to some family members. They were still "working out the details" of the weddings, according to Suzanne.

COMMON THEMES

Despite the fact that TLC3 is a more advantaged sample than PCFS, only a small minority of pregnancies in both samples was explicitly planned, and many occurred within the first few months of the couple being "together." This is consistent with mothers' reports in Edin and Kefalas's (2005) companion interviews in the PSFS neighborhoods, though mothers are more likely to characterize the pregnancies as at least "semi-planned" while fathers are more likely to say they were "just not thinking" at the time their partner became pregnant (see also Edin et al. 2007). This difference may reflect subtle differences in intentionality between mothers and fathers, or mere social desirability bias (i.e., mothers might: find it less socially acceptable to admit they were "just not thinking" when they became pregnant).

Once mothers learned they were pregnant, sharing the news with the father-to-be and deciding what to do about it were important defining moments for the couple. The pregnancy often prompted many of the men in PCFS, as well as some of the couples in TLC3, to think of themselves as a couple for the first time, or to reconsider a partner who had fallen out of favor. The decision whether to have the baby was usually left to the mother, with fathers typically agreeing to "support what she wants to do."

Pregnancy is a challenging time for most fathers' romantic relationships. In TLC3, several couples broke up owing to frequent arguments and other more serious problems, including infidelity and violent encounters, and then reconciled for the sake of the baby. In PCFS, where economic pressures were greater, such troubles were even more likely to break the couple up before the birth. Edin and Kefalas's (2005) interviews with mothers, described above, also highlighted pregnancy as a particularly volatile time. Among the couples in TLC3, however, both mothers and fathers typically blamed their problems during pregnancy on her "hormones" rather than on any fundamental problems with the relationship. This definition of the problem allowed the TLC3 couples to hang on to the idea that once the baby was born, everything would return to "normal"; this is despite the fact that many of these relationships were defined as "real relationships" only after the pregnancy had occurred. Naturally, the same problems tended to resurface soon after the child's birth and the mother and child's return home from the hospital. This is perhaps one reason why half of unmarried couples break up within one year of a child's birth (Center for Research on Child Wellbeing 2007). As Furstenberg points out (Chapter 8, this volume), breakup (e.g., divorce) was also exceedingly common among shotgun marriages of the 1950s.

As in PCFS, many TLC3 couples' troubles momentarily disappeared after the "magic moment" of their child's birth, as the fact of a shared child brought some measure of cohesion. Fathers who were still romantically involved, even if things were rough during the pregnancy, saw the baby as sufficient reason to renew their efforts to stay together with the mother. Especially for the somewhat more advantaged TLC3 sample, moving in together was an important part of the process of reorganizing their relationship around the baby. Of those who were living together when the TLC3 team interviewed them the first time, just a few months after their baby was born, nearly three-quarters (73 percent) had moved in together during the pregnancy or just after the child's birth.

Cohabitation in response to pregnancy was more common among TLC3 couples than among fathers in PCFS, reflecting the fact that the TLC3 couples were somewhat more economically advantaged and their relationships were, on average, a little more serious to begin with and became "family like" to a greater degree with pregnancy and birth. While entry into a "real relationship," sometimes symbolized by the move to cohabitation, may have indicated a growing level of commitment to the romantic partner, it also reflected a father's wish to be an involved parent. Usually, among fathers, the impulse to parent is at least as strong as, if not stronger than, the desire to remain partnered for the sake of the relationship. Work done by Edin and Kefalas (2005) on a companion sample of mothers in the PCFS communities shows that mothers share the desire for fathers to be involved, but view his involvement as a desirable, yet optional, complement to their mothering activities.

Cohabitation allows an unmarried father equal access to his child and a major caretaking role. Therefore, even among cohabiting couples, there was often ambiguity over whether the couple bond or the father-child bond was the primary motivating factor. In TLC3, this ambiguity sometimes led mothers to be unsure of how to gauge the depth of their partner's commitment. For their part, fathers in PCFS often worried that the women in their lives only wanted them for as long as they could provide, and underplayed the importance of their emotional contributions to their partner and parenting role.

These relationships, even those elevated to an especially high status by cohabitation, are quite different from marriage. While couples articulated a common view of the expectations, obligations, and roles they associated with marriage, they rarely discussed their expectations for a cohabiting relationship. Instead, unspoken assumptions were usually revealed only when they were violated by the partner, and if the transgressions were deemed serious enough, the relationship would end—though sometimes there was room for trial and error. Many of these more serious problems these partners faced centered on expectations of sexual fidelity. The twin problems of infidelity and sexual jealousy played a leading role in most breakups in both studies and were often the proverbial "last straw" that led parents to end relationships already plagued by multiple problems (see also Hill 2007).

In sum, for this group of mostly disadvantaged men parenting children outside of marriage, multiple and serious problems such as infidelity, sexual mistrust, substance abuse, domestic violence, criminal activity, and incarceration abound in their narratives about their experiences as romantic partners, though these men were far less likely than the mothers in TLC3 or Edin and Kefalas's female respondents to name violence as a cause of breakup (2005; see also Hill 2007).[2] Despite their desire to form strong relationships with their children, men found that in the aftermath of the breakup, staying in regular contact with their progeny was surprisingly difficult. A full discussion of barriers to father-child involvement is beyond the scope of this chapter.

What is evident from the narratives presented here is that the haphazard nature of the way that these families are formed places enormous pressure on already disadvantaged young people who don't know each other very well, but who nonetheless attempt to form "real" relationships, sometimes via cohabitation. Although pregnancy and birth do typically prompt relationship investment among men, their precarious economic situations and their mistrust of women prompt disinvestment. Men's behavior is usually the most proximate cause of a relationship's demise. Another significant factor is the ambiguous nature of the relationships themselves, where expectations are seldom revealed until they are violated. And though men may have believed they could have a direct relationship with their children with or without the mothers—"daddy baby, momma maybe"—accomplishing this feat is far more difficult than most had imagined.

References

Augustine, Jennifer March, Timothy Nelson, and Kathryn Edin. 2009. "Why Do Poor Men Have Children?" *Annals of the American Academy of Political and Social Science* 624 (July): 99–117.

Center for Research on Child Wellbeing. 2007. "Parents' Relationship Status Five Years after a Non-Marital Birth." Princeton, NJ: Center for research on Child Wellbeing, Research Brief 39 (August).

Davis, Allison, Burleigh B. Gardner, and Mary R. Gardner. 1941. *Deep South: A Social Anthropological Study of Caste and Class.* Chicago: University of Chicago Press.

Drake, St. Clair, and Horace R. Cayton. 1945. *Black Metropolis: A Study of Negro Life in a Northern City.* New York: Harcourt Brace.

Edin, Kathryn, and Maria J. Kefalas. 2005. *Promises I Can Keep: Why Poor Women Put Motherhood before Marriage.* Berkeley: University of California Press.

Edin, Kathryn, Paula England, Emily Fitzgibbons Shafer, and Joanna Reed. 2007. "Forging Fragile Families: Are the Pregnancies Planned, Unplanned, or In-Between?" In *Unmarried Couples with Children: The Unfolding Lives of New Unmarried Urban Parents*, edited by Paula England and Kathryn Edin. New York: Russell Sage Foundation.

Grail, Timothy S. 2007. "Custodial Mothers and Fathers and Their Child Support: 2005." *Current Population Reports* P60-234. Washington, DC: U.S. Census Bureau.

Furstenberg, Frank F., Jr. 2001. "The Fading Dream: Prospects for Marriage in the Inner City." In *Problem of the Century*, edited by Elijah Anderson and Douglas Massey, pp. 224–47. New York: Russell Sage Foundation.

Furstenberg, Frank F., Jr., and Andrew J. Cherlin. 1991. *Divided Families: What Happens to Children When Parents Part.* Cambridge, MA: Harvard University Press.

Hannerz, Ulf. 1969. *Soulside: Inquiries into Ghetto Culture and Community.* Chicago: University of Chicago Press.

Hill, Heather D. 2007. "Steppin' Out: Infidelity and Sexual Jealousy." In *Unmarried Couples with Children*, edited by Paula England and Kathryn Edin. New York: Russell Sage Foundation.

Hollingshead, A. B. 1949. *Elmtown's Youth: The Impact of Social Classes on Adolescents.* New York: Wiley.

Liebow, Eliot. 1967. *Tally's Corner.* Boston: Little, Brown.

Martin, Steven P. 2004. "Growing Evidence for a Divorce Divide? Education and Marital Dissolution Rates in the United States since the 1970's." New York, NY: Russell Sage Foundation Working Papers: Series on Social Dimensions of Inequality.

McLanahan, Sara. 2004. "Diverging Destinies: How Children Fare under the Second Demographic Transition." *Demography* 41(4): 607–27.

Moreland, John Kenneth. 1958. *Millways of Kent.* Chapel Hill: University of North Carolina Press.

Nelson, Timothy, and Kathryn Edin. Forthcoming. *Fragile Fatherhood: What Being a Daddy Means in the Lives of Low-Income Men.* New York: Russell Sage Foundation.

Nelson, Timothy J., Susan Clampet-Lundquist, and Kathryn Edin. 2002. "Sustaining Fragile Fatherhood: How Low-Income, Non-Custodial Fathers in Philadelphia Talk about Their Families." In *The Handbook of Father Involvement: Multidisciplinary Perspectives*, edited by Catherine Tamis-LeMonda and Natasha Cabrera, pp. 525–53. Mahwah, NJ: Lawrence Erlbaum Associates.

Nock, Stephen. 2007, "Marital and Unmarried Births to Men." Department of Health and Human Services Publication (PHS) 2006-1978. Hyattsville, MD: U.S. Department of Health and Human Services.

Powdermaker, Hortense. 1939, *After Freedom.* New York: Viking Press.

Rainwater, Lee. 1960. *And the Poor Get Children: Sex, Contraception, and Family Planning in the Working Class.* Chicago: Quadrangle Books.

———. 1970. *Behind Ghetto Walls*, Chicago: Aldine Press.

Reed, Joanna. 2007. "Anatomy of the Break-Up: How and Why Do Unmarried Parents Break Up?" In *Unmarried Couples with Children*, edited by Paula England and Kathryn Edin. New York: Russell Sage Foundation.

Roy, Kevin M., Nicole Buckmiller, and April McDowell. 2008. "Together but Not 'Together'; Trajectories of Relationship Suspension for Low-Income Unmarried Parents." *Family Relations* 57(2): 198–210.

Townsend, Nicholas W. 2002. *The Package Deal: Marriage: Work and Fatherhood in Men's Lines.* Philadelphia: Temple University Press.

Waller, Maureen R. 2002. *My Baby's Father: Unmarried Parents and Paternal Responsibility.* Ithaca, NY: Cornell University Press.

———. 2008. "How Do Disadvantaged Parents View Tensions in Their Relationships? Insights for Relationship Longevity among At-Risk Couples." *Family Relations* 57(2): 128–43.

William Julius Wilson. 1996. *When Work Disappears: The World of the New Urban Poor.* New York: Knopf.

Notes

1. Townsend, drawing on in-depth interviews with a group of Bay Area men who graduated from high school in 1972, showed that though fathers desired, in the abstract, to forge direct, intimate relationships with their children, their "package deal" definition of family life, in which fatherhood was part of a package that included marriage, breadwinning, and homeownership, limited them to demonstrating care through their breadwinning activities rather than forming the intimate father-child relationships they desired.

2. For a detailed analysis of breakups among TLC3 couples, see Reed 2007.

■ READING 16

Gay Parenthood and the End of Paternity as We Knew It

Judith Stacey

Do you [Adam] take [Eve] to be your wife—to live together after God's ordinance—in the holy estate of matrimony? Will you love her, comfort her, honor and keep her, in sickness and in health, for richer, for poorer, for better, for worse, in sadness and in joy, to cherish and continually bestow upon her your heart's deepest devotion, forsaking all others, keep yourself only unto her as long as you both shall live?

—*traditional Western wedding vows*

Because let's face it, if men weren't always hungry for it, nothing would ever happen. There would be no sex, and our species would perish.

—*Sean Elder, "Why My Wife Won't Sleep With Me," 2004*

Because homosexuals are rarely monogamous, often having as many as three hundred or more partners in a lifetime—some studies say it is typically more than one thousand—children in those polyamorous situations are caught in a perpetual coming and going. It is devastating to kids, who by their nature are enormously conservative creatures.

—*James Dobson, "Same-Sex Marriage Talking Points"*

Unlucky in love and ready for a family, [Christie] Malcomson tried for 4½ years to get pregnant, eventually giving birth to the twins when she was 38. Four years later, again without a mate, she had Sarah. "I've always known that I was meant to be a mother," Malcomson, 44, said. "I tell people, 'I didn't choose to be a single parent. I choose to be a parent.'"

—*Lornet Turnbull, "Family Is . . . Being Redefined All the Time," 2004*

GAY FATHERS WERE once as unthinkable as they were invisible. Now they are an undeniable part of the contemporary family landscape. During the same time that the marriage promotion campaign in the United States was busy convincing politicians and the public to regard rising rates of fatherlessness as a national emergency,[1] growing numbers of gay men were embracing fatherhood. Over the past two decades, they have built a cornucopia of family forms and supportive communities where they are raising children outside of the conventional family. Examining the experiences of gay men who have openly pursued parenthood against the odds can help us to understand forces that underlie the decline of paternity as we knew it. Contrary to the fears of many in the marriage-promotion movement, however, gay parenting is not a new symptom of the demise of fatherhood, but of its creative, if controversial, reinvention. When I paid close attention to gay men's parenting desires, efforts, challenges, and achievements, I unearthed crucial features of contemporary paternity and parenthood more generally. I also came upon some inspirational models of family that challenge widely held beliefs about parenthood and child welfare.

THE UNCERTAINTY OF PATERNITY

Access to effective contraception, safe abortions, and assisted reproductive technologies (ART) unhitches traditional links between heterosexual love, marriage, and baby carriages. Parenthood, like intimacy more generally, is now contingent. Paths to parenthood no longer appear so natural, obligatory, or uniform as they used to but have become voluntary, plural, and politically embattled. Now that children impose immense economic and social responsibilities on their parents, rather than promising to become a reliable source of family labor or social security, the pursuit of parenthood depends on an emotional rather than an economic calculus. "The men and women who decide to have children today," German sociologists Ulrich Beck and Elisabeth Beck-Gernsheim correctly point out, "certainly do not do so because they expect any material advantages. Other motives closely linked with the emotional needs of the parents play a significant role; our children mainly have 'a psychological utility.'"[2] Amid the threatening upheavals, insecurities, and dislocations of life under global market and military forces, children can rekindle opportunities for hope, meaning, and connection. Adults who wish to become parents today typically seek the intimate bonds that children seem to promise. More reliably than a lover or spouse, parenthood beckons to many (like Christie Malcomson in the third epigraph to this chapter) who hunger for lasting love, intimacy, and kinship—for that elusive "haven in a heartless world."[3]

Gay men confront these features of post-modern parenthood in a magnified mode. They operate from cultural premises antithetical to what U.S. historian Nicholas Townsend termed "the package deal" of (now eroding) modern masculinity—marriage, work, and fatherhood.[4] Gay men who choose to become primary parents challenge conventional definitions of masculinity and paternity and even dominant sexual norms of gay culture itself. Gay sex columnist Dan Savage mocked the cultural stakes involved when he and his partner were deciding to adopt a child: "Terry and I would be giving up certain things that, for better or worse, define what it means to be gay. Good things, things we enjoyed and that had value and meaning for us. Like promiscuity."[5]

Gay fatherhood represents "planned parenthood" in extremis. Always deliberate and often difficult, it offers fertile ground for understanding why and how people do and do not choose to become parents today. Unlike most heterosexuals or even lesbians, gay men have to struggle for access to "the means of reproduction" without benefit of default scripts for achieving or practicing parenthood. They encounter a range of challenging, risky, uncertain options—foster care, public and private forms of domestic and international adoption, hired or volunteered forms of "traditional" or gestational surrogacy, contributing sperm to women friends, relatives, or strangers who agree to co-parent with them, or even resorting to an instrumental approach to old-fashioned heterosexual copulation.

Compared with maternity, the social character of paternity has always been more visible than its biological status. Indeed, that's why prior to DNA testing, most modern societies mandated a marital presumption of paternity. Whenever a married woman gave birth, her husband was the presumed and legal father. Gay male paternity intensifies this emphasis on social rather than biological definitions of parenthood. Because the available routes to genetic parenthood for gay men are formidably expensive, very difficult to negotiate, or both, most prospective gay male parents pursue the purely social paths of adoption or foster care.[6]

Stark racial, economic, and sexual asymmetries characterize the adoption marketplace. Prospective parents are primarily white, middle-class, and relatively affluent, but the available children are disproportionately from poorer and darker races and nations. Public and private adoption agencies, as well as birth mothers and fathers, generally consider married heterosexual couples to be the most desirable adoptive parents.[7] These favored straight married couples, for their part, typically seek healthy infants, preferably from their own race or ethnic background. Because there are not enough of these to meet the demand, most states and counties allow single adults, including gay men, to shop for parenthood in their overstocked warehouse of "hard to place" children. This is an index of expediency more than tolerance. The state's stockpiled children have been removed from parents who were judged to be negligent, abusive, or incompetent. Disproportionate numbers are children of color, and the very hardest of these to place are older boys with "special needs," such as physical, emotional, and cognitive disabilities.

The gross disjuncture between the market value of society's adoptable children and the supply of prospective adoptive parents allows gay men to parent a hefty share of them. Impressive numbers of gay men willingly rescue such children from failing or devastated families. Just as in their intimate adult relationships, gay men more readily accept children across boundaries of race, ethnicity, class, and even health.[8]

The multi-racial membership of so many of gay men's families visually signals the social character of most gay fatherhood. In addition, as we will see, some gay men, like single-mother-by-choice Christie Malcomson, willingly unhitch their sexual and romantic desires from their domestic ones in order to become parents. For all of these reasons, gay men provide frontier terrain for exploring noteworthy changes in the meanings and motives for paternity and parenthood.

FINDING POP LUCK IN THE CITY OF ANGELS

Gay paternity is especially developed and prominent in L.A.—again, not the environment where most people would expect to find it, but which, for many reasons, became a multi-ethnic mecca for gay parenthood. According to data reported in Census 2000, both the greatest number of same-sex couple households in the United States and of such couples who were raising children were residing in Los Angeles County.[9] It is likely, therefore, that the numbers there exceeded those of any metropolis in the world.

Local conditions in Los Angeles have been particularly favorable for gay and lesbian parenthood. L.A. County was among the first in the United States to openly allow gay men to foster or adopt children under its custody, and numerous local, private adoption agencies, lawyers, and services emerged that specialized in facilitating domestic and international adoptions for a gay clientele. In 2001 California enacted a domestic-partnership law that authorized second-parent adoptions, and several family-court judges in California pioneered the still-rare practice of granting pre-birth custody rights to same-sex couples who planned to co-parent. Gay fatherhood became exceptionally institutionalized and visible in Los Angeles, as I indicated in Chapter 1. The City of Angels became the surrogacy capital of the gay globe, thanks especially to Growing Generations, the world's first gay- and lesbian-owned professional surrogacy agency founded to serve an international clientele of prospective gay parents.[10] The thriving Pop Luck Club (PLC), also mentioned earlier, sponsored monthly gatherings, organized special events, and provided information, referrals, support, and community to a membership that by the time I concluded my field research in 2003 included more than two hundred families of varying shapes, sizes, colors, and forms. A PLC subgroup of perhaps ten at-home dads and their children met for a weekly play date in a West Hollywood playground, followed by a "pop luck" lunch. Doting dads taught their young children to dig, slide, swing, teeter-totter, take turns, and make friends while swapping parenting advice, baby clothes, toys, and equipment and building a sustaining community. Single gay dads and "prospective SGDs seeking to meet others who understand how parenting affects our lives" held monthly mixers that featured "friendly folks, scintillating snacks, and brilliant banter—about the best brand of diapers!"[11] Additional PLC focus groups, for prospective gay dads or adoptive dads, for example, as well as satellite chapters in neighboring counties continually emerged.

The gay men I studied, as the stories in Chapter 1 revealed, were among the first cohort of gay men young enough to even imagine parenthood outside heterosexuality and mature enough to be in a position to choose or reject it. I intentionally over-sampled for gay fathers. Nationally 22 percent of male same-sex-couple households recorded in Census 2000 included children under the age of eighteen.[12] However, fathers composed half of my sample overall and more than 60 percent of the men who were then in same-sex couples. Depending on which definition of fatherhood one uses, between twenty-four and twenty-nine of my fifty primary interviewees were fathers of thirty-five children, and four men who were not yet parents declared their firm intention to become so.[13] Only sixteen men (32 percent), in contrast, depicted themselves as childless more or less by choice. Also by design, I sampled to include the full gamut of contemporary paths to gay paternity. Although most children with gay fathers in the United States were born within heterosexual marriages before their fathers came out, this was true for only six of the thirty-four children that the men in my study were raising. All of the others were among the pioneer generation of children with gay dads who chose to parent after they had come out of the closet. Fifteen of the children had been adopted (or were in the process of becoming so) through county and private agencies or via independent, open adoption agreements with birth mothers; four were foster-care children; five children had been conceived through surrogacy contracts, both gestational and "traditional"; and four children had been born to lesbians who conceived with sperm from gay men with whom they were co-parenting. In addition, five of the gay men in my study had served as foster parents to numerous teenagers, and several expected to continue to accept foster placements. Two men, however, were biological but not social parents, one by intention, the other unwittingly.[14]

The fathers and children in my study were racially and socially diverse, and their families, like gay-parent families generally, were much more likely to be multi-racial and multi-cultural than are other families in the United States, or perhaps anywhere in the world. Two-thirds of the gay-father families in my study were multi-racial. The majority (fifteen) of the twenty-four gay men who were parenting during the time of my study were white, but most (twenty-one) of their thirty-four children were not.[15] Even more striking, only two of the fifteen children they had adopted by 2003 were white, both of these through open adoption arrangements with birth mothers; seven adoptees were black or mixed race, and six were Latino. In contrast, nine of the twelve adoptive parents were white, and one each was black, Latino, and Asian American.

It is difficult to assess how racially representative this is of gay men, gay parents, and their families in the city, the state, or the nation. Although the dominant cultural stereotype of gay men and gay fathers is white and middle class, U.S. Census 2000 data surprisingly report that racial minorities represented a higher proportion of same-sex-couple-parent households in California than of heterosexual married couples.[16] The vast majority of the children in these families, however, were born within their gay parents' former heterosexual relationships.[17] Contemporary gay paths to paternity are far more varied and complex.

THE PASSION-FOR-PARENTHOOD CONTINUUM

The fifty gay men I interviewed in Los Angeles expressed attitudes toward parenthood that ranged from religious vocation to unabashed aversion. On one end of the passion-for-parenthood continuum clustered men I think of as "predestined parents." Compelled by a potent, irrepressible longing, these men said that they had always known that they wanted to become parents and that they had been prepared to move heaven and earth to do so. Few, if any, predestined parents consciously sought single parenthood, but like Christie Malcomson, they were willing to brave this trying trail rather than miss out on parenthood entirely. In fact, their desire to parent often trumped their desire for a partner, and a predestined parent would forsake a mate who forced him to choose between the two.

On the far opposite end of the spectrum lay the absolute "parental refuseniks," for whom parenthood held less than no appeal. A few gay men even viewed their freedom from the pressure to parent to be one of the compensatory rewards of their stigmatized sexual identity. With exactly inverse priorities to a predestined parent, a pure refusenik's aversion to parenthood was so potent that he would forfeit his couple relationship rather than go along with his mate's unequivocal yearning to become a parent. Arrayed between these two poles was a broad spectrum of inclinations held by less determined souls. Persuasive life partners or circumstances could recruit or divert these potential "situational parents" into or away from the world of Pampers and playgrounds that the two other groups fervently embraced or eschewed.

PREDESTINED PROGENITORS

Of the men I interviewed, eighteen who had become dads and four who planned to do so portrayed their passion for parenthood in terms so ardent that I classify them as predestined parents. A shared craving for parenthood united three fortunate pairs in my study, including Ossie and Harry, whom we met in Chapter 1. Five men sought to become parents without an intimate partner; five others persuaded situational partners to support their quest; and primordial parental desires had led two men to create married heterosexual-parent families before they came out—families that they later left. The following two stories illustrate typical challenges and triumphs of different paths to predestined parenthood. The first depicts another blessedly compatible and privileged couple, and the second is about a courageous, much less affluent gay man who was "single by chance, parent by choice," to paraphrase the title of a book about single women who choose to become mothers.[18]

PREDESTINED PAIRING

Eddie Leary and Charles Tillery, a well-heeled, white, Catholic couple, had three children born through gestational surrogacy. Their firstborn was a genetic half-sibling to a younger set of twins. The same egg donor and the same gestational surrogate conceived and bore the three children, but Charles is the genetic father of the first child, and Eddie's sperm conceived the twins. At the time I first interviewed them in 2002, their first child was three years old, the twins were infants, and the couple had been together for eighteen years. Eddie told me that they had discussed their shared desire to parent on their very first date, just as Ossie and Harry had done. In fact, by then Eddie had already entered a heterosexual marriage primarily for that purpose, but he came out to his wife and left the marriage before achieving it. Directly echoing Christie Malcomson, Eddie claimed that he always knew that he "was meant to be a parent." He recalled that during his childhood whenever adults had posed the clichéd question to him, "What do you want to be when you grow up?" his ready answer was "a daddy."

Charles and Eddie met and spent their first ten years together on the East Coast, where they built successful careers in corporate law and were gliding through the glamorous DINC (double income, no children) fast lane of life. By their mid-thirties, however, they were bored and began to ask themselves the existential question, "Is this all there is?" They had already buried more friends than their parents had by their sixties, which, Eddie believed, "gives you a sense of gravitas." In addition, he reported, "My biological clock was definitely ticking." In the mid-1990s, the couple migrated to L.A., lured by the kind of gay family life style and the ample job opportunities it seemed to offer. They spent the next five years riding an emotional roller coaster attempting to become parents. At first Eddie and Charles considered adoption, but they became discouraged when they learned that then-governor Pete Wilsons administration was preventing joint adoptions by same-sex couples. Blessed with ample financial and social resources, they decided to shift their eggs, so to speak, into the surrogacy basket. One of Charles's many cousins put the couple in touch with her college roommate, Sally, a married mother of two in her mid-thirties who lived in Idaho. Sally was a woman who loved both bearing and rearing children, and Charles's cousin knew that she had been fantasizing about bestowing the gift of parenthood on a childless couple. Although Sally's imaginary couple had not been gay, she agreed to meet them. Eddie and Sally both reported that they bonded instantly, and she agreed to serve as the men's gestational surrogate.

To secure an egg donor and manage the complex medical and legal processes that surrogacy requires at a moment just before Growing Generations had opened shop, Eddie and Charles became among the first gay clients of a surrogate parenthood agency that mainly served infertile heterosexual couples. Shopping for DNA in the agency's catalog of egg donors, they had selected Marya, a Dutch graduate student who had twice before served as an anonymous donor for married couples in order to subsidize her education. Marya had begun to long for maternity herself, however, and she was loathe to subject her body and soul yet again to the grueling and hormonally disruptive process that donating ova entails. Yet when she learned that the new candidates for her genes were gay men, she found herself taken with the prospect of openly aiding such a quest. Like Sally, she felt an immediate affinity with Eddie and agreed to enter a collaborative egg-donor relationship with him and Charles. When she had served as egg donor for infertile married couples, Marya explained, "the mother there can get a little jealous and a little threatened, because she's already feeling insecure about being infertile, and having another woman having that process and threatening the mother's role, I think is a big concern." With a gay couple, in contrast, "you get to be—there's no exclusion, and there's no threatened feelings."

Because Eddie is a few years older than Charles, he wanted to be the first to provide the sperm, and all four parties were thrilled when Sally became pregnant on the second in-vitro fertilization (IVF) attempt. Elation turned to despair, however, when the pregnancy miscarried in the thirteenth week. Eddie described himself as devastated, saying, "I grieved and mourned the loss of my child, just as if I'd been the one carrying it." In fact, Sally recovered from the trauma and was willing to try again before Eddie, who said, "I couldn't bear the risk of losing another of my children." Instead, Charles wound up supplying the sperm for what became the couples firstborn child, Heather. Two years later, eager for a second child, the couple had persuaded both reluctant women to subject their bodies to one more IVF surrogacy, this time with Eddie's sperm. A pair of healthy twin boys arrived one year later,[19] with all four procreative collaborators, as well as Sally's husband, present at the delivery to welcome the boys into what was to become a remarkable, surrogacy-extended family.

Occasionally Marya, the egg donor, continued to visit her genetic daughter, but Eddie and Sally quickly developed an extraordinary, deep, familial bond. They developed the habit of daily, long-distance phone calls that were often lengthy and intimate. "Mama Sally," as Heather started to call her, began to make regular use of the Leary-Tillery guest room, accompanied sometimes by her husband and their two children. Often she came to co-parent with Eddie as a substitute for Charles, who had to make frequent business trips. The two families began taking joint vacations skiing or camping together in the Rockies, and once Marya had come along. Sally's then ten-year-old daughter and eight-year-old son began to refer to Heather as their "surrogate sister."

Eddie and Charles jointly secured shared legal custody of all three children through some of the earliest pre-birth decrees granted in California. From the start, the couple had agreed that Eddie, a gourmet cook who had designed the family's state-of-the-culinary-art kitchen, would stay home as full-time parent, and Charles would be the family's sole breadwinner. After the twins arrived, they hired a daytime nanny to assist Eddie while Charles was out earning their sustenance, and she sometimes minded the twins when Eddie and Heather joined the weekly playgroup of PLC at-home dads and tots. Charles, for his part, blessed with Herculean energy and scant need for sleep, would plunge into his full-scale second shift of baby feedings, diapers, baths, and bedtime storytelling the moment he returned from the office. Although Eddie admitted to some nagging concerns that he "may have committed career suicide by joining the mom's club in the neighborhood," he also believed he'd met his calling: "I feel like this is who I was meant to be."

When I contacted Eddie again in late October 2008, he reported that he and Charles were among those thousands of same-sex couples in California who had just rushed to register their "shotgun weddings" before the November election. They would have preferred to wait until the following spring to celebrate the twenty-fifth anniversary of their union with a big wedding. Instead, they acted on what proved to be their prescient fear that voters would take away their new right to marry by passing Proposition 8, the initiative to insert a ban on same-sex marriage into the state constitution. Other than the hastily staged marriage, Eddie said that he had no momentous family changes to report:

> We are another of those boring families where little has changed other than our children are more beautiful and a little older, and Charles and I have more gray hair and feel a lot older. We live in a neighborhood filled with children (fifty of whom were here with their parents on Halloween night for our annual open house), and as far as I know, none of them have been traumatized living near a family headed by two gay men. Charles still works, and I still see my job as taking care of my family. We are fortunate to be able to afford this choice.

Of course, few readers would agree with Eddie that his is a boring family. In fact, its surrogacy-extended kin ties had expanded and deepened in the years since my research. Egg donor Marya was now a married mother of two after she too had held a shotgun wedding, but of a more old-fashioned sort. A few years earlier Marya had found herself accidentally, but not unhappily, pregnant after her fourth date with a lover who proved willing to jump-start a family. So the three Tillery-Leary children had acquired two more genetic half-siblings. Marya and her family were living in New Mexico and were about to come visit again, because, Eddie wrote, "Mama Marya and her husband believe it is important for the five kids to know they are siblings and that Marya is one of our three children's moms." In addition, Eddie announced that the children's other, more actively involved mom, gestational surrogate Mama Sally, and her husband were coming for Thanksgiving: "because we like spending as much time together as possible." The two surrogacy-linked couples and children celebrated holidays together regularly and had taken to spending their summers together as well on a ranch in south Texas that Sally and her husband had purchased.

Eddie and Charles were no longer active in the PLC, because they had neither time nor need for such organized support. Their children now went to school with several kids from the old PLC at-home dads' playground group. Their family and community life were so full, rich, rewarding, and integrated that being gay dads rarely seemed much of an issue anymore. In fact, Eddie reported that recently his aging Catholic mother had told him that he was the only person she knew who had gotten everything he had ever wanted in life.

PARENT SEEKING PARTNER

Armando Hidalgo, a Mexican immigrant, was thirty-four years old when I interviewed him in 2001. At that point, he was in the final stages of adopting his four-year-old black foster son, Ramón. Armando had been a teenage sexual migrant to Los Angeles almost twenty years earlier. He had run away from home when he was only fifteen in order to conceal his unacceptable sexual desires from his large, commercially successful, urban Mexican family. The youthful Armando had paid a coyote to help him cross the border. He had survived a harrowing illegal immigration experience which culminated in a Hollywood-style footrace across the California desert to escape an INS patrol in hot pursuit. By working at a Taco Bell in a coastal town, Armando put himself through high school. Drawing upon keen intelligence, linguistic facility, and a prodigious work ethic and drive, he had built a stable career managing a designer furniture showroom and he had managed to secure U.S. citizenship as well.

Four years after Armando's sudden disappearance from Mexico, he had returned there to come out to his family, cope with their painful reactions to his homosexuality and exile, and begin to restore his ruptured kinship bonds. He had made annual visits to his family ever since, and on one of these he fell in love with Juan, a Mexican language teacher. Armando said that he told Juan about his desire to parent right at the outset, and his new lover had seemed enthusiastic: "So, I thought we were the perfect match." Armando brought his boyfriend back to Los Angeles, and they lived together for five years.

However, when Armando began to pursue his lifelong goal of parenthood, things fell apart. To initiate the adoption process, Armando had enrolled the couple in the county's mandatory foster-care class. However, Juan kept skipping class and neglecting the homework, and so he failed to qualify for foster-parent status. This behavior jeopardized Armando's eligibility to adopt children as well as Juan's. The county then presented Armando with a "Sophie's choice." They would not place a child in his home unless Juan moved out. Despite Armando's primal passion for parenthood, "at the time," he self-critically explained to me, "I made the choice of staying with him, a choice that I regret. I chose him over continuing with my adoption." This decision ultimately exacted a fatal toll on the relationship. In Armando's eyes, Juan was preventing him from fulfilling his lifelong dream of having children. His resentment grew, but it took another couple of years before his passion for parenthood surpassed his diminishing passion for his partner. That is when Armando moved out and renewed the adoption application as a single parent.

Ramón was the first of three children that Armando told me he had "definitely decided" to adopt, whether or not he found another partner. His goal was to adopt two more children, preferably a daughter and another son, in that order. Removed at birth from crack-addicted parents, Ramón had lived in three foster homes in his first three years of life, before the county placed him with Armando through its fost-adopt program. Ramón had suffered from food allergies, anxiety, and hyperactivity when he arrived, and the social worker warned Armando to anticipate learning disabilities as well. Instead, after nine months under Armando's steady, patient, firm, and loving care, Ramón was learning rapidly and appeared to be thriving. And so was Armando. He felt so lucky to have Ramón, whom he no longer perceived as racially different from himself: "To me he's like my natural son. I love him a lot, and he loves me too much. Maybe I never felt so much unconditional love."

In fact, looking back, Armando attributed part of the pain of the years he spent struggling to accept his own homosexuality to his discomfort with gay male sexual culture and its emphasis on youth and beauty. "I think it made me fear that I was going to grow old alone," he reflected. "Now I don't have to worry that I'm gay and I'll be alone." For in addition to the intimacy that Armando savored with Ramón, his son proved to be a vehicle for building much closer bonds with most of his natal family. Several of Armando's eleven siblings had also migrated to Los Angeles. Among these were a married brother, his wife, and their children, who provided indispensable back-up support to the single working father. Ramón adored his cousins, and he and his father spent almost every weekend and holiday with them.

Ramón had acquired a devoted, long-distance *abuela* (grandmother) as well. Armando's mother had begun to travel regularly from Mexico to visit her dispersed brood, and, after years of disapproval and disappointment, she had grown to admire and appreciate her gay son above all her other children. Armando reported with sheepish pride that during a recent phone call his mother had stunned and thrilled him when she said, "You know what? I wish that all your brothers were like you. I mean that they liked guys." Astonished, Armando had asked her, "Why do you say that?" She replied, "I don't know. I just feel that you're really good to me, you're really kind. And you're such a good father." Then she apologized for how badly she had reacted when Armando told the family that he was gay, and she told him that now she was really proud of him. "'Now I don't have to accept it,'" Armando quoted her, "'because there's nothing to accept. You're natural, you're normal. You're my son, I don't have to accept you.' And she went on and on. It was so nice, it just came out of her. And now she talks about gay things, and she takes a cooking class from a gay guy and tells me how badly her gay cooking teacher was treated by his family when they found out and how unfair it is and all."

Although Armando had begun to create the family he always wanted, he still dreamt of sharing parenthood with a mate who would be more compatible than Juan: "I would really love to meet someone, to fall in love." Of course, the man of his dreams was someone family-oriented: "Now that's really important, family-oriented, because I am very close to my family. I always do family things, like my nephews' birthday parties, going to the movies with them, family dinners, etcetera. But these are things that many gay men don't like to do. If they go to a straight family party, they get bored." Consequently, Armando was pessimistic about finding a love match. Being a parent, moreover, severely constrained his romantic pursuits. He didn't want to subject Ramón, who had suffered so much loss and instability in his life, to the risk of becoming attached to yet another new parental figure who might leave him. In addition, he didn't want Ramón "to think that gay men only have casual relationships, that there's no commitment." "But," he observed, with disappointment, "I haven't seen a lot of commitment among gay men." Armando took enormous comfort, however, in knowing that even if he never found another boyfriend, he will "never really be alone": "And I guess that's one of the joys that a family brings." Disappointingly, I may never learn whether Armando found a co-parent and adopted a sister and brother for Ramón, because I was unable to locate him again in 2008.

ADOPTING DIVERSITY

While Eddie, Charles, and Armando all experienced irrepressible parental yearnings, they pursued very different routes to realizing this common "destiny." Gestational surrogacy, perhaps the newest, the most high-tech, and certainly the most expensive path to gay parenthood, is available primarily to affluent couples, the overwhelming majority of whom are white men who want to have genetic progeny.[20] Adoption, on the other hand, is one of the oldest forms of "alternative" parenthood. It involves bureaucratic and social rather than medical technologies, and the county fost-adopt program which Armando and six other men in my study employed is generally the least expensive, most accessible route to gay paternity. Like Armando, most single, gay prospective parents pursue this avenue and adopt "hard-to-place" children who, like Ramón, are often boys of color with "special needs."

The demographics of contrasting routes to gay parenthood starkly expose the race and class disparities in the market value of children. Affluent, mainly white couples, like Charles and Eddie, can purchase the means to reproduce white infants in their own image, or even an enhanced, eugenic one, by selecting egg donors who have traits they desire with whom to mate their own DNA. In contrast, for gay men who are single, less privileged, or both, public agencies offer a grab bag of displaced children who are generally older, darker, and less healthy.[21] Somewhere in between these two routes to gay paternity lie forms of "gray market," open domestic or international adoptions, or privately negotiated sperm-donor agreements with women, especially lesbians, who want to co-parent with men. Independent adoption agencies and the Internet enable middle-class gay men, again typically white couples, to adopt newborns in a variety of hues.

Bernardo Fernandez, a middle-class, black Latino, took the gray-market route to parenthood, and with intimate consequences almost opposite to Armando's. Bernardo adopted the first of two mixed-race children while he was single, but then he had the great fortune of falling in love with a gay man who also had always wanted to parent. Less fortunately, however, Bernardo's beloved was an Australian visitor to the United States, and U.S. immigration law does not grant family status to same-sex partners. His partner therefore applied for a work visa so that he could stay in the United States, but his tourist visa had expired, and he had been forced to return home. The prospects of receiving a work visa were not looking good, and Bernardo feared that in order to live together as a family, he and the children were going to have to migrate to Australia, because it did admit same-sex partners. In the meantime, Bernardo was spending the months between his lover's regular visits parenting alone.

Price does not always determine the route to parenthood that gay men choose, or the race, age, health, or pedigree of the children they agree to adopt. During the period of my initial research, only one white, middle-class couple in my study had chosen to adopt healthy white infants. Some affluent white men enthusiastically adopted children of color, even when they knew that the children had been exposed to drugs prenatally. Drew Greenwald, a very successful architect who could easily have afforded assisted reproductive technology (ART), was the most dramatic example of this. He claimed, "It never would have occurred to me to do surrogacy. I think it's outrageous because there are all these children who need good homes. And people have surrogacy, they say, in part it's because they want to avoid the complications of adoption, but in candor they are really in love with their own genes. . . . I just think there is a bit of narcissism about it." An observant Jew and the son of Holocaust survivors, Drew found gestational surrogacy particularly offensive. "The idea of having a different genetic mother and birth mother is a little too Nazi-esque for me, a little too much genetic engineering for me. I feel somewhat uncomfortable with that. I mean, someone can be good enough to carry the baby, but their genes aren't good enough? That's outrageous."

Drew had opted for independent, open, transracial adoption instead. When I first interviewed him in 2002, he had just adopted his second of two multi-racial babies born to two different women who both had acknowledged using drugs during their pregnancies. Drew, like Bernardo, had been single when he adopted his first child, and parenthood proved to be a route to successful partnership for him as well. Soon after adopting his first infant, Drew reunited with James, a former lover who had fallen "wildly in love" with Drew's new baby. James moved in while Drew was in the process of adopting a second child, and they have co-parented together ever since. Indeed, parenthood is the "glue" that cemented a relationship between the couple that Drew believed might otherwise have failed. Shared parenting provided them with a "joint project, a focus, and a source of commitment." Drew acknowledged that he was not a romantic. He had questions, in fact, "about the very term *intimacy*" and considered sex to be an important but minor part of life. He and James were very "efficient" in servicing their sexual needs, he quipped. They devoted perhaps "a few minutes" of their over-stuffed weekly schedule to this activity, "mainly on Shabbas, and then we're back to our family life."

I was indulging in my guilty pleasure of reading the Style section of the Sunday *New York Times* one morning in the fall of 2008, when I stumbled across a wedding photo and announcement that Drew and James, "the parents of five adopted children," had just married. Several weeks later, on a conference trip to Los Angeles, I visited the bustling, expanded family household. I learned that the white birth mother of their second child had since had two more unwanted pregnancies, one with the same African American man as before and one with a black Latino. She had successfully appealed to Drew and James to add both of these mixed-race siblings to their family. After the first of these two new brothers had joined their brood, Drew and James began to worry that because only one of their children was a girl, she would find it difficult to grow up in a family with two dads and only brothers. And so they turned to the Internet, where they found a mixed-race sister for their first daughter. Three of the five children suffered from learning or attention-deficit difficulties, but Drew took this in stride. He was aware, he said, that he and James had signed on "for all sorts of trauma, challenge, heartache" in the years ahead. He was both determined and financially able to secure the best help available for his children. Nonetheless, Drew acknowledged, "I fully expect that the kids will break my heart at some point in various ways, but it's so worth it." It was sufficiently worth it, apparently, that the year after my 2008 visit, I received an email from Drew announcing that their child head count had climbed to six, because their "jackpot birth mom" had given birth yet again. "We're up to four boys and two girls," Drew elaborated. "It's a lot, as you can imagine, but wonderful.". . . .

Two other predestined parents in my study were co-parenting with lesbian friends children who had been conceived through donor insemination.[22] Both have created multi-gay-parent families that I describe later in this chapter.

DADS-IN-WAITING

The final category of predestined parents consists of four men who were not yet parents but expressed irrepressible parental yearnings and had begun to actively weigh their options. Three of these men were white, and one black; two were coupled, and two single. And these social statuses influenced how they calculated the opportunities and risks that different strategies seemed to pose. Damian, for example, a thirty-four-year-old, white observant Catholic, was still struggling in 2001 to make his peace with what he viewed to be his "homosexual nature" and the barrier it posed to his potent conventional familial longings and values. Once again, like Christie Malcomson, Damian was unhappily single and discouraged about the prospects of finding the sort of committed relationship he desired, but he refused to forfeit his parental desires. He had been sorely tempted by the option of entering a heterosexual marriage of convenience. "I have a very close female friend," Damian reported, "who would marry me in a heartbeat if I wanted to marry and have a kid. I've actually thought about it, but then if I had a kid with Colleen, I'd have to share. And what if we broke up, or things fell apart? Then what?" To achieve a more secure form of primary parental status, Damian had decided to pursue some form of adoption.

Notes

1. I discuss the fatherlessness discourse and the history of the politics of family values in the conclusion. Also see Stacey, "Dada-ism in the Nineties."
2. Beck and Beck-Gernsheim, *The Normal Chaos of Love*, 105.
3. Lasch, Haven in a Heartless World.
4. Townsend, The Package Deal
5. Savage, *The Kid*, 26.
6. Here too, however, gays encounter discrimination. While one national study found that 60 percent of U.S. adoption agencies accept applications from homosexual clients, only 39 percent of the agencies in this group had placed at least one child with a gay or lesbian potential parent during the target period, and only 19 percent of these agencies actively recruit prospective gay and lesbian parents. Brodzinsky, Patterson, and Vaziri, "Adoption Agency Perspectives."
7. In Florida, although two pro-LGBT parenting bills died in committee, the strict law banning "homosexual" individuals from adopting has been struck down twice at the trial-court level, but the decisions have been stayed pending review by a state appellate court. Until its decision, the law remains in effect. In Arkansas, a law passed by voters went into effect January 1, 2009, that banned unmarried couples from becoming foster or adoptive parents. The law was challenged in state court, and a trial judge ruled it unconstitutional in April 2010. As this book goes to press, the state attorney general has not decided whether to appeal the trial court decision, but the conservative Family Council that spearheaded the ballot initiative has vowed to appeal. Moritz, "Judge Strikes Down Adoption Ban." In Tennessee, for the past three years, supporters of LGBT families have brushed back attempts to ban unmarried couples from adopting children, leaving in effect an opinion by the Tennessee attorney general stating that same-sex couples can legally adopt under state law. It is expected that anti-equality Tennessee state legislators will again attempt to pass the legislation in 2010. Human Rights Campaign, "Equality from State to State 2009."
8. Compared with children of married couples, children of same-sex couples were found in one study to be twice as likely to be adopted, and children of same-sex parents were disproportionately

of Hispanic and non-white race and ethnic origins. Sears and Badgett, "Same-Sex Couples and Same-Sex Couples Raising Children in California." Of the children adopted in California between October 1, 2001, and September 30, 2002, for example, 41 percent were Hispanic, 23 percent were non-Hispanic black, and only 29 percent were non-Hispanic white. U.S. Department of Health and Human Services, *The AFCARS Report*. Qualitative studies of gay fathers likewise report high percentages of cross-racial adoption. Sbordone, "Gay Men Choosing Fatherhood"; Schacher, Auerbach, and Silverstein, "Gay Fathers Expanding the Possibilities for Us All." Other, more recent studies show that gay parents are more likely to adopt non-white children, as well as children with disabilities. Gates et al., "Adoption and Foster Care by Lesbian and Gay Parents in the United States."

9. The 2000 Census reports 25,173 same-sex couples in Los Angeles County, of which 14,468 are male. With 8,015 of its reported same-sex couples raising children, Los Angeles County ranks first in the nation. Sears and Badgett, "Same-Sex Couples and Same-Sex Couples Raising Children in California." This vastly understates the incidence of gay parentage, because it does not include single parents, dual-household parents, or gay parents who did not report a same-sex partnership.

10. Growing Generations, http://www.growinggenerations.com; see also Strah and Margolis, *Gay Dads*.

11. Pop Luck Club, *Newsletter*.

12. Simmons and O'Connell, "Married-Couple and Unmarried-Partner Households: 2000," 10.

13. Twenty-four men were actively parenting children. In addition, two men were step-fathers to a partner's non-residential children; one man with his mother formerly co-foster-parented teenagers; four of the adoptive fathers had also formerly fostered teenagers, and two of these intended to resume this practice in the future; one man served as a known sperm donor for lesbian-couple friends; and one man was a genetic father who does not parent his offspring.

14. One man, a sperm dad who nicknamed himself a "spad," had facilitated a lesbian friends desire to conceive a child with a donor willing to be an avuncular presence in her child's life. The other unwittingly impregnated a former girlfriend who chose to keep the child and agreed not to reveal its paternity.

15. Of the gay parents, five are Latino, three are black or Caribbean, and one is Asian American. Thirteen of their thirty-four children are white; nine are Latino; eight are black, Caribbean, or mixed race; and four are multi-racial Asian.

16. Nearly 40 percent of same-sex parents in the state identified themselves as black, mixed race, or of another race, compared with 28 percent of married-couple parents; 53 percent of parents in same-sex couples were white, against 58 percent of married-couple parents. According to these census data, whites are slightly over-represented among individuals in same-sex couples in California, and Asian Americans are significantly under-represented, but percentages of Hispanic, black, and mixed-race individuals are proportional to their numbers in the state. Sears and Badgett, "Same-Sex Couples and Same-Sex Couples Raising Children in California."

17. In the 2000 Census, 76 percent of children residing in male same-sex-couple households were described as their "natural-born" children. Gary Gates, Distinguished Scholar at the Williams Institute, UCLA Law School, personal communication, May 17, 2005.

18. Hertz, *Single by Chance, Mothers by Choice*.

19. Multiple births occur frequently with IVF, because physicians implant multiple embryos to increase the odds of successful gestation.

20. In fact, the surrogacy agency that Charles and Eddie used did not accept single applicants.

21. Although non-Hispanic blacks represented only 12.5 percent of the U.S. population, 37 percent of children who entered the national foster-care system in September 2001 were non-Hispanic black. Blacks, moreover, disproportionately remain in the foster-care system—45 percent of the children who exited foster care during the 2000–2001 fiscal year were non-Hispanic white, while only 30 percent were non-Hispanic black. And although there are more black than white children waiting for adoption (45 percent of the children waiting to be adopted in September 2001 were non-Hispanic black, and 34 percent were non-Hispanic white), more white

than black children are adopted. Of the children adopted during the 2000–2001 fiscal year, 38 percent were white, and 35 percent were black. U.S. Department of Health and Human Services, Administration on Children, Youth, and Families, Children's Bureau, *The AFCARS Report*. Race has also been shown to affect the amount of time that children have to wait for adoption completion and legalization. Kapp, McDonald, and Diamond, "The Path to Adoption for Children of Color."

22. National cultural and institutional frameworks influence notable cross-national variations in preferred forms of gay and lesbian parenthood. Co-parenting arrangements between lesbians and gay male sperm donors, for example, appear to be more popular in Sweden than in the United States or Ireland. See Ryan-Flood, "Contested Heteronormativities."

8

Growing Up

■READING 17

Beyond Sentimentality: American Childhood as a Social and Cultural Construct

Steven Mintz

Nowhere is it easier to romanticize childhood than in Mark Twain's hometown of Hannibal, Missouri. In this small Mississippi riverfront town, where Mark Twain lived, off and on, from the age of four until he was seventeen, many enduring American fantasies about childhood come to life. There is a historical marker next to a fence like the one that Tom's friends paid him for the privilege of whitewashing. There is another marker pointing to the spot where Huck's cabin supposedly stood. There is also the window where Huck hurled pebbles to wake the sleeping Tom. Gazing out across the raging waters of the Mississippi, now unfortunately hidden behind a floodwall, one can easily imagine the raft excursion that Huck and Jim took seeking freedom and adventure.

Hannibal occupies a special place in our collective imagination as the setting of two of fiction's most famous depictions of childhood. Our cherished myth about childhood as a bucolic time of freedom, untainted innocence, and self-discovery comes to life in this river town. But beyond the accounts of youthful wonder and small-town innocence, Twain's novels teem with grim and unsettling details about childhood's underside. Huck's father Pap was an abusive drunkard who beat his son for learning how to read. When we idealize Mark Twain's Hannibal and its eternally youthful residents, we suppress his novels' more sinister aspects.[1]

Twain's real-life mid-nineteenth-century Hannibal was anything but a haven of stability and security. It was a place where a quarter of the children died before their first birthday, half before they reached the age of twenty-one. Twain himself experienced the death of two siblings. Although he was not physically abused like the fictional Huck, his father was emotionally cold and aloof. There were few open displays of affection in his boyhood home. Only once did he remember seeing his father and mother kiss, and that was at the deathbed of his brother Ben. Nor was his home a haven of economic security. His boyhood ended before his twelfth birthday when his father's death forced him to take up a series of odd jobs. Before he left home permanently at seventeen, he had already worked as a printer's apprentice; clerked in a grocery store, a bookshop, and a drug store; tried his hand at blacksmithing; and delivered newspapers. Childhood ended early in Twain's hometown, though full adulthood came no more quickly than it does today.[2]

A series of myths cloud public thinking about the history of American childhood. One is the myth of a carefree childhood. We cling to a fantasy that once upon a time childhood and youth were years of carefree adventure, despite the fact that for most children in the past, growing up was anything but easy. Disease, family disruption, and early entry into the world of work were integral parts of family life. The notion of a long childhood devoted to education and free from adult-like responsibilities is a very recent invention, a product of the past century and a half, and one that only became a reality for a majority of children after World War II.

Another myth is that of the home as a haven and bastion of stability in an ever-changing world. Throughout American history, family stability has been the exception, not the norm. At the beginning of the twentieth century, fully a third of all American children spent at least a portion of their childhood in a single-parent home, and as recently as 1940, one child in ten did not live with either parent—compared to one in twenty-five today.[3]

A third myth is that childhood is the same for all children, a status transcending class, ethnicity, and gender. In fact, every aspect of childhood is shaped by class—as well as by ethnicity, gender, geography, religion, and historical era. We may think of childhood as a biological phenomenon, but it is better understood as a life stage whose contours are shaped by a particular time and place. Childrearing practices, schooling, and the age at which young people leave home are all the products of particular social and cultural circumstances.

A fourth myth is that the United States is a peculiarly child-friendly society when, in actuality, Americans are deeply ambivalent about children. Adults envy young people their youth, vitality, and physical attractiveness, but they also resent children's intrusions on their time and resources and frequently fear their passions and drives. Many of the reforms that nominally have been designed to protect and assist the young were also instituted to insulate adults from children.

Lastly, the myth that is perhaps the most difficult to overcome is the myth of progress and its inverse, the myth of decline. There is a tendency to conceive of the history of childhood as a story of steps forward over time: of parental engagement replacing emotional distance, of kindness and leniency supplanting strict and stern punishment, of scientific enlightenment superceding superstition and misguided moralism. This progressivism is sometimes seen in reverse, that is, that childhood is disappearing: children are growing up too quickly and wildly and losing their innocence, playfulness, and malleability.

Various myths and misconceptions have contributed to this undue pessimism about the young. There has never been a golden age of childhood when the overwhelming majority of American children were well cared for and their experiences were idyllic. Nor has childhood ever been an age of innocence, at least not for the overwhelming majority of children. Childhood has never been insulated from the pressures and demands of the surrounding society and each generation of children has had to wrestle with the particular social, political, and economic constraints of its own historical period. In our own time, the young have had to struggle with high rates of family instability, a deepening disconnection from adults, and the expectation that all children should pursue the same academic path at the same pace, even as the attainment of full adulthood recedes ever further into the future.

THE SOCIAL AND CULTURAL CONSTRUCTION OF CHILDHOOD

The history of children is often treated as a marginal subject, and there is no question that the history of children is especially difficult to write. Children are rarely obvious historical actors. Compared to adults, they leave fewer historical sources, and their powerlessness makes them less visible than other social groups. Nevertheless, the history of childhood is inextricably bound up with the broader political and social events in the life of the nation—including colonization, revolution, slavery, industrialization, urbanization, immigration, and war—and children's experience embodies many of the key themes in American history, such as the rise of modern bureaucratic institutions, the growth of a consumer economy, and the elaboration of a welfare state. Equally important, childhood's history underscores certain long-term transformations in American life, such as an intensifying consciousness about age, a clearer delineation of distinct life stages, and the increasing tendency to organize institutions by age.

Childhood is not an unchanging, biological stage of life, and children are not just "grow'd," like Topsy in Harriet Beecher Stowe's *Uncle Tom's Cabin*. Rather, childhood is a social and cultural construct. Every aspect of childhood—including children's relationships with their parents and peers, their proportion of the population, and their paths through childhood to adulthood—has changed dramatically over the past four centuries. Methods of child rearing, the duration of schooling, the nature of children's play, young people's participation in work, and the points of demarcation between childhood, adolescence, and adulthood are products of culture, class, and historical era.[4]

Childhood in the past was experienced and conceived of in quite a different way than today. Just two centuries ago, there was far less age segregation than there is today and less concern with organizing experience by chronological age. There was also far less sentimentalization of children as special beings who were more innocent and vulnerable than adults. This does not mean that adults failed to recognize childhood as a stage of life, with its own special needs and characteristics, nor does it imply that parents were unconcerned about their children and failed to love them and mourn their deaths. Rather, it means that the experience of young people was organized and valued very differently than it is today.

Language itself illustrates shifts in the construction of childhood. Two hundred years ago, the words used to describe childhood were far less precise than those we use today. The word *infancy* referred not to the months after birth, but to the period in which children were under their mother's control, typically from birth to the age of 5 or 6. The word *childhood* might refer to someone as young as the age of 5 or 6 or as old as the late teens or early twenties. Instead of using our term adolescent or teenager, Americans two centuries ago used a broader and more expansive term *youth*, which stretched from the pre-teen years until the early or mid-20s. The vagueness of this term reflected the amorphousness of the life stages; chronological age was less important than physical strength, size, and maturity. A young person did not achieve full adult status until marriage and establishment of an independent farm or entrance into a full-time trade or profession. Full adulthood might be attained as early as the mid- or late teens, but usually did not occur until the late twenties or early thirties.[5]

How, then, has childhood changed over the past two hundred years? The transformations that have taken place might be grouped into three broad categories. The first involves shifts in the timing, sequence, and stages of growing up. Over the past two centuries, the stages of childhood have grown much more precise, uniform, and prescriptive. Before the Civil War, children and teens moved sporadically in and out of the parental home, schools, and jobs, in an irregular, episodic pattern that the historian Joseph F. Kett termed "semi-dependence." . . .

Beginning in the mid-nineteenth century, however, there were growing efforts to regularize and systematize childhood experiences. Unable to transmit their status position directly to their children, through bequests of family lands, transmission of craft skills, or selection of a marriage partner, middle-class parents adopted new strategies to assist their children, emphasizing birth control, maternal nurture, and prolonged schooling. Less formal methods of childrearing and education were replaced by intensive forms of childrearing and prescribed curricula in schools. Unstructured contacts with adults were supplanted by carefully age-graded institutions. Activities organized by young people themselves were succeeded by adult sponsored, adult-organized organization. Lying behind these developments was a belief that childhood should be devoted to education, play, and character-building activities; that children needed time to mature inside a loving home and segregated from adult affairs; and that precocious behavior needed to be suppressed.[6]

Demography is a second force for change. A sharp reduction in the birth rate substantially reduced the proportion of children in the general population, from half the population in the mid-nineteenth century to a third by 1900. A declining birth rate divided families into more distinct generations and allowed parents to lavish more time, attention, and resources on each child; it also made society less dependent on children's labor and allowed adult society to impose new institutional structures on young peoples' lives reflecting shifting notions about children's proper chronological development.

The third category is attitudinal. Adult conceptions of childhood have shifted profoundly over time, from the seventeenth-century Puritan image of the child as a depraved being who needed to be restrained; to the Enlightened notion of children as blank slates who could be shaped by environmental influences; to the Romantic conception of children as creatures with innocent souls and redeemable, docile wills; to the Darwinian emphasis on highly differentiated stages of children's cognitive, physiological, and emotional development; to the Freudian conception of children as seething cauldrons of instinctual drives; and to the contemporary notions that emphasize children's competence and capacity for early learning.

The history of childhood might be conceptualized in terms of three overlapping phases. The first, pre-modern childhood, which roughly coincides with the colonial era, was a period in which the young were viewed as adults in training. Religious and secular authorities regarded childhood as a time of deficiency and incompleteness, and adults rarely referred to their childhood with nostalgia or fondness. Infants were viewed as unformed and even animalistic due to their inability to speak or stand upright. A parent's duty was to hurry a child toward adult status, especially through early engagement in work responsibilities, both inside the parental home and outside it, as servants and apprentices.

The middle of the eighteenth century saw the emergence of a new set of attitudes, which came to define modern childhood. A growing number of parents began to regard children as innocent, malleable, and fragile creatures who needed to be sheltered from contamination. Childhood was increasingly viewed as a separate stage of life that required special care and institutions to protect it. During the nineteenth century, the growing acceptance of this new ideal among the middle class was evident in prolonged residence of young people within the parental home; longer periods of formal schooling; and an increasing consciousness about the stages of young peoples' development, culminating in the "discovery" (or, more accurately, the invention) of adolescence around the turn of the twentieth century.

Universalizing the modern ideal of a sheltered childhood was a highly uneven process and one that has never encompassed all American children. Indeed, it was not until the 1950s that the norms of modern childhood defined the modal experience of young people in the United States. But developments were already under way that would bring modern childhood to an end and replace it with something quite different, a new phase that might be called postmodern childhood. This term refers to the breakdown of dominant norms about the family, gender roles, age, and even reproduction, as they were subjected to radical change and revision. Age norms that many considered "natural" were thrown into question. Even the bedrock biological process of sexual maturation accelerated. Today's children are much more likely than the Baby Boomers to experience their parents' divorce; to have a working mother; to spend significant amounts of time unsupervised by adults; to grow up without siblings; and to hold a job during high school. Adolescent girls are much more likely to have sexual relations during their mid-teens.[7]

Superficially, postmodern childhood resembles premodern childhood. As in the seventeenth century, children are no longer regarded as the binary opposites of adults, nor are they considered naïve and innocent creatures. Today, adults quite rightly assume that even preadolescents are knowledgeable about the realities of the adult world. But unlike premodern children, postmodern children are independent consumers and participants in a separate, semi-autonomous youth culture. We still assume that the young are fundamentally different from adults; that they should spend their first eighteen years in the parents' home; and devote their time to education in age-graded schools. But it is also clear that basic aspects of the ideal of a protected childhood, in which the young are kept isolated from adult realities, have broken down.[8]

DIVERSITY

Diversity has always been the hallmark of American childhood. In seventeenth-century America, demographic, economic, religious, and social factors made geographical sub-cultures the most important markers of diversity in children's experience. In the early period of settlement, colonial childhood took profoundly different forms in New England, the Middle Colonies, and the Chesapeake and southernmost colonies. In seventeenth century New England, hierarchical, patriarchal Calvinist families shaped children's experiences. In the Chesapeake colonies of Maryland and Virginia, in contrast, families were highly unstable and indentured servitude shaped children's experience. Only in the Middle Colonies, from New York to Delaware, did a childhood emphasizing maternal nurture and an acceptance of early autonomy emerge, yet even here, large numbers of children experienced various forms of dependence, as household and indentured servants, apprentices, or slaves.[9]

In the nineteenth century, a highly uneven process of capitalist expansion made social class, gender, and race more salient contributors to childhood diversity. The children of the urban middle class, prosperous commercial farmers, and southern planters enjoyed increasingly longer childhoods, free from major household or work responsibilities until their late teens or twenties, whereas the offspring of urban workers, frontier farmers, and blacks, both slave and free, had briefer childhoods and became involved in work inside or outside the home before they reached their teens. Many urban working-class children contributed to the family economy through scavenging in the streets, vacant lots, or back alleys, collecting coal, wood, and other items that could be used at home or sold. Others took part in the street trades, selling gum, peanuts, and crackers. In industrial towns, young people under the age of 15 contributed on average about 20 percent of their family's income. In mining areas, boys as young as 10 or 12 worked as breakers, separating coal from pieces of slate and wood, before becoming miners in their mid- or late teens. On farms, children as young as 5 or 6 might pull weeds or chase birds and cattle away from crops. By the time they reached the age of 8, many tended livestock, and as they grew older they milked cows, churned butter, fed chickens, collected eggs, hauled water, scrubbed laundry, and harvested crops. A blurring of gender roles among children and youth was especially common on frontier farms. Schooling varied as widely as did work routines. In the rural North, the Midwest, and the Far West, most mid- and late-nineteenth-century students attended one-room schools for 3 to 6 months a year. In contrast, city children attended age-graded classes taught by professional teachers 9 months a year. In both rural and urban areas, girls tended to receive more schooling than boys.[10]

Late in the nineteenth century, self-described child-savers launched a concerted campaign to overcome diversity and universalize a middle-class childhood. This was a slow and bitterly resisted process. Not until the 1930s was child labor finally outlawed and not until the 1950s did high school attendance become a universal experience. Yet for all the success in advancing this middle-class ideal, even today, social class remains a primary determinant of children's well-being.[11]

In recent years, social conservatives have tended to fixate on family structure as a source of diversity in children's well-being, while political liberals have tended to focus on ethnicity, race, and gender. In fact, it is poverty that is the most powerful predictor of children's welfare. Economic stress contributes to family instability, inadequate health care, high degrees of mobility, poor parenting, and elevated levels of stress and depression. As in the nineteenth century, social class significantly differentiates contemporary American childhoods. There is a vast difference between the highly pressured, hyper-organized, fast-track childhoods of affluent children and the highly stressed childhoods of the one-third of children who live in poverty at some point before the age of eighteen. In many affluent families, the boundaries between work and family life have diminished, and parents manage by tightly organizing their children's lives. Yet, contradictorily, most affluent children have their own television and computer and therefore unmediated access to information and are unsupervised by their parents for large portions of the day. In many affluent families there are drastic swings between parental distance from children and parental indulgence, when fathers and mothers try to compensate for parenting too little. Yet at the same time, one-sixth of all children live in poverty at any one time, including 36 percent of black children and 34 percent of Hispanic children. This generally entails limited adult supervision, inferior schooling, and a lack of easy access to productive diversions and activities.

THE POLITICS OF CHILDHOOD

In recent years, two contrasting visions of childhood have collided. One is a vision of a protected childhood, in which children are to be sheltered from adult realities, especially from sex, obscenity, and death. The opposing vision is of a prepared childhood, of children who are exposed from a relatively early age to the realities of contemporary society, such as sexuality and diverse family patterns. Proponents of a prepared childhood argue that in a violent, highly commercialized, and hypersexualized society, a naïve child is a vulnerable child.

   Clashes between conflicting conceptions of childhood are not new. For four hundred years, childhood has been a highly contested category. The late twentieth-century culture war—pitting advocates of a "protected" childhood, who sought to shield children from adult realities, against proponents of a "prepared" childhood—was only the most recent in a long series of conflicts over the definition of a proper childhood. In the seventeenth century, there were bitter struggles between Puritans who regarded even newborn infants as sinful, humanistic educators who emphasized children's malleability, and Anglican traditionalists who considered children as symbols of values (including the value of deference and respect for social hierarchy) that were breaking down as England underwent the wrenching economic transformations that accompanied the rise of modern capitalist enterprise. In the late eighteenth century, battles raged over infant depravity and patriarchal authority, conflicts that gave added resonance to the American revolutionaries' struggle against royal authority. At the turn of the twentieth century, conflict erupted between the proponents of a useful childhood, which expected children to reciprocate for their parents' sacrifices, and advocates of a sheltered childhood, free from labor and devoted to play and education.[12]

PARENTING

Anxiety is the hallmark of modern parenthood. Today's parents agonize incessantly about their children's physical health, personality development, psychological well-being, and academic performance. From birth, parenthood is colored by apprehension. Contemporary parents worry about sudden infant death syndrome, stranger abductions, and physical and sexual abuse, as well as more mundane problems, such as sleep disorders and hyperactivity.

Parental anxiety about children's well-being is not a new development, but parents' concerns have taken dramatically different forms over time. Until the mid-nineteenth century, parents were primarily concerned about their children's health, religious piety, and moral development. In the late nineteenth century, parents became increasingly attentive to their children's emotional and psychological well-being, and during the twentieth century, parental anxieties dwelt on children's personality development, gender identity, and their ability to interact with peers. Today, much more than in the past, guilt-ridden, uncertain parents worry that their children not suffer from boredom, low self-esteem, or excessive school pressures.[13]

Today, we consider early childhood life's formative stage and believe that children's experiences during the first two or three years of life mold their personality, lay the foundation for future cognitive and psychological development, and leave a lasting imprint on their emotional life. We also assume that children's development proceeds through a series of physiological, psychological, social, and cognitive stages; that even very young children have a capacity to learn; that play serves valuable developmental functions; and that growing up requires children to separate emotionally and psychologically from their parents. These assumptions differ markedly from those held three centuries ago. Before the mid-eighteenth century, most adults betrayed surprisingly little interest in the very first years of life and autobiographies revealed little nostalgia for childhood. Also, adults tended to dismiss children's play as trivial and insignificant.

Parenting has evolved through a series of successive and overlapping phases, from a seventeenth-century view of children as "adults-in-training" to the early nineteenth-century emphasis on character formation; the late-nineteenth century notion of scientific childrearing, stressing regularity and systematization; the mid-twentieth century emphasis on fulfilling children's emotional and psychological needs; and the late twentieth century stress on maximizing children's intellectual and social development. Seventeenth-century colonists recognized that children differed from adults in their mental, moral, and physical capabilities and drew a distinction between childhood, an intermediate stage they called youth, and adulthood. But they did not rigidly segregate children by age. Parents wanted children to speak, read, reason, and contribute to their family's economic well-being as soon as possible. Infancy was regarded as a state of deficiency. Unable to speak or stand, infants lacked two essential attributes of full humanity. Parents discouraged infants from crawling and placed them in "walking stools," similar to today's walkers. To ensure proper adult posture, young girls wore leather corsets and parents placed rods along the spines of very young children of both sexes.

During the eighteenth century, a shift in parental attitudes took place. Fewer parents expected children to bow or doff their hats in their presence or stand during meals.

Instead of addressing parents as "sir" and "madam," children called them "papa" and "mama." By the end of the eighteenth century, furniture specifically designed for children, painted in pastel colors and decorated with pictures of animals or figures from nursery rhymes, began to be widely produced, reflecting the popular notion of childhood as a time of innocence and playfulness. There was a growing stress on implanting virtue and a capacity for self-government.

By the early nineteenth century, mothers in the rapidly expanding Northeastern middle class increasingly embraced an amalgam of earlier childrearing ideas. From John Locke, they absorbed the notion that children were highly malleable creatures and that a republican form of government required parents to instill a capacity for self-government in their children. From Jean-Jacques Rousseau and the Romantic poets, middle-class parents acquired the idea of childhood as a special stage of life, intimately connected with nature and purer and morally superior to adulthood. From the evangelicals, the middle class adopted the idea that the primary task of parenthood was to implant proper moral character in children and to insulate children from the corruptions of the adult world.

Toward the end of the nineteenth century, middle-class parents began to embrace the idea that childrearing needed to become more scientific. The Child Study movement, through which teachers and mothers under the direction of psychologists identified a series of stages of childhood development, culminating with the "discovery" of adolescence as a psychologically turbulent period that followed puberty. The belief that scientific principles had not been properly applied to childrearing produced new kinds of childrearing manuals, of which the most influential was Dr. Luther Emmett Holt's *The Care and Feeding of Children*, first published in 1894. Holt emphasized rigid scheduling of feeding, bathing, sleeping, and bowel movements and advised mothers to guard vigilantly against germs and undue stimulation of infants. At a time when a well-adjusted adult was viewed as a creature of habit and self-control, he stressed the importance of imposing regular habits on infants. He discouraged mothers from kissing their babies and told them to ignore their crying and to break such habits as thumb-sucking.[14]

During the 1920s and 1930s, the field of child psychology exerted a growing influence on middle-class parenting. It provided a new language to describe children's emotional problems, such as sibling rivalry, phobias, maladjustment, and inferiority and Oedipus complexes; it also offered new insights into forms of parenting (based on such variables as demandingness or permissiveness), the stages and milestones of children's development, and the characteristics of children at particular ages (such as the "terrible twos," which was identified by Arnold Gesell, Frances L. Ilg, and Louise Bates Ames). The growing prosperity of the 1920s made the earlier emphasis on regularity and rigid self-control seem outmoded. A well-adjusted adult was now regarded as a more easygoing figure, capable of enjoying leisure. Rejecting the mechanistic and behaviorist notion that children's behavior could be molded by scientific control, popular dispensers of advice favored a more relaxed approach to childrearing, emphasizing the importance of meeting babies' emotional needs. The title of a 1936 book by pediatrician C. Anderson Aldrich—*Babies Are Human Beings*—summed up the new attitude.[15]

The Great Depression of the 1930s and World War II greatly intensified parental anxieties about childrearing. During the postwar era, there was an intense fear that faulty mothering caused lasting psychological problems in children. Leading psychologists such as Theodore Lidz, Irving Bieber, and Erik Erikson linked schizophrenia, homosexuality, and identity diffusion to mothers who displaced their frustrations and needs for independence onto their children. A major concern was that many boys, raised almost exclusively by women, failed to develop an appropriate sex role identity. In retrospect, it seems clear that an underlying source of anxiety lay in the fact that mothers were raising their children with an exclusivity and in an isolation unparalleled in American history.[16]

Since the early 1970s, parental anxieties have greatly increased both in scope and intensity. Many parents sought to protect children from every imaginable harm by babyproofing their homes, using car seats, and requiring bicycle helmets. Meanwhile, as more mothers joined the labor force, parents arranged more structured, supervised activities for their children. A variety of factors contributed to a surge in anxiety. As parents had fewer children, they invested more emotion in each child. An increase in professional expertise about children, coupled with a proliferation of research and advocacy organizations, media outlets, and government agencies responsible for children's health and safety made parents increasingly aware of threats to children's well-being and of ways to maximize their children's physical, social, and intellectual development. Unlike postwar parents, who wanted to produce normal children who fit in, middle-class parents now wanted to give their child a competitive edge. For many middle-class parents, fears of downward mobility and anxiety that they would not be able to pass on their status and class to their children, made them worry that their offspring would underperform academically, athletically, or socially. . . .

MORAL PANICS OVER CHILDREN'S WELL-BEING

Americans are great believers in progress in all areas but one. For more than three centuries, Americans have feared that the younger generation is going to hell in a handbasket. Today, many adults mistakenly believe that compared to their predecessors, kids today are less respectful and knowledgeable, and more alienated, sexually promiscuous, and violent. They fear that contemporary children are growing up too fast and losing their sense of innocent wonder at too young an age. Prematurely exposed to the pressures, stresses, and responsibilities of adult life, they fear that the young mimic adult sophistication, dress inappropriately, and experiment with alcohol, drugs, sex, and tobacco before they are emotionally and psychologically ready.

A belief in the decline of the younger generation is one of this country's oldest convictions. In 1657, a Puritan minister, Ezekiel Rogers, admitted: "I find the greatest trouble and grief about the rising generation. . . . Much ado I have with my own family . . . the young breed doth much afflict me." For more than three centuries, American adults have worried that children are growing ever more disobedient and disrespectful. But wistfulness about a golden age of childhood is invariably misleading. Nostalgia almost always represents a yearning not for the past as it really was but rather for fantasies about the past. In 1820, children constituted about half of the workers in early factories. As recently as the 1940s, one child in ten lived apart from both parents and fewer than half of all high school students graduated. We forget that over the past century, the introduction of every new form of entertainment has generated intense controversy over its impact on children, and that the anxiety over video games and the Internet are only the latest in a long line of supposed threats to children that includes movies, radio, and even comic books. The danger of nostalgia is that it creates unrealistic expectations, guilt, and anger.[17]

Ever since the Pilgrims departed for Plymouth in 1620, fearful that "their posterity would be in danger to degenerate and be corrupted" in the Old World, Americans have experienced repeated panics over the younger generation. Sometimes these panics were indeed about children, such as the worries over polio in the early 1950s. More often, however, children stand in for some other issue, and the panics are more metaphorical than representational, such as the panic over teenage pregnancy, youth violence, and declining academic achievement in the late 1970s and 1980s, which reflected pervasive fears about family breakdown, crime, drugs, and America's declining competitiveness in the world.[18]

ABUSE OF CHILDREN

Concern about the abuse of children has waxed and waned over the course of American history. The seventeenth-century Puritans were the first people in the Western world to make the physical abuse of a children a criminal offense, though their concern with family privacy and patriarchal authority meant that these statutes were rarely enforced. During the pre-Civil War decades, temperance reformers argued that curbs on alcohol would reduce wife beating and child abuse. The first organizations to combat child abuse, which appeared in the 1870s, were especially concerned about abuse in immigrant, destitute, and foster families.[19]

Over half a century ago, Alfred Kinsey's studies found rates of sexual abuse similar to those reported today. His interviews indicated that exhibitionists had exposed themselves in front of 12 percent of preadolescent girls and that 9 percent of the girls had had their genitals fondled. But it was his findings about premarital and extramarital sex that grabbed the public's attention, not the sexual abuse of its children. Not until the publication of an influential article on "The Battered Child Syndrome" in 1962 was child abuse finally identified as a social problem demanding a significant governmental response. Even in succeeding years, however, public consciousness about abuse has fluctuated widely. In 1986, nearly a third of adults identified abuse as one of the most serious problems facing children and youth; in a survey a decade later abuse went unmentioned.[20]

We quite rightly focus on the way that young people are physically at risk, whether through physical or sexual abuse, neglect, or economic vulnerability. But across American history, some of the gravest threats to the young have involved their psychological vulnerability. Even worse than the physical sufferings under slavery were the psychological scars enslavement left. Worse than toiling in factories was the hidden curriculum that working class children were inferior to their supposed social betters, suited for little more than routine, repetitious labor. As the historian Daniel Kline has persuasively argued, contemporary American society subjects the young to three forms of psychological violence that we tend to ignore. First, there is the violence of expectations in which children are pushed beyond their social, physical, and academic capabilities, largely as an expression of their parents' needs. Then there is the violence of labeling that diagnoses normal childish behavior (for example, normal childhood exuberance or interest in sex) as pathological. Further, there is the violence of representation, the exploitation of children and adolescents by advertisers, marketers, purveyors of popular culture, and politicians, who exploit parental anxieties as well as young peoples' desire to be stylish, independent, and defiant, and eroticize teenage and preadolescent girls.

There is a fourth form of psychological abuse that is perhaps the most unsettling of all: the objectification of childhood. This involves viewing children as objects to be shaped and molded for their own good. Compared to its predecessors, contemporary American society is much more controlling in an institutional and ideological sense. We expect children to conform to standards that few adults could meet. Meanwhile, as the baby boom generation ages, we inhabit an increasingly adult-oriented society, a society that has fewer "free" spaces for the young, a society that values youth primarily as service workers and consumers and gawks at them as sex objects.

For more than three centuries, America has considered itself to be a particularly child-centered society despite massive evidence to the contrary. Today, no other advanced country allows as many young people to grow up in poverty or without health care, nor does any other western society make so poor a provision for child care or for paid parental leave. Still, Americans think of themselves as a child-centered nation. This paradox is not new. Beginning in the early nineteenth century, the United States developed a host of institutions for the young, ranging from the common school to the Sunday school, the orphanage, the house of refuge, and the reformatory, and eventually expanding to include the children's hospital, the juvenile court, and a wide variety of youth organizations. It was assumed that these institutions served children's interests, that they were caring, developmental, and educational. In practice, however, these institutions frequently proved to be primarily custodial and disciplinary. Indeed, many of the reforms that were supposed to help children were adopted partly because they served the adults' needs, interests, and convenience. The abolition of child labor removed competition from an overcrowded labor market. Age-grading not only made it much easier to control children within schools, it also divided the young into convenient market segments. One of the most serious challenges American society faces is to act on behalf of children's welfare rather than adults'.

The most important lesson that grows out of an understanding of the history of childhood is the simplest. While many fear that American society has changed too much, the sad fact is that it has changed too little. Americans have failed to adapt social institutions to the fact that the young mature more rapidly than they did in the past; that most mothers of preschoolers now participate in the paid workforce; and that a near majority of children will spend substantial parts of their childhood in a single-parent, cohabitating-parent, or stepparent household. How can we provide better care for the young, especially the one-sixth who are growing up in poverty? How can we better connect the worlds of adults and the young? How can we give the young more ways to demonstrate their growing competence and maturity? How can we tame a violence-laced, sex-saturated popular culture without undercutting a commitment to freedom and a respect for the free-floating world of fantasy? These are the questions we must confront as we navigate a new century of childhood.

Notes

1. Ron Powers, *Dangerous Water: A Biography of the Boy Who Became Mark Twain* (New York: Da Capo Press, 1999); Powers, *Tom and Huck Don't Live Here Anymore: Childhood and Murder in the Heart of America* (New York: St. Martin's Press, 2001), 2, 32–34, 40, 131; Shelley Fisher Fishkin, *Lighting Out for the Territories: Reflections on Mark Twain and American Culture* (New York: Oxford University Press, 1997).
2. Powers, *Dangerous Water*, 26, 84, 167; Powers, *Tom and Huck Don't Live Here Anymore*, 78.
3. Richard Weissbourd, *The Vulnerable Child: What Really Hurts America's Children and What We Can Do About It* (Reading, MA: Addison-Wesley, 1996), 48.
4. Colin Heywood, *A History of Childhood: Children and Childhood in the West from Medieval to Modern Times* (Cambridge, UK: Polity, 2001); Joseph Illick, *American Childhood* (Philadelphia: University of Pennsylvania Press, 2002); James A. Schultz, *The Knowledge of Childhood in the German Middle Ages*, 1100–1350 (Philadelphia: University of Pennsylvania Press, 1995), 11.
5. Howard P. Chudacoff, *How Old Are You? Age Consciousness in American Society* (Princeton: Princeton University Press, 1989); Joseph F. Kett, *Rites of Passage: Adolescence in America* (New York: Basic, 1977).
6. Kett, *Rites of Passage, passim*.
7. On changes in the onset of sexual maturation, see Marcia E. Herman-Giddens and others, "Secondary Sexual Characteristics and Menses in Young Girls Seen in Office Practice: A Study from the Pediatric Research in Office Settings Network," *Pediatrics*, Vol. 99, No. 4 (April 1997), 505–512. In 1890, the average age of menarche in the United States was estimated to be 14.8 years; by the 1990s, the average age had fallen to 12.5 (12.1 for African American girls and 12.8 for girls of northern European ancestry). According to the study, which tracked 17,000 girls to find out when they hit different markers of puberty, 15 percent of white girls and 48 percent of African American girls showed signs of breast development or pubic hair by age 8. For conflicting views on whether the age of menarche has fallen, see Lisa Belkin, "The Making of an 8-Year-Old Woman," *New York Times*, December 24, 2000; Gina Kolata, "Doubters Fault Theory Finding Earlier Puberty," *New York Times*, February 20, 2001; and "2 Endocrinology Groups Raise Doubt on Earlier Onset of Girls' Puberty," *New York Times*, March 3, 2001.
8. Stephen Robertson, "The Disappearance of Childhood," http://teaching.arts.usyd.edu.au /history/2044/.
9. Gerald F. Moran, "Colonial America, Adolescence in," *Encyclopedia of Adolescence*, edited by Richard Lerner, Anne C. Petersen, Jeanne Brooks-Gunn (New York: Garland Pub., 1991), I, 159–167.
10. Priscilla Clement, *Growing Pains: Children in the Industrial Age* (New York: Twayne, 1997); David Nasaw, *Children in the City: At Work and at Play* (Garden City, NY: Anchor Press/Doubleday, 1985); Christine Stansell, *City of Women: Sex and Class in New York*, 1789–1860 (New York: Knopf, 1986).
11. David I. Macleod, *The Age of the Child: Children in America*, 1890–1912 (New York: Twayne, 1998).
12. Viviana Zelizer, *Pricing the Priceless Child: The Changing Social Value of Children* (Princeton: Prince-ton University Press).
13. Peter N. Stearns, *Anxious Parents: A History of Modern Childrearing in America* (New York: New York University Press, 2002).
14. Ann Hulbert, *Raising America: Experts, Parents, and a Century of Advice about Children* (New York: Knopf, 2003); Julia Grant, *Raising Baby by the Book: The Education of American Mothers* (New Haven: Yale University Press, 1998).

15. Kathleen W. Jones, *Taming the Troublesome Child* (Cambridge, MA: Harvard University Press, 1999).
16. Steven Mintz and Susan Kellogg, *Domestic Revolutions: A Social History of American Family Life* (New York: Free Press, 1988), 189.
17. Rogers quoted in James Axtell, *School Upon a Hill: Education and Society in Colonial New England* (New Haven: Yale University Press, 1974), 28. Hard as it is to believe, in 1951 a leading television critic decried the quality of children's television. Jack Gould, radio and TV critic for *The New York Times* from the late 1940s to 1972, complained that there was "nothing on science, seldom anything on the country's cultural heritage, no introduction to fine books, scant emphasis on the people of other lands, and little concern over hobbies and other things for children to do themselves besides watch television." *Chicago Sun Times*, Aug. 9, 1998, 35; Phil Scraton, ed., *Childhood in "Crisis"* (London; Bristol, Penn.: UCL Press, 1997), 161, 164.
18. William Bradford, *Of Plymouth Plantation*, edited by Samuel Elliot Morrison (New York: Modern Library, 1952), 25; Moran, "Colonial America, Adolescence in," 159.
19. Linda Gordon, *Heroes of Their Own Lives: The Politics and History of Family Violence* (New York: Viking, 1988); Elizabeth Pleck, *Domestic Tyranny: the Making of Social Policy against Family Violence from Colonial Times to the Present* (New York: Oxford University Press, 1987).
20. William Feldman et al., "Is Childhood Sexual Abuse Really Increasing in Prevalence? An Analysis of the Evidence," *Pediatrics*, July 1991, Vol. 88, Issue 1, 29–34; Males, *Framing Youth*, 257. In 1998, government agencies substantiated over a million cases of child maltreatment, including approximately 101,000 cases of sexual abuse. About 51 percent of lifetime rapes occur prior to age 18 and 29 percent of lifetime rapes occur prior to age 12. Coordinating Council on Juvenile Justice and Delinquency Prevention, *Combating Violence and Delinquency: The National Juvenile Justice Action Plan: Report* (Washington DC: Coordinating Council on Juvenile Justice and Delinquency Prevention, 1996), 75; National Criminal Justice Reference Service, www.ncjrs.org/html/ojjdp /action_plan_2001_10/page1.html. The 1994 Sex in America study of the sex lives of 3,400 men and women reported that 17 percent of the women and 12 percent of the men reported childhood sexual abuse. See Males, *Scapegoat Generation*, 74.

■ READING 18

Diverging Development: The Not-So-Invisible Hand of Social Class in the United States

Frank Furstenberg

INTRODUCTION

America has never been a class conscientious society by the standards of the rest of the world. The notion that social class determines a person's life chances has always been an anathema in this country, flying in the face of our democratic ideology. Centuries ago, some of the earliest observers of American society, most notably Alexis de Tocqueville (1945) remarked upon the disdain for class distinctions in our early history compared to

France or the rest of Europe. To be sure, social class was far more prominent and salient in the U.S. at the time of Tocqueville's visit to this country in the 1830s than today; however, the seemingly boundless possibilities of land ownership and the ideology of upward mobility softened the contours of class distinctions in this country from its very inception. The idea that any hardworking American by dint of good character and hard work could rise up the social ladder has long been celebrated in the great American myth of Horatio Alger who rose from "rags to riches" providing a fictional example instructing young men—and it was men—of what they needed to do to make their fortunes in 19th Century America.

Curiously, the United States, long regarded as the land of opportunity, has never entirely lived up to its billing. Comparative studies on social mobility between the U.S. and our Western counterparts have failed to demonstrate that social mobility is especially higher here than in other industrialized nations (Bendix and Lipset 1966, Goldthorpe and Erickson 1993). Yet, Americans seem as oblivious to class gradations today as they have ever been. Most of us declare that we are middle-class and finer distinctions such as working-class and upper-middle class have all but vanished in the popular vernacular and even in social science research. While the salience of social class has declined in American society during the past several decades, we have witnessed a huge rise in economic inequality (Danziger and Gottschalk 1995; Levy 1999; Wolff 2002, 2004).

When I was entering academic sociology more than four decades ago, the social world was described very differently than it is today. Even while recognizing the muted notions of social class held by most Americans, social scientists were keenly attentive to, if not obsessed with, distinctions in values, life-style, and social practices inculcated in the family that were linked to social mobility (Hollingshead 1949, Lynd and Lynd 1929, Warner 1949). Indeed, the idea that parents in different social strata deliberately or unintentionally shaped their children's ambitions, goals, and habits, affecting the chances of moving up the social ladder was widely accepted, supported by a large body of literature in psychology, sociology, and economics showing how families situated at different rungs on the social ladder held distinctive world views and adhered to different ideas of development (Bernstein and Henderson 1969; Gans 1962; Komarovsky 1987; Miller and Swanson 1958). Most of all, social scientists believed that life chances were highly constrained by values and skills acquired in the family and structures of opportunity in the child's immediate environment that shaped his (and it usually was his) chances of economic success. Fine gradations of social class could be linked to virtually everything from toilet training to marriage practices (Blood and Wolfe 1960; Mead and Wolfenstein 1955).

Social class, not so long ago the most powerful analytic category in the researcher's conceptual toolbox has now been largely eclipsed by an emphasis on gender, race, and ethnicity. Socio-economic status has been reduced to a variable, mostly one that is often statistically controlled, to permit researchers to focus on the effect of determinants other than social class. We have stopped measuring altogether the finer grade distinctions of growing up with differential resources. True, we continue to look at poverty and economic disadvantage with no less interest than we ever have, and we certainly understand that affluence and education make a huge difference. Yet, most developmentalists view economic status as a continuum that defies qualitatively finer breakdowns. Consequently, working-class, lower-middle class families or even families in the middle of the income distribution are concealed rather than revealed in combinations of income, education, and occupation. (For exceptions, see Kefalas 2003 and Lareau 2003). In short, the idea of social class has largely been collapsed into rich and poor marked by education and earnings—above and below the poverty line. Think of the way we currently treat "single-parent families" as an example. They have become almost a proxy for poverty rather than a differentiated category of families that experiences life as differently as their two-parent counterparts.

The contention that contemporary developmental research downplays the influence of social class in no way is meant to imply that professional attention to gender or race/ethnicity is unwarranted or should be diminished. Without a firm grasp of social class differences in contemporary America, however, much of the current research on gender and ethnicity ignores class differences within the analytic categories of gender or ethnicity, blunting an understanding of how they shape social reality and social opportunities among men and women and across different racial and ethnic categories. Just as we have come to recognize the hazards of lumping together all Hispanics or Asians, I would suggest that we need a more nuanced understanding of what differences it makes to possess certain levels of education, occupation, income, and indeed a world view and life patterns attached to these constituent elements of socio-economic stratification.

Beyond a call to action, I want to outline a research agenda for examining social class in greater detail. Beginning with a brief discussion of developmental theories, I allude to some of the methodological obstacles to studying social class that must be attended to, and then turn to developmental processes that expose research questions I believe warrant greater attention by our society of scholars. My work nicely parallels observations recently put forth by Sara McLanahan (2004) in her Presidential Address to the Population Association of America on inequality and children's development though my attention is devoted more to the operation of stratification than to its implications for public policy. My central aim is to expose a series of developmental processes that work in tandem to fashion a stratification system operating from birth to maturity in this country that is pervasive, persistent, and far more powerful than we generally like to admit.

SOCIAL CLASS: A PROBLEMATIC CONSTRUCT

One reason why attention to social class has faded may be traced to the academic controversies surrounding the very idea that social classes exist in this country. If what is meant by social class is a closed set of life chances which people recognize and even affiliate with, then surely most would agree that America is a classless society. However, social class has been used in a different way to mark the structure of economic and social opportunities affecting individuals' behaviors and beliefs, networks and associations, and, ultimately, knowledge about and access to social institutions such as the family, education, and the labor market.

Viewed in this way, social classes are not tightly bounded categories; they are fuzzy sets created by experience and exposure to learning opportunities and selective social contacts that derive from resources that can be marshaled by individuals and their kinship networks. In this respect, the fuzzy nature of social class appears to differ from gender or ethnicity though both of these constructs have been appropriately critiqued when viewed as "naturally unambiguous" rather than "socially constructed" statuses. Still, there are no certain markers that identify individuals as belonging to one class or another; social class is probabilistically constructed and measured by particular constellations of socio-economic statuses. Thus, we might say that someone who has low education, works at a menial job which pays poorly is lower-class, a term that admittedly has become virtually taboo in the U.S. Nonetheless, we easily recognize that those possessing these attributes are socially isolated, often excluded from mainstream institutions, and limited in their access to mobility. Whether we refer to them as lower-class, poor, disadvantaged, or socially excluded, it really doesn't change their opportunities or their ability to confer opportunities to their children.

I will dodge the question in this paper of whether it makes sense to identify a particular number of social strata such as was common in social science a generation ago, designating four, five, or seven classes that possessed different family practices, values and beliefs, or lifestyles and cultural habits (Hollingshead 1949; Warner 1949). Instead, I merely want to observe how neglect of social class has created a void in attention by developmentalists in how stratification structures the first decades of the life course. Toward the end of this paper, I will reflect on what I and my colleagues on the MacArthur Network on Adult Transitions are learning about how social class shapes the transition to adulthood in myriad ways that have profound implications for the future of American society.

A DEVELOPMENTAL THEORY OF SOCIAL CLASS

Human development involves an ongoing interaction between individual level biological potentials and social processes shaped by children's multiple and changing social environments. Sometimes developmentalists make distinctions between maturation, regulated in part by biology, and socially arranged learning, the process that we generally refer to as socialization. One of the important legacies of late 20th Century developmental science was to put an end the useless debate between nature and nurture. Researchers initiated a theoretical re-orientation designed to explore ongoing interactions from birth to maturity in a nest of varying contexts—families, childcare settings, schools, communities, and the like to investigate how social context afforded or denied opportunities for optimal development, understanding that optimal development can vary according to children's innate abilities and their exposure to learning environments.

No one understood this scheme better or promoted it with more vigor than Urie Bronfenbrenner (1979), who, as it happens, was one of the pioneers in psychology in examining class differences in development. Bronfenbrenner's theory of development located the individual in an embedded set of contexts that extended from the intimate and direct to distant and indirect as they socially impinged and shaped the course of human development over the life span. Bronfenbrenner's ideas culled from the legacy of 19th and 20th century psychology closely parallel a tradition of sociological theory stemming from the work of George Herbert Mead (1934) and Charles Cooley (1902) that has come to be known as symbolic interaction. Like Bronfenbrenner, Mead and Cooley conceptualized human development as an ongoing process of engagement and response to social others—social exchange guided by feedback from the surrounding social system. As sociologists applied these ideas in practice, they quickly realized how differently it was possible to grow up in varying contexts and cultures, a lesson that is closely aligned with Bronfenbrenner's theory.

It was and, I believe still is, just a short step from this general theory of human development which features the ongoing interaction of children in local environments to seeing the pervasive influence of social class in shaping the course of development. That step involves a careful appraisal of how learning environments themselves are arranged to promote movement from one to the next. These more distal social arrangements are carefully regulated in all modern societies by gatekeepers who exercise presumably meritocratic standards based on a combination of talent, performance, and sponsorship (Buchmann 1989; Heinz and Marshall 2003). In all developed societies, parents cede direct control of their children's fates at an increasingly early age to others who become instrumental in guiding children through an age-graded system of opportunities. Parents train and coach their children, select and direct choices in this system, advocate when problems arise, and try to arrange for remediation when their children are not following an optimal path. So, as I have argued elsewhere (Furstenberg, et al. 1999), parents' managerial skills have become increasingly important in how well children navigate the institutional arrangements that affect their opportunities in later life.

Of course, parents themselves are embedded in very different opportunity systems; specifically they are more or less privileged in the knowledge, skills, and resources that they can provide to their children. Expressed in currently fashionable terms, they have different levels of human, social, cultural and psychological capital to invest in their children. Of course, parents are not the only agents that matter. By virtue of their social position at birth and during childhood, children have differential access to kin, friends, neighbors, teachers, and peers that can and do promote or diminish their chances of socio-economic attainment. So while differences in exposure to class-related opportunities might be relatively small, nonetheless they cumulate if they consistently favor or disadvantage children's life chances. Life chances are compounded positively or negatively as opportunities or their absence play out over time.

A century ago, Max Weber used a powerful metaphor for how history operates. Weber (1949) argued that it is like a pair of loaded dice that are weighted with each throw by the result of the previous one; constraints increase with repeated tosses of the dice, leading to a more and more skewed outcome. Social class can be conceptualized as just such a mechanism, establishing a set of life chances that become more sharply pronounced as they play out over time. Micro-interactions cumulate in a patterned and successively more consequential pattern, etching a probabilistically pre-ordained trajectory of success.

To be sure, when it comes to human development, an actor, let's say a child growing up in the U.S. today, exercises a certain level of discretion or influence by dint of his or her own abilities, talents, or needs facing contexts that may be tilted toward advantage or disadvantage. The outcome is always affected by how the child comes to interpret and act in these contexts. This might be an operational definition of resiliency or vulnerability as psychologists such as Rutter (2000; 1985), Garmezy (1993; 1991), and

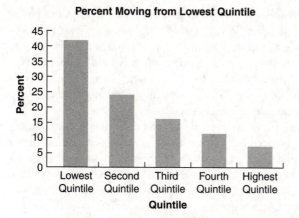

Percent Moving from Lowest Quintile

Werner (1995) have employed, the idea that some children are able to defy the odds. Interestingly, developmentalists in recent years have given at least as much, if not more, attention to research on beating the odds as on developing a careful understanding of how the structure of opportunities operates to create systematic advantage or disadvantage over time—or we might say why and how growing up in a certain social location establishes strong and long odds of departing from an expected pattern of success.

I suspect that most of us know just how strong the odds are for rising or falling substantially from the position at birth. Based on retrospective data that understates the amount of social mobility, current estimates suggest that 42 percent of children born into the bottom fifth of the income distribution will remain there as adults. Only 7 percent will make it into the top fifth of the income distribution. For those born into the top fifth of the income distribution, 40 percent remain there while just 6 percent fall into the lowest quintile (Hertz 2005).

METHODOLOGICAL OBSTACLES TO STUDY

Until very recently, we lacked the data and the methods to observe how social stratification shapes the course of human development. Longitudinal research really only became widely available in the latter decades of the last century though pioneering studies were done on relatively small samples such as Glen Elder's (1974, 1999) now classic work on the Berkeley and Oakland samples. Not until the introduction of the computer could we ever imagine more than cursory treatment of large-scale samples that might provide the kind of variation over time that permit us to examine the array of experiences that children have in the course of development that necessarily calls for merging of different waves of data collection, administrative records, blood samples, and the like that permit us to understand the numerous contingencies that make up children's lives.

Disciplinary rationale sometimes have steered us away from attention to social class as well. Psychologists have been actively discouraged from working on large existing data sets and instructed to collect their own data, thus restricting the range of problems that could be examined. Sociologists, beginning in the 1960s, turned away from studying children, ceding much work on socialization to psychologists. Disciplines have been organized to encourage work on specific life periods and younger researchers have been encouraged to become specialists in infancy, early or middle-childhood, or adolescence. To be sure, exceptions abound and I would be remiss if I did not acknowledge those researchers such as Eleanor Maccoby, John Clausen, Doris Entwisle, or Emmy Werner and others who broke out of the mold or, one might say, beat the odds of doing research in disciplines that discouraged such efforts.

Added to the problems stemming from data availability and disciplinary constraints are the methods, themselves, that are required to examine how trajectories of development unfold over time. Anyone who is familiar with my work will immediately know that I am probably the last person to discuss the new methodological frontiers in developmental science. However, even a methodological simpleton like me has become familiar with a host of novel techniques for analyzing and interpreting longitudinal data such as growth curves that are now available in our packaged software. No doubt, many more will be coming in the future as new and more powerful ways of understanding career contingencies, transitions, and the evolution of trajectories of development are invented and refined. The tools are now available to describe and explain how advantage and disadvantage along many dimensions configure and crystallize the developmental pathways from birth to maturity. In fact, I would contend that data availability and methods have outpaced our theoretical and substantive understanding of how social class influences human development.

THE ORIGIN OF SOCIAL CLASS DIFFERENCES

More sensitive analytic techniques will have to take account of several features that we already know about the influence of social class on development. *First and foremost, early patterns of development may be difficult to surmount once set in place for several different and perhaps overlapping reasons.* At this stage, we know relatively little about the way that brain development during infancy and early childhood takes place, but it is entirely possible that the architecture of early development could well preclude or, at least, compromise subsequent patterns of development. There is growing evidence that cognitive and emotional capacities that form early in life are foundational, providing a template or structure for later advances (Duncan and Brooks-Gunn 2000; Danziger and Waldfogel 2000; Haggerty, et al. 1994).

Exposure to these developmental influences begins before the child is born and is shaped in no small way by parents' prenatal experiences: their exposure to toxins, their diet, the quality of health care received during pregnancy and the neonatal health provided to them. Most children experience a normal delivery and are born in good health, but steep differences exist across social classes in all of these factors. The probability of pre-natal and neo-natal health problems are sharply structured by socio-economic status. Thus, children enter the world endowed unequally even if we discount any genetic variation by social class.

The families into which they are born provide vastly different opportunities to build on that endowment. Whether children are planned or unplanned, whether they must compete for limited family resources or have enough, and whether they will receive steady and sufficient attention from parent figures are but a few of the contingencies known to vary by social class (AG1 on planning, etc.). What is less well understood is how these early influences combine and cumulate creating developmental divides with lasting effects on children's prospects in later lives. Most of the work on the consequences of social attachment, for example, has not been traced for long enough periods to understand whether or how much it affects later transitions in adolescence and early adulthood.

The remarkable research on institutional care of children in Romania under the Communist regime by Charles Nelson and his colleagues provides evidence that something like a critical period exists for emotional development that, if breached, can lead to permanent impairment. Children raised in a collective setting with little or no opportunity to develop attachments with stable emotional figures were emotionally incapacitated. Nelson and his colleagues discovered that if placed in families with emotionally engaging surrogate parents by certain ages, the pattern of emotional disfigurement could be repaired, and perhaps even reversed if the placement occurred early in life. Now, an interesting question, relevant to the discussion here, is whether stimulation and human interaction in early childhood is dichotomous or multitiered, that is whether and how much early interaction sets the parameters for later growth by establishing a critical level or in a more graduated fashion that may still fall below the optimal amount. Few children in American society are impaired by lack of stimulation, but there seems little doubt that many children get less stimulation or fewer opportunities for emotional engagement than is optimal.

A series of experiments in neuropsychology conducted on barriers to reading reveal fascinating and perhaps parallel findings on brain development. It seems that middle-class and working-class children with reading difficulties may exhibit different neural responses when faced with a task of decoding words. The researchers making this discovery hypothesize that the amount of exposure to reading and remediation could account for the differences by social class, suggesting that the causes for reading problems could differ and the remedies might vary for children by social class.

Both these studies bring to mind the impressive qualitative study by Hart and Risley (1995). Home observation of family interactions among children and their families revealed gigantic variations in the range of words, expressions, and interaction styles creating, in effect, a continuous and mounting difference in verbal environments that appeared to be linked to the vocabularies that children acquired in the early years of life (Bernstein 1971; Bernstein and Henderson 1969; Farkas and Beron 2004). These varying cognitive contexts were later linked to reading skills and accordingly school success.

This study leads to a second observation relevant to developmental trajectories of children in different social classes. Small differences, if persistent, become larger and more consequential over time. A process of psychological and social accretion operates both at an internal and external level as children develop self concepts, styles of thought, and habits that shape their motivation and social interactions in ways that harden over time. If, for example, children are exposed to very modest differences in, let us say, language, reading practices, or interaction styles over long periods of time, the cumulative effects could be quite striking and large. Thus, if on average, years of education are linked to small differences in parental skills or practices, they could create significant effects on average in children's acquisition of cognitive and emotional skills. These

psychological and social styles create impressions on others that are reinforced and rei-
fied in informal and formal social settings. To answer this question, we need both stable
measures of social patterns established inside the home that are taken with sufficient frequency to permit us to examine growth curves of emotional and cognitive development
that extend beyond the early years of childhood into middle childhood, adolescence, and
early adulthood.

These styles that emerge in the home and are shaped to a great degree by class
differences in childrearing practices in the family establish what sociologists used to refer as "anticipatory socialization," advanced training for social roles outside the home,
especially entrance into pre-school programs that foreshadow and initiate social tracking
within the school system. Modest or perhaps not so modest differences that occur within
families are unlikely to be offset or compensated for by learning that takes place outside
the home. To the contrary, it is easy to demonstrate that they are greatly amplified by
differences in parents' capacities to locate, gain access to, and monitor settings outside
the home and by institutional practices that selectively recruit children from families that
have the resources and children who appear to exhibit the capabilities to perform well.

Parents, in all social strata, are well aware that beginning at an early age children
require and benefit from experiences outside the home that offer opportunities for learning offsetting or reinforcing patterns established in the family. We have rightly given a
good deal of attention to childcare settings (Chaudry 2004; Magnuson and Waldfogel
2005), but we have a lot less information on the impact of peer interactions or encounters with skill enhancing agencies such as recreational centers, libraries, museums and
the like. However, the likelihood of receiving a steady and stable exposure to these sorts
of social institutions vary tremendously by social class (Medrich et al. 1982). Qualitative studies have demonstrated large differences by social class in children's exposure
both to the amount and quality of these settings. The reasons why are pretty obvious.
Parents with better education are both more knowledgeable and therefore usually more
discriminating in locating high quality settings. Second, they have greater resources to
gain access to those settings such as time, transportation, and money to pay the cost
of admission. Finally, they have the ability to organize and implement on their children's behalf and to monitor ongoing engagements whether they be with the right kind
of peers, better classes, or high quality teachers, coaches or caregivers.

The other side of the coin of what happens to young children as a result of the
social class into which they are born is no less influential in channeling children from
different social classes into more or less favorable settings. *Settings find and recruit children from families of different social classes with varying levels of energy and enthusiasm.* In
many instances, settings regulate their clientele by the cost of services: the least affordable for parents attract mostly or exclusively children from affluent families whether we
are talking about prenatal health programs, childcare facilities, after school programs,
summer camps or Ivy League colleges. The availability of resources establishes to a large
extent the social class distribution of families who participate in social institutions in
American society. Those that can pay the cost of admission typically purchase better
teachers and peers who are more motivated and prepared. We have relatively little research on the social class networks of children that emerge over time, but it is certainly
a plausible hypothesis that most children in the U.S. grow up with little or no exposure

to peers outside their social class. Thus, their opportunities to acquire cultural and social capital are tremendously influenced the social class composition of kinship and peer networks. And, we have every reason to believe that money and education are playing an ever larger role in regulating the level of cross-class exposure and the composition of children's social networks.

THE IMPORTANCE OF PLACE

Most parents are well aware of this fact: this is why the primary mechanism of managing opportunities for children is choice of residence. Interestingly, we have all too little information on social class and residential decision making. Since schooling is generally determined by neighborhood, parents with more knowledge and resources can select neighborhoods that package together access to better schools, better peers, and, often, better recreational facilities. In the study that my colleagues and I did in Philadelphia on how families manage risk and opportunity, we discovered that parents were acutely aware of the opportunities attached to choice of neighborhood though their awareness of its importance often did not necessarily mean that they were able to exercise much discretion in where to live.

Most working-class families in Philadelphia could not afford to live in affluent sections of the city much less move to the suburbs where they knew that they would find better schools and more desirable peers. They often resorted to the second-best option, sending their children to parochial schools where children were monitored more closely, had a longer school day with more after-school activities, and attended school with like-minded peers.

Schools in turn were able to select families that enabled them to produce higher test-scores and hence greater academic success. A good portion of these outcomes were predetermined by the selection of parents and their children though clearly more able, prepared, and motivated students may help schools to recruit higher quality teachers and administrative staff. As I sometimes like to say, economists want to rule out selection as a methodological nuisance while sociologists regard selection as a fundamental social process that must be studied as a central feature of how things happen. In any event, social life is created by multiple and interacting influences that generally come in packages rather than operate as particular or singular influences as they are studied in experimental designs.

This is one of the larger lessons learned from the extensive experimental work on Moving to Opportunity, the government research study, that has followed families who participated in a random assignment experiment of public housing recipients who were given the opportunity to move to lower-poverty neighborhoods. Moving to lower poverty neighborhoods was not an event, as the researchers tended to regard it from the onset, but a succession of adaptations and interpretations that influenced its impact on particular family members differently depending on experiences prior to moving, new and old social networks, and demographic and unmeasured psychological characteristics of the movers and stayers. The net effects—important to policy makers—conceal a huge range of varied responses that unfortunately are only dimly understood.

SOCIAL REDUNDANCY IN MULTIPLE CONTEXTS

Perhaps, what I have written thus far might lead to the impression that opportunities at the family, school, and neighborhood levels are strongly correlated. However, important work by Tom Cook and his colleagues in their study of families in Prince Georges County reveals that, at an individual level, most children experience something of a mixture of social opportunities (Cook et al. 2002). There is only a modest correlation between the quality of parental resources, school resources, and neighborhood resources—surely the opposite conclusion from the idea that children grow up in an environment of class congruent settings.

However, the research by Cook and his colleagues also reveals that at the population level—when family characteristics, school, and neighborhood quality are considered in the aggregate—there is a much more powerful correlation among these arenas of social stratification. On average, children from better endowed families are very likely to attend better schools and live in better neighborhoods. It is as if the playing field for families is tilted in ways that are barely visible to the naked eye. Another way of looking at the stratification of social space is to imagine that families with more resources are able to arrange the world so that their children will have to be only ordinarily motivated and talented to succeed. Those with fewer resources are called upon to make more effort or have greater talent to succeed. Those with limited or meager resources must be highly gifted and super-motivated to achieve at a comparable levels. Developmentalists have often implicitly acknowledged the way the world works by valorizing the families and children that do manage to swim against the current, but we should be measuring the current as well as the swimmer's efforts, especially because there is every reason to believe that the current has become stronger in recent years.

Opportunity structures, made up of multiple and overlapping environments shaped by social position, are not accurately apprehended by individuals from different vantage points in the social system. They can only be understood by examining simultaneously what families see and respond to in their familiar settings, what they do not see but can be seen by other observers, and—most difficult of all—seeing what is *not* there. Take, for example, how much parents or children know about colleges and how they work. Most children in affluent families know more about this topic at age twelve, I would guess, than children in working class families when they are ready to enter college. Cultural capital—knowledge of how the world works—is acquired like vocabulary and speech practices in the family, schools, and from peers in the community (Bourdieu 1973, 1986; Lamont 2000; Lareau 1989, 2003). Class differences result from a process of social redundancy that exposes children to information, ideas, expectations, and navigational tools leading some children to know what they must do to get ahead and others merely to think that they know what to do. Cultural knowledge of the way the world works has surely been studied by developmentalists but we have a long way to go before we have a good map of what is and is not known by parents and children about the stratification system and how this knowledge changes over time as young people's impressions of how things work run up against how they actually work. With relatively few exceptions (Edin and Kefalas 2005; Newman 1993; Burton and

Stack 1993), we lack the kinds of cultural studies that peered inside the family, looking at the culture of families, that were far more common among past generations of social researchers.

THE SOCIAL CLASS DISTRIBUTION OF OBSTACLES

Social class position not only structures variations in opportunities for advancement, it also greatly influences the probability of untoward events and circumstances in the lives of children and their families. The likelihood of bad things happening to people varies enormously by social class though we know this more from inference and anecdote than we do from systematic studies of children's experiences in the course of growing up. Take, for example, the inventory of life events associated with sources of psychological stressors including mortality, serious morbidity, accidents, family dissolution, residential changes, job loss, and so on. Virtually all of these events occur much more frequently in highly disadvantaged than moderately advantaged families and least of all among the most privileged. Problems are more likely to happen to families who lack the educational, cultural, and social capital that I mentioned earlier. Lower-income families are more vulnerable than higher income-families to a host of troubles from credit loss, health problems, transportation breakdown, criminal victimization, divorce, mental health problems, and the list goes on. They also have fewer resources to prevent problems from happening in the first place by anticipating them or nipping them in the bud (preventive and ameliorative interventions). And, when they do occur, social class affects a family's ability to cushion their blow.

Anyone who has studied low-income households, as I have for so many decades, cannot help but notice that there is a steady stream of these events which constantly unsettle family functioning, requiring time, energy, and resources that often are in short supply or altogether unavailable. Life is simply harder and more brutish at the bottom, and, I suspect, it is more precarious in the middle than we ordinarily image. As developmentalists, I don't think that we have done a very good job in evaluating how such events affect the lives and life chances of children. They create wear and tear on families and often ignite a succession of subsequent difficulties. The problems may begin with job loss, which in turn results in marital strife or dissolution, and finally settle into long-term mental illness or substance abuse. Or this chain of events can just as easily be reversed. The point is that in the ordinary course of life, children at different social strata face vastly different probabilities of bad things happening to them and their parents and these events not infrequently spiral out of control.

Having spent part of my career examining the impact of marital disruption on children, I know all too well the difficulties of studying even single negative events if only because they are usually preceded and followed by other adversities. It clearly behooves us to give greater attention to the ways that these events are distributed and clustered in the lives of children and families. Social scientists are accustomed to describing these behaviors as "non-normative" events, but they may only be "non-normative"—at least in the statistical sense—in the lives of affluent families.

CLASS DIFFERENCES IN PROBLEM PREVENTION AND REMEDIATION

The distribution of obstacles, as I have suggested above, is negatively correlated with social class just as the distribution of means to prevent and remediate troubles is negatively related to class. Affluent families have access to a tremendous range of strategies for prevention. They purchase and practice preventive healthcare, they situate themselves in environments free of toxins, and their homes and streets are safer; when and if their children experience problems in school, they can exercise a range of actions from changing schools to procuring help in the form of tutoring, assessments, therapy, medication and so on. If their children happen to get in trouble in the community, they have means to minimize the trouble using informal contacts or legal interventions. We know a lot about the employment of these preventive and remedial strategies, but we have yet to put together a comprehensive picture of how troubles are avoided and deflected for children in different social classes. If we examined a sample of problem behaviors among adolescents, what would be the likelihood of adverse outcomes occurring from a series of incidents?

The criminological literature provides ample evidence that class (and race/ethnicity as well) accounts for a huge amount of the variation in outcomes of delinquency, for example. It is not that adolescents from affluent families do not commit delinquent acts, use drugs and alcohol, and engage in risky sex. Indeed, the evidence suggests that so-called problem behaviors are fairly evenly distributed by social class. However, the consequences of similar actions differ greatly by the capacities that families have to avert the negative sanctions that may follow or to avoid their adverse consequences. Families with greater assets and social connections can minimize the significance of troubles even when they occur, especially the more extreme sanctions such as going to court and being sentenced to incarceration.

Social class then provides a form of cover from negative events when they do occur. It provides a social airbrush for the privileged concealing mistakes and missteps that invariably occur in the course of growing up. The management of problem behavior by families, their access and use of professional delegates (doctors, lawyers, tutors, social service workers) across different social classes represents a neglected topic in adolescent development.

SOCIAL CLASS, SOCIAL CAPITAL AND SPONSORSHIP

We would miss a lot about the use of professional and non-professional agents in children's lives among different social classes were we to confine our attention to their role in problem intervention and remediation. This topic represents a broader exercise of what has come to be called social capital, the social resources that can be brought to bear by families, to promote positive development as well as prevent or correct negative courses of action. Recently, there has been considerable interest in mentoring and the roles that mentors play in children's development, especially in helping children who have limited access to positive role models, advisors, supporters and advocates, and sponsors.

Sponsors, of course, can be family members, but we generally think of them as agents outside the family who act on the behalf of children. They can be gatekeepers in institutions that allocate resources and access to programs, services and opportunities. More often, they are individuals who have connections to a range of different gatekeepers. Students of child and adolescent development know a lot less about how sponsorship operates in every day life than we should because it undoubtedly plays an important part in channeling children into successful pathways.

We know only a little bit about how various adults help to cultivate skills, talents, and special abilities such as art, music, theater, sports, and so on, but much less how sponsors operate to promote children's chances of getting ahead by non-academic means or in combination with formal schooling. This topic merits greater attention because, as I've said, sponsors can play an important role in facilitating social mobility. Less visible but perhaps equally prominent is the role that sponsors have in helping to guarantee that children in the more affluent classes retain their privileged position.

Some research exists on how young people enter the world of work and the role that families play in using contacts and connections to place adolescents in training, service, and work opportunities. Privileged parents understand that their children need to build portfolios of experience—resumes—in order to get ahead. Our research in Philadelphia on the less advantaged and the disadvantaged suggests much less understanding on the part of parents in how to connect their children to select institutions. Usually, it appears that children from less advantaged families are identified by sponsors by dint of their good efforts in school or perhaps community organizations. However, affluent parents do not simply rely on their children to attract sponsors. They actively recruit them or place their children in organizations, programs, and social arenas where sponsors are present and looking for motivated and talented prospects. Schools with well developed extra-curricular programs, after-school classes and activities, summer camps and educational courses are part of the stock and trade of growing up well off. Children in affluent families become practiced in relating to adults and in appreciating what adult sponsors, mentors, and coaches can do for them in middle childhood and adolescence. Increasingly, I would argue, the role of sponsors figures prominently in young people's ability to navigate successfully as they move from adolescence into early adulthood.

EARLY ADULTHOOD: THE EXTENSION OF INVESTMENT

Early adulthood, the period of life when youth enter adult roles and assume adult responsibilities—entering the labor force and becoming economically self-sufficient and forming families—has in recent decades become a less orderly and more protracted process than it was a half century ago. The driving force in the extension of the passage to adulthood has been the perceived need for a college education and, for the more privileged, an advanced degree often accompanied by a lengthy apprenticeship in a professional career. Related to this trend but not wholly because of it, young people put off more permanent relationship commitments and, generally, parenthood as well. Commitments to marriage and children, public opinion tells us, have become almost a second stage of the adult transition, often put off until education has been completed and some measure of job security is attained (Furstenberg et al. 1999; Settersten, Furstenberg, and Rumbaut 2005). Social class differences are no less prominent in this new stage of life than they are during childhood or adolescence. The current demands on young adults to attain more skills, be better prepared to enter the labor force, and postpone family formation play out quite differently in advantaged, middle-class, and disadvantaged families.

Let's begin with the obvious: the costs of higher education have become less and less affordable as grants and loans have not kept pace with college tuitions, much less the cost of professional education. Among families at the bottom of the income distribution, the debt taken on by parents and young adults can be crippling even though the long-term payoff theoretically makes borrowing for education economically rational (Rouse 2004). Add to the economic problems the academic liabilities that many, if not most, youth from disadvantaged families have accumulated in school brings us to the obvious fact that a very small proportion are academically, much less financially prepared to

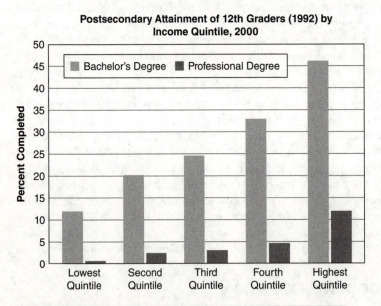

Postsecondary Attainment of 12th Graders (1992) by Income Quintile, 2000

Income Quintile	Bachelor's Degree	Professional Degree
Lowest Quintile	11.9	0.6
Second Quintile	20.2	2.4
Third Quintile	24.6	3.0
Fourth Quintile	33.0	4.6
Highest Quintile	46.2	11.9

From Table 1, Postsecondary Attainment, Attendance, Curriculum and Performance: Selected Results from the NELS:88/2000 Postsecondary Education Transcript Study (PETS), 2000 (NCES 2003-394)

endure a lengthy period of working and attending school (usually beginning with community college) as they work their way through college. It happens, but relatively rarely. Other events intrude: attachment to college is difficult in most community institutions because they lack the supportive staff and assistance offered by four-year institutions; financial crises arise siphoning off needed resources, parents cannot or will not offer aid or require support themselves, and so on.

Basically, among 12th graders likely to go to college, about 1 in 8 of those from families in the lowest quintile completed college compared to nearly 1 in 2 of those from families in the highest quintile. Only 1 in 4 of those in the middle quintile completed college.

Among middle-class families—let's say the third income quintile that ranges from $43,400 to $65,832 in 2004 (Census Historical Income Tables, Table F-1) few young adults can afford higher education without paying for it by working at the same time. Balancing school and work commitments in early adulthood is not an easy task, leading to high rates of school stop out and dropout. Thus, even when preparation for college is adequate and grants and loans can be managed, the process can be arduous and lengthy, partially accounting for the exceptionally high rates of some college—persons attending but not completing their college education—in the U.S. Many young people who enter college settle for, willingly or not, what amounts to post-secondary, technical training, often restricting mobility in their adult years.

The situation of the affluent families permits much greater latitude for families to help out during a longer and longer period of training. The prospect of attaining a high income job in the future, along with assistance offered by parents, sustains young adults through college and into professional careers. No doubt, too, young adults from affluent families who are generally better prepared academically are far more likely to qualify for financial aid packages that require taking on less debt.

Of course, this class-based profile is stereotypical to some degree. Talented individuals do rise from the bottom and untalented youth drift down. However, the social class mechanisms that I have described in this paper continue to play out during this period. The accumulation of deficits, the likelihood of problematic events, the availability of social capital and sponsorship continue to tilt the playing field as youth enter institutions with different levels of selectivity or work situations that permit or thwart opportunities for attaining further human capital.

I cannot leave the topic of early adulthood without mentioning how social class exposure in childhood, adolescence, and early adulthood affects partnerships and family formation. We have always known that social class is linked to the quality and stability of marriage though there was a time when divorce (not separation or marital unhappiness) occurred more frequently among the better off. This has not been true for some decades. Lower human capital is related to lower social, cultural, and psychological capital—the skills, knowledge of the world, social networks, and sponsorship all of which play some part in the ability to manage and sustain emotional relationships. Striking differences emerge in the occurrence of marriage, its stability, and in the incidence of non-marital childbearing by social class (Ellwood and Jencks 2001; Goldstein and Kenney 2001; Wu and Wolfe 2001).

These family patterns, so closely linked to class-related experiences in growing up, figure prominently in public discussions about the retreat from marriage among Americans. Curiously, the retreat has not occurred at all among the privileged and less so in the middle-class. Marriage, as I've written elsewhere, is increasingly a luxury good attainable only by those with the social, psychological, and material goods that make it happen and make it work.

References

Bendix, Reinhard, and Seymour Martin Lipset. 1966. *Class, Status, and Power*. New York: The Free Press.

Bernstein, Basil and Dorothy Henderson. 1969. "Social Class Differences and the Relevance of Language to Socialization. *Sociology* 3(1): 1–20.

Bernstein, Basil. 1971. *Class, Codes and Control: Theoretical Studies towards a Sociology of Language, Volume 1*. London: Routledge & Kegan Paul.

Blood, R. O., and D. Wolfe. 1960. *Husbands and Wives: The Dynamics of Married Living*. New York: The Free Press.

Bourdieu, Pierre. 1973. "Cultural Reproduction and Social Reproduction." In R. Brown (ed.), *Knowledge, Education, and Cultural Change*. London: Tavistock.

_____. 1986. "The Forms of Capital." In J. C. Richardson (ed.), *Handbook of Theory and Research for the Sociology of Education*. New York: Greenwood.

Bronfenbrenner, Uri. 1979. *The Ecology of Human Development: Experiments by Nature and Design*. Cambridge, MA: Harvard University Press.

Buchmann, Marlis. 1989. *The Script of Life in Modern Society: Entry into Adulthood in a Changing World*. Chicago: University of Chicago Press.

Burton, Linda and Carol Stack. 1993. "Conscripting Kin: Reflections on Family, Generation, and Culture." In *Family, Self, and Society: Toward a New Agenda for Family Research*. Cowan, Philip A.; Dorothy Field; Donald A. Hansen; Arlene Skolnick; and Guy E. Swanson (Eds). Hillsdale, NJ: Lawrence Erlbaum Associates.

Chaudry, Ajay. 2004. *Putting Children First: How Low-Income Working Mothers Manage Child Care*. New York: Russell Sage Foundation.

Cook, T. D., M. Herman, M. Phillips, and R. J. Setterson, Jr. 2002. "Some Ways in which Neighborhoods, Nuclear Families, Friendship Groups, and Schools Jointly Affect Changes in Early Adolescent Development." *Child Development* 73(4): 1283–1309.

Cooley, Charles H. 1902. *Human Nature and the Social Order*. New York: Scribners and Company.

Danziger, Sheldon H. and Peter Gottschalk. 1995. *America Unequal*. New York: Russell Sage Foundation.

Danziger, Sheldon H. and Jane Waldfogel. 2000. *Securing the Future: Investing in Children from Birth to College*. New York: Russell Sage Foundation.

Duncan, Greg J., W. Jean Yeung, Jeanne Brooks-Gunn and Judith R. Smith. 1998. "How much does childhood poverty affect the life chances of children?" *American Sociological Review* 63(3): 406–423.

Duncan, Greg and Jeanne Brooks-Gunn. 2000. *From Neurons to Neighborhoods: The Science of Early Childhood Development*. Washington, DC: National Academy Press.

Edin, Kathryn J. and Maria Kefalas. 2005. *Promises I Can Keep: Why Low-Income Women Put Motherhood Before Marriage*. Berkeley, CA: University of California Press.

Elder, Glen H., Jr. 1974. *Children of the Great Depression: Social change in Life Experience*. Chicago: University of Chicago Press. (Reissued as 25th Anniversary Edition, Boulder, CO: Westview Press, 1999).

———. 1999 (2nd ed). *Children of the Great Depression: Social change in Life Experience*. Chicago: University of Chicago Press.

Ellwood, David T. and Christopher Jencks. 2001. "The Spread of Single-Parent Families in the United States since 1960." Cambridge, MA: John F, Kennedy School of Government, Harvard University.

Farkas, George and Kurt Beron. 2004. "The Detailed Age Trajectory of Oral Vocabulary Knowledge: Differences by Class and Race." *Social Science Research* 33(3): 464–497.

Furstenberg, Jr., Frank F., Thomas D. Cook, Jacquelynne Eccles, Glen H. Edler, Jr. 1999. *Managing to Make It: Urban Families and Adolescent Outcomes*. (The John D. and Catherine T. MacArthur Foundation Series on Mental Health and Development). Chicago: University of Chicago Press.

Gans, Herbert J. 1962. *The Urban Villagers*. New York: The Free Press.

Garmezy, Norman. 1991. "Resilience and Vulnerability to adverse developmental outcomes associated with poverty." *American Behavioral Scientist* 34(4): 416–430.

Garmezy, Norman. 1993. "Vulnerability and Resilience." In *Studying Lives through Time: Personality and Development*. David C. Funder; Ross D. Parke; Carol Tomlinson-Keasey; Keith Widaman (eds). Washington, DC: American Psychological Association, pp. 377–398.

Goldstein, Joshua R. and Catherine T. Kenney. 2001. "Marriage Delayed or Marriage Forgone? New Cohort Forecasts of First Marriage for U.S. Women." *American Sociological Review* 66(4): 506–519.

Goldthorpe, J. and R. Erickson. 1993. *The Constant Flux: A Study of Class Mobility in Industrial Societies*. Oxford: Oxford University Press.

Haggerty, R. J., L. R. Sherrod, N. Garmezy, and M. Rutter. 1994. *Stress, Risk, and Resilience in Children and Adolescents*. New York: Cambridge University Press.

Hart, Betty and Todd R. Risley. 1995. *Meaningful Differences in the Everyday Experiences of Young American Children*. Baltimore, MD: Paul H. Brookes Publishing.

Heath, Shirley B. 1983. Ways with Words: Language, Life and Work in Communities and Classrooms. New York: Cambridge University Press.

Heinz, Walter R. and Victor W. Marshall (eds). 2003. *Social Dynamics of the Life Course: Transitions, Institutions and Interrelations*. Hawthorne, NY: Aldine De Gruyter.

Hertz, Tom. 2005. "Rags, Riches and Race: The Intergenerational Economic Mobility of Black and White Families in the United States." In Samuel Bowles, Herbert Gintis and Melissa Osborne Groves (eds.) *Unequal Chances: Family Background and Economic Success*. Princeton, NJ: Princeton University Press.

Hollingshead, A. de B. 1949. *Elmtown's Youth: The Impact of Social Classes on Adolescents*. New York: Wiley.

Komarovsky, Mira. 1987. *Blue-Collar Marriage*. 2nd ed. New Haven, CT: Yale University Press.

Kefalas, Maria. 2003. *Working Class Heroes: Protecting Home, Community and Nation in a Chicago Neighborhood*. Berkeley, CA: University of California Press.

Kohn, Melvin L. 1977. *Class and Conformity: A Study in Values (with a reassessment)*. 2nd edition. Chicago: University of Chicago Press.

Lamont, Michele. 2000. *The Dignity of Working Men: Morality and the Boundaries of Race, Class and Immigration*. Cambridge, MA: Harvard University Press.

Lareau, Annette. 1989. *Home Advantage: Social Class and Parental Intervention in Elementary Education*. New York: Falmer Press. (2nd Edition, 2000. Lanham, MD: Rowman and Littlefield Press).

Lareau, Annette. 2003. *Unequal Childhoods: Race, Class and Family Life*. Berkeley, CA: University of California Press.

Levy, Frank. 1999. *The New Dollars and Dreams*. New York: Russell Sage Foundation.

Lynd, Robert S. and Helen M. Lynd. 1929. *Middletown: A Study in Contemporary American Culture*. New York: Harcourt Brace & Company.

Magnuson, Katherine A. and Jane Waldfogel.2005. "Early Childhood Care and Education: Effects on Ethnic and Racial Gaps in School Readiness. *Future of Children* 15(1): 169–196.

McLanahan, Sara. 2004. "Diverging Destinies: How Children Fare Under the Second Demographic Transition." *Demography* 41(4): 607–627.

Mead, Margaret, and M. Wolfenstein. Eds. 1955. *Childhood in Contemporary Cultures*. Chicago: University of Chicago Press.

Medrich, E., J. Roizen, V. Rubin, with S. Buckley. 1982. *The Serious Business of Growing Up: A Study of Children's Lives Outside of School*. Berkeley: University of California Press.

Miller, Daniel R. and Guy E. Swanson. 1958. *The Changing American Parent*. New York: Wiley and Sons.

Newman, Katherine S. 1993. *Declining Fortunes: The Withering of the American Dream*. New York: Basic Books.

Rouse, Cecilia E. 2004. "Low Income Students and College Attendance: An Exploration of Income Expectations." *Social Science Quarterly* 85(5): 1299–1317.

Rutter, Michael. 1985. "Resilience in the Face of Adversity: Protective Factors and Resistance to Psychiatric Disorder. *British Journal of Psychiatry* 147: 598–611.

Rutter, Michael. 2000. "Resilience Reconsidered: Conceptual Considerations, Empirical Findings and Policy Implications. In *Handbook of Early Childhood Intervention*. (2nd edition). In Shenkoff, Jack P., and Samuel J. Meisels. (eds.). New York: Cambridge University Press. pp. 651–682.

Settersten, Richard A., Jr, Frank F. Furstenberg, and Ruben G. Rumbaut. 2005. *On the Frontier of Adulthood: Theory, Research, and Public Policy*. Chicago: University of Chicago Press.

Tocqueville, Alexis de. 1945. *Democracy in America*. New York: Knopf.

Warner, William Lloyd. 1949. *Social Class in America*. Chicago: Science Research Associates.

Weber, Max. 1949. *The Methodology of the Social Sciences*. New York: Free Press.

Werner, Emmy. 1995. "Resilience in Development." *Current Directions in Psychological Science* 4(3): 81–85.

Wolff, Edward N. 2002. *TOP HEAVY: A Study of Increasing Inequality of Wealth in America*. (The New Press).

Wolff, Edward N. 2004. "Changes in Household Wealth in the 1980s and 1990s in the U.S." *The Levy Economics Institute at Bard College*, Working Paper No. 407.

Wu, Lawrence, and Barbara Wolfe. Eds. 2001. *Out of Wedlock: Causes and Consequences of Nonmarital Fertility*. New York: Russell Sage Foundation.

■ READING 19

The Long and Twisting Path to Adulthood

Richard A. Settersten, Jr. and Barbara Ray

Becoming an adult has traditionally been understood as comprising five core transitions—leaving home, completing school, entering the workforce, getting married, and having children. Recent research on how young adults are handling these core transitions has yielded three important findings that contributors to this volume will explore in the pages to come. First, both in the United States and in many European countries, the process of becoming an adult is more gradual and varied today than it was half a century ago.[1] Social timetables that were widely observed in that era no longer seem relevant, and young people are taking longer to achieve economic and psychological autonomy than their counterparts did then. Experiences in early adulthood now also vary greatly by gender, race and ethnicity, and social class.

Second, families are often overburdened in extending support to young adult children as they make their way through this extended process. In the United States, in particular, parents contribute sizable material and emotional support through their children's late twenties and into their early thirties. Such flows are to be expected in more privileged families, but what is now striking are the significant flows—and associated strains—in middle-class families at a time when families themselves have become increasingly stressed or fractured. The heavier reliance on families exacerbates the already precarious plight of young people from a variety of vulnerable backgrounds.[2] It also raises complex questions about who is responsible for the welfare of young people and whether markets, families, or governments should absorb the risks and costs associated with the early adult years.

Third, there is a mismatch between young people making the transition to adulthood today and the existing institutional supports, including residential colleges and universities, community colleges, military and national service programs, work settings, and other environments. The policies, programs, and institutions that served young adults a half-century ago no longer meet the needs of youth today, either in the United States or Europe, and are based on assumptions that do not reflect the realities of the world today.[3]

Together, these three findings point to the need to strengthen the skills and capacities of young people on the path to adulthood and to improve the effectiveness of the institutions through which they move. Although some of the broad changes we describe are taking place in Canada and some Western European nations, as well as in the United States, the factors that explain them, the consequences of and responses to them, and the national histories in which they are embedded are often unique. For these reasons, we focus most of our attention on the story at home, in the United States. Because our aim is to provide an overview of changes and challenges in the contour and content of the early adult years, we focus on the larger story at the expense of more nuanced ones, which are told in the topic-focused articles that follow. We begin with a brief history of becoming an adult in the United States. We then take a closer look at a few particularly important shifts—in leaving the family home, in completing schooling, in securing work, in marriage and childbearing, and in the provision of family support. We close by illustrating the need to buttress or reform social institutions in light of a longer and more complex passage to adulthood.

BECOMING AN ADULT: A BRIEF HISTORY

During the first few decades of the twentieth century, the period known as "adolescence" was relatively brief. By their late teens, only a small fraction of the population was still in school, and most men had begun to work. While many left their natal homes early, surprisingly high shares of men and women nonetheless remained at home for a while, as we will later see, and marriage and child-bearing did not happen immediately. As the century progressed, however, growing proportions of young people had formed families by their late teens or early twenties. The Great Depression slowed the timing of family formation, but by the end of World War II, marriage and childbearing took place almost in lockstep with the conclusion of schooling. In the postwar boom that followed, high-paying industrial jobs were plentiful, and a prosperous economy enabled workers with high school degrees (or less) and college degrees alike to find secure employment with decent wages and benefits. Between 1949 and 1970, the income of earners in the lower and middle brackets grew 110 percent or more, while the income of those in the top brackets rose between 85 percent and 95 percent.[4]

These stable jobs made it possible for couples to marry and form families at young ages. By the 1950s and 1960s, most Americans viewed family roles and adult responsibilities as being nearly synonymous. For men, the defining characteristic of adulthood was having the means to marry and support a family. For women, it was getting married and becoming a mother; indeed, most women in that era married before they were twenty-one and had at least one child before they were twenty-three. By their early twenties, then, most young men and women were recognized as adults, both socially and economically.

In some ways, adult transitions today resemble those before industrialization, during the late nineteenth and early twentieth century, when the livelihoods of most families were bound to farms and agricultural jobs rather than the job market. Becoming an adult then, as now, was a gradual process characterized by "semi-autonomy," with youth waiting until they were economically self-sufficient to set up independent households, marry, and have children. There are important differences, however, in the ways young people today and in the recent and more distant past define and achieve adulthood.

How do Americans today define adulthood? To seek an answer, the MacArthur Research Network on Transitions to Adulthood developed a set of questions for the 2002 General Social Survey (GSS), an opinion poll administered to a nationally representative sample of Americans every two years by the National Opinion Research Center.[5] The survey asked nearly 1,400 Americans aged eighteen and older how important it was to reach certain traditional markers to be considered an adult: leaving home, finishing school, getting a full-time job, becoming financially independent from one's parents, being able to support a family, marrying, and becoming a parent.

Today, more than 95 percent of Americans consider the most important markers of adulthood to be completing school, establishing an independent household, and being employed full-time—concrete steps associated with the ability to support a family. But only about half of Americans consider it necessary to marry or to have children to be regarded as an adult. Unlike their parents' and grandparents' generations, for whom marriage and parenthood were prerequisites for adulthood, young people today more often view these markers as life choices rather than requirements, as steps that complete the process of becoming an adult rather than start it.

Definitions of adulthood also differ markedly by social class. For example, Americans who are less educated and less affluent give earlier deadlines for leaving home, completing school, obtaining full-time employment, marrying, and parenting. Around 40 percent of those in the bottom third of the economic distribution said that young adults should marry before they turn twenty-five, and one-third said they should have children by this age. Far fewer of the better-off respondents pointed to the early twenties, and about one-third of them said that these events could be delayed until the thirties.

Some important new realities underlie these definitions. First, becoming an adult today usually involves a period of living independently before marriage, even though growing shares of young people are staying at home longer or returning home later on. Second, the early adult years often involve the pursuit of higher education, as a decent standard of living today generally requires a college education, if not a professional degree. Third, regardless of whether young people enter college, it takes longer today to secure a full-time job that pays enough to support a family, and young people now have a greater range of employment experiences in getting there. Fourth, as a consequence of these changes, marriage and parenting now come significantly later in the life course. Finally, on each of these fronts, young adults often have starkly different sets of options and experiences depending on their family backgrounds and resources. Young adults today are also more likely to be black, Hispanic, immigrant, and multi-ethnic than any other of the nation's age groups.[6] They are also more likely to be foreign-born, a characteristic that in past generations was truer of families' oldest members. These shifts, too, have prompted new inequalities in early adult life.

LIVING INDEPENDENTLY

The post-World War II script for life left such an indelible mark that it often remains the benchmark against which individuals judge themselves and others, even today. Yet the postwar model was something of an aberration then as now. Families of the 1950s and 1960s did many things differently from their predecessors, including launching themselves into adulthood at very early ages. This is apparent in Figures 19.1 and 19.2, which show the proportion of men and women (single and without children) living with their parents at the ages of twenty, twenty-five, and thirty from 1900 to 2000, and Table 19.1, which adds a recent data point, 2007.

In 1900, roughly one-third of white men aged twenty-five were living at home with their parents—two and a half times the share in 1970.[7] By 2000, the share living at home was one-fifth; by 2007, it had increased to one-fourth. Since the 1970s, black men

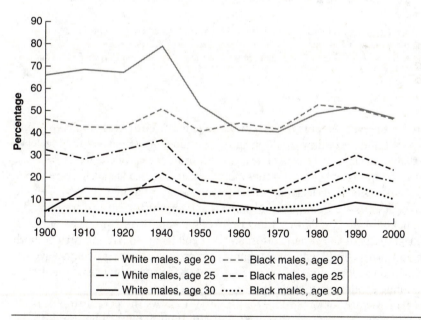

FIGURE 19.1 *Young Men Living at Home (Single, No Children), by Race and Age, 1900–2000*

Source: Adapted from data compiled in Elizabeth Fussell and Frank F. Furstenberg Jr., "The Transition to Adulthood during the Twentieth Century," In *On the Frontier of Adulthood: Theory, Research, and Public Policy*, edited by Richard A. Settersten Jr., Frank F. Furstenberg Jr., and Rubén G. Rumbaut (University of Chicago Press, 2005), pp. 29–75.

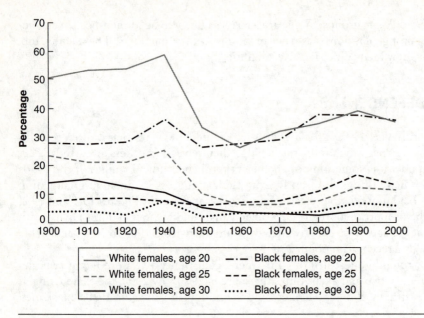

FIGURE 19.2   *Young Women Living at Home (Single, No Children), by Race and Age, 1900–2000*

Source: Adapted from data compiled in Elizabeth Fussell and Frank F. Furstenberg Jr., 'The Transition to Adulthood during the Twentieth Century," In *On the Frontier of Adulthood: Theory, Research, and Public Policy,* edited by Richard A. Settersten Jr., Frank F. Furstenberg Jr., and Rubén G. Rumbaut (University of Chicago Press, 2005), pp. 29–75.

have lived more often with parents than their white peers at both ages twenty-five and thirty. Figures 19.1 and 19.2 show that during this period women have tended to leave home earlier than men, and, as we show later, cohabit or marry earlier as well.

It might be tempting to infer from these figures that Americans have now returned to a more "normal" pattern of delayed home-leaving. That inference, however, would miss the important and often unique conditions that every historical era presents. To leave home quickly in the 1950s was "normal" because opportunities were plentiful and social expectations of the time reinforced the need to do so. At the turn of both the twentieth and twenty-first centuries, greater proportions of young people stayed at home longer than those who came of age at mid-century because they faced distinctive social and economic conditions of their own.

Carrying the picture forward to 2007, Table 19.1 shows the proportion of black and white young adults, at different ages, who live with their parents. The trends in co-residence with parents evidenced in Figures 19.1 and 19.2 have made dramatic leaps.[8] In every age bracket men are more likely than women to live with parents. Black men live with parents more often than white men, and more often than white and black women, at every age. Black women more often live with parents than do white women, again at

TABLE 19.1.   *Percentage of Young Adult Men and Women Living with Parents, 2007, by Race*

	Men			Women		
	All	*White*	*Black*	*All*	*White*	*Black*
Age 20–24	43.0	42.9	45.2	38.0	37.0	40.8
25–29	19.8	18.9	24.8	15.9	14.6	20.0
30–34	10.1	9.5	14.6	7.9	7.3	11.4
At age 20	54.0	54.3	54.6	48.1	47.2	51.5
At 25	26.3	25.5	30.2	21.4	20.1	25.1
At 30	12.1	11.4	18.4	9.7	8.8	13.7
At 35	7.5	6.8	12.1	6.1	5.8	9.5
At 40	5.8	5.8	7.5	4.4	4.0	7.7

Source: Authors' computations, 2007 American Community Survey, U.S. Bureau of the Census.

every age. The share of living with parents is particularly high for men and women in their early twenties, spanning 43 to 50 percent depending on the group, although proportions fall as the age rises. At each five-year mark—from age twenty, to twenty-five, to thirty—percentages are cut in half. Yet even at the ages of thirty-five and forty, between 4 and 12 percent of adult children live with their parents, depending on the group.

Comparisons between native-born whites and blacks overlook the very sizable group of young people from other ethnic and immigrant populations who live at home. In 2008, among young men and women aged eighteen to twenty-four across ten distinct immigrant groups, second-generation youth (those born in the United States to foreign-born parents) are consistently more likely to be living at home than first-generation or so-called 1.5-generation youth (those who arrived at age thirteen or older, or age twelve or younger, respectively).[9] Immigrants of the second generation are more likely to live at home than native-born blacks and especially whites, and some groups show very high rates of home-staying (for example, between 64 and 75 percent of young adults from Indian, Dominican, Chinese, Filipino, and Salvadoran/Guatemalan backgrounds live at home).

Although residential independence has been and continues to be one of the markers of attaining adulthood in the United States, particularly among native-born youth, recent downturns in the economy may create pressure on families to house adult children. Growing numbers of young people have also been staying at home while enrolled in school or to make ends meet while working.[10]

For women, it was not until the 1960s that large numbers began to live on their own before marriage, thus creating a critical "hiatus" (as sociologist Frances Goldscheider has called it) that allowed women to become more fully integrated into the paid labor market and college classrooms.[11] By 1970, the share of twenty-year-olds who were living on their

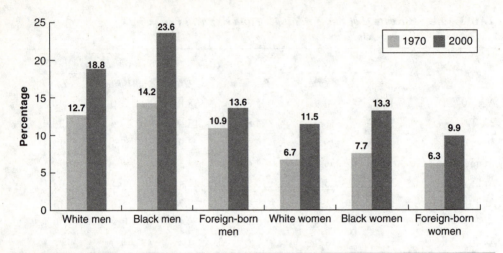

FIGURE 19.3 *Share of Men and Women Aged Twenty-Five Living with Parents,*
1970 and 2000

Source: Adapted from data compiled in Elizabeth Fussell and Fank F. Furstenberg Jr., "The Transition to
Adulthood during the Twentieth Century," In *On the Frontier of Adulthood: Theory, Research, and Public Policy*,
edited by Richard A. Settersten Jr., Frank F. Furstenberg Jr., and Rubén G. Rumbaut (University of Chicago
Press, 2005), pp. 29–75.

own before marrying was more than double that for both white men and women at the
turn of the century.[12] As we show later, marriage was becoming less urgent and desirable
for a host of reasons, and when young people did not marry, they still considered moving
out and living on their own—and women *en masse* did so for the first time. During this
era, housing was also inexpensive, and staying with parents humiliating.

Figures 19.3 through 19.6 demonstrate how much has changed in just a generation
or so. These snapshots show that in 1970, only 13 percent of white males were living
with their parents at age twenty-five, compared with 19 percent in 2000. Only about
10 percent were living on their own or with roommates in 1970, compared with one-third
in 2000. Most profoundly, nearly seven in ten were married in 1970, compared with
only one-third by 2000. The trend, then, has been for men to move out of their parents'
homes, but not into marriages or even cohabitation; by contrast, the proportion living
with parents has grown only modestly. Trends are similar for women and for those of
other racial and ethnic groups at age twenty-five. Half as many black men, for example,
were living at home with parents in 1970 as in 2000. Likewise, the share married at age
twenty-five in 1970 was triple that in 2000.

It is clear that the emergence of a period of independent living—despite more
recent social concerns about young people staying at home longer or returning home
later—is one of the most profound changes in the experiences of young adults in the past
several decades.[13] This significant shift coincides with a few other major transformations
in the early adult years, including the rising demand for, and attainment of, advanced
education, to which we now turn.

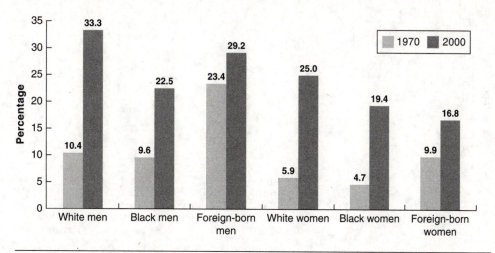

FIGURE 19.4 *Share of Men and Women Aged Twenty-Five Living Independently, 1970 and 2000*

Source: Adapted from data compiled in Elizabeth Fussell and Frank F. Furstenberg Jr., "The Transition to Adulthood during the Twentieth Century," In *On the Frontier of Adulthood: Theory, Research, and Public Policy*, edited by Richard A. Settersten Jr., Frank F. Furstenberg Jr., and Rubén G. Rumbaut (University of Chicago Press, 2005), pp. 29–75.

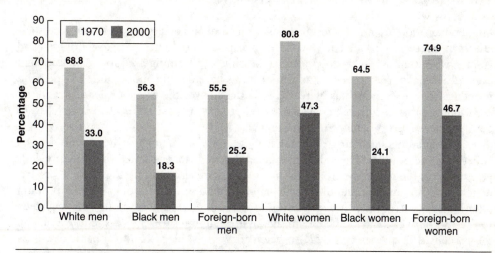

FIGURE 19.5 *Share of Married Couples Aged Twenty-Five Living Independently, 1970 and 2000*

Source: Adapted from data compiled in Elizabeth Fussell and Frank F. Furstenberg Jr., "The Transition to Adulthood during the Twentieth Century," In *On the Frontier of Adulthood: Theory, Research, and Public Policy*, edited by Richard A. Settersten Jr., Frank F. Furstenberg Jr., and Rubén G. Rumbaut (University of Chicago Press, 2005), pp. 29–75.

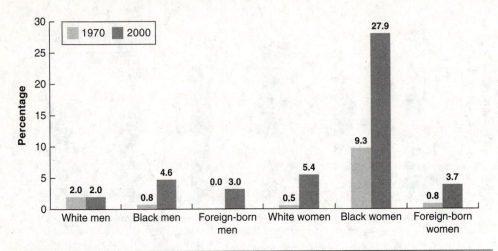

FIGURE 19.6 *Share of Singles with Own Children Aged Twenty-Five Living Independently, 1970 and 2000*

Source: Adapted from data compiled in Elizabeth Fussell and Frank F. Furstenberg Jr., "The Transition to Adulthood during the Twentieth Century," In *On the Frontier of Adulthood: Theory, Research, and Public Policy*, edited by Richard A. Settersten Jr., Frank F. Furstenberg Jr., and Rubén G. Rumbaut (University of Chicago Press, 2005), pp. 29–75.

THE RISING DEMAND FOR EDUCATION

Higher education has flourished in all post-industrial and emerging post-industrial societies. Once reserved for the elite, a college education is now a necessity for both men and women who want access to good jobs. Education and training are more valuable than ever because jobs are less secure and work careers have become more fluid. The demand for education and training has increased relentlessly over the past four decades, and the economic returns to education have grown in recent years, even after the higher costs of getting an education are taken into account.[14]

Young adults have heard the message loud and clear: to get ahead, one needs a college degree. And, in fact, today's young adults are better educated than any previous generation in the nation's history. Yet many youth are also floundering badly. Approximately eight in ten high school seniors plan to attend some form of college or training after high school.[15] But even high school dropout rates are high: among people sixteen to twenty-four years old in 2006, high school dropout rates were 9.3 percent overall and 5.8 percent, 10.7 percent, and 22.1 percent for whites, blacks, and Hispanics, respectively.[16] More disturbing estimates suggest that as many as three in ten ninth graders today will not graduate from high school four years later; for Hispanics, blacks, and Native Americans, the figures hover around a disturbing five in ten.[17]

"College for all" may be a salient cultural message, but only one-quarter of young adults between the ages of twenty-five and thirty-four have a bachelor's degree today, and only 5 percent have graduate degrees.[18] Popular perceptions to the contrary, these shares have not changed significantly in the past three decades. The breakdown of degree holders has changed, however, by gender and by race and ethnicity. Women have now surpassed men in college graduation rates and in educational attainment generally.[19] Asians are most likely to have bachelor's degrees or higher, followed by whites. Hispanics are least likely. Only 9 percent of Hispanics between the ages of twenty-five and thirty-four had a bachelor's degree in 2005. Asians are four times more likely than Hispanics to have a bachelor's degree.[20] Among whites, the share with a bachelor's degree is 27 percent; among blacks, the share is 15 percent.[21]

It is telling that only 40 percent of those who enter four-year institutions earn degrees within six years—and the rest are unlikely ever to earn degrees, as six years is generally understood to be the point of no return.[22] The children of parents who have themselves graduated from college are far more likely to have both the skills and the resources to enter and complete college. Although six in ten students whose parents have college degrees finish college in four years, only about one in ten students whose parents lack college degrees finishes in four years.[23]

The gap between young adults' high aspirations for college and their low graduation rates sounds an important alarm. Youth who are ill-prepared for the rigors of higher education may start school, but they are also more likely to have unclear plans and inadequate skills, veer off course, cycle in and out, or drop out altogether.[24] The growth of the "nontraditional" student (one who is older, working, or parenting) is also a key reason why it now takes longer to get a "four-year" degree.[25] Youth who have dropped out of four-year colleges or who are not seeking four-year degrees often find their way to community colleges. In his article in this volume, Thomas Brock explores the formidable challenges these students and these institutions now face.

More worrisome is the plight of young adults who have no education beyond high school and who are largely disengaged from social institutions and economic life—schools, the labor market, and the military. In 2005, even before the current recession and during the height of the Iraq war, roughly three in ten white men between ages sixteen and twenty-four with only a high school degree were not in school, in the military, or at work.[26] For young black men, the proportion is staggering: more than half were not in school, in the military, or at work.

Of even more concern is the high probability that poorly educated men, particularly black men, will be imprisoned in early adulthood. Economist Steven Raphael estimates that 90 percent of black male high school dropouts in California aged forty-five to fifty-four have histories of imprisonment.[27] Other studies using national data have found similar, but lower, probabilities of imprisonment.[28] The most conservative estimates, from the U.S. Department of Justice, though nonetheless startling, are that about one in three black men and one in six Latino men are expected to go to prison during their lifetime—compared with one in seventeen white men—if current incarceration rates remain unchanged.[29] Among all American men in their twenties in 2008, 1.5 percent of whites, 4 percent of Latinos, and fully 10 percent of blacks were incarcerated.[30] These are very high rates of incarceration for all groups, but far higher for blacks than for others. These data highlight just how difficult the adult experiences and circumstances of black and Latino men are, particularly for those with the least education, for whom risks grow in the late adolescent and early adult years.

GETTING AHEAD GETS HARDER

The prosperity that made it possible for young adults to move quickly into adult roles continued for several decades after World War II. During the 1970s, however, wages stagnated and inflation rose. The manufacturing sector that had been the backbone of the middle class and had ensured lives of relative security for the working class crumbled. For the next thirty years, wages for workers without college degrees stagnated, and the pensions and benefits that they had once enjoyed began to vanish. Globalization increased competition, markets became internationalized, and new technologies spread networks and knowledge.[31] All these forces gave rise to new economic and employment uncertainties that now complicate young adults' decisions about living arrangements, educational investments, and family formation.

At mid-century a high school degree was enough to establish a solid standard of living; today not even a college degree guarantees success. As shown in Figure 19.7, young men (aged twenty-five to thirty-four) with a high school degree or less earned about $4,000 less in 2002 than in 1975 (with earnings adjusted for inflation).[32] Men with some college also lost ground, earning about $3,500 a year less in 2002 than in 1975. College graduates made gains, but the big winners were men who had completed at least some graduate school, whose earnings grew by about $19,000.[33] And even small gains, of course, have significant effects on lifetime earnings.

Over the past quarter-century, the earnings of women, unlike those of men, have risen (see Figure 19.8). Figures 19.7 and 19.8 indicate that women's earnings have grown faster than those of men—although men have continued to outearn women. In part

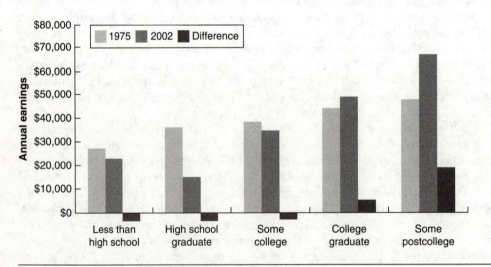

FIGURE 19.7 *Earnings of Men Aged Twenty-Five to Thirty-Four, by Education Level, 1975 and 2002*

Source: Adapted from data compiled in Sheldon Danzlger, "Earning by Education for Young Workers: 1975 and 2002," *Data Brief* 17 (Philadelphia: MacArthur Network on Transitions to Adulthood, 2004). Earnings adjusted for Inflation.

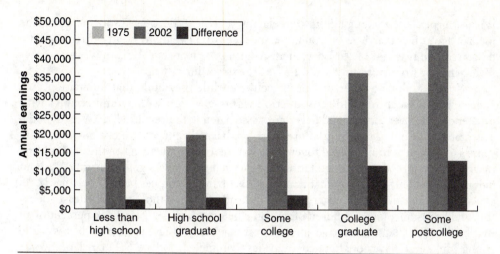

FIGURE 19.8 *Earnings of Women Aged Twenty-Five to Thirty-Four, by Education Level, 1975 and 2002*

Source: Adapted from data compiled in Sheldon Danziger, "Earning by Education for Young Workers: 1975 and 2002," *Data Brief* 17 (Philadelphia: MacArthur Network on Transitions to Adulthood, 2004). Earnings adjusted for Inflation.

because women's wages were much lower to start, their average earnings have remained well below those of men. In 1975, a female high school graduate earned about 46 percent as much during the year as a male; by 2002, she earned 62 percent as much. As with men, the most educated women saw the largest earnings gains. Finally, for each group (except those with some graduate-level education), the share whose earnings were below poverty levels (about $19,000 for a family of four in 2002) was greater in 2002 than in 1975.

Having an income—or at least the ability to earn an income—has always been a precursor to being independent and taking on adult roles, such as marrying and settling down. In 1969, only about 10 percent of men in their early thirties had wages that were below poverty level. By 2004, the share had more than doubled. Women fared a little better over the same time span, but nearly half were still earning poverty-level wages by their mid-thirties.[34] Overall, the share of young adults in 2005 living in poverty was higher than the national average.[35] Given these and a host of other new economic vulnerabilities, it is perhaps not so surprising that by age thirty, only half as many young adults in 2005 as in 1960 had achieved all the traditional markers of adulthood—particularly marriage and parenthood.[36]

DELAYING "I DO"

Young adults today take a different view of marriage than their counterparts did in times past.[37] Whereas once couples came together to build a life together, today couples build their own lives separately and then marry. Because acquiring educational credentials and work experience—a key part of the foundation to be built before marriage—takes time, it is no surprise that young adults are delaying marriage. Between 1960 and 1980, the median age at first marriage for young people rose from twenty to twenty-three; by 2000 it had reached twenty-five.[38] Today, median age at first marriage for men is over twenty-seven, and for women, twenty-six.[39] These are extraordinary leaps.

Young adults, however, are hardly celibate while they build that foundation. Advances in contraception and reproduction rights have left women and couples with greater control over fertility and fewer risks associated with premarital sex. Views on the acceptability of living together before marriage have also become more positive. Fifty years ago, very few couples lived together before marrying; today, more than half of first marriages are preceded by cohabitation, a trend that shows no signs of abating.[40] About half of high school seniors say that they plan to cohabit as couples before they marry.[41]

For young adults with fewer prospects ahead of them—those with the least education and lowest incomes—children often come before marriage. Nearly 40 percent of all first births occur before marriage, and the vast majority of these premarital births are to young adults who have not attended, much less completed, college.[42] The risk of divorce is also consistently highest for couples who marry earliest. Sixty percent of those who marry before age eighteen will be divorced by age thirty-four. Forty percent of those who marry by age twenty will not make it to their tenth wedding anniversary, compared with roughly 25 percent of those who wait until twenty-five.[43]

For those who bemoan the demise of marriage, there is heartening news. Young adults may be postponing marriage, but they are not abandoning it altogether. By age thirty-four, seven in ten have tied the knot.[44] At the same time, the proportions of young people who are single and have never married, by age and race, are striking, as shown in Table 19.2.

In 2007, men in every age bracket through age thirty-four were more likely to be single and never-married than women. Black men and black women were consistently more likely to be single and never-married than whites, with Hispanic men and women

TABLE 19.2.   *Percentage of Young Adult Men and Women, Single and Never Married, 2007, by Race*

	Men			Women		
	All	*White*	*Black*	*All*	*White*	*Black*
Age 20–24	88.0	87.3	92.5	79.6	78.0	89.9
25–29	58.9	55.8	73.8	47.0	42.2	71.4
30–34	35.8	33.0	52.4	27.3	22.8	52.9
At 20	95.2	95.0	97.0	91.1	90.7	96.2
At 25	70.6	68.0	82.5	58.4	54.6	78.5
At 30	43.8	41.4	49.2	33.3	29.0	50.8
At 35	27.8	25.4	42.5	21.1	16.7	43.0
At 40	21.5	19.2	34.2	16.1	12.5	34.6

Source: Authors' computations, 2007 *American Community Survey*, U.S. Bureau of the Census.

falling in between. As the table shows, the proportions of single and never-married peo- ple drop by age for all groups, although less dramatically for black men and women than for whites. In their early thirties, more than half of black men and women are single and never-married. Even later, at age forty, sizable proportions of men and women, and especially black men and women, are still single and never-married. The percentages of people who have never married, and who are intentionally childless, are higher now than at any other time in American history—and policy makers have not yet begun to antici- pate the future social ramifications of this profound fact.[45]

THE CRUCIAL ROLE OF FAMILIES AND SOCIAL RELATIONSHIPS

Both the government and the general public in the United States place a high premium on personal responsibility and self-reliance.[46] The prevailing "sink or swim" philosophy leaves it up to young people and their families to take advantage of the opportunities they encounter or actively create, and to shoulder responsibility for problems that ensue as they navigate markets for education, jobs, and partners using their own knowledge and resources.

Stark inequalities therefore exist in the skills, resources, and opportunities of young people, depending on what parents can provide during their children's third decade and what they provided in the first two decades. To understand these inequalities, one need only look at the financial supports that parents provide to their young adult children. U.S. data from 1988—seemingly outdated but the best available over a long time span— showed that parents spent about one-third of the total cost of raising a child from birth to age eighteen again between eighteen and thirty-four. This support included the pro- vision of material assistance (in the form of housing, food, and educational expenses) and direct cash assistance, although support diminished as adult children grew older.[47] Even more striking, children from families in the top quarter of the income distribu- tion received at least 70 percent more in material assistance than children in the bottom quarter.

One can safely assume that these outlays have only increased dramatically since those data were collected in 1988. A 2005 update of that study, based on parents of youth aged eighteen to twenty-one, shows that, regardless of income, parents are spend- ing 10 percent of their annual incomes to help their young adult children. All families are thus devoting similar proportions of their resources to their young adult children, although the amounts they spend are obviously drastically different (10 percent of $40,000 is considerably different from 10 percent of $200,000). The higher transfers in financially well-positioned families give a further boost to children who are already better off going into adulthood.

This expensive new stage of life is creating some consternation for families that have to adjust to the changing pace of adult transitions. For the most privileged young adults—those who receive ample support from their parents—the new, extended path to adulthood is a time of unparalleled freedom: freedom to proceed directly through college, travel or work for a few years, or perhaps participate in community service, and then enter graduate or professional school. Relatively few Americans, however, have this good fortune. Youth from less well-off families shuttle back and forth between work and school or combine both while they gradually gain their credentials; they wait for jobs that can support the families they wish to start or perhaps have already started; and they feel little control over their lives.

More than at any time in recent history, then, parents are being called on to provide material and other types of assistance to their young adult children. A century ago, it was the other way around: young adults typically helped their parents when they first went to work, particularly if they still lived together. Now, many young adults continue to receive support from their parents even after they begin working. The exceptions seem to be in immigrant families, where young adult children stay in the parental home and feel strong obligations to help support parents.[48]

The challenges of a longer transition to adulthood pose chronic dilemmas for families with limited means that must find ways to support their children, especially in a course of extended education. Of course, it has always been true that some youth do well and others do not, regardless of resources. Having resources is no guarantee of success, just as the absence of resources is no guarantee of failure. But having additional resources would surely seem to foster positive outcomes in early adulthood. Resources may also soften the consequences of poor judgments and mistakes, which seem more perilous today as the safety nets on which post-World War II generations could rely—pensions and health insurance, steady work with benefits, company loyalty—are fraying.

The weakened position of families in the current volatile economy exacerbates the challenges to populations of young people who are already vulnerable going into adulthood—those whose skills and resources are less than adequate, whose family relationships are absent or fragile, or who have long been in foster care, special education, or juvenile justice systems only to be abruptly cut off from support when they reach the legal ages of adulthood, eighteen or in some cases twenty-one.[49] Most supports for these youth now end at age eighteen—a time when, as noted, their more advantaged peers are continuing to receive sizable assistance from their families of origin. For these populations, maintaining supports is an important priority, even—or especially—in times of economic hardship.

Even middle-class families that once seemed strongly positioned to invest in young adult children may now be experiencing new vulnerabilities amid the "Great Recession" that began in 2008. As the middle class shrinks and family incomes fluctuate from year to year in an uncertain economy, families cannot offer the same set of resources to their children.[50] Families on the low end of middle-income seem especially vulnerable—they have some, but not ample, resources, and their incomes are just high enough to make them ineligible for government support.

Young people who can build stronger and wider connections to adults *other than* parents (for example, teachers and adult mentors) also end up faring better than those who do not. Especially for those young people with limited or absent relationships with their parents, relationships with other adults are invaluable in replacing or compensating for the support that their parents cannot or do not provide. The presence of meaningful relationships with adults significantly bolsters school achievement, success in jobs, emotional maturity, and satisfaction with life, and keeps in check problematic behaviors such as substance abuse.[51] Relationships with adults other than parents are also important in opening opportunities and resources by connecting young people to the larger and loosely connected social networks in which these adults are embedded.[52]

In the United States, the solutions for managing this extended transition are, to a great degree, private ones, made possible by whatever social connections or resources young people and their parents happen to have or can create. But the transition takes place within multiple institutional contexts, and the investments that society makes in the institutions around young people and their parents are also important. These supports are particularly important for families that are unable to extend help because of limited resources or because they lack the knowledge and skills to help their children move forward.

BEYOND PERSONAL SOLUTIONS: STRENGTHENING SOCIAL INSTITUTIONS

As the transition to adulthood evolves, so too must society's institutions. As young people and their families struggle with the new reality of a longer and more demanding pathway into adult life, existing institutions may need to change and new ones may have to be developed. Which institutions are most important to a successful transition, which will reach the largest share of young adults in meaningful ways, and which are most open to intervention and reform? We highlight three institutions: community colleges, service learning programs, and the military.

Community colleges are an ideal target for intervention. These two-year colleges touch large numbers and a wide variety of young people, serve many purposes, are flexible, and offer connections to a range of potential career paths. Yet they are seriously in need of support and reform if they are to meet the needs of youth in transition to adulthood. Four-year residential colleges and universities, by contrast, provide a perfect example of how a social institution can successfully address the needs of young adults—by providing shelter, directed activities, adult and peer support, health care, and entertainment. Explicitly designed as a bridge between a student's family and the wider society, four-year colleges have increasingly been tailored to provide the sort of semi-autonomy that characterizes early adulthood. In his article on community colleges in this issue, Thomas Brock notes the irony that the most selective institutions of higher education take the most capable students and wrap them in support, while community colleges are the least selective institutions and provide the least support.

Community colleges, however, can be restructured to provide these same kinds of services. The Obama administration has already recognized the important role that community colleges can play in strengthening the skills and opportunities of youth who do not or cannot go on to four-year colleges. It has proposed $12 billion in additional funding, with the goal of graduating 5 million more community college students by 2020. It also aims to forge tighter links between community colleges and employers.

The second institution, service learning programs in schools and workplaces, provides important networks and opportunities for young people to "take stock" of themselves and of society, wrestle with social and political attitudes and values, explore their identities, build skills, contribute to their communities, and develop a larger sense of purpose beyond the pursuit of individual gain.[53] For young people, the new Edward M. Kennedy Serve America Act (PL 111-13) increases the numbers of slots in AmeriCorps programs and adds several new corps and fellowships. It also increases the education award and adds flexibility in how young people can get engaged in service and balance service with their other responsibilities. Finally, it targets the needs of low-income communities and prioritizes the inclusion of marginalized youth.[54]

Targeting marginalized youth is especially important because research has consistently shown that youth from disadvantaged backgrounds have few opportunities to gain civic skills and be recruited into civic action. They are much less likely to have parents who participate in community organizations; to have peers who are incorporated into mainstream institutions; to live in neighborhoods that are safe and include opportunities to be involved in civic life; and to attend schools that have strong civic programming, teachers, counselors, and parent participation.[55] National service can serve as an important bridge to jobs, not only in building job-related skills and experience, but also in fostering connections to adult mentors, social networks, and organizations.

The third institution, the military, also serves many young people. For the majority of enlistees, the military is not a second-chance institution, but a first choice—though it too is in need of significant reform.[56] Still, the military, like four-year residential colleges and universities, is designed to shape the futures of young adults by providing a setting in which they can successfully live, work, and learn. By coupling expectations and demands with guidance, mentoring, and other resources, military service helps young adults acquire skills and fosters a sense of competence, like national service programs, it also provides a bridge from school to higher education or the labor force by providing tuition credits, loan forgiveness, financial stipends, access to jobs, or health insurance and other benefits.

By strengthening community colleges, service learning programs, and military service, the nation can establish clearer and more viable paths into adulthood for those who are not college bound and engage these young people positively in social institutions. College is not the only route to a successful adulthood, but alternatives are few and must be improved. Although youth with a bachelor's degree clearly have multiple advantages, the "college for all" mentality does a disservice to many young adults who simply do not have the intellectual, motivational, and economic resources to complete a four-year (or more) program of higher education.

These are but a few examples of the existing institutions that must be reformed or buttressed in response to the longer and more complex transition to adulthood today. And because this new, lengthened transition is not a passing phenomenon and is likely to grow yet more complicated, it may be necessary to create new institutions, especially ones that can better support middle- and working-class families alongside populations that have traditionally been viewed as socially or economically disadvantaged. The inability to reform existing institutions and create new ones carries significant costs for young people, their families, and our society.

Although many policy makers in Washington are now focused on programs designed for the early years of a child's life (the critical "zero to three" years), it remains important to offer supports as youth make their way into adulthood. Without discounting the importance of services in infancy and early childhood, we stress that young adults make and take exceedingly consequential decisions and actions that carry strong and cumulative effects—on schooling, work, marriage, and parenthood—over the many decades of life ahead. Only by continuing or increasing investments in young people after the age of eighteen can policy makers implement the supports needed to make the road to adulthood less perilous.

THE GOOD WITH THE BAD

Much of the media attention and public debate on the subject of the changing transition to adulthood start from the assumption that something is wrong with young people today as they take longer to "grow up," that the "fault" is of their own doing. To counter that assumption, we have pointed to some of the large cultural, economic, and demographic forces that have altered the landscape of the early adult years and complicated young people's efforts to leave home, finish school, look for jobs, find partners, and start families.

We would be remiss, however, in not acknowledging that we see some benefits to the way this period of life is being shaken up and to the more varied pathways to adulthood that young people are adopting as a consequence. The rigid three-part model of life (education-work-retirement) through which men born in the first half of the past century marched lockstep, has loosened. So, too, have the family constraints known to those same cohorts of women.[57] Educational attainment has expanded dramatically, and a college education is now within reach for many. Many young people now have more time to build their skills and earn credentials, to pursue activities meant for personal growth, to experience multiple jobs, and to experiment in romantic relationships before they settle in.

As we have noted, the story of the changing transition to adulthood is not just one of privileged youth versus underprivileged youth—that is, those who have the luxury to use the early adult years for exploration versus those who have limited opportunities, inadequate personal resources, or fragile family circumstances. It is also a story of the middle class, which is increasingly losing institutional support at precisely the same time as it takes on the heavy burden of supporting young people in the face of dwindling public resources.

Of some things we can be certain. Little about education, work, and family life today comes close to what past generations have known. In some ways life is better, in some ways it is worse, but in most ways it is different. Societies have not yet become fully aware of, or begun fully to address, the ramifications of the longer and more varied transition into adult life. Social institutions, much like young people and their families, are without a clear script for a new era and need to be refashioned to better reflect the times. Finally, for most young people, whether by choice or by circumstance, adulthood no longer begins when adolescence ends.

Notes

1. See Hans-Peter Blossfeld and others, eds., *Globalization, Uncertainty, and Youth in Society* (New York Routledge, 2005); M. Corijn and Erik Klijzing, eds., *Transitions to Adulthood in Europe* (London: Kluwer Academic Publishers, 2001); Frank F. Furstenberg Jr., ed., "Early Adulthood in Cross-National Perspective," *Annals of the American Academy of Political and Social Science* (London: Sage, 2002); Anne H. Gauthier, ed., "Becoming a Young Adult: An International Perspective on the Transitions to Adulthood," *European Journal of Population* 23, nos. 3–4 (October 2007); Cynthia B. Lloyd, ed., *Growing Up Global* (Washington: National Academies Press, 2005); Richard A. Settersten Jr., Frank F Furstenberg Jr., and Rubén G. Rumbaut, eds., *On the Frontier of Adulthood: Theory, Research, and Public Policy* (University of Chicago Press, 2005).

2. For illustrations, see *On Your Own without a Net: The Transition to Adulthood for Vulnerable Populations*, edited by D. Wayne Osgood and others (University of Chicago Press, 2005).

3. For illustrations, see Richard A. Settersten Jr., "Social Policy and the Transition to Adulthood," in *On the Frontier of Adulthood*, edited by Settersten, Furstenberg, and Rumbaut (see note 1). Richard A. Settersten Jr., "Passages to Adulthood," *European Journal of Population* 23, nos. 3–4: 251–72.

4. Robert Frank, *Falling Behind: How Rising Inequality Harms the Middle Class* (University of California Press, 2007).

5. Information about the MacArthur Research Network on Transitions to Adulthood can be found at: www.transad.pop.upenn.edu.

6. Rubén G. Rumbaut and Golnaz Komaie, "Young Adults in the United States: A Mid-Decade Profile" (Philadelphia: MacArthur Network on Transitions to Adulthood, September 2007).

7. Ibid.

8. It is important to note, however, that the data source for the recent update differs from the continuous data source for the century-long view found in Figures 19.1 and 19.2. The 2007 data point comes from the American Community Survey of the U.S. Bureau of the Census, available through the Integrated Public Use Microdata Series (IPUMS), whereas the 1900–2000 data points come from the decennial Census, which is also available through IPUMS. Because the data sources are different, and because the leaps from 2000 to 2007 are in some cases rather large, we have not added the 2007 data point directly to the figure. Instead, we use the 2007 data source as a window into the contemporary context until the 2010 decennial Census data are available.

9. Rubén G. Rumbaut and Golnaz Komaie, "Immigration and Adult Transitions" *Future of Children* 20, no. 1 (2010), pp. 43–66.

10. See *On the Frontier of Adulthood*, edited by Settersten, Furstenberg, and Rumbaut (see note 1); see also Sheldon Danziger and Cecelia Rouse, eds., *The Price of Independence: The Economics of Early Adulthood* (New York: Russell Sage Foundation, 2007).

11. Frances K. Goldscheider and Calvin Goldscheider, "Moving Out and Marriage: What Do Young Adults Expect?" *American Sociological Review* 52 (April 1987): 278–85. Women in the 1930s also worked, largely to support their parents during the Depression and later to support the country in the war effort in the 1940s. With prosperity following the war, they would leave the workforce for homemaking. Their absence from the workforce in large numbers was once again a blip on the historical radar. Furthermore, African American women had always worked.

12. These early trends toward greater independence at the cusp of the twenties were similar for black men and women, with one exception. Black men and women were more often becoming parents (married or not).

13. For more information on this topic, see Michael Rosenthal, *The Age of Independence: Interracial Unions, Same-Sex Unions, and the Changing American Family* (Harvard University Press, 2007).

14. Lisa Barrow and Cecilia Rouse, "Does College Still Pay?" *Economist's Voice* 2, no. 4 (2005): 1–8.

15. National data show that between 85 and 93 percent of high school graduates plan to pursue college degrees, and all but 10 percent of them enroll in postsecondary education. See Charles Adelman, "The Toolbox Revisited: Paths to Degree Completion from High School through College" (Washington: U.S. Department of Education, Office of Educational Research and Improvement, 2006); U.S. Department of Education, National Center for Education Statistics, *The Condition of Education* 2004, NCES 98-013 (Washington: U.S. Government Printing Office,

2004). See also Barbara Schneider and David Stevenson, *The Ambitious Generation* (Yale University Press, 1999).

16. "Dropouts" are those who are not enrolled in school and who have not earned a high school diploma or equivalent credential, such as a GED. See the National Center for Education Statistics, *Digest of Education Statistics: 2007* (Washington: National Center for Education Statistics, 2008). Some dropouts will, of course, go on to receive a GED. See Dan Bloom, "Programs and Policies to Assist High School Dropouts in the Transition to Adulthood," *Future of Children* 20, no. 1 (2010): 89–108.

17. Fifty-eight percent of Hispanics, 55 percent of African Americans, and 51 percent of Native Americans graduate from high school. Gates Foundation, "Diplomas Count" (Seattle: Bill and Melinda Gates Foundation, 2008). The Gates method results in higher estimates.

18. Rumbaut and Komaie, "Young Adults in the United States" (see note 6).

19. Claudia Goldin, Lawrence F. Katz, and Ilyana Kuziemko, "The Homecoming of American College Women: The Reversal of the College Gender Gap," *Journal of Economic Perspectives* 20 (Fall 2006): 133–56. For women, gains in education were particularly dramatic in the final few decades of the past century. For example, the share of women completing college by age thirty-five quadrupled for those born between 1940 and 1975; for men, it rose by 50 percent.

20. Rumbaut and Komaie also emphasize that, for most adult transitions, the differences between native-born whites and blacks are often more narrow than the gap between Asians, on the upper end, and Hispanics, and especially Mexicans and Puerto Ricans, on the lower. This is especially true where educational attainment is concerned.

21. Rumbaut and Komaie, "Young Adults in the United States" (see note 6).

22. Sara Goldrick-Rab and Josipa Roksa, "A Federal Agenda for Promoting Student Success and Degree Completion" (Washington: Center for American Progress, 2008). Also, the methods of calculating dropout rates vary across studies, and therefore studies often arrive at slightly different figures.

23. U.S. Department of Education, National Center for Education Statistics, 2001 *Baccalaureate and Beyond Longitudinal Study* (Washington: NCES, 2002), table II.11.

24. See Thomas Brock, "Young Adults and Higher Education: Barriers and Breakthroughs to Success," *Future of Children* 20, no. 1 (2010): 109–32.

25. Maria Fitzpatrick and Sarah E. Turner, "Blurring the Boundary: Changes in Collegiate Participation and the Transition to Adulthood," in *The Price of Independence*, edited by Danziger and Rouse (see note 10).

26. The numbers are significantly underestimated because the tallies exclude those who are sent to prison. The reasons for the disparity between black and white young men are many, and include a very different set of advantages and blocked opportunities. While lack of education is a common obstacle for both white and black men who are struggling to get started in life, black men have the added burden of racism, greater social isolation in inner cities, and an all-too-tempting drug and gang trade that quickly fills the void of lost jobs.

27. Steven Raphael, "Early Incarceration Spells and the Transition to Adulthood," in *The Price of Independence*, edited by Danziger and Rouse (see note 10).

28. For example, Becky Pettit and Bruce Western, "Mass Imprisonment and the Life Course: Race and Class Inequality in U.S. Incarceration," *American Sociological Review* 69 (2004): 151–69.

29. Department of Justice, Bureau of Justice Statistics, "Prevalence of Imprisonment in the U.S. Population, 1974–2001," Special Report, August 2003, NCJ 197976.

30. Heather C. West and William J. Sabol, "Prison Inmates and Mid-Year 2008," Special Report, NCJ 225619, Department of Justice (Washington: Bureau of Justice Statistics, March 2009).

31. Blossfeld and others, eds., *Globalization, Uncertainty, and Youth in Society* (see note 1).

32. Of course, this difference also reflects the fact that education has also been inflated: a high school graduate was at a lower percentile in the educational distribution of the population in 2002 than in 1975.

33. Sheldon Danziger, "Earnings by Education for Young Workers, 1975 and 2002," Data Brief 17 (Philadelphia: MacArthur Network on Transitions to Adulthood, November 2004).

34. Ibid.

35. Rumbaut and Komaie, "Young Adults in the United States" (see note 6). In 2005, 14.9 percent of young adults aged eighteen to thirty-four were in poverty, by government standards. The

national poverty rate in 2005 was 12.6 percent. Women were more likely than men to live in poverty (17.7 percent versus 12.1 percent).

36. Ibid.

37. Andrew Cherlin, "American Marriage in the Early 21st Century," *Future of Children* 15, no. 2 (2005): 33–55. See also Frank Furstenberg, "On a New Schedule: Transitions to Adulthood and Family Change," *Future of Children* 20, no. 1 (2010): 67–87.

38. Ibid.

39. Ibid.

40. Suzanne Bianchi and Lynne Casper, "American Families," *Population Bulletin* (December 2000).

41. Wendy Manning, Monica Longmore, and Peggy Giordano, "The Changing Institution of Marriage: Adolescents' Expectations to Cohabit and Marry," Working Paper 2005–11 (Bowling Green, Ohio: Center for Family and Demographic Research, Bowling Green State University, 2005). These plans vary slightly by religion (far fewer from more religions backgrounds plan to live together), and by education. Among women aged twenty-two to forty-four in 2002, roughly 69 percent with a high school degree or less had ever lived together compared with 46 percent among college-educated women. U.S. Department of Health and Human Services, "Fertility, Family Planning, and the Health of U.S. Women: Data from the 2002 National Survey of Family Growth" (Hyattsville, M.D.: National Center for Health Statistics, 2006).

42. See Furstenberg, "On a New Schedule" (see note 37).

43. Centers for Disease Control, "Probability of First Marriage Disruption by Duration of Marriage and Wife's Age at Marriage," Advance Data 323 (Atlanta: CDC, May 31, 2001), table 3.

44. Rumbaut and Komaie, "Young Adults in the United States" (see note 6).

45. See Furstenberg, "On a New Schedule" (see note 37).

46. Jacob Hacker, *The Great Risk Shift* (Oxford University Press, 2006). For a cross-national description of different types of welfare states, see Karl Ulrich Mayer, "Whose Lives? How History, Societies and Institutions Define and Shape Life Courses," *Research in Human Development* 1, no. 3 (2003): 161–87. On welfare states and the transition to adulthood, see Settersten, "Social Policy and the Transition to Adulthood" (see note 3).

47. Robert Schoeni and Karen Ross, "Material Assistance from Families during the Transition to Adulthood," in *On the Frontier of Adulthood*, edited by Settersten, Furstenberg, and Rumbaut (see note 1). Adult children are financially supported by parents through their twenties. The network's study using 1988 data found that amounts drop off after age twenty-two, but even at age thirty, young adults received about $1,600 from their parents in the previous year. Data from the Youth Development Survey at the University of Minnesota also show that even at age twenty-nine to thirty, 13 percent of respondents received at least some economic support (covering living expenses) from their parents, a drop from 20 percent at age twenty-five to twenty-six, and 39 percent at age twenty-three to twenty-four (Jeylan Mortimer, personal communication). This general trend is echoed in new international evidence, which shows significant declines in economic self-sufficiency among youth in Belgium, Canada, Germany, Italy, the United Kingdom, and the United States from the mid-1980s through 2000. See Lisa Bell and others, "A Cross-National Survey of Trends in the Transition to Economic Independence," in *The Price of Independence*, edited by Danziger and Rouse (see note 10).

48. See Rumbaut and Komaie, "Immigration and Adult Transitions" (see note 9).

49. For American illustrations across a wide range of vulnerable populations, see *On Your Own without a Net*, edited by Osgood and others (see note 2). See also D. Wayne Osgood, E. Michael Foster, and Mark E. Courtney, "Vulnerable Populations and the Transition to Adulthood," *Future of Children* 20, no. 1 (2010): 209–29.

50. Peter Gosselin, *Hire Wire: The Precarious Financial Lives of American Families* (New York: Basic Books, 2009).

51. Jean Rhodes and Sarah Lowe, "Mentoring in Adolescence," in *Handbook of Adolescent Psychology*, edited by Richard Lerner and Lawrence Steinberg (Hoboken, N.J.: Wiley), 152–90.

52. Mark Granovetter, "The Strength of Weak Ties," *American Journal of Sociology* 78, no. 6 (1973): 1360–80.

53. See Constance Flanagan and Peter Levine, "Civic Engagement and the Transition to Adulthood," *Future of Children* 20, no. 1 (2010): 159–79. See also Constance Flanagan, Peter Levine, and Richard A. Settersten Jr., "Civic Engagement and the Changing Transition to Adulthood," Working Paper (Boston: Tufts University Center for Information and Research on Civic Learning and Engagement, 2009).

54. Ibid.

55. Ibid.

56. See Ryan Kelty, Meredith Kleykamp, and David Segal "The Military and the Transition to Adulthood," *Future of Children* 20, no. 1 (2010): 181–207.

57. Richard A. Settersten Jr., "The New Landscape of Adult Life," *Research in Human Development* 4, nos. 3–4: 239–52.

IV

Families in Society

Although social scientists have often emphasized the diversity of U.S. society in terms of ethnic groups, religion, social class, and geographic region, the concept of diversity had rarely been applied to the family. In the wake of the social upheavals of the 1960s and 1970s, middle-class "mainstream" attitudes toward women's roles, sexuality, and family living arrangements were transformed. In fact, there is now a tendency to go to the other extreme and overstate how much family patterns have changed.

The selections in this part of the book discuss not only diversity in families, but also the reality that families are embedded in and sensitive to changes in the social structure and economics of the U.S. life. The Great Recession of 2008 hit American families hard because of layoffs, pay cuts, home foreclosures, lost pensions, and investments. But economic pressures on families have been increasing since the mid-1970s and have done as much as if not more than feminism to draw women into the paid workforce.

What really does happen in the family as women and men share the role of the family breadwinner? Arlie Hochschild and Anne Machung take a close look at the emotional dynamics inside the family when both parents work full time and the "second shift"—the work of caring for children and maintaining the home—is not shared equitably.

The selection from their book portrays a painful dilemma common to many couples in their study: The men saw themselves as living up to the idea of equal marriage; they were doing more work around the house than their fathers had ever done and more than they thought other men were doing.

But women, whose lives were very different from their own mothers', saw their husbands' contributions as falling far short of true equality. They resented having to carry more than their share of the "second shift," yet they stifled their angry feelings in order to preserve their marriages. Still, this strategy took its toll on love and intimacy.

Despite the great changes in women's lives and the rise of the two-earner family, most workplaces still adhere to the old model of the ideal worker as someone without responsibilities outside the job. This means someone who can work long hours, be available for meetings or business trips with little or no notice. This lack of flexibility in the workplace is one source of what has been called the "the opt-out revolution"—professional women supposedly leaving the workplace in droves to become full-time mothers. Pamela Stone's research was aimed at understanding the reality behind the rhetoric.

Are professional women really choosing to "opt out"? Are they really trying to return to the "feminine mystique" model of the family? Stone found a more complicated reality. Rather than "choosing" to become full-time homemakers, she discovered that these women actually faced a "choice gap": The kind of work-and-family balance they really wanted was simply not available to them. Instead, they were caught between the demands of "intensive mothering"—the new and higher standards of middle-class childrearing—and the demands of today's high-pressure workplaces. Stone concludes that the opting-out notion is a myth that harms not just women, but society. Employers need the skills of high-achieving women, but they have created toxic work environments that are incompatible with family life.

Of course, it's not only professionals facing the pressures of the new economy. How do less affluent working parents, and especially working mothers, cope with the conflicting demands of family and workplace responsibilities? What obstacles do they face? In her article here, Joan Williams shows that these workers face special hurdles.

While professional and managerial employees often have some degree of flexibility to take care of family matters, many working-class parents are literally "one sick child away from being fired." A parent can be fired or disciplined for refusing overtime, or for coming in a few minutes late after spending a night caring for a baby. Even calling home during work hours—a right that professionals take for granted—can get an ordinary worker fired.

American parents lack the kinds of family support policies that parents in other postindustrial societies take for granted—high quality, affordable childcare, paid maternity and sick leave, and job flexibility. The lack of such policies threatens the jobs of fathers as well as mothers.

The effects of economic insecurity were already clear long before the Great Recession. Lillian Rubin's study of working-class families in the 1990s found that downsizing, restructuring, and reengineering were becoming too familiar and even terrifying to the people she interviewed.

Two decades earlier, Rubin carried out a similar study of working-class families. She found then that while these families were never entirely secure, back in the 1970s they felt they had a grasp of the American dream. Most owned their own homes, and expected that their children would do as well or even better.

In a more recent study, the people Rubin interviewed sensed that something had gone very wrong in the country. Thirty-five percent of the men in the study were either unemployed at the time or had experienced bouts of unemployment. Parents and adult children had given up hope of upward mobility, or even the hope that the children could own homes comparable to the ones they had grown up in. The families, particularly the men, were angry, but perplexed about who or what to blame for their economic decline—the government, high taxes, immigrants, minorities, working women.

Not even the solid middle class is immune from the stresses of the current economy. Before proceeding, a word about what we talk about when we talk about the "middle class." It's a elusive term. Sociologists have disagreed about the definition of "class" in general, and of "middle class" in particular.

Some scholars define middle class literally as the exact middle of the income distribution—the median. Most recently, in practice, researchers, define middle class as having a college degree.

No matter how we define the term, the middle class has been losing ground economically in recent decades. The recession that began in 2008 may be officially over, but for most families good jobs and steady work are hard to find. Income inequality has soared, with the very rich—the 1 percent—pulling away from everyone else. As the article by Arlene Skolnick shows, economic insecurity has become pervasive up and down the income scale, except at the very top. Middle class and even affluent families are leading precarious economic lives.

Not only is the secure job a thing of the past, but public and private safety nets have also been frayed. One barometer of middle-class economic distress is soaring rates of bankruptcy. American children are more likely to see their parents file for bankruptcy than for divorce. And the idea that Americans are spending themselves into financial ruin for luxuries they don't really need is wrong. Instead, the rising costs of housing, medical care, decent elementary schools, and college tuition have placed middle-class parents at greater risk than in earlier generations.

The next group of articles addresses family diversity along several dimensions—race, ethnicity, age, and sexual orientation. In recent years, family researchers have recognized that diversity is more complicated than previously thought. It's too simple to sort people into distinct ethnic or cultural categories—African Americans, Latinos, Asian Americans, European Americans, or gays. There is also great diversity within groups.

In his article, Ronald L. Taylor explores diversity among African American families. He recalls being troubled that the stereotypes of African Americans in the media as well as in social science did not reflect the families he knew growing up in a small southern city.

The dominant image of African American families remains the low-income, single-parent family living in a crime-ridden inner-city neighborhood. Yet only a quarter of African American families fit that description. All African Americans share a common history of slavery and segregation, and they still face discrimination in housing and employment. Taylor discusses the impact of these past and present features on African American family life.

Latino families are now emerging as America's largest "minority." They are even more diverse than other groups, as Maxine Baca Zinn and Barbara Wells show in their article. Mexican Americans are the largest group among Latinos and have been the most studied, but Puerto Ricans, Cubans, and Central and South Americans differ from those of Mexican background and among themselves. These differences are not only cultural, but also reflect the immigrants' social and economic statuses in their home countries as well as the reasons for and the timing of their departures for the United States.

In her reading here, Min Zhou examines the often difficult parent—child relations in today's Chinese immigrant families. The pattern of Chinese immigration to the United States was changed dramatically by the new immigration law passed by Congress in 1965. The law ended tight limits on Chinese immigration and allowed for family reunification.

As a result, Chinese communities shifted from being "bachelor" to family societies. The new Chinese immigrants are no longer mainly poor as was the older wave, and are more spread out in mainstream American society. As a result, there is more of a generation gap now. Young Chinese are freer to "become American" and to rebel against their parents' traditional ways. Many describe their homes as "pressure cookers," with conflicts over their parents' expectations of obedience to their parents' authority, and good grades at school. Parents typically view dating as a waste of time, and especially dangerous to the reputations of daughters. But the many Chinese community institutions, such as schools that teach the language and customs of China, help to resolve parent–child conflicts.

America's population is not only becoming more diverse ethnically, it is also "graying" as the aging population continues to grow. Ann Bookman and Delia Krimble discuss an important family issue that is less publically discussed than it should be. By 2030, people over 65 years of age are expected to grow to 20 percent of the American population. Caring for elders has always been a family matter, and usually assigned to women. But changes in work, family, the economy, and demography have greatly complicated caring for elders.

Most women are, of course, now in the paid workforce, largely because most families have come to need two incomes to make ends meet. Further, people are living to much older ages; across the twentieth century, the over 65-year-old population has increased elevenfold. But the trend in birth rates has been in the opposite direction, except during the baby-boom years after World War II. So, in general, there are fewer adult children to care for a growing number of elders.

Also, we have seen that in today's economy, the path from adolescence to adulthood has become longer and more uncertain. Thus, young adults need more support from their parents for much longer than in past decades, and they are disadvantaged if their parents are unable to help.

But middle-class families sandwiched between the needs of their children and their parents are stressed as well. Unable to afford the array of paid care services that richer families can provide their elders, they are not eligible for the public supports that help the poor. Bookman and Kimbrel conclude that we need a society friendlier to the aging, and friendlier to people at all stages of life.

In the final chapter, we look at several kinds of family trouble. First, we consider an issue that is rarely thought of as a family problem: the huge spike in the prison population in recent decades, due to the "war on drugs" and other get-tough-on-crime policies. The United States now locks up a higher proportion of its citizens than any other country in the world. People who commit violent crimes should go to prison, both as punishment and to protect the community, but about half of those now in prison for long sentences are not there for violent acts. As Jeremy Travis points out, prison places a huge burden on the families of prisoners, especially on relationships with partners and children. He also spells out the ripple effects that high rates of imprisonment have on poor and minority communities—for example, creating a shortage of marriageable men.

Travis partially answers the questions that Kathryn Edin and Maria Kefalas address in their article on poor unmarried young mothers. Why do they have babies when they know they will have to struggle to support them? Have they given up the marriage norm? When George W. Bush was in power, his administration funded efforts to promote marriage as a poverty policy, on the theory that if low-income people marry they will no longer be poor.

In contrast, Edin and Kefalas find that this kind of thinking is backward—their research shows that these women revere marriage, and about 70 percent will eventually marry. But in America's poor neighborhoods, plagued by joblessness, drug and alcohol abuse, as well as high rates of crime and imprisonment, a good man is hard to find. Edin and Kefalas conclude that the real cure for poverty and "too-early" motherhood is access to good jobs for both men and women.

Is family violence mostly violence against women? Or are women just as likely as men to assault their spouses? Should the legal system recognize a "battered husband syndrome"? There is a debate among researchers on this issue. Demie Kurz examines the evidence, and concludes that the terms like "family violence" or "spouse abuse" are misleading.

She finds that when some researchers claim women are as violent as men, they rely on questionnaires where equal numbers of men and women confess they have hit or assaulted their spouse. But Kurz argues that real-life data from the criminal justice system and hospitals, as well as interviews with victims of battering and batterers show a different picture: Women are overwhelmingly the victims, and men the batterers.

Women's violence against men is mostly defensive, and not as severe as men's. Further, Kurz links men's violence to cultural assumptions about masculinity; men are most likely to be violent when their control and dominance over their partners is challenged.

Work and Family Life

The Second Shift: Working Parents and the Revolution at Home

Arlie Hochschild, with Anne Machung

Between 8:05 A.M. and 6:05 P.M., both Nancy and Evan are away from home, working a "first shift" at full-time jobs. The rest of the time they deal with the varied tasks of the second shift: shopping, cooking, paying bills; taking care of the car, the garden, and yard; keeping harmony with Evan's mother who drops over quite a bit, "concerned" about Joey, with neighbors, their voluble babysitter, and each other. And Nancy's talk reflects a series of second-shift thoughts: "We're out of barbecue sauce. . . . Joey needs a Halloween costume. . . . The car needs a wash. . . ." and so on. She reflects a certain "second-shift sensibility," a continual attunement to the task of striking and restriking the right emotional balance between child, spouse, home, and outside job.

When I first met the Holts, Nancy was absorbing far more of the second shift than Evan. She said she was doing 80 percent of the housework and 90 percent of the childcare. Evan said she did 60 percent of the housework, 70 percent of the childcare. Joey said, "I vacuum the rug, and fold the dinner napkins," finally concluding, "Mom and I do it all." A neighbor agreed with Joey. Clearly, between Nancy and Evan, there was a "leisure gap": Evan had more than Nancy. I asked both of them, in separate interviews, to explain to me how they had dealt with housework and childcare since their marriage began.

One evening in the fifth year of their marriage, Nancy told me, when Joey was two months old and almost four years before I met the Holts, she first seriously raised the issue with Evan. "I told him: 'Look, Evan, it's not working. I do the housework, I take the major care of Joey, *and* I work a full-time job. I get pissed. This is *your* house too. Joey is *your* child too. It's not all *my* job to care for them.' When I cooled down I put to him, 'Look, how about this: I'll cook Mondays, Wednesdays, and Fridays. You cook Tuesdays, Thursdays, and, Saturdays. And we'll share or go out Sundays.'"

According to Nancy, Evan said he didn't like "rigid schedules." He said he didn't necessarily agree with her standards of housekeeping, and didn't like that standard "imposed" on him, especially if she was "sluffing off" tasks on him which from time to time he felt she was. But he went along with the idea in principle. Nancy said the first week of the new plan went as follows: On Monday, she cooked. For Tuesday, Evan planned a meal that required shopping for a few ingredients, but on his way home he forgot to shop for them. He came home, saw nothing he could use in the refrigerator or in the cupboard and suggested to Nancy that they go out for Chinese food. On Wednesday, Nancy cooked. On Thursday morning, Nancy reminded Evan, "Tonight it's your turn." That night Evan fixed hamburgers and french fries and Nancy was quick to praise him. On Friday, Nancy cooked. On Saturday, Evan forgot again.

As this pattern continued, Nancy's reminders became sharper. The sharper they became, the more actively Evan forgot—perhaps anticipating even sharper reprimands if he resisted more directly. This cycle of passive refusal followed by disappointment and anger gradually tightened, and before long the struggle had spread to the task of doing the laundry. Nancy said it was only fair that Evan share the laundry. He agreed in principle, but anxious that Evan would not share, Nancy wanted a clear, explicit agreement. "You ought to wash and fold every other load," she had told him. Evan experienced this "plan" as a yoke around his neck. On many weekdays, at this point, a huge pile of laundry sat like a disheveled guest on the living-room couch.

In her frustration, Nancy began to make subtle emotional jabs at Evan. "I don't know *what's* for dinner," she would say with a sigh. Or "I can't cook now, I've got to deal with this pile of laundry." She tensed at the slightest criticism about household disorder; if Evan wouldn't do the housework, he had absolutely *no* right to criticize how she did it. She would burst out angrily at Evan. She recalled telling him: "After work *my* feet are just as tired as *your* feet. I'm just as wound up as you are. I come home. I cook dinner. I wash and I clean. Here we are, planning a second child, and I can't cope with the one we have."

About two years after I first began visiting the Holts, I began to see the problem in a certain light: as a conflict between their two gender ideologies. Nancy wanted to be the sort of woman who was needed and appreciated both at home and at work—like Lacey, she told me, on the television show "Cagney and Lacey." She wanted Evan to appreciate her for being a caring social worker, a committed wife, and a wonderful mother. But she cared just as much that she be able to appreciate *Evan* for what *he* contributed at home, not just for how he supported the family. She would feel proud to explain to women friends that she was married to one of these rare "new men."

A gender ideology is often rooted in early experience, and fueled by motives formed early on and such motives can often be traced to some cautionary tale in early life. So it was for Nancy. Nancy described her mother:

> My mom was wonderful, a real aristocrat, but she was also terribly depressed being a housewife. My dad treated her like a doormat. She didn't have any self-confidence. And growing up, I can remember her being really depressed. I grew up bound and determined not to be like her and not to marry a man like my father. As long as Evan doesn't do the housework, I feel it means he's going to be like my father—coming home, putting his feet up, and hollering at my mom to serve him. That's my biggest fear. I've had *bad* dreams about that.

Nancy thought that women friends her age, also in traditional marriages, had come to similarly bad ends. She described a high school friend: "Martha barely made it through City College. She had no interest in learning anything. She spent nine years trailing around behind her husband [a salesman]. It's a miserable marriage. She hand washes all his shirts. The high point of her life was when she was eighteen and the two of us were running around Miami Beach in a Mustang convertible. She's gained seventy pounds and she hates her life." To Nancy, Martha was a younger version of her mother, depressed, lacking in self-esteem, a cautionary tale whose moral was "if you want to be happy, develop a career and get your husband to share at home." Asking Evan to help again and again felt like "hard work" but it was essential to establishing her role as a career woman.

For his own reasons, Evan imagined things very differently. He loved Nancy and if Nancy loved being a social worker, he was happy and proud to support her in it. He knew that because she took her caseload so seriously, it was draining work. But at the same time, he did not see why, just because she chose this demanding career, *he* had to change *his own* life. Why should her personal decision to work outside the home require him to do more inside it? Nancy earned about two-thirds as much as Evan, and her salary was a big help, but as Nancy confided, "If push came to shove, we could do without it." Nancy was a social worker because she loved it. Doing daily chores at home was thankless work, certainly not something Evan needed her to appreciate about him. Equality in the second shift meant a loss in his standard of living, and despite all the high-flown talk, he felt he hadn't *really* bargained for it. He was happy to help Nancy at home if she needed help; that was fine. That was only decent. But it was too risky a matter "committing" himself to sharing.

Two other beliefs probably fueled his resistance as well. The first was his suspicion that if he shared the second shift with Nancy, she would "dominate him." Nancy would ask him to do this, ask him to do that. It felt to Evan as if Nancy had won so many small victories that he had to draw the line somewhere. Nancy had a declarative personality; and as Nancy said, "Evan's mother sat me down and told me once that I was too forceful, that Evan needed to take more authority." Both Nancy and Evan agreed that Evan's sense of career and self was in fact shakier than Nancy's. He had been unemployed. She never had. He had had some bouts of drinking in the past. Drinking was foreign to her. Evan thought that sharing housework would upset a certain balance of power that felt culturally "right." He held the purse strings and made the major decisions about large purchases (like their house) because he "knew more about finances" and because he'd chipped in more inheritance than she when they married. His job difficulties had lowered his self-respect, and now as a couple they had achieved some ineffable "balance"—tilted in his favor, she thought—which, if corrected to equalize the burden of chores, would result in his giving in "too much." A certain driving anxiety behind Nancy's strategy of actively renegotiating roles had made Evan see agreement as "giving in." When he wasn't feeling good about work, he dreaded the idea of being under his wife's thumb at home.

Underneath these feelings, Evan perhaps also feared that Nancy was avoiding taking care of *him*. His own mother, a mild-mannered alcoholic, had by imperceptible steps phased herself out of a mother's role, leaving him very much on his own. Perhaps a personal motive to prevent that happening in his marriage—a guess on my part, and unarticulated on his—underlay his strategies of passive resistance. And he wasn't altogether wrong to fear this. Meanwhile, he felt he was "offering" Nancy the chance to stay home, or cut back her hours, and that she was refusing his "gift;" while Nancy felt that, given her feelings about work, this offer was hardly a gift.

In the sixth year of her marriage, when Nancy again intensified her pressure on Evan to commit himself to equal sharing, Evan recalled saying, "Nancy, why don't you cut back to half time, that way you can fit everything in." At first Nancy was baffled: "We've been married all this time, and you *still* don't get it. Work is important to me. I worked *hard* to get my MSW. Why *should* I give it up?" Nancy also explained to Evan and later to me, "I think my degree and my job has been my way of reassuring myself that I won't end up like my mother." Yet she'd received little emotional support in getting her degree from either her parents or in-laws. (Her mother had avoided asking about her thesis, and her in-laws, though invited, did not attend her graduation, later claiming they'd never been invited.)

In addition, Nancy was more excited about seeing her elderly clients in tenderloin hotels than Evan was about selling couches to furniture salesmen with greased-back hair. Why shouldn't Evan make as many compromises with his career ambitions and his leisure as she'd made with hers? She couldn't see it Evan's way, and Evan couldn't see it hers.

In years of alternating struggle and compromise, Nancy had seen only fleeting mirages of cooperation, visions that appeared when she got sick or withdrew and disappeared when she got better or came forward.

After seven years of loving marriage, Nancy and Evan had finally come to a terrible impasse. Their emotional standard of living had drastically declined, they began to snap at each other, to criticize, to carp. Each felt taken advantage of. Evan, because his offering of a good arrangement was deemed unacceptable, and Nancy, because Evan wouldn't do what she deeply felt was "fair."

This struggle made its way into their sexual life—first through Nancy directly, and then through Joey. Nancy had always disdained any form of feminine wiliness or manipulation. Her family saw her as "a flaming feminist" and that was how she saw herself. As such, she felt above the underhanded ways traditional women used to get around men. She mused, "When I was a teenager, I vowed I would *never* use sex to get my way with a man. It is not self-respecting; it's demeaning. But when Evan refused to carry his load at home, I did, I used sex, I said, 'Look, Evan, I would not be this exhausted and asexual every night if I didn't have so much to face every morning.'" She felt reduced to an old "strategy," and her modern ideas made her ashamed of it. At the same time, she'd run out of other, modern ways.

The idea of a separation arose, and they became frightened. Nancy looked at the deteriorating marriages and fresh divorces of couples with young children around them. One unhappy husband they knew had become so uninvolved in family life (they didn't know whether his unhappiness made him uninvolved, or whether his lack of involvement had caused his wife to be unhappy) that his wife left him. In another case, Nancy felt the wife had "nagged" her husband so much that he abandoned her for another woman. In both cases, the couple was less happy after the divorce than before, and both wives took the children and struggled desperately to survive financially. Nancy took stock. She asked herself, "Why wreck a marriage over a dirty frying pan?" Is it really worth it?

UPSTAIRS-DOWNSTAIRS: A FAMILY MYTH AS "SOLUTION"

Not long after this crisis in the Holts' marriage, there was a dramatic lessening of tension over the issue of the second shift. It was as if the issue was closed. Evan had won. Nancy would do the second shift. Evan expressed vague guilt but beyond that he had nothing to say. Nancy had wearied of continually raising the topic, wearied of the lack of resolution. Now in the exhaustion of defeat, she wanted the struggle to be over too. Evan was "so good" in *other* ways, why debilitate their marriage by continual quarreling. Besides, she told me, "Women always adjust more, don't they?"

One day, when I asked Nancy to tell me who did which tasks from a long list household chores, she interrupted me with a broad wave of her hand and said, "I do the upstairs, Evan does the downstairs." What does that mean? I asked. Matter-of-factly, she explained that the upstairs included the living room, the dining room, the kitchen, two bedrooms, and two baths. The downstairs meant the garage, a place for storage and hobbies—Evan's hobbies. She explained this was a "sharing" arrangement, without humor or irony—just as Evan did later. Both said they had agreed it was the best solution to their dispute. Evan would take care of the car, the garage, and Max, the family dog. As Nancy explained, "the dog is all Evan's problem. I don't have to deal with the dog." Nancy took care of the rest.

For purposes of accommodating the second shift, then, the Holts' garage was elevated to the full moral and practical equivalent of the rest of the home. For Nancy and Evan, "upstairs and downstairs," "inside and outside," were vaguely described like "half and half," a fair division of labor based on a natural division of their house.

The Holts presented their upstairs-downstairs agreement as a perfectly equitable solution to a problem they "once had." This belief is what we might call "family myth," even a modest delusional system. Why did they believe it? I think they believed it because they needed to believe it, because it solved a terrible problem. It allowed Nancy to continue thinking of herself as the sort of woman whose husband didn't abuse her—a self-conception that mattered a great deal to her. And it avoided the hard truth that, in his stolid, passive way, Evan had refused to share. It avoided the truth, too, that in their showdown, Nancy was more afraid of divorce than Evan was. This outer cover to their family life, this family myth was jointly devised. It was an attempt to agree that there was no conflict over the second shift, no tension between their versions of manhood and womanhood, that the powerful crisis that had arisen was temporary and minor.

The wish to avoid such a conflict is natural enough. But their avoidance tacitly supported by the surrounding culture, especially the image of the woman with the flying hair. After all, this admirable woman also proudly does the "upstairs" each day without a husband's help and without conflict.

After Nancy and Evan reached their upstairs-downstairs agreement, the confrontations ended. They were nearly forgotten. Yet, as she described daily life months after the agreement, Nancy's resentment still seemed alive and well. For example, she said:

> Evan and I eventually divided the labor so that I do the upstairs and Evan does the downstairs and the dog. So the dog is my husband's problem. But when I was getting the dog outside and getting Joey ready for childcare, and cleaning up the mess, feeding the cat, and getting the lunches together, and having my son wipe his nose on my outfit so I would have to change—then I was pissed! I felt that I was doing *everything*. All Evan was doing was getting up, having coffee, reading the paper, saying, "Well, I have to go now," and often forgetting the lunch I'd bothered to make.

She also mentioned that she had fallen into the habit of putting Joey to bed in a certain way: he asked to be swung around by the arms, dropped on the bed and nuzzled and hugged, whispered to in his ear. Joey waited for her attention. He didn't go to sleep without it. But, increasingly, when Nancy tried it at eight and nine, the ritual didn't put Joey to sleep. On the contrary, it woke him up. It was then that Joey began to say he could only go to sleep in his parents' bed, that he began to sleep in their bed and to encroach on their sexual life.

Near the end of my visits, it struck me that Nancy was putting Joey to bed in an "exciting" way, later and later at night, in order to tell Evan something important: "You win, I'll go on doing all the work at home, but I'm angry about it and I'll make you pay." Evan had won the battle but lost the war. According to the family myth, all was well: the struggle had been resolved by the upstairs-downstairs agreement. But suppressed in one area of their marriage, this struggle lived on in another—as Joey's Problem, and as theirs.

NANCY'S "PROGRAM" TO SUSTAIN THE MYTH

There was a moment, I believe, when Nancy seemed to *decide* to give up on this one. She decided to try not to resent Evan. Whether or not other women face a moment just like this, at the very least they face the need to deal with all the feelings that naturally arise from a clash between a treasured ideal and an incompatible reality. In the age of a stalled revolution, it is a problem a great many women face.

Emotionally, Nancy's compromise from time to time slipped; she would forget and grow resentful again. Her new resolve needed maintenance. Only half aware that she was doing so, Nancy went to extraordinary lengths to maintain it. She could tell me now, a year or so after her "decision," in a matter-of-fact and noncritical way: "Evan likes to come home to a hot meal. He doesn't like to clear the table. He doesn't like to do the dishes. He likes to go watch TV. He likes to play with his son when he feels like it and not feel like he should be with him more." She seemed resigned.

Everything was "fine." But it had taken an extraordinary amount of complex "emotion work"—the work of *trying* to feel the "right" feeling, the feeling she wanted to feel—to make and keep everything "fine." Across the nation at this particular time in history, this emotion work is often all that stands between the stalled revolution on the one hand, and broken marriages on the other.

HOW MANY HOLTS?

In one key way the Holts were typical of the vast majority of two-job couples: their family life had become the shock absorber for a stalled revolution whose origin lay far outside it—in economic and cultural trends that bear very differently on men and women. Nancy was reading books, newspaper articles, and watching TV programs on the changing role of women. Evan wasn't. Nancy felt benefited by these changes; Evan didn't. In her ideals and in reality, Nancy was more different from her mother than Evan was from his father, for the culture and economy were in general pressing change faster upon women like her than upon men like Evan. Nancy had gone to college; her mother hadn't. Nancy had a professional job; her mother never had. Nancy had the idea that she should be equal with her husband; her mother hadn't been much exposed to that idea in her day. Nancy felt she should share the job of earning money, and that Evan should share the work at home; her mother hadn't imagined that was possible. Evan went to college, his father (and the other boys in his family, though not the girls) had gone too. Work was important to Evan's identity as a man as it had been for his father before him. Indeed, Evan felt the same way about family roles as his father had felt in his day. The new job opportunities and the feminist movement of the 1960s and '70s had transformed Nancy but left Evan pretty much the same. And the friction created by this difference between them moved to the issue of second shift as metal to a magnet. By the end, Evan did less housework and childcare than most men married to working women—but not much less. Evan and Nancy were also typical of nearly 40 percent of the marriages studied in their clash of gender ideologies and their corresponding difference is a notion about what constituted a "sacrifice" and what did not. By far the most common form of mismatch was like that between Nancy, an egalitarian, and Evan, a transitional.

But for most couples, the tensions between strategies did not move so quickly and powerfully to issues of housework and childcare. Nancy pushed harder than most women to get her husband to share the work at home, and she also lost more overwhelmingly than the few other women who fought that hard. Evan pursued his strategy of passive resistance with more quiet tenacity then most men, and he allowed himself to become far more marginal to his son's life than most other fathers. The myth of the Holts' "equal" arrangement seems slightly more odd than other family myths that encapsulated equally powerful conflicts.

Beyond their upstairs-downstairs myth, the Holts tell us a great deal about the subtle ways a couple can encapsulate the tension caused by a struggle over the second shift without resolving the problem or divorcing. Like Nancy Holt, many women struggle to avoid, suppress, obscure, or mystify a frightening conflict over the second shift. They do not struggle like this because they start off wanting to, or because such struggle is inevitable or because women inevitably lose, but because they are forced to choose between equality and marriage. And they choose marriage. When asked about "ideal" relations between men and women in general, about what they want for their daughters or about what "ideally" they'd like in their own marriage, most working mothers "wished" their men would share the work at home.

But many "wish" it instead of "want" it. Other goals—like keeping peace at home—come first. Nancy Holt did some extraordinary behind-the-scenes emotion work to prevent her ideals from clashing with her marriage. In the end she had confined and miniaturized her ideas of equality successfully enough to do two things she badly wanted to do: feel like a feminist, and live at peace with a man who was not. Her program had "worked." Evan won on the reality of the situation, because Nancy did the second shift. Nancy won on the cover story, they would talk about it as if they shared.

Nancy wore the upstairs-downstairs myth as an ideological cloak to protect her from the contradictions in her marriage and from the cultural and economic forces that press upon it. Nancy and Evan Holt were caught on opposite sides of the gender revolution occurring all around them. Through the 1960s, 1970s, and 1980s masses of women entered the public world of work—but went only so far up the occupational ladder. They tried for "equal" marriages, but got only so far in achieving it. They married men who liked them to work at the office and who wouldn't share the extra month a year at home. When confusion about the identity of the working woman created a cultural vacuum in the 1970s and 1980s, the image of the supermom quietly glided in. She made the "stall" seem normal and happy. But beneath the happy image of the woman with the flying hair are modern marriages like the Holts', reflecting intricate webs of tension, and the huge, hidden emotional cost to women, men, and children of having to "manage" inequality. Yet on the surface, all we might see would be Nancy Holt bounding confidently out the door at 8:30 A.M. briefcase in one hand, Joey in the other. All we might hear would be Nancy's and Evan's talk about their marriage as happy, normal, even "equal"—because equality was so important to Nancy.

■ READING 21

The Rhetoric and Reality of "Opting Out"

Pamela Stone

As a senior publicist at a well-known media conglomerate, Regina Donofrio had one of the most coveted, glamorous jobs in New York. A typical workday might include riding around Manhattan in limousines with movie stars. She loved her job, had worked "a long time," and felt "comfortable" in it. So when the time came to return to work after the birth of her first child, Regina did not hesitate. "I decided I would go back to work, because the job was great, basically," she told me. Before long, Regina found herself "crying on the train," torn between wanting to be at home with her baby and wanting to keep up her successful, exciting career. She started feeling she was never in the right place at the right time. "When I was at work, I should have been at home. When I was at home, I felt guilty because I had left work a little early to see the baby, and I had maybe left some things undone." Ever resourceful, she devised a detailed job-share plan with a colleague who was also a first-time mother. But their proposal was denied. Instead, Regina's employer offered her more money to stay and work full time, and Regina left in a huff, incensed that her employer, with whom she had a great track record, would block her from doing what she wanted to do—continue with her career and combine it with family.

Despite mainstream media portrayals to the contrary, Regina's reasons for quitting are all too typical of what I found in my study of high-achieving, former professionals who are now at-home moms. While Regina did, in fact, feel a strong urge to care for her baby, she decided to quit because of an inflexible workplace, not because of her attraction to home and hearth. She gave up her high-powered career as a last resort, after agonized soul-searching and exhausting her options. Her story differs from the popular depiction of similar, high-achieving, professional women who have headed home. Media stories typically frame these women's decisions as choices about family and see them as symptomatic of a kind of sea-change among the daughters of the feminist revolution, a return to traditionalism and the resurgence of a new feminine mystique. The quintessential article in this prevailing story line (and the one that gave the phenomenon its name) was published in 2003 by the *New York Times*'s work-life columnist, Lisa Belkin, titled "The Opt-Out Revolution." "Opting out" is redolent with overtones of lifestyle preference and discretion, but Regina's experience counters this characterization; her decision to quit was not a lifestyle preference, nor a change in aspirations, nor a desire to return to the 1950s family. Regina did not "opt out" of the workplace because she chose to, but for precisely the opposite reason: because she had no real options and no choice.

High-achieving women's reasons for heading home are multilayered and complex, and generally counter the common view that they quit because of babies and family. This is what I found when I spoke to scores of women like Regina: highly educated, affluent, mostly white, married women with children who had previously worked as professionals or managers and whose husbands could support their being at home. Although many of these women speak the language of choice and privilege, their stories reveal a choice gap—the disjuncture between the rhetoric of choice and the reality of constraints like those Regina encountered. The choice gap reflects the extent to which high achieving women like Regina are caught in a double bind: spiraling parenting (read "mothering") demands on the home front collide with the increasing pace of work in the gilded cages of elite professions.

SOME SKEPTICISM

I approached these interviews with skepticism tempered by a recognition that there might be some truth to the popular image of the "new traditionalist." But to get beyond the predictable "family" explanation and the media drumbeat of choice, I thought it was important to interview women in some depth and to study women who, at least theoretically, could exercise choice. I also gave women full anonymity, creating fictitious names for them so they would speak to me as candidly as possible. The women I interviewed had outstanding educational credentials; more than half had graduate degrees in business, law, medicine, and other professions, and had once had thriving careers in which they had worked about a decade. By any measure, these were work-committed women, with strong reasons to continue with the careers in which they had invested so much. Moreover, they were in high-status fields where they had more control over their jobs and enjoyed (at least relative to workers in other fields) more family-friendly benefits.

While these women had compelling reasons to stay on the job, they also had the option not to, by virtue of their own past earnings and because their husbands were also high earners. To counter the potential criticism that they were quitting or being let go because they were not competent or up to the job, I expressly chose to study women with impeccable educational credentials, women who had navigated elite environments with competitive entry requirements. To ensure a diversity of perspectives, I conducted extensive, in-depth interviews with 54 women in a variety of professions—law, medicine, business, publishing, management consulting, nonprofit administration, and the like—living in major metropolitan areas across the country, roughly half of them in their 30s, half in their 40s.

To be sure, at-home moms are a distinct minority. Despite the many articles proclaiming a trend of women going home, among the demographic of media scrutiny—white, college-educated women, 30–54 years old—fully 84 percent are now in the workforce, up from 82 percent 20 years ago. And the much-discussed dip in the labor-force participation of mothers of young children, while real, appears to be largely a function of an economic downturn, which depresses employment for all workers.

Nevertheless, these women are important to study. Elite, educated, high-achieving women have historically been cultural arbiters, defining what is acceptable for all women in their work and family roles. This group's entrance into high-status, formerly male professions has been crucial to advancing gender parity and narrowing the wage gap, which stubbornly persists to this day. At home, moreover, they are rendered silent and invisible, so that it is easy to project and speculate about them. We can see in them whatever we want to, and perhaps that is why they have been the subject of endless speculation—about mommy wars, a return to traditionalism, and the like. While they do not represent all women, elite women's experiences provide a glimpse into the work-family negotiations that all women face. And their stories lead us to ask, "If the most privileged women of society cannot successfully combine work and family, who can?"

MOTHERHOOD PULLS

When Regina initially went back to work, she had "no clue" that she would feel so torn. She advises women not to set "too much in stone," because "you just don't know, when a human being comes out of your body, how you're going to feel." For some women, the pull of children was immediate and strong. Lauren Quattrone, a lawyer, found herself "absolutely besotted with this baby. . . . I realized that I just couldn't bear to leave him." Women such as Lauren tended to quit fairly soon after their first child was born. For others, like Diane Childs, formerly a nonprofit executive, the desire to be home with the kids came later. "I felt that it was easy to leave a baby for twelve hours a day. That I could do. But to leave a six-year-old, I just thought, was a whole different thing."

But none of these women made their decisions to quit in a vacuum. In fact, they did so during a cultural moment when norms and practices for parents—mothers—are very demanding. These women realized they would rear children very differently from the way their own mothers raised them, feeling an external, almost competitive pressure to do so. Middle- and upper-middle-class women tend to be particularly mindful of expert advice, and these women were acutely aware of a well-documented intensification in raising children, which sociologist Sharon Hays calls an "ideology of intensive mothering." This cultural imperative, felt by women of all kinds, "advises mothers to expend a tremendous amount of time, energy and money in raising their children."

A corollary is what Annette Lareau terms "concerted cultivation," a nonstop pace of organized activities scheduled by parents for school-age children. Among the women I spoke to, some, like Diane, felt the urgency of "concerted cultivation" and reevaluated their childcare as the more sophisticated needs of their older children superseded the simpler, more straightforward babysitting and physical care required for younger children. Marina Isherwood, a former executive in the health care industry, with children in the second and fourth grades, became convinced that caregivers could not replace her own parental influence:

> There isn't a substitute, no matter how good the childcare. When they're little, the fact that someone else is doing the stuff with them is fine. It wasn't the part that I loved anyway. But when they start asking you questions about values, you don't want your babysitter telling them. . . . Our children come home, and they have all this homework to do, and piano lessons and this and this, and it's all a complicated schedule. And, yes, you could get an au pair to do that, to balance it all, but they're not going to necessarily teach you how to think about math. Or help you come up with mnemonic devices to memorize all of the countries in Spain or whatever.

Because academic credentials were so important to these women's (and their husband's) career opportunities, formal schooling was a critical factor in their decisions to quit. For some, the premium they placed on education and values widened the gap between themselves and their less educated caregivers.

Depending on the woman, motherhood played a larger or smaller role in her decision whether and when to quit. Children were the main focus of women's caregiving, but other family members needed care as well, for which women felt responsible. About 10 percent of the women spoke of significant elder-care responsibilities, the need for which was especially unpredictable. This type of caregiving and mothering made up half of the family/career double bind. More important, though, motherhood influenced women's decision to quit as they came to see the rhythms and values of the workplace as antagonistic to family life.

WORKPLACE PUSHES

On top of their demanding mothering regime, these women received mixed messages from both their husbands and their employers. Husbands offered emotional support to wives who were juggling career and family. Emily Mitchell, an accountant, described her marriage to a CPA as "a pretty equal relationship," but when his career became more demanding, requiring long hours and Saturdays at work, he saw the downside of egalitarianism:

> I think he never minded taking my daughter to the sitter, that was never an issue, and when he would come home, we have a pretty equal relationship on that stuff. But getting her up, getting her ready, getting himself ready to go into work, me coming home, getting her, getting her to bed, getting unwound from work, and then he would come home, we'd try to do something for dinner, and then there was always something else to do—laundry, cleaning, whatever—I think he was feeling too much on a treadmill.

But husbands did little to share family responsibilities, instead maintaining their own demanding careers full-speed ahead.

Similarly, many workplaces claimed to be "family friendly" and offered a variety of supports. But for women who could take advantage of them, flexible work schedules (which usually meant working part-time) carried significant penalties. Women who shifted to part-time work typically saw their jobs gutted of significant responsibilities and the once-flourishing careers derailed. Worse, part-time hours often crept up to the equivalent of full time. When Diane Childs had children, she scaled back to part time and began to feel the pointlessness of continuing:

> And I'm never going to get anywhere—you have the feeling that you just plateaued professionally because you can't take on the extra projects; you can't travel at a moment's notice; you can't stay late; you're not flexible on the Friday thing because that could mean finding someone to take your kids. You really plateau for a much longer period of time than you ever realize when you first have a baby. It's like you're going to be plateaued for thirteen to fifteen years.

Lynn Hamilton, an M.D., met her husband at Princeton, where they were both undergraduates. Her story illustrates how family pulls and workplace pushes (from both her career and her husband's) interacted in a marriage that was founded on professional equality but then devolved to the detriment of her career:

> We met when we were 19 years old, and so, there I was, so naive, I thought, well, here we are, we have virtually identical credentials and comparable income earnings. That's an opportunity. And, in fact, I think our incomes were identical at the time I quit. To the extent to which we have articulated it, it was always understood, well, with both of us working, neither of us would have to be working these killer jobs. So, what was happening was, instead, we were both working these killer jobs. And I kept saying, "We need to reconfigure this." And what I realized was, he wasn't going to.

Meanwhile, her young daughter was having behavioral problems at school, and her job as a medical director for a biomedical start-up company had "the fax machine going, the three phone lines upstairs, they were going." Lynn slowly realized that the only reconfiguration possible, in the face of her husband's absence, was for her to quit.

Over half (60 percent) of the women I spoke to mentioned their husbands as one of the key reasons why they quit. That not all women talked about their husbands' involvement, or lack thereof, reveals the degree to which they perceived the work-family balancing act to be their responsibility alone. But women seldom mentioned their husbands for another reason: they were, quite literally, absent.

Helena Norton, an educational administrator who characterized her husband as a "workaholic," poignantly described a scenario that many others took for granted and which illustrates a pattern typical of many of these women's lives: "He was leaving early mornings; 6:00 or 6:30 before anyone was up, and then he was coming home late at night. So I felt this real emptiness, getting up in the morning to, not necessarily an empty house, because my children were there, but I did, I felt empty, and then going to bed, and he wasn't there."

In not being there to pick up the slack, many husbands had an important indirect impact on their wives' decisions to quit. Deferring to their husbands' careers and exempting them from household chores, these women tended to accept this situation. Indeed, privileging their husbands' careers was a pervasive, almost tacit undercurrent of their stories.

When talking about their husbands, women said the same things: variations on "he's supportive," and that he gave them a "choice." But this hands-off approach revealed husbands to be bystanders, not participants, in the work family bind. "It's your choice" was code for "it's your problem." And husbands' absences, a direct result of their own high-powered careers, put a great deal of pressure on women to do it all, thus undermining the façade of egalitarianism.

Family pulls—from children and, as a result of their own long work hours, their husbands—exacerbated workplace pushes; and all but seven women cited features of their jobs—the long hours, the travel—as another major motivation in quitting. Marketing executive Nathalie Everett spoke for many women when she remarked that her full-time workweek was "really 60 hours, not 40. Nobody works nine-to-five anymore."

Surprisingly, the women I interviewed, like Nathalie, neither questioned nor showed much resentment toward the features of their jobs that kept them from fully integrating work and family. They routinely described their jobs as "all or nothing" and appeared to internalize what sociologists call the "ideal worker" model of a (typically male) worker unencumbered by family demands. This model was so influential that those working part time or in other flexible arrangements often felt stigmatized. Christine Thomas, a marketing executive and job-sharer, used imagery reminiscent of *The Scarlet Letter* to describe her experience: "When you job share, you have 'MOMMY' stamped in huge letters on your forehead."

While some women's decisions could be attributed to their unquestioning acceptance of the status quo or a lack of imagination, the unsuccessful attempts of others who tried to make it work by pursuing alternatives to full-time, like Diane, serve as cautionary tales. Women who made arrangements with bosses felt like they were being given special favors. Their part-time schedules were privately negotiated, hence fragile and unstable, and were especially vulnerable in the context of any kind of organizational restructuring such as mergers.

THE CHOICE GAP

Given the incongruity of these women's experiences—they felt supported by "supportive" yet passive husbands and pushed out by workplaces that once prized their expertise—how did these women understand their situation? How did they make sense of professions that, on the one hand, gave them considerable status and rewards, and, on the other hand, seemed to marginalize them and force them to compromise their identity as mothers?

The overwhelming majority felt the same way as Melissa Wyatt, the 34-year-old who gave up a job as a fund-raiser: "I think today it's all about choices, and the choices we want to make. And I think that's great. I think it just depends where you want to spend your time." But a few shared the outlook of Olivia Pastore, a 42-year-old ex-lawyer:

> I've had a lot of women say to me, "Boy, if I had the choice of, if I could balance, if I could work part-time, if I could keep doing it." And there are some women who are going to stay home full-time no matter what and that's fine. But there are a number of women, I think, who are home because they're caught between a rock and a hard place. . . . There's a lot of talk about the individual decisions of individual women. "Is it good? Is it bad? She gave it up. She couldn't hack it." . . . And there's not enough blame, if you will, being laid at the feet of the culture, the jobs, society.

My findings show that Olivia's comments—about the disjuncture between the rhetoric of choice and the reality of constraint that shapes women's decisions to go home—are closer to the mark. Between trying to be the ideal mother (in an era of intensive mothering) and the ideal worker (a model based on a man with a stay-at-home wife), these high-flying women faced a double bind. Indeed, their options were much more limited than they seemed. Fundamentally, they faced a "choice gap": the difference between the decisions women could have made about their careers if they were not mothers or caregivers and the decisions they had to make in their circumstances as mothers married to high-octane husbands in ultimately unyielding professions. This choice gap obscures individual preferences, and thus reveals the things Olivia railed against—culture, jobs, society—the kinds of things sociologists call "structure."

Overall, women based their decisions on mutually reinforcing and interlocking factors. They confronted, for instance, two sets of trade-offs: kids versus careers, and their own careers versus those of their husbands. For many, circumstances beyond their control strongly influenced their decision to quit. On the family side of the equation, for example, women had to deal with caregiving for sick children and elderly parents, children's developmental problems, and special care needs. Such reasons figured in one-third of the sample. On the work side, women were denied part-time arrangements, a couple were laid off, and some had to relocate for their own careers or their husbands'.

A total of 30 women, a little more than half the sample, mentioned at least one forced-choice consideration.

But even before women had children, the prospect of pregnancy loomed in the background, making women feel that they were perceived as flight risks. In her first day on the job as a marketing executive, for example, Patricia Lambert's boss asked her: "So, are you going to have kids?" And once women did get pregnant, they reported that they were often the first in their office, which made them feel more like outsiders. Some remarked that a dearth of role models created an atmosphere unsympathetic to work-family needs. And as these women navigated pregnancy and their lives beyond, their stories revealed a latent bias against mothers in their workplaces. What some women took from this was that pregnancy was a dirty little secret not to be openly discussed. The private nature of pregnancy thus complicated women's decisions regarding their careers once they became mothers, which is why they often waited until the last minute to figure out their next steps. Their experiences contrasted with the formal policies of their workplaces, which touted themselves as "family friendly."

THE RHETORIC OF CHOICE

Given the indisputable obstacles—hostile workplaces and absentee husbands—that stymied a full integration of work and family, it was ironic that most of the women invoked "choice" when relating the events surrounding their decision to exit their careers. Why were there not more women like Olivia, railing against the tyranny of an outmoded workplace that favored a 1950s-era employee or bemoaning their husbands' drive for achievement at the expense of their own?

I found that these women tended to use the rhetoric of choice in the service of their exceptionality. Women associated choice with privilege, feminism, and personal agency, and internalized it as a reflection of their own perfectionism. This was an attractive combination that played to their drive for achievement and also served to compensate for their loss of the careers they loved and the professional identities they valued. Some of these women bought into the media message that being an at-home mom was a status symbol, promoted by such cultural arbiters as *New York Magazine* and the *Wall Street Journal*. Their ability to go home reflected their husbands' career success, in which they and their children basked. Living out the traditional lifestyle, male breadwinner and stay-at-home-mom, which they were fortunate to be able to choose, they saw themselves as realizing the dreams of third-wave feminism. The goals of earlier, second-wave feminism, economic independence and gender equality, took a back seat, at least temporarily.

CHALLENGING THE MYTH

These strategies and rhetoric, and the apparent invisibility of the choice gap, reveal how fully these high-achieving women internalized the double bind and the intensive mothering and ideal-worker models on which it rests. The downside, of course, is that they blamed themselves for failing to "have it all" rather than any actual structural constraints.

That work and family were incompatible was the overwhelming message they took from their experiences. And when they quit, not wanting to burn bridges, they cited family obligations as the reason, not their dissatisfaction with work, in accordance with social expectations. By adopting the socially desirable and gender-consistent explanation of "family," women often contributed to the larger misunderstanding surrounding their decision. Their own explanations endorsed the prevalent idea that quitting to go home is a choice. Employers rarely challenged women's explanations. Nor did they try to convince them to stay, thus reinforcing women's perception that their decision was the right thing to do as mothers, and perpetuating the reigning media image of these women as the new traditionalists.

Taken at face value, these women do seem to be traditional. But by rejecting an intransigent workplace, their quitting signifies a kind of silent strike. They were not acquiescing to traditional gender roles by quitting, but voting with their feet against an outdated model of work. When women are not posing for the camera or worried about offending former employers (from whom they may need future references), they are able to share their stories candidly. From what I found, the truth is far different and certainly more nuanced than the media depiction.

The vast majority of the type of women I studied do not want to choose between career and family. The demanding nature of today's parenting puts added pressure on women. Women do indeed need to learn to be "good enough" mothers, and their husbands need to engage more equally in parenting. But on the basis of what they told me, women today "choose" to be home full-time not as much because of parenting overload as because of work overload, specifically long hours and the lack of flexible options in their high-status jobs. The popular media depiction of a return to traditionalism is wrong and misleading. Women are trying to achieve the feminist vision of a fully integrated life combining family and work. That so many attempt to remain in their careers when they do not "have to work" testifies strongly to their commitment to their careers, as does the difficulty they experience over their subsequent loss of identity. Their attempts at juggling and their plans to return to work in the future also indicate that their careers were not meant to be ephemeral and should not be treated as such. Rather, we should regard their exits as the miner's canary—a frontline indication that something is seriously amiss in many workplaces. Signs of toxic work environments and white-collar sweatshops are ubiquitous. We can glean from these women's experiences the true cost of these work conditions, which are personal and professional, and, ultimately, societal and economic.

Our current understanding of why high-achieving women quit—based as it is on choice and separate spheres—seriously undermines the will to change the contemporary workplace. The myth of opting out returns us to the days when educated women were barred from entering elite professions because "they'll only leave anyway." To the extent that elite women are arbiters of shifting gender norms, the opting out myth also has the potential to curtail women's aspirations and stigmatize those who challenge the separate-spheres ideology on which it is based. Current demographics make it clear that employers can hardly afford to lose the talents of high-achieving women. They can take a cue from at-home moms like the ones I studied: Forget opting out; the key to keeping professional women on the job is to create better, more flexible ways to work.

Recommended Resources

Mary Blair-Loy. *Competing Devotions: Career and Family among Women Executives* (Harvard University Press, 2003). Argues for a cultural, less materialist, understanding of contemporary work-family conflict among high-achieving working women.

Sharon Hays. *The Cultural Contradictions of Motherhood* (Yale University Press, 1995). Describes the historical emergence and contemporary internalization of motherhood norms that are at odds with the realities of women's changing lives, with powerful theorizing as to why.

Arlie Hochschild. *The Second Shift* (Viking, 1989). Still the defining classic of the work-family field, identifying women's work at home another problem that had no name.

Jerry A. Jacobs and Kathleen Gerson. *The Time Divide: Work, Family and Gender Inequality* (Harvard University Press, 2004). Makes the case for time as the newly emerging basis of gender and class inequality, with lots of hard-to-find facts and good policy prescriptions.

Phyllis Moen and Patricia Roehling. *The Career Mystique: Cracks in the American Dream* (Rowman and Littlefield, 2005). A masterful exploration of the creation, maintenance, and consequences of the high-demand, all-consuming workplace, whose title consciously echoes Friedan's *The Feminine Mystique*.

■ READING 22

One Sick Child Away from Being Fired

Joan C. Williams

> I've done my fair share of agonizing in print about the implacable tensions between work and family, but I'm moved this Mother's Day to feel rather sheepish about such laments. The reason for my embarrassment is [the Center for WorkLife Law's Report] *One Sick Child Away from Being Fired: When Opting Out Is Not an Option*. With that stark title, the report punctures the entitled, self-referential perspective from which journalists tend to write about working mothers . . . Guilty as charged.
>
> —Ruth Marcus, *Washington Post*

Professional-Managerial women are not the only Americans affected by work-family conflict. In fact, they are the lucky ones. They can afford high-quality child care and can outsource much of the housekeeping. Or they can afford to stay home to ensure high-quality care.[1]

Not so with less-affluent families, who often face steep hurdles in balancing work and family. Thus when an employer ordered some factory workers to work overtime, they had their babysitters drop off the children at the factory. When the managers confronted the women, the women said, "I would be put in prison and my children would be taken away from me if I leave them home alone—I cannot do that. You told me to stay, so they're going to come here."[2] This is just one example of the kinds of quandaries faced by nonprofessionals. A packer was fired when she left work in response to a call that her preschooler was in the emergency room with a head injury. A newspaper press operator, who was the mother of a one-year-old as well as the primary caregiver for her own mother, came to work late because she overslept after a night spent caring for both baby and mother. Although she called ahead, she was fired when she arrived twenty minutes late.[3]

For families dealing with a child's serious illness or chronic disease, Americans' lack of child care and social services, along with job inflexibility, creates a toxic mixture that threatens the jobs of fathers as well as mothers. Consider these cases: a divorced father with custody of an asthmatic son; the father of a severely disabled son; the step-father of a young man paralyzed as the result of a gunshot wound; a male train operator with a diabetic son; a male rental car shuttle driver whose son had a serious heart condition; the father of a child who needed a ventilator in order to breathe; a father of a child with special needs; and a janitor whose son had severe mental and physical disabilities. All were disciplined or fired due to work-family conflicts.[4]

Twenty percent of American families are caring for a child with special needs; 30% of these caregivers either reduce their hours or end up without work as a result of their conflicting responsibilities. When family crises strike, these families do not have the resources to hire help or seek out professional care for ill or troubled family members. Offering a window on this problem are the phone company workers fired for monitoring their own home telephones, worried over drug-dealing teenagers, family members who have threatened suicide, asthmatic children home alone, or elders endangered by dementia and living in violent neighborhoods. These cases reveal the lack of an important right that professional employees take for granted: the chance to make a personal phone call at work. Especially in the summer, when one in ten children aged six to twelve is home alone or in the company of a sibling under thirteen, all working parents need to be able to make a call home.[5]

The Center for WorkLife Law studied ninety-nine union arbitrations to examine the problems working-class parents face as they try to juggle the competing demands of their jobs and their family responsibilities. The cases offer a unique glimpse of how these two sets of responsibilities clash in the lives of men as well as women—bus drivers, telephone workers, construction linemen, carpenters, welders, and others. Also represented are nurses' aides and janitors, whose low-wage jobs place them among the working poor. The grievants all faced a similar and deeply troubling dilemma: their efforts to meet crucial family responsibilities jeopardized the jobs that were essential for supporting their families. These workers had far more protection than the average Joe: they were unionized, and their unions chose to challenge (or "grieve") their discipline. The scenario for the 87.6% of American workers who are not unionized is quite different. In nonunionized workplaces, employees typically have fewer rights and fewer protections.[6]

The stories that unfolded represent ripples on the surface of a deeper struggle. This face of work-family conflict in the United States is unknown to many professionals. It is not captured in uplifting stories of professional mothers who "discover their inner housewife." Nor has it been a cause célèbre for unions. Here are important messages both for the press—which should start covering how workplace-workforce mismatch differs across class—and for unions. Unions have mandates to serve their members, to organize more workers into unions, and to affect the political process in ways that benefit workers. Addressing workplace-workforce mismatch has powerful potential for helping achieve all three goals. Union women have long argued that work-family issues are useful in organizing women, but the fact is that that work-family issues are also of pressing concern to many unionized men.[7] Unions need a new message of manly solidarity: "Just because the boss gives me a job doesn't mean he can forbid me from putting family first." "Providing," for most working-class men today, requires them to provide care as well as cash.

Stories of work-family conflict among the working class have the potential to change the national debate. This potential cuts across party lines; the Department of Labor under George W. Bush found the Center for WorkLife Law's *One Sick Child* report useful in the controversy over whether to eliminate workers' right to take federal Family and Medical Leave Act (FMLA) leave in short periods (e.g., taking time off twice a week for kidney dialysis or taking off a week three times a year to care for a child hospitalized for a serious, chronic condition). The report buttressed the position of those who were arguing that the reason workers take intermittent FMLA leave is that they urgently need it—not because they are "gaming the system," as some economists were arguing. *One Sick Child* also has played a role in the current campaign to gain a minimum number of paid sick days for American workers. Publicizing the acute work-family conflicts faced by workers is essential; helping workers to address these conflicts should be seen as a core part of the union movement—not a frill. After all, no amount of wages or benefits helps a worker who was fired for putting family first.

THE NEW FACE OF WORK-FAMILY CONFLICT

Working-class Americans typically lack the kind of flexibility those in professional and managerial jobs take for granted.

Upper-middle-class workers can take time off to attend a child's school event, are permitted to use the telephone or even leave work to check on a sick child, and often can arrange their work day to enable them to take a family member to the doctor. Things are different for blue- and pink-collar workers. They are closely supervised. Typically they must "punch in" and adhere to rigid schedules. Arriving late or leaving work even a few minutes early may lead to dismissal. Personal business often is prohibited except during lunch and designated breaks. One study found that one-third of working-class employees—men as well as women—cannot decide when to take breaks, nearly 60% cannot choose starting or quitting times, and 53% cannot take time off to care for sick children.[8]

Nearly three-quarters of employed adults say they have little or no control over their work schedules. In addition, among the working class, 87% of families have two weeks or less of vacation and sick leave *combined*. Nearly 70% of working-class parents report having paid time off for family emergencies, but only about 34% of fathers and 39% of mothers report actually using the leave. "It's hard to get a day off," one working mother explained. "If you want a day off you put a request slip in and nine times out of 10 it gets denied because of short staff." Because only 10% of all employed mothers have paid maternity leave (apart from their sick and vacation time), they are vulnerable to discipline or dismissal if emergencies arise that require them to take additional time off.[9]

Workplace inflexibility has a particularly harsh impact on American families with children. Despite the oft-repeated idea that only rich women can afford to work part-time, many working-class women work reduced hours. One qualitative study found that in two-thirds of two-job working-class families, wives typically worked shorter hours for pay than husbands did. But, as noted earlier, American workers pay dearly for taking part-time work—the wage penalty for part-time work is a whopping 21% per hour worked. Nevertheless, one recent survey found higher demand for part-time work among U.S. hourly workers than among professionals. Given the trade-off between hours and income, this indicates the desperate hunger for family time. Fully 95% of women and 90% of men in the United States wish they had more time with family.[10]

Inflexible schedules work in combination with what are known as "no-fault" progressive discipline systems. Under these systems, workers accumulate points for absenteeism—regardless of the cause—unless the situation is specifically covered by work rules or union contract. A worker who garners a particular number of points is first disciplined and then fired, regardless of the reasons for the accrued absences. Some of the workers in the arbitrations discussed in this chapter had excellent attendance records, while many others struggled with child care, elder care, transportation, and other problems that resulted in unenviable absenteeism records. At issue is not whether employers have a right to count on employees to show up—clearly they do. Yet two questions emerge. The first is whether employees who have done everything they could to put in place dependable routine and backup family care should be fired when an emergency triggers the final point that leads to dismissal. The second issue is whether absences covered by the FMLA can be legitimately treated as garnering points under a no-fault system.[11]

CRAZY QUILTS AND TAG TEAMS

The twenty-four-hour economy means that many people work what Europeans call "unsocial hours": hours outside the generally recognized working day that encroach on time traditionally reserved for family and friends. In fact, for 40% of employed Americans, most of their work time occurs outside of standard daylight hours. And 51% of two-job families with children have at least one parent working a nonday shift. Almost 30% report variable starting and stopping times, typically with the employer setting those times at will. Ten percent of Americans have schedules so unpredictable that, when asked, they tell researchers they do not know from one week to the next what their weekly schedule will be. The evening shift is the most common alternative work schedule, accounting for 40% of all nonstandard work shifts among full-time workers and more than half of those among part-time workers.[12]

Nonstandard working hours are especially prevalent in low-level service and laborer jobs and increasingly in retail, where many low-wage mothers who can least afford to pay for child care are employed. People working unsocial hours, not surprisingly, tend to have strained relationships. These schedules are associated with higher work-family conflict, lower marital quality, and reduced time spent with children. They are also associated with a lower likelihood of eating meals together, providing homework supervision, and sharing leisure. Workers with nonstandard shifts face special hardships if they divorce. One divorcing mother lost her job at a factory due to a shift change when she refused to report to work in time for her new shift because she believed she would lose custody of her children if she did.[13]

Inflexible work schedules work in poisonous combination with American workers' unusually heavy reliance on family members for child care. In the United States, child care is both expensive and of highly variable quality. Consequently, working-class families typically patch together a crazy quilt of family-delivered care that may include, in addition to parents' shift work, drafting grandparents and other family members to help with child care. These fragile, patched-together systems often break down. One study found that 30% of workers surveyed had to cut back on work for at least one day during the week in order to care for family members: nearly one-quarter of men as well as over one-third of women. These cutbacks were more frequent among lower-income workers with the most inflexible schedules, presumably because they were only half as likely to rely on child care centers as were professional-managerial workers.[14]

Among the arbitrations we examined, many that were settled in the worker's favor involved parents whose well-laid plans for both regular child care and backup care went awry. For example, in *Princeton City School District Board of Education*, a teacher requested a personal leave day when her normal day care provider suddenly became sick. Her husband was out of town, and her mother-in-law was scheduled to work. School officials denied leave in the absence of proof that she had tried to arrange for backup through a commercial day care center. She had not tried to do so on the date in question because she had learned, several years earlier, that the local centers (like most centers in the United States) did not accept short-notice, one-day clients. The arbitrator held that the personal day should have been granted because the teacher had a backup plan—relying on her husband and mother-in-law—that had worked in the past.[15]

In *General Telephone Company of Indiana*, an arbitrator ruled in favor of a service clerk who had just had a baby and was ordered, the day she returned from maternity leave, to attend a two-week out-of-town training course. Because the clerk was given less than a week's notice, she was unable to get a babysitter, and her husband was on a work assignment out of town. She asked that the class be scheduled when she had sufficient time to arrange babysitting. The supervisor suggested that she start the class several months later; she agreed. A few days later, she was informed that attending the training program was a job requirement and that she would be terminated if she did not go. After a few more days, she was given the choice of being demoted to an operator job or fired. The arbitrator reinstated this worker with full back pay, benefits, and seniority, noting that "no effort whatever was made to accommodate [her] very real child care needs," despite the fact that two other employees had been excused from the same training for compelling personal reasons. If the inability to find a suitable babysitter when neither spouse nor relatives are available "is not a compelling personal reason," the arbitrator opined, "it is hard to imagine what sort of excuse would be acceptable."[16]

An arbitrator also found in favor of the worker in *Social Security Administration, Westminster Teleservice Center*, another situation involving backup child care. The case concerned a contact representative who was treated as absent without leave when she did not report to work because her regular babysitter had car problems and her backup babysitter's husband was hospitalized with a heart attack. The worker, a single mother with no relatives nearby, made persistent efforts to reach her supervisor, expressing mounting anxiety over the cost of her long-distance calls. Her direct supervisor never returned her calls. She ultimately used foul language in frustration and remained at home. She was disciplined for her absence, a decision that was overturned by the arbitrator, who held that she was entitled to emergency annual leave under the contract because

> [She] had met the commonly understood meaning of "emergency": She had a childcare emergency. It is not disputed that the two people she reasonably and legitimately depended upon for childcare were suddenly and unexpectedly unavailable . . . Indeed, her circumstances exactly met the situation described in [the contract]; that is, there was an unexpected change in her childcare arrangements.[17]

Men as well as women are affected by child care breakdowns, in significant part because of "tag teaming," an arrangement where parents work different shifts so that each parent can care for the children while the other is at work. Among "tag teamers," fathers act as primary caregivers when their wives are at work.[18] Describing his own experience, John Goldstein, past president of the Milwaukee Labor Council, said,

> When I was a young bus driver and my children were very small (ages 4, 2, and 1), I worked the late shift and my wife went to school during the day. We couldn't afford child care, and this way one of us was always home. One day in the middle of winter, I was scheduled to work at 4 pm. The babysitter didn't show up or call to say she wasn't coming. I had to bundle up the kids and take them to work. They had to ride my bus with me. After about two hours I was lucky enough to see my wife studying in a coffee shop, so I stopped the bus and ran in and handed her the kids.[19]

Tag teaming exists in professional families, but it is far more common in nonprofessional families, especially among young, lower-income families. This way of covering child care is driven in part by simple economics. Given the lack of government subsidies, in every state the average price for child care for a one-year-old is higher than the average cost of college tuition at the state's university. Most experts estimate that more than half of paid care in the United States is "poor" to "adequate," and only about 10% of paid care is developmentally enriching. In other words, out-of-family child care is either prohibitively expensive or poor quality; tag teaming is a way to avoid inferior care. But family-delivered care can have steep costs and dangers of its own. A tag-teaming parent or grandparent who is forbidden to leave the workplace or is ordered to stay overtime faces a no-win situation. Those who leave without their supervisors' consent can expect discipline or even job loss.[20]

When faced with child care emergencies, tag-teaming families must make difficult choices as to whether the mother or the father will face discipline or discharge for taking time off to care for children. In *U.S. Steel Corp.*, a factory worker whose regular babysitter was in the hospital took off work because his wife's employer had a stricter absenteeism policy than his did. Another case involved the father of a toddler, who started his warehouse job at 7 A.M. to be available to pick up his daughter from preschool at 3 P.M.; his wife brought the child to preschool in the mornings. The father won a grievance challenging his employer's attempt to change him to a 9-to-5 schedule, on the grounds that the union contract did not allow the company to unilaterally change start times. (Without a union, the worker most likely would have lost his job.) In a third case, the arbitrator reduced a father's discharge to a one-month suspension for refusing to take an assignment because he had to pick up his daughter. In yet another arbitration, when a carpenter left work to pick up his children, the employer argued that he should have obeyed the order to stay and grieved later (that is, challenged the employer's order). The arbitrator disagreed: "the 'work now, grieve later' rule has no application. [He] could not both continue working and pick up his children."[21]

The cases we examined also revealed an unexpected finding: men's work-family conflicts stem not just from tag teaming but also from divorce. One example involved a twenty-two-year employee who explained that his stay-at-home wife had left him and their four-year-old son. He was notified that social service authorities were investigating him for child neglect. They found no grounds for the charge and subsequently tried to help him find day care for his son, but it took nearly three months of struggling with unreliable babysitters before he was able to place his son with an approved day care provider. In the meantime, he had been fired for excessive absenteeism under his employer's no-fault policy, *Interlake Conveyors* involved a material handler who was fired when he was not allowed to produce documentation that, as the divorced father of an asthmatic son, he needed to stay home because his son was ill.[22] Both fathers later were reinstated by arbitrators but would have been out of luck had they not belonged to a union.

Even when families are able to rely on child care centers or family day care, they still must cope with paid providers' often-inflexible hours and policies. Most centers close before the end of normal business hours, and most charge steep fees (often one dollar per minute) if children are picked up late. Even more important, because child-care staff become unhappy when children are not picked up on time, parents who arrive late risk losing their child care arrangement. That often means losing their jobs. In five of the arbitrations we examined, workers lost their jobs after they lost their child care.[23]

Another common scenario is when an employer unilaterally changes a worker's starting and stopping times, often without much notice, and the parent's child care provider cannot, or will not, take the child at the new time. Sometimes a schedule change affects not child care but elder care, as in *Simpson v. District of Columbia Office of Human Rights*. A secretary challenged her employer's insistence that she start work an hour and a half earlier, thereby making it impossible for her to care for her elderly and ailing father before she arrived at work. In certain jobs, an employer is not in a position to offer flexibility—obviously, one cannot stop a factory line to accommodate a babysitter. But many employers could offer far more flexibility than they do without jeopardizing business needs.[24]

FAMILIES IN CRISIS, EMPLOYERS IN DENIAL

The vision of families in crisis emerges strongly in the arbitration mentioned above that involved more than thirty phone company workers fired for tapping telephone lines. One reported having a mentally unstable son who had threatened to kill her, her family, and himself. Three different workers had children whom they said had threatened and/or attempted suicide. Another had a stepdaughter who was physically threatening her daughter. Another became worried and called her house fifty-two times in a single day; when she broke in to monitor the line, she heard her son acknowledging taking drugs. Two workers monitored the phones of their parents. One had a mother who was "suffering from confusion"; the other's father was ill and, according to the worker, had been threatened with harm from other tenants in the building. In another arbitration, an employee with twenty-five years' tenure was fired for monitoring her phone to check up on her young children, one of whom was asthmatic. Finally, an employee with fourteen years' service, who was on probation for absenteeism, was fired when he failed to report to work. He had stayed home because his pregnant wife, who subsequently died of a brain hemorrhage, had broken a phone in a fit of rage, and he decided he could not leave his children alone with her.[25]

In addition to child care breakdowns and family crises, family illness may lead to discipline or job loss because family members lack sick leave they can use to care for family members who are ill. Routine childhood illness is a major concern. Families with infants with special needs visit the doctor an average of eleven times a year; other infants visit the doctor an average of four to six times a year. For children aged two to four, the number of yearly doctors' visits falls to seven for kids with special needs and to four for others. In the 70% of families in which all adults are employed, one working parent needs to stay home when a child is sick—but that parent may lose his or her job for doing so. For example, in *Naval Air Rework Facility*, the grievant and her husband both worked, one as a machinist and one at an aerospace plant. Since the child care facility would not accept their child because he had chicken pox, the mother stayed home with her ill child. She was denied sick leave upon returning to work and as a result was discharged. The arbitrator held for the employer, finding that the employee did not provide the necessary documentation from the local health authorities that her child's illness required isolation.[26]

Under the FMLA, workers caring for an immediate family member (spouse, child, or parent) with a serious health condition are entitled to up to twelve weeks of unpaid leave each year, so long as they have worked for at least one year at an employer with fifty or more employees (and 1,250 hours in the year prior to the leave). Workers can take this leave in an intermittent pattern, which is particularly useful for those who need to take family members to doctors' appointments or those who have family members with chronic diseases. Yet many workers are not covered: only 11% of private-sector workplaces meet the act's minimum size requirements and fully 40% of workers are not covered. Workers who are covered sometimes fail to request FMLA leave in a manner the employer can recognize, or they fail to obtain the necessary medical documentation. In other cases, it is unclear whether the workers ever considered the FMLA.[27]

Even in the best of circumstances, FMLA leave covers only a small proportion of the time off families require in order to negotiate the joys and travails of everyday life. Children need adult attention long after they leave preschool. During children's adolescence, high parental involvement can significantly help build self-esteem and educational accomplishment. Active parental involvement and supervision also can help prevent juvenile crime and other risky behavior: most teenage pregnancies and teen violence occur between 3 P.M. and 6 P.M., when most schools have been dismissed but when parents are often still at work. Several of the arbitrations we analyzed involved workers' adolescent children (suicidal daughters; a son injured in a gang beating; a father fired for absences caused by family illnesses and "delinquent children"; a father fired for absenteeism caused, among other things, by the drug overdoses of his daughter).[28]

Grandparents, too, face workplace discipline and/or job loss when they give priority to the needs of their families. Because the average age at which Americans become grandparents for the first time is now forty-seven, three-fourths of grandmothers and almost nine out of ten grandfathers are in the labor force. Thus the more than one-third of grandmothers who provide care for preschool-aged children typically are otherwise employed. Many grandmothers tag team with their daughters, but these older family caregivers are vulnerable to the same work-family conflicts faced by parents. In *Department of Veterans Affairs Medical Center*, a grandmother was suspended from her job as a nursing assistant when she was unable to work her scheduled shift (3:30 P.M. to midnight) because she could not find child care. In another case, a grandmother bus driver lost her chance at promotion because she had been absent for a significant period caring for her adult son, who was injured. In yet another, a steel plant worker was fired when she stayed home to care for her adult daughter, who had been injured in a car accident. *Mercer County* involved a grandmother who needed time off to care for her grandchildren. She happened to have legal custody, but grandparents frequently provide regular child care even when they are not the legal guardians of their grandchildren: over one-fifth of preschool-aged children are cared for primarily by grandparents when their parents are at work. A recent study reports that 2.4 million grandparents have primary responsibility for the care of their grandchildren—and over one-fourth had cared for their grandchildren for five or more years.[29]

Grandparents sometimes ease parents' work-family conflicts, but eventually parents, as well as children, need care: one in four families care for elderly relatives. Among people aged fifty to sixty-four who need support for their health and emotional needs, 84% rely on informal caregiving networks. Almost one in five caregivers say they provide forty-plus hours of care per week, and the average length of care is 4.3 years. In *Sprint/Central Telephone Co. of Texas*, a phone customer service representative failed to meet her sales quota because of the stress caused by caring for her mother, who had died by the time of the arbitration. Fully 57% of working caregivers say that they have had to go to work late, leave early, or take time off during the day to provide care. This is a face of work-family conflict that is not well known and is rarely reported in the mainstream press. Unions, too, may not fully grasp the range and depth of family crises that their members must balance with their jobs.[30]

THE BURDEN OF MANDATORY OVERTIME

One form of workplace inflexibility shows up again and again in the arbitrations: mandatory overtime. The design of mandatory overtime systems can make or break workers' ability to avoid discipline or discharge when work and family conflict. The overtime issue is important, in part, because Americans work among the longest hours of any other developed economy. Long hours are largely the province of men: 95% of mothers aged twenty-five to forty-four years old work fewer than fifty hours per week, year-round. While managerial and professional men are most likely to work fifty-plus hours per week (38% do), nearly one in four (23%) men in middle-income families (with incomes between $35,000 and $101,000) do so, too. Working-class men average forty-two to forty-three hours per week, far longer than their European counterparts.[31]

Mandatory overtime leaves single parents and tag team families in jeopardy of losing their jobs. Until the union negotiated a solution, for example, members of the Amalgamated Transit Union were being fired when they refused to stay for mandatory drug and alcohol tests, which last up to three hours. Said Robert Molofsky, who was General Counsel of the ATU at the time, "They had no problem taking the tests; the problem was that they were triggered at or near the end of their shifts. And with little or no advance notice they could not stay even as paid overtime, because they had to get home to take care of their kids." In other words, they were tag team dads.[32]

Recall *U.S. Steel Corp.*, a tag team situation in which a factory worker stated that when his family's regular babysitter was sick, he took off work because his wife's employer had a stricter absenteeism policy; he was suspended for fifteen days for an unexcused absence. While his frankness was unusual, the family-care hardships mandatory overtime present are widespread and need to be addressed.[33]

Another example involved a janitor who was divorced and the mother of a seventeen-year-old son with the mental capacity of an eighteen-month-old child. In *Tenneco Packaging Burlington Container Plant*, she was fired after twenty-seven years' service for failing to report one Saturday when her son's caregiver could not work because of a sick child. All of the evidence indicated that this was an isolated incident. The janitor had worked sixty hours a week, including all but one Saturday, in the four months before she was fired, and she called in twice and left a message telling her employer she could not work on the day of the absence that led to her termination. When she returned the following Monday, she was denied her request for a vacation day to excuse her Saturday absence. Instead she was fired. The arbitrator who reinstated her said:

> The Company had been scheduling six-day work weeks for an extended period of time. This heavy work schedule was likely to have a substantial impact on any single-parent employees, and would have a particularly heavy impact on an employee with a child in need of permanent care and assistance, [The worker] had legitimate reasons for missing two of the 2.3 Saturdays when she had been scheduled to work overtime.

He continued, "the demands of a regular six day work week would be a strain on a caregiver," especially given the "10-hour days . . . Under such circumstances, it is not surprising that there would be problems in persuading the caregiver to regularly work on the weekends, as well as long days, with some regularity even if her child had not become ill." The arbitrator ordered that this employee be reinstated with full back pay. Most U.S. workers, being nonunionized, would have been fired without appeal.[34]

In *State of New York, Rochester Psychiatric Center*, another arbitrator took a proactive role on behalf of a single mother. This case involved a health center that fired a mental health aide who had worked for her employer for nine years. The aide had a history of attendance problems, almost all of which stemmed from her status as a single parent.

Due to understaffing and the need for around-the-clock care, aides at the center were expected to work mandatory overtime on a regular basis. If an employee refused overtime, she remained at the top of the list until she took it, which is why, after the aide refused to work overtime, she was ordered five days later to work an additional eight hours after her regular shift ended at 11:20 P.M. The aide's sitter could not stay because she had a day job. The aide asked her supervisor if she knew anyone who could watch her children at such short notice. The supervisor, while sympathetic, did not. Then the aide said she could stay at work if she could bring her children in so they could sleep at the center but that she could not leave her children alone: "If I have to stay, my kids have to stay here." Once again, she was fired; once again, the arbitrator overturned the worker's discharge, opining that the situation was

> shocking to one's sense of fairness . . . The [worker] may not be a woman of means, but she is a woman of substance . . . She does not hold a high-paying job. She would probably be better off financially if she chose to stay home, watch her kids, and go on the dole. However, instead of becoming a public charge, she has chosen to make a public contribution . . . Her recent performance evaluation indicates "she can function well on any ward she is assigned." As the parties are aware, I take a very dim view of time and attendance infractions and insubordination . . . However, [she] deserves every conceivable "break" . . . Her children were well-groomed, neatly dressed, and well-behaved. It is her efforts to be a good parent that have created her problems at work.

The arbitrator directed the aide to identify, thirty days in advance, three days a month when she could work overtime given that aides typically worked overtime two to three days a month. This is an example of how to design an overtime system that does not have a punitive impact on adults with family responsibilities—particularly if this approach is combined, to the maximum extent possible, with a system that relies on voluntary overtime. In two other arbitrations, nurses' aides were not so lucky. Both were fired, and not reinstated, when they refused mandatory overtime because they had no one to care for their children.[35]

In *GTE California, Inc.*, a single-parent telephone installer was fired when she left work in defiance of a new telephone company policy that workers had to stay until every customer who had called before 3 P.M. had been served. The installer's supervisor had a policy that only one person per shift could refuse overtime; if more than one person requested to leave without working overtime, all workers requesting to do so had to come to an agreement as to who could leave and who would stay. The installer was fired for insubordination when she left work after being ordered to stay because she and a coworker both wanted to leave without working overtime. The arbitrator overturned her dismissal, saying that the worker was entitled to leave rather than obeying the supervisor's order and filing a grievance later, because her situation was covered by a rule concerning safety. The arbitrator held that a parent could be disciplined if she left unjustifiably, but she need not "obey now, grieve later" in the face of an unreasonable system that placed a child at risk:

> I do not know what would have happened to the child if [her mother] had not arrived to pick her up. Chances are that the child would have been cared for. However, it was clear

that the [worker] also did not know what would happen to the child, although she did know that she was running the risk of losing day care service. In these circumstances, the [worker] did what I believe any unintimidated parent would have done. She ran the risk of discipline.[36]

Single fathers as well as single mothers are sanctioned for refusing overtime, which makes sense, given that (outside of nursing) overtime is largely a masculine phenomenon. In *Bryant v. Bell Atlantic Maryland*, an African-American construction lineman who was the single father of two children was fired for refusing overtime. The arbitrator held that the employer lacked just cause to terminate and strongly suggested that Bryant be placed "in a position that did not require overtime" or, as an alternative, that "Bryant be scheduled for overtime in a manner that would allow him to meet his workplace and child care obligations." This arbitration was reported in a court case; the court noted Bryant's claim that child care difficulties of white workers had been accommodated, while his had not.[37]

In *Marion Composites*, a factory worker whose wife had recently left him was suspended three days for insubordination when he left after eight hours of a twelve-hour overtime shift. He was, according to the arbitrator, "an excellent employee who consistently worked overtime when asked to do so . . . He was never absent. He accepted overtime whenever the Company needed him. Indeed, his dedication to his work placed him in a situation that may have jeopardized his family responsibilities." When first asked to work overtime, he said he could not because he was "tired and worn out"—he had been so upset by his wife's departure that he had been feeling ill. Later that afternoon, he said he would help out the company but that he could only stay for eight hours because he had to get home to care for his two children. He stayed after the eight hours was up but became "distraught" after receiving a call from his wife and left after eight hours and twenty minutes. In the *Suprenant Cable Corp.* case (discussed earlier), a single father with a four-year-old son was fired for excessive absenteeism under the employer's no-fault policy as the result of the worker's inability to find child care. Said the arbitrator:

> Such policies are not best suited to dealing with long-term employees who, like [this worker), have overall good records and who run into an unusual period of bad luck and hard times. Anyone can—most of us will—experience at least one period of adversity in a lifetime. Otherwise good, long-term employees are entitled to understanding and sympathy during those rare periods. Their seniority does not exempt them from the expectations of the workplace but may require that they be applied more flexibly and sensitively.[38]

Some cases of family needs that conflict with unscheduled overtime involve care for ill spouses. In *Allied Paper*, a plant worker refused a Saturday callback because his water pump had broken, and he did not want to leave his wife, who had cancer and was severely depressed, "without water, in case of a fire." He was so concerned about his wife's cancer and depression that he had previously sacrificed thousands of dollars to avoid overtime that would have left her home alone. Said the arbitrator, "his wife had stood by him in sickness and tragedy, and he was trying to return it. He owed it to her."[39]

*Notes*_____

1. Ruth Marcus, "The Family as Firing Offense; for Too Many Workers, Emergencies at Home Force Stark Choices," *Washington Post*, May 14, 2006, at B7 (epigraph). © 2006 The Washington Post. All rights reserved. Used by permission and protected by the Copyright Laws of the United States. The printing, copying, redistribution, or retransmission of the Material without express written permission is prohibited.

2. Naomi Gerstel & Dan Clawson, "Union's Responses to Family Concerns," 48 *Social Problems* 284–285 (2001).

3. ATU database: *Chicago Transit Authority*, case no. *97-0166* (Hayes, 1999) (arbitrator reinstated a female bus driver with no loss of seniority but put her on probation and gave her partial back pay, after she was discharged because of absences due to a flat tire, a family funeral, misunderstandings about a vacation day and extra board duty, a suspended driver's license, and time lost spent taking her son to a high school placement test); *Knauf Fiber Glass*, 81 LA 333 (Abrams, 1983) (arbitrator reinstated the grievant without back pay and put her on probation, concluding: "[The grievant] felt deeply about her personal obligations and responsibilities as the unwed mother of three children. While understandably her son and daughters may be of paramount importance to her, her employer can insist that she meet reasonable attendance requirements. The grievant can meet those requirements, keep her job and support her children. If she cannot meet those requirements now and in the future, she will lose her job and her children will suffer as a result. It will require great effort on her part to meet her dual responsibilities, but it certainly is worth the effort."); *Chicago Tribune Co.*, 119 LA 1007 (Nathan, 2003) (arbitrator reinstated the grievant after holding that her oversleeping, which led to her tardiness, was an FMLA-qualified event because it resulted) from exhaustion from her responsibilities as primary caregiver for her mother).

4. *Interlake Material Handling Div.*, *Interlake Material Handling Div.*, *Interlake Conveyors Inc.*, 113 LA 1120 (Lalka, 2000) (arbitrator reinstated grievant when he was not allowed to show that he needed to stay home because his asthmatic son was sick); Boise *Cascade Corp.*, *Insulite Div. International*, 77 LA 28 (Fogelberg, 1981) (severely handicapped son); *State of NY, Dept. of Correctional Services*, 89 LA 122 (Handsaker, 1987) (paralyzed stepson); ATU database: *Massachusetts Bay Transportation Authority* (Hodlen, 2001) (diabetic son); *Budget Rent-A-Car Systems*, 115 LA 1745 (Suardi, 2001) (son with heart condition); ATU database: *Chicago Transit Authority*, case no. 99-155 (Patterson, 2001) (child on ventilator); ATU database: *Massachusetts Bay Authority* (Dunn, 2000) (special needs child); *Tenneco Packaging, Burlington Container Plant*, 112 LA 761 (Kessler, 1999) (arbitrator reinstated with full back pay the grievant, a single parent of a mentally handicapped son, who was terminated after twenty-seven years for failing to report to work when her son's caregiver could not work); *Mercer County Association for the Retarded & American Federation of State, County and Municipal Employees AFL-CIO*, 1996 WL 492101 (Hewitt, 1996) (mentally disabled son).

5. Netsy Firestein, *A Job and a Life: Organizing & Bargaining for Work Family Issues: A Union Guide*, Labor Project for Working Families 17 (2005), available to order at http://www.laborproject.org /bargaining/guide.html (20% caring for a child with special needs); CWA database: *Ameritech*, case no. 4-99-39 (Bellman, 2001) (arbitrator reinstated a twenty-five-year employee, without back pay, discharged for monitoring her phone to check up on her young children, one of whom was asthmatic); Firestein, *supra* note 5, at 15 (one in ten children aged six to twelve is home alone).

6. United States Department of Labor, Bureau of Labor Statistics, *Union Members Summary*, January 28, 2009, http://www.bls.gov/news/release/union2.nro.htm. In a unionized workplace, when a worker is disciplined or fired, the union may file a grievance on the worker's behalf, arguing that the employer lacked "just cause." If the union and employer's attempts to negotiate a settlement are unsuccessful, the case goes to arbitration. Most arbitrations are not public, but in some cases the decisions are published. This chapter draws on several sources. It uses published cases analyzed in the Center for WorkLife Law's initial report on union arbitrations, *Work/Family Conflict, Union Style*, which was written by Martin H. Malin, Maureen K. Milligan, Mary C. Still, and Joan C. Williams and published on the Web in 2004. It also uses other published arbitrations we found after publication of that initial report and taps databases of unpublished

arbitration made available to us through the generosity of three unions: the Communication Workers of America (CWA), the Amalgamated Transit Union (ATU), and the Teamsters (UPS database only). We are currently seeking access to other arbitration databases; please contact the author for more information.

7. Marion Crane, "Feminizing Unions: Challenging the Gendered Structure of Wage Labor," 89 *Mich. L. Rev.* 1155–1156 (1991).

8. Jody Heymann, *The Widening Gap: Why America's Working families Are in Jeopardy and What Can Be Done about It* 115, Figure 6.1 (2000).

9. AFL-CIO, *Work and Family*, available at http://www.aflcio.org/issues/workfamily; Heymann, *supra* note 8 at 133 (87% have two weeks or less combined); Maureen Perry-Jenkins, Heather Bourne, & Karen Meteyer, "Work-Family Challenges for Blue-Collar Families," in *The Future of Work in Massachusetts*, 185–204, 191, 193 (Tom Juravich ed., 2007) (70% of working-class parents; "hard to get time off";10% of mothers).

10. Fancine Deutsch, *Halving It All: How Equally Shared Parenting Works* 172, 186–189 (1999) (wives typically worked shorter hours); Janet C. Gornick & Marcia K. Meyers, *Families That Work: Policies for Reconciling Parenthood and Employment* 63 (2003) (wage penalty is 21%); Corporate Voices for Working Families (WFD Consulting), *Business Impacts of Flexibility: An Imperative for Expansion 16* (November 2005), available for download from http://www.cvwf.org/ (higher demand for part-time work); Gornick & Meyers, *supra* note 10 at 81 (wish they had more time with family).

11. See, e.g., Jeanne M. Vonhoff & Martin H. Malin, "What a Mess! The FMLA, Collective Bargaining and Attendance Control Plans," 21 *Ill. Pub. Employee Rel. Rep.* 1 (2004).

12. Deutsch, *supra* note 10 at 170 (1999) (at least one parent working nonday shift); Heymann, *supra* note 8 at 48 (evening shift most common alternative work schedule).

13. Julia R. Henly, H. Luke Schaefer, & Elaine Waxman, "Nonstandard Work Schedules: Employer- and Employee-Driven Flexibility in Retail Jobs," 80 *Social Service Rev.* at 609, 610 (December 2006) (citing studies); *ITT Industries, Night Vision Roanoke Plant*, 118 LA 1504 (Cohen, 2003) (arbitrator reinstated grievant after the employer did not allow grievant to revoke her resignation that she had submitted after the employer changed its shift schedules).

14. Heymann, *supra* note 8 at 24–25 (30% had to cut back); *Id.* at 36, 126 (cutbacks more frequent among low-income workers).

15. *Princeton City School District Board of Education*, 101 LA 789 (Paolucci, 1993) (arbitrator held that the personal day should have been granted after grievant was denied leave when her child day care provider became sick).

16. CWA database: *General Telephone Company of Indiana*, case no. 5-80-934 (Walt, 1981) (arbitrator reinstated the grievant who was terminated after not attending an out-of-town training program that began the day she returned from maternity leave).

17. *Social Security Administration, Westminster Teleservice Ctr.*, 93 LA 687 (Feigenbaum, 1989) (arbitrator held that grievant was entitled to emergency annual leave after she was disciplined for being AWOL when her regular babysitting arrangement broke down).

18. Harriet B. Presser, "Toward a 24-Hour Economy," 284 *Science* 1778, 1779 (June 11, 1999).

19. Firestein, *supra* note 5 at 7.

20. Heather Boushey, *Tag Team Parenting*, Washington, DC: Center for Economic and Policy Research 3 (2006) (Boushey concluded that "lower income families simply cannot afford to buy formal childcare" and that "the older a family is, the more likely it is that the spouses have similar schedules"); Heymann, *supra* note 8 at 50 (average price of child care for one-year old); Gornick & Meyers, *supra* note 10 at 53 (only 10% of paid child care is developmentally enriching).

21. *U.S. Steel Corp.*, 95 LA 610 (Das, 1990) (factory worker took off work for child care because wife's employer's absentee policy was stricter, and arbitrator sustained the grievant's suspension for failure to report to mandatory overtime due to child care difficulties); *Central Beverage*, 110 LA 104 (Brunner, 1998) (arbitrator held that unilateral change of grievant's working hours violated the contract); *Jefferson Partners*, 109 LA 335 (Bailey, 1997) (arbitrator reduced a father's discharge to a one-month suspension for refusing to take an assignment because he had to pick up his daughter); *Ashland Oil, Inc.*, 91 LA 1101 (Volz, 1988) (arbitrator reduced a three-day suspension to one day for a carpenter who left job early to pick up his child from day care).

22. CWA database: *Suprenant Cable Corp.*, case no. 1-95-85 (Bornstein, 1995) (arbitrator reinstated grievant without back pay after he was discharged for excessive absenteeism due to caring for his son after his wife left him); *Inter-lake Material Handling Div.*, *supra* note 4 (arbitrator reinstated grievant when he was not allowed to show that he needed to stay home because his son was sick).

23. *Naval Air Rework Facility*, 86 LA 1129 (Hewitt, 1986) (arbitrator upheld the discharge of grievant who was denied sick leave to care for a child with chicken pox); *Piedmont Airlines Inc.*, 103 LA 751, 753; *Southern Champion Tray Co.*, 96 LA 633 (Nolan, 1991) (arbitrator upheld the discharge of a mechanic whom he faulted for failing to make backup child care arrangements after two warnings from his supervisor that he needed to do so); *Sutter Roseville Medical Center*, 116 LA 621 (Staudohar, 2001) (arbitrator upheld the discharge of a nuclear medicine technician who was charged with insubordination by a new supervisor after refusing to be placed on standby because he lived far away and had to care for his son); *Town of Stratford*, 97 LA 513 (Stewart, 1991) (arbitrator upheld a five-day suspension of a police officer when she failed to report for an "orderback" because she could not without notice find child care).

24. *Simpson v. District of Columbia Office of Human Rights*, 597 A.2d 392 (D.C. Cir. 1991).

25. CWA database: *U.S. West Communications*, case no. 7-95-93 (Rinaldo, 1999) (arbitrator upheld the discharge of seven workers because they were not facing an "immediate, overwhelming threat to safety" and reduced to final warnings the dismissals of nine cases that met the threat-to-safety test); *Ameritech*, *supra* note 5 (employee monitored her phone to check on her asthmatic child); ATU database: *Chicago Transit Authority*, case no. 98-080 (Goldstein, 1997) (arbitrator reinstated without back pay a fourteen-year employee when he failed to report to work because he did not want to leave his children with his pregnant wife after she broke the phone in a fit of rage).

26. Heymann, *supra* note 8 at 73 (routine childhood illness stats); *Naval Air Rework Facility*, *supra* note 23.

27. Family and Medical Leave Act of 1993, Pub. L. No. 103-3, 107 Stat. 6 (codified at 29 U.S.C. Sect. 2601-2654 (1994)); 29 USC § 2612(b)(1), 29 CFR § 25.203(a); Susan J. Lambert & Anna Haley-Lock, "The Organizational Stratification of Opportunities for Work-Life Balance," 7 *Community, Work & Family* 179 (2004); Gornick & Meyers, *supra* note 10, at 114 (10% and 60%); ATU database: *Chicago Transit Authority*, case no. 00-373 (Gundermann, 2001) (employee failed to request FMLA leave in a way the employer could understand); *Budget Rent-A-Car Systems*, *supra* note 4 (some employees failed to provide the necessary medical documentation); Boise *Cascade Corp., Insulite Div. International*, *supra* note 4 (was unclear whether workers considered using FMLA leave).

28. Barbara Schneider & David Stevenson, *The Ambitious Generation: America's Motivated but Directionless* 145 (1999) (parental involvement can build self-esteem); Stanford A. Newman et al., *America's After-School Choice: The Prime Time for Juvenile Crime, or Youth Achievement and Enrichment*, Fight Crime: Invest in Kids, 2–3 (2000), available at http://www.fightcrime.org (active parental involvement can help prevent juvenile crime); ATU database: *Transit Management of Decatur* (Perkovich, 1998) (suicidal daughters); *Chicago Transit Authority*, *supra* note 27 (gang beating); *Greater Cleveland Regional Transit Authority*, 106 LA 807 (Duda, 1996) (arbitrator upheld the discharge of a brake mechanic who did not request family and medical leave despite being notified that he could do so, did not use the resources of the Employee Assistance Program although he was repeatedly urged to do so, and failed to provide proper documentation for an illness even when given an extra two weeks to accomplish this); and ATU Database: *Regional Transit Authority* (Vernon, 1983) (daughter's drug overdose).

29. *Columbiana County Brd. of Mental Retardation & Disabilities*, 117 LA 13 (Skulina, 2002) (arbitrator upheld the county's decision to pass over grievant, a senior employee, for a position because the junior employee had a better attendance record; grievant had a significant amount of absences due to caring for her injured son); Heymann, *supra* note 8 at 166 (three of four grandmothers and nine of ten grandfathers in labor force); Presser, *supra* note 18 at 1779 (one out of three care-providing grandmothers are in labor force); Harriet B. Presser & Amy G. Cox, "The Work Schedules of Low-Income American Women and Welfare Reform," *Monthly Lab. Rev.* 26 (April 1997) (grandmothers tag team with daughters); *Dept. of Veterans Affairs Medical Ctr.*, 100 LA 233 (Nicholas, 1992) (arbitrator reduced a fourteen-day suspension to five days); *Federal Mogul Corporation*, WL. 2003: 23531172 (Cohen, 2003) (arbitrator reinstated a factory worker after her employer refused to revoke her resignation);*Mercer County Association for the Retarded*, *supra* note

4 (arbitrator upheld a three-day suspension of a residential worker in a home for the mentally handicapped who refused to work overtime because her husband was not at home and she could not leave her own mentally handicapped son alone); U.S. Census Bureau, *Who's Minding the Kids?* Table 2 (Fall 1995, issued October 2000), available at http://www.census.gov/prod/2000pubs /p70-70.pdf (21.7% of preschool-aged children are cared for by a grandparent); U.S. Census Bureau, *Grandparents Living with Grandchildren*: 2000, at 3 (2000, issued October 2003), available at http://www.census.gov/prod/2003pubs/c2kbr-31.pdf (2.4 million grandparents).

30. Heymann, *supra* note 8 at 2 (one in four families take care of elderly relatives); Mary Jo Gibson, American Association of Retired Persons,*Beyond 50.03: A Report to the Nation on Independent Living and Disability* 59 (2003), available at http://research.aarp.org/il/beyond_50_il.html (84% rely on informal arrangements); Firestein, *supra* note 5 at 16 (one in five caregivers provide forty-plus hours per week); *Id.* at 14 (4.3 years); *Sprint/Central Telephone Company of Texas, Inc.*, 117 LA 1321 (Baroni, 2002) (arbitrator upheld the discharge of a customer service representative who had cared for a dying mother because the grievant did not have the skills and temperament to do her job well); Firestein, *supra* note 5 at 14 (57% of working caregivers).

31. Gornick & Meyers, *supra* note 10 at 59 (Americans work longer hours); Mary C. Still, *Litigating the Maternal Wall: U.S. Lawsuits Charging Discrimination against Workers with Family Responsibilities*, Center for WorkLife Law Report, University of California, Hastings College of the Law (2006), available at http://www.worklifelaw.org/pubs/FRDreport.pdf (95% of mothers); Joan C. Williams & Heather Boushey, *The Three Faces of Work-Family Conflict: The Poor, the Professionals and the Missing Middle*, report by the Center for American Progress and the Center for WorkLife Law, University of California, Hastings College of the Law, Table 3, 7–8 (2010) available at http://www.worklifelaw.org/pubs/ThreeFacesofWork-FamilyConflict.pdf (38% and 23%); Gornick & Meyers, *supra* note 10 at 156–163 (working-class men work forty-two to forty-three hours per week; in interpreting Gornick's statistics, I have defined working class as men with high school but not college degrees).

32. Joan C. Williams, *One Sick Child Away from Being Fired: When Opting Out Is Not an Option*, Center for WorkLife Law Report, University of California, Hastings College of the Law (2006), available at http://www.uchastings.edu/site_files/WLL/onesickchild.pdf.

33. *U.S. Steel Corp.*, 95 LA 610 (Das, 1990) (arbitrator sustained the grievant's suspension for failure to report to mandatory overtime due to child care difficulties).

34. *Tenneco Packaging Burlington Container Plant*, *supra* note 4 at 765–766.

35. *State of New York, Rochester Psychiatric Ctr.*, 87 LA 725 (Babiskin, 1986) (arbitrator reinstated grievant) (Based on information from the Rochester Psychiatric Center website, available at http://www.omh.state.ny.us/omhweb/facilities/ropc/facility.htm, MHTA is either "Mental Hygiene Therapy Assistant" or "Mental Health Therapy Aide."); *Id.* at 726, 727; *Rock County, Wisconsin*, 1993 WL 835474 (McAlpin, 1993) (arbitrator sustained the discharge); *Fairmont General Hospital, Inc.*, 2004 WL 3422192 (Miles, 2004) (arbitrator sustained grievant's discharge for refusal to work overtime because grievant's childcare arrangement broke down and she made no effort to make alternative arrangements).

36. CWA database: GTE *California, Inc.*, case no. 11-91-86 (Miller, 1992) (Arbitrator overturned grievant's dismissal because the employee was entitled to leave rather than obeying the supervisor's order and filing a grievance later because her situation was covered by a rule concerning safety. If more than one person wanted to avoid overtime work on a given day, the rule was that they had to agree which of them would not work overtime. If they could not agree, then both had to work overtime.).

37. Gornick & Meyers, *supra* note 10 at 247 (overtime largely masculine phenomenon); *Bryant v. Bell Atlantic Maryland*, 288 F.3d 124, 129 (4th Cir. 2002) (single father construction lineman fired for refusing overtime).

38. *Marion Composites*, 115 LA 95 (Wren, 2001) (arbitrator reduced the grievant's suspension to a written warning and awarded him back pay after the grievant was suspended for insubordination for leaving after eight hours of a twelve-hour overtime shift to care for his children); *Suprenant Cable Corp.*, *supra* note 22 at 14.

39. *Allied Paper*, 80 LA 435, 44 (Mathews, 1983) (arbitrator reduced the suspension to a written warning).

Chapter 10

Family and the Economy

Families on the Fault Line

Lillian B. Rubin

THE BARDOLINOS

It has been more than three years since I first met the Bardolino family, three years in which to grow accustomed to words like *downsizing*, *restructuring*, or the most recent one, *reengineering*; three years in which to learn to integrate them into the language so that they now fall easily from our lips. But these are no ordinary words, at least not for Marianne and Tony Bardolino.

The last time we talked, Tony had been unemployed for about three months and Marianne was working nights at the telephone company and dreaming about the day they could afford a new kitchen. They seemed like a stable couple then—a house, two children doing well in school, Marianne working without complaint, Tony taking on a reasonable share of the family work. Tony, who had been laid off from the chemical plant where he had worked for ten years, was still hoping he'd be called back and trying to convince himself their lives were on a short hold, not on a catastrophic downhill slide. But instead of calling workers back, the company kept cutting its work force. Shortly after our first meeting, it became clear: There would be no recall. Now, as I sit in the little cottage Marianne shares with her seventeen-year-old daughter, she tells the story of these last three years.

"When we got the word that they wouldn't be calling Tony back, that's when we really panicked; I mean *really* panicked. We didn't know what to do. Where was Tony going to find another job, with the recession and all that? It was like the bottom really dropped out. Before that,

341

we really hoped he'd be called back any day. It wasn't just crazy; they told the guys when they laid them off, you know, that it would be three, four months at most. So we hoped. I mean, sure we worried; in these times, you'd be crazy not to worry. But he'd been laid off for a couple of months before and called back, so we thought maybe it's the same thing. Besides, Tony's boss was so sure the guys would be coming back in a couple of months; so you tried to believe it was true."

She stops speaking, takes a few sips of coffee from the mug she holds in her hand, then says with a sigh, "I don't really know where to start." So much happened, and sometimes you can't even keep track. Mostly what I remember is how scared we were. Tony started to look for a job, but there was nowhere to look. The union couldn't help; there were no jobs in the industry. So he looked in the papers, and he made the rounds of all the places around here. He even went all the way to San Francisco and some of the places down near the airport there. But there was nothing.

"At first, I kept thinking, *Don't panic; he'll find something*. But after his unemployment ran out, we couldn't pay the bills, so then you can't help getting panicked, can you?"

She stops again, this time staring directly at me, as if wanting something. But I'm not sure what, so I sit quietly and wait for her to continue. Finally, she demands, "Well, can you?"

I understand now; she wants reassurance that her anxiety wasn't out of line, that it's not she who's responsible for the rupture in the family. So I say, "It sounds as if you feel guilty because you were anxious about how the family would manage."

"Yeah, that's right," she replies as she fights her tears. "I keep thinking maybe if I hadn't been so awful, I wouldn't have driven Tony away." But as soon as the words are spoken, she wants to take them back. "I mean, I don't know, maybe I wasn't that bad." We were both so depressed and scared, maybe there's nothing I could have done. But I think about it a lot, and I didn't have to blame him so much and keep nagging at him about how worried I was. It wasn't his fault; he was trying.

"It was just that we looked at it so different. I kept thinking he should take anything, but he only wanted a job like the one he had. We fought about that a lot. I mean, what difference does it make what kind of job it is? No, I don't mean that; I know it makes a difference. But when you have to support a family, that should come first, shouldn't it?"

As I listen, I recall my meeting with Tony a few days earlier and how guiltily he, too, spoke about his behavior during that time. "I wasn't thinking about her at all," he explained. "I was just so mad about what happened; it was like the world came crashing down on me. I did a little too much drinking, and then I'd just crawl into a hole, wouldn't even know whether Marianne or the kids were there or not. She kept saying it was like I wasn't there. I guess she was right, because I sure didn't want to be there, not if I couldn't support them."

"Is that the only thing you were good for in the family?" I asked him.

"Good point," he replied laughing. "Maybe not, but it's hard to know what else you're good for when you can't do that."

I push these thoughts aside and turn my attention back to Marianne. "Tony told me that he did get a job after about a year," I remark.

"Yeah, did he tell you what kind of job it was?"

"Not exactly, only that it didn't work out."

"Sure, he didn't tell you because he's still so ashamed about it. He was out of work so long that even he finally got it that he didn't have a choice. So he took this job as a dishwasher in this restaurant. It's one of those new kind of places with an open kitchen, so there he was, standing there washing dishes in front of everybody. I mean, we used to go there to eat sometimes, and now he's washing the dishes and the whole town sees him doing it. He felt so ashamed, like it was such a comedown, that he'd come home even worse than when he wasn't working."

"That's when the drinking really started heavy. Before that he'd drink, but it wasn't so bad. After he went to work there, he'd come home and drink himself into a coma. I was working days by then, and I'd try to wait up until he came home. But it didn't matter; all he wanted to do was go for that bottle. He drank a lot during the day, too, so sometimes I'd come home and find him passed out on the couch and he never got to work that day. That's when I was maddest of all. I mean, I felt sorry for him having to do that work. But I was afraid he'd get fired."

"Did he?"

"No, he quit after a couple of months. He heard there was a chemical plant down near L.A. where he might get a job. So he left. I mean, we didn't exactly separate, but we didn't exactly not. He didn't ask me and the kids to go with him; he just went. It didn't make any difference. I didn't trust him by then, so why would I leave my job and pick up the kids and move when we didn't even know if he'd find work down there?

"I think he went because he had to get away. Anyway, he never found any decent work there either. I know he had some jobs, but I never knew exactly what he was doing. He'd call once in awhile, but we didn't have much to say to each other then. I always figured he wasn't making out so well because he didn't send much money the whole time he was gone."

As Tony tells it, he was in Los Angeles for nearly a year, every day an agony of guilt and shame. "I lived like a bum when I was down there. I had a room in a place that wasn't much better than a flop house, but it was like I couldn't get it together to go find something else. I wasn't making much money, but I had enough to live decent. I felt like what difference did it make how I lived?"

He sighs—a deep, sad sound—then continues, "I couldn't believe what I did, I mean that I really walked out on my family. My folks were mad as hell at me. When I told them what I was going to do, my father went nuts, said I shouldn't come back to his house until I got some sense again. But I couldn't stay around with Marianne blaming me all the time."

He stops abruptly, withdraws to someplace inside himself for a few moments, then turns back to me. "That's not fair. She wasn't the only one doing the blaming. I kept beating myself up, too, you know, blaming myself, like I did something wrong.

"Anyhow, I hated to see what it was doing to the kids; they were like caught in the middle with us fighting and hollering, or else I was passed out drunk. I didn't want them to have to see me like that, and I couldn't help it. So I got out."

For Marianne, Tony's departure was both a relief and a source of anguish. "At first I was glad he left; at least there was some peace in the house. But then I got so scared; I didn't know if I could make it alone with the kids. That's when I sold the house. We were behind in our payments, and I knew we'd never catch up. The bank was okay; they said they'd give us a little more time. But there was no point.

"That was really hard. It was our home; we worked so hard to get it. God, I hated to give it up. We were lucky, though. We found this place here. It's near where we used to live, so the kids didn't have to change schools, or anything like that. It's small, but at least it's a separate little house, not one of those grungy apartments." She interrupts herself with a laugh, "Well, 'house' makes it sound a lot more than it is, doesn't it?"

"How did your children manage all this?"

"It was real hard on them. My son had just turned thirteen when it all happened, and he was really attached to his father. He couldn't understand why Tony left us, and he was real angry for a long time. At first, I thought he'd be okay, you know, that he'd get over it. But then he got into some bad company. I think he was doing some drugs, although he still won't admit that. Anyway, one night he and some of his friends stole a car. I think they just wanted to go for a joyride; they didn't mean to really steal it forever. But they got caught, and he got sent to juvenile hall.

"I called Tony down in L.A. and told him what happened. It really shocked him; he started to cry on the phone. I never saw him cry before, not with all our trouble. But he just cried and cried. When he got off the phone, he took the first plane he could get, and he's been back up here ever since.

"Jimmy's trouble really changed everything around. When Tony came back, he didn't want to do anything to get Jimmy out of juvy right away. He thought he ought to stay there for a while; you know, like to teach him a lesson. I was mad at first because Jimmy wanted to come home so bad; he was so scared. But now I see Tony was right.

"Anyhow, we let Jimmy stay there for five whole days, then Tony's parents lent us the money to bail him out and get him a lawyer. He made a deal so that if Jimmy pleaded guilty, he'd get a suspended sentence. And that's what happened. But the judge laid down the law, told him if he got in one little bit of trouble again, he'd go to jail. It put the fear of God into the boy."

For Tony, his son's brush with the law was like a shot in the arm. "It was like I had something really important to do, to get that kid back on track. We talked it over and Marianne agreed it would be better if Jimmy came to live with me. She's too soft with the kids; I've got better control. And I wanted to make it up to him, too, to show him he could count on me again. I figured the whole trouble came because I left them, and I wanted to set it right.

"So when he got out of juvy, he went with me to my folks' house where I was staying. We lived there for awhile until I got this job. It's no great shakes, a kind of general handyman. But it's a job, and right from the start I made enough so we could move into this here apartment. So things are going pretty good right now."

"Pretty good" means that Jimmy, now sixteen, has settled down and is doing well enough in school to talk about going to college. For Tony, too, things have turned around. He set up his own business as an independent handyman several months ago and, although the work isn't yet regular enough to allow him to quit his job, his reputation as a man who can fix just about anything is growing. Last month the business actually made enough money to pay his bills. "I'll hang onto the job for a while, even if the business gets going real good, because we've got a lot of catching up to do. I don't mind working hard; I like it. And being my own boss, boy, that's really great," he concludes exultantly.

"Do you think you and Marianne will get together again?"

"I sure hope so; it's what I'm working for right now. She says she's not sure, but she's never made a move to get a divorce. That's a good sign, isn't it?"

When I ask Marianne the same question, she says, "Tony wants to, but I still feel a little scared. You know, I never thought I could manage without him, but then when I was forced to, I did. Now, I don't know what would happen if we got together again. It wouldn't be like it was before. I just got promoted to supervisor, so I have a lot of responsibility on my job. I'm a different person, and I don't know how Tony would like that. He says he likes it fine, but I figure we should wait a while and see what happens. I mean, what if things get tough again for him? I don't ever want to live through anything like these last few years."

"Yet you've never considered divorce."

She laughs, "You sound like Tony." Then more seriously, "I don't want a divorce if I can help it. Right now, I figure if we got through these last few years and still kind of like each other, maybe we've got a chance."

* * *

When the economy falters, families tremble. The Bardolinos not only trembled, they cracked. Whether they can patch up the cracks and put the family back together again remains an open question. But the experience of families like those on the pages of this book provides undeniable evidence of the fundamental link between the public and private arenas of modern life.

No one has to tell the Bardolinos or their children about the many ways the structural changes in the economy affect family life. In the past, a worker like Tony Bardolino didn't need a high level of skill or literacy to hold down a well-paying semiskilled job in a steel mill or an automobile plant. A high school education, often even less, was enough. But an economy that relies most heavily on its service sector needs highly skilled and educated workers to fill its better-paying jobs, leaving people like Tony scrambling for jobs at the bottom of the economic order.

The shift from the manufacturing to the service sector, the restructuring of the corporate world, the competition from low-wage workers in underdeveloped countries that entices American corporations to produce their goods abroad, all have been going on for decades; all are expected to accelerate through the 1990s. The manufacturing sector, which employed just over 26 percent of American workers in 1970, already had fallen to nearly 18 percent by 1991. And experts predict a further drop to 12.5 percent by the year 2000. "This is the end of the post-World War boom era. We are never going back to what we knew," says employment analyst Dan Lacey, publisher of the newsletter *Workplace Trends*.

Yet the federal government has not only failed to offer the help working-class families need, but as a sponsor of a program to nurture capitalism elsewhere in the world it has become party to the exodus of American factories to foreign lands. Under the auspices of the U.S. Agency for International Development (AID), for example, Decaturville Sportswear, a company that used to be based in Tennessee, has moved to El

Salvador. AID not only gave grants to trade organizations in El Salvador to recruit Decaturville but also subsidized the move by picking up the $5 million tab for the construction of a new plant, footing the bill for over $1 million worth of insurance, and providing low-interest loans for other expenses involved in the move.

It's a sweetheart deal for Decaturville Sportswear and the other companies that have been lured to move south of the border under this program. They build new factories at minimal cost to themselves, while their operating expenses drop dramatically. In El Salvador, Decaturville is exempted from corporate taxes and shipping duties. And best of all, the hourly wage for factory workers there is forty-five cents an hour; in the United States the minimum starting wage for workers doing the same job is $4.25.

True, like Tony Bardolino, many of the workers displaced by downsizing, restructuring, and corporate moves like these will eventually find other work. But like him also, they'll probably have to give up what little security they knew in the past. For the forty-hour-a-week steady job that pays a decent wage and provides good benefits is quickly becoming a thing of the past. Instead, as part of the new lean, clean, mean look of corporate America, we now have what the federal government and employment agencies call "contingent" workers—a more benign name for what some labor economists refer to as "disposable" or "throwaway" workers.

It's a labor strategy that comes in several forms. Generally, disposable workers are hired in part-time or temporary jobs to fill an organizational need and are released as soon as the work load lightens. But when union contracts call for employees to join the union after thirty days on the job, some unscrupulous employers fire contingent workers on the twenty-ninth day and bring in a new crew. However it's done, disposable workers earn less than those on the regular payroll and their jobs rarely come with benefits of any kind. Worse yet, they set off to work each morning fearful and uncertain, not knowing how the day will end, worrying that by nightfall they'll be out of a job.

The government's statistics on these workers are sketchy, but Labor Secretary Robert Reich estimates that they now make up nearly one-third of the existing work force. This means that about thirty-four million men and women, most of whom want steady, full-time work, start each day as contingent and/or part-time workers. Indeed, so widespread is this practice now that in some places temporary employment agencies are displacing the old ones that sought permanent placements for their clients.

Here again, class makes a difference. For while it's true that managers and professionals now also are finding themselves disposable, most of the workers who have become so easily expendable are in the lower reaches of the work order. And it's they who are likely to have the fewest options. These are the workers, the unskilled and the semi-skilled—the welders, the forklift operators, the assemblers, the clerical workers, and the like—who are most likely to seem to management to be interchangeable. Their skills are limited; their job tasks are relatively simple and require little training. Therefore, they're able to move in and perform with reasonable efficiency soon after they come on the job. Whatever lost time or productivity a company may suffer by not having a steady crew of workers is compensated by the savings in wages and benefits the employment of throwaway workers permits. A resolution that brings short-term gains for the company at the long-term expense of both the workers and the nation. For when a person can't count on a permanent job, a critical element binding him or her to society is lost.

THE TOMALSONS

When I last met the Tomalsons, Gwen was working as a clerk in the office of a large Manhattan company and was also a student at a local college where she was studying nursing. George Tomalson, who had worked for three years in a furniture factory, where he laminated plastic to wooden frames, had been thrown out of a job when the company went bankrupt. He seemed a gentle man then, unhappy over the turn his life had taken but still wanting to believe that it would come out all right.

Now, as he sits before me in the still nearly bare apartment, George is angry. "If you're a black man in this country, you don't have a chance, that's all, not a chance. It's like no matter how hard you try, you're nothing but trash. I've been looking for work for over two years now, and there's nothing. White people are complaining all the time that black folks are getting a break. Yeah, well, I don't know who those people are, because it's not me or anybody else I know. People see a black man coming, they run the other way, that's what I know."

"You haven't found any work at all for two years?" I ask.

"Some temporary jobs, a few weeks sometimes, a couple of months once, mostly doing shit work for peanuts. Nothing I could count on."

"If you could do any kind of work you want, what would you do?"

He smiles, "That's easy; I'd be a carpenter. I'm good with my hands, and I know a lot about it," he says, holding his hands out, palms up, and looking at them proudly. But his mood shifts quickly; the smile disappears; his voice turns harsh. "But that's not going to happen. I tried to get into the union, but there's no room there for a black guy. And in this city, without being in the union, you don't have a chance at a construction job. They've got it all locked up, and they're making sure they keep it for themselves."

When I talk with Gwen later, she worries about the intensity of her husband's resentment. "It's not like George; he's always been a real even guy. But he's moody now, and he's so angry, I sometimes wonder what he might do. This place is a hell hole," she says, referring to the housing project they live in. "It's getting worse all the time; kids with guns, all the drugs, grown men out of work all around. I'll bet there's hardly a man in this whole place who's got a job, leave alone a good one."

"Just what is it you worry about?"

She hesitates, clearly wondering whether to speak, how much to tell me about her fears, then says with a shrug, "I don't know, everything, I guess. There's so much crime and drugs and stuff out there. You can't help wondering whether he'll get tempted." She stops herself, looks at me intently, and says, "Look, don't get me wrong; I know it's crazy to think like that. He's not that kind of person. But when you live in times like these, you can't help worrying about everything.

"We both worry a lot about the kids at school. Every time I hear about another kid shot while they're at school, I get like a raving lunatic. What's going on in this world that kids are killing kids? Doesn't anybody care that so many black kids are dying like that? It's like a black child's life doesn't count for anything. How do they expect our kids to grow up to be good citizens when nobody cares about them?

"It's one of the things that drives George crazy, worrying about the kids. There's no way you can keep them safe around here. Sometimes I wonder why we send them to school. They're not getting much of an education there. Michelle just started, but Julia's in the fifth grade, and believe me she's not learning much.

"We sit over her every night to make sure she does her homework and gets it right. But what good is it if the people at school aren't doing their job. Most of the teachers there don't give a damn. They just want the paycheck and the hell with the kids. Everybody knows it's not like that in the white schools; white people wouldn't stand for it.

"I keep thinking we've got to get out of here for the sake of the kids. I'd love to move someplace, anyplace out of the city where the schools aren't such a cesspool. But," she says dejectedly, "we'll never get out if George can't find a decent job." I'm just beginning my nursing career, and I know I've got a future now. But still, no matter what I do or how long I work at it, I can't make enough for that by myself."

George, too, has dreams of moving away, somewhere far from the city streets, away from the grime and the crime. "Look at this place," he says, his sweeping gesture taking in the whole landscape. "Is this any place to raise kids? Do you know what my little girls see every day they walk out the door? Filth, drugs, guys hanging on the corner waiting for trouble.

"If I could get any kind of a decent job, anything, we'd be out of here, far away, someplace outside the city where the kids could breathe clean and see a different life. It's so bad here, I take them over to my mother's a lot after school; it's a better neighborhood. Then we stay over there and eat sometimes. Mom likes it; she's lonely, and it helps us out. Not that she's got that much, but there's a little pension my father left."

"What about Gwen's family? Do they help out, too?"

"Her mother doesn't have anything to help with since her father died. He's long gone; he was killed by the cops when Gwen was a teenager," he says as calmly as if reporting the time of day.

"Killed by the cops." The words leap out at me and jangle my brain. But why do they startle me so? Surely with all the discussion of police violence in the black community in recent years, I can't be surprised to hear that a black man was "killed by the cops."

It's the calmness with which the news is relayed that gets to me. And it's the realization once again of the distance between the lives and experiences of blacks and others, even poor others. Not one white person in this study reported a violent death in the family. Nor did any of the Latino and Asian families, although the Latinos spoke of a difficult and often antagonistic relationship with Anglo authorities, especially the police. But four black families (13 percent) told of relatives who had been murdered, one of the families with two victims—a teenage son and a twenty-two-year-old daughter, both killed in violent street crimes.

But I'm also struck by the fact that Gwen never told me how her father died. True, I didn't ask. But I wonder now why she didn't offer the information. "Gwen didn't tell me," I say, as if trying to explain my surprise.

"She doesn't like to talk about it. Would you?" he replies somewhat curtly.

It's a moment or two before I can collect myself to speak again. Then I comment, "You talk about all this so calmly."

He leans forward, looks directly at me, and shakes his head. When he finally speaks, his voice is tight with the effort to control his rage. "What do you want? Should I rant and rave? You want me to say I want to go out and kill those mothers? Well, yeah, I do.

They killed a good man just because he was black. He wasn't a criminal; he was a hard-working guy who just happened to be in the wrong place when the cops were looking for someone to shoot," he says, then sits back and stares stonily at the wall in front of him.

We both sit locked in silence until finally I break it. "How did it happen?"

He rouses himself at the sound of my voice. "They were after some dude who robbed a liquor store, and when they saw Gwen's dad, they didn't ask questions; they shot. The bastards. Then they said it was self-defence, that they saw a gun in his hand. That man never held a gun in his life, and nobody ever found one either. But nothing happens to them; it's no big deal, just another dead nigger," he concludes, his eyes blazing.

It's quiet again for a few moments, then, with a sardonic half smile, he says, "What would a nice, white middle-class lady like you know about any of that? You got all those degrees, writing books and all that. How are you going to write about people like us?"

"I was poor like you once, very poor," I say somewhat defensively.

He looks surprised, then retorts, "Poor and white; it's a big difference."

* * *

Thirty years before the beginning of the Civil War, Alexis de Tocqueville wrote: "If ever America undergoes great revolutions, they will be brought about by the presence of the black race on the soil of the United States; that is to say they will owe their origin, not to the equality, but to the inequality of condition." One hundred and sixty years later, relations between blacks and whites remain one of the great unresolved issues in American life, and "the inequality of condition" that de Tocqueville observed is still a primary part of the experience of black Americans.

I thought about de Tocqueville's words as I listened to George Tomalson and about how the years of unemployment had changed him from, as Gwen said, "a real even guy" to an angry and embittered one. And I was reminded, too, of de Tocqueville's observation that "the danger of conflict between the white and black inhabitants perpetually haunts the imagination of the [white] Americans, like a painful dream." Fifteen generations later we're still paying the cost of those years when Americans held slaves—whites still living in fear, blacks in rage. "People see a black man coming, they run the other way," says George Tomalson.

Yet however deep the cancer our racial history has left on the body of the nation, most Americans, including many blacks, believe that things are better today than they were a few decades ago—a belief that's both true and not true. There's no doubt that in ending the legal basis for discrimination and segregation, the nation took an important step toward fulfilling the promise of equality for all Americans. As more people meet as equals in the workplace, stereotypes begin to fall away and caricatures are transformed into real people. But it's also true that the economic problems of recent decades have raised the level of anxiety in American life to a new high. So although virtually all whites today give verbal assent to the need for racial justice and equality, they also find ways to resist the implementation of the belief when it seems to threaten their own status or economic well-being.

Our schizophrenia about race, our capacity to believe one thing and do another, is not new. Indeed, it is perhaps epitomized by Thomas Jefferson, the great liberator. For surely, as Gordon Wood writes in an essay in the *New York Review of Books*, "there is no greater irony in American history than the fact that America's supreme spokesman for liberty and equality was a lifelong aristocratic owner of slaves."

Jefferson spoke compellingly about the evils of slavery, but he bought, sold, bred, and flogged slaves. He wrote eloquently about equality but he was convinced that blacks were an inferior race and endorsed the racial stereotypes that have characterized African-Americans since their earliest days on this continent. He believed passionately in individual liberty, but he couldn't imagine free blacks living in America, maintaining instead that if the nation considered emancipating the slaves, it must also prepare for their expulsion.

No one talks seriously about expulsion anymore. Nor do many use the kind of language to describe African-Americans that was so common in Jefferson's day. But the duality he embodied—his belief in justice, liberty, and equality alongside his conviction of black inferiority—still lives.

THE RIVERAS

Once again Ana Rivera and I sit at the table in her bright and cheerful kitchen. She's sipping coffee; I'm drinking some bubbly water while we make small talk and get reacquainted. After a while, we begin to talk about the years since we last met. "I'm a grandmother now," she says, her face wreathed in a smile. "My daughter Karen got married and had a baby, and he's the sweetest little boy, smart, too. He's only two and a half, but you should hear him. He sounds like five."

"When I talked to her the last time I was here, Karen was planning to go to college. What happened?" I ask.

She flushes uncomfortably. "She got pregnant, so she had to get married. I was heartbroken at first. She was only nineteen, and I wanted her to get an education so bad. It was awful; she had been working for a whole year to save money for college, then she got pregnant and couldn't go."

"You say she had to get married. Did she ever consider an abortion?"

"I don't know; we never talked about it. We're Catholic," she says by way of explanation. "I mean, I don't believe in abortion." She hesitates, seeming uncertain about what more she wants to say, then adds, "I have to admit, at a time like that, you have to ask yourself what you really believe. I don't think anybody's got the right to take a child's life. But when I thought about what having that baby would do to Karen's life, I couldn't help thinking, *What if* . . . ?" She stops, unable to bring herself to finish the sentence.

"Did you ever say that to Karen?"

"No, I would *never* do that. I didn't even tell my husband I thought such things. But, you know," she adds, her voice dropping to nearly a whisper, "if she had done it, I don't think I would have said a word."

"What about the rest of the kids?"

"Paul's going to be nineteen soon; he's a problem," she sighs. "I mean, he's got a good head, but he won't use it. I don't know what's the matter with kids these days; it's like they want everything but they're not willing to work for anything. He hardly finished high school, so you can't talk to him about going to college. But what's he going to do? These days if you don't have a good education, you don't have a chance. No matter what we say, he doesn't listen, just goes on his smart-alecky way, hanging around the neighborhood with a bunch of no-good kids looking for trouble.

"Rick's so mad, he wants to throw him out of the house. But I say no, we can't do that because then what'll become of him? So we fight about that a lot, and I don't know what's going to happen."

"Does Paul work at all?"

"Sometimes, but mostly not. I'm afraid to think about where he gets money from. His father won't give him a dime. He borrows from me sometimes, but I don't have much to give him. And anyway, Rick would kill me if he knew."

I remember Paul as a gangly, shy sixteen-year-old, no macho posturing, none of the rage that shook his older brother, not a boy I would have thought would be heading for trouble. But then, Karen, too, had seemed so determined to grasp at a life that was different from the one her parents were living. What happens to these kids?

When I talk with Rick about these years, he, too, asks in bewilderment: What happened? "I don't know; we tried so hard to give the kids everything they needed. I mean, sure, we're not rich, and there's a lot of things we couldn't give them. But we were always here for them; we listened; we talked. What happened? First my daughter gets pregnant and has to get married; now my son is becoming a bum."

"Roberto—that's what we have to call him now," explains Rick, "he says it's what happens when people don't feel they've got respect. He says we'll keep losing our kids until they really believe they really have an equal chance. I don't know; I knew I had to *make* the Anglos respect me, and I had to make my chance. Why don't my kids see it like that?" he asks wearily, his shoulders seeming to sag lower with each sentence he speaks.

"I guess it's really different today, isn't it?" he sighs. "When I was coming up, you could still make your chance. I mean, I only went to high school, but I got a job and worked myself up. You can't do that anymore. Now you need to have some kind of special skills just to get a job that pays more than the minimum wage.

"And the schools, they don't teach kids anything anymore. I went to the same public schools my kids went to, but what a difference. It's like nobody cares anymore."

"How is Roberto doing?" I ask, remembering the hostile eighteen-year-old I interviewed several years earlier.

"He's still mad; he's always talking about injustice and things like that. But he's different than Paul. Roberto always had some goals. I used to worry about him because he's so angry all the time. But I see now that his anger helps him. He wants to fight for his people, to make things better for everybody. Paul, he's like the wind; nothing matters to him.

"Right now, Roberto has a job as an electrician's helper, learning the trade. He's been working there for a couple of years; he's pretty good at it. But I think—I hope—he's going to go to college. He heard that they're trying to get Chicano students to go to the university, so he applied. If he gets some aid, I think he'll go," Rick says, his face radiant at the thought that at least one of his children will fulfill his dream. "Ana and me, we tell him even if he doesn't get aid, he should go. We can't do a lot because we have to help Ana's parents and that takes a big hunk every month. But we'll help him, and he could work to make up the rest. I know it's hard to work and go to school, but people do it all the time, and he's smart; he could do it."

His gaze turns inward; then, as if talking to himself, he says, "I never thought I'd say this but I think Roberto's right. We've got something to learn from some of these kids. I told that to Roberto just the other day. He says Ana and me have been trying to pretend we're one of them all of our lives. I told him, 'I think you're right.' I kept thinking if I did everything right, I wouldn't be a 'greaser.' But after all these years, I'm still a 'greaser' in their eyes. It took my son to make me see it. Now I know. If I weren't I'd be head of the shipping department by now, not just one of the supervisors, and maybe Paul wouldn't be wasting his life on the corner."

* * *

We keep saying that family matters, that with a stable family and two caring parents children will grow to a satisfactory adulthood. But I've rarely met a family that's more constant or more concerned than the Riveras. Or one where both parents are so involved with their children. Ana was a full-time homemaker until Paul, their youngest, was twelve. Rick has been with the same company for more than twenty-five years, having worked his way up from clerk to shift supervisor in its shipping department. Whatever the conflicts in their marriage, theirs is clearly a warm, respectful, and caring relationship. Yet their daughter got pregnant and gave up her plans for college, and a son is idling his youth away on a street corner.

Obviously, then, something more than family matters. Growing up in a world where opportunities are available makes a difference. As does being able to afford to take advantage of an opportunity when it comes by. Getting an education that broadens horizons and prepares a child for a productive adulthood makes a difference. As does being able to find work that nourishes self-respect and pays a living wage. Living in a world that doesn't judge you by the color of your skin makes a difference. As does feeling the respect of the people around you.

This is not to suggest that there aren't also real problems inside American families that deserve our serious and sustained attention. But the constant focus on the failure of family life as the locus of both our personal and social difficulties has become a mindless litany, a dangerous diversion from the economic and social realities that make family life so difficult today and that so often destroy it.

THE KWANS

It's a rare sunny day in Seattle, so Andy Kwan and I are in his backyard, a lovely showcase for his talents as a landscape gardener. Although it has been only a few years since we first met, most of the people to whom I've returned in this round of interviews seem older, grayer, more careworn. Andy Kwan is no exception. The brilliant afternoon sunshine is cruel as it searches out every line of worry and age in his angular face. Since I interviewed his wife the day before, I already know that the recession has hurt his business. So I begin by saying, "Carol says that your business has been slow for the last couple of years."

"Yes," he sighs. "At first when the recession came, it didn't hurt me. I think Seattle didn't really get hit at the beginning. But the summer of 1991, that's when I began to feel it. It's as if everybody zipped up their wallets when it came to landscaping.

"A lot of my business has always been when people buy a new house. You know, they want to fix up the outside just like they like it. But nobody's been buying houses lately, and even if they do, they're not putting any money into landscaping. So it's been tight, real tight."

"How have you managed financially?"

"We get by, but it's hard. We have to cut back on a lot of stuff we used to take for granted, like going out to eat once in a while, or going to the movies, things like that. Clothes, nobody gets any new clothes anymore.

"I do a lot of regular gardening now—you know, the maintenance stuff. It helps; it takes up some of the slack, but it's not enough because it doesn't pay much. And the competition's pretty stiff, so you've got to keep your prices down. I mean, everybody knows that it's one of the things people can cut out when things get tough, so the gardeners around here try to hold on by cutting their prices. It gets pretty hairy, real cutthroat."

He gets up, walks over to a flower bed, and stands looking at it. Then, after a few quiet moments, he turns back to me and says, "It's a damned shame. I built my business like you build a house, brick by brick, and it was going real good. I finally got to the point where I wasn't doing much regular gardening anymore. I could concentrate on landscaping, and I was making a pretty good living. With Carol working, too, we were doing all right. I even hired two people and was keeping them busy most of the time. Then all of a sudden, it all came tumbling down.

"I felt real bad when I had to lay off my workers. They have families to feed, too. But what could I do? Now it's like I'm back where I started, an ordinary gardener again and even worrying about how long that'll last," he says disconsolately.

He walks back to his seat, sits down, and continues somewhat more philosophically, "Carol says I shouldn't complain because, with all the problems, we're lucky. She still has her job, and I'm making out. I mean, it's not great, but it could be a lot worse." He pauses, looks around blankly for a moment, sighs, and says, "I guess she's right. Her sister worked at Boeing for seven years and she got laid off a couple of months ago. No notice, nothing; just the pink slip. I mean, everybody knew there'd be layoffs there, but you know how it is. You don't think it's really going to happen to you.

"I try not to let it get me down. But it's hard to be thankful for not having bigger trouble than you've already got," he says ruefully. Then, a smile brightening his face for the first time, he adds, "But there's one thing I can be thankful for, and that's the kids; they're doing fine. I worry a little bit about what's going to happen, though. I guess you can't help it if you're a parent. Eric's the oldest; he's fifteen now, and you never know. Kids get into all kinds of trouble these days. But so far, he's okay. The girls, they're good kids. Carol worries about what'll happen when they get to those teenage years. But I think they'll be okay. We teach them decent values; they go to church every week. I have to believe that makes a difference."

"You say that you worry about Eric but that the girls will be fine because of the values of your family. Hasn't he been taught the same values?"

He thinks a moment, then says, "Did I say that? Yeah, I guess I did. I think maybe there's more ways for a boy to get in trouble than a girl." He laughs and says again, "Did I say *that*?" Then, more thoughtfully, "I don't know. I guess I worry about them all, but if you don't tell yourself that things'll work out okay, you go nuts. I mean, so much can go wrong with kids today.

"It used to be the Chinese family could really control the kids. When I was a kid, the family was law. My father was Chinese-born; he came here as a kid. My mother was born right here in this city. But the grandparents were all immigrants; everybody spoke Chinese at home; and we never lived more than a couple of blocks from both sides of the family. My parents were pretty Americanized everywhere but at home, at least while their parents were alive. My mother would go clean her mother's house for her because that's what a Chinese daughter did."

"Was that because your grandmother was old or sick?"

"No," he replies, shaking his head at the memory. "It's because that's what her mother expected her to do; that's the way Chinese families were then. We talk about that, Carol and me, and how things have changed. It's hard to imagine it, but that's the kind of control families had then.

"It's all changed now. Not that I'd want it that way. I want my kids to know respect for the family, but they shouldn't be servants. That's what my mother was, a servant for her mother.

"By the time my generation came along, things were already different. I couldn't wait to get away from all that family stuff. I mean, it was nice in some ways; there was always this big, noisy bunch of people around, and you knew you were part of something. That felt good. But Chinese families, boy, they don't let go. You felt like they were choking you.

"Now it's *really* different; it's like the kids aren't hardly Chinese any more. I mean, my kids are just like any other American kids. They never lived in a Chinese neighborhood like the one I grew up in, you know, the kind where the only Americans you see are the people who come to buy Chinese food or eat at the restaurants."

"You say they're ordinary American kids. What about the Chinese side? What kind of connection do they have to that?"

"It's funny," he muses. "We sent them to Chinese school because we wanted them to know about their history, and we thought they should know the language, at least a little bit. But they weren't really interested; they wanted to be like everybody else and eat peanut butter and jelly sandwiches. Lately it's a little different, but that's because they feel like they're picked on because they're Chinese. I mean, everybody's worrying about the Chinese kids being so smart and winning all the prizes at school, and the kids are angry about that, especially Eric. He says there's a lot of bad feelings about Chinese kids at school and that everybody's picking on them—the white kids and the black kids, all of them.

"So all of a sudden, he's becoming Chinese. It's like they're making him think about it because there's all this resentment about Asian kids all around. Until a couple of years ago, he had lots of white friends. Now he hangs out mostly with other Asian kids. I guess that's because they feel safer when they're together."

"How do you feel about this?"

The color rises in his face; his voice takes on an edge of agitation. "It's too bad. It's not the way I wanted it to be. I wanted my kids to know they're Chinese and be proud of it, but that's not what's going on now. It's more like . . . ," he stops, trying to find the words, then starts again. "It's like they have to defend themselves *because* they're Chinese. Know what I mean?" he asks. Then without waiting for an answer, he explains, "There's all this prejudice now, so then you can't forget you're Chinese.

"It makes me damn mad. You grow up here and they tell you everybody's equal and that any boy can grow up to be president. Not that I ever thought a Chinese kid could ever be president; any Chinese kid knows that's fairy tale. But I did believe the rest of it, you know, that if you're smart and work hard and do well, people will respect you and you'll be successful. Now, it looks like the smarter Chinese kids are, the more trouble they get."

"Do you think that prejudice against Chinese is different now than when you were growing up?"

"Yeah, I do. When I was a kid like Eric, nobody paid much attention to the Chinese. They left us alone, and we left them alone. But now all these Chinese kids are getting in the way of the white kids because there's so many of them, and they're getting better grades, and things like that. So then everybody gets mad because they think our kids are taking something from them."

He stops, weighs his last words, then says, "I guess they're right, too. When I was growing up, Chinese kids were lucky to graduate from high school, and we didn't get in anybody's way. Now so many Chinese kids are going to college that they're taking over places white kids used to have. I can understand that they don't like that. But that's not our problem; it's theirs. Why don't they work hard like Chinese kids do?

"It's not fair that they've got quotas for Asian kids because the people who run the colleges decided there's too many of them and not enough room for white kids. Nobody ever worried that there were too many white kids, did they?"

* * *

"It's not fair"—a cry from the heart, one I heard from nearly everyone in this study. For indeed, life has not been fair to the working-class people of America, no matter what their color or ethnic background. And it's precisely this sense that it's not fair, that there isn't enough to go around, that has stirred the racial and ethnic tensions that are so prevalent today.

In the face of such clear class disparities, how is it that our national discourse continues to focus on the middle class, denying the existence of a working class and rendering them invisible?

Whether a family or a nation, we all have myths that play tag with reality—myths that frame our thoughts, structure our beliefs, and organize our systems of denial. A myth encircles reality, encapsulates it, controls it. It allows us to know some things and to avoid knowing others, even when somewhere deep inside we really know what we don't want to know. Every parent has experienced this clash between myth and reality. We see signals that tell us a child is lying and explain them away. It isn't that we can't know; it's that we won't, that knowing is too difficult or painful, too discordant with the myth that defines the relationship, the one that says: *My child wouldn't lie to me.*

The same is true about a nation and its citizens. Myths are part of our national heritage, giving definition to the national character, offering guidance for both public and private behavior, comforting us in our moments of doubt. Not infrequently our myths trip over each other, providing a window into our often contradictory and ambivalently held beliefs. The myth that we are a nation of equals lives side-by-side in these United States with the belief in white supremacy. And, unlikely as it seems, it's quite possible to believe both at the same time. Sometimes we manage the conflict by shifting from one side to the other. More often, we simply redefine reality. The inequality of condition between whites and blacks isn't born in prejudice and discrimination, we insist; it's black inferiority that's the problem. Class distinctions have nothing to do with privilege, we say; it's merit that makes the difference.

It's not the outcome that counts, we maintain; it's the rules of the game. And since the rules say that everyone comes to the starting line equal, the different results are merely products of individual will and wit. The fact that working-class children usually grow up to be working-class parents doesn't make a dent in the belief system, nor does it lead to questions about why the written rule and the lived reality are at odds. Instead, with perfect circularity, the outcome reinforces the reasoning that says they're deficient, leaving those so labeled doubly wounded—first by the real problems in living they face, second by internalizing the blame for their estate.

Two decades ago, when I began the research for *Worlds of Pain*, we were living in the immediate aftermath of the civil rights revolution that had convulsed the nation since the mid-1950s. Significant gains had been won. And despite the tenacity with which this headway had been resisted by some, most white Americans were feeling good about themselves. No one expected the nation's racial problems and conflicts to dissolve easily or quickly. But there was also a sense that we were moving in the right direction, that there was a national commitment to redressing at least some of the worst aspects of black-white inequality.

In the intervening years, however, the national economy buckled under the weight of three recessions, while the nation's industrial base was undergoing a massive restructuring. At the same time, government policies requiring preferential treatment were enabling African-Americans and other minorities to make small but visible inroads into what had been, until then, largely white terrain. The sense of scarcity, always a part of American life but intensified sharply by the history of these economic upheavals, made minority gains seem particularly threatening to white working-class families.

It isn't, of course, just working-class whites who feel threatened by minority progress. Wherever racial minorities make inroads into formerly all-white territory, tensions increase. But it's working-class families who feel the fluctuations in the economy most quickly and most keenly. For them, these last decades have been like a bumpy roller coaster ride. "Every time we think we might be able to get ahead, it seems like we get knocked down again," declares Tom Ahmundsen, a forty-two-year-old white construction worker. "Things look a little better; there's a little more work; then all of a sudden, boom, the economy falls apart and it's gone. You can't count on anything; it really gets you down."

This is the story I heard repeatedly: Each small climb was followed by a fall, each glimmer of hope replaced by despair. As the economic vise tightened, despair turned to anger. But partly because we have so little concept of class resentment and conflict in America, this anger isn't directed so much at those above as at those below. And when whites at or near the bottom of the ladder look down in this nation, they generally see blacks and other minorities.

True, during all of the 1980s and into the 1990s, white ire was fostered by national administrations that fanned racial discord as a way of fending off white discontent—of diverting anger about the state of the economy and the declining quality of urban life to the foreigners and racial others in our midst. But our history of racial animosity coupled with our lack of class consciousness made this easier to accomplish than it might otherwise have been.

The difficult realities of white working-class life not withstanding, however, their whiteness has accorded them significant advantages—both materially and psychologically—over people of color. Racial discrimination and segregation in the workplace have kept competition for the best jobs at a minimum. They do, obviously, have to compete with each other for the resources available. But that's different. It's a competition among equals; they're all white. They don't think such things consciously, of course; they don't have to. It's understood, rooted in the culture and supported by the social contract that says they are the superior ones, the worthy ones. Indeed, this is precisely why, when the courts or the legislatures act in ways that seem to contravene that belief, whites experience themselves as victims.

From the earliest days of the republic, whiteness has been the ideal, and freedom and independence have been linked to being white. "Republicanism," writes labor historian David Roediger, "had long emphasized that the strength, virtue and resolve of a people guarded them from enslavement." And it was whites who had these qualities in abundance, as was evident, in the peculiarly circuitous reasoning of the time, in the fact that they were not slaves.

By this logic, the enslavement of blacks could be seen as stemming from their "slavishness" rather than from the institution of slavery. Slavery is gone now, but the reasoning lingers on in white America, which still insists that the lowly estate of people of color is due to their deficits, whether personal or cultural, rather than to the prejudice, discrimination, and institutionalized racism that has barred them from full participation in the society.

This is not to say that culture is irrelevant, whether among black Americans or any other group in our society. The lifeways of a people develop out of their experiences—out of the daily events, large and small, that define their lives; out of the resources that are available to them to meet both individual and group needs; out of the place in the social, cultural, and political systems within which group life is embedded. In the case of a significant proportion of blacks in America's inner cities, centuries of racism and economic discrimination have produced a subculture that is both personally and socially destructive. But to fault culture or the failure of individual responsibility without understanding the larger context within which such behaviors occur is to miss a vital piece of the picture. Nor does acknowledging the existence of certain destructive subcultural forms among some African-Americans disavow or diminish the causal connections between the structural inequalities at the social, political, and economic levels and the serious social problems at the community level.

In his study of "working-class lads" in Birmingham, England, for example, Paul Willis observes that their very acts of resistance to middle-class norms—the defiance with which these young men express their anger at class inequalities—help to reinforce the class structure by further entrenching them in their working-class status. The same can be said for some of the young men in the African-American community, whose active rejection of white norms and "in your face" behavior consigns them to the bottom of the American economic order.

To understand this doesn't make such behavior, whether in England or the United States, any more palatable. But it helps to explain the structural sources of cultural forms and to apprehend the social processes that undergird them. Like Willis's white "working-class lads," the hip-hoppers and rappers in the black community who are so determinedly "not white" are not just making a statement about black culture. They're also expressing their rage at white society for offering a promise of equality, then refusing to fulfill it. In the process, they're finding their own way to some accommodation and to a place in the world they can call their own, albeit one that ultimately reinforces their outsider status.

But, some might argue, white immigrants also suffered prejudice and discrimination in the years after they first arrived, but they found more socially acceptable ways to accommodate. It's true—and so do most of today's people of color, both immigrant and native born. Nevertheless, there's another truth as well. For wrenching as their early experiences were for white ethnics, they had an out. Writing about the Irish, for example, Roediger shows how they were able to insist upon their whiteness and to prove it by adopting the racist attitudes and behaviors of other whites, in the process often becoming leaders in the assault against blacks. With time and their growing political power, they won the prize they sought—recognition as whites. "The imperative to define themselves as white," writes Roediger, "came from the particular 'public and psychological wages' whiteness offered to a desperate rural and often preindustrial Irish population coming to labor in industrializing American cities."

Thus does whiteness bestow its psychological as well as material blessings on even the most demeaned. For no matter how far down the socioeconomic ladder whites may fall, the one thing they can't lose is their whiteness. No small matter because, as W. E. B. DuBois observed decades ago, the compensation of white workers includes a psychological wage, a bonus that enables them to believe in their inherent superiority over nonwhites.

It's also true, however, that this same psychological bonus that white workers prize so highly has cost them dearly. For along with the importation of an immigrant population, the separation of black and white workers has given American capital a reserve labor force to call upon whenever white workers seemed to them to get too "uppity." Thus, while racist ideology enables white workers to maintain the belief in their superiority, they have paid for that conviction by becoming far more vulnerable in the struggle for decent wages and working conditions than they might otherwise have been. . . .

■ READING 24

Middle-Class Families in the Age of Insecurity

Arlene Skolnick

In the fall of 2009, Brian Lawler was a 34-year-old airline pilot living in Virginia with his four children and his schoolteacher wife. Until recently, he had been a captain earning $68,000 a year, and expecting a raise. But suddenly, in a cost-cutting move, his airline demoted him and other captains to the rank of first officer. His salary was cut in half, to less than what his wife makes.

Lawler's story appeared on the front page of the *New York Times* on October 14, 2009, to illustrate a trend: Paycuts, downgrades, and shortened workweeks were occurring more often than at any time since the Great Depression. The economic meltdown was hitting not just people who actually lost their jobs, but those who still had them. Employers usually prefer to lay people off, rather than cut their pay, the article notes, because then the "demoralized" workers are gone.

Brian Lawler's frank description of his own "demoralization" gives a glimpse of the emotional toll that downgrading takes on workers and their families, a milder version of what has been called the "normal pathology" of job loss or other economic slides.

Not allowed to wear his captain's uniform, or command an airliner, and no longer the major breadwinner in the family, he feels, he says, "diminished." It bothers him that he can no longer pick up the check when the family goes out to dinner with his parents.

A more practical worry is that the mortgage on the family home is now more than he and his wife can afford. He worries that the children, who have not been told of change in home economics, will be disappointed when Santa brings them fewer Christmas gifts.

Though Lawler is often angry and upset, he prides himself on not showing it. But he regrets having recently blown up twice—once at his 3 year old for fussing about taking a nap, and once at his wife one day for not appreciating the effort and stress involved making it home early. "My mind is always on 20 different things," he told the reporter. ". . . Rush, rush, rush, and then somebody makes the wrong comment and I get uncorked." (Uchitelle, 2009).

The troubles Lawler mentions hit harder when somebody actually loses a job, and harder still when the months go by and joblessness drags on. That can be devastating for a family and for the future of the children. A large body research reveals that job loss or other financial setbacks can have profound effects on the mental and physical health of the unemployed person, on marriage, on parent-child relationships, and on children's well-being and their success at school. Stress in families can be highly contagious; one study found that college students who perceived their parents to be anxious about work were distracted and their academic performance declined (see Kalil, 2009). Another study found that children in families where the head of the household became unemployed were 15 percent more likely to repeat a grade (Luo 2009).

Though the two-earner family has become the norm, unemployment seems to be harder on everyone when the husband and father loses his job. A man's identity and sense of self-worth are still bound up with his work and ability to earn a living. The men feel diminished, as did Brian Lawler. They feel a loss of authority and respect in the household. Especially if he is at home all day, he is likely to become irritable with his wife and especially the children. If he remains out of work, he may become clinically depressed. The risk of suicide increases with every rise in unemployment rates.

With a strong marriage, supportive relatives, a roof over their heads and a still decent two-earner income, the Lawlers are obviously not the hardest hit victims of the recent recession. And of course Brian still has a job. But the family could be poster children for the economic forces that have made even solid middle-class lives far more uncertain and stressful. And the trouble started decades before the financial meltdown of 2008.

A QUIET DEPRESSION

The great untold story of the past four decades is the steady erosion of the economic underpinnings of American families, up and down the income scale, even while the national economy itself seemed to be thriving. Many of the family problems Americans worry about—single motherhood, teen pregnancy, twenty somethings seemingly unable to launch themselves into adulthood—have more to do with an unfriendly economic landscape than any lack of family values.

Actually, the story of middle-class economic decline *has* been told—by academics and journalists, but never became part of the public discussion of the changing family. A small but growing library of books and articles has documented the revolution in Americans' economic circumstances. The financial meltdown of 2007–08 did not mark a break from the stresses of recent decades so much as a worsening of a chronic condition. The economic lives of Americans up and down the income scale had become more precarious even when the economy seemed to be good and getting better according to standard indicators.

Almost three decades ago, in 1986, a British research firm, Oxford Analytica published a book entitled, *America in Perspective*. Five years earlier, at the start of the Reagan era, the firm, Oxford Analytica, had been commissioned by three major corporations—American Express, Sun Oil, and Bristol Meyers—to map the economic, social, and political trends likely to shape American society in the 1980s and beyond. The book was a compilation of many specific findings; it attracted little notice.

But it presented a remarkably prescient overview of how Americans would live and work in the coming era. The nation, the researchers concluded, was becoming a "high-risk, high-stress society." The postwar boom was over. Family incomes had stopped growing. The future would offer less opportunity, wider insecurity, greater risks of downward mobility, a widening gap between haves and have-nots, and fewer public efforts to respond to social needs.

The United States would become less "exceptional" than ever, and more like the older class-ridden nations of Europe. As a result, Americans would experience greater stress and anxiety than at any time since World War II. *"Tension between work, in the broad sense, and family will probably be the central dynamic of American society."*

More recently, a cover story in the March 2010 issue of *The Atlantic Magazine*, described "How a New Jobless Era will Transform America." The writer, Don Peck, cites a long line of social science research on the impact of hard times on individuals and families, starting with classic studies of families in the Great Depression. Peck predicted that the current era of high unemployment would not end soon, and more than more than five and half years after the meltdown, his prediction has turned out to be right. He argues that this period of sustained joblessness "will likely change the life course and character of a generation of young adults. It will leave an indelible imprint on many blue collar men. It could cripple marriage as an institution in many communities . . ."

Peck's article did not get much attention from the public and the media, especially in comparison to an earlier cover story in *The Atlantic*—"Dan Quayle was Right"—the 1993 assault on single motherhood and divorce that sold a record number of copies, and helped to launch the "marriage movement" of the 1990s.

As of now, however, policy makers still seem oblivious to how much harm the trouble in the larger economy is inflicting on well-being of children and families. Globalization, the computer revolution, and new technologies were the driving forces behind the upheaval, but politics set the tone and defined the limits of public policy. The result was an extreme disconnect between the nation's complacent conversation about the economy and its worried talk about family decline.

You would think that in a country deeply anxious about the "breakdown" in American family life, where any statistical blip in rates of marriage or divorce or births to unwed mothers, or of women supposedly "opting out" of the workforce makes headlines, that a decades-long decline of family security and opportunity would be big news.

But somehow such stories don't strike nerves attuned more to tremors in the nation's moral foundations than its home economics. The conventional wisdom has been that feminism, along with the hedonism and sexual excesses of the "the sixties" lured women away from home and family, and made marriage an endangered institution.

Even the Great Recession has been reshaped into a moral tale. A great "Myth of Over-consumption" (Warren and Tyagi, 2003) has spread through America to explain why so many families are in financial trouble. Why have they run up so much debt on their credit cards? Why are they behind on their mortgage payments? Why haven't they saved more?

The myth says that families have been blowing their paychecks on things they don't really need: McMansions, granite countertops, designer clothes and shoes, eating out too much, fancy vacations, and too many lattes at Starbucks. In fact, however, there are government records going back a century containing detailed information about spending patterns.

There is no evidence of more frivolous spending today than there was in the last generation. It turns out, according to Warren, that we are spending less on some things, and more on others. We are spending less on clothing and food than in the past and more on such things as phone services. The problem is that middle-class incomes have not kept pace with the rising costs of the basics of middle-class life: The price of housing has soared, as has the costs of medical care, and college.

The U.S. economy has changed in some disturbing ways since the 1970s. To this day, however, there has been a strange disconnect between the public discussion of the economics and debates about family change. The nation faces three major economic challenges. The most urgent problem the nation faces is the widespread joblessness that persists more than five years after the financial meltdown. The second problem is the extreme inequality that now sets us apart from other rich democracies: increasing poverty rates, a shrinking middle class, and the growing gulf between the very rich—the 1 percent—and everyone else.

The third major problem is economic insecurity—a quiet revolution in risk that has placed families of all income levels on a financial tightrope, one lost job, or major illness, away from disaster (Gosselin, 2008; Hacker, 2006). While there has been too little public discussion about all these problems, this new insecurity is discussed the least.

The problem is not that our political leaders ignore the state of the economy, or the struggles of the middle class. During 2012 presidential campaign, those topics were often at the center of angry debates. But what's not commonly recognised is how profoundly the economy's problems are affecting the lives of American families up and down the income scale. And even worse, the remedy that most pundits and politicians endorse can only make things worse: slashing government spending and cutting social safety nets—unemployment insurance, Social Security, Medicare.

Talking about poverty and unwed motherhood is useful for pundits and politicians, especially conservative ones. That's because the poor, especially the inner city poor, can be blamed for their own predicaments. They suffer from a "poverty of values" and personal responsibility. If only they had not dropped out of school, not got themselves pregnant before being married, not used drugs, not gotten arrested, or done something else risky and impulsive. But for middle-class families, such as the Lawlers, who suddenly fell from grace for no fault of their own, blaming their plight on bad values and bad choices just doesn't work.

Economic security was once the defining feature of middle-class life; it is no longer. The middle class is now exposed to the kind of financial upheavals that the poor and working classes have always lived with in more extreme form. The era of the steady blue collar job is over, and the threat of being replaced by a machine or a worker in India or China has advanced through the ranks of white-collar work and is moving through the professions.

Consider personal bankruptcy. Elizabeth Warren, formerly a law professor, now a Massachusetts Senator, has been studying bankruptcy since she graduated from law school. She and her colleagues have found that filings for bankruptcy more than quadrupled between 1980 and 2005. (In 2005, Congress made it harder for families to obtain relief from their debts through bankruptcy.) Then they discovered that the people in such deep financial trouble were ordinary middle-class families with children. These are families "who spent every last penny and then some" (2003, p. 10) to give their children a middle-class life.

Concerned about their children's futures in a global, high tech economy, these parents want their children to go to schools where they can get a solid education. That means living in a suburb or neighborhood known for having good public schools. The problem is that the demand for homes in such places has resulted in a bidding war, driving up real estate prices. As a result, the average middle-class family can only afford a home near good schools if both parents work. The second income is needed to pay the bills, not to serve as a cushion in times of special need. So family can be in trouble if either job is lost.

Soaring rates of bankruptcy are a barometer of middle-class economic distress. More children in a given year will live through their parent's bankruptcy than a parental divorce. There are more bankruptcies in a year than heart attacks. Like divorce, they have become a routine, rather than a rare event in middle-class life. And like divorce, "bankruptcy is about a destabilized family" (Warren and Tyagi, 2003, p. 177). But while the impact of divorce on children has been a much debated issue in the culture wars, the disruptions of family life children face because of financial losses are rarely discussed.

Part of the reason is that middle-class families feel that serious money troubles are shameful: There is a "code of silence" about the issue. Bankrupt families may feel that they don't know any other family in the same situation, while they may be surrounded by others who are in as much trouble as they are.

CONCLUSION

We badly need a new conversation about "family values," and a new definition of the term for the twenty-first century. The Oxford researchers did not predict the long-term outcome of the shift from postwar prosperity to the high-risk, high-stress society. The future, they argue, would depend on which of the two contrasting traditions the nation would embrace: the "business of American is business" tradition, versus the more egalitarian American dream of widespread opportunity and shared prosperity.

For anyone born since about 1980, today's economy appears to be a natural habitat. Even for the older generations who actually remember living in postwar America, it's hard to believe that from the late 1940s to the early 1980s America was once a country in which the majority of people enjoyed a middle-class standard of living.

When I tell people in their twenties and thirties that you could once get a good college education for free, or close to it, they can scarcely believe it. There is much else that is hard to believe about the era that has been labeled "The Great Prosperity." Top tax rates for the wealthy were 70 to 90 percent, for example; and this in the Republican administration of Dwight Eisenhower. Working 40 hours a week was considered full time. And most middle-class employees enjoyed job security, good pay, and benefits such as health insurance and pensions.

By the 1950s, 60 percent of the population had attained a middle-class standard of living, in contrast to only 31 percent in the last year of prosperity before the Great Depression. The unionized working class, particularly white workers, experienced the greatest change of fortune, being able to move from urban slums to the new suburbia springing up all over.

Postwar America was not a Utopia, however. Affluence was never as widespread as many people assumed there was. There were still people living in what was called "pockets of poverty"; Michael Harrington's 1960 book *The Other America* was credited with the "discovery" of poverty. Racism and discrimination were rampant, and not only in the South. And women were constrained by "the feminine mystique."

The Great Prosperity was fuelled by the spectacular growth of the American economy, the strength of the labor movement, and massive government spending, much of it justified as defense spending. While it lasted, it nurtured a sense that the end of scarcity was here to stay. It encouraged a readiness to tackle longstanding problems such as poverty and racial inequality. Government investments in education, scientific research, new technologies, and infrastructure also had social consequences: increased levels of education for both men and women, longer, healthier lives—all these were part of the boom.

We need a drastically altered definition of family values and new thinking about the role of government as well as business in sustaining the well-being of parents and children. We can't banish the computer and the Internet, and restore the industrial economy as it was in the fifties. We need new family policies geared to the realities of a fast changing global economy and an irreversible shift in gender relations.

All the advanced countries have experienced technological change and globalization, but none has experienced the levels of inequality, instability, family stress, and poverty we have. Nor have they lost the basic protections Americans once had against job loss, disability, illness and old age, at a time when they are needed the most. In short, the new U.S. economy has undermined the conditions that enable children and families to thrive.

But this is unsustainable. In a postindustrial information society, the family's role is more central than ever; only families can create, nurture, and sustain the human capital that an advanced economy needs today to remain competitive. Sooner or later, attention must be paid to the profound impact that the high-risk, high-stress winner take all economy inflicts on families and on the development of children and young people.

References

Gosselin, P. (2008). *High Wire: The Precarious Financial Lives of American Families.* New York: Basic Books.

Hacker, J. (2006). *The Great Risk Shift: The Assault on American Jobs, Families, Health Care and Retirement—And How You Can Fight Back.* New York: Oxford.

Kalil, A. (2009) "Joblessness, family relations and children's deveopment" In *Family Matters: Australian Institute of Family Studies Journal. No. 83.*

Luo, M. (2009) "Job Woes Exacting a Toll on Family Life." *New York Times,* Nov. 11.

Uchitelle, L. (2009). "Still on the Job at Half the Pay." *New York Times,* Oct. 14.

Warren E., and Tyagi, A.E. (2003) *The Two Income Trap: Why Middle Class Parents are Going Broke.* New York: Basic Books.

11

Dimensions of Diversity

■ READING 25

Diversity within African American Families

Ronald L. Taylor

PERSONAL REFLECTIONS

My interest in African American families as a topic of research was inspired more than two decades ago by my observation and growing dismay over the stereotypical portrayal of these families presented by the media and in much of the social science literature. Most of the African American families I knew in the large southern city in which I grew up were barely represented in the various "authoritative" accounts I read and other scholars frequently referred to in their characterizations and analyses of such families. Few such accounts have acknowledged the regional, ethnic, class, and behavioral diversity within the African American community and among families. As a result, a highly fragmented and distorted public image of African American family life has been perpetuated that encourages perceptions of African American families as a monolith. The 1986 television documentary *A CBS Report: The Vanishing Family: Crisis in Black America*, hosted by Bill Moyers, was fairly typical of this emphasis. It focused almost exclusively on low-income, single-parent households in inner cities, characterized them as "vanishing" non-families, and implied that such families represented the majority of African American families in urban America. It mattered little that poor, single-parent households in the inner cities made up less than a quarter of all African American families at the time the documentary was aired.

As an African American reared in the segregated South, I was keenly aware of the tremendous variety of African American families in composition, lifestyle, and socioeconomic status. Racial segregation ensured that African American families, regardless of means or circumstances, were constrained to live and work in close proximity to one another. Travel outside the South made me aware of important regional differences among African American families as well. For example, African American families in the Northeast appeared far more segregated by socioeconomic status than did families in many parts of the South with which I was familiar. As a graduate student at Boston University during the late 1960s, I recall the shock I experienced upon seeing the level of concentrated poverty among African American families in Roxbury, Massachusetts, an experience duplicated in travels to New York, Philadelphia, and Newark. To be sure, poverty of a similar magnitude was prevalent throughout the South, but was far less concentrated and, from my perception, far less pernicious.

As I became more familiar with the growing body of research on African American families, it became increasingly clear to me that the source of a major distortion in the portrayal of African American families in the social science literature and the media was the overwhelming concentration on impoverished inner-city communities of the Northeast and Midwest to the near exclusion of the South, where more than half the African American families are found and differences among them in family patterns, lifestyles, and socioeconomic characteristics are more apparent.

In approaching the study of African American families in my work, I have adopted a *holistic* perspective. This perspective, outlined first by DuBois (1898) and more recently by Billingsley (1992) and Hill (1993), emphasizes the influence of historical, cultural, social, economic, and political forces in shaping contemporary patterns of family life among African Americans of all socioeconomic backgrounds. Although the impact of these external forces is routinely taken into account in assessing stability and change among white families, their effects on the structure and functioning of African American families are often minimized. In short, a holistic approach undertakes to study African American families *in context*. My definition of the *family*, akin to the definition offered by Billingsley (1992), views it as an intimate association of two or more persons related to each other by blood, marriage, formal or informal adoption, or appropriation. The latter term refers to the incorporation of persons in the family who are unrelated by blood or marital ties but are treated as though they are family. This definition is broader than other dominant definitions of families that emphasize biological or marital ties as defining characteristics.

This [reading] is divided into three parts. The first part reviews the treatment of African American families in the historical and social sciences literatures. It provides a historical overview of African American families, informed by recent historical scholarship, that corrects many of the misconceptions about the nature and quality of family life during and following the experience of slavery. The second part examines contemporary patterns of marriage, family, and household composition among African Americans in response to recent social, economic, and political developments in the larger society. The third part explores some of the long-term implications of current trends in marriage and family behavior for community functioning and individual well-being, together with implications for social policy.

THE TREATMENT OF AFRICAN AMERICAN FAMILIES IN AMERICAN SCHOLARSHIP

As an area of scientific investigation, the study of African American family life is of recent vintage. As recently as 1968, Billingsley, in his classic work *Black Families in White America*, observed that African American family life had been virtually ignored in family studies and studies of race and ethnic relations. He attributed the general lack of interest among white social scientists, in part, to their "ethnocentrism and intellectual commitment to peoples and values transplanted from Europe" (p. 214). Content analyses of key journals in sociology, social work, and family studies during the period supported Billingsley's contention. For example, a content analysis of 10 leading journals in sociology and social work by Johnson (1981) disclosed that articles on African American families constituted only 3% of 3,547 empirical studies of American families published between 1965 and 1975. Moreover, in the two major journals in social work, only one article on African American families was published from 1965 to 1978. In fact, a 1978 special issue of the *Journal of Marriage and the Family* devoted to African American families accounted for 40% of all articles on these families published in the 10 major journals between 1965 and 1978.

Although the past two decades have seen a significant increase in the quantity and quality of research on the family lives of African Americans, certain features and limitations associated with earlier studies in this area persist (Taylor, Chatters, Tucker, & Lewis, 1990). In a review of recent research on African American families, Hill (1993) concluded that many studies continue to treat such families in superficial terms; that is, African American families are not considered to be an important unit of focus and, consequently, are treated peripherally or omitted altogether. The assumption is that African American families are automatically treated in all analyses that focus on African Americans as individuals; thus, they are not treated in their own right. Hill noted that a major impediment to understanding the functioning of African American families has been the failure of most analysts to use a theoretical or conceptual framework that took account of the totality of African American family life. Overall, he found that the preponderance of recent studies of African American families are

(a) fragmented, in that they exclude the bulk of Black families by focusing on only a subgroup; (b) ad hoc, in that they apply arbitrary explanations that are not derived from systematic theoretical formulations that have been empirically substantiated; (c) negative, in that they focus exclusively on the perceived weaknesses of Black families; and (d) internally oriented, in that they exclude any systematic consideration of the role of forces in the wider society on Black family life. (p. 5)

THEORETICAL APPROACHES

The study of African American families, like the study of American families in general, has evolved through successive theoretical formulations. Using white family structure as the norm, the earliest studies characterized African American families as impoverished versions of white families in which the experiences of slavery, economic deprivation, and racial discrimination had induced pathogenic and dysfunctional features (Billingsley, 1968). The classic statement of this perspective was presented by Frazier, whose study, *The Negro Family in the United States* (1939), was the first comprehensive analysis of African American family life and its transformation under various historical conditions— slavery, emancipation, and urbanization (Edwards, 1968).

It was Frazier's contention that slavery destroyed African familial structures and cultures and gave rise to a host of dysfunctional family features that continued to undermine the stability and well-being of African American families well into the 20th century. Foremost among these features was the supposed emergence of the African American "matriarchal" or maternal family system, which weakened the economic position of African American men and their authority in the family. In his view, this family form was inherently unstable and produced pathological outcomes in the family unit, including high rates of poverty, illegitimacy, crime, delinquency, and other problems associated with the socialization of children. Frazier concluded that the female-headed family had become a common tradition among large segments of lower-class African American migrants to the North during the early 20th century. The two-parent male-headed household represented a second tradition among a minority of African Americans who enjoyed some of the freedoms during slavery, had independent artisan skills, and owned property.

Frazier saw an inextricable connection between economic resources and African American family structure and concluded that as the economic position of African Americans improved, their conformity to normative family patterns would increase. However, his important insight regarding the link between family structure and economic resources was obscured by the inordinate emphasis he placed on the instability and "self-perpetuating pathologies" of lower-class African American families, an emphasis that powerfully contributed to the pejorative tradition of scholarship that emerged in this area. Nonetheless, Frazier recognized the diversity of African American families and in his analyses, "consistently attributed the primary sources of family instability to external forces (such as racism, urbanization, technological changes and recession) and not to internal characteristics of Black families" (Hill, 1993, pp. 7–8).

During the 1960s, Frazier's characterization of African American families gained wider currency with the publication of Moynihan's *The Negro Family: The Case for National Action* (1965), in which weaknesses in family structure were identified as a major source of social problems in African American communities. Moynihan attributed high rates of welfare dependence, out-of-wedlock births, educational failure, and other problems to the "unnatural" dominance of women in African American families. Relying largely on the work of Frazier as a source of reference, Moynihan traced the alleged "tangle of pathology" that characterized urban African American families to the experience of slavery and 300 years of racial oppression, which, he concluded, had caused "deep-seated structural distortions" in the family and community life of African Americans.

Although much of the Moynihan report, as the book was called, largely restated what had become conventional academic wisdom on African American families during the 1960s, its generalized indictment of all African American families ignited a firestorm of criticism and debate and inspired a wealth of new research and writings on the nature and quality of African American family life in the United States (Staples & Mirande, 1980). In fact, the 1970s saw the beginning of the most prolific period of research on African American families, with more than 50 books and 500 articles published during that decade alone, representing a fivefold increase over the literature produced in all the years since the publication of DuBois's (1909) pioneering study of African American family life (Staples & Mirande, 1980). To be sure, some of this work was polemical and defensively apologetic, but much of it sought to replace ideology with research and to provide alternative perspectives for interpreting observed differences in the characteristics of African American and white families (Allen, 1978).

Critics of the deficit or pathology approach to African American family life (Scanzoni, 1977; Staples, 1971) called attention to the tendency in the literature to ignore family patterns among the majority of African Americans and to overemphasize findings derived from studies of low-income and typically problem-ridden families. Such findings were often generalized and accepted as descriptive of the family life of all African American families, with the result that popular but erroneous images of African American family life were perpetuated. Scrutinizing the research literature of the 1960s, Billingsley (1968) concluded that when the majority of African American families was considered, evidence refuted the characterization of African American family life as unstable, dependent on welfare, and matriarchal. In his view, and in the view of a growing number of scholars in the late 1960s and early 1970s, observed differences between white and African American families were largely the result of differences in socioeconomic position and of differential access to economic resources (Allen, 1978; Scanzoni, 1977).

Thus, the 1970s witnessed not only a significant increase in the diversity, breadth, and quantity of research on African American families, but a shift away from a social pathology perspective to one emphasizing the resilience and adaptiveness of African American families under a variety of social and economic conditions. The new emphasis reflected what Allen (1978) referred to as the "cultural variant" perspective, which treats African American families as different but legitimate functional forms. From this perspective, "Black and White family differences [are] taken as given, without the presumption of one family form as normative and the other as deviant" (Farley & Allen, 1987, p. 162). In accounting for observed racial differences in family patterns, some researchers have taken a *structural perspective*, emphasizing poverty and other socioeconomic factors as key processes (Billingsley, 1968). Other scholars have taken a *cultural approach*, stressing elements of the West African cultural heritage, together with distinctive experiences, values, and behavioral modes of adaptation developed in this country, as major determinants (Nobles, 1978; Young, 1970). Still others (Collins, 1990; Sudarkasa, 1988) have pointed to evidence supporting both interpretations and have argued for a more comprehensive approach.

Efforts to demythologize negative images of African American families have continued during the past two decades, marked by the development of the first national sample of adult African Americans, drawn to reflect their distribution throughout the United States (Jackson, 1991), and by the use of a variety of conceptualizations, approaches, and methodologies in the study of African American family life (Collins, 1990; McAdoo, 1997). Moreover, the emphasis in much of the recent work

> has not been the defense of African American family forms, but rather the identification of forces that have altered long-standing traditions. The ideological paradigms identified by Allen (1978) to describe the earlier thrust of Black family research—cultural equivalence, cultural deviance, and cultural variation—do not fully capture the foci of this new genre of work as a whole. (Tucker & Mitchell-Kernan, 1995, p. 17)

Researchers have sought to stress balance in their analyses, that is, to assess the strengths and weaknesses of African American family organizations at various socioeconomic levels, and the need for solution-oriented studies (Hill, 1993). At the same time, recent historical scholarship has shed new light on the relationship of changing historical circumstances to characteristics of African American family organization and has underscored the relevance of historical experiences to contemporary patterns of family life.

AFRICAN AMERICAN FAMILIES IN HISTORICAL PERSPECTIVE

Until the 1970s, it was conventional academic wisdom that the experience of slavery decimated African American culture and created the foundation for unstable female—dominated households and other familial aberrations that continued into the 20th century. This thesis, advanced by Frazier (1939) and restated by Moynihan (1965), was seriously challenged by the pioneering historical research of Blassingame (1972), Furstenberg, Hershberg, and Modell (1975), and Gutman (1976), among others. These works provide compelling documentation of the centrality of family and kinship among African Americans during the long years of bondage and how African Americans created and sustained a rich cultural and family life despite the brutal reality of slavery.

In his examination of more than two centuries of slave letters, autobiographies, plantation records, and other materials, Blassingame (1972) meticulously documented the nature of community, family organization, and culture among American slaves. He concluded that slavery was not "an all-powerful, monolithic institution which strip[ped] the slave of any meaningful and distinctive culture, family life, religion or manhood" (p. vii). To the contrary, the relative freedom from white control that slaves enjoyed in their quarters enabled them to create and sustain a complex social organization that incorporated "norms of conduct, defined roles and behavioral patterns" and provided for the traditional functions of group solidarity, defense, mutual assistance, and family organization. Although the family had no legal standing in slavery and was frequently disrupted, Blassingame noted its major role as a source of survival for slaves and as a mechanism of social control for slaveholders, many of whom encouraged "monogamous mating arrangements" as insurance against runaways and rebellion. In fashioning familial and community organization, slaves drew upon the many remnants of their African heritage (e.g., courtship rituals, kinship networks, and religious beliefs), merging those elements with American forms to create a distinctive culture, features of which persist in the contemporary social organization of African American family life and community.

Genovese's (1974) analysis of plantation records and slave testimony led him to similar conclusions regarding the nature of family life and community among African Americans under slavery. Genovese noted that, although chattel bondage played havoc with the domestic lives of slaves and imposed severe constraints on their ability to enact and sustain normative family roles and functions, the slaves "created impressive norms of family, including as much of a nuclear family norm as conditions permitted and . . . entered the postwar social system with a remarkably stable base" (p. 452). He attributed this stability to the extraordinary resourcefulness and commitment of slaves to marital relations and to what he called a "paternalistic compromise," or bargain between masters and slaves that recognized certain reciprocal obligations and rights, including recognition of slaves' marital and family ties. Although slavery undermined the role of African American men as husbands and fathers, their function as role models for their children and as providers for their families was considerably greater than has generally been supposed. Nonetheless, the tenuous position of male slaves as husbands and fathers and the more visible and nontraditional roles assumed by female slaves gave rise to legends of matriarchy and emasculated men. However, Genovese contended that the relationship between slave men and women came closer to approximating gender equality than was possible for white families.

Perhaps the most significant historical work that forced revisions in scholarship on African American family life and culture during slavery was Gutman's (1976) landmark study, *The Black Family in Slavery and Freedom*. Inspired by the controversy surrounding the Moynihan report and its thesis that African American family disorganization was a legacy of slavery, Gutman made ingenious use of quantifiable data derived from plantation birth registers and marriage applications to re-create family and kinship structures among African Americans during slavery and after emancipation. Moreover, he marshaled compelling evidence to explain how African Americans developed an autonomous and complex culture that enabled them to cope with the harshness of enslavement, the massive relocation from relatively small economic units in the upper South to vast plantations in the lower South between 1790 and 1860, the experience of legal freedom in the rural and urban South, and the transition to northern urban communities before 1930.

Gutman reasoned that, if family disorganization (fatherless, matrifocal families) among African Americans was a legacy of slavery, then such a condition should have been more common among urban African Americans closer in time to slavery—in 1850 and 1860—than in 1950 and 1960. Through careful examination of census data, marriage licenses, and personal documents for the period after 1860, he found that stable, two-parent households predominated during slavery and after emancipation and that families headed by African American women at the turn of the century were hardly more prevalent than among comparable white families. Thus "[a]t all moments in time between 1860 and 1925 . . . the typical Afro-American family was lower class in status and headed by two parents. That was so in the urban and rural South in 1880 and 1900 and in New York City in 1905 and 1925" (p. 456). Gutman found that the two-parent family was just as common among the poor as among the more advantaged, and as common among southerners as those in the Northeast. For Gutman, the key to understanding the durability of African American families during and after slavery lay in the distinctive African American culture that evolved from the cumulative slave experiences that provided a defense against some of the more destructive and dehumanizing aspects of that system. Among the more enduring and important aspects of that culture are the enlarged kinship network and certain domestic arrangements (e.g., the sharing of family households with nonrelatives and the informal adoption of children) that, during slavery, formed the core of evolving African American communities and the collective sense of interdependence.

Additional support for the conclusion that the two-parent household was the norm among slaves and their descendants was provided by Furstenberg et al. (1975) from their study of the family composition of African Americans, native-born whites, and immigrants to Philadelphia from 1850 to 1880. From their analysis of census data, Furstenberg et al. found that most African American families, like those of other ethnic groups, were headed by two parents (75% for African Americans versus 73% for native whites). Similar results are reported by Pleck (1973) from her study of African American family structure in late 19th-century Boston. As these and other studies (Jones, 1985; White, 1985) have shown, although female-headed households were common among African Americans during and following slavery, such households were by no means typical. In fact, as late as the 1960s, three fourths of African American households were headed by married couples (Jaynes & Williams, 1989; Moynihan, 1965).

However, more recent historical research would appear to modify, if not challenge, several of the contentions of the revisionist scholars of slavery. Manfra and Dykstra (1985) and Stevenson (1995), among others, found evidence of considerably greater variability in slave family structure and in household composition than was reported in previous works. In her study of Virginia slave families from 1830 to 1860, Stevenson (1995) discovered evidence of widespread matrifocality, as well as other marital and household arrangements, among antebellum slaves. Her analysis of the family histories of slaves in colonial and antebellum Virginia revealed that many slaves did not have a nuclear "core" in their families. Rather, the "most discernible ideal for their principal kinship organization was a malleable extended family that provided its members with nurture, education, socialization, material support, and recreation in the face of the potential social chaos the slavemasters' power imposed" (1995, p. 36).

A variety of conditions affected the family configurations of slaves, including cultural differences among the slaves themselves, the state or territory in which they lived, and the size of the plantation on which they resided. Thus, Stevenson concluded that

> the slave family was not a static, imitative institution that necessarily favored one form of family organization over another. Rather, it was a diverse phenomenon, sometimes assuming several forms even among the slaves of one community. . . . Far from having a negative impact, the diversity of slave marriage and family norms, as a measure of the slave family's enormous adaptive potential, allowed the slave and the slave family to survive. (p. 29)

Hence, "postrevisionist" historiography emphasizes the great diversity of familial arrangements among African Americans during slavery. Although nuclear, matrifocal, and extended families were prevalent, none dominated slave family forms. These postrevisionist amendments notwithstanding, there is compelling historical evidence that

African American nuclear families and kin-related households remained relatively intact and survived the experiences of slavery, Reconstruction, the Great Depression, and the transition to northern urban communities. Such evidence underscores the importance of considering recent developments and conditions in accounting for changes in family patterns among African Americans in the contemporary period.

CONTEMPORARY AFRICAN AMERICAN FAMILY PATTERNS

Substantial changes have occurred in patterns of marriage, family, and household composition in the United States during the past three decades, accompanied by significant alterations in the family lives of men, women, and children. During this period, divorce rates have more than doubled, marriage rates have declined, fertility rates have fallen to record levels, the proportion of "traditional" families (nuclear families in which children live with both biological parents) as a percentage of all family groups has declined, and the proportion of children reared in single-parent households has risen dramatically (Taylor, 1997).

Some of the changes in family patterns have been more rapid and dramatic among African Americans than among the population as a whole. For example, while declining rates of marriage and remarriage, high levels of separation and divorce, and higher proportions of children living in single-parent households are trends that have characterized the U.S. population as a whole during the past 30 years, these trends have been more pronounced among African Americans and, in some respects, represent marked departures from earlier African American family patterns. A growing body of research has implicated demographic and economic factors as causes of the divergent marital and family experiences of African Americans and other populations.

In the following section, I examine diverse patterns and evolving trends in family structure and household composition among African Americans, together with those demographic, economic, and social factors that have been identified as sources of change in patterns of family formation.

Diversity of Family Structure

Since 1960, the number of African American households has increased at more than twice the rate of white households. By 1995, African American households numbered 11.6 million, compared with 83.7 million white households. Of these households, 58.4 million white and 8.0 million African American ones were classified as family households by the U.S. Bureau of the Census (1996), which defines a *household* as the person or persons occupying a housing unit and a *family* as consisting of two or more persons who live in the same household and are related by birth, marriage, or adoption. Thus, family households are households maintained by individuals who share their residence with one or more relatives, whereas nonfamily households are maintained by individuals with no relatives in the housing unit. In 1995, 70% of the 11.6 million African American households were family households, the same proportion as among white households (U.S. Bureau of the Census, 1996). However, nonfamily households have been increasing at a faster rate than family households among African Americans because of delayed marriages among young adults, higher rates of family disruption (divorce and separation), and sharp increases in the number of unmarried cohabiting couples (Cherlin, 1995; Glick, 1997).

Family households vary by type and composition. Although the U.S. Bureau of the Census recognizes the wide diversity of families in this country, it differentiates between three broad and basic types of family households: married-couple or husband-wife families, families with female householders (no husband present), and families with male householders (no wife present). Family composition refers to whether the household is *nuclear*, that is, contains parents and children only, or extended, that is, nuclear plus other relatives.

To take account of the diversity in types and composition of African American families, Billingsley (1968; 1992) added to these conventional categories *augmented* families (nuclear plus nonrelated persons), and modified the definition of nuclear family to include *incipient* (a married couple without children), *simple* (a couple with children), and *attenuated* (a single parent with children) families. He also added three combinations of augmented families: *incipient extended augmented* (a couple with relatives and nonrelatives), *nuclear extended augmented* (a couple with children, relatives, and nonrelatives), and *attenuated extended augmented* (a single parent with children, relatives, and nonrelatives). With these modifications, Billingsley identified 32 different kinds of nuclear, extended, and augmented family households among African Americans. His typology has been widely used and modified by other scholars (see, for example, Shimkin, Shimkin, & Frate, 1978; Stack, 1974). For example, on the basis of Billingsley's typology, Dressler, Haworth-Hoeppner, and Pitts (1985) developed a four-way typology with 12 subtypes for their study of household structures in a southern African American community and found a variety of types of female-headed households, less than a fourth of them consisting of a mother and her children or grandchildren.

However, as Staples (1971) pointed out, Billingsley's typology emphasized the household and ignored an important characteristic of such families—their "extendedness." African Americans are significantly more likely than whites to live in extended families that "transcend and link several different households, each containing a separate . . . family" (Farley & Allen, 1987, p. 168). In 1992, approximately 1 in 5 African American families was extended, compared to 1 in 10 white families (Glick, 1997). The greater proportion of extended households among African Americans has been linked to the extended family tradition of West African cultures (Nobles, 1978; Sudarkasa, 1988) and to the economic marginality of many African American families, which has encouraged the sharing and exchange of resources, services, and emotional support among family units spread across a number of households (Stack, 1974).

In comparative research on West African, Caribbean, and African American family patterns some anthropologists (Herskovits, 1958; Sudarkasa, 1997) found evidence of cultural continuities in the significance attached to coresidence, formal kinship relations, and nuclear families among black populations in these areas. Summarizing this work, Hill (1993, pp. 104–105) observed that, with respect to

co-residence, the African concept of family is not restricted to persons living in the same household, but includes key persons living in separate households. . . . As for defining kin relationships, the African concept of family is not confined to relations between formal kin, but includes networks of unrelated [i.e., "fictive kin"] as well as related persons living in separate households. . . . Herskovits (1941), the African nuclear family unit is not as central to its family organization as is the case for European nuclear families: "The African immediate family, consisting of a father, his wives, and their children, is but a part of a larger unit. This immediate family is generally recognized by Africanists as belonging to a local relationship group termed the 'extended family.'"

Similarly, Sudarkasa (1988) found that unlike the European extended family, in which primacy is given to the conjugal unit (husband, wife, and children) as the basic building block, the African extended family is organized around blood ties (consanguineous relations).

In their analysis of data from the National Survey of Black Americans (NSBA) on household composition and family structure, Hatchett, Cochran, and Jackson (1991) noted that the extended family perspective, especially kin networks, was valuable in describing the nature and functioning of African American families. They suggested that the "extended family can be viewed both as a family network in the physical-spatial sense and in terms of family relations or contact and exchanges. In this view of extendedness, family structure and function are interdependent concepts" (p. 49). Their examination of the composition of the 2,107 households in the NSBA resulted in the identification of 12 categories, 8 of which roughly captured the "dimensions of household family structure identified in Billingsley's typology of Black families (1968)—the incipient nuclear family, the incipient nuclear extended and/or augmented nuclear family, the simple nuclear family, the simple extended and/or augmented nuclear family, the attenuated nuclear family, and the attenuated extended and/or augmented family, respectively" (p. 51). These households were examined with respect to their *actual kin networks*, defined as subjective feelings of emotional closeness to family members, frequency of contact, and patterns of mutual assistance, and their *potential kin networks*, defined as the availability or proximity of immediate family members and the density or concentration of family members within a given range.

Hatchett et al. (1991) found that approximately 1 in 5 African American households in the NSBA was an extended household (included other relatives—parents and siblings of the household head, grandchildren, grandparents, and nieces and nephews). Nearly 20% of the extended households with children contained minors who were not the head's; most of these children were grandchildren, nieces, and nephews of the head. The authors suggested that "[t]hese are instances of informal fostering or adoption— absorption of minor children by the kin network" (p. 58).

In this sample, female-headed households were as likely to be extended as male-headed households. Hatchett et al. (1991) found little support for the possibility that economic hardship may account for the propensity among African Americans to incorporate other relatives in their households. That is, the inclusion of other relatives in the households did not substantially improve the overall economic situation of the households because the majority of other relatives were minor children, primarily grandchildren of heads who coresided with the household heads' own minor and adult children. Moreover, they stated, "household extendedness at both the household and extra-household levels appears to be a characteristic of black families, regardless of socioeconomic level" (p. 81), and regardless of region of the country or rural or urban residence.

The households in the NSBA were also compared in terms of their potential and actual kin networks. The availability of potential kin networks varied by the age of the respondent, by the region and degree of urban development of the respondent's place of residence, and by the type of household in which the respondent resided (Hatchett et al., 1991). For example, households with older heads and spouses were more isolated from kin than were younger households headed by single mothers, and female-headed households tended to have greater potential kin networks than did individuals in nuclear households. With respect to region and urbanicity, the respondents in the Southern and North Central regions and those in rural areas had a greater concentration of relatives closer at hand than did the respondents in other regions and those in urban areas. However, proximity to relatives and their concentration nearby did not translate directly into actual kin networks or extended family functioning:

> Complex relationships were found across age, income, and type of household. From these data came a picture of the Black elderly with high psychological connectedness to family in the midst of relative geographical and interactional isolation from them. The image of female single-parent households is, on the other hand, the reverse or negative of this picture. Female heads were geographically closer to kin, had more contact with them, and received more help from family but did not perceive as much family solidarity or psychological connectedness. (Hatchett et al., 1991, p. 81)

The nature and frequency of mutual aid among kin were also assessed in this survey. More than two thirds of the respondents reported receiving some assistance from family members, including financial support, child care, goods and services, and help during sickness and at death. Financial assistance and child care were the two most frequent types of support reported by the younger respondents, whereas goods and services were the major types reported by older family members. The type of support the respondents received from their families was determined, to some extent, by needs defined by the family life cycle.

In sum, the results of the NSBA document the wide variety of family configurations and households in which African Americans reside and suggest, along with other studies, that the diversity of structures represents adaptive responses to the variety of social, economic, and demographic conditions that African Americans have encountered over time (Billingsley, 1968; Farley & Allen, 1987).

Although Hatchett et al. (1991) focused on extended or augmented African American families in their analysis of the NSBA data, only 1 in 5 households in this survey contained persons outside the nuclear family. The majority of households was nuclear, containing one or both parents with their own children.

Between 1970 and 1990, the number of all U.S. married-couple families with children dropped by almost 1 million, and their share of all family households declined from 40% to 26% (U.S. Bureau of the Census, 1995). The proportion of married-couple families with children among African Americans also declined during this period, from 41% to 26% of all African American families. In addition, the percentage of African

American families headed by women more than doubled, increasing from 33% in 1970 to 57% in 1990. By 1995, married-couple families with children constituted 36% of all African American families, while single-parent families represented 64% (U.S. Bureau of the Census, 1996). The year 1980 was the first time in history that African American female-headed families with children outnumbered married-couple families. This shift in the distribution of African American families by type is associated with a number of complex, interrelated social and economic developments, including increases in age at first marriage, high rates of separation and divorce, male joblessness, and out-of-wedlock births.

Marriage, Divorce, and Separation

In a reversal of a long-time trend, African Americans are now marrying at a much later age than are persons of other races. Thirty years ago, African American men and women were far more likely to have married by ages 20–24 than were white Americans. In 1960, 56% of African American men and 36% of African American women aged 20–24 were never married; by 1993, 90% of all African American men and 81% of African American women in this age cohort were never married (U.S. Bureau of the Census, 1994).

The trend toward later marriages among African Americans has contributed to changes in the distribution of African American families by type. Delayed marriage tends to increase the risk of out-of-wedlock childbearing and single parenting (Hernandez, 1993). In fact, a large proportion of the increase in single-parent households in recent years is accounted for by never-married women maintaining families (U.S. Bureau of the Census, 1990).

The growing proportion of never-married young African American adults is partly a result of a combination of factors, including continuing high rates of unemployment, especially among young men; college attendance; military service; and an extended period of cohabitation prior to marriage (Glick, 1997; Testa & Krogh, 1995; Wilson, 1987). In their investigation of the effect of employment on marriage among African American men in the inner city of Chicago, Testa and Krogh (1995) found that men in stable jobs were twice as likely to marry as were men who were unemployed, not in school, or in the military. Hence, it has been argued that the feasibility of marriage among African Americans in recent decades has decreased because the precarious economic position of African American men has made them less attractive as potential husbands and less interested in becoming husbands, given the difficulties they are likely to encounter in performing the provider role in marriage (Tucker & Mitchell-Kernan, 1995).

However, other research has indicated that economic factors are only part of the story. Using census data from 1940 through the mid-1980s, Mare and Winship (1991) sought to determine the impact of declining employment opportunities on marriage rates among African Americans and found that although men who were employed were more likely to marry, recent declines in employment rates among young African American men were not large enough to account for a substantial part of the declining trend in their marriage rates. Similarly, in their analysis of data from a national survey of young African American adults, Lichter, McLaughlin, Kephart, and Landry (1992) found that lower employment rates among African American men were an important contributing factor to delayed marriage—and perhaps to nonmarriage—among African American women. However, even when marital opportunities were taken into account, the researchers found that the rate of marriage among young African American women in the survey was only 50% to 60% the rate of white women of similar ages.

In addition to recent declines in employment rates, an unbalanced sex ratio has been identified as an important contributing factor to declining marriage rates among African Americans. This shortage of men is due partly to high rates of mortality and incarceration of African American men (Kiecolt & Fossett, 1995; Wilson & Neckerman, 1986). Guttentag and Secord (1983) identified a number of major consequences of the shortage of men over time: higher rates of singlehood, out-of-wedlock births, divorce, and infidelity and less commitment among men to relationships. Among African Americans, they found that in 1980 the ratio of men to women was unusually low; in fact, few populations in the United States had sex ratios as low as those of African Americans. Because African American women outnumber men in each of the age categories 20 to 49, the resulting "marriage squeeze" puts African American women at a significant disadvantage in the marriage market, causing an unusually large proportion of them to remain unmarried. However, Glick (1997) observed a reversal of the marriage squeeze among African Americans in the age categories 18 to 27 during the past decade: In 1995, there were 102 African American men for every 100 African American women in this age range. Thus, "[w]hereas the earlier marriage squeeze made it difficult for Black women to marry, the future marriage squeeze will make it harder for Black men" (Glick, 1997, p. 126). But, as Kiecolt and Fossett (1995) observed, the impact of the sex ratio on marital outcomes for African Americans may vary, depending on the nature of the local marriage market. Indeed, "marriage markets are local, as opposed to national, phenomena which may have different implications for different genders . . . [for example,] men and women residing near a military base face a different sex ratio than their counterparts attending a large university" (Smith, 1995, p. 137).

African American men and women are not only delaying marriage, but are spending fewer years in their first marriages and are slower to remarry than in decades past. Since 1960, a sharp decline has occurred in the number of years African American women spend with their first husbands and a corresponding rise in the interval of separation and divorce between the first and second marriages (Espenshade, 1985; Jaynes & Williams, 1989). Data from the National Fertility Surveys of 1965 and 1970 disclosed that twice as many African American couples as white couples (10% versus 5%) who reached their 5th wedding anniversaries ended their marriages before their 10th anniversaries (Thornton, 1978), and about half the African American and a quarter of the white marriages were dissolved within the first 15 years of marriage (McCarthy, 1978). Similarly, a comparison of the prevalence of marital disruption (defined as separation or divorce) among 13 racial-ethnic groups in the United States based on the 1980 census revealed that of the women who had married for the first time 10 to 14 years before 1980, 53% of the African American women, 48% of the Native American women, and 37% of the non-Hispanic white women were separated or divorced by the 1980 census (Sweet & Bumpass, 1987).

Although African American women have a higher likelihood of separating from their husbands than do non-Hispanic white women, they are slower to obtain legal divorces (Chertin, 1996). According to data from the 1980 census, within three years of separating from their husbands, only 55% of the African American women had obtained divorces, compared to 91% of the non-Hispanic white women (Sweet & Bumpass, 1987). Cherlin speculated that, because of their lower expectations of remarrying, African American women may be less motivated to obtain legal divorces. Indeed, given the shortage of African American men in each of the age categories from 20 to 49, it is not surprising that the proportion of divorced women who remarry is lower among African American than among non-Hispanic white women (Glick, 1997). Overall, the remarriage rate among African Americans is about one fourth the rate of whites (Staples & Johnson, 1993).

Cherlin (1996) identified lower educational levels, high rates of unemployment, and low income as important sources of differences in African American and white rates of marital dissolution. However, as he pointed out, these factors alone are insufficient to account for all the observed difference. At every level of educational attainment, African American women are more likely to be separated or divorced from their husbands than are non-Hispanic white women. Using data from the 1980 census, Jaynes and Williams (1989) compared the actual marital-status distributions of African Americans and whites, controlling for differences in educational attainment for men and women and for income distribution for men. They found that when differences in educational attainment were taken into account, African American women were more likely to be "formerly married than White women and much less likely to be living with a husband" (p. 529). Moreover, income was an important factor in accounting for differences in the marital status of African American and white men. Overall, Jaynes and Williams found that socioeconomic differences explained a significant amount of the variance in marital status differences between African Americans and whites, although Bumpass, Sweet, and Martin (1990) noted that such differences rapidly diminish as income increases, especially for men. As Glick (1997) reported, African American men with high income levels are more likely to be in intact first marriages by middle age than are African American women with high earnings. This relationship between income and marital status, he stated, is strongest at the lower end of the income distribution, suggesting that marital permanence for men is less dependent on their being well-to-do than on their having the income to support a family.

As a result of sharp increases in marital disruption and relatively low remarriage rates, less than half (43%) the African American adults aged 18 and older were currently married in 1995, down from 64% in 1970 (U.S. Bureau of the Census, 1996). Moreover, although the vast majority of the 11.6 million African Americans households in 1995 were family households, less than half (47%) were headed by married couples, down from 56% in 1980. Some analysts expect the decline in marriage among African Americans to continue for some time, consistent with the movement away from marriage as a consequence of modernization and urbanization (Espenshade, 1985) and in response to continuing economic marginalization. But African American culture may also play a role. As a number of writers have noted (Billingsley, 1992; Cherlin, 1996), blood ties and extended families have traditionally been given primacy over other types of relationships, including marriage, among African Americans, and this emphasis may have influenced the way many African Americans responded to recent shifts in values in the larger society and the restructuring of the economy that struck the African American community especially hard.

Such is the interpretation of Cherlin (1992, p. 112), who argued that the institution of marriage has been weakened during the past few decades by the increasing economic independence of women and men and by a cultural drift "toward a more individualistic ethos, one which emphasized self-fulfillment in personal relations." In addition, Wilson (1987) and others described structural shifts in the economy (from manufacturing to service industries as a source of the growth in employment) that have benefited African American women more than men, eroding men's earning potential and their ability to support families. According to Cherlin, the way African Americans responded to such broad sociocultural and economic changes was conditioned by their history and culture:

> Faced with difficult times economically, many Blacks responded by drawing upon a model of social support that was in their cultural repertoire. . . . This response relied heavily on extended kinship networks and deemphasized marriage. It is a response that taps a traditional source of strength in African-American society: cooperation and sharing among a large network of kin. (p. 113)

Thus, it seems likely that economic developments and cultural values have contributed independently and jointly to the explanation of declining rates of marriage among African Americans in recent years (Farley & Allen, 1987).

Single-Parent Families

Just as rates of divorce, separation, and out-of-wedlock childbearing have increased over the past few decades, so has the number of children living in single-parent households. For example, between 1970 and 1990, the number and proportion of all U.S. single-parent households increased threefold, from 1 in 10 to 3 in 10. There were 3.8 million single-parent families with children under 18 in 1970, compared to 11.4 million in 1994. The vast majority of single-parent households are maintained by women (86% in 1994), but the number of single-parent households headed by men has more than tripled: from 393,000 in 1970 to 1.5 million in 1994 (U.S. Bureau of the Census, 1995).

Among the 58% of African American families with children at home in 1995, more were one-parent families (34%) than married-couple families (24%). In 1994, single-parent families accounted for 25% of all white family groups with children under age 18, 65% of all African American family groups, and 36% of Hispanic family groups (U.S. Bureau of the Census, 1995).

Single-parent families are created in a number of ways: through divorce, marital separation, out-of-wedlock births, or death of a parent. Among adult African American women aged 25–44, increases in the percentage of never-married women and disrupted marriages are significant contributors to the rise in female-headed households; for white women of the same age group, marital dissolution or divorce is the most important factor (Demo, 1992; Jaynes & Williams, 1989). Moreover, changes in the living arrangements of women who give birth outside marriage or experience marital disruption have also been significant factors in the rise of female-headed households among African

American and white women. In the past, women who experienced separation or divorce, or bore children out of wedlock were more likely to move in with their parents or other relatives, creating subfamilies; as a result, they were not classified as female headed. In recent decades, however, more and more of these women have established their own households (Parish, Hao, & Hogan, 1991).

An increasing proportion of female-headed householders are unmarried teenage mothers with young children. In 1990, for example, 96% of all births to African American teenagers occurred outside marriage; for white teenagers, the figure was 55% (National Center for Health Statistics, 1991). Although overall fertility rates among teenage women declined steadily from the 1950s through the end of the 1980s, the share of births to unmarried women has risen sharply over time. In 1970, the proportion of all births to unmarried teenage women aged 15–19 was less than 1 in 3; by 1991, it had increased to 2 in 3.

Differences in fertility and births outside marriage among young African American and white women are accounted for, in part, by differences in sexual activity, use of contraceptives, the selection of adoption as an option, and the proportion of premarital pregnancies that are legitimated by marriage before the children's births (Trusell, 1988). Compared to their white counterparts, African American teenagers are more likely to be sexually active and less likely to use contraceptives, to have abortions when pregnant, and to marry before the babies are born. In consequence, young African American women constitute a larger share of single mothers than they did in past decades. This development has serious social and economic consequences for children and adults because female-headed households have much higher rates of poverty and deprivation than do other families (Taylor, 1991b).

Family Structure and Family Dynamics

As a number of studies have shown, there is a strong correspondence between organization and economic status of families, regardless of race (Farley & Allen, 1987). For both African Americans and whites, the higher the income, the greater the percentage of families headed by married couples. In their analysis of 1980 census data on family income and structure, Farley and Allen (1987) found that "there were near linear decreases in the proportions of households headed by women, households where children reside with a single parent, and extended households with increases in economic status" (p. 185). Yet, socioeconomic factors, they concluded, explained only part of the observed differences in family organization between African Americans and whites. "Cultural factors—that is, family preferences, notions of the appropriate and established habits—also help explain race differences in family organization" (p. 186).

One such difference is the egalitarian mode of family functioning in African American families, characterized by complementarity and flexibility in family roles (Billingsley, 1992; Hill, 1971). Egalitarian modes of family functioning are common even among low-income African American families, where one might expect the more traditional patriarchal pattern of authority to prevail. Until recently, such modes of family functioning were interpreted as signs of weakness or pathology because they were counternormative to the gender-role division of labor in majority families (Collins, 1990).

Some scholars have suggested that role reciprocity in African American families is a legacy of slavery, in which the traditional gender division of labor was largely ignored by slaveholders, and Black men and women were "equal in the sense that neither sex wielded economic power over the other" (Jones, 1985, p. 14). As a result of historical experiences and economic conditions, traditional gender distinctions in the homemaker and provider roles have been less rigid in African American families than in white families (Beckett & Smith, 1981). Moreover, since African American women have historically been involved in the paid labor force in greater numbers than have white women and because they have had a more significant economic role in families than their white counterparts, Scott-Jones and Nelson-LeGall (1986, p. 95) argued that African Americans "have not experienced as strong an economic basis for the subordination of women, either in marital roles or in the preparation of girls for schooling, jobs, and careers."

In her analysis of data from the NSBA, Hatchett (1991) found strong support for an egalitarian division of family responsibilities and tasks. With respect to attitudes toward the sharing of familial roles, 88% of the African American adults agreed that women and men should share child care and housework equally, and 73% agreed that both men and women should have jobs to support their families. For African American men, support for an egalitarian division of labor in the family did not differ by education or socioeconomic level, but education was related to attitudes toward the sharing of family responsibilities and roles among African American women. College-educated women were more likely than were women with less education to support the flexibility and interchangeability of family roles and tasks.

Egalitarian attitudes toward familial roles among African Americans are also reflected in child-rearing attitudes and practices (Taylor, 1991a). Studies have indicated that African American families tend to place less emphasis on differential gender-role socialization than do other families (Blau, 1981). In her analysis of gender-role socialization among southern African American families, Lewis (1975) found few patterned differences in parental attitudes toward male and female roles. Rather, age and relative birth order were found to be more important than gender as determinants of differential treatment and behavioral expectations for children. Through their socialization practices, African American parents seek to inculcate in both genders traits of assertiveness, independence, and self-confidence (Boykin & Toms, 1985; Lewis, 1975). However, as children mature, socialization practices are adapted to reflect "more closely the structure of expectations and opportunities provided for Black men and women by the dominant society" (Lewis, 1975, p. 237)—that is, geared to the macrostructural conditions that constrain familial role options for African American men and women.

However, such shifts in emphasis and expectations often lead to complications in the socialization process by inculcating in men and women components of gender-role definitions that are incompatible or noncomplementary, thereby engendering a potential source of conflict in their relationships. Franklin (1986) suggested that young African American men and women are frequently confronted with contradictory messages and dilemmas as a result of familial socialization. On the one hand, men are socialized to embrace an androgynous gender role within the African American community, but, on the other hand, they are expected to perform according to the white masculine gender-role paradigm in some contexts. According to Franklin, this dual orientation tends to foster confusion in some young men and difficulties developing an appropriate gender identity. Likewise, some young African American women may receive two different and contradictory messages: "One message states, 'Because you will be a Black woman, it is imperative that you learn to take care of yourself because it is hard to find a Black man who will take care of you.' A second message . . . that conflicts with the first . . . is 'your ultimate achievement will occur when you have snared a Black man who will take care of you'" (Franklin, 1986, p. 109). Franklin contended that such contradictory expectations and mixed messages frequently lead to incompatible gender-based behaviors among African American men and women and conflicts in their relationships.

Despite the apparently greater acceptance of role flexibility and power sharing in African American families, conflict around these issues figures prominently in marital instability. In their study of marital instability among African American and white couples in early marriages, Hatchett, Veroff, and Douvan (1995) found young African American couples at odds over gender roles in the family. Anxiety over their ability to function in the provider role was found to be an important source of instability in the marriages for African American husbands, but not for white husbands. Hatchett (1991) observed that marital instability tended to be more common among young African American couples if the husbands felt that their wives had equal power in the family and if the wives felt there was not enough sharing of family tasks and responsibilities. Hatchett et al. (1991) suggested that African American men's feelings of economic anxiety and self-doubt may be expressed in conflicts over decisional power and in the men's more tenuous commitment to their marriages vis-à-vis African American women. Although the results of their study relate to African American couples in the early stages of marriage, the findings may be predictive of major marital difficulties in the long term. These and other findings (see, for example, Tucker & Mitchell-Kernan, 1995) indicate that changing attitudes and definitions of familial roles among young African American couples are tied to social and economic trends (such as new and increased employment opportunities for women and new value orientations toward marriage and family) in the larger society.

African American Families, Social Change, and Public Policy

Over the past three decades, no change in the African American community has been more fundamental and dramatic than the restructuring of families and family relationships. Since the 1960s, unprecedented changes have occurred in rates of marriage, divorce, and separation; in the proportion of single and two-parent households and births to unmarried mothers; and in the number of children living in poverty. To be sure, these changes are consistent with trends for the U.S. population as a whole, but they are more pronounced among African Americans, largely because of a conflux of demographic and economic factors that are peculiar to the African American community.

In their summary of findings from a series of empirical studies that investigated the causes and correlates of recent changes in patterns of African American family formation, Tucker and Mitchell-Kernan (1995) came to several conclusions that have implications for future research and social policy. One consistent finding is the critical role that sex ratios—the availability of mates—play in the formation of African American families. Analyzing aggregate-level data on African American sex ratios in 171 U.S. cities, Sampson (1995) found that these sex ratios were highly predictive of female headship, the percentage of married couples among families with school-age children, and the percentage of African American women who were single. In assessing the causal effect of sex ratios on the family structure of African Americans and whites, he showed that the effect is five times greater for the former than the latter. Similarly, Kiecolt and Fossett's (1995) analysis of African American sex ratios in Louisiana cities and counties disclosed that they had strong positive effects on the percentage of African American women who were married and had husbands present, the rate of marital births per thousand African American women aged 20–29, the percentage of married-couple families, and the percentage of children living in two-parent households.

Another consistent finding is the substantial and critical impact of economic factors on African American family formation, especially men's employment status. Analyses by Sampson (1995) and Darity and Myers (1995) provided persuasive evidence that economic factors play a major and unique role in the development and maintenance of African American families. Using aggregate data, Sampson found that low employment rates for African American men in cities across the United States were predictive of female headship, the percentage of women who were single, and the percentage of married-couple families among family households with school-age children. Moreover, comparing the effect of men's employment on the family structure of African American and white families, he found that the effect was 20 times greater for African Americans than for whites. Similar results are reported by Darity and Myers, who investigated the effects of sex ratio and economic marriageability—Wilson and Neckerman's (1986) Male Marriageability Pool Index—on African American family structure. They found that, although both measures were independently predictive of female headship among African Americans, a composite measure of economic and demographic factors was a more stable and effective predictor. Moreover, Sampson found that the strongest independent effect of these factors on family structure was observed among African American families in poverty. That is, "the lower the sex ratio and the lower the male employment rate the higher the rate of female-headed families with children and in poverty" (p. 250). It should be noted that neither rates of white men's employment nor white sex ratios was found to have much influence on white family structure in these analyses, lending support to Wilson's (1987) hypothesis regarding the structural sources of family disruption among African Americans.

Although the findings reported here are not definitive, they substantiate the unique and powerful effects of sex ratios and men's employment on the marital behavior and family structure of African Americans and point to other problems related to the economic marginalization of men and family poverty in African American communities. Some analysts have predicted far-reaching consequences for African Americans and for society at large should current trends in marital disruption continue unabated. Darity and Myers (1995) predicted that the majority of African American families will be headed by women by the beginning of the next decade if violent crime, homicide, incarceration, and other problems associated with the economic marginalization of African American men are allowed to rob the next generation of fathers and husbands. Moreover, they contended, a large number of such families are likely to be poor and isolated from the mainstream of American society.

The growing economic marginalization of African American men and their ability to provide economic support to families have contributed to their increasing estrangement from family life (Bowman, 1989; Tucker & Mitchell-Kernan, 1995) and are identified as pivotal factors in the development of other social problems, including drug abuse, crime, homicide, and imprisonment, which further erode their prospects as marriageable mates for African American women.

In addressing the structural sources of the disruption of African American families, researchers have advanced a number of short- and long-term proposals. There is considerable agreement that increasing the rate of marriage alone will not significantly improve the economic prospects of many poor African American families. As Ehrenreich (1986) observed, given the marginal economic position of poor African American men, impoverished African American women would have to be married to three such men—simultaneously—to achieve an average family income! Thus, for many African American women, increasing the prevalence of marriage will not address many of the problems they experience as single parents.

With respect to short-term policies designed to address some of the more deleterious effects of structural forces on African American families, Darity and Myers (1995) proposed three policy initiatives that are likely to produce significant results for African American communities. First, because research has indicated that reductions in welfare benefits have failed to stem the rise in female-headed households, welfare policy should reinstate its earlier objective of lifting the poor out of poverty. In Darity and Myers's view, concerns about the alleged disincentives of transfer payments are "moot in light of the long-term evidence that Black families will sink deeper into a crisis of female headship with or without welfare. Better a world of welfare-dependent, near-poor families than one of welfare-free but desolate and permanently poor families" (p. 288). Second, programs are needed to improve the health care of poor women and their children. One major potential benefit of such a strategy is an improvement in the sex ratio because the quality of prenatal and child care is one of the determinants of sex ratios. "By assuring quality health care now, we may help stem the tide toward further depletion of young Black males in the future" (p. 288). A third strategy involves improvements in the quality of education provided to the poor, which are key to employment gains.

Although these are important initiatives with obvious benefits to African American communities, in the long term, the best strategy for addressing marital disruptions and other family-related issues is an economic-labor market strategy. Because much of current social policy is ideologically driven, rather than formulated on the basis of empirical evidence, it has failed to acknowledge or address the extent to which global and national changes in the economy have conspired to marginalize significant segments of the African American population, both male and female, and deprive them of the resources to form or support families. Although social policy analysts have repeatedly substantiated the link between the decline in marriages among African Americans and fundamental changes in the U.S. postindustrial economy, their insights have yet to be formulated into a meaningful and responsive policy agenda. Until these structural realities are incorporated into governmental policy, it is unlikely that marital disruption and other adverse trends associated with this development will be reversed.

There is no magic bullet for addressing the causes and consequences of marital decline among African Americans, but public policies that are designed to improve the economic and employment prospects of men and women at all socioeconomic levels have the greatest potential for improving the lot of African American families. Key elements of such policies would include raising the level of education and employment training among African American youth, and more vigorous enforcement of antidiscrimination laws, which would raise the level of employment and earnings and contribute to higher rates of marriage among African Americans (Burbridge, 1995). To be sure, many of the federally sponsored employment and training programs that were launched during the 1960s and 1970s were plagued by a variety of administrative and organizational problems, but the effectiveness of some of these programs in improving the long-term employment prospects and life chances of disadvantaged youth and adults has been well documented (Taylor et al., 1990).

African American families, like all families, exist not in a social vacuum but in communities, and programs that are designed to strengthen community institutions and provide social support to families are likely to have a significant impact on family functioning. Although the extended family and community institutions, such as the church, have been important sources of support to African American families in the past, these community support systems have been overwhelmed by widespread joblessness, poverty, and a plethora of other problems that beset many African American communities. Thus, national efforts to rebuild the social and economic infrastructures of inner-city communities would make a major contribution toward improving the overall health and well-being of African American families and could encourage more young people to marry in the future.

Winning support for these and other policy initiatives will not be easy in a political environment that de-emphasizes the role of government in social policy and human welfare. But without such national efforts, it is difficult to see how many of the social conditions that adversely affect the structure and functioning of African American families will be eliminated or how the causes and consequences of marital decline can be ameliorated. If policy makers are serious about addressing conditions that destabilize families, undermine communities, and contribute to a host of other socially undesirable outcomes, new policy initiatives, such as those just outlined, must be given higher priority.

References

Allen, W. (1978). The search for applicable theories of black family life. *Journal of Marriage and the Family, 40,* 117–129.

Beckett, J., & Smith, A. (1981). Work and family roles: Egalitarian marriage in black and white families. *Social Service Review, 55,* 314–326.

Billingsley, A. (1968). *Black families in white America.* Englewood Cliffs, NJ: Prentice Hall.

Billingsley, A. (1992). *Climbing Jacob's ladder: The enduring legacy of African American families.* New York: Simon & Schuster.

Blassingame, J. (1972). *The slave community.* New York: Oxford University Press.

Blau, Zena. (1981). *Black children/white socialization.* New York: Free Press.

Bowman, P. J. (1989). Research perspectives on black men: Role strain and adaptation across the life cycle. In R. L. Jones (Ed.), *Black adult development and aging* (pp. 117–150). Berkeley, CA: Cobb & Henry.

Boykin, A. W., & Toms, F. D. (1985). Black child socialization: A conceptual framework. In H. P. McAdoo & J. L. McAdoo (Eds.), *Black children* (pp. 33–54). Beverly Hills, CA: Sage.

Bumpass, L., Sweet, J., & Martin, T. C. (1990). Changing patterns of remarriage. *Journal of Marriage and the Family, 52*, 747–756.

Burbridge, L. C. (1995). Policy implications of a decline in marriage among African Americans. In M. B. Tucker & C. Mitchell-Kernan (Eds.), *The decline in marriage among African Americans* (pp. 323–344). New York: Russell Sage Foundation.

Cherlin, A. (1992). *Marriage, divorce, remarriage* (rev. ed.). Cambridge, MA: Harvard University Press.

Cherlin, A. (1995). Policy issues of child care. In P. Chase-Lansdale & J. Brooks-Gunn (Eds.), *Escape from poverty* (pp. 121–137). New York: Cambridge University Press.

Cherlin, A. (1996). *Public and private families*. New York: McGraw-Hill.

Collins, P. (1990). *Black feminist thought*. Boston, MA: Unwin Hyman.

Darity, W., & Myers, S. (1995). Family structure and the marginalization of black men: Policy implications. In M. B. Tucker & C. Mitchell-Kernan (Eds.), *The decline in marriage among African Americans* (pp. 263–308). New York: Russell Sage Foundation.

Demo, D. (1992). Parent-child relations: Assessing recent changes. *Journal of Marriage and the Family, 54*, 104–117.

Dressler, W., Haworth-Hoeppner, S., & Pitts, B. (1985). Household structure in a southern black community. *American Anthropologist, 87*, 853–862.

DuBois, W. E. B. (1898). The study of the Negro problem. *Annals, 1*, 1–23.

DuBois, W. E. B. (1909). *The Negro American family*. Atlanta: Atlanta University Press.

Edwards, G. F. (1968). *E. Franklin Frazier on race relations*. Chicago: University of Chicago Press.

Ehrenreich, B. (1986, July-August). Two, three, many husbands. *Mother Jones*, 8–9.

Espenshade, T. (1985). Marriage trends in America: Estimates, implications, and underlying causes. *Population and Development Review, 11*, 193–245.

Farley, R., & Allen, W. (1987). *The color line and the quality of life in America*. New York: Oxford University Press.

Franklin, C. (1986). Black male-Black female conflict: Individually caused and culturally nurtured. In R. Staples (Ed.), *The black family* (3rd ed., pp. 106–113). Belmont, CA: Wadsworth.

Frazier, E. F. (1939). *The Negro family in the United States*. Chicago: University of Chicago Press.

Furstenberg, F., Hershberg, T., & Modell, J. (1975). The origins of the female-headed black family: The impact of the urban experience. *Journal of Interdisciplinary History, 6*, 211–233.

Genovese, E. (1974). *Roll Jordan roll: The world slaves made*. New York: Pantheon.

Glick, P. (1997). Demographic pictures of African American families. In H. McAdoo (Ed.), *Black families* (3rd ed., pp. 118–138). Thousand Oaks, CA: Sage.

Gutman, H. (1976). *The black family in slavery and freedom, 1750–1925*. New York: Pantheon.

Guttentag, M., & Secord, P. F. (1983). *Too many women*. Beverly Hills, CA: Sage.

Hatchett, S. (1991). Women and men. In J. Jackson (Ed.), *Life in black America* (pp. 84–104). Newbury Park, CA: Sage.

Hatchett, S., Cochran, D., & Jackson, J. (1991). In J. Jackson (Ed.), *Life in black America* (pp. 46–83). Newbury Park, CA: Sage.

Hatchett, S., Veroff, J., & Douvan, E. (1995). Marital instability among black and white couples in early marriage. In M. B. Tucker & C. Mitchell-Kernan (Eds.), *The decline in marriage among African Americans* (pp. 177–218). New York: Russell Sage Foundation.

Hernandez, D. J. (1993). *America's children*. New York: Russell Sage.

Herskovits, M. J. (1958). *The myth of the Negro past* (Beacon Paperback No. 69). Boston: Beacon Press.

Hill, R. (1971). *The strengths of black families*. New York: Emerson Hall.

Hill, R. (1993). *Research on the African American family: A holistic perspective*. Westport, CT: Auburn House.

Jackson, J. (Ed.). (1991). *Life in black America*. Newbury Park, CA: Sage.

Jaynes, G., & Williams, R. (1989). *A common destiny: Blacks and American society*. Washington, DC: National Academy Press.

Johnson, L. B. (1981). Perspectives on black family empirical research: 1965–1978. In H. P. McAdoo (Ed.), *Black families* (pp. 252–263). Beverly Hills, CA: Sage.

Jones, J. (1985). *Labor of love, labor of sorrow: Black women, work, and the family from slavery to the present*. New York: Basic Books.

Kiecolt, K., & Fossett, M. (1995). Mate availability and marriage among African Americans: Aggregate-and individual-level analysis. In M. B. Tucker & C. Mitchell-Kernan (Eds.), *The decline in marriage among African Americans* (pp. 121–135). New York: Russell Sage Foundation.

Lewis, D. (1975). The black family: Socialization and sex roles. *Phylon, 36,* 221–237.

Lichter, D. T., McLaughlin, D. K., Kephart, G., & Landry, G. (1992). Race and the retreat from marriage: A shortage of marriageable men? *American Sociological Review, 57,* 781–799.

Manfra, J. A. & Dykstra, R. P. (1985). Serial marriage and the origins of the black stepfamily: The Rowanty evidence. *Journal of American History, 7,* 18–44.

Mare, R., & Winship, C. (1991). Socioeconomic change and the decline of marriage for blacks and whites. In C. Jencks & P. E. Peterson (Eds.), *The urban underclass* (pp. 175–204). Washington, DC: Brookings Institute.

McAdoo, H. P. (Ed.). (1997). *Black families* (3rd ed.). Thousand Oaks, CA: Sage.

McCarthy, J. (1978). A comparison of the probability of the dissolution of first and second marriages. *Demography, 15,* 345–359.

Moynihan, D. P. (1965). *The Negro family: The case for national action.* Washington, DC: U.S. Government Printing Office.

National Center for Health Statistics. (1991). *Monthly Vital Statistics Report* (Vol. 35, No. 4, Suppl.). Washington, DC: U.S. Department of Health and Human Services.

Nobles, W. (1978). Toward an empirical and theoretical framework for defining black families. *Journal of Marriage and the Family, 40,* 679–688.

Parish, W. L., Hao, L., & Hogan, D. P. (1991). Family support networks, welfare, and work among young mothers. *Journal of Marriage and the Family, 53,* 203–215.

Pleck, E. (1973). The two-parent household: Black family structure in late nineteenth-century Boston. In M. Gordon (Ed.), *The American family in socio-historical perspective* (pp. 152–178). New York: St. Martin's Press.

Sampson, R. J. (1995). Unemployment and unbalanced sex ratios: Race-specific consequences for family structure and crime. In M. B. Tucker & C. Mitchell-Keman (Eds.), *The decline in marriage among African Americans* (pp. 229–254). New York: Russell Sage Foundation.

Scanzoni, J. (1977). *The black family in modern society.* Chicago: University of Chicago Press.

Scott-Jones, D., & Nelson-LeGall, S. (1986). Defining black families: Past and present. In E. Seidman & J. Rappaport (Eds.), *Redefining social problems* (pp. 83–100). New York: Plenum.

Shimkin, D., Shimkin, E. M., & Frate, D. A. (Eds.). (1978). *The extended family in black societies.* The Hague, the Netherlands: Mouton.

Smith, A. W. (1995). Commentary. In M. B. Tucker & C. Mitchell-Kernan (Eds.), *The decline in marriage among African Americans* (pp. 136–141). New York: Russell Sage Foundation.

Stack, C. (1974). *All our kin.* New York: Harper & Row.

Staples, R. (1971). Toward a sociology of the black family: A decade of theory and research. *Journal of Marriage and the Family, 33,* 19–38.

Staples, R., & Johnson, L. B. (1993). *Black families at the crossroads.* San Francisco: Jossey-Bass.

Staples, R., & Mirande, A. (1980). Racial and cultural variations among American families: A decennial review of the literature on minority families. *Journal of Marriage and the Family, 42,* 157–173.

Stevenson, B. (1995). Black family structure in colonial and antebellum Virginia: Amending the revisionist perspective. In M. B. Tucker & C. Mitchell-Kernan (Eds.), *The decline in marriage among African Americans* (pp. 27–56). New York: Russell Sage Foundation.

Sudarkasa, N. (1988). Interpreting the African heritage in Afro-American family organization. In H. P. McAdoo (Ed.), *Black families* (pp. 27–42). Newbury Park, CA: Sage.

Sudarkasa, N. (1997). African American families and family values. In H. P. McAdoo (Ed.), *Black families* (pp. 9–40). Thousand Oaks, CA: Sage.

Sweet, J., & Bumpass, L. (1987). *American families and households.* New York: Russell Sage Foundation.

Taylor, R. L. (1991a). Child rearing in African American families. In J. Everett, S. Chipungu, & B. Leashore (Eds.), *Child welfare: An Africentric perspective* (pp. 119–155). New Brunswick, NJ: Rutgers University Press.

Taylor, R. L. (1991b). Poverty and adolescent black males: The subculture of disengagement. In P. Edelman & J. Ladner (Eds.), *Adolescence and poverty: Challenge for the 1990s* (pp. 139–162). Washington, DC: Center for National Policy Press.

Taylor, R. L. (1997). Who's parenting? Trends and Patterns. In T. Arendell (Ed.), *Contemporary parenting: Challenges and issues* (pp. 68–91). Thousand Oaks, CA: Sage.

Taylor, R. J., Chatters, L., Tucker, M. B., & Lewis, E. (1990). Developments in research on black families: A decade review. *Journal of Marriage and the Family*, *52*, 993–1014.

Testa, M., & Krogh, M. (1995). The effect of employment on marriage among black males in inner-city Chicago. In M. B. Tucker & C. Mitchell-Kernan (Eds.), *The decline in marriage among African Americans* (pp. 59–95). New York: Russell Sage Foundation.

Thornton, A. (1978). Marital instability differentials and interactions: Insights from multivariate contingency table analysis. *Sociology and Social Research*, *62*, 572–595.

Trusell, J. (1988). Teenage pregnancy in the United States. *Family Planning Perspectives*, *20*, 262–272.

Tucker, M. B., & Mitchell-Kernan, C. (1995). Trends in African American family formation: A theoretical and statistical overview. In M. B. Tucker & C. Mitchell Kernan (Eds.), *The decline in marriage among African Americans* (pp. 3–26). New York: Russell Sage Foundation.

U.S. Bureau of the Census. (1990). Marital status and living arrangements: March 1989. *Current Population Reports* (Series P-20, No. 445). Washington, DC: U.S. Government Printing Office.

U.S. Bureau of the Census. (1994). Marital status and living arrangements: March 1993. *Current Population Reports* (Series P-20, No. 478). Washington, DC: U.S. Government Printing Office.

U.S. Bureau of the Census. (1995). Household and family characteristics: March 1994. *Current Population Reports* (Series P-20, No. 483). Washington, DC: U.S. Government Printing Office.

U.S. Bureau of the Census. (1996). *Statistical abstract of the United States: 1996*. Washington, DC: U.S. Government Printing Office.

White, D. G. (1985). *Ain't I a woman? Female slaves in the plantation South*. New York: W. W. Norton.

Wilson, W. J. (1987). *The truly disadvantaged: The inner city, the underclass and public policy*. Chicago: University of Chicago Press.

Wilson, W. J., & Neckerman K. (1986). Poverty and family structure: The widening gap between evidence and public policy issues. In S. Danziger & D. Weinberg (Eds.), *Fighting poverty: What works and what doesn't* (pp. 232–259). Cambridge, MA: Harvard University Press.

Young, V. H. (1970). Family and childhood in a southern Negro community. *American Anthropologist*, *72*, 269–288.

■ READING 26

Diversity within Latino Families: New Lessons for Family Social Science

Maxine Baca Zinn and Barbara Wells

Who are Latinos? How will their growing presence in U.S. society affect the family field? These are vital questions for scholars who are seeking to understand the current social and demographic shifts that are reshaping society and its knowledge base. Understanding family diversity is a formidable task, not only because the field is poorly equipped to deal with differences at the theoretical level, but because many decentering efforts are themselves problematic. Even when diverse groups are included, family scholarship can distort and misrepresent by faulty emphasis and false generalizations.

Latinos are a population that can be understood only in terms of increasing hetero-geneity. Latino families are unprecedented in terms of their diversity. In this [reading], we examine the ramifications of such diversity on the history, boundaries, and dynamics of family life. We begin with a brief look at the intellectual trends shaping Latino family research. We then place different Latino groups at center stage by providing a framework that situates them in specific and changing political and economic settings. Next, we apply our framework to each national origin group to draw out their different family experi-ences, especially as they are altered by global restructuring. We turn, then, to examine family structure issues and the interior dynamics of family living as they vary by gender and generation. We conclude with our reflections on studying Latino families and remaking family social science. In this [reading], we use interchangeably terms that are commonly used to describe Latino national-origin groups. For example, the terms Mexican Ameri-can, Mexican, and Mexican-origin population will be used to refer to the same segment of the Latino population. Mexican-origin people may also be referred to as Chicanos.

INTELLECTUAL TRENDS, CRITIQUES, AND CHALLENGES

Origins

The formal academic study of Latino families originated in the late 19th and early 20th centuries with studies of Mexican immigrant families. As the new social scientists of the times focused their concerns on immigration and social disorganization, Mexican-origin and other ethnic families were the source of great concern. The influential Chicago School of Sociology led scholars to believe that Mexican immigration, settlement, and poverty cre-ated problems in developing urban centers. During this period, family study was emerging as a new field that sought to document, as well as ameliorate, social problems in urban set-tings (Thomas & Wilcox, 1987). Immigrant families became major targets of social reform.

Interwoven themes from race relations and family studies gave rise to the view of Mexicans as particularly disorganized. Furthermore, the family was implicated in their plight. As transplants from traditional societies, the immigrants and their children were thought to be at odds with social requirements in the new settings. Their family arrange-ments were treated as cultural exceptions to the rule of standard family development. Their slowness to acculturate and take on Western patterns of family development left them behind as other families modernized (Baca Zinn, 1995).

Dominant paradigms of assimilation and modernization guided and shaped re-search. Notions of "traditional" and "modern" forms of social organization joined the new family social science's preoccupation with a standard family form. Compared to mainstream families, Mexican immigrant families were analyzed as traditional cultural forms. Studies of Mexican immigrants highlighted certain ethnic lifestyles that were said to produce social disorganization. Structural conditions that constrained families in the new society were rarely a concern. Instead, researchers examined (1) the families' foreign patterns and habits, (2) the moral quality of family relationships, and (3) the prospects for their Americanization (Bogardus, 1934).

Cultural Preoccupations

Ideas drawn from early social science produced cultural caricatures of Mexican families that became more exaggerated during the 1950s, when structural functionalist theories took hold in American sociology. Like the previous theories, structural functionalism's strategy for analyzing family life was to posit one family type (by no means the only family form, even then) and define it as "the normal family" (Boss & Thorne, 1989). With an emphasis on fixed family boundaries and a fixed division of roles, structural functionalists focused their attention on the group-specific characteristics that deviated from the normal or standard family and predisposed Mexican-origin families to deficiency. Mexican-origin families were analyzed in isolation from the rest of social life, described in simplistic terms of rigid male dominance and pathological clannishness. Although the earliest works on Mexican immigrant families reflected a concern for their eventual adjustment to American society, the new studies virtually abandoned the social realm. They dealt with families as if they existed in a vacuum of backward Mexican traditionalism. Structural functionalism led scholars along a path of cultural reductionism in which differences became deficiencies.

The Mexican family of social science research (Heller, 1966; Madsen, 1973; Rubel, 1966) presented a stark contrast with the mythical "standard family." Although some studies found that Mexican family traditionalism was fading as Mexicans became acculturated, Mexican families were stereotypically and inaccurately depicted as the chief cause of Mexican subordination in the United States.

New Directions

In the past 25 years, efforts to challenge myths and erroneous assumptions have produced important changes in the view of Mexican-origin families. Beginning with a critique of structural functionalist accounts of Mexican families, new studies have successfully challenged the old notions of family life as deviant, deficient, and disorganized.

The conceptual tools of Latino studies, women's studies, and social history have infused the new scholarship to produce a notable shift away from cultural preoccupations. Like the family field in general, research on Mexican-origin families has begun to devote greater attention to the "social situations and contexts that affect Mexican families" (Vega, 1990, p. 1015). This "revisionist" strategy has moved much Latino family research to a different plane—one in which racial-ethnic families are understood to be constructed by powerful social forces and as settings in which different family members adapt in a variety of ways to changing social conditions.

Current Challenges

Despite important advances, notable problems and limitations remain in the study of Latino families. A significant portion of scholarship includes only Mexican-origin groups (Massey, Zambrana, & Bell, 1995) and claims to generalize the findings to other Latinos. This practice constructs a false social reality because there is no Latino population in the same sense that there is an African American population. However useful the terms *Latino* and *Hispanic* may be as political and census identifiers, they mask extraordinary diversity. The category

Hispanic was created by federal statisticians to provide data on people of Mexican, Cuban, Puerto Rican, and other Hispanic origins in the United States. There is no precise definition of group membership, and Latinos do not agree among themselves on an appropriate group label (Massey, 1993). While many prefer the term *Latino*, they may use it interchangeably with *Hispanic* to identify themselves (Romero, 1996). These terms are certainly useful for charting broad demographic changes in the United States, but when used as panethnic terms, they can contribute to misunderstandings about family life.

The labels Hispanic or Latino conceal variation in the family characteristics of Latino groups whose differences are often greater than the overall differences between Latinos and non-Latinos (Solis, 1995). To date, little comparative research has been conducted on Latino subgroups. The systematic disaggregation of family characteristics by national-origin groups remains a challenge, a necessary next step in the development of Latino family research.

We believe that the lack of a comprehensive knowledge base should not stand in the way of building a framework to analyze family life. We can use the burgeoning research on Latinos in U.S. social life to develop an analytical, rather than just a descriptive, account of families. The very complexity of Latino family arrangements begs for a unified (but not unitary) analysis. We believe that we can make good generalizations about Latino family diversity. In the sections that follow, we use a structural perspective grounded in intergroup differences. We make no pretense that this is an exhaustive review of research. Instead, our intent is to examine how Latino family experiences differ in relation to socially constructed conditions.

CONCEPTUAL FRAMEWORK

Conventional family frameworks, which have never applied well to racial-ethnic families, are even less useful in the current world of diversity and change. Incorporating multiplicity into family studies requires new approaches. A fundamental assumption guiding our analysis is that Latino families are not merely an expression of ethnic differences but, like all families, are the products of social forces.

Family diversity is an outgrowth of distinctive patterns in the way families and their members are embedded in environments with varying opportunities, resources, and rewards. Economic conditions and social inequalities associated with race, ethnicity, class, and gender place families in different "social locations." These differences are the key to understanding family variation. They determine labor market status, education, marital relations, and other factors that are crucial to family formation.

Studying Latino family diversity means exposing the structural forces that impinge differently on families in specific social, material, and historical contexts. In other words, it means unpacking the structural arrangements that produce and often require a range of family configurations. It also requires analyzing the cross-cutting forms of difference that permeate society and penetrate families to produce divergent family experiences. Several macrostructural conditions produce widespread family variations across Latino groups: (1) the sociohistorical context; (2) the structure of economic opportunity; and (3) global reorganization, including economic restructuring and immigration.

The Sociohistorical Context

Mexicans, Puerto Ricans, Cubans, and other Latino groups have varied histories that distinguish them from each other. The timing and conditions of their arrival in the United States produced distinctive patterns of settlement that continue to affect their prospects for success. Cubans arrived largely between 1960 and 1980; a group of Mexicans indigenous to the Southwest was forcibly annexed into the United States in 1848, and another has been migrating continually since around 1890; Puerto Ricans came under U.S. control in 1898 and obtained citizenship in 1917; Salvadorans and Guatemalans began to migrate to the United States in substantial numbers during the past two decades.

The Structure of Economic Opportunity

Various forms of labor are needed to sustain family life. Labor status has always been the key factor in distinguishing the experiences of Latinos. Mexicans, Puerto Ricans, Cubans, and others are located in different regions of the country where particular labor markets and a group's placement within them determine the kind of legal, political, and social supports available to families. Different levels of structural supports affect family life, often producing various domestic and household arrangements. Additional complexity stems from gendered labor markets. In a society in which men are still assumed to be the primary breadwinners, jobs generally held by women pay less than jobs usually held by men. Women's and men's differential labor market placement, rewards, and roles create contradictory work and family experiences.

Global Reorganization, Including Economic Restructuring and Immigration

Economic and demographic upheavals are redefining families throughout the world. Four factors are at work here: new technologies based primarily on the computer chip, global economic interdependence, the flight of capital, and the dominance of the information and service sectors over basic manufacturing industries (Baca Zinn & Eitzen, 1998). Latino families are profoundly affected as the environments in which they live are reshaped and they face economic and social marginalization because of under-employment and unemployment. Included in economic globalization are new demands for immigrant labor and the dramatic demographic transformations that are "Hispanicizing" the United States. Family flexibility has long been an important feature of the immigrant saga. Today, "Latino immigration is adding many varieties to family structure" (Moore & Vigil, 1993, p. 36).

The macrostructural conditions described earlier provide the context within which to examine the family experiences of different Latino groups. They set the foundation for comparing family life across Latino groups. These material and economic forces help explain the different family profiles of Mexicans, Puerto Ricans, Cubans, and others. In other words, they enable sociologists to understand how families are bound up with the unequal distribution of social opportunities and how the various national-origin groups develop broad differences in work opportunities, marital patterns, and household structures. However, they do not explain other important differences in family life that cut across national-origin groups. People of the same national origin may experience family differently, depending on their location in the class structure as unemployed, poor, working class or professional; their location in the gender structure as female or male; and their location in the sexual orientation system as heterosexual, gay, lesbian, or bisexual (Baca Zinn & Dill, 1996). In addition to these differences, family life for Latinos is shaped by age, generation living in the United States, citizenship status, and even skin color. All these differences intersect to influence the shape and character of family and household relations.

While our framework emphasizes the social context and social forces that construct families, we do not conclude that families are molded from the "outside in." What happens on a daily basis in family relations and domestic settings also constructs families. Latinos themselves—women, men, and children—have the ability actively to shape their family and household arrangements. Families should be seen as settings in which people are agents and actors, coping with, adapting to, and changing social structures to meet their needs (Baca Zinn & Eitzen, 1996).

Sociohistorical Context for Family Diversity among Mexicans

Families of Mexican descent have been incorporated into the United States by both conquest and migration. In 1848, at the end of the Mexican War, the United States acquired a large section of Mexico, which is now the southwestern United States. With the signing of the Treaty of Guadalupe Hidalgo, the Mexican population in that region became residents of U.S. territory. Following the U.S. conquest, rapid economic growth in that region resulted in a shortage of labor that was resolved by recruiting workers from Mexico. So began the pattern of Mexican labor migration that continues to the present (Portes & Rumbaut, 1990). Some workers settled permanently in the United States, and others continued in cycles of migration, but migration from Mexico has been continuous since around 1890 (Massey et al., 1995).

Dramatic increases in the Mexican-origin population have been an important part of the trend toward greater racial and ethnic diversity in the United States. The Mexican population tripled in size in 20 years, from an estimated 4.5 million in 1970 to 8.7 million in 1980 to 13.5 million in 1990 (Rumbaut, 1995; Wilkinson, 1993). At present, approximately two thirds of Mexicans are native born, and the remainder are foreign born (Rumbaut, 1995). Important differences are consistently found between the social experiences and economic prospects of the native born and the foreign born (Morales & Ong, 1993; Ortiz, 1996). While some variation exists, the typical Mexican migrant to the United States has low socioeconomic status and rural origins (Ortiz, 1995; Portes & Rumbaut, 1990). Recent immigrants have a distinct disadvantage in the labor market because of a combination of low educational attainment, limited work skills, and limited English language proficiency. Social networks are vital for integrating immigrants into U.S. society and in placing them in the social class system (Fernandez-Kelly & Schauffler, 1994). Mexicans are concentrated in barrios that have social networks in which vital information is shared, contacts are made, and job referrals are given. But the social-class context of these Mexican communities is overwhelmingly poor and working class. Mexicans remain overrepresented in low-wage occupations, especially service, manual labor, and low-end manufacturing. These homogeneous lower-class communities lack the high-quality resources that could facilitate upward mobility for either new immigrants or second- and later-generation Mexicans.

The common assumption that immigrants are assimilated economically by taking entry-level positions and advancing to better jobs has not been supported by the Mexican experience (Morales & Ong, 1993; Ortiz, 1996). Today's Mexican workers are as likely as ever to be trapped in low-wage unstable employment situations (Ortiz, 1996; Sassen, 1993). Studies (Aponte, 1993; Morales & Ong, 1993; Ortiz, 1996) have found that high labor force participation and low wages among Mexicans have created a large group of working poor. Households adapt by holding multiple jobs and pooling wages (Velez-Ibañez & Greenberg, 1992).

Mexicans are the largest Latino group in the United States; 6 of 10 Latinos have Mexican origins. This group has low family incomes, but high labor force participation for men and increasing rates for women. Mexicans have the lowest educational attainments and the largest average household size of all Latino groups. (See Table 26.1 and Figure 26.1 for between-group comparisons.)

Puerto Ricans

The fortunes of Puerto Rico and the United States were joined in 1899 when Puerto Rico became a U.S. possession in the aftermath of Spain's defeat in the Spanish-American War. Puerto Ricans are U.S. citizens and, as such, have the right to migrate to the mainland without regulation. A small stream of migrants increased dramatically after World War II for three primary reasons: high unemployment in Puerto Rico,

TABLE 26.1 *Social and Economic Population Characteristics*

			Labor Force Participation				
	Median Income	Poverty	% Female Head of Household	Male	Female	High School Graduate	Average Household
Mexican	23,609	29.6	19.9	80.9	51.8	46.5	3.86
Puerto Rican	20,929	33.2	41.2	70.6	47.4	61.3	2.91
Cuban	30,584	13.6	21.3	69.9	50.8	64.7	2.56
Central/South American	28,558	23.9	25.4	79.5	57.5	64.2	3.54
Other Hispanic	28,658	21.4	29.5			68.4	
All Hispanic	24,313	27.8	24	79.1	52.6	53.4	2.99
All U.S.	38,782	11.6	12	75	58.9	81.7	2.65
	1994	1994	1995	1995	1995	1995	1995

Source: U.S. Bureau of the Census, Statistical Abstract of the United States: 1996 (116th ed.), Washington, D.C.: U.S. Government Printing Office, 1996, Tables 53, 68, 241, 615, 622, 723, 738.

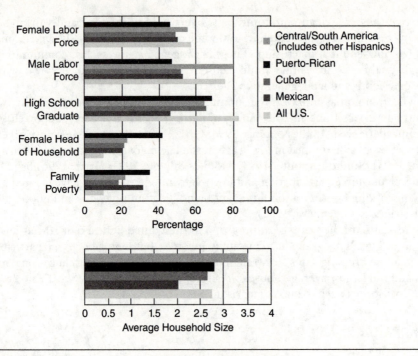

FIGURE 26.1   *Social and Economic Population Characteristics*

the availability of inexpensive air travel between Puerto Rico and the United States, and labor recruitment by U.S. companies (Portes & Rumbaut, 1990). Puerto Ricans were concentrated in or near their arrival point—New York City—although migrant laborers were scattered throughout the Northeast and parts of the Midwest. They engaged in a variety of blue-collar occupations; in New York City, they were particularly drawn into the textile and garment industries (Torres & Bonilla, 1993). The unique status of Puerto Rico as a commonwealth of the United States allows Puerto Ricans to engage in a circulating migration between Puerto Rico and the mainland (Feagin & Feagin, 1996).

Puerto Ricans are the most economically disadvantaged of all major Latino groups. The particular context of Puerto Ricans' entry into the U.S. labor market helps explain this group's low economic status. Puerto Ricans with limited education and low occupational skills migrated to the eastern seaboard to fill manufacturing jobs (Ortiz, 1995); their economic well-being was dependent on opportunities for low-skill employment (Aponte, 1993). The region in which Puerto Ricans settled has experienced a major decline in its manufacturing base since the early 1970s. The restructuring of the economy means that, in essence, the jobs that Puerto Ricans came to the mainland to fill have largely disappeared. Latinos who have been displaced from manufacturing have generally been unable to gain access to higher-wage service sector employment (Carnoy, Daley, & Ojeda, 1993).

Compared to Mexicans and Cubans, Puerto Ricans have the lowest median family incomes and the highest unemployment and poverty rates. Puerto Ricans also have a high rate of female-headed households.

Cubans

The primary event that precipitated the migration of hundreds of thousands of Cubans to the United States was the revolution that brought Fidel Castro to power in 1959. This revolution set off several waves of immigration, beginning with the former economic and political elite and working progressively downward through the class structure. Early Cuban immigrants entered the United States in a highly politicized cold-war context as political refugees from communism. The U.S. government sponsored the Cuban Refugee Program, which provided massive supports to Cuban immigrants, including resettlement assistance, job training, small-business loans, welfare payments, and health care (Dominguez, 1992; Perez-Stable & Uriarte, 1993). By the time this program was phased out after the mid-1970s, the United States had invested nearly $1 billion in assistance to Cubans fleeing from communism (Perez-Stable & Uriarte, 1993, p. 155). Between 1960 and 1980, nearly 800,000 Cubans immigrated to the United States (Dominguez, 1992).

The Cuban population is concentrated in south Florida, primarily in the Miami area, where they have established a true ethnic enclave in which they own businesses; provide professional services; and control institutions, such as banks and newspapers (Perez, 1994). The unique circumstances surrounding their immigration help explain the experience of Cubans. U.S. government supports facilitated the economic successes of early Cuban immigrants (Aponte, 1993; Fernandez-Kelly & Schauffler, 1994). High rates of entrepreneurship resulted in the eventual consolidation of an enclave economy (Portes & Truelove, 1987).

Immigrants, women, and minorities have generally supplied the low-wage, flexible labor on which the restructured economy depends (Morales & Bonilla, 1993). However, Cubans "embody a privileged migration" in comparison to other Latino groups (Morales & Bonilla, 1993, p. 17). Their social-class positions, occupational attainments, and public supports have insulated them from the effects of restructuring. Yet Cubans in Miami are not completely protected from the displacements of the new economic order. As Perez-Stable and Uriarte (1993) noted, the Cuban workforce is polarized, with one segment moving into higher-wage work and the other remaining locked in low-wage employment.

Cuban families have higher incomes and far lower poverty rates than do other major Latino groups. Cubans are the most educated major Latino group and have the smallest average household size.

Other Latinos

In each national-origin group discussed earlier, one finds unique socioeconomic, political and historical circumstances. But the diversity of Latinos extends beyond the differences between Mexican Americans, Cuban Americans, and mainland Puerto Ricans. One finds further variation when one considers the experiences of other Latino national-origin groups. Although research on "other Latinos" is less extensive than the literature cited earlier, we consider briefly contexts for diversity in Central American and Dominican families.

Central Americans.   Political repression, civil war, and their accompanying economic dislocations have fueled the immigration of a substantial number of Salvadorans, Guatemalans, and Nicaraguans since the mid-1970s (Hamilton & Chinchilla, 1997). The U.S. population of Central Americans more than doubled between the 1980 and 1990 censuses and now outnumbers Cubans (U.S. Bureau of the Census, 1993). These Latinos migrated under difficult circumstances and face a set of serious challenges in the United States (Dorrington, 1995). Three factors render this population highly vulnerable: (1) a high percentage are undocumented (an estimated 49% of Salvadorans and 40% of Guatemalans), (2) they have marginal employment and high poverty rates, and (3) the U.S. government does not recognize them as political refugees (Lopez, Popkin, & Telles, 1996).

The two largest groups of Central Americans are Salvadorans and Guatemalans, the majority of whom live in the Los Angeles area. Lopez et al.'s (1996) study of Central Americans in Los Angeles illumined the social and economic contexts in which these Latinos construct their family lives. In general, the women and men have little formal education and know little English, but have high rates of labor force participation. Salvadorans and Guatemalans are overrepresented in low-paying service and blue-collar occupations. Salvadoran and Guatemalan women occupy a low-wage niche in private service (as domestic workers in private homes). Central Americans, especially the un-documented who fear deportation and usually have no access to public support, are desperate enough to accept the poorest-quality, lowest-paying work that Los Angeles has to offer. These immigrants hold the most disadvantageous position in the regional economy (Scott, 1996). Lopez et al. predicted that in the current restructured economy, Central Americans will continue to do the worst of the "dirty work" necessary to support the lifestyles of the high-wage workforce.

Dominicans.   A significant number of Dominicans began migrating to the U.S. in the mid-1960s. What Grasmuck and Pessar (1996) called the "massive displacement" of Dominicans from their homeland began with the end of Trujillo's 30-year dictator-ship and the political uncertainties that ensued. Dominican immigrant families did not fit the conventional image of the unskilled, underemployed peasant. They generally had employed breadwinners who were relatively well educated by Dominican standards; the majority described themselves as having urban middle-class origins (Mitchell, 1992).

The Dominican population is heavily concentrated in New York City. They entered a hostile labor market in which their middle class aspirations were to remain largely unfulfilled because the restructured New York economy offers low-wage, mar-ginal, mostly dead-end employment for individuals without advanced education (Torres & Bonilla, 1993). Dominicans lacked the English language competence and educational credentials that might have facilitated their upward mobility (Grasmuck & Pessar, 1996). More than two thirds of the Dominican-origin population in the United States is Dominican born. As a group, Dominicans have high rates of poverty and female-headed families. Approximately 4 in 10 family households are headed by women.

THE STRUCTURE OF ECONOMIC OPPORTUNITY

Latino families remain outside the economic mainstream of U.S. society. Their median family income stands at less than two thirds the median family income of all U.S. families (U.S. Bureau of the Census, 1996). But the broad designation of "Latino" obscures important differences among national-origin groups. In this section, we explore variations in the structure of economic opportunity and consider how particular economic contexts shape the lives of different groups of Latino families.

Class, Work, and Family Life

A number of studies (see, for example, Cardenas, Chapa, & Burek, 1993; Grasmuck & Pessar, 1996; Lopez et al., 1996; Ortiz, 1995; Perez, 1994) have documented that diverse social and economic contexts produce multiple labor market outcomes for Latino families. The quality, availability, and stability of wage labor create a socioeconomic context in which family life is constructed and maintained. Cuban American families have fared far better socioeconomically than have other Latino families. Scholars consistently cite the role of the Cuban enclave in providing a favorable economic context with advantages that other groups have not enjoyed (Morales & Bonilla, 1993; Perez, 1994; Perez-Stable & Uriarte, 1993). Cuban families have the highest incomes, educational attainments, and levels of upper-white-collar employment. Puerto Rican, Mexican, and Central American families cluster below Cubans on these socioeconomic indicators, with Puerto Ricans the most disadvantaged group.

The structure of Mexican American economic opportunity stands in sharp contrast to that of Cubans. Betancur, Cordova, and Torres (1993) documented the systematic exclusion of Mexicans from upward-mobility ladders, tracing the incorporation of Mexican Americans into the Chicago economy to illustrate the historic roots of the concentration of Mexicans in unstable, poor-quality work. Throughout the 20th century Mexican migrants have constituted a transient workforce that has been continually vulnerable to fluctuations in the labor market and cycles of recruitment and deportation. Betancur et al.'s study highlighted the significance of the bracero program of contract labor migration in institutionalizing a segmented market for labor. The bracero program limited Mexican workers to specific low-status jobs and industries that prohibited promotion to skilled occupational categories. Mexicans were not allowed to compete for higher-status jobs, but were contracted to fill only the most undesirable jobs. Although formal bracero-era regulations have ended, similar occupational concentrations continue to be reproduced among Mexican American workers.

The effects of these diverging social-class and employment contexts on families are well illustrated by Fernandez-Kelly's (1990) study of female garment workers—Cubans in Miami and Mexicans in Los Angeles—both of whom placed a high value on marriage and family; however, contextual factors shaped differently their abilities to sustain marital relationships over time. Fernandez-Kelly contended that the conditions necessary for maintaining long-term stable unions were present in middle-class families but were absent in poor families. That is, the marriages of the poor women were threatened by unemployment and underemployment. Among these Mexican women, there was a high rate of poor female-headed households, and among the Cuban women, many were members of upwardly mobile families.

Women's Work

Several studies (Chavira-Prado, 1992; Grasmuck & Pessar, 1991; Lamphere, Zavella, Gonzales, & Evans, 1993; Stier & Tienda, 1992; Zavella, 1987) that have explored the intersection of work and family for Latinas have found that Latinas are increasingly likely to be employed. Labor force participation is the highest among Central American women and the lowest among Puerto Rican women, with Mexican and Cuban women equally likely to be employed. Not only do labor force participation rates differ by national origin, but the meaning of women's work varies as well. For example, Fernandez-Kelly's (1990) study demonstrated that for Cuban women, employment was part of a broad family objective to reestablish middle-class status. Many Cuban immigrants initially experienced downward mobility, and the women took temporary jobs to generate income while their husbands cultivated fledgling businesses. These women often withdrew from the workforce when their families' economic positions had been secured. In contrast, Mexican women in Los Angeles worked because of dire economic necessity. They were drawn into employment to augment the earnings of partners who were confined to secondary-sector work that paid less than subsistence wages or worse, to provide the primary support for their households. Thus, whereas the Cuban women expected to work temporarily until their husbands could resume the role of middle-class breadwinner, the Mexican women worked either because their partners could not earn a family wage or because of the breakdown of family relationships by divorce or abandonment.

GLOBAL REORGANIZATION

Economic Restructuring

The economic challenges that Latinos face are enormous. A workforce that has always been vulnerable to exploitation can anticipate the decline of already limited mobility prospects. A recent body of scholarship (see, for example, Lopez et al., 1996; Morales & Bonilla, 1993; Ortiz, 1996) has demonstrated that the restructuring of the U.S. economy has reshaped economic opportunities for Latinos.

Torres and Bonilla's (1993) study of the restructuring of New York City's economy is particularly illustrative because it focused on Puerto Ricans, the Latino group hit hardest by economic transformations. That study found that restructuring in New York City is based on two processes that negatively affect Puerto Ricans. First, stable jobs in both the public and private sectors have eroded since the 1960s because many large corporations that had provided long-term, union jobs for minorities left the New York area and New York City's fiscal difficulties restricted the opportunities for municipal employment. Second, the reorganization of light manufacturing has meant that new jobs offer low wages and poor working conditions; new immigrants who are vulnerable to exploitation by employers generally fill these jobs. The restructuring of the economy has resulted in the exclusion or withdrawal of a substantial proportion of Puerto Ricans from the labor market (Morales & Bonilla, 1993).

Families are not insulated from the effects of social and economic dislocations. Research that has tracked this major social transformation has considered how such changes affect family processes and household composition (Grasmuck & Pessar, 1996; Lopez et al., 1996; Rodriguez & Hagan, 1997). What Sassen (1993) called the "informalization" and "casualization" of urban labor markets will, in the end, shape families in ways that deviate from the nuclear ideal. The marginalization of the Puerto Rican workforce is related not only to high unemployment and poverty rates, but to high rates of nonmarital births and female-headed households (Fernandez-Kelly, 1990; Morrissey, 1987).

Contrasting the experience of Dominicans to that of Puerto Ricans indicates that it is impossible to generalize a unitary "Latino experience" even within a single labor market—New York City. Torres and Bonilla (1993) found that as Puerto Ricans were displaced from manufacturing jobs in the 1970s and 1980s, new Dominican immigrants came into the restructured manufacturing sector to fill low-wage jobs. Dominicans were part of a pool of immigrant labor that entered a depressed economy, was largely ineligible for public assistance, and was willing to accept exploitative employment. Grasmuck and Pessar (1991, 1996) showed how the incorporation of Dominicans into the restructured New York economy has affected families. Although the rate of divorce among early immigrants was high, relationships have become increasingly precarious as employment opportunities have become even more constrained. Currently, rates of poverty and female-headed households for Dominicans approximate those of Puerto Ricans (Rumbaut, 1995).

A Latino Underclass?   Rising poverty rates among Latinos, together with the alarmist treatment of female-headed households among "minorities," have led many policy makers and media analysts to conclude that Latinos have joined inner-city African Americans to form part of the "underclass." According to the underclass model, inner-city men's joblessness has encouraged nonmarital childbearing and undermined the economic foundations of the African American family (Wilson, 1987, 1996). Researchers have also been debating for some time whether increases in the incidence of female-headed households and poverty among Puerto Ricans are irreversible (Tienda, 1989). Recent thinking, however, suggests that applying the underclass theory to Latinos obscures more than it reveals and that a different analytical model is needed to understand poverty and family issues in each Latino group (Massey et al., 1995). Not only do the causes of poverty differ across Latino communities, but patterns of social organization at the community and family levels produce a wide range of responses to poverty. According to Moore and Pinderhughes (1993), the dynamics of poverty even in the poorest Latino barrios differ in fundamental ways from the conventional portrait of the under-class. Both African Americans and Puerto Ricans have high rates of female-headed households. However, Sullivan's (1993) research in Brooklyn indicated that Puerto Ricans have high rates of cohabitation and that the family formation processes that lead to these household patterns are different from those of African Americans. Other case studies have underscored the importance of family organization. For example, Velez-Ibañez (1993) described a distinctive family form among poor Mexicans of South Tucson—cross-class household clusters surrounded by kinship networks that stretch beyond neighborhood boundaries and provide resources for coping with poverty.

Immigration

Families migrate for economic reasons, political reasons, or some combination of the two. Immigration offers potential and promise, but one of the costs is the need for families to adapt to their receiving community contexts. A growing body of scholarship has focused on two areas of family change: household composition and gender relations.

Household Composition.   Immigration contributes to the proliferation of family forms and a variety of household arrangements among Latinos (Vega, 1995). Numerous studies have highlighted the flexibility of Latino family households. Chavez (1990, 1992) identified transnational families, binational families, extended families, multiple-family households, and other arrangements among Mexican and Central American immigrants. Landale and Fennelly (1992) found informal unions that resemble marriage more than cohabitation among mainland Puerto Ricans, and Guarnizo (1997) found binational households among Dominicans who live and work in both the United States and the Dominican Republic. Two processes are at work as families adapt their household structures. First, family change reflects, for many, desperate economic circumstances (Vega, 1995), which bring some families to the breaking point and lead others to expand their household boundaries. Second, the transnationalization of economies and labor has created new opportunities for successful Latino families; for example, Guarnizo noted that Dominican entrepreneurs sometimes live in binational households and have "de facto binational citizenship" (p. 171).

Immigration and Gender.   Several important studies have considered the relationship between immigration and gender (Boyd, 1989; Grasmuck & Pessar, 1991; Hondagneu-Sotelo, 1994). In her study of undocumented Mexican immigrants, Hondagneu-Sotelo (1994) demonstrated that gender shapes migration and immigration shapes gender relations. She found that family stage migration, in which husbands migrate first and wives and children follow later, does not fit the household-strategy model. Often implied in this model is the assumption that migration reflects the unanimous and rational collective decision of all household members. However, as Hondagneu-Sotelo observed, gender hierarchies determined when and under what circumstances migration occurred; that is, men often decided spontaneously, independently, and unilaterally to migrate north to seek employment. When Mexican couples were finally reunited in the United States, they generally reconstructed more egalitarian gender relations. Variation in the form of gender relations in the United States is partially explained by the circumstances surrounding migration, such as the type and timing of migration, access to social networks, and U.S. immigration policy.

FAMILY DYNAMICS ACROSS LATINO GROUPS

Familism

Collectivist family arrangements are thought to be a defining feature of the Latino population. Presumably, a strong orientation and obligation to the family produces a kinship structure that is qualitatively different from that of all other groups. Latino familism, which is said to emphasize the family as opposed to the individual, "is linked to many of the pejorative images that have beset discussions of the Hispanic family" (Vega, 1990, p. 1018). Although themes of Latino familism figure prominently in the social science literature, this topic remains problematic owing to empirical limitations and conceptual confusion.

Popular and social science writing contain repeated descriptions of what amounts to a generic Latino kinship form. In reality, a Mexican-origin bias pervades the research on this topic. Not only is there a lack of comparative research on extended kinship structures among different national-origin groups, but there is little empirical evidence for all but Mexican-origin families. For Mexican-origin groups, studies are plentiful (for reviews, see Baca Zinn, 1983; Vega, 1990, 1995), although they have yielded inconsistent evidence about the prevalence of familism, the forms it takes, and the kinds of supportive relationships it serves.

Among the difficulties in assessing the evidence on extended family life are the inconsistent uses of terms like *familism* and *extended family system*. Seeking to clarify the multiple meanings of familism, Ramirez and Arce (1981) treated familism as a multidimensional concept comprised of such distinct aspects as structure, behavior, norms and attitudes, and social identity, each of which requires separate measurement and analysis. They proposed that familism contains four key components: (1) demographic familism, which involves such characteristics as family size; (2) structural familism, which measures the incidence of multigenerational (or extended) households; (3) normative families, which taps the value that Mexican-origin people place on family unity and solidarity; and (4) behavioral familism, which has to do with the level of interaction between family and kin networks.

Changes in regional and local economies and the resulting dislocations of Latinos have prompted questions about the ongoing viability of kinship networks. Analyzing a national sample of minority families, Rochelle (1997) argued that extended kinship networks are declining among Chicanos, Puerto Ricans, and African Americans. On the other hand, a large body of research has documented various forms of network participation by Latinos. For three decades, studies have found that kinship networks are an important survival strategy in poor Mexican communities (Alvirez & Bean, 1976; Hoppe & Heller, 1975; Velez-Ibañez, 1996) and that these networks operate as a system of cultural, emotional, and mental support (Keefe, 1984; Mindel, 1980; Ramirez, 1980), as well as a system for coping with socioeconomic marginality (Angel & Tienda, 1982; Lamphere et al., 1993).

Research has suggested, however, that kinship networks are not maintained for socioeconomic reasons alone (Buriel & De Ment, 1997). Familistic orientation among Mexican-origin adults has been associated with high levels of education and income

(Griffith & Villavicienco, 1985). Familism has been viewed as a form of social capital that is linked with academic success among Mexican-heritage adolescents (Valenzuela & Dornbusch, 1994).

The research on the involvement of extended families in the migration and settlement of Mexicans discussed earlier (Chavez, 1992; Hondagneu-Sotelo, 1994; Hondagneu-Sotelo & Avila, 1997) is profoundly important. In contrast to the prevailing view that family extension is an artifact of culture, this research helps one understand that the structural flexibility of families is a social construction. Transnational families and their networks of kin are extended in space, time, and across national borders. They are quintessential adaptations—alternative arrangements for solving problems associated with immigration.

Despite the conceptual and empirical ambiguities surrounding the topic of familism, there is evidence that kinship networks are far from monolithic. Studies have revealed that variations are rooted in distinctive social conditions, such as immigrant versus nonimmigrant status and generational status. Thus, even though immigrants use kin for assistance, they have smaller social networks than do second-generation Mexican Americans who have broader social networks consisting of multigenerational kin (Vega, 1990). Studies have shown that regardless of class, Mexican extended families in the United States become stronger and more extensive with generational advancement, acculturation, and socioeconomic mobility (Velez-Ibañez, 1996). Although an assimilationist perspective suggests that familism fades in succeeding generations, Velez-Ibañez found that highly elaborated second- and third-generation extended family networks are actively maintained through frequent visits, ritual celebrations, and the exchange of goods and services. These networks are differentiated by the functions they perform, depending on the circumstances of the people involved.

Gender

Latino families are commonly viewed as settings of traditional patriarchy and as different from other families because of machismo, the cult of masculinity. In the past two decades, this cultural stereotype has been the impetus for corrective scholarship on Latino families. The flourishing of Latina feminist thought has shifted the focus from the determinism of culture to questions about how gender and power in families are connected with other structures and institutions in society. Although male dominance remains a central theme, it is understood as part of the ubiquitous social ordering of women and men. In the context of other forms of difference, gender exerts a powerful influence on Latino families.

New research is discovering gender dynamics among Latino families that are both similar to and different from those found in other groups. Similarities stem from social changes that are reshaping all families, whereas differences emerge from the varied locations of Latino families and the women and men in them. Like other branches of scholarship on Latino families, most studies have been conducted with Mexican-origin populations. The past two decades of research have shown that family life among all Latino groups is deeply gendered. Yet no simple generalizations sum up the essence of power relations.

Research has examined two interrelated areas: (1) family decision making and (2) the allocation of household labor. Since the first wave of "revisionist works" (Zavella, 1987) conducted in the 1970s and 1980s (Baca Zinn, 1980; Ybarra, 1982), researchers have found variation in these activities, ranging from patriarchal role-segregated patterns to egalitarian patterns, with many combinations in between. Studies have suggested that Latinas' employment patterns, like those of women around the world, provide them with resources and autonomy that alter the balance of family power (Baca Zinn, 1980; Coltrane & Valdez, 1993; Pesquera, 1993; Repack, 1997; Williams, 1990; Ybarra, 1982; Zavella, 1987). But, as we discussed earlier, employment opportunities vary widely, and the variation produces multiple work and family patterns for Latinas. Furthermore, women's employment, by itself, does not eradicate male dominance. This is one of the main lessons of Zavella's (1987) study of Chicana cannery workers in California's Santa Clara Valley. Women's cannery work was circumscribed by inequalities of class, race, and gender. As seasonal, part-time workers, the women gained some leverage in the home, thereby creating temporary shifts in their day-to-day family lives, but this leverage did not alter the balance of family power. Fernandez-Kelly and Garcia's (1990) comparative study of women's work and family patterns among Cubans and Mexican Americans found strikingly different configurations of power. Employed women's newfound rights are often contradictory. As Repack's study (1997) of Central American immigrants revealed, numerous costs and strains accompany women's new roles in a new landscape. Family relations often became contentious when women pressed partners to share domestic responsibilities. Migration produced a situation in which women worked longer and harder than in their countries of origin.

Other conditions associated with varying patterns in the division of domestic labor are women's and men's occupational statuses and relative economic contributions to their families. Studies by Pesquera (1993), Coltrane and Valdez (1993), and Coltrane (1996) found a general "inside/outside" dichotomy (wives doing most housework, husbands doing outside work and sharing some child care), but women in middle-class jobs received more "help" from their husbands than did women with lower earnings.

"Family power" research should not be limited to women's roles, but should study the social relations between women and men. Recent works on Latino men's family lives have made important strides in this regard (Coltrane & Valdez, 1993; Shelton & John, 1993). Still, there is little information about the range and variety of Latino men's family experiences (Mirande, 1997) or of their interplay with larger structural conditions. In a rare study of Mexican immigrant men, Hondagneu-Sotelo and Messner (1994) discussed the diminution of patriarchy that comes with settling in the United States. They showed that the key to gender equality in immigrant families is women's and men's relative positions of power and status in the larger society. Mexican immigrant men's status is low owing to racism, economic marginality, and possible undocumented status. Meanwhile, as immigrant women move into wage labor, they develop autonomy and economic skills. These conditions combine to erode patriarchal authority.

The research discussed earlier suggested some convergences between Latinos and other groups in family power arrangements. But intertwined with the shape of domestic power are strongly held ideals about women's and men's family roles. Ethnic gender identities, values, and beliefs contribute to gender relations and constitute an important but little understood dimension of families. Gender may also be influenced by Latinos' extended family networks. As Lamphere et al. (1993) discovered, Hispanas in Albuquerque were living in a world made up largely of Hispana mothers, sisters, and other relatives. Social scientists have posited a relationship between dense social networks and gender segregation. If this relationship holds, familism could well impede egalitarian relations in Latino families (Coltrane, 1996; Hurtado, 1995).

Compulsory heterosexuality is an important component of both gender and family systems. By enforcing the dichotomy of opposite sexes, it is also a form of inequality in its own right, hence an important marker of social location. A growing literature on lesbian and gay identity among Latinas and Latinos has examined the conflicting challenges involved in negotiating a multiple minority status (Alarcon, Castillo, & Moraga, 1989; Almaguer, 1991; Anzaldúa, 1987; Carrier, 1992; Moraga, 1983; Morales, 1990). Unfortunately, family scholarship on Latinos has not pursued the implications of lesbian and gay identities for understanding family diversity. In fact, there have been no studies in the social sciences in the area of sexual orientation and Latino families (Hurtado, 1995). But although the empirical base is virtually nonexistent and making *families* the unit of analysis no doubt introduces new questions (Demo & Allen, 1996), we can glean useful insights from the discourse on sexual identity. Writing about Chicanos, Almaguer (1991) identified the following obstacles to developing a safe space for forming a gay or lesbian identity: racial and class subordination and a context in which ethnicity remains a primary basis of group identity and survival. "Moreover Chicano *family life* [italics added] requires allegiance to patriarchal gender relations and to a system of sexual meanings that directly mitigate against the emergence of this alternative basis of self identity" (Almaguer, p. 88). Such repeated references to the constraints of ethnicity, gender, and sexual orientation imposed by Chicano families (Almaguer, 1991; Moraga, 1983) raise important questions. How do varied family contexts shape and differentiate the development of gay identities among Latinos? How do they affect the formation of lesbian and gay families among Latinas and Latinos? This area is wide open for research.

Children and Their Parents

Latinos have the highest concentration of children and adolescents of all major racial and ethnic groups. Nearly 40% of Latinos are aged 20 or younger, compared to about 26% of non-Hispanic whites (U.S. Bureau of the Census, 1996). Among Latino subgroups, the highest proportions of children and adolescents are among Mexicans and Puerto Ricans and the lowest among Cubans (Solis, 1995).

Latino socialization patterns have long held the interest of family scholars (Martinez, 1993). Most studies have focused on the child-rearing practices of Mexican families. Researchers have questioned whether Mexican families have permissive or authoritarian styles of child rearing and the relationship of childrearing styles to social class and cultural factors (Martinez, 1993). Patterns of child rearing were expected to reveal the level of acculturation to U.S. norms and the degree of modernization among traditional immigrant families. The results of research spanning the 1970s and 1980s were mixed and sometimes contradictory.

Buriel's (1993) study brought some clarity to the subject of child-rearing practices by situating it in the broad social context in which such practices occur. This study of Mexican families found that child-rearing practices differ by generation. Parents who were born in Mexico had a "responsibility-oriented" style that was compatible with their own life experience as struggling immigrants. U.S.-born Mexican parents had a "concern-oriented" style of parenting that was associated with the higher levels of education and income found among this group and that may also indicate that parents compensate for their children's disadvantaged standing in U.S. schools.

Mainstream theorizing has generally assumed a middle-class European-American model for the socialization of the next generation (Segura & Pierce, 1993). But the diverse contexts in which Latino children are raised suggest that family studies must take into account multiple models of socialization. Latino children are less likely than Anglo children to live in isolated nuclear units in which parents have almost exclusive responsibility for rearing children and the mothers' role is primary. Segura and Pierce contended that the pattern of nonexclusive mothering found in some Latino families shapes the gender identities of Latinos in ways that conventional thinking does not consider. Velez-Ibañez & Greenberg (1992) discussed how the extensive kinship networks of Mexican families influence child rearing and considered the ramifications for educational outcomes. Mexican children are socialized into a context of "thick" social relations. From infancy onward, these children experience far more social interaction than do children who are raised in more isolated contexts. The institution of education—second only to the family as an agent of socialization—is, in the United States, modeled after the dominant society and characterized by competition and individual achievement. Latino students who have been socialized into a more cooperative model of social relations often experience a disjuncture between their upbringing and the expectations of their schools (Velez-Ibañez & Greenberg, 1992).

Social location shapes the range of choices that parents have as they decide how best to provide for their children. Latino parents, who are disproportionately likely to occupy subordinate social locations in U.S. society, encounter severe obstacles to providing adequate material resources for their children. To date, little research has focused on Latino fathers (Powell, 1995). Hondagneu-Sotelo and Avila's (1997) study documented a broad range of mothering arrangements among Latinas. One such arrangement is transnational mothering, in which mothers work in the United States while their children remain in Mexico or Central America; it is accompanied by tremendous costs and undertaken when options are extremely limited. The researchers found that transnational mothering occurred among domestic workers, many of whom were live-in maids or child care providers who could not live with their children, as well as mothers who could better provide for their children in their countries of origin because U.S. dollars stretched further in Central America than in the United States. Other mothering arrangements chosen by Latinas in the study included migrating with their children, migrating alone and later sending for their children, and migrating alone and returning to their children after a period of work.

Intrafamily Diversity

Family scholars have increasingly recognized that family experience is differentiated along the lines of age and gender (Baca Zinn & Eitzen, 1996; Thorne, 1992). Members of particular families—parents and children, women and men—experience family life differently. Scholarship that considers the internal differentiation of Latino families is focused on the conditions surrounding and adaptations following immigration.

While immigration requires tremendous change of all family members, family adaptation to the new context is not a unitary phenomenon. Research has found patterns of differential adjustment as family members adapt unevenly to an unfamiliar social environment (Gold, 1989). Gil and Vega's (1996) study of acculturative stress in Cuban and Nicaraguan families in the Miami area identified significant differences in the adjustment of parents and their children. For example, Nicaraguan adolescents reported more initial language conflicts than did their parents, but their conflicts diminished over time, whereas their parents' language conflicts increased over time. This difference occurred because the adolescents were immediately confronted with their English language deficiency in school, but their parents could initially manage well in the Miami area without a facility with English. The authors concluded that family members experience "the aversive impacts of culture change at different times and at variable levels of intensity" (p. 451).

Differential adjustment creates new contexts for parent-child relations. Immigrant children who are school-aged generally become competent in English more quickly than do their parents. Dorrington (1995) found that Salvadoran and Guatemalan children often assume adult roles as they help their parents negotiate the bureaucratic structure of their new social environment; for example, a young child may accompany her parents to a local utility company to act as their translator.

Immigration may also create formal legal distinctions among members of Latino families. Frequently, family members do not share the same immigration status. That is, undocumented Mexican and Central American couples are likely, over time, to have children born in the United States and hence are U.S. citizens; the presence of these children then renders the "undocumented family" label inaccurate. Chavez (1992, p. 129) used the term *binational family* to refer to a family with both members who are undocumented and those who are citizens or legal residents.

Not only do family members experience family life differently, but age and gender often produce diverging and even conflicting interests among them (Baca Zinn & Eitzen, 1996). Both Hondagneu-Sotelo's (1994) and Grasmuck and Pessar's (1991) studies of family immigration found that Latinas were generally far more interested in settling permanently in the United States than were their husbands. In both studies, the women had enhanced their status by migration, while the men had lost theirs. Hondagneu-Sotelo noted that Mexican women advanced the permanent settlement of their families by taking regular, nonseasonal employment; negotiating the use of public and private assistance; and forging strong community ties. Grasmuck and Pessar observed that Dominican women tried to postpone their families' return to the Dominican Republic by extravagantly spending money that would otherwise be saved for their return and by establishing roots in the United States.

DISCUSSION AND CONCLUSION

The key to understanding diversity in Latino families is the uneven distribution of constraints and opportunities among families, which affects the behaviors of family members and ultimately the forms that family units take (Baca Zinn & Eitzen, 1996). Our goal in this review was to call into question assumptions, beliefs, and false generalizations about the way "Latino families are." We examined Latino families not as if they had some essential characteristics that set them apart from others, but as they are affected by a complex mix of structural features.

Our framework enabled us to see how diverse living arrangements among Latinos are situated and structured in the larger social world. Although this framework embraces the interplay of macro- and microlevels of analysis, we are mindful that this review devoted far too little attention to family experience, resistance, and voice. We do not mean to underestimate the importance of human agency in the social construction of Latino families, but we could not devote as much attention as we would have liked to the various ways in which women, men, and children actively produce their family worlds. Given the sheer size of the literature, the "non-comparability of most contemporary findings and the lack of a consistent conceptual groundwork" (Vega, 1990, p. 102), we decided that what is most needed is a coherent framework within which to view and interpret diversity. Therefore, we chose to focus on the impact of social forces on family life.

The basic insights of our perspective are sociological. Yet a paradox of family sociology is that the field has tended to misrepresent Latino families and those of other racial-ethnic groups. Sociology has distorted Latino families by generalizing from the experience of dominant groups and ignoring the differences that make a difference. This is a great irony. Family sociology, the specialty whose task it is to describe and understand social diversity, has marginalized diversity, rather than treated it as a central feature of social life (Baca Zinn & Eitzen, 1993).

As sociologists, we wrote this [reading] fully aware of the directions in our discipline that hinder the ability to explain diversity. At the same time, we think the core insight of sociology should be applied to challenge conventional thinking about families. Reviewing the literature for this [reading] did not diminish our sociological convictions, but it did present us with some unforeseen challenges. We found a vast gulf between mainstream family sociology and the extraordinary amount of high-quality scholarship on Latino families. Our review took us far beyond the boundaries of our discipline, making us "cross disciplinary migrants" (Stacey, 1995). We found the new literature in diverse and unlikely locations, with important breakthroughs emerging in the "borderlands" between social science disciplines. We also found the project to be infinitely more complex than we anticipated. The extensive scholarship on three national-origin groups and "others" was complicated by widely varying analytic snapshots. We were, in short, confronted with a kaleidoscope of family diversity. Our shared perspective served us well in managing the task at hand. Although we have different family specializations and contrasting family experiences, we both seek to understand multiple family and household forms that emanate from structural arrangements.

What are the most important lessons our sociological analysis holds for the family field? Three themes offer new directions for building a better, more inclusive, family social science. First, understanding Latino family diversity does not mean simply appreciating the ways in which families are different; rather, it means analyzing how the formation of diverse families is based on and reproduces social inequalities. At the heart of many of the differences between Latino families and mainstream families and the different aggregate family patterns among Latino groups are structural forces that place families in different social environments. What is not often acknowledged is that the same social structures—race, class, and other hierarchies—affect *all* families, albeit in different ways. Instead of treating family variation as the property of group difference, recent sociological theorizing (Baca Zinn, 1994; Dill, 1994; Glenn, 1992; Hill Collins, 1990, 1997) has conceptualized diverse family arrangements in *relational* terms, that is, mutually dependent and sustained through interaction across racial and class boundaries. The point is not that family differences based on race, class, and gender simply coexist. Instead, many differences in family life involve relationships of domination and subordination and differential access to material resources. Patterns of privilege and subordination characterize the historical relationships between Anglo families and Mexican families in the Southwest (Dill, 1994). Contemporary diversity among Latino families reveals *new* interdependences and inequalities. Emergent middle-class and professional lifestyles among Anglos and even some Latinos are interconnected with a new Latino servant class whose family arrangements, in turn, must accommodate to the demands of their labor.

Second, family diversity plays a part in different economic orders and the shifts that accompany them. Scholars have suggested that the multiplicity of household types is one of the chief props of the world economy (Smith, Wallerstein, & Evers, 1985). The example of U.S.-Mexican cross-border households brings this point into full view. This household arrangement constitutes an important "part of the emerging and dynamic economic and technological transformations in the region" (Velez-Ibañez, 1996, p. 143). The structural reordering required by such families is central to regional economic change.

Finally, the incredible array of immigrant family forms and their enormous capacity for adaptation offer new departures for the study of postmodern families. "Binational," "transnational," and "multinational" families, together with "border balanced households" and "generational hopscotching," are arrangements that remain invisible even in Stacey's (1996) compelling analysis of U.S. family life at the century's end. And yet the experiences of Latino families—flexible and plastic—as far back as the late 1800s (Griswold del Castillo, 1984), give resonance to the image of long-standing family fluidity and of contemporary families lurching backward and forward into the postmodern age (Stacey, 1990). The shift to a postindustrial economy is not the only social transformation affecting families. Demographic and political changes sweeping the world are engendering family configurations that are yet unimagined in family social science.

These trends offer new angles of vision for thinking about family diversity. They pose new opportunities for us to remake family studies as we uncover the mechanisms that construct multiple household and family arrangements.

References

Alarcon, N., Castillo, A., & Moraga, C. (Eds.). (1989). *Third woman: The sexuality of Latinas*. Berkeley, CA: Third Woman.

Almaguer, T. (1991). Chicano men: A cartography of homosexual identity and behavior. *Differences: A Journal of Feminist Cultural Studies, 3*, 75–100.

Alvirez, D., & Bean, F. (1976). The Mexican American family. In C. Mindel & R. Habenstein (Eds.), *Ethnic families in America* (pp. 271–292). New York: Elsevier.

Angel, R., & Tienda, M. (1982). Determinants of extended household structure: Cultural pattern or economic need? *American Journal of Sociology*, 87, 1360–1383.

Anzaldúa, G. (1987). *Borderlands/La Frontera: The new meztiza*. San Francisco: Spinsters, Aunt Lute Press.

Aponte, R. (1993). Hispanic families in poverty: Diversity, context, and interpretation. *Families in Society: The Journal of Contemporary Human Services*, 36, 527–537.

Baca Zinn, M. (1980). Employment and education of Mexican American women: The interplay of modernity and ethnicity in eight families. *Harvard Educational Review*, 50, 47–62.

Baca Zinn, M. (1983). Familism among Chicanos: A theoretical review. *Humboldt Journal of Social Relations*, 10, 224–238.

Baca Zinn, M. (1994). Feminist rethinking from racial-ethnic families. In M. Baca Zinn & B. T. Dill (Eds.), *Women of color in U.S. society* (pp. 303–312). Philadelphia: Temple University Press.

Baca Zinn, M. (1995). Social science theorizing for Latino families in the age of diversity. In R. E. Zambrana (Ed.), *Understanding Latino families* (pp. 177–187). Thousand Oaks, CA: Sage.

Baca Zinn, M., & Dill, B. T. (1996). Theorizing difference from multiracial feminism. *Feminist Studies*, 22, 321–332.

Baca Zinn, M., & Eitzen, D. S. (1993). The demographic transformation and the sociological enterprise. *American Sociologist*, 24, 5–12.

Baca Zinn, M., & Eitzen, D. S. (1996). *Diversity in families* (4th ed.). New York: HarperCollins.

Baca Zinn, M., & Eitzen, D. S. (1998). Economic restructuring and systems in inequality. In M. L. Andersen & P. H. Collins (Eds.), *Race, class and gender* (3rd ed., pp. 233–237). Belmont, CA: Wadsworth.

Betancur, J. J., Cordova, T., & Torres, M. L. A. (1993). Economic restructuring and the process of incorporation of Latinos into the Chicago economy. In R. Morales & F. Bonilla (Eds.), *Latinos in a changing U.S. economy: Comparative perspectives on growing inequality* (pp. 109–132). Newbury Park, CA: Sage.

Bogardus, A. (1934). *The Mexican in the United States*. Los Angeles: University of Southern California Press.

Boss, P., & Thorne, B. (1989). Family sociology and family therapy. In M. McGoldrick, C. M. Anderson, & F. Walsh (Eds.), *Women in families* (pp. 78–96). New York: W. W. Norton.

Boyd, M. (1989). Family and personal networks in international migration: Recent developments and new agendas. *International Migration Review*, 23, 638–670.

Buriel, R. (1993). Childrearing orientations in Mexican American families: The influence of generation and sociocultural factors. *Journal of Marriage and the Family*, 55, 987–1000.

Buriel, R., & De Ment, T. (1997). Immigration and sociocultural change in Mexican, Chinese, and Vietnamese American families. In A. Booth, A. C. Crouter, & N. Landale (Eds.), *Immigration and the family: Research and policy on U.S. immigrants* (pp. 165–200). Mahwah, NJ: Lawrence Erlbaum.

Cardenas, G., Chapa, J., & Burek, S. (1993). The changing economic position of Mexican Americans in San Antonio. In R. Morales & F. Bonilla (Eds.), *Latinos in a changing U.S. economy: Comparative perspectives on growing inequality* (pp. 160–183). Newbury Park, CA: Sage.

Carnoy, M., Daley, H. M., & Ojeda, R. H. (1993). The changing economic position of Latinos in the U.S. labor market since 1939. In R. Morales & F. Bonilla (Eds.), *Latinos in a changing U.S. economy: Comparative perspectives on growing inequality* (pp. 28–54). Newbury Park, CA: Sage.

Carrier, J. (1992). Miguel: Sexual life history of a gay Mexican American. In G. Herdt (Ed.), *Gay culture in America* (pp. 202–224). Boston: Beacon Press.

Chavez, L. R. (1990). Coresidence and resistance: Strategies for survival among undocumented Mexicans and Central Americans in the United States. *Urban Anthropology*, 19, 31–61.

Chavez, L. R. (1992). *Shadowed lives: Undocumented immigrants in American society*. Fort Worth, TX: Holt, Rinehart, & Winston.

Chavira-Prado, A. (1992). Work, health, and the family: Gender structure and women's status in an undocumented migrant population. *Human Organization*, 51, 53–64.

Coltrane, S. (1996). *Family man*. New York: Oxford University Press.

Coltrane, S., & Valdez, E. O. (1993). Reluctant compliance: Work-family role allocation in dual earner Chicano families. In J. Hood (Ed.), *Men, work, and family* (pp. 151–175). Newbury Park, CA: Sage.

Demo, D. H., & Allen, K. R. (1996). Diversity within gay and lesbian families: Challenges and implications for family theory and research. *Journal of Social and Personal Relationships, 13*, 415–434.

Dill, B. T. (1994). Fictive kin, paper sons, and compadrazgo: Women of color and the struggle for survival. In M. Baca Zinn & B. T. Dill (Eds.), *Women of color in U.S. society* (pp. 149–169). Philadelphia: Temple University Press.

Dominguez, J. I. (1992). Cooperating with the enemy? U.S. immigration policies toward Cuba. In C. Mitchell (Ed.), *Western hemisphere immigration and United States foreign policy* (pp. 31–88). University Park, PA: Pennsylvania State University Press.

Dorrington, C. (1995). Central American refugees in Los Angeles: Adjustment of children and families. In R. Zambrana (Ed.), *Understanding Latino families: Scholarship, policy, and practice* (pp. 107–129). Thousand Oaks, CA: Sage.

Feagin, J. R., & Feagin, C. B. (1996). *Racial and ethnic relations*. Upper Saddle River, NJ: Prentice Hall.

Fernandez-Kelly, M. P. (1990). Delicate transactions: Gender, home, and employment among Hispanic women. In F. Ginsberg & A. L. Tsing (Eds.), *Uncertain terms* (pp. 183–195). Boston: Beacon Press.

Fernandez-Kelly, M. P., & Garcia, A. (1990). Power surrendered and power restored: The politics of home and work among Hispanic women in southern California and southern Florida. In L. Tilly & P. Gurin (Eds.), *Women and politics in America* (pp. 130–149). New York: Russell Sage Foundation.

Fernandez-Kelly, M. P., & Schauffler, R. (1994). Divided fates: Immigrant children in a restructured U.S. economy. *International Migration Review, 28*, 662–689.

Gil, A. G., & Vega, W. A. (1996). Two different worlds: Acculturation stress and adaptation among Cuban and Nicaraguan families. *Journal of Social and Personal Relationships, 13*, 435–456.

Glenn, E. N. (1992). From servitude to service work: Historical continuities in the racial division of paid reproductive labor. *Signs: Journal of Women in Culture and Society, 18*, 1–43.

Gold, S. J. (1989). Differential adjustment among new immigrant family members. *Journal of Contemporary Ethnography, 17*, 408–434.

Grasmuck, S., & Pessar, P. R. (1991). *Between two islands: Dominican international migration*. Berkeley: University of California Press.

Grasmuck, S., & Pessar, P. R. (1996). Dominicans in the United States: First- and second-generation settlement, 1960–1990. In S. Pedraza & R. G. Rumbaut (Eds.), *Origins and destinies: Immigration, race, and ethnicity in America* (pp. 280–292). Belmont, CA: Wadsworth.

Griffith, J., & Villavicienco, S. (1985). Relationships among culturation, sociodemographic characteristics, and social supports in Mexican American adults. *Hispanic Journal of Behavioral Science, 7*, 75–92.

Griswold del Castillo, R. (1984). *La familia*. Notre Dame, IN: University of Notre Dame Press.

Guarnizo, L. E. (1997). Los Dominicanyorks: The making of a binational society. In M. Romero, P. Hondagneu-Sotelo, & V. Ortiz (Eds.), *Challenging fronteras: Structuring Latina and Latino lives in the U.S.* (pp. 161–174). New York: Routledge.

Hamilton, N., & Chinchilla, N. S. (1997). Central American migration: A framework for analysis. In M. Romero, P. Hondagneu-Sotelo, & V. Ortiz (Eds.), *Challenging fronteras: Structuring Latina and Latino lives in the U.S.* (pp. 81–100). New York: Routledge.

Heller, C. (1966). *Mexican American youth: Forgotten youth at the crossroads*. New York: Random House.

Hill Collins, P. (1990). *Black feminist thought: Knowledge, consciousness and the politics of empowerment*. Boston: Unwin Hyman.

Hill Collins, P. (1997). African-American women and economic justice: A preliminary analysis of wealth, family, and black social class. Unpublished manuscript, Department of African American Studies. University of Cincinnati.

Hondagneu-Sotelo, P. (1994). *Gendered transitions: Mexican experiences of migration*. Berkeley: University of California Press.

Hondagneu-Sotelo, P., & Avila, E. (1997). "I'm here, but I'm there": The meanings of transnational motherhood. *Gender and Society, 11*, 548–571.

Hondagneu-Sotelo, P., & Messner, M. A. (1994). Gender displays and men's power: The "new man" and the Mexican immigrant man. In H. Brod & M. Kaufman (Eds.), *Theorizing masculinities* (pp. 200–218). Newbury Park, CA: Sage.

Hoppe, S. K., & Heller, P. L. (1975). Alienation, familism and the utilization of health services by Mexican-Americans. *Journal of Health and Social Behavior, 16*, 304–314.

Hurtado, A. (1995). Variations, combinations, and evolutions: Latino families in the United States. In R. E. Zambrana (Ed.), *Understanding Latino families* (pp. 40–61). Thousand Oaks, CA: Sage.

Keefe, S. (1984). Deal and ideal extended familism among Mexican Americans and Anglo Americans: On the meaning of "close" family ties. *Human Organization, 43*, 65–70.

Lamphere, L., Zavella, P., & Gonzales F., with Evans, P. B. (1993). *Sunbelt working mothers: Reconciling family and factory.* Ithaca, NY: Cornell University Press.

Landale, N. S., & Fennelly, K. (1992). Informal unions among mainland Puerto Ricans: Cohabitation or an alternative to legal marriage? *Journal of Marriage and the Family, 54*, 269–280.

Lopez, D. E., Popkin, E., & Telles, E. (1996). Central Americans: At the bottom, struggling to get ahead. In R. Waldinger & M. Bozorgmehr (Eds.), *Ethnic Los Angeles* (pp. 279–304). New York: Russell Sage Foundation.

Madsen, W. (1973). *The Mexican-Americans of south Texas.* New York: Holt, Rinehart & Winston.

Martinez, E. A. (1993). Parenting young children in Mexican American/Chicago families. In H. P. McAdoo (Ed.), *Family ethnicity: Strength in diversity* (pp. 184–194). Newbury Park, CA: Sage.

Massey, D. S. (1993). Latino poverty research: An agenda for the 1990s. Items, *Social Science Research Council Newsletter, 47*(l), 7–11.

Massey, D. S., Zambrana, R. E., & Bell, S. A. (1995). Contemporary issues for Latino families: Future directions for research, policy, and practice. In R. E. Zambrana (Ed.), *Understanding Latino families* (pp. 190–204). Thousand Oaks, CA: Sage.

Mindel, C. H. (1980). Extended familism among urban Mexican-Americans, Anglos and blacks. *Hispanic Journal of Behavioral Sciences, 2*, 21–34.

Mirande, A. (1997). *Hombres y machos: Masculinity and Latino culture.* Boulder, CO: Westview Press.

Mitchell, C. (1992). U.S. foreign policy and Dominican migration to the United States. In C. Mitchell (Ed.), *Western hemisphere immigration and United States foreign policy* (pp. 89–123). University Park: Pennsylvania State University Press.

Moore, J. W., & Pinderhughes, R. (Eds.). (1993). *In the barrios: Latinos and the underclass debate.* New York: Russell Sage Foundation.

Moore, J. W., & Vigil, J. D. (1993). Barrios in transition. In J. W. Moore & R. Pinderhughes (Eds.), *In the barrios: Latinos and the underclass debate* (pp. 27–50). New York: Russell Sage Foundation.

Moraga, C. (1983). *Loving in the war years: Lo que nunca paso por sus labios.* Boston: South End Press.

Morales, E. S. (1990). Ethnic minority families and minority gays and lesbians. In F. W. Bozett & M. B. Sussman (Eds.), *Homosexuality and family relations* (pp. 217–239). New York: Harrington Park Press.

Morales, R., & Ong, P. M. (1993). The illusion of progress: Latinos in Los Angeles. In R. Morales & F. Bonilla (Eds.), *Latinos in a changing U.S. economy: Comparative perspectives on growing inequality* (pp. 55–84). Newbury Park, CA: Sage.

Morales, R., & Bonilla, F. (1993). Restructuring and the new inequality. In R. Morales & F. Bonilla (Eds.), *Latinos in a changing U.S. economy: Comparative perspectives on growing inequality* (pp. 1–27). Newbury Park, CA: Sage.

Morrissey, M. (1987). Female-headed families: Poor women and choice. In N. Gerstel & H. Gross (Eds.), Families and work (pp. 302–314). Philadelphia: Temple University Press.

Ortiz, V. (1995). The diversity of Latino families. In R. Zambrana (Ed.), *Understanding Latino families: Scholarship, policy, and practice* (pp. 18–30). Thousand Oaks, CA: Sage.

Ortiz, V. (1996). The Mexican-origin population: Permanent working class or emerging middle class? In R. Waldinger & M. Bozorgmehr (Eds.), *Ethnic Los Angeles* (pp. 247–277). New York: Russell Sage Foundation.

Perez, L. (1994). Cuban families in the United States. In R. L. Taylor (Ed.), *Minority families in the United States: A multicultural perspective.* Englewood Cliffs, NJ: Prentice Hall.

Perez-Stable, M., & Uriarte, M. (1993). Cubans and the changing economy of Miami. In R. Morales & F. Bonilla (Eds.), *Latinos in a changing U.S. economy: Comparative perspectives on growing inequality* (pp. 133–159). Newbury Park, CA: Sage.

Pesquera, B. M. (1993). In the beginning he wouldn't lift even a spoon: The division of household labor. In A. de la Torre & B. M. Pesquera (Eds.), *Building with our hands* (pp. 181–198). Berkeley: University of California Press.

Portes, A., & Rumbaut, R. G. (1990). *Immigrant America: A portrait.* Berkeley: University of California Press.

Portes, A., & Truelove, C. (1987). Making sense of diversity: Recent research on Hispanic minorities in the United States. *Annual Review of Sociology, 13,* 357–385.

Powell, D. R. (1995). Including Latino fathers in parent education and support programs: Development of a program model. In R. E. Zambrana (Ed.), *Understanding Latino families* (pp. 85–106). Thousand Oaks, CA: Sage.

Ramirez, O. (1980, March). Extended family support and mental health status among Mexicans in -Detroit. *Micro, Onda, LaRed, Monthly Newsletter of the National Chicano Research Network,* p. 2.

Ramirez, O., & Arce, C. H. (1981). The contemporary Chicano family: An empirically based review. In A. Baron, Jr. (Ed.), *Explorations in Chicano Psychology* (pp. 3–28). New York: Praeger.

Repack, T. A. (1997). New rules in a new landscape. In M. Romero, P. Hondagneu-Sotelo, & V. Ortiz (Eds.), *Challenging fronteras: Structuring Latina and Latino lives in the U.S.* (pp. 247–257). New York: Routledge.

Rochelle, A. (1997). *No more kin: Exploring race, class, and gender in family networks.* Thousand Oaks, CA: Sage.

Rodriguez, N. P., & Hagan, J. M. (1997). Apartment restructuring and Latino immigrant tenant struggles: A case study of human agency. In M. Romero, P. Hondagneu-Sotelo, & V. Ortiz (Eds.), *Challenging fronteras: Structuring Latina and Latina lives in the U.S.* (pp. 297–309). New York: Routledge.

Romero, M. (1996). Introduction. In M. Romero, P. Hondagneu-Sotelo, & V. Ortiz (Eds.), *Challenging fronteras: Structuring Latina and Latino lives in the U.S.* (pp. xiii–xix). New York: Routledge.

Rubel, A. J. (1966). *Across the tracks: Mexican Americans in a Texas city.* Austin: University of Texas Press.

Rumbaut, R. G. (1995). *Immigrants from Latin America and the Caribbean: A socioeconomic profile* (Statistical Brief No. 6). East Lansing: Julian Samora Research Institute, Michigan State University.

Sassen, S. (1993). Urban transformation and employment. In R. Morales & F. Bonilla (Eds.), *Latinos in a changing U.S. economy: Comparative perspectives on growing inequality* (pp. 194–206). Newbury Park, CA: Sage.

Scott, A. J. (1996). The manufacturing economy: Ethnic and gender divisions of labor. In R. Waldinger & M. Bozorgmehr (Eds.), *Ethnic Los Angeles.* New York: Russell Sage Foundation.

Segura, D. A., & Pierce, J. L. (1993). Chicana/o family structure and gender personality: Chodorow, familism, and psychoanalytic sociology revisited. *Signs, 19,* 62–91.

Shelton, B. A., & John, D. (1993). Ethnicity, race, and difference: A comparison of white, black, and Hispanic men's household labor time. In J. Hood (Ed.), *Men, work, and family* (pp. 1–22). Newbury Park, CA: Sage.

Smith, J., Wallerstein, I., & Evers, H. D. (1985). *The household and the world economy.* Beverly Hills, CA: Sage.

Solis, J. (1995). The status of Latino children and youth: Challenges and prospects. In R. E. Zambrana (Ed.), *Understanding Latino families* (pp. 62–84). Thousand Oaks, CA: Sage.

Stacey, J. (1990). *Brave new families: Stories of domestic upheaval in late twentieth century America.* New York: Basic Books.

Stacey, J. (1995). Disloyal to the disciplines: A feminist trajectory in the border lands. In D. C. Stanton & A. Stewart (Eds.), *Feminisms in the academy* (pp. 311–330). Ann Arbor: University of Michigan Press.

Stacey, J. (1996). *In the name of the family: Rethinking family values in the postmodern age.* Boston: Beacon Press.

Stier, H., & Tienda, M. (1992). Family, work, and women: The labor supply of Hispanic immigrant wives. *International Migration Review, 26,* 1291–1313.

Sullivan, M. L. (1993). Puerto Ricans in Sunset Park, Brooklyn: Poverty amidst ethnic and economic diversity. In J. W. Moore & R. Pinderhughes (Eds.), *In the barrios: Latinos and the underclass debate* (pp. 1–26). New York: Russell Sage Foundation.

Thomas, D., & Wilcox, J. E. (1987). The rise of family theory. In M. B. Sussman & S. Steinmetz (Eds.), *Handbook of marriage and the family* (pp. 81–102). New York: Plenum.

Thorne, B. (1992). Feminism and the family: Two decades of thought. In B. Thorne & M. Yalom (Eds.), *Rethinking the family: Some feminist questions* (pp. 3–30). Boston: Northeastern University Press.

Tienda, M. (1989). Puerto Ricans and the underclass debate. *Annals of the American Association of Political and Social Sciences, 501,* 105–119.

Torres, A., & Bonilla, F. (1993). Decline within decline: The New York perspective. In R. Morales & F. Bonilla (Eds.), *Latinos in a changing U.S. economy: Comparative perspectives on growing inequality* (pp. 85–108). Newbury Park, CA: Sage.

U.S. Bureau of the Census. (1993). *1990 census of the population: Persons of Hispanic origin in the United States.* Washington, DC: U.S. Government Printing Office.

U.S. Bureau of the Census. (1996). *Statistical abstract Of the United States: 1996.* Washington DC: U.S. Government Printing Office.

Valenzuela, A., & Dornbusch, S. (1994). Familism and social capital in the academic achievement of Mexican origin and Anglo adolescents. *Social Science Quarterly, 75,* 18–36.

Vega, W. (1990). Hispanic families in the 1980s: A decade of research. *Journal of Marriage and the Family, 52,* 1015–1024.

Vega, W. A. (1995). The study of Latino families: A point of departure. In R. E. Zambrana (Ed.), *Understanding Latino families* (pp. 3–17). Thousand Oaks, CA: Sage.

Velez-Ibañez, C. (1993). U.S. Mexicans in the borderlands: Being poor without the underclass. In J. Moore & R. Pinderhughes (Eds.), *In the barrios: Latinos and the underclass debate* (pp. 195–220). New York: Russell Sage Foundation.

Velez-Ibañez, C. (1996). *Border visions.* Tucson: University of Arizona Press.

Velez-Ibañez, C. G., & Greenberg, J. B. (1992). Formation and transformation of funds of knowledge among U.S.-Mexican households. *Anthropology and Education Quarterly, 23,* 313–335.

Williams, N. (1990). *The Mexican American family: Tradition and change.* Dix Hills, NY: General Hall.

Wilkinson, D. (1993). Family ethnicity in America. In H. P. McAdoo (Ed.), *Family ethnicity: Strength in diversity* (pp. 15–59). Newbury Park, CA: Sage.

Wilson, W. J. (1987). *The truly disadvantaged. The inner city, the underclass, and public policy.* Chicago: University of Chicago Press.

Wilson, W. J. (1996). *When work disappears: The world of the new urban poor.* New York: Alfred A. Knopf.

Ybarra, L. (1982). When wives work: The impact on the Chicano family. *Journal of Marriage and the Family, 44,* 169–178.

Zavella, P. (1987). *Women's work and Chicano families: Cannery workers of the Santa Clara Valley.* Ithaca, NY: Cornell University Press.

■ READING 27

Conflict, Coping, and Reconciliation: Intergenerational Relations in Chinese Immigrant Families

Min Zhou

Chinese Americans are by far the oldest and largest ethnic group of Asian ancestry in the United States. Their long history of migration and settlement dates back to the late 1840s, including some sixty years of legal exclusion. With the lifting of legal barriers to Chinese immigration during World War II and especially following the 1965 Hart-Celler Act, which abolished the national-origins quota system and emphasized family reunification and the importation of skilled labor, the Chinese American community increased dramatically—from 237,000 in 1960 to more than three million (including half a million mixed-race persons) in 2005. Much of this extraordinary growth is due to immigration. Between 1961 and 2005, more than 1.8 million immigrants were admitted to the United States as permanent residents from China, Hong Kong, and Taiwan.[1,2,3] The foreign born accounted for more than two-thirds of the ethnic Chinese population in the United States. Today's second generation is still very young and has not yet come of age in significant numbers.[4] The 2000 Current Population Survey indicates that 44 percent of the U.S.-born Chinese are under the age of eighteen and another 10 percent are between eighteen and twenty-four.[5]

After 1965, the Chinese American community was transformed from a bachelors' society to a family community. There have been other significant changes as well. Unlike earlier Chinese immigrants, post-1965 Chinese arrivals have come not only from mainland China, but also from the greater Chinese Diaspora—Hong Kong, Taiwan, Vietnam, Cambodia, Malaysia, and the Americas. Diverse national origins entail diverse cultural patterns. Linguistically, for example, Chinese immigrants come from a much wider variety of dialect groups than in the past. While all Chinese share a single ancestral written language, they speak numerous regional dialects—Cantonese, Mandarin, Minnanese, Hakkaese, Chaozhounese, and Shanghainese.

Post-1965 Chinese immigrants also have diverse socioeconomic backgrounds. Like those in the past, some arrive in the United States with little money, minimum education, few job skills, and from rural areas, but a significant number now come with considerable family savings, education, and skills far above the levels of average Americans. The 2004 American Community Survey reports that 50 percent of adult Chinese Americans (age twenty-five or older) in the United States have attained four or more years of college education, compared to 30 percent of non-Hispanic whites. Immigrants from Taiwan displayed the highest levels of educational attainment, with nearly two-thirds completing at least four years of college, followed by those from Hong Kong (just shy of half) and from mainland China (about a third). Professional occupations were also more common among Chinese American workers (age sixteen or older) than non-Hispanic white workers (52 percent versus 38 percent). The annual median household income for Chinese Americans was $57,000 in 2003 dollars, compared to $49,000 for non-Hispanic whites. While major socioeconomic indicators are above the national average and above those for non-Hispanic whites, the poverty rate for Chinese Americans was also higher (13 percent) than for non-Hispanic whites (9 percent), and the homeownership rate was lower (63 percent) than for non-Hispanic whites (74 percent).[6]

In terms of settlement patterns, Chinese Americans have continued to concentrate in the western United States and in urban areas. California alone accounts for nearly 40 percent of all Chinese Americans (1.1 million); New York comes in second with 16 percent, followed by Hawaii with 6 percent. At the same time, other states that historically received few Chinese immigrants, such as Texas, New Jersey, Massachusetts, Illinois, Washington, Florida, Maryland, and Pennsylvania, have now witnessed phenomenal growth. Traditional urban enclaves, such as Chinatowns in San Francisco, New York,

Los Angeles, Chicago, and Boston, still receive new immigrants, but they are no longer the primary centers of initial settlement now that many new immigrants, especially the affluent and highly skilled, go straight to the suburbs on arrival. Currently, only 2 percent of the Chinese in Los Angeles, 8 percent in San Francisco, and 14 percent in New York City live in old Chinatowns. Half of all Chinese Americans live in suburbs. A good number live in the new multiethnic, immigrant-dominant suburban municipalities, often referred to as "ethnoburbs," that have appeared since the 1980s.[7] In 2000, there were eleven cities in the United States—all in California and all but San Francisco in the suburbs—in which Chinese Americans made up more than 20 percent of the population.

These demographic changes in the Chinese American community have created multiple contexts in which the new second generation (the U.S.-born or -raised children of post-1965 Chinese immigrants) is coming of age. Three main neighborhood contexts—the traditional ethnic enclaves such as inner-city Chinatowns, the ethnoburbs, and the white middle-class suburbs—are particularly important in understanding the challenges confronting new Chinese immigrant families.

COMMUNITY TRANSFORMATIONS AND CONTEXTS

During the era of legal exclusion, most Chinese immigrants were isolated in inner-city ethnic enclaves that were characterized as bachelors' societies. Many Chinatown "bachelor" workers were actually married but had left their wives, children, and parents behind in their villages in China. The few "normal" families in the bachelors' society often were those of merchants or workers who, for immigration purposes, claimed to be partners of merchants. In old Chinatowns, individuals and families were enmeshed in and highly dependent upon the ethnic community for social, economic, and emotional support, while also subject to its control. Chinatown children grew up in an extended family environment surrounded by and under the watchful eyes of many "grandpas" and "uncles" who were not actually related by blood but were part of an intricate system of family, kin or parental friendship associations.

The behavior of both children and parents in old Chinatowns was carefully monitored by a closely knit ethnic community. Children were either "good" kids—loyal, *guai* (obedient), and *you-chu-xi* (promising)—or "bad" kids, disrespectful, *bai-jia-zi* (family failure), and *mei-chu-xi* (good-for-nothing). They grew up speaking fluent Chinese, mostly in local dialects, going to Chinese schools, working in Chinese-owned businesses in the community, and interacting intimately with other Chinese in the ethnic enclave. Many wished to become like other American children but faced resistance from the larger society as well as from their own families. The larger society looked down on the Chinese and set barriers to keep them apart, such as segregation in schools and workplaces. The Chinese family tied children to Chinatown and its ethnic institutions, Chinese school being the most important, to shield them from overt discrimination. Despite considerable adolescent rebellion and generational conflict within the family, the children often found themselves dependent on ethnic networks without much scope to break free.

Whereas members of the old second generation grew up in ethnic enclaves isolated from middle-class America, those of the new second generation come from more diverse socioeconomic backgrounds and have settled in a wider range of neighborhoods. Those who reside in inner-city Chinatowns are generally from low-income families who have recently arrived. Like the old second generation, they speak Chinese fluently, interact primarily with people in a Chinese-speaking environment, and participate in various cultural and social institutions in the ethnic community. However, they no longer live in a hostile environment that socially and legally excludes the Chinese. Even though they may go to neighborhood schools with mostly immigrant Chinese and other minority children, they have more opportunities to interact with non-coethnic children and adults and a wider range of occupational choices.

Members of the new second generation who reside in multiethnic ethnoburbs are mainly from upper- and middle-income families. They generally go to higher-quality suburban public schools. They also have access to ethnic institutions unavailable, or less available, in old Chinatown, such as after-school tutoring (*buxiban*), academic enrichment, sports, and music programs offered by Chinese-owned private businesses. Although they speak Chinese fluently, interact with other Chinese, and are involved with things "Chinese," including food, music, and customs, they also interact regularly with people of diverse racial/ethnic backgrounds.

The children of Chinese immigrants in suburban white middle-class neighborhoods tend to have parents who have achieved high levels of education, occupation, income, and English proficiency and who are bicultural, transnational, cosmopolitan, and highly assimilated. These children attend schools where white students are in the majority and have few primary contacts with coethnic peers. Many grow up speaking only English at home and have mostly white friends.

Overall, compared to the old, pre-1965, second generation, members of the new second generation are growing up in a more open society. They do not face the kinds of legal barriers to educational and occupational attainment that blocked the mobility of the old second generation. They tend to live in family neighborhoods and have more sources of social support beyond the ethnic community. They also have much more freedom to "become American" and more leverage to rebel against their parents if they choose. They can even report their parents to government authorities if they feel they have been "abused" at home, because social institutions and the legal system in the larger society provide support. And to take another extreme measure, should they decide to run away from home, they have more options to get by. In today's more open society, immigrant parents often find it harder than in the isolated enclave to raise children "the Chinese way" because of the more intense conflicts between the parents' social world and the mainstream society.

CHALLENGES CONFRONTING THE CHINESE IMMIGRANT FAMILY

Post-1965 Chinese immigrants confront profound challenges when they move to America. One such challenge has to do with structural changes in the immigrant family. In Taiwan, Hong Kong, and the mainland, Chinese families are often extended in form, with grandparents or other relatives living in the home or in close contact. When family members arrive in the United States, their extended kin and friendship networks, and the associated support and control mechanisms, are disrupted. When immigrant families locate first in ethnic enclaves or ethnoburbs, they may be able to reconnect to, or rebuild, ethnic networks, but these new ethnic networks tend to be composed of coethnic "strangers" rather than close kin and friends and tend to be more instrumental than emotionally intimate. Those who go to white middle-class suburbs are more detached from the existing ethnic community and have a harder time rebuilding social networks based on common origins and a common cultural heritage. Even though affluent Chinese immigrant families may have less need of ethnic networks and ethnic resources than their working-class counterparts, many find them comforting and, at times, helpful in enforcing traditional Chinese values to which they are still closely attached.

A second challenge is the change in roles within the immigrant family. In most Chinese immigrant families, both parents work full time, and some hold several jobs on different shifts. Because of the disadvantages associated with immigrant status, many Chinese immigrant men experience downward mobility and have difficulty obtaining jobs that enable them to be the main breadwinners. Women have to work outside the home, and many contribute equally, if not more, to the family income while also assuming the principal responsibility for child-rearing. That women work outside the home often creates difficulties for children in the family. Without the help of grandparents, relatives, and other close friends, many of them become latch-key children, staying home alone after school hours. Immigration affects parent-child roles in another way, particularly in families where the parents have low levels of education and job skills and speak little or no English. Often, these parents have to depend on their children as translators and brokers between home and the outside world, which typically diminishes parental authority.

A third challenge is the generation gap between parents and children, which is exacerbated by a cultural divide between the immigrant family and the larger society. There is a pronounced discrepancy in goal orientation—and views of the means of achieving goals—between immigrant parents and their U.S.-born or -raised children. Most immigrants structure their lives primarily around three goals—as one Chinese immigrant put it, "to live in your own house, to be your own boss, and to send your children to the Ivy League." They try to acculturate or assimilate into American society, but only in ways that facilitate the attainment of these goals. The children, in contrast, want more. They aspire to be fully American. In the words of a U.S.-born high school student in Los Angeles's Chinatown, ". . . Looking cool, going to the ball games, eating hamburgers and french fries, taking family vacations, having fun . . . feeling free to do whatever you like rather than what your parents tell you to."

This cultural gap sets the parents and children apart and increases what are often already-strained parent-child relations. Children frequently view their immigrant parents as *lao-wan-gu* and consciously rebel against familial traditions. The parents, aside from juggling work and household responsibilities that devour most of their waking hours, are worried that their children have too much freedom, too little respect for authority, and too many unfavorable stimuli in school, on the street, and on the television screen at home. They are horrified when their children are openly disrespectful, for example, or aggressively disobey their orders. Intergenerational strains are further intensified because parents have difficulty communicating with their Americanized children. To make matters worse, the parents' customary ways of exercising authority or disciplining children—physical punishment by beating, for example—which were considered normative and acceptable in the old world, have suddenly become obsolete and even illegal, further eroding parental power in parent-child relations.

Immigrant children who arrive in the United States as teenagers have additional problems that affect relations with their parents. They have spent their formative years in a different society, were schooled in a different language, and were immersed in a different youth culture than that of the United States. In their homeland, they played a leading role in defining what was *in*, what was cool, and what was trendy, and many were average students in their schools. However, once in the United States, they find themselves standing out the wrong way, becoming the objects of mockery and ridicule and being referred to derogatively as "FOB" (fresh-off-boat) by their U.S.-born or raised coethnic peers. They also experience problems in school. Because of language difficulties, many are unable to express themselves and are misunderstood by their teachers and fellow students; they are often teased, mocked, or harassed by other students because of their different look, accent, and dress; and they worry that if they bring up these problems at home their parents will get upset or blame them. When their problems are unaddressed by schools or parents, the youth become discouraged. This discouragement is sometimes followed by loss of interest in school and plunging grades, and some eventually drop out and join gangs.

SENSITIVE PRESSURE POINTS

The generation gap between parents and children that I have described is particularly acute in Chinese immigrant families because Chinese cultural norms are so different from those that dominate in the United States and because Chinese parents are often afraid of losing their children to Americanization. Second-generation Chinese, born and raised in the United States, find themselves straddling two social-cultural worlds—Chinese and American—which is at the core of head-on intergenerational conflicts within the Chinese immigrant family. Lacking meaningful connections to their parents' countries of origin, they rarely consider the homeland as a point of reference and generally evaluate themselves against and adopt American standards and values.[8]

This is clearly different for immigrant parents who remain oriented to the homeland and, especially relevant here, to Chinese notions of filial piety. In the Chinese cultural context, filial piety is at the core of parent-child relationships. In its ideal form, the child's filial responsibility is the debt of life owed to parents; a child is expected to suppress his or her own self-interests to satisfy parental needs, whether or not these needs are appropriate or rational.[9] Related to filial piety is the notion of unconditional obedience, or submission, to authority—to the parent, the elder, and the superior. The parent is the authority in the home, as is the teacher in the school. The parent, often the father, is not supposed to show too much affection to his children, to play with them, or treat them as equals. This stone-faced, authoritative image often inhibits children from questioning, much less challenging, their parents. Furthermore, in the traditional

Chinese family, there is little room for individualism. All family members are tied to one another, and every act of individual members is considered to bring honor or shame to the whole family. Thus, Chinese parents are expected to bring up their children in ways that honor the family.

Asymmetric filial piety, unconditional submission to authority, and face-saving override other familial values in the traditional Chinese family. Even though modernization has brought changes to the family in China, these traditional influences still loom large among Chinese immigrants. The problem is that in the American context, these practices and values are frowned upon, and children and parents are expected to be independent individuals on equal terms.

The immigrant Chinese family is often referred to by the children as a "pressure cooker," where intense intergenerational conflicts accumulate and sometimes boil to the point of explosion. Issues related to education, work ethic, consumption behavior, and dating, among others, are sensitive pressure points that can create potentially intense conflicts. For example, a young Chinese American who returned to college to complete her associate degree recalled:

> I never felt I was good enough to live up to my parents' expectations. So I fought them non-stop through high school. A war broke out when I got accepted into a few UC [University of California] schools but decided not to enroll in any one of them. I got kicked out of home. I moved in with my white boyfriend and started to work to support myself. I felt that the only way to get back at my parents was to make them feel ashamed. With a rebellious daughter, they had nothing to brag about and they lost the war. It may seem silly now, but at that time I really liked what I did.

Chinese parents who were raised in the Confucian tradition tend to be particularly demanding and unyielding about their children's educational achievement. While education is generally considered a primary means to upward social mobility in all American families, it is emphasized in some unique ways in the immigrant Chinese family. First and foremost, the children's success in school is tied to face-saving for the family. Parents consistently remind their children that achievement is a duty and an obligation to the family goal, and that if they fail they will bring shame to the family. Not surprisingly, children are under tremendous pressure to succeed.

Immigrant parents also have a pragmatic view of education. They see education as not only the most effective means to achieve success in society but also the *only* means. The parents are keenly aware of their own limitations as immigrants and the structural constraints blocking their own mobility—for example, limited family wealth even among middle-income immigrants, lack of access to social networks connecting them to the mainstream economy and various social and political institutions, and entry barriers to certain occupations because of racial stereotyping and discrimination. Their own experience tells them that a good education in certain fields will allow their children to get good jobs in the future. These fields include science, math, engineering, medicine, and, to a lesser extent, business and law. Parents are more concerned with their children's academic coursework, grades, and majors in these preferred fields than with a well-rounded learning experience and extracurricular activities. They actively discourage their children from pursuing interests in history, literature, music, dance, sports, or any subject that they consider unlikely to lead to well-paid, stable jobs. Involvement in these academic fields and extracurricular activities is only encouraged to the extent that it will improve their children's chances of getting into an Ivy League college. The children are often frustrated—sometimes deeply resentful—that their parents choose the type of education they are to pursue and make decisions for their future. At college, many Chinese American students pursue double majors, one in science or engineering for their parents and the other in history, literature, or Asian American studies for themselves.

Another sensitive issue is the work ethic. Immigrant Chinese parents believe that hard work, rather than natural ability or innate intelligence, is the key to educational success. Regardless of socioeconomic background, they tend to think that their children can get A's on all their exams if they just work hard, and if the children get lower grades they will be scolded for not working hard enough. The parents also believe that by working twice as hard it is possible to overcome structural disadvantages associated with immigrant and/or racial minority status. They tend to ignore the fact that not everybody learns English, catches up with school work, and establishes productive relationships with teachers and fellow students at the same rate. As a result, the children often find themselves working at least twice as hard as their American peers and simultaneously feeling that their parents never think that they work hard enough.

A third sensitive issue is related to the value of thrift.[10] Immigrant Chinese parents emphasize savings as a means of effectively deploying available family resources. They often bluntly reject their children's desire for material possessions and view spending money on name-brand clothes, stylish accessories, and fashionable hairstyles as a sign of corruption, or as becoming "too American." At the same time, these parents seldom hesitate to spend money on whatever they consider good for their children, such as books and computer software, after-school programs, Chinese lessons, private tutors, private lessons on the violin or the piano, and other education-oriented activities.

The fourth sensitive issue is dating, particularly at an early age. Chinese parents, especially newer arrivals, consider dating in high school not only a wasteful distraction from academics, but also a sign of unhealthy, promiscuous behavior, especially for girls. They are concerned about the potential risks of unwanted pregnancy—and that this will interfere with their daughters' educational progress. Over time, parents' attitudes toward dating in high school may grow more ambivalent, and it may be interracial dating, rather than early dating in general, that "freaks them out."

These sensitive pressure points have become the sources of parent-child conflicts as the children rapidly acculturate into American ways, and as parents, in a position of authority, insist on their values and practices. These conflicts seem to be especially severe in the case of working-class Chinese immigrant parents, who are unusually demanding and unbending when it comes to their children's education and behavioral standards because they lack the time, patience, cultural sensitivity, and financial and human capital to be more compromising. Middle-class Chinese immigrant parents are also demanding and have high expectations for their children. But owing to their higher socioeconomic status and higher level of acculturation, they consciously try to be more like American parents in some ways. Some middle-class parents develop a sense of guilt for not being like American parents and become more easygoing and less strict with their children. For example, when a child refuses to do schoolwork on weekends as the father demands, and talks back by saying that "nobody works on weekends," a middle-class suburban Chinese immigrant father might simply shrug and let his child run off with his friends, because he himself doesn't have to work on weekends. A working-class Chinese immigrant father is more likely to get angry and make the child feel guilty about his own sacrifice, since he has to work on weekends to support the family.

ETHNIC NETWORKS AND INSTITUTIONS AS SOURCES OF CONCILIATION AND MEDIATING GROUNDS

Tremendous parental pressures to achieve and behave in the Chinese way can lead children to rebellious behavior, withdrawal from school, and alienation from ethnic networks. Alienated children fall easy prey to street gangs. Even those children who do well in school and hope to make their parents proud are at risk for rebellious and disrespectful behavior and for flouting their parents' rules and regulations. A high school student said, "But that [doing well to make parents happy] never happens. My mother is never satisfied no matter what you do and how well you do it." This remark echoes a frustration felt by many other Chinatown youths, who are torn between wanting to please their parents and succeed educationally, but who feel overwhelmed and constrained by parental pressures, rules, and orders. Tensions in the home may seethe beneath the surface—often to a point that parents and children feel they have no room to breathe.

Yet despite these intense pressures, and the strains between the children and their parents, there is rarely an all-out war between them. And despite severe bicultural conflicts—and the challenges that American popular culture poses to Chinese immigrant parents' values—many Chinese immigrant children, whatever their socioeconomic background, seem to live up to their parents' expectations. Involvement in the Chinese ethnic community is critical in explaining why this is so.

Most remarkable is the educational success of Chinese immigrant children, who significantly outperform other Americans, including non-Hispanic whites. They score exceptionally well on standardized tests and are overrepresented in the nation's elite universities as well as in the top lists of many national or regional academic competitions. They have appeared repeatedly in the top-ten award winners' list of the Westinghouse Science Talent Search, now renamed the Intel Science Talent Search, one of the country's most prestigious high school academic prizes. At the University of California, Los Angeles, where I teach, the proportion of Chinese Americans in the entering class in the past few years has been 18 percent higher than that of blacks and Latinos combined.

Is the extraordinary educational achievement of Chinese Americans a result of the parental pressure for success and enforcement of Confucian values? There is no simple answer. A more appropriate question is: How is it possible for parents in the Chinese immigrant family, plagued with intergenerational strains, to exercise authority and enforce Confucian values on education? Why do children end up doing what their parents expect them to do? My research in the Chinese immigrant community points to the important role of an ethnic institutional environment and multiple ethnic involvements.

In Chinatowns or Chinese ethnoburbs, an ethnic enclave economy and a range of ethnic social and cultural institutions have developed to support the daily needs of Chinese immigrants. As the community changed from a bachelor society to a family community, traditional ethnic institutions also shifted their functions to serve families and children. Among the programs they offer are weekend Chinese schools and a variety of educational and recreational enterprises, such as daily afterschool classes that match formal school curricula, academic tutoring and English enhancement classes, "exam-cram" schools, college prep schools, and music/dance/sports studios.

Consider the Chinese language school. In New York City, the Chinese Language School (*Zhongwen xuexiao*), run by the Chinese Consolidated Benevolent Association (CCBA), is perhaps the largest children- and youth-oriented organization in the nation's Chinatowns.[11] The school enrolls about four thousand Chinese children annually (not including summer), from pre-school to twelfth grade, in its 137 Chinese language classes and other specialty classes (including band, choir, piano, cello, violin, T'ai chi, ikebana, dancing, and Chinese painting). The Chinese language classes run from 3:00 to 6:30 p.m. daily after regular school hours. Students usually spend one hour on regular school homework and two hours on Chinese language or other selected specialties. The school also has English classes for immigrant youths and adult immigrant workers.

As Chinese immigrants have become dispersed residentially, Chinese language schools have also sprung up in the suburbs. As of the mid-1990s, there were approximately 635 Chinese language schools in the United States (with 189 in California alone), enrolling nearly 83,000 students.[12] The Chinese language school provides an ethnically affirming experience for most Chinese immigrant children. In response to the question, "What makes you Chinese?" many Chinese students say that it is "going to Chinese school." In Chinese language school, Chinese immigrant children come to understand that their own problems with their parents are common in Chinese families and that their parents are simply acting like other Chinese parents. They come to terms with the fact that growing up in Chinese families is different. As Betty Lee Sung observes:

> For Chinese immigrant children who live in New York's Chinatown or in satellite Chinatowns, these [bi-cultural] conflicts are moderated to a large degree because there are other Chinese children around to mitigate the dilemmas that they encounter. When they are among their own, the Chinese ways are better known and better accepted. The Chinese customs and traditions are not denigrated to the degree that they would be if the immigrant child were the only one to face the conflict on his or her own.[13]

Ethnic institutions also allow the children to develop strategies to cope with parental constraints. For example, a girl can tell her parents that she is going out with someone at the Chinese school whom her parents know, while she actually goes to a movie with her white boyfriend. Her friends at the Chinese school will provide cover for her, confirming her story when her parents check. Chinese parents usually trust their children's friends from Chinese schools because they know the parents of the Chinese school friends.

The Chinese schools and various after-school programs not only ensure that the children spend time on homework or other constructive activities, they also help to keep children off the streets and reduce the anxieties and worries of working parents. More important, these ethnic institutions offer some space where children can share their feelings. A Chinese school teacher said, "It is very important to allow youths to express themselves in their own terms without parental pressures. Chinese parents usually have very high expectations of their children. When children find it difficult to meet these expectations and do not have an outlet for their frustration and anxiety, they tend to become alienated and lost on the streets."

Ethnic institutions also serve as a bridge between a seemingly closed immigrant community and the mainstream society. Immigrant parents and the children who live in ethnic enclaves or ethnoburbs are relatively isolated and their daily exposure to the larger American society is limited. Many parents, usually busy working, expect their children to do well in school and have successful careers in the future, but are unable to give specific directions to guide their children's educational and career plans, leaving a gap between high expectations and feasible means of meeting them. Ethnic institutions fill this gap by helping young people to become better aware of their choices and to find realistic means of moving up socioeconomically in mainstream society. After-school programs, tutor services, and test preparation programs are readily available in the ethnic community, making school after school an accepted norm. An educator said, "When you think of how much time these Chinese kids put in their studies after regular school, you won't be surprised why they succeed at such a high rate."

At the same time, ethnic institutions function as cultural centers, where Chinese traditional values and a sense of ethnic identity are nurtured. Students who participate in the after-school programs, especially those born and raised in the United States, often speak English to one another in their Chinese classes, but they learn a limited number of Chinese words each day. In the after-school programs, they are able to relate to Chinese "stuff" without being teased as they might be in school. They listen to stories and sing songs in Chinese, which reveal different aspects of Chinese history and culture. Children and youths learn to write in Chinese such phrases as "I am Chinese" and "My home country is in China" and to recite classical Chinese poems and Confucian sayings about family values, behavioral and moral guidelines, and the importance of schooling. A Chinese school principal made it clear that "these kids are here because their parents sent them. They are usually not very motivated to learn Chinese per se, and we do not push them too hard. Language teaching is only part of our mission. An essential part of our mission is to enlighten these kids about their own cultural heritage, so that they show respect for their parents and feel proud of being Chinese."

Despite differences in origin, socioeconomic backgrounds, and geographic dispersion, Chinese immigrants have many opportunities to interact with one another as they participate in the ethnic community in multiple ways. Working, shopping, and socializing in the community tie immigrants to a closely knit system of ethnic social relations. Social networks, embedded in the broader Chinese immigrant community, reinforce norms and standards and operate as a means of control over those who are connected to them. Especially pertinent here is that involvement in different types of ethnic institutions also helps children to cope with—and indeed has the effect of alleviating—parental pressure.

CONCLUSION

A complex and often contradictory set of forces affect parents and children in Chinese immigrant families and their relations with each other. Many Chinese immigrant parents expect the children to attain the highest levels of achievement possible and rely on them to move the family into middle-class status as a way to repay parental sacrifices and to honor the family name. Deviation from these cultural values, standards, and expectations is considered shameful or "losing face" and is strongly criticized, indeed censured, by the family and the ethnic community. Still, parents have trouble enforcing these values and behavioral standards—and guaranteeing that familial expectations are met. Both parents and children struggle constantly to negotiate cultural differences, make compromises, and resolve conflicts in order to navigate the "right" way into mainstream American society.

This undertaking is by no means limited to the family arena, nor is it simply a matter of having the right cultural values. As I have emphasized, Chinese immigrant families cannot be viewed in isolation. Many are intricately and closely connected to broader networks in the wider ethnic community. Ethnic educational institutions and children-oriented programs, as I have shown, not only provide tangible resources in the form, for example, of educational training, but also serve as effective mechanisms of social control, thereby reinforcing parental values. At the same time, they give young people a socially accepted place to develop their own coping strategies as well as social relationships with peers experiencing the same dilemmas at home. One of the many factors that set parachute kids apart is their lack of access to these kinds of support and control because they are less connected to the ethnic community than young people in immigrant families. It is also important to stress that the mobilization of educational resources in the immigrant family and community is heavily affected by immigration selectivity, in that those with education, professional skills, and money comprise a significant proportion of the Chinese migrant inflow.

The children of Chinese immigrants are motivated to learn and do well in school because they believe that education is the most effective route for them to do better than their parents—and also a way to free themselves from their parents' control. Whatever the children's motivation, parental pressure—which is supported and strengthened through participation in the ethnic community—reinforces educational goals and often leads to positive outcomes. A community youth program organizer put it this way: "Well, tremendous pressures create problems for sure. However, you've got to realize that we are not living in an ideal environment. Without these pressures, you would probably see as much adolescent rebellion in the family, but a much *larger* proportion of kids failing. Our goal is to get these kids out into college, and for that, we have been very successful."

While intense parent–child and community pressure pushes children to work hard to succeed, there are limits to its effectiveness. Beyond high school, the social capital available in the Chinese-American community is not sufficient to help children choose appropriate academic and career paths. When applying to college, many children of Chinese immigrants are forced by parents to choose institutions close to home, which can limit chances for significant social mobility. At college, the children tend to concentrate in science and engineering because their families want them to and their friends are doing it—even if this is something they are not interested or lack talent in. After graduation from college, they often lack the type of networks that facilitate job placement and occupational mobility.

A whole series of additional issues arise as the children of Chinese immigrants enter adulthood. What will their relationships with their parents be like then? Will the children be grateful to parents for pushing them to succeed? Will sources of conflict prominent in adolescence be less acute in adulthood? Will there be new sources of tension, for example, disagreements with parents over family finances, marriage, and childbearing or child-rearing methods? In the case of the parachute kids, if they stay in the United States and their parents remain in the homeland, will the children become even more emotionally distant from parents—or will some return to their homeland and reestablish close bonds with parents? These are among the many questions that deserve further research.

Notes

1. This chapter draws on my previously published work; see Zhou 1997; 1998; 2006.
2. Foner 1999; Mahalingam 2006.
3. USDHS 2006.
4. Estimated from the Current Population Survey (CPS) data 1998–2000. See Logan et al. 2001.
5. Compared to 8 percent under age eighteen and 8 percent between ages eighteen and twenty-four in the first generation.
6. U.S. Census Bureau 2007.
7. "Ethnoburb" is a term developed by Wei Li (1997) to refer to suburban ethnic clustering of diverse groups with no single racial ethnic group dominating. Los Angeles's Monterey Park is a typical ethnoburb.
8. Gans 1992; Portes and Zhou 1993; Zhou 1997.
9. Yeh and Bedford 2003.
10. Sung 1987.
11. The Chinese Consolidated Benevolent Association (CCBA) is a quasi-government in Chinatown. It used to be an apex group representing some sixty different family and district associations, guilds, tongs, the Chamber of Commerce, and the Nationalist Party, and it has remained the most influential ethnic organization in the Chinese immigrant community.
12. Chao 1996.
13. Sung 1987: 126.

References

Chao, Teresa Hsu. 1996. "Overview." Pp. 7–13 in Xueying Wang (ed.), *A View from Within: A Case Study of Chinese Heritage Community Language Schools in the United States*. Washington, DC: The National Foreign Language Center.

Foner, Nancy. 1999. "The Immigrant Family: Cultural Legacies and Cultural Changes." Pp. 257–74 in C. Hirschman, P. Kasinitz and J. DeWind (eds.), *The Handbook of International Migration: The American Experience*. New York: Russell Sage Foundation.

Gans, Herbert J. 1992. "Second-Generation Decline: Scenarios for the Economic and Ethnic Futures of the Post-1965 American Immigrants." *Ethnic and Racial Studies* 15 (2): 173–92.

Li, Wei. 1997. "Spatial Transformation of an Urban Ethnic Community from Chinatown to Chinese Ethnoburb in Los Angeles." Ph.D. Dissertation, Department of Geography. University of Southern California.

Logan, John R., with Jacob Stowell and Elena Vesselinov. 2001. "From Many Shores: Asians in Census 2000." A report by the Lewis Mumford Center for Comparative Urban and Regional Research, State University of New York at Albany, accessed on October 6, 2001, at http://mumford1 .dyndns.org/cen2000/report.html.

Mahalingam, Ram (ed.). 2006. *Cultural Psychology of Immigrants*. Mahwah, NJ: Lawrence Erlbaum.

Portes, Alejandro, and Min Zhou. 1993. "The New Second Generation: Segmented Assimilation and Its Variants." *Annals of the American Academy of Political and Social Science* 530 (November): 74–96.

Sung, Betty Lee. 1987. *The Adjustment Experience of Chinese Immigrant Children in New York City*. New York: Center for Migration Studies.

U.S. Census Bureau. 2007. *The American Community, Asians: 2004*. American Community Survey Reports (acs-05), accessed on September 6, 2007, at http://www.census.gov/prod/2007pubs/acs-05.pdf.

U.S. Department of Homeland Security (USDHS). 2006. *Yearbook of Immigration Statistics, 2006*. Accessed on October 9, 2007, at http://www.dhs.gov/ximgtn/statistics/publications/LPR06.shtm.

Wang, Xueying (ed.). 1996. *A View from Within: A Case Study of Chinese Heritage Community Language Schools in the United States*. Washington, DC: The National Foreign Language Center.

Yeh, Kuang-Hui, and Olwen Bedford. 2003. "Filial Piety and Parent-Child Conflict." Paper presented at the International Conference on Intergenerational Relations in Families' Life Course, co-sponsored by the Institute of Sociology, Academie Sinica, Taiwan, and the Committee on Family Research, International Sociological Association, March 12–14, Taipei.

Zhou, Min. 1992. *Chinatown: The Socioeconomic Potential of an Urban Enclave*. Philadelphia: Temple University Press.

———. 1997. "Social Capital in Chinatown: the Role of Community-Based Organizations and Families in the Adaptation of the Younger Generation." Pp. 181–206 in Lois Weis and Maxine S. Seller (eds.), *Beyond Black and White: New Faces and Voices in U.S. Schools*. Albany, NY: State University of New York Press.

———. 1998. "'Parachute Kids' in Southern California: The Educational Experience of Chinese Children in Transnational Families." *Educational Policy* 12 (6): 682–704.

———. 2006. "Negotiating Culture and Ethnicity: Intergenerational Relations in Chinese Immigrant Families in the United States." Pp. 315–36 in Ram Mahalingam, ed., *Cultural Psychology of Immigrants*. Mahwah, NJ: Lawrence Erlbaum.

Zhou, Min, and Xiyuan Li. 2003. "Ethnic Language Schools and the Development of Supplementary Education in the Immigrant Chinese Community in the United States." Pp. 57–73 in Carola Suarez-Orozco and Irina L.G. Todorova (eds.), *New Directions for Youth Development: Understanding the Social Worlds of Immigrant Youth*. San Francisco: Jossey-Bass.

■**READING 28**

Families and Elder Care in the Twenty-First Century

Ann Bookman and Delia Kimbrel

For most of the nation's history, caring for the elderly was a family affair carried out largely by women in the home. As the twenty-first century unfolds, however, elder care in the United States is an increasingly complex enterprise, with much personal care "outsourced" to paid nonfamily caregivers. Today elder care is a multisector undertaking with six key stakeholder groups—health care providers, nongovernmental community-based service agencies, employers, government, families, and elders themselves. The six groups, however, often work separately, or even at cross-purposes. They must be better integrated and resourced to ensure that seniors can age with dignity, families can receive appropriate supports, and society can manage the costs associated with geriatric health care and elder economic security.

In this article we examine the changing demographics of elders and families; what it means to engage in care work of an elderly parent or relative; how caregiving varies by race, gender, and socioeconomic status; and institutional responses to the challenges of caregiving from employers and the government. We close with reflections on the need for a coordinated, cross-sector movement to create an "aging-friendly" society in the United States—a society that values well-being across the life course and seeks multi-generational solutions.

CHANGING DEMOGRAPHICS

With the numbers of older Americans rapidly growing ever larger, the landscape of elder care in the United States is changing. During the past century, the population of Americans aged sixty-five and older increased elevenfold.[1] According to the 2010 census, 13 percent of the population, or 40.3 million individuals, were sixty-five or older.[2] The population share of those aged eighty-five and older, sometimes called the "oldest old," was 1.1 percent. By 2030 approximately 80 million Americans, or 20 percent of the population, are projected to be sixty-five or older, and 2.3 percent of the population will be eighty-five and older.[3]

In addition to its increasing numbers over the coming decades, the elderly population will change in a variety of ways—more people will five longer and healthier lives, the number of older males will grow, and the group's racial and ethnic diversity will increase.[4] But not all trends are positive. Although the poverty rate among the elderly fell from 25 percent in 1970 to 13 percent in 1992, as the real median income of both males and females increased,[5] in 2009, approximately 12.9 percent of people 65 and older still had incomes at the poverty level.[6] The Great Recession that began in 2007 eroded the economic status of moderate-income and middle-class elders, many of whom saw their pensions and 401(k)s decrease, the value of their homes decline, and their other financial investments lose value.[7]

Clearly these changes in the nation's elderly population will present challenges to family members who help provide elder care. And other national demographic shifts—delayed marriage and childbearing for young adults, decreased family size, and changes in family composition and structure—are complicating that challenge. Increased longevity among elders not only extends the years of caregiving by their adult children but may require their grandchildren to become caregivers as well. Married couples may have as many as four elderly parents living; in fact, they may have more parents or relatives in need of care than they have children living at home or on their own. In the past, research on elder care focused on the challenges facing working adults who were caring for both children and elderly parents—the so-called *sandwich generation*—a term coined by sociologist Dorothy Miller to refer to specific generational inequalities in the exchange of resources and support.[8] Miller's research highlighted the stress on the middle generation of employees who are caring for two groups of dependents while receiving little support. The sandwich metaphor, however, is outmoded in several respects: it does not convey that more than one generation may provide elder care or that members of any generational cohort can be both caregivers and care receivers. Nor does the image of static layers do justice to the dynamic interaction between generations, such as transfers of financial aid, sharing residential space, or exchanging personal and emotional care.

Today researchers are increasingly finding that adults may spend more years caring for their parents than caring for their children.[9] And because families today tend to be small, middle-aged adults may have smaller sibling networks to share elder care responsibilities. In short, elder care in the United States is a demanding task, and caregivers, especially the almost 60 percent of family caregivers who are employed, are finding it harder to undertake that task alone.[10]

CARE WORK AND THE DIMENSIONS OF ELDER CAREGIVING

There is an extensive body of research on family "care work" dating back to the 1960s with a study that challenged the "myth of the abandoned elderly" and showed that families were still caring for elders, but that changes in external conditions in the family, the workplace, and the community were making caregiving more challenging.[11]

One of the contributions of recent care work research is to draw attention to the "work" aspects of caregiving. This framing contradicts personal and cultural ideas about why families care for elders and makes two related arguments: the first is that because family caregiving is largely done by women and is unpaid, it is often devalued; the second is that despite this devaluing, unpaid care work adds huge value to U.S. society in providing much needed care and "services" to the most vulnerable in the nation's population. Some scholars have tried to calculate the monetary value of unpaid care work to strengthen the argument about its value. Estimates vary from $196 billion a year, calculated in 1997,[12] to $257 billion a year based on a subsequent study by the United Hospital Fund in 2004.[13] In either case, the numbers far exceed what the United States spends on home health care and nursing home care, underscoring the importance of family care.

To differentiate the work families provide from the work that professionals and paraprofessionals provide, many studies of caregiving use the terms "informal care" to refer to the care provided by families and "formal care" to refer to that provided by trained health and social service staff. The distinction creates a sharp line between the informal care that is unpaid and takes place in private homes and the formal care that is paid and takes place in institutional and community settings. The distinction, however, has been challenged by some elder care scholars who find that family caregivers of elders provide care in hospitals, rehabilitation facilities, outpatient clinics, and community agencies. Family caregivers are a "shadow workforce" in the geriatric health care system.[14] Some states are piloting "cash and counseling" programs to pay families for the elder care they do, so the paid-unpaid distinction is being challenged in public policies.

Elder care entails a variety of supports and responsibilities, many of which can change in intensity and complexity over time. Cultural differences unique to elders and their families shape their views on what aging, health, and end of life mean and thus affect expectations about who provides care and what is provided.[15] The variations in elder care are numerous, as the following eight dimensions illustrate.

Time Dimension

Elder care takes three forms: short-term, intermittent, and long-term. Elderly parents may, for example, have surgery that immobilizes them temporarily, but restores them to a high level of daily functioning. In such cases the care needed may be fairly intense but of short duration, and so it disrupts the caregiver's job, family, and personal life, but only temporarily. In contrast, the seven in ten care recipients who have chronic health conditions[16] may require intermittent care that entails regular trips to one or more specialists, medication management, and adjustments to household and personal routines. In such cases, the caregiver is needed frequently over a longer period and may be hard pressed to integrate caregiving demands with paid work. In other cases elder care may be long-term, lasting for months or years. Such caregiving may be required on a daily basis and can seriously complicate the caregiver's ability to maintain a job, provide care for other family members, and maintain personal and community involvement.

Since 1987 the American Association of Retired Persons (now called AARP) and the National Alliance for Caregiving (NAC) have conducted several national surveys tracking the time Americans invest in elder care.[17] The most recent survey, in 2009, found intermittent elder care to be the type most commonly provided. Caregivers surveyed in that poll report providing such care for an average of 4.6 years; 31 percent report giving such care for more than five years.[18] Half of all of caregivers spend eight hours or less a week, while 12 percent spend more than forty hours. Short-term or intermittent care may evolve into long-term care as an elder's physical or mental function, or both, deteriorates.

Geographic Dimension

The distance between an elder's place of residence and that of the caregiver has a major effect on the type and frequency of care. Because some American families are mobile—about 16 percent of families move each year[19]—adult children sometimes five in different cities, states, or even regions from their elderly parents. According to the most recent AARP-NAC survey data, 23 percent of caregivers five with the elder for whom they are caring (co-residence is particularly common among low-income caregivers) and 51 percent live twenty minutes away.[20]

Long-distance caregiving, however, has been on the rise over the past fifteen years.[21] One study by MetLife finds that at least 5 million caregivers live an hour or more away from the elder for whom they care.[22] Of this group, about 75 percent provide help with daily activities, such as shopping, transportation, and managing household finances. Most long-distance caregivers share responsibilities with siblings or paid caregivers, or both. Several studies document that adult children who live near an elderly relative are most likely to provide the majority of elder care,[23] underscoring the importance of geographic location.

Residential Dimension

To move, or not to move? Many elders struggle with this question, and often turn to family caregivers for help with the answer. Most elders want to live in their own homes and neighborhoods; for some, safety and accessibility require home renovations. Family caregivers may plan, organize, and finance adaptations in an elder's living space. Not all elders and all caregivers are homeowners (some are renters), which can pose particular challenges for all parties.[24] When it is not feasible for elders to adapt their dwelling, moving becomes necessary. In that case, caregivers often research, plan, and organize the move. Some elders move to continuing care retirement communities that provide different types of units for residents of different abilities.[25] Although such communities have grown in popularity, and may relieve families of some responsibilities, the units are expensive to buy, and monthly maintenance fees are costly, thus making this option unaffordable for most elders.

A small share of elders lives in rehabilitation faculties, usually on a short-term basis. Between 5 and 6 percent of elders live in a long-term-care facility or nursing home, with caregivers making regular or intermittent trips to visit and monitor the care being provided. Most elders live in their own homes,[26] which must be constantly assessed for safety and the availability of community services such as transportation, social services, and recreational opportunities. Nongovernmental organizations (NGOs) help maintain more than 10 million elders a day with long-term care supports and services so they can continue to live in their homes independently.[27] To help caregivers assess what is required for independent living, researchers have developed tools that can aid in choosing appropriate housing and support services.[28]

Financial Dimension

The economic resources available to caregiving families vary widely. Upper-middle-class and affluent families usually have adequate funds to pay for elder care services, while poor families are usually eligible for a variety of subsidized services, such as home health care. The hardest-hit families are the working poor and those with moderate incomes, who are too "rich" to qualify for subsidized services but unable to pay for care themselves. Many families caring for elderly relatives encounter this type of "middle-class squeeze."

Researchers who explore the financial dimension of elder care find that cross-generational transfers are fairly common. In a 2005 study, 29 percent of baby boomers provided financial assistance to a parent in the previous year, while about a fifth received financial support from a parent.[29] A recent nationally representative survey of elders over sixty-five offers a slightly different picture: half of these elders say they have given money to their adult children, while about a third say they help their adult children with child care, errands, housework, and home repairs. When asked what their adult children give them, more than 40 percent report receiving help with errands and rides to appointments; about a third, help with housework and home repairs; and about a fifth, help with bill paying and direct financial support.[30] What is striking is that care, time, and money are being exchanged between the generations, going both ways.

Health Dimension

Some caregivers provide help in a short-term acute health care crisis, others care for elders with one or more chronic diseases, and a third group cares for elders with long-term incurable or progressive diseases. Families are a critical resource for the nation's health care system when they care for a relative with a debilitating disease, such as dementia or Alzheimer's, for which paid care is very expensive. Giving such care, however, is a major burden on these families, who frequently find that caregiver training—both how to manage the behavior and symptoms of the elder and how to cope with their own feelings—is often not available.[31]

The health status of an elder determines the extent of a caregiver's involvement with personal care, often referred to as activities of daily living, such as eating, bathing, toileting, and dressing, or as instrumental activities of daily living, such as cooking, shopping, and bill paying. The health status of the elder also shapes the extent of caregivers' involvement in medical tasks such as giving medications; dressing wounds after surgery; checking weight, blood pressure, and blood sugar levels; and monitoring medical equipment. A national survey of caregivers found that more than 40 percent helped with one or more medical tasks, even though only one-third reported that they had the training to do so.[32] That finding underscores the "medicalization" of the care work that families are providing for elders.

One elderly cohort that is growing is "frail elders," defined as those sixty-five and older who do not live in nursing homes, but have difficulty with at least one aspect of independent living or are severely disabled, or both. This group numbered about 10.7 million people in 2002.[33] Analyses of a national data set showed that two-thirds of frail elders receive help—an average of 177 hours a month—with personal care from an unpaid family caregiver. More than half of that help comes from their daughters, most of whom are working.[34]

Legal and Ethical Dimension

When significant declines in physical and mental health compromise elders' ability to manage their own affairs, it is usually the family caregiver who assumes some level of control, decision-making power, and ultimately legal authority such as power of attorney. Studies on the legal issues of elders often focus, particularly when financial resources are involved, on the caregiver as a source of interfamilial conflict and even elder abuse. A recent study of financial elder abuse, however, found that only 16.9 percent of the perpetrators were family members.[35]

Legal issues may also require caregivers to take on complex health-related roles, such as acting as health care proxy or setting up an advance directive or DNR (do not resuscitate) order. These steps can involve complex ethical questions and decisions, such as when to discontinue life supports for a terminally ill parent. Studies on elders at the end of life show the critical role that family caregivers play once palliative care is chosen, including assisting elders with daily living, handling medications, and making medical decisions.[36] Using ethnographic data, a study of one elderly mother and her daughter documents how this family navigated the health care system and brought their own cultural meaning to end-of-life care.[37] Other studies emphasize the high degree of stress on families with terminally ill elders, showing the unresponsiveness of some health care systems, as well as the ways in which community services can ease stress.[38]

Emotional, Moral, and Spiritual Dimension

Much of the research on elder care explores the practical daily routines involved in personal care, health care, and housing. The emotional care that families provide, although essential to the well-being of elders, is less studied and is difficult to define. The medical anthropologist Arthur Kleinman, a caregiver for his wife with Alzheimer's, argues that the emotional part of caregiving is in essence a moral act—"an existential quality of *what it is to be a human being*."[39]

Attending to the spiritual needs of elders for whom religious experience, practice, and faith have been important is also critical to sustaining their physical and mental health and longevity.[40] For these elders, caregivers' tasks include: spiritual and well-being assessments; using a reminiscence-and-life-review approach; identifying and facilitating contact with religious services, organizations, and clergy; and discussing end-of-life issues.[41] Tailoring these tasks to an individual elder's particular faith tradition is both time-consuming and extremely meaningful.

Outsourcing Elder Care and Care Coordination

When family members cannot provide care, particularly if they are full-time workers or long-distance caregivers, or both, their job is to find an agency close to where the elder lives that will provide services for a fee. It takes time and effort to find an appropriate multiservice or aging service agency,[42] to provide the agency with detailed personal and health information about the elder to ensure a good "client-provider fit," and to monitor services to be sure that needs are met and the elder is comfortable with the provider. Carrying out all these tasks to find just one type of service is difficult enough; if an elder needs multiple services, the work for the family can be significant.

Many studies have documented the fragmentation in the geriatric health care and social services system, and others have called for greater care coordination to support caregivers.[43] The handoffs between hospitals and families, or between rehabilitation facilities and families, can often be unsafe and unsatisfying, and the need for improved communication is widely documented.[44] Given the cross-institutional complexities, some caregivers hire a geriatric care manager—often a trained social worker—to identify, monitor, and coordinate services. Hiring a care manager requires research by the family caregiver, as well as ongoing monitoring and extensive communication. The work of care coordination is a significant, often unnoticed, aspect of care many families do themselves, either because they cannot afford to hire a geriatric care manager or because they prefer to keep an eye on things themselves.[45]

ELDER CAREGIVING AND DIVERSITY

Most studies on aging and elder care treat elders and their caregivers as monolithic groups. But as the nation has become more diverse, so too has the population of elders. Elder caregiving varies by gender, race, and socioeconomic status, and families from African American, Latino, Asian, Native American, and other groups bring their own strengths and needs to the caregiving experience. Although gender, race, and socioeconomic status are treated separately below, it is important to note that these variables often intersect in powerful and important ways in the lives of caregivers. An "intersectionality" approach shows how unequal opportunity over the life course shapes trajectories of advantage and disadvantage for elders and the families who care for them. Future research must explore multiple aspects of diversity in order to develop new policies that address the interaction between socioeconomic inequality and differences based on gender, race, and culture.

Gender and Elder Care

Elderly women live longer than do elderly men, and despite a lifetime of providing care to others, they are more likely than men to live alone, live in poverty, and lack care themselves when they are elderly.[46] Research on gender and caregiving has two major themes. First, the majority (67 percent) of family caregivers are women,[47] with wives providing care to spouses and adult daughters providing the majority of care to elderly parents. Second, given the persistence of gender inequality in the workforce, including the gender gap in wages, women caregivers are more likely than men to cut back on work hours or quit their jobs because of their caregiving duties and are thus left with less income, small savings, and reduced pensions.

Although women in the general population have greater elder care responsibilities than do men, recent studies reveal that employed women and employed men provide care in roughly equal numbers.[48] But gender differences persist nonetheless: employed women are more likely than employed men to provide family care on a regular basis, they spend more hours providing care, and they spend more time providing direct care such as meal preparation, household work, physical care, and transportation.[49] This finding is consistent with other evidence on gender trends in elder care showing that women tend to perform household and personal care tasks that are physically draining and likely to interrupt daily activities, while men tend to give periodic assistance.[50] Both working and nonworking male caregivers receive more assistance with their caregiving efforts than do women; they also tend to delegate their tasks to others and to seek paid assistance to alleviate some of their caregiving responsibilities.[51]

Despite the growing number of men balancing work and elder care responsibilities, women are particularly vulnerable to negative work-related consequences.[52] Women who are caring for elders generally reduce their work hours, leave the workforce, or make other adjustments that have negative financial or career implications. Some refuse overtime and pass up promotions, training, assignments that are more lucrative, jobs requiring travel, and other challenging but time-consuming job opportunities.[53] Many low-income women and women of color who are employed do not have sufficient flexibility or autonomy in their jobs to be able to take an elderly parent to the doctor or attend to other needs.[54]

Despite feelings of satisfaction from their care, caregivers can sometimes feel burdened, socially isolated, strained, and hopeless. A recent MetLife study of working caregivers, based on a large corporate employer's health risk appraisal database of roughly 17,000 respondents, found that employed women are significantly more likely than employed men caregivers to self-report negative effects on personal well-being.[55] Caregivers in general report more physical and mental health problems than noncaregivers,[56] and more female caregivers (58 percent) report negative health effects than male caregivers (42 percent).[57] In a study assessing gender differences in caregiver health, Martin Pinquart and Silvia Sörensen found that women had lower scores for subjective well-being and perceived physical health, as well as higher scores for burden and depression than men. The effects for women caregivers indicated a positive and statistically significant relationship.[58]

Race, Ethnicity, and Elder Care

The growing diversity of the United States makes it important for researchers to consider how race and ethnicity—both socially constructed categories—shape aging and the caregiving experience. The nation s legacy of racial oppression and structural inequality has created socioeconomic inequities in education, health, housing, income, and wealth. Many low-income men and women of color enter old age after a lifetime of cumulative disadvantage, during which limited access to economic opportunity has obstructed efforts to accumulate savings for retirement and limited access to health care has led to poorer health.

Few families from racial and ethnic minority groups use paid or outsourced care, and those who do can sometimes face structural barriers in accessing them. Although most Americans refrain from putting their elderly kin in nursing homes, Latinos, African Americans, and Asians are least likely to do so.[59] Even elders of color with greater care needs, such as those afflicted with dementia or chronic illnesses, are more likely than whites to receive care from their children and live in the community with them.[60]

Many studies show that families of color rely on extended kin networks and friends for financial assistance, material goods, domestic duties, and other supports.[61] African Americans, especially, rely on networks of neighbors, friends, and fellow congregants. Language and cultural barriers often lead Chinese American and Puerto Rican caregivers to use ethnically oriented organizations in their communities for support.[62]

Extensive social support may partially explain why racial and ethnic minority groups tend to have more favorable attitudes toward caregiving and higher caregiving satisfaction.[63] Studies suggest that many groups of color value mutual exchange, reciprocity, filial responsibility, and interdependence, whereas Western European and white ethnic groups value self-reliance and independence. Using well-established positive appraisal scales and coping questionnaires, several studies find a significant "race" effect, with caregivers of color such as African Americans and Latinos showing the highest appraisals of positive aspects of caregiving and higher scores on well-being measures.[64]

Among some Latino groups, the extended family is expected to provide care to older relatives,[65] and Native Americans strongly value giving back to those who have provided for them, reinforcing the value of reciprocity in their culture.[66] White caregivers report greater depression and view caregiving as more stressful than do caregivers of color.[67] Studies that have addressed racial and ethnic differences among caregivers generally have not focused on working caregivers. One that does finds that employed white caregivers report significantly higher work demand and strain than Latino and black working caregivers.[68]

Although research consistently reveals significant differences in caregiver outcomes by race, findings may vary because of differences in recruitment strategies, in criteria for inclusion and exclusion, in construct measurement, in research instruments, and in statistical techniques. The studies also vary in sample size and sampling strategy and rarely use random assignment or national probability sampling to posit any causal relationships between variables. To strengthen generalizability, accuracy of statistical findings, and comparability across studies, researchers will have to use more diverse and random sampling strategies as well as experimental and mixed qualitative and quantitative methodologies.[69]

Socioeconomic Status and Elder Care

Although researchers do not often explore the implications of socioeconomic status—defined by education, occupational status, family income, net worth, and financial assets—for elder care, it can nevertheless have important effects on elders' quality of life and the kind of care their families can provide.

In the first place, many low-income elders have insufficient resources. More than half of all senior households (54 percent) cannot meet their expenses even using their combined financial net worth, Social Security benefits, and pension incomes.[70] Among older persons reporting income in 2008, 20.3 percent had less than $10,000.[71] Such economic challenges often increase the financial burden, hardship, and strain on their families. Many studies do show that families with higher socioeconomic status tend not to provide physical care themselves, and instead tend to purchase elder care services, provide financial gifts, buy alternative lodging, and remodel homes to accommodate an elder.[72]

A scarcity of resources makes working poor and working-class caregivers more likely to provide direct care themselves rather than to hire professional care managers. When low-income families do purchase formal services, they use them only for short periods. Middle-class and higher-income caregivers hire elder care assistance for longer periods or until their resources run out.[73]

RESPONSES FROM EMPLOYERS AND GOVERNMENT

Researchers have also investigated how employers and government are responding to the challenges families face in providing elder care. Are employers, for example, providing working caregivers of elders with "family-friendly" benefits and policies? Are federal,

state, and local governments meeting the needs of elders and caregivers with public policies? We explore the adequacy of their responses to the needs of both elders and family
caregivers to gain insight into what policy changes may be needed in the future.

Responses from Employers

Given the aging of the population and the high rate of female labor force participation,
the share of elder caregivers who are employed has been growing over the past thirty
years and is expected to continue, nearing the percentage of employees with child care
responsibilities. One of the earliest national estimates, based on data from the 1982
National Long-Term Care Survey and its companion National Informal Caregivers
Survey, was that 15.8 percent of elder caregivers were employed,[74] 9 percent had quit
their jobs because of elder care responsibilities, and 20 percent were experiencing conflict between work and elder care.[75] Surveys conducted in the late 1980s and 1990s found
the share of employed caregivers rising significantly, up to 64 percent in 1997.[76] One
2010 study found that six in ten family caregivers are employed;[77] another found that
considered as a group, 50 percent of employed caregivers of elders work full time, and
11 percent work part time. In the coming years, employers will need to respond to the elder
care needs of their workforce lest they compromise the performance of their firms and
the retention of some of their most valued employees.

Research on work and family conflict is extensive, and many studies focus on work
and elder care for employees.[78] Beyond general feelings of role conflict, working caregivers in one study report using their own sick leave or vacation hours to accommodate
elder care needs (48 percent), cutting back on hours or quitting their job (37 percent),
taking an additional job or increasing their hours to get funds for elder care expenses
(17 percent), taking unpaid leave (15 percent), and leaving their job for a different one
(14 percent).[79] Many studies report negative health consequences for employed caregivers, including increased risk of stress and depression, diabetes, hypertension, and even
premature death.[80] If caregivers cut back work hours, take unpaid leaves, or leave their
jobs, the negative effects can go beyond the individual caregivers themselves to include
whole families. For example, a MetLife study documented negative financial repercus-
sions for families from short-term income losses, long-term losses of retirement savings, and lost opportunities for career advancement.[81] Researchers are also examining
the policies and programs of employers to address their employees' elder care needs;
rough estimates are that from 25 to 50 percent of employers offer these programs.[82]
Large firms are more likely than small companies to have elder care programs, and a
2003 study estimates that 50 percent of large corporations offer such programs.[83] For
small and mid-sized firms, the estimate was 26 percent in 2006 and 22 percent in 2007.[84]
Studies on how the recent recession affected elder care programs are just now becoming available; one, for example, shows that most employers are maintaining workplace
flexibility, although reduction of hours may translate into reduction in pay, so increased
flexibility entails both costs and benefits.[85]

Elder Care Assistance Programs, introduced by companies during the late 1980s,
have grown in scope. The early programs—paralleling those developed to support workers with young children—included resource and referral services to locate elder care

services in the elder's community, and flexible spending accounts for putting aside funds on a pre-tax basis to cover elder care expenses.[86] During the 1990s, some companies expanded elder care benefits through Employee Assistance Programs or new "work-life programs" to include flexible work arrangements (58 percent), personal or sick leaves (16 percent), and access to short-term emergency backup care when a paid caregiver was unexpectedly absent (4 percent).[87]

During the mid-1990s, some researchers began exploring the question of whether employees made use of elder care benefits. Early studies found that use rates were low, although the range was fairly wide—from 2 to 34 percent—with use by employees in private-sector firms lower than use by public-sector employees.[88] Most scholars and human resource managers hypothesize that rates were low because employers had not publicized the programs that were available. A 2007 survey of human resource managers at Fortune 500 companies found that flexible work arrangements and leave programs were the most highly utilized and had the best use-to-cost ratio.[89] Emergency short-term home care had the lowest use rates and highest cost, and thus the worst use-to-cost ratio. In open-ended questions, respondents focused on the need for better communication about elder care programs; the importance of supervisors actively encouraging the use of these programs; and the difficulty of countering negative perceptions about these programs.[90] Although elder care benefits appear to boost employee recruitment and retention, that link has not been conclusively demonstrated.[91]

To date, the needs of employed elder caregivers far exceed the employer response, and elder care assistance tends to be offered only by the largest employers. Some studies about "family-responsive" workplaces do not even mention elder care as a benefit needed by families,[92] and the findings of studies that do focus on elder care have less than encouraging findings. The 2009 Age and Generations study found that employees who are caring for elders had less access to flexible work arrangements than did employees who were caring for their children or who had no dependent care responsibilities, that employees in the sandwich generation were less likely to be included in new projects based on teamwork than workers with no elder care demands,[93] and that employees who provide elder care had lower job security than other groups.[94] Elder care programs are still less frequently offered than child care programs, and a 2006 study found that although almost three-quarters of employers offered some child care assistance, only one-third offered elder care assistance.[95]

What accounts for employers' lag in offering elder care assistance? And how can workplaces make elder care a key component of the work-family or work-life agenda? Elder care may have received less attention than child care because ageism and denial about aging is deeply entrenched in U.S. culture. As Muriel Gillick, a palliative care physician, argues, "Contemporary Americans are eager to prevent, obliterate, or at least conceal old age . . . in keeping with the belief that we can control our destiny."[96] This denial can lead employers to ignore or minimize the elder care needs of their workforce, using arguments about high costs and low utilization to justify having few elder care programs.

Some work-family scholars argue that developing a family-friendly workplace is a long-term process with three distinct stages. In the first stage the goal is to promote the recognition of a particular work-family issue as a visible, legitimate need. In the second stage the goal is to implement and then refine specific programs, including effective communication and supervisor training. The third stage involves institutionalizing the new work-family programs into the culture of the workplace to heighten program reach and effectiveness.[97] In this evolutionary paradigm, different percentages of companies are at different stages in responding to elder care. Many private-sector firms and the majority of small and mid-sized firms are still in the first stage, struggling to recognize elder care programs as a legitimate need of the workforce. Roughly a third of firms are in the second stage, starting, developing, and retaining elder care programs. Only a minority of firms—mainly large companies—are in the third stage. Making the "family-friendly workplace" an "elder-care-friendly workplace" remains an unrealized project for many employers.

Responses from Government

During the nineteenth and twentieth centuries the United States gradually transferred responsibility for elder care from the family to the government, from the private sphere to the public sphere.[98] But despite landmark twentieth-century legislation, it can be argued that the United States lacks the full range of public policies needed to address the aging of the population, and that families still bear the primary responsibility.

Table 29.1 briefly summarizes six public policies that are key to the well-being of elders and their family caregivers. Some have enhanced health and income security for elders; others have enhanced the supports available to both employed and nonemployed family caregivers. We briefly address the strengths and weaknesses of some of these policies to suggest possible areas for policy expansion.

Social Security is critical to providing a basic level of financial support and security to elders. Several issues, however, weaken its effectiveness. Initially the system strengthened intergenerational ties because those who retired—only 5.2 percent of the population was sixty-five or older in 1930—were reaping benefits based on the productivity of younger workers. But in the decades ahead, more people will be needing retirement income, and fewer young workers will be available to replenish Social Security funds, thus putting pressure on the younger generation and creating tension between generations.[99] In addition, because Social Security is based on wages in the paid labor force, women who delayed work, interrupted work, or never entered the workforce because of family caregiving responsibilities have smaller benefits in old age than men (though at the death of her spouse, a woman is eligible to collect a "survivor" Social Security benefit).

Medicare, a second foundational piece of economic security for elders, ensures coverage of many health care costs. It, too, however, is problematic. Originally enacted to cover the costs of acute care and hospitalization, Medicare does not provide adequate insurance for chronic illnesses, those common to most elders. Medicare does not reimburse hospitals fully for the care they provide, so many hospitals have shortened patient stays, creating difficulties for caregivers when an elder is prematurely discharged to rehab or to home. Medicare will cover a stay in a skilled nursing facility only if daily nursing or rehab services are needed, and will cover ten hours a week of home care only if skilled nursing care is required. Finally, Medicare does not cover the cost of long-term care.

TABLE 29.1 *Institutional Responses to Aging and Elder Care from Government*

Name of policy	Year started	Basic goal	Eligibility	Source of funds
Social Security Act	1935	Provide Income for people who have retired from paid employment	Work in a Social Security-covered Job for 10 years or more, can start collecting at age 62 up to age 70, widow(er)s at 60, disabled at 50	Payroll taxes and self-employment contributions, paid Into Social Security Trust Fund by employees and employers
Medicare	1965	Coverage of health care costs, Including Part A: hospital care, Part B: outpatient care, and Part D: prescription drugs	People 65 and older, who had Medicare-covered employment, not linked to Income earned	Employers and employees pay taxes for Part A, funds from SSI checks cover Part B, and Part D paid for by Medicare plus private Insurance
Medicaid	1965	Cover health care costs for low-Income children and families, long-term care for elderly and/or disabled	Pregnant women, children, teens, elders, blind, and disabled with low Incomes	Means-tested, funded by state and federal funds, managed by states
Older Americans Act (OAA)	1965	Promote the delivery of social services to aging population via Administration on Aging (AoA) and state agencies	National Elder Locator for all families, some meal programs, housing, and services for low-Income elders	Taxes and other government funds, most funding for social service programs, rest goes to Jobs program, research, and training
Family and Medical Leave Act	1993	Twelve weeks of Job-protected unpaid leave with continuation of health benefits for own serious health condition, and/or care of seriously Ill parent child or spouse, and child rearing	Workers at firms with 50 or more employees within 75-mile radius, who worked 1,250 hours and 12 consecutive months	Payroll tax in California and New Jersey, otherwise unpaid Administrative costs funded by states and U.S. Department of Labor
National Family Caregiver Support Program	2000, under OAA reauthorization	Referrals for services/ respite care, Information, counseling, training, and support groups for family caregivers	Persons of any age who serve as unpaid caregivers for persons 60 years or older	Funds from Older Americans Act, Title III E

Medicaid, the third key government policy, is the largest source of payment for nursing home care, and it will become increasingly important as the nations population ages. In 2008, nearly 41 percent of the nations nursing facility care was paid by Medicaid, averaging nearly $30,000 for each beneficiary.[100] In most states, Medicaid also pays for some long-term care services at home and in the community. Although eligibility varies from state to state, those elders who are eligible for Medicaid assistance must have limited assets and incomes below the poverty line. They also must contribute all or most of their available income toward the cost of their care. Many elderly who enter nursing homes pay for their own care initially. Once their resources have been depleted, however, they are covered by Medicaid. According to a study by Brenda Spillman and Peter Kemper, 16 percent of Medicaid users began by paying their own way in long-term nursing facilities, exhausted their resources, and converted to Medicaid; 27 percent were covered by Medicaid when they were admitted to the nursing home.[101]

Medicaid often provides supplemental services to fill gaps left by Medicare. The Centers for Medicare and Medicaid Services estimated that Medicaid provided some additional health coverage for 8.5 million Medicare beneficiaries in 2009.[102] In addition, Medicare and Medicaid jointly fund a model program called PACE (Program of All-inclusive Care for the Elderly), in which an interdisciplinary team, consisting of professional and paraprofessional staff, assesses participants' needs, develops care plans, and delivers all services (including acute care services and nursing facility services when necessary), which are integrated for a seamless provision of total care. The program is available to individuals fifty-five and older who are certified by the state as nursing home eligible and meet the income and assets requirements to qualify for Medicaid.[103]

Despite their many provisions for elder support, Medicaid and Medicare leave significant gaps in coverage. The new Patient Protection and Affordable Care Act of 2010 should ease some of the burdens by expanding drugs covered by Medicare Part D, the prescription drug program, improving prevention benefits such as free annual wellness visits, and changing the cost of Medicare Advantage plans. Mechanisms to control or reduce Medicare spending may or may not benefit elders, and a new Medicare and Medicaid Innovations Center holds promise of testing new payment and service delivery models that could benefit elders and their families.

A fourth important policy with implications for elder care is the Older Americans Act (OAA), passed as part of Lyndon Johnsons "Great Society" reforms and the first public policy to recognize the importance of community-based NGOs in the elder care system. Although the OAA signaled a significant effort to systematize and broaden access to elder services, studies evaluating its effectiveness have had mixed findings. For example, studies of home care programs have found that although providers have had some success in managing the daily practical needs of elders, they have been less successful in dealing with emergencies or significant health issues or levels of impairment.[104] Studies have shown that home care is more effective than inpatient care and reduces the length of hospital stays, but little data are available on how OAA programs affect measures of quality of life for elders or caregivers.[105] A book on OAA's Long-Term Care Ombudsman Program summarizes a number of issues cited in studies of other OAA programs. These include: a misalignment of resources and goals, which compromises program effectiveness; a lack of coordination between OAA programs and resources, which diminishes program effectiveness; and a lack of elder or caregiver empowerment to take control of elders' health care or make positive programs more sustainable and cost-effective.[106]

The Family and Medical Leave Act (FMLA) is the only law that deals specifically with the challenges of working and providing elder care. A bipartisan commission that conducted two nationally representative random-sample surveys to study the impact of the FMLA on employers and employees reported to Congress in 1996 that the law was not the burden to business that some had anticipated.[107] In terms of ease of administration and impact on productivity, profitability, and performance, the law was found either to have "no noticeable effect" or, in some cases, to produce cost savings. On the employee side, the FMLA was found to be a boon to families in their caregiving roles. Most leaves were short, and concerns that employees would abuse the law and use it for recreational time off proved unwarranted. In fact, some "leave-needers" did not take advantage of the law because they could not afford an unpaid leave. The surveys were repeated in 2000 with largely comparable results for employers and employees.[108] The major complaint from the employer community was the difficulty of administering "intermittent leaves," although employees find that type of leave useful for chronic health problems. Between the 1995 and 2000 surveys there was a statistically significant increase in the use of FMLA for elder care.[109]

From a policy perspective, the FMLA is like a minimum labor standard. It provides valuable protections to workers, but has limitations that hamper its effectiveness. Access to FMLA, for example, is restricted to about 55 percent of the workforce because of eligibility requirements for firms and employees. The definition of "family" is limited to parent, child, and spouse, depriving many elderly relatives such as grandparents or aunts and uncles, as well as those who are members of the lesbian, gay, bisexual, and transgendered (LGBT) community or who are not legally married, of coverage. And because the leave provided is unpaid, it is difficult for low-income workers to use. Recently two states, California and New Jersey, passed laws to establish paid leave programs, and a new study of the California law yields useful information about the applicability of these models for other states.[110] These new state policies are contemporary examples of the historical research of sociologist Theda Skocpol, who showed that federal policy is often driven by demands from local citizen associations and the actions of state legislatures.[111]

Finally, the National Family Caregiver Support Program (NFCSP) is the first federal law to acknowledge fully the needs of caregivers regardless of their employment status. Preliminary studies have shown that the program is expanding caregivers' access to elder care information and providing needs assessments, support groups, and stress reduction programs.[112] Although NFCSP offers many excellent services, such as respite care, counseling, and training for family caregivers, the funds available to deliver them are limited, particularly in the area of respite care.[113] As with many OAA programs, the goals of the statute are not matched by the resources needed for nongovernmental agencies to carry them out. Although the NFCSP has brought greater attention and supports to families caring for elders, particularly resources to promote caregiver health and prevent caregiver burnout, inadequate resources impair its effectiveness. Proposals for tax-based supports for caregivers or programs to pay family caregivers are appearing in state legislatures, but have yet to gain traction in Congress.

When government and employers cannot provide adequate support for elder care, family caregivers often rely on nongovernmental organizations, such as health care providers and community-based aging service agencies. Although NGOs are often created and funded by government, they are not direct policy-making organizations, and their role is beyond the scope of this article. Caregivers do, however, receive significant support, information, and services from these groups, including faith-based organizations, neighborhood centers in communities of color, LGBT advocacy organizations, and educational organizations. Because so many elder caregivers are employed, NGOs that provide services for elders and their caregivers must take the needs of employees into account.

CREATING AN AGING-FRIENDLY SOCIETY

The challenges faced today by elders and their family caregivers are enormous and will continue to increase during the twenty-first century as the population ages. Families alone cannot provide elder care, employers alone cannot provide all the supports employed caregivers need, and the government alone cannot provide or fund all the elder policies required. A large-scale, cross-sector initiative is needed to coordinate efforts at the national, state, and local level and to support all citizens from diverse cultures and income levels as they age.

Public policies must move in a universal direction, like Social Security and Medicare, to help transform U.S. communities and make housing, transportation, and open space accessible to all elders. There is a pressing need to better integrate nongovernmental organizations in the health care and social service sectors and to ensure they are culturally responsive. Employers must be encouraged to give employees in both professional and hourly jobs access to flexible work arrangements including part-time work, paid leave policies, paid sick days, and other "elder-friendly" workplace benefits. Overall, these groups must work together to create a culture in which aging is seen as a natural part of the life course and caregiving is seen as a multigenerational enterprise of great value to children, adults, elders, and society.

Elders themselves and their family caregivers, as well as the public and private sectors, must build support for social investment in the next generation. Today's children will be the workers, citizens, and family caregivers who will care for the growing U.S. elderly population tomorrow. Focusing on children's healthy development and education will build their capacity to provide supportive care for the elders of future generations.

Notes

1. Frank B. Hobbs, "Population Profile of the United States: The Elderly Population," U.S. Census Bureau (vvvw.census.gov/population/www/pop-profile/elderpop.htrnl).
2. Census 2000 Brief, C2KBR/01-12, U.S. Census Bureau (2001).
3. Jennifer Cheeseman Day, *Population Projections of the United States by Age, Sex, Race, and Hispanic Origin: 1993–2050*, Current Population Reports, P25-1104, U.S. Census Bureau (1993);

Administration on Aging, Table 12, "Older Population as a Percentage of the Total Population, 1900-2050" (www.aoa.gov/aoaroot/aging_statistics/future_growth/future_growth.aspx#age).

4. U.S. Census Bureau, "Age: 2000," Census 2000 Brief, October 2001 (www.census.gov /prod/2001pubs/c2kbr01-12.pdf).

5. Wan He and others, "Sixty-Five Plus in the United States," *Current Population Reports, Special Studies*, Series P23-209 (Washington: December 2005).

6. U.S. Census Bureau, Current Population Survey, Annual Social and Economic Supplements (www.census.gov/hhes/www/poverty/histpov/hstpov5.xls); U.S. Census Bureau, Historical Poverty Tables, table C, "Poverty Rates for Elderly and Non-Elderly Adults, 1966–2009."

7. The percentage of homeless adults fifty and older appears to be increasing, particularly in cities. M. William Sermons and Meghan Henry, "Demographics of Homelessness Series: The Rising Elderly Population," National Alliance to End Homelessness (April 2010).

8. Dorothy A. Milller, "The 'Sandwich' Generation: Adult Children of the Aging," *Social Work* 26, no. 5 (September, 1981): 419–23.

9. Leslie Foster Stebbins, *Work and Family in America: A Reference Handbook* (Santa Barbara, Calif.: ABC-CLIO, 2001), p. 40.

10. National Alliance for Caregiving and AARP, *Caregiving in the United States* (Washington: 2009), p. 53.

11. E. Shanas and G. F. Streib, eds., *Social Structure and the Family: Generational Relations* (Englewood Cliffs, N.J.: Prentice-Hall, 1965).

12. Peter S. Amo, Carol Levine, and M. N. Memmott, "The Economic Value of Informal Caregiving," *Health Affairs* 18, no. 2 (1999): 182–88.

13. Carol Levine, ed. *Always on Call: When Illness Turns Families into Caregivers* (Vanderbilt University Press, 2004), p. 5.

14. Ann Bookman and Mona Harrington, "Family Caregivers: A Shadow Workforce in the Geriatric Health Care System?" *Journal of Health Policy, Politics and Law* 32, no. 6 (2007): 1026.

15. Carol Levine and Thomas H. Murray, eds., *The Cultures of Caregiving: Conflict and Common Ground among Families, Health Professionals and Policy Makers* (Johns Hopkins University Press, 2004).

16. *Family Caregiving in the U.S.: Findings from a National Survey* (Washington: National Alliance for Caregiving and the American Association of Retired Persons, 1997).

17. Donna Wagner, *Comparative Analysis of Caregiver Data for Caregivers to the Elderly, 1987 and 1997* (Bethesda, Md.: National Alliance for Caregiving, June 1997).

18. National Alliance for Caregiving, *Caregiving in the U.S.*, National Alliance for Caregiving in collaboration with the AARP (November 2009), p. 5.

19. "What Moves Americans to Move?" Census 2000, U.S. Census Bureau (http://usgovinfo.about .com/library/weekly/aa060401a.htm).

20. National Alliance for Caregiving, *Caregiving in the U.S.* (see note 18), p. 14.

21. Linda K. Bledsoe, Sharon E. Moore, and Lott Collins, "Long Distance Caregiving: An Evaluative Review of the Literature," *Ageing International* (New York: Springer Science, 2010); Beverly Koerin and Marcia Harrigan, "P.S. I Love You: Long Distance Caregiving," *Journal of Gerontological Social Work* 40, no. 1/2 (2003): 63–81.

22. MetLife, *Miles Away: The MetLife Study of Long-Distance Caregiving* (Westport, Conn.: MetLife Mature Market Institute, July 2004).

23. S. H. Matthews and T. T. Rosner, "Shared Filial Responsibility: The Family as the Primary Caregiver," *Journal of Marriage and the Family* 50, no. 1 (1998): 278–86; E. P. Stoller, L. E. Forster, and T. S. Duniho, "Systems of Parent Care within Sibling Networks," *Research on Aging* 14, no. 1 (1992): 472–92.

24. E. Fuller-Thompson and M. Minkler, "Housing Issues and Realities Faced by Grandparent Caregivers Who Are Renters," *Gerontologist* 43, no. 1 (2003): 92–98.

25. Continuing care retirement communities include "independent living" units for those who can still care for themselves; "assisted living" units for those who need some daily help with personal care; and "long-term-care" beds for those who are no longer able to take care of themselves.

26. National Alliance for Caregiving, *Caregiving in the U.S.* (see note 18), p. 14.

27. National Council on Aging, "Long-Term Services and Supports" (www.ncoa.org/independence
-diginry/long-term-services-supports.html).

28. J. Keefe and others, "Caregivers' Aspirations, Realities, and Expectations: The CARE Tool,"
Journal of Applied Gerontology 27, no. 3 (2008): 286–308.

29. Pew Research Center, "From the Age of Aquarius to the Age of Responsibility: Baby Boomers
Approach Age 60, A Social Trends Report" (2005), pp. 10–13.

30. Pew Research Center; *Growing Old in America: Expectations vs. Reality*, A Social and Demographic
Trends Report (June 2009), p. 11.

31. E. Papastavrou and others, "Caring for a Relative with Dementia: Family Caregiver Burden"
(JAN Original Research, Blackwell Publishing, Ltd., 2007).

32. Karen Donelan and others, "Challenged to Care: Informal Caregivers in a Changing Health
Care System," *Health Affairs* 21, no. 4 (2002): 222–31.

33. R. Johnson and J. Wiener, *A Profile of Frail Older Americans and Their Caregivers*, The Retirement
Project, Occasional Paper 8 (Washington: Urban Institute, 2006).

34. Ibid, p. 24.

35. MetLife, *Broken Trust: Elders, Family, and Finances* (Westport, Conn.: MetLife Mature Market
Institute, 2009), p. 12.

36. Joshua Hauser and Betty Kramer, "Family Caregivers in Palliative Care," *Clinics in Geriatric Medicine* 20, no. 4 (November 2004): 671–88.

37. Luisa Margulies, *My Mother's Hip: Lessons from the World of Elder Care* (Philadelphia: Temple
University Press, 2004).

38. Kevin Brazil, Daryl Bainbridge, and Christine Rodriguez, "The Stress Process in Palliative Cancer Care: A Qualitative Study on Informal Caregiving and Its Implication for the Delivery of
Care," *American Journal of Hospice and Palliative Medicine* 27, no. 2 (2010): 111–16.

39. Arthur Kleinman, "On Caregiving: A Scholar Experiences the Moral Acts That Come Before—
and Go Beyond—Modern Medicine," *Harvard Magazine* (July–August 2010): 27.

40. David O. Moberg, ed., *Aging and Spirituality: Spiritual Dimensions of Aging Theory, Research, Practice, and Policy* (Binghamton, N.Y.: Haworth Press, 2001).

41. M. Crowther and others, "Spiritual and Emotional Well-Being Tasks Associated with Elder
Care," *Geriatric Care Management Journal* 13, no. 1 (Winter/Spring 2003): 15–21.

42. The Administration on Aging has a website to help families find an agency near where their
elderly relative lives (www.eldercare.gov/Eldercare.NET/Public/Home.aspx).

43. T. Semla, "How to Improve Coordination of Care," *Annals of Internal Medicine* 148, no. 8 (April 15,
2008): 627–28.

44. Grif Alspach, "Handing Off Critically Ill Patients to Family Caregivers: What Are Your Best
Practices?" *Critical Care Nurse* 29, no. 3 (2009): 12–22.

45. Bookman and Harrington, "Family Caregivers" (see note 14).

46. Laura Katz Olsen, *The Not-So-Golden Years: Caregiving, the Frail Elderly, and the Long-Term
Care Establishment* (Lanham, Md.: Rowman & Litdefield Publishers, Inc., 2003), p. 98; Nancy
R. Hooyman, "Research on Older Women: Where Is Feminism?" *Gerontologist* 39, no.1(1999):
115–18.

47. National Alliance for Caregiving and AARP, *Caregiving in the U.S.: A Focused Look at Those Caring
for Someone Age 50 or Older* (Washington, 2009), p. 22.

48. Kerstin Aumann and others, *Working Family Caregivers of the Elderly: Everyday Realities and Wishes
for Change* (New York: Families and Work Institute, 2010), p. 2.

49. Ibid.

50. Lynn M. Martire and Mary Ann Parris Stephens, "Juggling Parent Care and Employment Responsibilities: The Dilemmas of Adult Daughter Caregivers in the Workforce," *Sex Roles* 48,
no. 3/4 (2003): 167–73.

51. Olsen, *The Not-So-Golden Years* (see note 46).

52. Margaret B. Neal and Donna L. Wagner, "Working Caregivers: Issues, Challenges, and Opportunities for the Aging Network," *National Family Caregiver Support Program Issue Brief* (2002): 1–31.

53. Susan C. Eaton, "Eldercare in the United States: Inadequate, Inequitable, but Not a Lost Cause,"
Feminist Economics 11, no. 2 (2005): 37–51; MetLife Mature Market Institute, *Employer Costs for*

Working Caregivers (Washington: MetLife Mature Market Institute and National Alliance for Caregivers, 1997).

54. Karen Bullock, Sybil L. Crawford, and Sharon L. Tennstedt, "Employment and Caregiving: Exploration of African American Caregivers," *Social Work* 48, no. 2 (2003): 150–62.

55. MetLife, *MetLife Study of Working Caregivers and Employer Health Costs* (Westport, Conn.: National Alliance for Caregiving and MetLife Mature Market Institute, February 2010).

56. Peter P. Vitaliano, Jianping Zhang, and James M. Scanlan, "Is Caregiving Hazardous to One's Physical Health? A Meta-Analysis," *Psychological Bulletin* 129, no. 6 (2003): 946–72.

57. Martin Pinquart and Silvia Sörensen, "Gender Differences, Caregiver Stressors, Social Resources, and Health: An Updated Meta-Analysis," *Journals of Gerontology Series B: Psychological Sciences & Social Sciences* 61, no. 1 (2006): 33–45.

58. Ibid.

59. Sara Torres, "Barriers to Mental-Health Care Access Faced by Hispanic Elderly," in *Servicing Minority Elders in the Twenty-First Century*, edited by Mary L. Wykle and Amasa B. Ford (New York: Springer, 1999), pp. 200–18.

60. Sarah J. Yarry, Elizabeth K. Stevens, and T. J. McCallum, "Cultural Influences on Spousal Caregiving," *American Society on Aging* 31, no. 3 (2007): 24–30.

61. James Jackson, "African American Aged," in the Encyclopedia of Aging, 2nd ed., edited by George L. Maddox (New York: Springer, 1995), pp. 30–80; Sharon L. Tennstedt, Bei-Hung Chang, and Melvin Delgado, "Patterns of Long-Term Care: A Comparison of Puerto Rican, African-American, and Non-Latino White Elders," *Journal of Gerontological Social Work* 30, no. 1/2 (1998): 179–99.

62. Sue Levkoff, Becca Levy, and Patricia Flynn Weitzmann, "The Role of Religion and Ethnicity in the Help Seeking of Family Caregivers of Elders with Alzheimer's Disease and Related Disorders," *Journal of Cross-Cultural Gerontology* 14, no. 4 (1999): 335.

63. Martin Pinquart and Silvia Sörensen, "Associations of Stressors and Uplifts of Caregiving with Caregiver Burden and Depressive Mood: A Meta-Analysis," *Journals of Gerontology Series B: Psychological Sciences & Social Sciences* 58B, no. 2 (2003): 112; D. W. Coon and others, "Well-Being, Appraisal, and Coping in Latina and Caucasian Female Dementia Caregivers: Findings from the REACH Study," *Aging & Mental Health* 8, no. 4 (2004): 330–45.

64. W. E. Haley and others, "Weil-Being, Appraisal, and Coping in African-American and Caucasian Dementia Caregivers: Findings from the REACH Study," *Aging & Mental Health* 8, no. 4 (2004): 316–29; Coon and others, "Well-Being, Appraisal, and Coping in Latina and Caucasian Female Dementia Caregivers" (see note 63).

65. Tennstedt, Chang, and Delgado, "Patterns of Long-Term Care" (see note 61).

66. Catherine Hagan Hennessey and Robert John, "American Indian Family Caregivers' Perceptions of Burden and Needed Support Services," *Journal of Applied Gerontology* 15, no. 3 (1996): 275–93.

67. Martin Pinquart and Silvia Sörensen, "Ethnic Differences in Stressors, Resources, and Psychological Outcomes of Family Caregiving: A Meta-Analysis," *Gerontologist* 45, no. 1 (2005): 90–106; M. R. Janevic and M. C. Connell, "Racial, Ethnic, and Cultural Differences in the Dementia Caregiving Experience: Recent Finding," *Gerontologist* 41, no. 3 (2001): 334–47.

68. Karen I. Fredriksen-Goldsen and Nancy Farwell, "Dual Responsibilities among Black, Hispanic, Asian, and White Employed Caregivers," *Journal of Gerontological Social Work* 43, no. 4 (2004): 25–44.

69. Peggye Dilworth-Anderson, Ishan Canty Williams, and Brent E. Gibson, "Issues of Race, Ethnicity, and Culture in Caregiving Research: A 20-Year Review (1980–2000)," *Gerontologist* 42, no. 2 (2002): 237–72.

70. Tatjana Meschede, Thomas M. Shapiro, and Jennifer Wheary, *Living Longer on Less: The New Economic Insecurity of Seniors* (Institute on Assets and Social Policy and Demos, 2009).

71. Administration on Aging, *A Profile of Older Americans: 2009* (www.aoa.gov/AoAroot/Aging _Staristics/Profile/2009/docs/2009profile_508.pdf).

72. Deborah M. Merrill, *Caring for Elderly Parents: Juggling Work, Family, and Caregiving in Middle and Working Class Families* (Westport: Auburn House, 1997), pp. 13–15.

73. Ibid.

74. Rachel F. Boaz, "Full-Time Employment and Informal Caregiving in the 1980s," *Medical Care* 34, no. 6 (1996): 524–36.

75. Robyn Stone, Gail Lee Cafferata, and Judith Sangl, "Caregivers of the Frail Elderly: A National Profile," *Gerontologist* 27, no. 5 (1987): 616–26.

76. Wagner, *Comparative Analysis of Caregiver Data for Caregivers to the Elderly*, 1987 and 1997 (see note 17), p. 2.

77. MetLife, *MetLife Study of Working Caregivers and Employer Health Costs* (see note 55).

78. Margaret B. Neal and others, *Balancing Work and Caregiving for Children, Adults, and Elders* (Newbury Park, Calif.: Sage, 1993); Urie Bronfenbrenner and others, *The State of Americans: This Generation and the Next* (New York: Free Press, 1996); J. L. Gibeau, J. W. Anastas, and P. J. Larson, "Breadwinners, Caregivers, and Employers: New Alliances in an Aging America," *Employee Benefits Journal* 12, no. 3 (1987): 6–10; Andrew E. Scharlach, "Caregiving and Employment: Competing or Complementary Roles?" *Gerontologist* 34, no. 3 (1994): 378–85.

79. Evercare, *Family Caregivers—What They Spend, What They Sacrifice* (Minnetonka, Minn.: 2007), p. 21.

80. R. Schudtz and S. Beach, "Caregiving as a Risk Factor for Mortality: The Caregiver Health Effects Study," *Journal of the American Medical Association* 282, no. 23 (1999): 2215–19; R. Schutlz,, P. Visintainer, and G. M. Williamson, "Psychiatric and Physical Morbidity Effect of Caregiving," *Journal of Gerontology* 45, no. 5 (1990): 181–91.

81. National Alliance for Caregiving and the National Center for Women and Aging at Brandeis University, *The MetLife Juggling Act Study: Balancing Caregiving with Work and the Costs Involved* (New York: The MetLife Mature Market Institute, 1999).

82. Society for Human Resource Management (SHRM), 2007 *Employee Benefits Survey* (Alexandria, Va.: 2007).

83. Hewitt Associates, *Work/Life Benefits Provided by Major U.S. Employers in 2003-2004* (Lincolnshire, Ill: 2003)

84. SHRM, 2007 *Employee Benefits Survey* (see note 82).

85. Ellen Galinsky and James T. Bond, *The Impact of the Recession on Employers* (New York: Families and Work Institute, 2009), p. 7.

86. Allarde Dembe and others, "Employer Perceptions of Elder Care Assistance Programs," *Journal of Workplace Behavioral Health* 23, no. 4 (2008): 360.

87. SHRM, 2007 *Employee Benefits Survey* (see note 82).

88. Donna Wagner and Gail Hunt, "The Use of Workplace Eldercare Programs by Employed Caregivers," *Research on Aging* 16, no. 1 (March 1994): 69–84.

89. Dembe and others, "Employer Perceptions of Elder Care Assistance Programs" (see note 86), p. 371.

90. Ibid., p. 373.

91. Terry Bond and others, *The National Study of Employers: Highlights of Findings* (New York: Families and Work Institute, 2006).

92. J. L. Class and A. Finley, "Coverage and Effectiveness of Family Responsive Workplace Policies," *Human Resources Management Review* 12, no. 3 (Autumn 2002): 313–37.

93. Marcie Pitt-Catsouphes, Christina Matz-Costa, and Elyssa Besen, *Age and Generations: Understanding Experiences at the Workplace* (Chestnut Hill, Mass.: Boston College, 2009), p. 17.

94. Ibid.

95. Bond, *The National Study of Employers* (see note 91).

96. Muriel Gillick, *The Denial of Aging: Perpetual Youth, Eternal Life, and Other Dangerous Fantasies* (Harvard University Press, 2006), pp. 4, 6.

97. Ellen Galinsky, Dana Friedman, and C. Hernandez, *The Corporate Reference Guide to Work-Family Programs* (New York: Families and Work Institute, 1991).

98. Tamara Haraven, "The Changing Patterns of Family Life as They Affect the Aged," *Families and Older Persons: Policy Research and Practice*, edited by G. K. Maddox, I. C. Siegler, and D. G. Blazer (Durham, N.C.: Duke University Center for the Study of Aging and Human Development, 1980), pp. 31–41.

99. Nancy Folbre, *The Invisible Heart* (New York: The New Press, 2001), p. 102.

100. Centers for Medicare and Medicaid Services, "National Health Accounts" (http://cms.hhs.gov/statistics/nhe).
101. Brenda Spillman and Peter Kemper, "Lifetime Patterns of Payment for Nursing Home Care," *Medical Care* 33, no. 3 (1995): 280–96.
102. Centers for Medicare and Medicaid Services, Brief Summaries of Medicare and Medicaid, 2010 (www.cms.gov/MedicareProgramRatesStats/downloads/MedicareMedicaidSummaries2010.pdf).
103. Carol Levine, ed., *Always on Call: When Illness Turns Families into Caregivers* (New York: United Hospital Fund, 2004), p. 137.
104. L. W. Kaye, "The Adequacy of the Older Americans Act Home Care Mandate: A Front Line View from Three Programs," *Home Health Care Service Quarterly* 5, no. 1 (Spring 1984): 75–87.
105. T. Burns and others, "Home Treatment for Mental Health Problems: A Systemic Review," *Health Technology Assessment* 5, no. 15 (2001): 1–139.
106. Jo Harris-Wehling and others, *Real Problems, Real People: An Evaluation of the Long-Term Care Ombudsman Programs of the Older Americans Act* (Washington: Division of Health Care Services, Institute of Medicine, 1995).
107. Commission on Leave, *A Workable Balance: A Report to Congress on Family and Medical Leave Policies* (Washington: U.S. Department of Labor, May 1996).
108. David Cantor and others, *Balancing the Needs of Families and Employers: Family and Medical Leave Surveys* (Bethesda, Md.: Westat, 2001).
109. Jane Waldfogel, "Family and Medical Leave: Evidence from the 2000 Surveys," *Monthly Labor Review* 124, no. 9 (September 2001): 17–23.
110. Ruth Milkman and Eileen Applebaum, "Leaves That Pay: Employer and Worker Experiences with Paid Family Leave in California" (Center for Research on Economic Policy, January 2011), pp. 1–36.
111. Theda Skocpol, *Protecting Soldiers and Mothers: The Political Origins of Social Policy in the United States* (Harvard University Press, 1992), pp. 46–47.
112. Stephanie Whittier, Andrew Scharlach, and Teresa S. Dal Santo, "Availability of Caregiver Support Services: Implications for Implementation of the National Family Caregiver Support Program," *Journal of Aging and Social Policy* 17, no. 1 (2005): 45–62.
113. In 2006, Congress passed the "Lifespan Respite Care Act" (Public Law 109–442), but no funds have been allocated for implementation.

Chapter 12

Trouble in the Family

■READING 29

Prisoners' Families and Children

Jeremy Travis

As the nation debates the wisdom of a fourfold increase in our incarceration rate over the past generation, one fact is clear: Prisons separate prisoners from their families. Every individual sent to prison leaves behind a network of family relationships. Prisoners are the children, parents, siblings, and kin to untold numbers of relatives who are each affected differently by a family member's arrest, incarceration, and ultimate homecoming.

Little is known about imprisonment's impact on these family networks. Descriptive data about the children of incarcerated parents only begin to tell the story. During the 1990s, as the nation's prison population increased by half, the number of children who had a parent in prison also increased by half—from 1 million to 1.5 million. By the end of 2002, 1 in 45 minor children had a parent in prison (Mumola 2004).[1] These children represent 2 percent of all minor children in America, and a sobering 7 percent of all African-American children (Mumola 2000). With little if any public debate, we have extended prison's reach to include hundreds of thousands of young people who were not the prime target of the criminal justice policies that put their parents behind bars.

In the simplest human terms, prison places an indescribable burden on the relationships between these parents and their children. Incarcerated fathers and mothers must learn to cope with the loss of normal contact with their children, infrequent visits in inhospitable surroundings, and lost opportunities to contribute to their children's development. Their children must come to terms with the reality of an absent parent, the stigma of parental imprisonment, and an altered support system that may include

452 Part IV • Families in Society

grandparents, foster care, or a new adult in the home. In addition, in those communities where incarceration rates are high, the experience of having a mother or father in prison is now quite commonplace, with untold consequences for foster care systems, multigenerational households, social services delivery, community norms, childhood development, and parenting patterns.

Imprisonment profoundly affects families in another, less tangible way. When young men and women are sent to prison, they are removed from the traditional rhythms of dating, courtship, marriage, and family formation. Because far more men than women are sent to prison each year, our criminal justice policies have created a "gender imbalance" (Braman 2002), a disparity in the number of available single men and women in many communities. In neighborhoods where incarceration and reentry have hit hardest, the gender imbalance is particularly striking. Young women complain about the shortage of men who are suitable marriage prospects because so many of the young men cycle in and out of the criminal justice system. The results are an increase in female-headed households and narrowed roles for fathers in the lives of their children and men in the lives of women and families in general. As more young men grow up with fewer stable attachments to girlfriends, spouses, and intimate partners, the masculine identity is redefined.

The family is often depicted as the bedrock of American society. Over the years, we have witnessed wave after wave of social policy initiatives designed to strengthen, reunite, or simply create families. Liberals and conservatives have accused each other of espousing policies that undermine "family values." In recent years, policymakers, foundation officers, and opinion leaders have also decried the absence of fathers from the lives of their children. These concerns have translated into a variety of programs, governmental initiatives, and foundation strategies that constitute a "fatherhood movement." Given the iconic stature of the family in our vision of American life and the widespread consensus that the absence of father figures harms future generations, our national experiment with mass incarceration seems, at the very least, incongruent with the rhetoric behind prevailing social policies. At worst, the imprisonment of millions of individuals and the disruption of their family relationships has significantly undermined the role that families could play in promoting our social well-being.

The institution of family plays a particularly important role in the crime policy arena. Families are an integral part of the mechanisms of informal social control that constrain antisocial behavior. The quality of family life (e.g., the presence of supportive parent-child relationships) is significant in predicting criminal delinquency. Thus, if families suffer adverse effects from our incarceration policies, we would expect these harmful effects to be felt in the next generation, as children grow up at greater risk of engaging in delinquent and criminal behavior. The institution of marriage is another important link in the mechanism of informal social control. Marriage reduces the likelihood that ex-offenders will associate with peers involved in crime, and generally inhibits a return to crime (Laub, Nagin, and Sampson 1998). In fact, marriage is a stronger predictor of desistance from criminal activity than simple cohabitation, and a "quality" marriage—one based on a strong mutual commitment—is an even stronger predictor (Horney, Osgood, and Marshall 1995). Thus, criminal justice policies that weaken marriage and inhibit spousal commitments are likely to undermine the natural processes of desistance, thereby causing more crime. In short, in developing crime policies, families matter. If our crime policies have harmful consequences for families, we risk undermining the role families can play in controlling criminal behavior.

This [reading] examines the impact of incarceration and reentry on families. We begin by viewing the antecedents to the creation of families—the relationships between young men and young women—in communities where the rates of arrest, removal, incarceration, and reentry are particularly high. Then we discuss imprisonment's impact on relationships between an incarcerated parent and his or her children. Next we examine the effects of parental incarceration on the early childhood and adolescent development of children left behind. We then observe the family's role in reentry. We close with reflections on the impact of imprisonment on prisoners' family life, ways to mitigate incarceration's harmful effects, and ways to promote constructive connections between prisoners and their families.

THE "GENDER IMBALANCE"

To understand the magnitude of the criminal justice system's impact on the establishment of intimate partner relationships, we draw upon the work of Donald Braman (2002, 2004), an anthropologist who conducted a three-year ethnographic study of incarceration's impact on communities in Washington, D.C. In the District of Columbia, 7 percent of the adult African-American male population returns to the community from jail or prison each year. According to Braman's estimates, more than 75 percent of African-American men in the District of Columbia can expect to be incarcerated at some point during their lifetime. One consequence of these high rates of incarceration is what Braman calls a "gender imbalance," meaning simply that there are fewer men than women in the hardest hit communities. Half of the women in the nation's capital live in communities with low incarceration rates. In these communities, there are about 94 men for every 100 women. For the rest of the women in D.C.—whose neighborhoods have higher incarceration rates—the ratio is about 80 men for every 100 women. Furthermore, 10 percent of the District's women live in neighborhoods with the highest incarceration rates, where more than 12 percent of men are behind bars. In these neighborhoods, there are fewer than 62 men for every 100 women.

This gender imbalance translates into large numbers of fatherless families in communities with high rates of incarceration. In neighborhoods with a 2 percent male incarceration rate, Braman (2002) found that fathers were absent from more than one-half of the families. But in the communities with the highest male incarceration rates—about 12 percent—more than three-quarters of the families had a father absent. This phenomenon is not unique to Washington, D.C., however. In a national study, Sabol and Lynch (1998) also found larger numbers of female-headed families in counties receiving large numbers of returning prisoners.

Clearly, mass incarceration results in the substantial depletion in the sheer numbers of men in communities with high rates of imprisonment. For those men who are arrested, removed, and sent to prison, life in prison has profound and long-lasting consequences for their roles as intimate partners, spouses, and fathers. In the following sections, we will document those effects. Viewing this issue from a community perspective, however, reminds us that incarceration also alters the relationships between the men and women who are not incarcerated. In her research on the marriage patterns of low-income mothers, Edin (2000) found that the decision to marry (or remarry) depends, in part, on the economic prospects, social respectability, and reliability of potential husbands—attributes that are adversely affected by imprisonment. Low marriage rates, in turn, affect the life courses of men who have been imprisoned, reducing their likelihood of desistance from criminal activity. Thus, the communities with the highest rates of incarceration are caught in what Western, Lopoo, and McLanahan (2004, 21) call the "high-crime/low-marriage equilibrium." In these communities, women "will be understandably averse to marriage because their potential partners bring few social or economic benefits to the table. Men, who remain unmarried or unattached to stable households, are likely to continue their criminal involvement."

Braman quotes two of his community informants to illustrate these ripple effects of the gender imbalance. "David" described how the shortage of men affected dating patterns:

> Oh, yeah, everybody is aware of [the male shortage]. . . . And the fact that [men] know the ratio, and they feel that the ratio allows them to take advantage of just that statistic. 'Well, this woman I don't want to deal with, really because there are six to seven women to every man.' (2002, 166)

The former wife of a prisoner commented that women were less discerning in their choices of partners because there were so few men:

> Women will settle for whatever it is that their man [wants], even though you know that man probably has about two or three women. Just to be wanted, or just to be held, or just to go out and have a date makes her feel good, so she's willing to accept. I think now women accept a lot of things—the fact that he might have another woman or the fact that they can't clearly get as much time as they want to. The person doesn't spend as much time as you would [like] him to spend. The little bit of time that you get you cherish. (2002, 167)

The reach of our incarceration policies thus extends deep into community life. Even those men and women who are never arrested pay a price. As they are looking for potential partners in marriage and parenting, they find that the simple rituals of dating are darkened by the long shadow of imprisonment.

THE IMPACT OF INCARCERATION ON PARENT-CHILD RELATIONSHIPS

The Family Profile of the Prisoner Population

Before turning to a closer examination of the effects of imprisonment on the relationships between incarcerated parents and their children, we should first describe the family circumstances of the nation's prisoners. In 1997, about half (47 percent) of state prisoners reported they had never been married. Only 23 percent reported they were married at the time of their incarceration, while 28 percent said they were divorced or separated

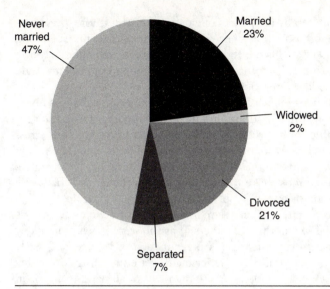

FIGURE 29.1 *Marital Status of Parents in State Prison, 1997*
Source: Mumola (2000).

(Figure 29.1). Yet most prisoners are parents. More than half (55 percent) of all state prisoners reported having at least one minor child. Because the overwhelming majority of state prisoners are men, incarcerated parents are predominantly male (93 percent). The number of incarcerated mothers, however, has grown dramatically in the past decade. Between 1991 and 2000, the number of incarcerated mothers increased by 87 percent, compared with a 60 percent increase in the number of incarcerated fathers. Of the men in state prison, 55 percent have children—a total of about 1.2 million—under the age of 18. About 65 percent of women in state prison are mothers to children younger than 18; their children number about 115,500 (Mumola 2000).

A mother's incarceration has a different impact on living arrangements than does that of a father. Close to two-thirds (64 percent) of mothers reported living with their children before incarceration, compared with slightly less than half (44 percent) of fathers in 1997. Therefore, as the percentage of women in prison increases, more children experience a more substantial disruption. We should not conclude, however, that the imprisonment of a nonresident father has little impact on his children. Research has shown that nonresident fathers can make considerable contributions to the development and well-being of their children (Amato and Rivera 1999; Furstenberg 1993). They contribute to their children's financial support, care, and social support even when they are not living in the children's home (Edin and Lein 1997; Hairston 1998; Western and McLanahan 2000). Therefore, a depiction of families' living arrangements only begins to describe the nature of the parenting roles played by fathers before they were sent to prison.

The national data on incarcerated parents also fail to capture the diversity of parent-child relationships. According to research conducted by Denise Johnston (2001) at the Center for Children of Incarcerated Parents, it is not uncommon for both incarcerated fathers and mothers to have children by more than one partner. Furthermore, these parents may have lived with some but not all of their children prior to their incarceration. This perspective leads to another conclusion: Individuals who are incarcerated may also have served as parent figures to children not their own—as stepparents or surrogate parents in families that blend children into one household.

We know little about the nature of these parent-child relationships. As was noted above, even absent fathers can provide emotional and financial support prior to their incarceration. However, the profiles of incarcerated parents also point to indicia of stress and dysfunction within these families. More than three-quarters of parents in state prison reported a prior conviction and, of those, more than half had been previously incarcerated. During the time leading up to their most current arrest and incarceration, nearly half were out of prison on some type of conditional release, such as probation or parole, in 1997. Nearly half (46 percent) of incarcerated fathers were imprisoned for a violent crime, as were one-quarter (26 percent) of the mothers. Mothers in prison were much more likely than fathers to be serving time for drug offenses (35 percent versus 23 percent). Nearly one-third of the mothers reported committing their crime to get either drugs or money for drugs, compared with 19 percent of fathers. More than half of all parents in prison reported using drugs in the month before they were arrested, and more than a third were under the influence of alcohol when they committed the crime. Nearly a quarter of incarcerated mothers (23 percent) and about a tenth (13 percent) of incarcerated fathers reported a history of mental illness (Mumola 2000). Clearly, these individuals were struggling with multiple stressors that, at a minimum, complicated their role as parents.

The portrait of prisoners' extended family networks is also sobering. According to findings from the Urban Institute's *Returning Home* (Visher, La Vigne, and Travis 2004) study in Maryland, these networks exhibit high rates of criminal involvement, substance abuse, and family violence (La Vigne, Kachnowski, et al. 2003). In inte rviews conducted with a sample of men and women just prior to their release from prison and return to homes in Baltimore, the Institute's researchers found that about 40 percent of the prisoners reported having at least one relative currently serving a prison sentence. Nine percent of the women said they had been threatened, harassed, or physically hurt by their husband, and 65 percent of those who reported domestic violence also reported being victimized by a nonspouse intimate partner. No male respondents reported this kind of abuse. The women reported that, other than their partners, the highest level of abuse came from other women in their families—their mothers, stepmothers, or aunts. Nearly two-thirds of inmates (62 percent) reported at least one family member with a substance abuse or alcohol problem and more than 16 percent listed four or more family members with histories of substance abuse. These characteristics highlight the high levels of risks and challenges in the families prisoners leave behind.

The Strain of Incarceration on Families

We turn next to a discussion of the impact of parental incarceration on the families left behind. One obvious consequence is that the families have fewer financial resources. According to the Bureau of Justice Statistics, in 1997 most parents in state prison (71 percent) reported either full-time or part-time employment in the month preceding their current arrest (Mumola 2002). Wages or salary was the most common source of income among incarcerated fathers before imprisonment, 60 percent of whom reported having a full-time job. Mothers, on the other hand, were less likely to have a full-time job (39 percent). For them, the most common sources of income were wages (44 percent) or public assistance (42 percent). Very few mothers reported receiving formal child support payments (6 percent) (Mumola 2000). During incarceration, the flow of financial support from the incarcerated parent's job stops, leaving the family to either make do with less or make up the difference, thereby placing added strains on the new caregivers. Eligibility for welfare payments under the TANF (Temporary Assistance for Needy Families) program ceases as soon as an individual is no longer a custodial parent—i.e., upon incarceration. In some cases, a caregiver may continue to receive TANF payments when the incarcerated parent loses eligibility, but because these benefits are now "child-only," they are lower than full TANF benefits. Food stamps are also unavailable to incarcerated individuals.

New caregivers often struggle to make ends meet during the period of parental incarceration. Bloom and Steinhart (1993) found that in 1992 nearly half (44 percent) of families caring for the children of an incarcerated parent were receiving welfare payments under TANF's predecessor program, AFDC (Aid to Families with Dependent Children). Under the recent welfare reform laws, however, TANF support is more limited than in the past, as lifetime eligibility has been capped at 60 months, work requirements have been implemented, and restrictions have been placed on TANF funds for those who have violated probation or parole, or have been convicted of certain drug crimes (Phillips and Bloom 1998). Even under the old AFDC program, most caregivers reported that they did not have sufficient resources to meet basic needs (Bloom and Steinhart 1993). Moreover, these economic strains affect more than the family's budget. According to several studies, financial stress can produce negative consequences for caretakers' behavior, including harsh and inconsistent parenting patterns, which, in turn, cause emotional and behavioral problems for the children (McLoyd 1998).

Other adjustments are required as well. Because most prisoners are men, and 55 percent of them are fathers, the first wave of impact is felt by the mothers of their children. Some mothers struggle to maintain contact with the absent father, on behalf of their children as well as themselves. Others decide that the incarceration of their children's father is a turning point, enabling them to start a new life and cut off ties with the father. More fundamentally, Furstenberg (1993) found that a partner left behind often becomes more independent and self-sufficient during the period of incarceration, changes that may ultimately benefit the family unit or lead to the dissolution of the relationship. At a minimum, however, these changes augur a significant adjustment in roles when the incarcerated partner eventually returns home.

In some cases, the incarceration period can have another, longer-lasting effect on the legal relationships between parents and children. In 1997, Congress enacted the Adoption and Safe Families Act (ASFA) to improve the safety and well-being of children in the foster care system as well as to remove barriers to the permanent placement, particularly adoption, of these children.[2] The ASFA stipulates that "permanency" decisions (determinations about a child's ultimate placement) should be made within 12 months of the initial removal of the child from the home. With limited exceptions, foster care placements can last no longer than 15 months, and if a child has been in foster care for 15 out of the previous 22 months, petitions must be filed in court to terminate parental rights. At least half the states now include incarceration as a reason to terminate parental rights (Genty 2001).

This new legislation has far-reaching consequences for the children of incarcerated parents. According to BJS, 10 percent of mothers in prison, and 2 percent of fathers, have at least one child in foster care (Mumola 2000). Because the average length of time served for prisoners released in 1997 was 28 months (Sabol and Lynch 2001), the short timelines set forth in ASFA establish a legal predicate that could lead to increases in the termination of parental rights for parents in prison (Lynch and Sabol 2001). Philip Genty (2001), a professor at Columbia University Law School, made some rough calculations of ASFA's impact. Looking only at reported cases discoverable through a Lexis search, he found, in the five years following ASFA's enactment, a 250 percent increase in cases terminating parental rights due to parental incarceration, from 260 to 909 cases.

In addition to those legal burdens placed on incarcerated parents, the new family caregivers face challenges in forging relationships with the children left behind. Some of these new caregivers may not have had much contact with the children before the parent's incarceration, so they must establish themselves as de facto parents and develop relationships with the children. Contributing to the trauma of this changing family structure, prisoners' children are sometimes separated from their siblings during incarceration because the new network of caregivers cannot care for the entire sibling group.

In short, when the prison gates close and parents are separated from their children, the network of care undergoes a profound realignment. Even two-parent families experience the strain of lost income, feel the remaining parent's sudden sole responsibility for the children and the household, and suffer the stigma associated with imprisonment. However, prisoners' family structures rarely conform to the two-parent model and are more often characterized by nonresident fathers, children living with different parents, and female-headed households. In these circumstances, the ripple effects of a mother or father going to prison reach much farther, and grandparents, aunts and uncles, and the foster care system must step into the breach. In addition, these extended networks feel the financial, emotional, and familial weight of their new responsibilities.

Incarceration has yet one more effect on the structure of prisoners' families. One of the important functions that families perform is to create assets that are passed along to the next generation. These assets are sometimes quite tangible: Money is saved, real estate appreciates in value, and businesses are built. These tangible assets can typically be transferred to one's children. Sometimes the assets are intangible: Social status is achieved, professional networks are cultivated, and educational milestones are reached. These intangible assets can also translate into economic advantage by opening doors for the next generation. Braman asks whether the minimal intergenerational transfer of wealth in black families is related to the high rates of incarceration among black men. Taking a historical view, he concludes:

> The disproportionate incarceration of black men . . . helps to explain why black families are less able to save money and why each successive generation inherits less wealth than their white counterparts. Incarceration acts like a hidden tax, one that is visited disproportionately on poor and minority families; and while its costs are most directly felt by

the adults closest to the incarcerated family member, the full effect is eventually felt by the next generation as well. (2004, 156)

The ripple effects of incarceration on the family are far-reaching. The gender imbalance disturbs the development of intimate relationships that might support healthy families. Families' financial resources and relationship capabilities are strained at the same time they are scrambling for more assets to support their incarcerated loved one. Yet, despite the hardships of incarceration, families can play an important role in improving outcomes for prisoners and prisoners' children. Several studies have shown that the "quality of care children receive following separation and their ongoing relationships with parents" are "instrumental forces in shaping outcomes for children" (Hairston 1999, 205). According to one study (Sack 1977), the behavioral problems displayed by children of incarcerated fathers diminished once the children got to spend time with their fathers.

On the other hand, in a small percentage of cases, continued parental involvement may not be in the child's best interests. For example, BJS (Greenfeld et al. 1998) reports that 7 percent of prisoners convicted of violent crimes were convicted of intimate partner violence. Even more disturbing are those cases involving child abuse and neglect, where the child's best interests argue against parental involvement. According to BJS, among inmates who were in prison for a sex crime against a child, the child was the prisoner's own child or stepchild in a third of the cases (Langan, Schmitt, and Durose 2003). Yet there has been very little research on the nexus between this form of family violence, incarceration, and reentry.

Discussion of prisoners convicted of violence within the family only raises larger questions—questions not answered by current research—about whether some parent-child relationships are so troubled and so characterized by the patterns of parental substance abuse, criminal involvement, mental illness, and the intrusions of criminal justice supervision that parental removal is a net benefit for the child. It is undoubtedly true that removing a parent involved in certain types of child abuse is better for the child. But we know little about the critical characteristics of the preprison relationships between children and their incarcerated parents, especially as to what kind of parents they were, and how their removal affects their children.

Even without a deeper understanding of the parenting roles played by America's prisoners, we still must face several incontrovertible, troubling facts. First, expanding the use of prison to respond to crime has put more parents in prison. Between 1991 and 1999, a short eight-year period, the number of parents in state and federal prisons increased by 60 percent, from 452,500 to 721,500 (Mumola 2000). By the end of 2002, 3.7 million parents were under some form of correctional supervision (Mumola 2004). Second, many children are left behind when parents are incarcerated. By 1999, 2 percent of all minor children in the United States—about 1.5 million—had a parent in state or federal prison. (If we include parents who are in jail, on probation or parole, or recently released from prison, the estimate of children with a parent involved in the criminal justice system reaches 7 million, or nearly 10 percent of all minor children in America [Mumola 2000].) Third, the racial disparities in America's prison population translate into substantial, disturbing racial inequities in the population of children affected by our current levels of imprisonment. About 7 percent of all African-American minor children and nearly 3 percent of all Hispanic minor children in America have a parent in prison.

In comparison, barely 1 percent of all Caucasian minor children have a parent in prison (Mumola 2000). Finally, most of the children left behind are quite young. Sixty percent are under age 10, while the average child left behind is 8 years old.

In this era of mass incarceration, our criminal justice system casts a wide net that has altered the lives of millions of children, disrupting their relationships with their parents, altering the networks of familial support, and placing new burdens on such governmental services as schools, foster care, adoption agencies, and youth-serving organizations. As Phillips and Bloom succinctly concluded, "by getting tough on crime, the United States has gotten tough on children" (1998, 539). These costs are rarely included in our calculations of the costs of justice.

Parent-Child Relationships during Imprisonment

When a parent is arrested and later incarcerated, the child's world undergoes significant, sometimes traumatic, disruption. Most children are not present at the time of their parent's arrest, and arrested parents typically do not tell the police that they have minor children (American Bar Association 1993). Family members are often reluctant to tell the children that their parent has been incarcerated because of social stigma. Therefore, the immediate impact of an arrest can be quite traumatizing—a child is abruptly separated from his or her parent, with little information about what happened, why it happened, or what to expect.

The arrest and subsequent imprisonment of a parent frequently results in a significant realignment of the family's arrangements for caring for the child, depicted in Figure 29.2. Not surprisingly, the nature of the new living arrangements depends heavily on which parent is sent to prison. Recall that about two-thirds of incarcerated mothers in state prison lived with their children before they were imprisoned. Following the mother's incarceration, about a quarter (28 percent) of their children remain with their fathers. Most children of incarcerated mothers, however, are cared for by an extended family that is suddenly responsible for another mouth to feed and child to raise. More than half of these children (53 percent) will live with a grandparent, adding burdens to a generation that supposedly has already completed its child-rearing responsibilities. Another quarter of these children (26 percent) will live with another relative, placing new duties on the extended family. Some children have no familial safety net: almost 10 percent of incarcerated mothers reported that their child was placed in foster care (Mumola 2000).[3]

The story for incarcerated fathers is quite different. Less than half (44 percent) lived with their children before prison; once they are sent to prison, most of their children (85 percent) will live with the children's mother. Grandparents (16 percent) and other relatives (6 percent) play a much smaller role in assuming child care responsibilities when a father is incarcerated. Only 2 percent of the children of incarcerated men enter the foster care system. In sum, a child whose father is sent to prison is significantly less likely to experience a life disruption, such as moving in with another family member or placement in a foster home.

The nation's foster care system has become a child care system of last resort for many children with parents in prison. Research by the Center for Children of Incarcerated Parents (Johnston 1999) found that, at any given time, 10 percent of children in foster care currently have a mother—and 33 percent have a father—behind bars. Even

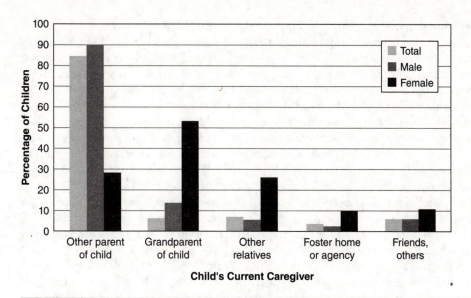

FIGURE 29.2 *Living Arrangements of Minor Children of State Inmates prior to Incarceration*

Figures do not total 100 percent because some prisoners had children living with multiple caregivers.

Source: Mumola (2000).

more striking, 70 percent of foster children have had a parent incarcerated at one time or another during their time in foster care.

When a parent goes to prison, the separation between parent and child is experienced at many levels. First, there is the simple fact of distance. The majority of state prisoners (62 percent) are held in facilities located more than 100 miles from their homes (Mumola 2000). Because prison facilities for women are scarce, mothers are incarcerated an average of 160 miles away from their children (Hagan and Coleman 2001). The distance between prisoners and their families is most pronounced for District of Columbia residents. As a result of the federal takeover of the District's prison system, defendants sentenced to serve felony time are now housed in facilities that are part of the far-flung network of federal prisons. In 2000, 12 percent of the District's inmates were held in federal prisons more than 500 miles from Washington. By 2002, that proportion had risen to 30 percent. Nineteen percent are in prisons as far away as Texas and California (Santana 2003). Not surprisingly, in an analysis of BJS data, Hairston and Rollin (2003, 68) found a relationship between this distance and family visits: "The distance prisoners were from their homes influenced the extent to which they saw families and friends. The farther prisoners were from their homes, the higher the percentage of prisoners who had no visitors in the month preceding the survey. . . . Those whose homes were closest to the prison had the most visits."

Geographic distance inhibits families from making visits and, for those who make the effort, imposes an additional financial burden on already strained family budgets. Donald Braman tells the story of Lilly, a District resident whose son Anthony is incarcerated in Ohio (Braman 2002). When Anthony was held in Lorton, a prison in Virginia that formerly housed prisoners from the District, she visited him once a week. Since the federal takeover, she manages to make only monthly visits, bringing her daughter, Anthony's sister. For each two-day trip, she spends between $150 and $200 for car rental, food, and a motel. Added to these costs are her money orders to supplement his inmate account and the care packages that she is allowed to send twice a year. She also pays about $100 a month for the collect calls he places. She lives on a fixed income of $530 a month.

Given these realities, the extent of parent-child contact during incarceration is noteworthy. Mothers in prison stay in closer contact with their children than do fathers. According to BJS, nearly 80 percent of mothers have monthly contact and 60 percent have at least weekly contact. Roughly 60 percent of fathers, by contrast, have monthly contact, and 40 percent have weekly contact with their children (Mumola 2000). These contacts take the form of letters, phone calls, and prison visits. Yet, a large percentage of prisoners serve their entire prison sentence without ever seeing their children. More than half of all mothers, and 57 percent of all fathers, never receive a personal visit from their children while in prison.

Particularly disturbing is Lynch and Sabol's finding (2001) that the frequency of contact decreases as prison terms get longer. Between 1991 and 1997, as the length of prison sentences increased, the level of contact of all kinds—calls, letters, and visits—decreased (Figure 29.3). This is especially troubling in light of research showing that the average length of prison sentences is increasing in America, reflecting more stringent sentencing policies. Thus, prisoners coming home in the future are likely to have had fewer interactions with their children, a situation that further weakens family ties and makes family reunification even more difficult.

In addition to the significant burden imposed by the great distances between prisoners and their families, corrections policies often hamper efforts to maintain family ties across the prison walls. The Women's Prison Association (1996) has identified several obstacles to constructive family contacts, some of which could easily be solved. The association found that it is difficult to get simple information on visiting procedures, and correctional administrators provide little help in making visiting arrangements. The visiting procedures themselves are often uncomfortable or humiliating. Furthermore, little attention is paid to mitigating the impact on the children of visiting a parent in prison.

Elizabeth Gaynes, director of the Osborne Association in New York City, tells a story that captures the emotional and psychological impact of a particular correctional policy upon a young girl who had come to visit her father. Because inmates were not allowed to handle money, the prison had drawn a yellow line three feet in front of the soda vending machines. Only visitors could cross that line. The father could not perform the simple act of getting his daughter a soda. If he wanted one, he had to ask his daughter to get it. According to Ms. Gaynes, this interaction represented an unnecessary and damaging role transformation; the child had become the provider, the parent had become the child.[4]

Family Contact during Imprisonment: Obstacles and Opportunities

For a number of reasons, it is difficult to maintain parent-child contact during a period of incarceration. For one thing, many prisons narrowly define the family members who

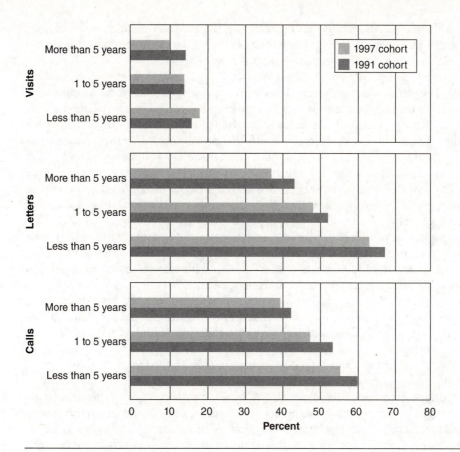

FIGURE 29.3   *Level of Prisoners' Weekly Contact with Children, by Method and Length of Stay, 1991 and 1997*

Prisoners to be released in the next 12 months.

Source: Lynch and Sabol (2001).

are granted visiting privileges. The State of Michigan's corrections department, for example, promulgated regulations in 1995 restricting the categories of individuals who are allowed to visit a prisoner. The approved visiting list may include minor children under the age of 18, but only if they are the prisoner's children, stepchildren, grandchildren, or siblings. Prisoners who are neither the biological parents nor legal stepparents of the children they were raising do not have this privilege. Finally, a child authorized to visit must be accompanied by either an adult who is an immediate family member of the child or of the inmate, or who is the child's legal guardians.[5] Many prisoners' extended family networks, including girlfriends and boyfriends who are raising prisoners' children, are not recognized in these narrow definitions of "family."[6] Limitations on visiting privileges are commonly justified on security or management grounds, but fail to recognize the complexity of the prisoner's familial networks. Rather than allowing the prisoner to define the "family" relationships that matter most, the arbitrary distinctions of biology or legal status are superimposed on the reality of familial networks, limiting meaningful contact that could make a difference to both prisoner and child.

Telephone contact is also burdened by prison regulations and by controversial relationships between phone companies and corrections departments. Prisoners are typically limited in the number of calls they can make. Their calls can also be monitored. The California Department of Corrections interrupts each call every 20 seconds with a recorded message: "This is a call from a California prison inmate." Most prisons allow prisoners to make only collect calls, and those calls typically cost between $1 and $3 per minute, even though most phone companies now charge less than 10 cents per minute for phone calls in the free society (Petersilia 2003). Telephone companies also charge between $1.50 and $4 just to place the collect call, while a fee is not charged for collect calls outside of prison.

The high price of collect calls reflects sweetheart arrangements between the phone companies and corrections agencies, under which the prisons receive kickbacks for every collect call, about 40 to 60 cents of every dollar. This arrangement translates into a substantial revenue source for corrections budgets. In 2001, for example, California garnered $35 million, based on $85 million of total revenue generated from prison calls. Some states require, by statute or policy, that these revenues pay for programs for inmates. Most states simply deposit this money into the general budget for their department of corrections.

Yet who bears these additional costs for maintaining phone contact with prisoners? The families of prisoners do, of course. In a study conducted by the Florida House of Representatives Corrections Committee (1998), family members reported spending an average amount of $69.19 per month accepting collect phone calls. According to this report, "Several family members surveyed stated that, although they wanted to continue to maintain contact with the inmate, they were forced to remove their names from the inmate's approved calling list because they simply could not afford to accept the calls" (1998, 23).

This monopolistic arrangement between phone companies and prisons makes families the unwitting funders of the prisons holding their loved ones. In essence, the states have off-loaded upwards of hundreds of millions of dollars of prison costs on to prisoners' families. Subsequently, families are placed in the unacceptable position of either agreeing to accept the calls, thereby making contributions to prison budgets, or ceasing phone contact with their loved ones. Of course, there are other, deeper costs attached to this practice. If a family chooses to limit (or stop) these phone calls, then family ties are weakened and the support system that could sustain the prisoner's reintegration is damaged. If the family chooses to pay the phone charges, then those financial resources are not available for other purposes, thereby adding to the strain the household experiences. In recent years, efforts to reform prison telephone policies have been successful in several states.[7] Yet, while these reform efforts are under way, tens of thousands of families are setting aside large portions of their budgets to pay inflated phone bills to stay in touch with their imprisoned family members.

Fortunately, a number of communities have implemented programs designed to overcome the barriers of distance, cost, and correctional practices that reduce contact between prisoners and their families. For example, Hope House, an organization in

Washington, D.C., that connects incarcerated fathers with their children in the District, hosts summer camps at federal prisons in North Carolina and Maryland where children spend several hours a day for a week visiting with their fathers in prison. Hope House has also created a teleconference hookup with federal prisons in North Carolina, Ohio, and New Mexico so that children can go to a neighborhood site to talk to their fathers in prison. In another instance, a Florida program called "Reading and Family Ties—Face to Face" also uses technology to overcome distance. Incarcerated mothers and their children transmit live video recordings via the Internet. These sessions occur each week, last an hour, and are available at no cost to the families. In addition, the U.S. Department of Justice in 1992 initiated the Girl Scouts Beyond Bars program, the first mother-daughter visitation program of its kind. Twice a month, more than 500 girls across the country, much like other girls their age, participate in Girl Scout programs, but in this program these Girl Scouts meet their mothers in prison. Finally, in Washington State, the McNeil Island Correction Center has launched a program that teaches incarcerated fathers the skills of active and involved parenting, encourages them to provide financial support for their children, and facilitates events to bring prisoners together with their families.

These programs—and many others like them—demonstrate that, with a little creativity and a fair amount of commitment, corrections agencies can find ways to foster ongoing, constructive relationships between incarcerated parents and their children. It seems particularly appropriate, in an era when technology has overcome geographical boundaries, to harness the Internet to bridge the divide between prisons and families. Yet the precondition for undertaking such initiatives is the recognition that corrections agencies must acknowledge responsibility for maintaining their prisoners' familial relationships. If these agencies embraced this challenge for all inmates—and were held accountable to the public and elected officials for the results of these efforts—the quality of family life for prisoners and their extended family networks would be demonstrably improved.

Notes

1. This is a single-day prevalence and does not take into account minor children whose parents were previously incarcerated; it accounts only for those who are currently incarcerated in state and federal prisons in 2002.
2. Public Law 105–89.
3. Figures do not total 100 percent because some prisoners had children living with multiple caregivers.
4. Elizabeth Gaynes, conversation with the author, June 22, 2004. Cited with permission.
5. The Michigan restrictions were challenged in court as unconstitutional because they violated the Fourteenth Amendment's guarantee of due process, the First Amendment's guarantee of free association, and the Eighth Amendment's prohibition against cruel and unusual punishment. The Supreme Court upheld the regulations, finding that the restrictions "bear a rational relation to the [department of correction's] valid interests in maintaining internal security and protecting child visitors from exposure to sexual or other misconduct or from accidental injury. . . . To reduce the number of child visitors, a line must be drawn, and the categories set out by these regulations are reasonable" (*Overton v. Bazzetta*, 539 U.S. 94 [2003]).
6. The definition of who can visit or take children to visit is an even bigger problem in light of cultural traditions, i.e., the extended family network and fictive kin arrangements that exist in many African-American families. Family duties and responsibilities are shared among a group of

individuals; e.g., a young uncle may be expected to take on the father's role and do things such as take the child to a game or on a prison visit while the grandmother provides day-to-day care and an aunt with a "good" job provides financial subsidies. Apparently this perspective was either not presented or ignored as unimportant in the Michigan case (Personal communication with Creasie Finney Hairston, January 6, 2004).

7. Missouri has announced that its next contract with prison telephone systems will not include a commission for the state. The Ohio prison system entered into a contract that will reduce the cost of prison phone calls by 15 percent. California will reduce most prisoner phone calls by 25 percent. In 2001, the Georgia Public Service Commission ordered telephone providers to reduce the rates for prisoner calls from a $3.95 connection fee and a rate of $0.69 per minute to a $2.20 connection fee and a rate of $0.35 per minute. The new telephone contract for the Pennsylvania Department of Corrections will reduce the average cost of a 15-minute telephone call by 30 percent. And litigation has been initiated in a number of states—including Illinois, Indiana, Kentucky, Ohio, New Hampshire, New Mexico, New York, South Dakota, Washington, Wisconsin, and the District of Columbia—to reduce the cost of prison phone calls and kickbacks to the state (eTc Campaign 2003).

References

Amato, Paul R., and Fernando Rivera. 1999. "Paternal Involvement and Children's Behavior Problems." *Journal of Marriage and the Family* 61(2): 375–84.

American Bar Association. 1993. *ABA Standards for Criminal Justice*. Chicago: American Bar Association.

Bloom, Barbara, and David Steinhart. 1993. *Why Punish the Children? A Reappraisal of the Children of Incarcerated Mothers in America*. San Francisco: National Council on Crime and Delinquency.

Braman, Donald. 2002. "Families and Incarceration." In *Invisible Punishment: The Collateral Consequences of Mass Imprisonment*, edited by Marc Mauer and Meda Chesney-Lind (117–35). New York: The New Press.

———. 2004. *Doing Time on the Outside: Incarceration and Family Life in Urban America*. Ann Arbor: University of Michigan Press.

Edin, Kathryn. 2000. "Few Good Men: Why Poor Mothers Don't Marry or Remarry." *The American Prospect* 11(4): 26–31.

Edin, Kathryn, and Laura Lein. 1997. *Making Ends Meet: How Single Mothers Survive Welfare and Low-Wage Work*. New York: Russell Sage Foundation.

eTc Campaign. 2003. "The Campaign to Promote Equitable Telephone Charges." http://www.curenational.org/~etc/. (Accessed April 5, 2004.)

Florida House of Representatives, Justice Council, Committee on Corrections. 1998. *Maintaining Family Contact When a Family Member Goes to Prison: An Examination of State Policies on Mail, Visiting, and Telephone Access*. http://www.fcc.state.fl.us/fcc/reports/family.pdf. (Accessed February 8, 2005.)

Furstenberg, Frank F. 1993. "How Families Manage Risk and Opportunity in Dangerous Neighborhoods." In *Sociology and the Public Agenda*, edited by William J. Wilson (231–58). Newbury Park, CA: Sage Publications.

Genty, Philip M. 2001. "Incarcerated Parents and the Adoption and Safe Families Act: A Challenge for Correctional Service Providers." *International Community Corrections Association Journal*, 44–47.

Greenfeld, Lawrence A., Michael R. Rand, Diane Craven, Patsy A. Klaus, Craig A. Perkins, Cheryl Ringel, Greg Warchol, Cathy Maston, and James Alan Fox. 1998. "Violence by Intimates: Analysis of Data on Crimes by Current or Former Spouses, Boyfriends, and Girlfriends." NCJ 167237. U.S. Department of Justice, Bureau of Justice Statistics.

Hagan, John, and Juleigh Petty Coleman. 2001. "Returning Captives of the American War on Drugs: Issues of Community and Family Reentry." *Crime and Delinquency* 47(3): 352–67.

Hairston, Creasie Finne. 1998. "The Forgotten Parent: Understanding the Forces that Influence Incarcerated Fathers' Relationships with Their Children." *Child Welfare: Journal of Polity, Practice and Program* 77(5): 617–39.

———. 1999. "Kinship Care When Parents Are Incarcerated." In *Kinship Care Research: Improving Practice through Research*, edited by James P. Gleeson and Creasie Finney Hairston (189–212). Washington, DC: Child Welfare League of America.

Hairston, Creasie Finney, and James Rollin. 2003. "Social Capital and Family Connections." *Women, Girls & Criminal Justice* 4(5): 67–69.

Horney, Julie, D. Wayne Osgood, and Ineke Haen Marshall. 1995. "Criminal Careers in the Short-Term: Infra-Individual Variability in Crime and Its Relation to Local Life Circumstances." *American Sociological Review* 60(5): 655–73.

Johnston, Denise. 1999. "Children of Criminal Offenders and Foster Care." Presented at the Child Welfare League of America National Conference on Research, Seattle.

———. 2001. "Incarceration of Women and Effects on Parenting." Paper prepared for a conference: *The Effects of Incarceration on Children and Families*, sponsored by the Program on Child, Adolescent, and Family Studies, Institute for Policy Research, Northwestern University, Evanston, IL, May 5.

La Vigne, Nancy G., Vera Kachnowski, Jeremy Travis, Rebecca Naser, and Christy Visher. 2003. *A Portrait of Prisoner Reentry in Maryland*, Washington, DC: The Urban Institute. http://www.ur-ban.org/url.cfm?ID=410655. (Accessed April 5, 2004.)

Langan, Patrick A., Erica L. Schmitt, and Matthew R. Durose. 2003. *Recidivism of Sex Offenders Released from Prison in 1994*. NCJ 198281. Washington, DC: U.S. Department of Justice, Bureau of Justice Statistics.

Laub, John H., Daniel S. Nagin, and Robert J. Sampson. 1998. "Trajectories of Change in Criminal Offending: Good Marriages and the Desistance Process." *American Sociological Review* 63(2): 225–38.

Lynch, James P., and William J. Sabol. 2001. *Prisoner Reentry in Perspective*. Crime Policy Report, vol. 3. Washington, DC: The Urban Institute.

McLoyd, Vonnie C. 1998. "Socioeconomic Disadvantage and Child Development." *American Psychologist* 53(2): 185–204.

Mumola, Christopher. 2000. "Incarcerated Parents and Their Children." NCI 182335. Washington, DC: U.S. Department of Justice, Bureau of Justice Statistics.

———. 2002. "Survey of Inmates in State and Federal Correctional Facilities, 2001 Annual Survey of Jails, and the 2001 National Prisoners Statistics Program." Paper presented at the National Center for Children and Families, Washington, DC, October 31.

———. 2004. "Incarcerated Parents and Their Children." Presented at the annual Administration for Children and Families Welfare Research and Evaluation Conference, U.S. Department of Health and Human Services, Washington, DC, May 28.

Petersilia, Joan. 2003. *When Prisoners Come Home: Parole and Prisoner Reentry*. New York: Oxford University Press.

Phillips, Susan, and Barbara Bloom. 1998. "In Whose Best Interest? The Impact of Changing Public Policy on Relatives Caring for Children with Incarcerated Parents." *Child Welfare* 77(5): 531–42.

Sabol, William J., and James P. Lynch. 1998. "Assessing the Longer-run Consequences of Incarceration: Effects on Families and Employment." Paper presented at the 20th Annual APPAM (Association for Public Policy Analysis and Management) Research Conference, New York, October 29–31.

Sack, W. 1977. "Children of Imprisoned Fathers." *Psychiatry* 40: 163–74.

Santana, Arthur. 2003. "Locked Dow and Far From Home." *Washington Post*, April 24.

Visher, Christy, Nancy La Vigne, and Jeremy Travis. 2004. Returning Home: Understanding the Challenges of Prisoner Reentry: Maryland Pilot Study: Findings from Baltimore. Washington, DC: The Urban Institute.

Western, Bruce, and Sarah McLanahan. 2000. "Fathers Behind Bars: The Impact of Incarceration on Family Formation." *Contemporary Perspectives in Family Research* 2: 307–22.

Western, Bruce, Leonard M. Lopoo, and Sarah McLanahan. 2004. "Incarceration and the Bonds Between Parents in Fragile Families." In *Imprisoning America: The Social Effects of Mass Incarceration*, edited by Mary Pattillo, David Weiman, and Bruce Western (21–45). New York: Russell Sage Foundation.

Women's Prison Association. 1996. *When a Mother Is Arrested: How the Criminal Justice and Child Welfare Systems Can Work Together More Effectively*. Baltimore: Maryland Department of Human Resources.

Unmarried with Children

Kathryn Edin and Maria Kefalas

Jen Burke, a white tenth-grade dropout who is 17 years old, lives with her stepmother, her sister, and her 16-month-old son in a cramped but tidy row home in Philadelphia's beleaguered Kensington neighborhood. She is broke, on welfare, and struggling to complete her GED. Wouldn't she and her son have been better off if she had finished high school, found a job, and married her son's father first?

In 1950, when Jen's grandmother came of age, only 1 in 20 American children was born to an unmarried mother. Today, that rate is 1 in 3—and they are usually born to those least likely to be able to support a child on their own. In our book, *Promises I Can Keep: Why Poor Women Put Motherhood Before Marriage*, we discuss the lives of 162 white, African American, and Puerto Rican low-income single mothers living in eight destitute neighborhoods across Philadelphia and its poorest industrial suburb, Camden. We spent five years chatting over kitchen tables and on front stoops, giving mothers like Jen the opportunity to speak to the question so many affluent Americans ask about them: Why do they have children while still young and unmarried when they will face such an uphill struggle to support them?

ROMANCE AT LIGHTNING SPEED

Jen started having sex with her 20-year-old boyfriend Rick just before her 15th birthday. A month and a half later, she was pregnant. "I didn't want to get pregnant," she claims. "He wanted me to get pregnant." "As soon as he met me, he wanted to have a kid with me," she explains. Though Jen's college-bound suburban peers would be appalled by such a declaration, on the streets of Jen's neighborhood, it is something of a badge of honor. "All those other girls he was with, he didn't want to have a baby with any of them," Jen boasts. "I asked him, 'Why did you choose me to have a kid when you could have a kid with any one of them?' He was like, 'I want to have a kid with you.'" Looking back, Jen says she now believes that the reason "he wanted me to have a kid that early is so that I didn't leave him."

In inner-city neighborhoods like Kensington, where child-bearing within marriage has become rare, romantic relationships like Jen and Rick's proceed at lightning speed. A young man's avowal, "I want to have a baby by you," is often part of the courtship ritual from the beginning. This is more than idle talk, as their first child is typically conceived within a year from the time a couple begins "kicking it." Yet while poor couples' pillow talk often revolves around dreams of shared children, the news of a pregnancy—the first indelible sign of the huge changes to come—puts these still-new relationships into overdrive. Suddenly, the would-be mother begins to scrutinize her mate as never before, wondering whether he can "get himself together"—find a job, settle down, and become a family man—in time. Jen began pestering Rick to get a real job instead of picking up day-labor jobs at nearby construction sites. She also wanted him to stop hanging out with his ne'er-do-well friends, who had been getting him into serious trouble for more than a decade. Most of all, she wanted Rick to shed what she calls his "kiddie mentality"—his habit of spending money on alcohol and drugs rather than recognizing his growing financial obligations at home.

Rick did not try to deny paternity, as many would-be fathers do. Nor did he abandon or mistreat Jen, at least intentionally. But Rick, who had been in and out of juvenile detention since he was 8 years old for everything from stealing cars to selling drugs, proved unable to stay away from his unsavory friends. At the beginning of her seventh month of pregnancy, an escapade that began as a drunken lark landed Rick in jail on a carjacking charge. Jen moved back home with her stepmother, applied for welfare, and spent the last two-and-a-half months of her pregnancy without Rick.

Rick sent penitent letters from jail. "I thought he changed by the letters he wrote me. I thought he changed a lot," she says. "He used to tell me that he loved me when he was in jail. . . . It was always gonna be me and the baby when he got out." Thus, when Rick's alleged victim failed to appear to testify and he was released just days before Colin's birth, the couple's reunion was a happy one. Often, the magic moment of childbirth calms the troubled waters of such relationships. New parents typically make amends and resolve to stay together for the sake of their child. When surveyed just after a child's birth, eight in ten unmarried parents say they are still together, and most plan to stay together and raise the child.

Promoting marriage among the poor has become the new war on poverty, Bush style. And it is true that the correlation between marital status and child poverty is strong. But poor single mothers already believe in marriage. Jen insists that she will walk down the aisle one day, though she admits it might not be with Rick. And demographers still project that more than seven in ten women who had a child outside of marriage will eventually wed someone. First, though, Jen wants to get a good job, finish school, and get her son out of Kensington.

Most poor, unmarried mothers and fathers readily admit that bearing children while poor and unmarried is not the ideal way to do things. Jen believes the best time to become a mother is "after you're out of school and you got a job, at least, when you're like 21. . . . When you're ready to have kids, you should have everything ready, have your house, have a job, so when that baby comes, the baby can have its own room." Yet given their already limited economic prospects, the poor have little motivation to time their births as precisely as their middle-class counterparts do. The dreams of young people like Jen and Rick center on children at a time of life when their more affluent peers plan for college and careers. Poor girls coming of age in the inner city value children highly, anticipate them eagerly, and believe strongly that they are up to the job of mothering—even in difficult circumstances. Jen, for example, tells us, "People outside the neighborhood, they're like, 'You're 15! You're pregnant?' I'm like, it's not none of their business. I'm gonna be able to take care of my kid. They have nothing to worry about." Jen says she has concluded that "some people . . . are better at having kids at a younger age. . . . I think it's better for some people to have kids younger."

WHEN I BECAME A MOM

When we asked mothers like Jen what their lives would be like if they had not had children, we expected them to express regret over foregone opportunities for school and careers. Instead, most believe their children "saved" them. They describe their lives as spinning out of control before becoming pregnant—struggles with parents and peers, "wild," risky behavior, depression, and school failure. Jen speaks to this poignantly. "I was just real bad. I hung with a real bad crowd. I was doing pills. I was really depressed. . . . I was drinking. That was before I was pregnant." "I think," she reflects, "if I never had a baby or anything, . . . I would still be doing the things I was doing. I would probably still be doing drugs. I'd probably still be drinking." Jen admits that when she first became pregnant, she was angry that she "couldn't be out no more. Couldn't be out with my friends. Couldn't do nothing." Now, though, she says, "I'm glad I have a son . . . because I would still be doing all that stuff."

Children offer poor youth like Jen a compelling sense of purpose. Jen paints a before-and-after picture of her life that was common among the mothers we interviewed. "Before, I didn't have nobody to take care of. I didn't have nothing left to go home for. . . . Now I have my son to take care of. I have him to go home for. . . . I don't have to go buy weed or drugs with my money. I could buy my son stuff with my money! . . . I have something to look up to now." Children also are a crucial source of relational intimacy, a self-made community of care. After a nasty fight with Rick, Jen recalls, "I was crying. My son came in the room. He was hugging me. He's 16 months and he was hugging me with his little arms. He was really cute and happy, so I got happy. That's one of the good things. When you're sad, the baby's always gonna be there for you no matter what." Lately she has been thinking a lot about what her life was like back then, before the baby. "I thought about the stuff before I became a mom, what my life was like back then. I used to see pictures of me, and I would hide in every picture. This baby did so much for me. My son did a lot for me. He helped me a lot. I'm thankful that I had my baby."

Around the time of the birth, most unmarried parents claim they plan to get married eventually. Rick did not propose marriage when Jen's first child was born, but when she conceived a second time, at 17, Rick informed his dad, "It's time for me to get married. It's time for me to straighten up. This is the one I wanna be with. I had a baby with her, I'm gonna have another baby with her." Yet despite their intentions, few of these couples actually marry. Indeed, most break up well before their child enters preschool.

I'D LIKE TO GET MARRIED, BUT . . .

The sharp decline in marriage in impoverished urban areas has led some to charge that the poor have abandoned the marriage norm. Yet we found few who had given up on the idea of marriage. But like their elite counterparts, disadvantaged women set a high financial bar for marriage. For the poor, marriage has become an elusive goal—one they feel ought to be reserved for those who can support a "white picket fence" lifestyle: a mortgage on a modest row home, a car and some furniture, some savings in the bank, and enough money left over to pay for a "decent" wedding. Jen's views on marriage provide a perfect case in point. "If I was gonna get married, I would want to be married like my Aunt Nancy and my Uncle Pat. They live in the mountains. She has a job. My Uncle Pat is a state trooper; he has lots of money. They live in the [Poconos]. It's real nice out there. Her kids go to Catholic school. . . . That's the kind of life I would want to have. If I get married, I would have a life like [theirs]." She adds, "And I would wanna have a big wedding, a real nice wedding."

Unlike the women of their mothers' and grandmothers' generations, young women like Jen are not merely content to rely on a man's earnings. Instead, they insist on being economically "set" in their own right before taking marriage vows. This is partly because they want a partnership of equals and they believe money buys say-so in a relationship. Jen explains, "I'm not gonna just get into marrying him and not have my own house! Not have a job! I still wanna do a lot of things before I get married. He [already] tells me I can't do nothing. I can't go out. What's gonna happen when I marry him? He's gonna say he owns me!"

Economic independence is also insurance against a marriage gone bad. Jen explains, "I want to have everything ready, in case something goes wrong. . . . If we got a divorce, that would be my house. I bought that house, he can't kick me out or he can't take my kids from me." "That's what I want in case that ever happens. I know a lot of people that happened to. I don't want it to happen to me." These statements reveal that despite her desire to marry, Rick's role in the family's future is provisional at best. "We get along, but we fight a lot. If he's there, he's there, but if he's not, that's why I want a job . . . a job with computers . . . so I could afford my kids, could afford the house. . . . I don't want to be living off him. I want my kids to be living off me."

Why is Jen, who describes Rick as "the love of my life," so insistent on planning an exit strategy before she is willing to take the vows she firmly believes ought to last "forever?" If love is so sure, why does mistrust seem so palpable and strong? In relationships among poor couples like Jen and Rick, mistrust is often spawned by chronic violence and infidelity, drug and alcohol abuse, criminal activity, and the threat of imprisonment. In these tarnished corners of urban America, the stigma of a failed marriage is far worse than an out-of-wedlock birth. New mothers like Jen feel they must test the relationship over three, four, even five years' time. This is the only way, they believe, to insure that their marriages will last.

Trust has been an enormous issue in Jen's relationship with Rick. "My son was born December 23rd, and [Rick] started cheating on me again . . . in March. He started cheating on me with some girl—Amanda. . . . Then it was another girl, another girl, another girl after. I didn't wanna believe it. My friends would come up to me and be like, 'Oh yeah, your boyfriend's cheating on you with this person.' I wouldn't believe it. . . . I would see him with them. He used to have hickies. He used to make up some excuse that he was drunk—that was always his excuse for everything." Things finally came to a head when Rick got another girl pregnant. "For a while, I forgave him for everything. Now, I don't forgive him for nothing." Now we begin to understand the source of Jen's hesitancy. "He wants me to marry him, [but] I'm not really sure. . . . If I can't trust him, I can't marry him, 'cause we would get a divorce. If you're gonna get married, you're supposed to be faithful!" she insists. To Jen and her peers, the worst thing that could happen is "to get married just to get divorced."

Given the economic challenges and often perilously low quality of the romantic relationships among unmarried parents, poor women may be right to be cautious about marriage. Five years after we first spoke with her, we met with Jen again. We learned that Jen's second pregnancy ended in a miscarriage. We also learned that Rick was out of the picture—apparently for good. "You know that bar [down the street] It happened in that bar. . . . They were in the bar, and this guy was like badmouthing [Rick's friend] Mikey, talking stuff to him or whatever. So Rick had to go get involved in it and start with this guy. . . . Then he goes outside and fights the guy [and] the guy dies of head trauma. They were all on drugs, they were all drinking, and things just got out of control, and that's what happened. He got fourteen to thirty years."

THESE ARE CARDS I DEALT MYSELF

Jen stuck with Rick for the first two and a half years of his prison sentence, but when another girl's name replaced her own on the visitors' list, Jen decided she was finished with him once and for all. Readers might be asking what Jen ever saw in a man like Rick. But Jen and Rick operate in a partner market where the better-off men go to the better-off women. The only way for someone like Jen to forge a satisfying relationship with a man is to find a diamond in the rough or improve her own economic position so that she can realistically compete for more upwardly mobile partners, which is what Jen is trying to do now. "There's this kid, Donny, he works at my job. He works on C shift. He's a supervisor! He's funny, three years older, and he's not a geek or anything, but he's not a real preppy good boy either. But he's not [a player like Rick] and them. He has a job, you know, so that's good. He doesn't do drugs or anything. And he asked my dad if he could take me out!"

These days, there is a new air of determination, even pride, about Jen. The aimless high school dropout pulls ten-hour shifts entering data at a warehouse distribution center Monday through Thursday. She has held the job for three years, and her aptitude and hard work have earned her a series of raises. Her current salary is higher than anyone in her household commands—$10.25 per hour, and she now gets two weeks of paid vacation, four personal days, 60 hours of sick time, and medical benefits. She has saved up the necessary $400 in tuition for a high school completion program that offers evening and weekend classes. Now all that stands between her and a diploma is a passing grade in mathematics, her least favorite subject. "My plan is to start college in January. [This month] I take my math test . . . so I can get my diploma," she confides.

Jen clearly sees how her life has improved since Rick's dramatic exit from the scene. "That's when I really started [to get better] because I didn't have to worry about what he was doing, didn't have to worry about him cheating on me, all this stuff. [It was] then I realized that I had to do what I had to do to take care of my son. . . . When he was there, I think that my whole life revolved around him, you know, so I always messed up somehow because I was so busy worrying about what he was doing. Like I would leave the [GED] programs I was in just to go home and see what he was doing. My mind was never concentrating." Now, she says, "a lot of people in my family look up to me now, because all my sisters dropped out from school, you know, nobody went back to school. I went back to school, you know? . . . I went back to school, and I plan to go to college, and a lot of people look up to me for that, you know? So that makes me happy . . . because five years ago nobody looked up to me. I was just like everybody else."

Yet the journey has not been easy. "Being a young mom, being 15, it's hard, hard, hard, you know." She says, "I have no life. . . . I work from 6:30 in the morning until 5:00 at night. I leave here at 5:30 in the morning. I don't get home until about 6:00 at night." Yet she measures her worth as a mother by the fact that she has managed to provide for her son largely on her own. "I don't depend on nobody. I might live with my dad and them, but I don't depend on them, you know." She continues, "There [used to] be days when I'd be so stressed out, like, 'I can't do this!' And I would just cry and cry and cry. . . . Then I look at Colin, and he'll be sleeping, and I'll just look at him and think I don't have no [reason to feel sorry for myself]. The cards I have I've dealt myself so I have to deal with it now. I'm older. I can't change anything. He's my responsibility—he's nobody else's but mine—so I have to deal with that."

Becoming a mother transformed Jen's point of view on just about everything. She says, "I thought hanging on the corner drinking, getting high—I thought that was a good life, and I thought I could live that way for eternity, like sitting out with my friends. But it's not as fun once you have your own kid. . . . I think it changes [you]. I think, 'Would I want Colin to do that? Would I want my son to be like that . . .?' It was fun to me but it's not fun anymore. Half the people I hung with are either . . . Some have died from drug overdoses, some are in jail, and some people are just out there living the same life that they always lived, and they don't look really good. They look really bad." In the end, Jen believes, Colin's birth has brought far more good into her life than bad. "I know I could have waited [to have a child], but in a way I think Colin's the best thing that could have happened to me. . . . So I think I had my son for a purpose because I think Colin changed my life. He saved my life, really. My whole life revolves around Colin!"

PROMISES I CAN KEEP

There are unique themes in Jen's story—most fathers are only one or two, not five years older than the mothers of their children, and few fathers have as many glaring problems as Rick—but we heard most of these themes repeatedly in the stories of the 161 other poor, single mothers we came to know. Notably, poor women do not reject marriage; they revere it. Indeed, it is the conviction that marriage is forever that makes them think that divorce is worse than having a baby outside of marriage. Their children, far from being liabilities, provide crucial social-psychological resources—a strong sense of purpose and a profound source of intimacy. Jen and the other mothers we came to know are coming of age in an America that is profoundly unequal—where the gap between rich and poor continues to grow. This economic reality has convinced them that they have little to lose and, perhaps, something to gain by a seemingly "ill-timed" birth.

The lesson one draws from stories like Jen's is quite simple: Until poor young women have more access to jobs that lead to financial independence—until there is reason to hope for the rewarding life pathways that their privileged peers pursue—the poor will continue to have children far sooner than most Americans think they should, while still deferring marriage. Marital standards have risen for all Americans, and the poor want the same things that everyone now wants out of marriage. The poor want to marry too, but they insist on marrying well. This, in their view, is the only way to avoid an almost certain divorce. Like Jen, they are simply not willing to make promises they are not sure they can keep.

Recommended Resources

Kathryn Edin and Maria Kefalas. *Promises I Can Keep: Why Poor Women Put Motherhood Before Marriage* (University of California Press, 2005). An account of how low-income women make sense of their choices about marriage and motherhood.

Christina Gibson, Kathryn Edin, and Sara McLanahan. "High Hopes but Even Higher Expectations: A Qualitative and Quantitative Analysis of the Marriage Plans of Unmarried Couples Who Are New Parents." Working Paper 03-06-FF, Center for Research on Child Wellbeing, Princeton University, 2004. Online at http://crcw.princeton.edu/workingpapers/WP03-06-FF-Gibson.pdf. The authors examine the rising expectations for marriage among unmarried parents.

Sharon Hays. *Flat Broke with Children: Women in the Age of Welfare Reform* (Oxford University Press, 2003). How welfare reform has affected the lives of poor moms.

Annette Lareau. *Unequal Childhoods: Class, Race, and Family Life* (University of California Press, 2003). A fascinating discussion of different childrearing strategies among low-income, working-class, and middle-class parents.

Timothy J. Nelson, Susan Clampet-Lundquist, and Kathryn Edin. "Fragile Fatherhood: How Low-Income, Non-Custodial Fathers in Philadelphia Talk About Their Families." In *The Handbook of Father Involvement: Multidisciplinary Perspectives*, ed. Catherine Tamis-LeMonda and Natasha Cabrera (Lawrence Earlbaum Associates, 2002). What poor, single men think about fatherhood.

■ **READING 31**

Violence Against Women or Family Violence? Current Debates and Future Directions

Demie Kurz

In recent years, due to the efforts of the battered women's movement and other reformers, much more public attention has been focused on the physical abuse of women at the hands of male partners (Dobash and Dobash 1992). The problems of "woman abuse" or "wife abuse" are now recognized as widespread and as having serious consequences. Advocates for battered women in many professions and organizations have worked to make legal, medical, and social service agencies more responsive to battered women (American Medical Association 1992; Dobash and Dobash 1992; Jones 1994; Koss 1990; Novello et al. 1992).

Despite increased recognition of the problem of male violence toward women, however, much of the research on violence in intimate relationships focuses not on woman abuse, but on "spouse abuse" or "partner abuse." Many researchers have argued that we should focus our attention on "family violence," and that adult family members are equally violent toward each other (Straus 1993). Thus, those who are interested in researching the question of wife abuse find instead data on "spouse abuse," which claims that men are victims of violence equally with women (Kurz 1993).

What lies behind this confusing discrepancy between the widely perceived view that women are the targets of violence at the hands of male partners, and the view held by some researchers that violence against women is really a "family violence" problem? It is not often recognized that differences in language reflect two sharply different views among researchers concerning the nature of violence in intimate relationships, particularly the question of whether women are violent toward men. In this chapter [reading] I will examine these two different perspectives on the issue of violence against women.

One group of social scientists adopts what has been called the "violence against women" perspective (Dobash and Dobash 1992) and argues that women are the victims of violence in relationships with men (Daly and Wilson 1988; Ellis and DeKeseredy 1996; Dobash and Dobash 1992; Kurz 1995; Loseke 1992; Saunders 1988; Stanko 1987; Yllö and Bograd 1988; Yllö 1993). Among these researchers, those who identify with the feminist tradition claim that, historically, the law has promoted women's subordination and condoned husbands' use of force in marriage. The other group of social scientists are the "family violence" researchers (Brinkerhoff and Lupri 1988; Gelles 1993; Gelles and Cornell 1985; Gelles and Straus 1988; McNeely and Mann 1990; McNeely and Robinson-Stimpson 1987; Shupe, Stacey, and Hazelwood 1987; Stets 1990; Straus 1993; Straus and Gelles 1990), who argue that the real problem is "spouse abuse" and "family violence." These researchers believe that women, as well as men, are violent, and some claim that women "initiate and carry out physical assaults on their partner as often as men" (Straus 1993, 67).

This debate over men's and women's use of violence has significant consequences for popular and academic conceptions of battered women, as well as for social policy. How a problem is framed determines the amount of concern that is generated and the solutions that are proposed for that problem. Research findings influence whether the media and the public take battered women seriously, or whether they view them as equally blameworthy partners in "family violence." Violence-against women researchers fear that framing the problem as "spouse abuse" will lead to decreased funding for shelters, a diversion of resources to "battered men," and increased arrest of women in "domestic disputes" under mandatory arrest policies. More generally, violence-against-women researchers fear that the discourse of "spouse abuse" obscures the cause of violence against women—inequality and male dominance.

I argue that the violence against women point of view best explains the nature and the extent of violence between men and women in intimate relationships. Violence-against-women researchers argue that violence between intimates takes place within a context of inequality between men and women in marriage, while family violence proponents promote a gender-neutral view of power in intimate relationships. I will compare the evidence and theories presented by the proponents of each perspective, and I will argue that the family violence view is based on false assumptions about the nature of marriage and of equality between men and women.

A VIOLENCE AGAINST WOMEN PERSPECTIVE

Researchers who take a violence against women perspective argue that overwhelmingly it is women, not men, who are the victims of violence. They support their point of view with official crime statistics, data from the criminal justice system and hospitals, interviews with victims of battering and batterers, and historical evidence. As Dobash and Dobash (1992, 265) note, data from victimization surveys, court statistics, and police files in North America and Canada indicate that women are the victims of male violence in 90 to 95 percent of assaults within a family context. A number of researchers have examined National Crime Survey data and found that wives were the victims of violence at the hands of their husbands in the overwhelming majority of cases. In his analysis of National Crime Survey data, Schwartz (1987) found that only 4 percent of men claimed to be victims of violence at the hands of their wives. In the remaining 96 percent of cases, wives claimed to be the victims of violence at the hands of their husbands. Other researchers who have analyzed National Crime Survey data have reported similar findings (McLeod 1984; Gaquin 1977/78). In their study of police records in Scotland, Dobash and Dobash (1979) found that when gender was known, women were targets in 94 percent and offenders in 3 percent of cases. Other studies based on data from the criminal justice system show similar results (Kincaid 1982; Quarm and Schwartz 1985).

Data on injury patterns confirm that it is women, not men, who sustain injuries in conflicts between males and females in intimate relationships. Brush (1990), in an analysis of NSFH (National Survey of Families and Households) data, found that women were significantly more likely to be injured than men in disputes involving violent tactics. Berk and his colleagues (1983), based on their examination of police records, concluded that in 95 percent of cases it is the woman who is injured and that, even when both partners are injured, the woman's injuries are nearly three times as severe as the man's. Data from hospitals (JAMA 1990; Kurz 1990; McLeer and Anwar 1989; Stark and Flitcraft 1996) show women to be overwhelmingly the injured party. These data lead violence-against-women researchers to reject the concept of "spouse abuse," the idea that women are equally as violent as men.

Data from divorcing couples also provide evidence that women are more frequently the targets of violence than men. In their study of 362 separating husbands and wives, Ellis and Stuckless (1993) report that more than 40 percent of separating wives and 17 percent of separating husbands state that they were injured by their partners at some time during the relationship. In a random sample of divorced women with children from Philadelphia County, Kurz (1995) found that 70 percent of women reported experiencing violence at least once during their marriage, 54 percent two to three times, and 37 percent more than two to three times, findings similar to those found in other studies (Fields 1978; Parker and Schumacher 1977).

Researchers have also reported high rates of abuse after separation. Indeed, most surveys of post-separation abuse report more violence after separation than during relationships (Wilson and Daly 1993). Further, during separation women are not only at greater risk of injury, they are also at greater risk of death. Data gathered in Canada; New South Wales, Australia; and Chicago demonstrate that women are much more likely to be killed by their husbands after separating from them than when they are still living with them (Wilson and Daly 1993). These wives are at significantly high risk within the first two months of leaving a relationship (Wilson and Daly 1993; Schwartz 1987). Data indicate that separated and divorced women are also at increased risk of rape (Bowker 1981; Solicitor General of Canada 1985; U.S. Department of Justice 1987).

Researchers who take a violence against women perspective claim that the use of violence by men to control female intimates has long been condoned by major social institutions. The first law in the United States to recognize a husband's right to control his wife with physical force was an 1824 ruling by the Supreme Court of Mississippi permitting the husband "to exercise the right of moderate chastisement in cases of great emergency" (quoted in Browne 1987, 166). This and similar rulings in Maryland and Massachusetts were based on English common law, which gave a husband the right of "correction" of his wife, although he was supposed to use it in moderation.

> In 1871 wife beating was made illegal in Alabama. The court stated: The privilege, ancient though it be, to beat her with a stick, to pull her hair, choke her, spit in her face or kick her about the floor, or to inflict upon her like indignities, is not now acknowledged by our law. . . . [T]he wife is entitled to the same protection of the law that the husband can invoke for himself. (Quoted in Browne 1987, 167)

A North Carolina court made a similar decision in 1874, but limited the kinds of cases in which the court should intervene:

> If no permanent injury has been inflicted, nor malice, cruelty nor dangerous violence shown by the husband, it is better to draw the curtain, shut out the public gaze, and leave the parties to forget and forgive. (Quoted in Browne 1987, 167)

Until recent legal reforms were enacted, the "curtain rule" was widely used by the legal system to justify its nonintervention in wife-abuse cases.

The law and the nature of marriage have changed dramatically since the early twentieth century; however, violence-against-women researchers claim that these institutions continue to condone violence against women. New laws have criminalized battering, but we do not know whether these laws will be enforced (Buzawa and Buzawa 1996; Kurz 1992). One study suggests that even police who receive training in how to respond to battering cases as crimes may continue to view battered women as unfortunate victims of personal and social problems such as poverty and, in the absence of strong police department support, view arrests as low priority and not part of their "real" work (Ferraro 1989). To the extent that these laws are not taken seriously, the legal system will continue to treat battering as an individual problem rather than as criminal behavior.

As for marriage, violence-against-women researchers, particularly those who are feminists, argue that it still institutionalizes the control of wives by husbands through the structure of husband-wife roles. As long as women are responsible for domestic work, child care, and emotional and psychological support, and men's primary identity is that of provider and revolves around employment, the husband has the more important status and also controls the majority of decisions in the family (Kurz 1995). It is through such a system, coupled with the acceptance of physical force as a means of control, that, in the words of the Dobashes (1979), the wife becomes an "appropriate victim" of physical and psychological abuse. Feminists argue further that the use of violence for control in marriage is perpetuated not only through norms about a man's rights in marriage, but also through women's continued economic dependence on their husbands, which makes it difficult to leave a violent relationship. This dependence is increased by the lack of adequate child care and job training, which would enable women to get jobs with which they could support themselves.

Citing interview data from men and women that demonstrate that battering incidents occur when husbands try to make their wives comply with their wishes, violence-against-women researchers believe that men still use violence as a way to control female partners. Based on data from interviews with 109 battered women, Dobash and Dobash (1979) demonstrate how batterers, over the course of their marriages, increasingly control wives through intimidation and isolation, findings confirmed by other interview studies (Kurz 1995; Pagelow 1981; Walker 1984). Violence, therefore, is just one of a variety of controls that men try to exercise over female partners; others are anger and psychological abuse (Dobash and Dobash 1992; Mederos 1987; Yllö 1993). Interviews with batterers (Adams 1988; Dobash and Dobash 1979; Ptacek 1988) show that men believe they are justified in their use of violence, particularly when their wives do not conform to the ideal of "good wife."

Finally, violence-against-women researchers demonstrate that a variety of institutions, in addition to the law and the family, condone male dominance and reinforce battering on an ongoing, everyday basis. Some have demonstrated how this occurs through the labeling and processing of abused women by front-line workers who have the most contact with these women. Stark and Flitcraft (1996) have argued that due to patriarchal medical ideologies and practices, health care practitioners have failed to recognize battering and instead label battered women as having psychological or psychosomatic problems. These researchers claim that the actions of health care workers serve to perpetuate battering relationships and argue that the medical system duplicates and reinforces the patriarchal structure of the family. Kurz (1990) has documented how individual staff in emergency rooms come to define battered women not as "true medical cases," but as "social" ones, and feel they make extra work and trouble for medical practitioners. Battered women who do not look like "typical victims" are frequently not recognized as battered and are sent back home, without any recognition of or attention to their battering.

Other studies address the issue of how violence against women is taught and reinforced in institutions such as the military (Russell 1989) and sports (Messner 1989). Sanday (1990) and others (Martin and Hummer, 1989) have studied the ways in which fraternity practices and rituals, in promoting loyalty to a brotherhood of men, legitimate gang rape and other types of violence against women. Kanin (1984) suggests that the college date rapists he studied came from a more highly sexualized subculture than men who did not commit date rape.

THE FAMILY VIOLENCE PERSPECTIVE AND ITS CRITICS

In stark contrast to violence-against-women researchers, family-violence researchers focus on what they see as the problem of "spouse abuse" on women's as well as men's use of violence. They claim that women as well as men are perpetrators of physical violence (McNeeley and Mann 1990; McNeely and Robinson-Simpson 1987; Steinmetz and Lucca 1988), and some claim that women are as violent within the family as men (Shupe, Stacey, and Hazelwood 1987; Stets and Straus 1990; Straus 1993; Straus and Gelles 1986). In this section, I argue that when researchers claim that women are as violent as men, they do so on the basis of faulty data and assumptions about gender and the family.

Family-violence researchers typically base their claims about women's use of violence on data collected using the Conflict Tactics Scales (CTS) (Straus 1979), instruments that require respondents to identify conflict tactics they have used in the previous year. These range from nonviolent tactics (calm discussion) to the most violent tactics (use of a knife or gun). Using this scale, family-violence researchers (Straus 1993; Straus and Gelles 1986; Straus et al. 1980) find similar percentages of husbands and wives using violent tactics. On the basis of these data, some family-violence researchers conclude that "husband battering" is a serious problem and even that there is a "battered husband syndrome" (Stemmetz and Lucca 1988; Steinmetz 1977/78, 1988). Findings based on the CTS have been replicated by a number of researchers here and abroad (Brinkerhoff and Lupri 1988; Nisonoff and Bitman 1979; Stets 1990), including for dating relationships (Arias et al. 1987; DeMaris 1987; Lane and Gwartney-Gibbs 1985).

Findings from the 1985 National Family Violence Survey (NFVS), based on women's responses to the Conflict Tactics Scales, show that both wife and husband were violent in 48.6 percent of cases, the husband only was violent in 25.9 percent of cases, and the wife only was violent in 25.5 percent of cases (Straus 1993). Straus concludes from these data that "regardless of whether the analysis is based on all assaults, or is focused on dangerous assaults, about as many women as men attacked a spouse who had *not* hit them during the one year referent period." Citing other studies that show the same results, he concludes that these figures are "inconsistent with the 'self-defense' explanation for the high rate of domestic assault by women" (1993, 74).

Violence-against-women researchers (Berk et al. 1983; Dobash et al. 1992; Saunders 1989; Stark and Flitcraft 1996; Yllö 1993) argue that the data showing that women are as violent as men, particularly data based on the Conflict Tactics Scales, are misleading and flawed. These researchers believe that the validity of the scales is undermined because the continuum of violence in the scales is so broad that it fails to discriminate among different kinds of violence (Dobash and Dobash 1979, 1992; Stark and Flitcraft 1985). For example, the CTS contains an item "bit, kicked, or hit with a fist." Thus, a woman who bites is equated with a man who kicks or hits with a fist. Another item, "hit or tried to hit with an object," which is counted as severe violence, is similarly ambiguous. Further, critics argue, the scale does not take self-defense into account.

In support of their position, violence-against-women researchers also point to the findings of studies in which women were asked about their use of violence. For example, Saunders (1988) found that in the vast majority of cases, women attributed their use of violent tactics to self-defense and fighting back. Emery et al. (1989), in an interview study based on a small sample of women who were victims of dating violence, found that most women spoke of self-defense. Some women also spoke of using violence in frustration and anger at being dominated by their partners and in retaliation for their partners' violent behavior.

Further, violence-against-women researchers point out that the CTS focuses narrowly on counting acts of violence. Such as focus draws attention away from related patterns of control and abuse in relationships, including psychological abuse and sexual abuse, and does not address other means of nonviolent intimidation and domination including verbal abuse, the use of suicide threats, or the use of violence against property, pets, children, or other relatives. Similarly, the conception of violence as a "conflict tactic" fails to convey the connection between the use of violence and the exercise of power. Yllö (1993, 53) argues that violence is better conceptualized as a "tactic of coercive control to maintain the husband's power."

In addition to their view that women commit as many violent acts as men, family-violence researchers claim that women initiate violence as frequently as men. They draw this conclusion on the basis of responses to a question in the National Family Violence Survey about who initiated conflicts in the relationship. The NFVS, based on the CTS, found that in the case of wives who were involved in "violent relationships," 53 percent reported that they hit first, while their partners initiated the violence in 42 percent of cases (Straus 1993, 74). These findings have led family-violence researchers to a new focus on women's use of violence (Straus 1993). Even though husbands use more serious types of violence, these researchers now claim that violence by women against their husbands must be considered a serious problem.

Let us briefly examine the logic of the family-violence position that women initiate violence as often as men. Straus (1993, 79) turns our attention to occasions when a woman slaps a man. He refers to a "typical case" in which a woman uses acts of violence because a man who is acting like a "cad" has done something offensive to her. "Let us assume that most of the assaults by women are the 'slap the cad' genre and are not intended to, and only rarely cause physical injury." He then focuses on the woman's "assaults" and goes on to argue that a woman who "slaps the cad" is in effect provoking her partner by providing him with a justification for hitting:

> Such morally correct slapping acts out and reinforces the traditional tolerance of assault in marriage. The moral justification of assault implicit when a woman slaps or throws something at a partner for something outrageous reinforces the moral justification for slapping her when *she* is doing something outrageous, being obstinate, nasty, or "not listening to reason" as he sees it.

After claiming that assaults by wives are one of the "causes" of assaults by husbands, he concludes with a stern warning that all women must forsake violence:

> One of the many steps needed for primary prevention of assaults on wives is for women to forsake even "harmless" physical attacks on male partners and children. Women must insist on non-violence by their sisters, just as they rightfully insist on it by men.

In a few sentences, Straus proceeds from women's defensive behavior to a focus on women as provoking the violence. What is wrong with this logic? Although eliminating violence should be a high-priority goal for all men, women, and children, this reframing of the issue puts the blame and responsibility for the violence on the woman. Targeting women's behavior removes the focus from what men might be doing to women. What does it mean that he is acting like a "cad"? Does this refer to unwanted sexual advances, the belittling of a woman, verbal intimidation, drunken frenzy? Who is responsible here? Focusing on the woman's behavior provides support for typical excuses and justifications by batterers, such as "she provoked me to do this" (Ptacek 1988).

Another problem with asking a single question about who initiated the violence is that it does not focus on the meaning and context of female violence against male partners. For example, there were no questions asked about women's motives for striking first. We know that male physical and sexual violence against women is often preceded by name-calling and other types of psychological abuse (Browne 1987), and that women may view these behaviors as early warning signs of violence and hit first in hopes of preventing their partners from using violence (Saunders 1989). Hanmer and Saunders (1984) have noted that many women hit first because of a "well-founded fear" of being beaten or raped by their husbands or male intimates. Thus, even when women do initiate violence, it may very well be an act of self-defense.

In my view, there are many reasons why it would be better if we all could be nonviolent—it may well be true that violence provokes more violence. However, we must understand the power dynamics behind the use of violence in particular types of relationships; we must examine who feels entitled to use violence and why. The violence against women perspective addresses these critical questions about the context of violence.

A brief examination of the theoretical perspective of family-violence researchers shows the faulty assumptions that guide their interpretation of the data. As one would expect from their findings, as well as their use of the terms "family violence" and "spouse abuse," family-violence researchers take a family systems approach to analyzing husbands' and wives' use of violence. They believe that the origins of the problem of violence lie in the nature of the family, not in the relationship between husband and wife (Gelles and Straus 1988; Straus 1993), and that violence affects all family relationships. According to Straus, Gelles, and Steinmetz (1980, 44):

> A fundamental solution to the problem of wife-beating has to go beyond a concern with how to control assaulting husbands. It seems as if violence is built into the very structure of the society and family system itself. . . . (Wife-beating) is only one aspect of the general pattern of family violence, which includes parent-child violence, child-to-child violence, and wife-to-husband violence.

Family-violence researchers (Gelles and Cornell 1985; Gelles and Straus 1988) believe that violence in the contemporary American family is caused by a variety of social-structural factors, including stresses from difficult working conditions, unemployment, financial insecurity, and health problems. They also believe that husbands and wives are affected by wider social norms condoning violence as a means of solving conflict, and they see evidence of the cultural acceptance of violence in television programming, folklore, and fairy tales (Straus 1980), and in surveys showing widespread public acceptance of violence. Straus and his colleagues also cite sexism as a factor in family violence; while

they believe men and women are equally violent, they believe women are more victimized by family violence because of "the greater physical, financial, and emotional injury
suffered by women" (Straus 1993).

Proponents of the family violence perspective make some important points about
the prevalence of violence in American society; however, from a violence against women
perspective, the family violence view is seriously flawed. Although cultural norms of
violence and stressful living conditions may influence individuals' use of violence, these
wider cultural norms and social conditions are mediated by the norms of particular institutions. In the case of marriage, norms promoting male dominance in heterosexual
relationships and males' right to use force have a direct influence on how people behave
in marriage.

Family-violence researchers do acknowledge male dominance when they argue
that sexism is an important factor in domestic violence and that women are the ones who
are most seriously hurt in battering relationships. However, from the perspective of a
violence-against-women researcher, sexism is not just "a" factor in domestic violence.
Rather, gender is one of the fundamental organizing principles of society. It is a social
relation that enters into and partially constitutes all other social relations and activities,
and pervades the entire social context in which a person lives. Thus, violence-against-
women researchers criticize family-violence researchers for equating "spouse abuse,"
elder abuse, and child abuse, because women become just one of a number of victims.
Violence-against-women researchers believe that wife abuse should be compared to related types of violence against women such as rape, marital rape, sexual harassment, and
incest (Wardell et al. 1983), all of which are also products of male dominance.

Violence-against-women researchers believe that family-violence researchers disregard the influence of gender on marriage and heterosexual relationships and see power
in the family as a gender-neutral phenomenon. Family-violence researchers claim that
"violence is used by the most powerful family member as a means of legitimizing his or
her dominant position" (Straus et al. 1980, 193) and believe that power can as easily be
held by a wife as by a husband. According to violence-against-women researchers, this
view of the exercise of power as gender-neutral misrepresents the nature of marriage
as a partnership of equals. As discussed above, marriage has been and still is structured
so that husbands have more power than wives. Men are the primary wage earners and
women, as those responsible for childrearing and household work, do not typically have
the same bargaining power as their husbands. Thus power is not gender-neutral; it is
structured into the institution of marriage in such a way that women are disadvantaged.

The basic assumptions of the family violence and violence against women approaches to domestic violence are irreconcilable. Further, each group has voiced strong
disagreements with the other. Family-violence researchers argue that the legitimate sociological approach to the issue of violence in the family should be a "multicausal" one
and believe that violence against women perspectives, particularly those identified as
feminist, are biased by a single-minded focus on gender (Straus 1991). Further, family-
violence researchers criticize feminist work as "political" (Gelles 1983; Straus 1991) and
charge that they have been harrassed for studying violent women (Gelles and Straus
1988, 106; Straus 1991). They believe that findings about women's violence have been
"suppressed" because they are not "politically correct" (Straus 1993). Such statements

posit a conspiracy of feminists to keep the "truth" from being known, rather than an understanding that different theories and methods lead to different conclusions.

Violence-against-women researchers fear that the family-violence approach will reinforce existing popular conceptions that women cause their own victimization by provoking their male partners. They fear that such views will lead to policy outcomes that are harmful to women. Family-violence researchers acknowledge that their research has been used to provide testimony against battered women in court cases and to minimize the need for shelters (Straus and Gelles 1986, 471; Gelles and Straus 1988, 90); however, they argue that this is less "costly" than the "denial and suppression" of violence by women (Straus and Gelles 1986, 471). The question is, costly for whom?

Further, these researchers are concerned that if funders come to believe that family violence is a "mutual" occurrence between "spouses," or that there is a "battered husband syndrome," there will be decreased support for shelters for battered women. Violence-against-women researchers also fear a diversion of resources to shelters for "battered men." Straus's work has been cited to provide evidence that women assault men (Lewin 1992, 12). Men's rights groups cite the "battered husband syndrome" when lobbying for custody and child support issues from a men's rights perspective (Ansberry 1988; Fathers for Equal Rights Organization 1988; McNeely and Robinson-Simpson 1987).

Violence-against-women researchers also fear that the family-violence perspective will reinforce the individualist bias in the field of counseling—that counselors will focus on clients' individual and personal problems without identifying the inequality between men and women that provides the context for battering (Adams 1988). They disagree with those family-violence researchers who argue that violence is caused primarily by frustration, poor social skills, or inability to control anger (Hotaling, Straus, and Lincoln 1990; Shupe, Stacey, and Hazelwood 1987; Steinmetz 1986). Finally, violence-against-women researchers worry that a belief in "spouse abuse" or a "battered husband syndrome" will encourage police who operate under mandatory arrest statutes to arrest women in "domestic disputes."

CONCLUSION

In this chapter I have argued that research that promotes a gender-neutral view of "family violence" misrepresents the nature of violence against women. Women are typically the victims, not the perpetrators, of violence in intimate relationships. A violence against women perspective much more accurately explains the nature of violence in intimate relationships. It is norms and practices of male dominance that promote the use of violence by men toward female intimates. The proponents of the family violence perspective, in arguing that women are violent toward men, disregard gender and its determining role in structuring marital and other heterosexual relationships. Existing data on the use of conflict tactics and acts of violence must be interpreted in the context of power differences in male-female relationships. Abstracted from their context, data on who initiates and uses violence promote faulty conclusions. Fortunately, some have begun to develop new ways of measuring the use of violence and control that take into account how gender shapes the exercise of power in heterosexual relationships (Yllö 1990).

One important direction for future research is to demonstrate how male dominance produces male violence against women on an ongoing, everyday basis (Hood 1989). One way to do this is to devote greater attention to the study of the major institutions in which males learn violence, such as the military (Russell 1989), sports (Messner 1992), and fraternities (Martin and Hummer 1993; Sanday 1991). Another is to investigate how major institutions, through their ideologies and practices, define the abuse of women by male intimates and respond to women who have experienced abuse. Researchers should focus both on institution wide policies and practices and on the labeling and processing of abused women by front-line workers who have the most contact with abused women. In studying the institutional response to violence, it would be profitable to compare responses to the range of violence against women, including rape, marital rape, sexual harassment, and incest (Stanko 1985; Wardell et al. 1983).

One institution that is central in the labeling and processing of woman battering is the legal system. Traditionally, the legal system has defined woman battering as a private, family matter and has been instrumental in enforcing its privatization. Although new laws have criminalized woman battering, the critical question is whether these laws will be enforced. If these laws are not taken seriously, the legal system will continue to treat the problem of woman battering as an individual one and return battered women to the private sphere.

Another institution that is key in the identification of abuse is the health care system. We must analyze how current medical ideologies (Stark and Flitcraft 1996) and practices (Kurz 1990) ignore the problem of battering, or redefine it as a problem caused by women's own individual problems and therefore outside the purview of the health care system. We must also analyze how medical language and discourse render the problem of battering invisible. In a study of the medical records of women who had been physically abused, Warshaw (1993) found that physicians, through their use of disembodied language that focused on injuries caused by nameless forces, obscured the fact that women had been abused. Lamb (1991, 1995) found that when newspaper writers and even scholars write about physical abuse, they use vague language that fails to specify who is responsible for the abuse.

We need a major reexamination of those norms of male-female intimates and family relationships that promote and condone violence. One approach would be to place the study of woman battering in the context of other strategies of power and control in male-female relationships. Mederos (1987) suggests that there is a continuum of strategies that husbands use to control wives, from anger to emotional abuse to physical violence.

We would also profit from an understanding of women's responses to violence and their control strategies in intimate relationships. There are strong indications that men and women see violent acts differently (Adams 1988). Some argue that women minimize and rationalize the violence done to them (Greenblat 1983). Several studies (Dobash and Dobash 1979; Ferraro and Johnson 1983; Mills 1985) have documented a progression in women's outlook from an initial view of the violence as an aberrant, occasional event to a view of the violence as a serious problem. Mills (1985) describes how the women she interviewed minimized the problematic aspects of their husband's violence by ignoring it and focusing on the positive aspects of their relationship with their husband or by justifying their husband's behavior as beyond his control. As the violence in these relationships increased, however, the women became increasingly anxious. But women's perceptions that something is wrong must be validated by someone outside the situation in order for them to define the situation as one in which they are victims of physical abuse.

In the case of men, some argue that batterers have either a set of explanations by which they deny their abusive behavior or a set of rationalizations by which they legitimize their violent behavior (Okun 1986; Ptacek 1988), Understanding these control strategies would provide a greater understanding of power in marriage, of the origins of violence, and of the possibilities of reducing male violence toward female intimates.

A focus on power in the family also provides an opportunity to examine changes in rates of violence along with changes in family power. For example, it is widely accepted that when wives work, they increase their power in the family (Collins 1988; Scanzoni 1982). Does male violence against women increase or decrease as a result of this shift in power? Does it make a difference whether the wife works with mostly women or mostly men?

Finally, it would be very useful to have cross-cultural data on rates of violence and variations in institutional responses to violence. In a cross-cultural study of rape, Sanday . . . found that a combination of economic and cultural factors contributes to variations in rates of rape. In societies in which women are included in religious and cultural institutions and in which women's economic and reproductive contributions are recognized, there is less violence and rape against women. Cross-cultural data would provide useful information on the relative importance of a variety of factors influencing all the forms of violence against women: norms and practices of male domination, norms of violence, cultural production, and economic and family systems.

References

Please see original article for references.

Credits

pp. 15–26: William J. Goode, "The Theoretical Importance of the Family" from *The Family*, second edition. Copyright © 1982. Reproduced by permission of Pearson Education, Upper Saddle River, New Jersey.

pp. 27–33: Anthony Giddens, "The Global Revolution in Family and Personal Life" from *Runaway World: How Globalization is Reshaping Our Lives*. Copyright © 1999. Reprinted by permission of the author.

pp. 35–54: Sharon Hays, "The Mommy Wars: Ambivalence, Ideological Work, and the Cultural Contradictions of Motherhood" from *The Cultural Contradictions of Motherhood*, pp. 131–151. Copyright © 1996. Published by Yale University Press. Reprinted by permission of the publisher.

pp. 54–74: Janet Z. Giele, "Decline of the Family: Conservative, Liberal, and Feminist Views" from *Promises to Keep: Decline and Renewal of Marriage in America*, edited by David Popenoe, Jean Bethke Elshtain and David Blankenhorn, pp. 89–115. Copyright © 1996. Reprinted by permssion of Rowman & Littlefield Publishers.

pp. 79–87: Robert M. Jackson, "Destined for Equality" from *Destined for Equality: The Inevitable Rise of Women's Status*, pp. 1–23, 157–171. Cambridge, Mass: Harvard University Press. Copyright © 1998 by Robert Max Jackson.

pp. 87–101: Kathleen Gerson, "Falling Back on Plan B: The Children of the Gender Revolution Face Uncharted Territory" from *Families as They Really Are*, edited by Barbara J. Risman. Copyright © 2010 by W.W. Norton & Company, Inc. Used by permission of W.W. Norton & Company, Inc.

pp. 103–108: Elizabeth A. Armstrong, Laura Hamilton, and Paula England, "Is Hooking Up Bad for Women?" from *Contexts*, Vol. 9, No. 3, pp. 22–27. Copyright © 2010. Reprinted by permission of SAGE Publications.

pp. 109–118: Mark Regnerus and Jeremy Uecker, "Sex and Marriage in the Minds of Emerging Adults" in *Premarital Sex in America: How Young Americans Meet, Mate, and Think about Marrying*, pp. 169–182. Copyright © 2010. Reprinted by permission of Oxford University Press.

pp. 119–140: Andrew J. Cherlin, "American Marriage in the Early Twenty-First Century" from *The Future of Children*, a publication of the Woodrow Wilson School of Public and International Affairs at Princeton University and the Brookings Institute. Copyright © 2005. Reprinted with permission.

pp. 140–149: Arlene Skolnick, "Grounds for Marriage: How Relationships Succeed or Fail" from *Inside the American Couple: New Thinking/New Challenges*, edited by Margaret Yalom and Laura L. Carstensen. Copyright © 2002. The regents of the University of California Press. Used with permission of the University of California Press.